About the author and his memoirs

"Lee Kuan Yew is one of the brightest, ablest men I have ever met. *The Singapore Story* is a must read for people interested in a true Asian success story. From this book we also learn a lot about the thinking of one of this century's truly visionary statesmen." — *George Bush, US President, 1989–93*

"In office, I read and analysed every speech of Harry's. He had a way of penetrating the fog of propaganda and expressing with unique clarity the issues of our times and the way to tackle them. He was never wrong ..."
— *Margaret Thatcher, British Prime Minister, 1979–90*

"Lee Kuan Yew is one of the seminal figures of Asia, and this book does justice to his extraordinary accomplishments. Describing the motivations and concepts that have animated his conduct and explaining specific actions, he will undoubtedly raise many controversies. But whether one agrees or not, one will learn a great deal."
— *Dr Henry A. Kissinger, US Secretary of State, 1973–77*

"Candid, informed, forceful, brilliant: these attributes explain why leaders throughout the world have sought out Lee Kuan Yew – and the words apply to his great memoir. You can learn the fascinating story of Singapore from this book, (and) how to think about power and politics in the world, how to analyse intricate problems, how to lead a people. A powerful book written by an extraordinary man." — *George P. Shultz, US Secretary of State, 1982–89*

"Your memoirs strike me as excellent stuff, far better than the normal run of autobiographies, which are usually full of post hoc justifications. The treatment of events is refreshing. No one can accuse you of unfairness to your adversaries. I thoroughly enjoyed reading it."
— *Dr Goh Keng Swee, Singapore Deputy Prime Minister, 1973–84*

"In the many years I have known him, Senior Minister Lee Kuan Yew has become a valued friend and counsellor. His resoluteness, energy and vision have left a deep impression on Singapore, making it a political and economic powerhouse whose influence extends far beyond its own region.

"Lee Kuan Yew is not only a remarkable political figure but a challenging thinker. He has much of moment to say to us as we steer our course into the future. I hope his memoirs and ideas will find a wide and receptive public." — *Helmut Kohl, German Chancellor since 1992*

"Lee Kuan Yew is a statesman who created a successful nation. He has known everybody. He has achieved impossible things and his memoirs tell the truth." — *William Rees-Mogg, Editor of The Times of London, 1967–81*

"Lee Kuan Yew is fascinating due to his grasp of the world's political and economic fabric. Many American and European leaders have profited from his wisdom, particularly by his evaluation of China as a world power and by his analysis and explanation of Asian values."

— *Helmut Schmidt, German Chancellor, 1974–82*

"For a country to rise from the threshold of subsistence to one of the highest living standards in the world in 30 years is no common achievement. At the root of this success lies the genius of one man, Mr Lee Kuan Yew. ... He has turned a city into a state. ... Mr Lee has gathered around himself the most brilliant minds, transforming the most exacting standards into a system of government. Under his leadership, the primacy of the general interest, the cult of education, work and saving, the capacity to foresee the needs of the city have enabled Singapore to take what I call 'shortcuts to progress'.

"... Through these memoirs, the reader will gain deep insight into the highly singular character of Singapore. He will discover the most perfect possible encounter between East and West, between Europe and Asia.

"Enabling individuals to develop the peculiar genius of each of the cultures of Singapore: Chinese, Malay, Indian and European, is surely one of the challenges facing us on a worldwide scale ... Does not development and peace among nations develop upon the success of this undertaking?"

— *Jacques Chirac, French President since 1995*

"Senior Minister Lee Kuan Yew is one of the pivotal figures in the modern history of Southeast Asia. His actions have shaped the course of events in this region. His vision and ideas continue to enrich intellectual debate and influence policy-makers worldwide. This seminal work is an invaluable account of the history of Singapore and the region."

— *Prem Tinsulanonda, Thai Prime Minister, 1980–88*

"This is a personal history of a man who, almost single-handedly, built a great nation from a small island ... this is the first textbook in the world on how to build a nation. Mr Lee has also been a great friend and often an astute observer of Japan. Japanese readers will learn in this book not only about their present image but also about their future portrait as seen through the penetrating eyes of this great political leader." — *Kiichi Miyazawa, Japanese Prime Minister, 1991–93 and Finance Minister since July 1998*

"These memoirs provide a unique insight into the history of modern Singapore and the thinking of one of the great Asian leaders of the 20th century. I am sure everyone who reads them will enjoy them immensely."

— *Tony Blair, British Prime Minister since 1997*

"He always commands an attentive audience amongst Western leaders. This book shows why." — *James Callaghan, British Prime Minister, 1976–79*

"Harry Lee has been and remains one of the most distinguished leaders of the last half century. He was fortunate in being supported by a group of ministers of extraordinary ability who would have graced the cabinet room of any major country.

"As a current history, *The Singapore Story* is without equal. ... It was impossible to put the book down. It is a commanding story of a man and a country." — *Malcolm Fraser, Australian Prime Minister, 1975–83*

"This is a remarkable autobiography by any standards ... distinguished by its clarity, thought and expression as well as by the breadth of its coverage.

"His judgments of those in high places with whom he had to deal during his long period in office, in particular with British Prime Ministers and American Presidents, are fascinating. Equally so, is his account of his first contacts with China." — *Edward Heath, British Prime Minister, 1970–74*

"Lee's vision, astute political judgement and strategy turned Singapore from a trading post into the successful thriving nation that it is today, respected by others. For those interested in politics and economic development, his memoirs should be required reading." — *Tun Daim Zainuddin, Malaysian Finance Minister, 1984–91 and Special Functions Minister since June 1998*

"His memoirs are more than the story of his own career, fascinating though that is ... They are the reflections on the international scene of one of the clearest political minds of our time." — *Percy Cradock, Foreign Policy Adviser to the British Prime Minister, 1984–92*

"Combining what is best in the Chinese and British traditions, his penetrating intellect gives political pragmatism a unique edge which has made the city state of Singapore a model far beyond Asia. The memoirs provide a mine of wisdom and information which politicians would be wise to quarry."
— *Denis Healey, British Chancellor of the Exchequer, 1974–79*

"This is the story of a man and his country. He returned to it when it was the rump of empire. He and it are now critical geopolitical pivots. They are now indivisible because of his unique ability to draw on the best of eastern and western cultures, to yield to objectivity rather than populism, to create a nation in his own image and having done so to be revered rather than despised. ... I am lost in awe of the man and his works. These writings are as economic, modest and understated as he is. He learned from history how to make it. It is good that he shares the way with us."
— *David Lange, New Zealand Prime Minister, 1984–89*

"How to turn a crisis into positive benefit distinguishes an able statesman from the ordinary. *The Singapore Story* reflects this great leader's life and vision. Everyone can learn from these most interesting memoirs." — *Siddhi Savetsila, Thai Foreign Minister, 1980–90*

The Singapore Story

At work on my drafts on home PC (Oxley Road).

The Singapore Story

Memoirs of
LEE KUAN YEW

Singapore
Press
Holdings

TIMES EDITIONS

Published by
Times Editions Pte Ltd
a member of the Times Publishing Group
Times Centre, 1 New Industrial Road
Singapore 536196
Tel: (65) 2848844   Fax: (65) 2854871
E-mail: te@corp.tpl.com.sg
Online Bookstore:
http://www.timesone.com.sg/te
and
The Straits Times Press
a member of Singapore Press Holdings
Times House
390 Kim Seng Road
Singapore 239495

Book and jacket design by Tuck Loong
Dust jacket photographs by George Gascon

Reprinted 1998

Printed by Times Offset Malaysia

ISBN 981 204 983 5

To my wife and partner,
Choo

Contents

Preface

I had not intended to write my memoirs and did not keep a diary. To do so would have inhibited my work.

Five years after I stepped down as prime minister, my old friend and colleague, Lim Kim San, chairman of Singapore Press Holdings (SPH), convinced me that the young would read my memoirs since they were interested in a book of my old speeches that SPH had published in Chinese. I was also troubled by the apparent over-confidence of a generation that has only known stability, growth and prosperity. I thought our people should understand how vulnerable Singapore was and is, the dangers that beset us, and how we nearly did not make it. Most of all, I hope that they will know that honest and effective government, public order and personal security, economic and social progress did not come about as the natural course of events.

This is not an official history. It is the story of the Singapore I grew up in, the placid years of British colonial rule, the shock of war, the cruel years of Japanese occupation, communist insurrection and terrorism against the returning British, communal riots and intimidation during Malaysia, and the perils of independence. This book deals with the early years which ended with our sudden independence in 1965. My next book will describe the long, hard climb over the next 25 years from poverty to prosperity.

Many, not born or too young when I took office in 1959, do not know how a small country with no natural resources was cut off from its natural hinterland and had to survive in a tough world of nationalistic new states in Southeast Asia. They take it as quite normal that in less than 40 years the World Bank has reclassified Singapore from a less developed to a developed country.

To write this book I had to revive memories of events long forgotten, reading through minutes of meetings, letters written and received, and oral history transcripts of colleagues. It was psychological stocktaking, and I was surprised how disturbing it was occasionally although these events were past and over with.

I had one powerful critic and helper, my wife, Choo. She went over every word that I wrote, many times. We had endless arguments. She is a conveyancing lawyer by profession. I was not drafting a will or a conveyance to be scrutinised by a judge. Nevertheless she demanded precise, clear and unambiguous language. Choo was a tower of strength, giving me constant emotional and intellectual support.

I have not written, except incidentally, about what was an important part of my life, our three children. They have been a source of joy and satisfaction as Choo and I watched them grow up and, like their peers, build successful careers in the Singapore my policies had transformed.

For my cabinet colleagues and me, our families were at the heart of our team efforts to build a nation from scratch. We wanted a Singapore that our children and those of our fellow citizens would be proud of, a Singapore that would offer all citizens equal and ample opportunities for a fulfilling future. It was this drive in an immigrant Asian society that spurred us on to fight and win against all odds.

Lee Kuan Yew
Singapore, July 1998

Acknowledgements

I was fortunate in 1995 to gather a team of young researchers. Andrew Tan Kok Kiong, seconded to SPH from the Singapore Administrative Service, was helped by Pang Gek Choo, who worked for the *Straits Times*, and Alan Chong. They made a thorough search of government archives and ferreted out my correspondence, minutes of important meetings and other relevant documents. Andrew Tan was my most valuable aide; able and resourceful, he coordinated the work of the researchers, organised the material, and made my task easier. Pang Gek Choo was quick and efficient in tracing reports of events and speeches in Straits Times' archives of the last 40 years. After two years, as the work expanded, Walter Fernandez and Yvonne Lim from SPH and Dr Goh Ai Ting from the National University of Singapore (NUS) joined my researchers.

They had help from officers like Panneer Selvan of the Ministry of Foreign Affairs. The registry officer in the Prime Minister's Office, Florence Ler Chay Keng, and her assistants, Wendy Teo Kwee Geok and Vaijayanthimala, were amazingly successful in locating my letters and notes as far back as the 1960s.

Lily Tan, director of the National Archives, helped my researchers in their requests for documents and oral history transcripts of those persons who had given me permission to read them. The staff at the NUS library, the National Library and the Straits Times editorial library were equally helpful.

The prime minister, Goh Chok Tong, allowed me access to all records and documents in the government ministries and in the archives.

The British Public Record Office in Kew, Richmond yielded Colonial Office and Commonwealth Office documents which gave interesting insights from a British perspective on events from 1955 to 1965.

Dennis Bloodworth, an old friend, once foreign correspondent for the *London Observer* newspaper, went through my drafts. He was thorough in deleting repetitions and suggesting alternatives to my overworked favourite expressions. However, Bloodworth left me to decide what went into my book.

A younger generation of editorial writers and journalists – from the *Straits Times*, Cheong Yip Seng (editor in chief), Han Fook Kwang (political editor), Warren Fernandez, Sumiko Tan and Zuraidah Ibrahim; from the *New Paper*, Irene Ng; from the *Zaobao*, Lim Jim Koon (editor) and Seng Han Thong – read my drafts. They suggested many improvements so that those not yet born when the events I described happened could understand the background against which they took place. Han Fook Kwang and Warren Fernandez improved the flow of my narrative. Shova Loh, line editor in Times Editions, meticulously tightened my sentences and removed errors.

To avoid being unwittingly insensitive on Malay issues, I had all my draft chapters relating to Malays read by Guntor Sadali (editor of *Berita Harian*), People's Action Party MPs Yaacob Ibrahim, Mohamad Maidin and Zainul Abidin Rasheed, and minister for community development, Abdullah Tarmugi. I did not want to hurt Malay feelings and have tried not to do so.

Old colleagues, including Goh Keng Swee, Lim Kim San, Ong Pang Boon, Othman Wok, Lee Khoon Choy, Rahim Ishak, Maurice Baker, Sim Kee Boon, S.R. Nathan and Ngiam Tong Dow, read the relevant parts of my drafts and helped to confirm or correct my recollection of events.

Tommy Koh, ambassador-at-large, Chan Heng Chee, ambassador to Washington, Kishore Mahbubani, permanent secretary (policy), ministry of foreign affairs, and Bilahari Kausikan, deputy secretary, ministry of foreign affairs, read the page proofs and made many useful suggestions.

I am grateful to them and to the many others who gave freely of their time and advice from which I have benefited. But the responsibility for the final result with all its shortcomings is mine alone.

I had visitors and other duties to attend to during the day. I did most of my uninterrupted work on the PC at night after the day's work was done. Several of the young men and women to whom I sent my drafts asked if the time-stamp on my PC was wrong, because they were frequently stamped as 3 or 4 am. I assured them that it was correct.

My long-time personal assistants, Cheong Cheng Hoon and Wong Lin Hoe, had the hard work of typing and retyping my drafts. They helped me out when I ran into problems with my PC. Cheong retired when the book was three-quarters done, and two others, Loh Hock Teck and Koh Kiang Chay, took over. All had to adjust to my difficult hours requiring them to work well past dinner-time.

I am indebted and grateful to all of them.

1. Suddenly, Independence

It was like any other Monday morning in Singapore until the music stopped. At 10 am, the pop tunes on the radio were cut off abruptly. Stunned listeners heard the announcer solemnly read out a proclamation – 90 words that changed the lives of the people of Singapore and Malaysia:

> "Whereas it is the inalienable right of a people to be free and independent, I, Lee Kuan Yew, prime minister of Singapore, do hereby proclaim and declare on behalf of the people and the government of Singapore that as from today, the ninth day of August in the year one thousand nine hundred and sixty-five, Singapore shall be forever a sovereign, democratic and independent nation, founded upon the principles of liberty and justice and ever seeking the welfare and happiness of her people in a more just and equal society."

Two hundred and fifty miles to the north, in peninsular Malaysia, Tunku Abdul Rahman was making his own proclamation, declaring that "Singapore shall cease to be a state of Malaysia and shall forever be an independent and sovereign state and nation separate from and independent of Malaysia, and that the government of Malaysia recognises the government of Singapore as an independent and sovereign government of Singapore and will always work in friendship and cooperation with it."

Separation! What I had fought so hard to achieve was now being dissolved. Why? And why so suddenly? It was only two years since the island of Singapore had become part of the new Federation of Malaysia (which also included the North Borneo territories of Sarawak and Sabah).

At 10 am the same day, in the Malaysian capital, Kuala Lumpur, the Tunku explained to parliament:

> "In the end we find that there are only two courses open to us: to take repressive measures against the Singapore government or their leaders for the behaviour of some of their leaders, and the course of action we are taking now, to sever with the state government of Singapore that has ceased to give a measure of loyalty to the central government."

The House listened in utter silence. The Tunku was speaking at the first reading of a resolution moved by Tun Abdul Razak, the deputy prime minister, to pass the Constitution of Malaysia (Singapore Amendment) Bill, 1965, immediately. By 1:30 pm, the debate on the second and third readings had ended, and the bill was sent to the senate. The senate started its first reading at 2:30 and completed the third reading by 4:30. The head of state, the Yang di-Pertuan Agong, gave his royal assent that same day, concluding the constitutional formalities. Singapore was cast out.

Under Malay-Muslim custom, a husband, but not the wife, can declare "*Talak*" (I divorce thee) and the woman is divorced. They can reconcile and he can remarry her, but not after he has said "*Talak*" three times. The three readings in the two chambers of parliament were the three *talaks* with which Malaysia divorced Singapore. The partners – predominantly Malay in Malaya, predominantly Chinese in Singapore – had not been compatible. Their union had been marred by increasing conjugal strife over whether the new Federation should be a truly multiracial society, or one dominated by the Malays.

Singapore went for the substance of the divorce, not its legal formalities. If there was to be separation, I wanted to ensure that the terms were practical, workable and final. To make certain there could be no doubt as to their finality, the Singapore government published the two proclamations in a special government gazette that morning. I had asked for – and the Tunku had given – his proclamation with his personal signature so that there could be no reversal, even if other Malaysian leaders or members of parliament disagreed with it. P.S. Raman, director of Radio & Television Singapore, had received these documents from the secretary of the Cabinet Office. He decided to have them read in full, in Malay, Mandarin and English, on the three different language channels and repeated every half hour. Within minutes, the news agencies had cabled the news to the world.

I had started the day, Monday, 9 August, with a series of meetings with key civil servants, especially those under federal jurisdiction, to inform them that Singapore ministers would now assume control. Just before 10 o'clock, when the announcement was to be made, I met those members of the diplomatic corps in Singapore who could be gathered at short notice. I told them of the separation and Singapore's independence, and requested recognition from their governments.

As the diplomats left, I drew aside the Indian deputy high commissioner and the UAR (Egyptian) consul-general and gave them letters for Prime Minister Shastri and President Nasser. India and Egypt were then, with Indonesia, the leading countries in the Afro-Asian movement. In my letters, I sought their recognition and support. From India, I asked for advisers to train an army, and from Egypt, an adviser to build a coastal defence force.

Before noon, I arrived at the studios of Radio & Television Singapore for a press conference. It had an unintended and unexpected result. After a few opening questions and answers, a journalist asked, "Could you outline for us the train of events that led to this morning's proclamation?"

I recounted my meetings with the Tunku in Kuala Lumpur during the previous two days:

"But the Tunku put it very simply that there was no way, and that there would be a great deal of trouble if we insisted on going on. And I would like to add ... You see, this is a moment of ... every time we look back on this moment when we signed this agreement, which severed Singapore from Malaysia, it will be a moment of anguish because all my life I have believed in merger and the unity of these two territories. It's a people connected by geography, economics, and ties of kinship ... Would you mind if we stop for a while?"

At that moment, my emotions overwhelmed me. It was only after another 20 minutes that I was able to regain my composure and resume the press conference.

It was not a live telecast, as television transmissions then started only at 6 pm. I asked P.S. Raman to cut the footage of my breakdown. He strongly advised against it. The press, he said, was bound to report it, and if he edited it out, their descriptions of the scene would make it appear worse. I had found Raman, a Tamil Brahmin born in Madras and a loyal Singaporean, a shrewd and sound adviser. I took his advice. And so, many people in Singapore and abroad saw me lose control of my emotions. That evening, Radio & Television Malaysia in Kuala Lumpur telecast my press conference, including this episode. Among Chinese, it is unbecoming to exhibit such a lack of manliness. But I could not help myself. It was some consolation that many viewers in Britain, Australia and New Zealand sympathised with me and with Singapore. They were interested in Malaysia because their troops were defending it against armed "Confrontation", the euphemism President Sukarno of Indonesia used to describe his small-scale undeclared war against the new and expanded "neo-colonialist" Federation.

I was emotionally overstretched, having gone through three days and nights of a wrenching experience. With little sleep since Friday night in Kuala Lumpur, I was close to physical exhaustion. I was weighed down by a heavy sense of guilt. I felt I had let down several million people in Malaysia: immigrant Chinese and Indians, Eurasians, and even some Malays. I had aroused their hopes, and they had joined people in

Singapore in resisting Malay hegemony, the root cause of our dispute. I was ashamed that I had left our allies and supporters to fend for themselves, including party leaders from other states of Malaysia – Sabah, Sarawak, Penang, Perak, Selangor and Negeri Sembilan. Together we had formed the Malaysian Solidarity Convention, which had been meeting and coordinating our activities to mobilise the people to stand up for a non-communal society. We had set out to create a broad coalition that could press the Alliance government in Kuala Lumpur for a "Malaysian Malaysia", not a Malay Malaysia – no easy matter, since the ruling Alliance itself was dominated by the Tunku's United Malays National Organisation (UMNO).

I was also filled with remorse and guilt for having had to deceive the prime ministers of Britain, Australia and New Zealand. In the last three weeks, while they had been giving me and Singapore their quiet and powerful support for a peaceful solution to Malaysia's communal problems, I had been secretly discussing this separation.

All these thoughts preyed on me during the three weeks of our negotiations with Razak, the Tunku's deputy. As long as the battle of wills was on, I kept my cool. But once the deed was done, my feelings got the better of me.

While I was thus overwhelmed, the merchants in Singapore's Chinatown were jubilant. They set off firecrackers to celebrate their liberation from communal rule by the Malays from Kuala Lumpur, carpeting the streets with red paper debris. The Chinese language newspaper *Sin Chew Jit Poh*, reporting that people had fired the crackers to mark this great day, said with typical Chinese obliqueness, "It could be that they were anticipating Zhong Yuan Jie (the Festival of the Hungry Ghosts)." It added an enigmatic phrase, "In each individual's heart is his own prayer." The *Nanyang Siang Pau* wrote, "The heart knows without having to announce it."

The president of the Singapore Chinese Chamber of Commerce, Soon Peng Yam, publicly welcomed the news of Singapore's separation from Malaysia. His committee would meet the next day to discuss sponsoring a joint celebration of the island's independence by all registered trade associations, unions, guilds, and other civic organisations. He said, "Businessmen in general feel very much relieved at the latest political developments."

Investors did not feel my anguish either. Separation set off a tremendous burst of activity in the share market. On that first day, the trading rooms of the still joint Singapore-Malaysia Stock Exchange in Singapore and Kuala Lumpur recorded twice the volume of transactions of the most active days of the previous week. By the next day, investors had decided independence was good for the economy, and there was an even larger turnover. The value of 25 out of 27 industrial stocks rose.

In the city centre, by contrast, the streets were deserted by the afternoon of 9 August. The night before, I had informed John Le Cain, the Singapore police commissioner, of the impending announcement, and had handed him a letter from Dato Dr Ismail bin Dato Abdul Rahman, the federal minister for home affairs, telling him to take his instructions from the Singapore government in future. Le Cain had deployed his Police Reserve Units, paramilitary squads specially trained to deal with violent rioters, just in case pro-UMNO Malay activists in Singapore went on a rampage to protest against separation. People were quick to sense the danger, having experienced two bloody Malay-Chinese riots the previous year, 1964. The presence of the riot squads and their special vans, equipped with water hoses and fitted with wire netting over glass windows and windscreens to protect them from missiles, encouraged caution. Many decided to leave their offices and go home early.

The day was hot and humid, typical August weather. By the time the earth cooled that evening, I was weary. But I was determined to keep to my routine of daily exercise to remove my tensions. I spent more than an hour hitting 150 golf balls from the practice tee in front of Sri Temasek, my official residence in the grounds of the Istana (formerly Government House). It made me feel better and gave me an appetite for dinner before my meeting with Viscount Head, the British high commissioner to Kuala Lumpur.

My secretary had taken a telephone call from Antony Head's office that morning at 9:30, and since it was only 30 minutes before the proclamation was to be made, he had said that I was not immediately available. Head asked if he could see me that afternoon. I sent back a message offering 8 pm. We settled for ten to eight.

At 7:50 pm, he arrived at Sri Temasek (for security reasons I was not staying at my home in Oxley Road), to be greeted by my daughter Wei Ling, all of 10 years old and dressed in tee-shirt and shorts, who was playing under the porch.

"Do you want to see my father?" she asked Lord Head.

It was a suitably informal welcome, for with independence my relations with him had suddenly become equivocal. I reached the porch in time to greet him as he got out of the car, and asked him, "Who are you talking on behalf of?"

He replied, "Well, of course, you know, I am accredited to a foreign government."

"Exactly. And have you got specific authority to speak to me about Singapore's relationship with Britain?"

"No."

"Then this is a tête-à-tête – it is just a chit-chat."

"If you like to put it that way."

It was that way.

When describing this meeting to a group of British and Australian foreign correspondents later that month, I tried to give the impression of an encounter between two adversaries. In truth, I had a heavy heart throughout. Head's bearing impressed me. His demeanour was worthy of a Sandhurst-trained officer in the Life Guards. He had been defence minister at the time of the Anglo-French invasion of Suez in 1956, and had resigned along with Anthony Eden, accepting responsibility for the débâcle. He was British upper class, good at the stiff upper lip.

He had tried his best to prevent this break. He had done his utmost to get the Tunku and the federal government to adopt policies that could build up unity within Malaysia. Both he, as British high commissioner in constant touch with the Tunku and his ministers, and his prime minister in London, Harold Wilson, had given me unstinting support for a constitutional solution to the dispute between Kuala Lumpur and Singapore. They had insisted, successfully, that force should not be used. Had they not done this, the outcome would have been different. Separation was certainly not the solution he had worked so hard for.

But despite the presence of some 63,000 British servicemen, two aircraft carriers, 80 warships and 20 squadrons of aircraft in Southeast Asia to defend the Federation, he could not prevail against the force of Malay communalism. The Malay leaders, including the Tunku, feared that if ever they shared real political power with the non-Malays, they would be overwhelmed. That was the crux of the matter. Head did not understand this. Nor had I originally, but I came to do so before he did because I had spent more time interacting with the Tunku, Razak and Ismail. And I spoke Malay, which Head did not. I could also recall incidents of friction and rivalry between Malays and non-Malays from my past, especially during my student days at Raffles College in 1940 and 1941. I knew the Malays better. So when, at the end of June 1965, I read that the Tunku had gone down with shingles in London, I suspected he was reaching breaking point.

Head and I met for about an hour, and I tried to make all this clear to him. But how could I explain that, after the one-on-one meeting I had had with Razak on 29 June, in his office in Kuala Lumpur, I had seen little hope of a peaceful solution to our problems? Head and I were both controlled and restrained in our exchanges. He uttered no recriminations, but simply expressed his regret that I had not informed him or his government of what was happening. On my part, I was filled with sadness for having had to conceal from him the final developments of the past three weeks that had ended in separation. I thought he looked sad too. But if I had told Head that the Tunku wanted us out of Malaysia, although what I wanted was a looser federation, he would have found a way to stop the Tunku as it was against British interests to have Singapore separated and independent. Then race riots could not have been ruled out. Seventeen hours after we met, the British government extended recognition to independent Singapore.

After Head left, I had innumerable discussions on the phone with my cabinet colleagues to compare notes on how the day had turned out and to check on developments. Fearful of a deep split in the cabinet and among the MPs, I had wanted every minister to sign the Separation Agreement precisely because I knew that several would have opposed it tooth and nail.

But I had to get on with the business of governing this new Singapore. I had spent most of my time that day with my close colleague Goh Keng Swee. First, we had to sort out the problems of internal security and defence. I decided to amalgamate the ministry of home affairs with the new ministry of defence, with him in charge. But then who was to take his job as finance minister? We settled on Lim Kim San. The next problem was international recognition and good relations with those who could help ensure our security and survival. We agreed that S. Rajaratnam, a founder member of our People's Action Party (PAP), should take over foreign affairs. We were in a daze, not yet adjusted to the new realities and fearful of the imponderables ahead.

We faced a bleak future. Singapore and Malaya, joined by a causeway across the Straits of Johor, had always been governed as one territory by the British. Malaya was Singapore's hinterland, as were the Borneo territories of Sarawak, Brunei and Sabah. They were all part of the British Empire in Southeast Asia, which had Singapore as its administrative and commercial hub. Now we were on our own, and the Malaysian government was out to teach us a lesson for being difficult, and for not complying with their norms and practices and fitting into their set-up. We could expect them to cut us off from our role as their traditional outlet for imports and exports and as the provider of many other services. In a world of new nation states, all pursuing nationalistic economic policies, all wanting to do everything themselves and to deal directly with their principal buyers and sellers in Europe, America or Japan, how was Singapore going to survive without its hinterland? Indeed, how were we to live? Even our water came from the neighbouring Malaysian state of Johor. I remembered vividly how, in early February 1942, the Japanese army had captured our reservoirs there, demoralising the British defenders by that act, even though there was still some water in the reservoirs in Singapore.

Some countries are born independent. Some achieve independence. Singapore had independence thrust upon it. Some 45 British colonies had held colourful ceremonies to formalise and celebrate the transfer of sovereign power from imperial Britain to their indigenous governments. For Singapore, 9 August 1965 was no ceremonial occasion. We had never sought independence. In a referendum less than three years ago, we had persuaded 70 per cent of the electorate to vote in favour of merger with Malaya. Since then, Singapore's need to be part and parcel of the Federation in one political, economic, and social polity had not changed. Nothing had changed – except that we were out. We had said that an independent Singapore was simply not viable. Now it was our unenviable task to make it work. How were we to create a nation out of a polyglot collection of migrants from China, India, Malaysia, Indonesia and several other parts of Asia?

Singapore was a small island of 214 square miles at low tide. It had thrived because it was the heart of the British Empire in Southeast Asia; with separation, it became a heart without a body. Seventy-five per cent of our population of two million were Chinese, a tiny minority in an archipelago of 30,000 islands inhabited by more than 100 million Malay or Indonesian Muslims. We were a Chinese island in a Malay sea. How could we survive in such a hostile environment?

There was no doubt about the hostility. To add to our problems, the Indonesians had mounted their aggressive "Confrontation" against Malaysia when it came into being in September 1963, a low-level war that included an economic boycott, acts of terrorism with commandos infiltrating Singapore to explode bombs and military incursions involving the dropping of paratroops in Johor. The Chinese in Malaya and Singapore knew the Indonesian government was against even its own three million ethnic Chinese in Indonesia.

Meanwhile, not only did the entrepot trade on which Singapore had depended ever since it was founded in 1819 face a doubtful future, but our strategic value to Britain in holding the empire together was vanishing as the empire dissolved. Singapore's economy would be hard hit by any sudden scaling down of the British presence. British defence spending in Singapore accounted for about 20 per cent of our GDP; their military gave employment, directly to 30,000 workers, and indirectly to another 10,000 domestic help, besides those who catered to their other needs. They created employment for more than 10 per cent of the work force at a time when a high population growth of 2.5 per cent per annum was putting enormous pressure on the government for jobs as well as education, health services and housing.

But for the moment, I was grateful and relieved that we had got through the day without disturbances. I went to bed well past midnight, weary but not sleepy. It was not until two or three in the morning that I finally dropped off exhausted, still disturbed from time to time as my subconscious wrestled with our problems. How could I overcome them? Why had we come to this sorry pass? Was this to be the end result after 40 years of study, work and struggle? What did the future hold for Singapore? I would spend the next 40 years finding answers to these difficult questions.

2. Growing Up

My earliest and most vivid recollection is of being held by my ears over a well in the compound of a house where my family was then living, at what is now Tembeling Road in Singapore. I was about 4 years old.

I had been mischievous and had messed up an expensive jar of my father's *4711* pale green scented brilliantine. My father had a violent temper, but that evening his rage went through the roof. He took me by the scruff of the neck from the house to this well and held me over it. How could my ears have been so tough that they were not ripped off, dropping me into that well? Fifty years later, in the 1970s, I read in the *Scientific American* an article explaining how pain and shock released neuropeptides in the brain, stamping the new experience into the brain cells and thus ensuring that the experience would be remembered for a long time afterwards.

I was born in Singapore on 16 September 1923, in a large two-storey bungalow at 92 Kampong Java Road. My mother, Chua Jim Neo, was then 16 years old. My father, Lee Chin Koon, was 20. Their parents had arranged the marriage a year previously. Both families must have thought it an excellent match, for they later married my father's younger sister to my mother's younger brother.

My father had been brought up a rich man's son. He used to boast to us that, when he was young, his father allowed him a limitless account at Robinsons and John Little, the two top department stores in Raffles Place, where he could charge to this account any suit or other items he fancied. He was educated in English at St Joseph's Institution, a Catholic mission school founded by the De La Salle Brothers in 1852. He said he completed his Junior School Certificate, after which he ended his formal education – to his and my mother's eternal regret. Being without a profession, he could only get a job as a storekeeper with the Shell Oil Company when the fortunes of both families were destroyed in the Great Depression.

My family history in Singapore began with my paternal great-grandfather, Lee Bok Boon, a Hakka. The Hakkas are Han Chinese from the northern and central plains of China who migrated to Fujian, Guangdong and other provinces in the south some 700 to 1,000 years ago, and as latecomers were only able to squeeze themselves into the less fertile and more hilly areas unoccupied by the local inhabitants. According to the inscription on the tombstone on his grave behind the house he built in China, Lee Bok Boon was born in 1846 in the village of Tangxi in the Dabu prefecture of Guangdong. He had migrated to Singapore on a Chinese junk. Little is known of him after that until 1870, when he married a Chinese girl, Seow Huan Neo, born in Singapore to a Hakka shopkeeper.

In 1882 he decided that he had made enough money to return to his ancestral village in China, build himself a large house, and set himself up as local gentry. His wife, however, did not want to leave her family in Singapore and go to some place she had never seen. According to my grandfather, who was then about ten, the children and their mother went into hiding with her family in Ah Hood Road. Lee Bok Boon went back to China alone. There he married again, built his large house, and duly bought a minor mandarinate. He had a portrait done of himself in mandarin robes, which he sent to Singapore, together with another painting of an impressive-looking Chinese traditional-style house complete with courtyard and grey-tiled roofs. The painting of the house has been lost, but the portrait of my great-grandfather still exists.

My grandfather, Lee Hoon Leong – whom I addressed as Kung or "grandfather" in Chinese – was born in Singapore in 1871, and according to my father was educated at Raffles Institution up to standard V, which would be today's lower secondary school. He himself told me he worked as a dispenser (an unqualified pharmacist) when he left school, but after a few years became a purser on board a steamer plying between Singapore and the Dutch East Indies. The ship was part of a fleet belonging to the Heap Eng Moh Shipping Line, which was owned by the Chinese millionaire sugar king of Java, Oei Tiong Ham.

In between his travels he married my grandmother, Ko Liem Nio, in Semarang, a city in central Java. There is a document in Dutch, dated 25 March 1899, issued by the Orphan's Court in Semarang, giving consent to Ko Liem Nio, age 16, to marry Lee Hoon Leong, age 26. An endorsement on this document states that the marriage was solemnised on 26 March 1899. My father was born in Semarang in 1903, in the Dutch East Indies. But he was a British subject by descent, because his father – Kung – was from Singapore. Kung brought his wife and baby son back to the island for good soon after the child's birth.

His fortunes rose as he gained the confidence of Oei Tiong Ham, who appointed him his attorney to manage his affairs in Singapore. Kung told me how he was so trusted that in 1926, on his own authority, he donated $150,000, then a princely sum, from Oei's funds towards the foundation of Raffles College.

Between my father and my grandfather, there was no question as to whom I admired more. My grandfather loved and pampered me. My father, the disciplinarian in the family, was tough with me. My grandfather had acquired great wealth. My father was just a rich man's son, with little to show for himself.

When the family fortunes declined during the Great Depression, which caused rubber prices to fall from a high of 80 cents per pound to some 20 cents between 1927 and 1930, Kung was badly hit. He must have had less business sense than my mother's father, Chua Kim Teng. The Chua fortunes also suffered because Chua had invested in rubber estates and had speculated on the rubber market. But he had gone into property as well. He owned markets and shophouses and he was not wiped out, as Kung was. So it was that by 1929 my parents had moved from Kung's home to Chua's large rambling house in Telok Kurau.

Kung was very Westernised, the result of his years as a purser on board ships with British captains, first officers and chief engineers. He used to recount to me his experiences, stories of how rigidly discipline was maintained on board a ship. For example, despite the heat and humidity of the tropics, the captain, the other officers and he, as purser, dressed in buttoned-up white cotton drill suits for dinner, which was served with plates, forks, knives and napkins, all properly laid out. From his accounts of his journeys in the region, the British officers left him with a lasting impression of order, strength and efficiency.

When I was born, the family consulted a friend knowledgeable in these matters for an auspicious name for me. He suggested "Kuan Yew", the dialect rendering of the Mandarin *guang yao*, meaning "light and brightness". But my grandfather's admiration for the British made him add "Harry" to my name, so I was Harry Lee Kuan Yew. My two younger brothers, Kim Yew and Thiam Yew, were also given Christian names – Dennis and Freddy respectively. At that time few non-Christian Chinese did this, and at school later I was to find myself the odd boy out with a personal name like "Harry". When my youngest brother, Suan Yew, was born in 1933, I persuaded my parents not to give him a Christian name since we were not Christians.

Although Kung had lost the money that had enabled him to live and dress in style, he still retained remnants of his former wealth, including some handsome solid furniture of the early 1910s imported from England. He was, moreover, a gourmet. A meal with him was a treat. My grandmother was a good cook. She would fry a steak seasoned with freshly grated nutmeg to a succulent, sizzling brown, and serve it with potato chips, also fried to a golden brown but never oily, something Kung was particular about. I was impressed: here was a man who had made his way up in the world, who knew how to live the good life.

He was in marked contrast to my maternal grandfather. Chua Kim Teng had no formal English schooling nor had he associated with British sea captains and Chinese sugar millionaires. He was born in Singapore in 1865, into a Hokkien Chinese family that came from Malacca. He had grown wealthy through hard work and frugal living, saving his money for judicious investments in rubber and property.

He had married three times. His first two wives had died and the third was my grandmother, Neo Ah Soon, a large, broad-shouldered Hakka from Pontianak in Dutch Borneo, who spoke the Hakka dialect and Indonesian Malay. When she married Chua, she was a young widow with two children by her first husband, who had died soon after the younger son was born. She bore Chua seven children before dying in 1935. He died in 1944 during the Japanese occupation of Singapore.

My mother was the eldest child of this union, and when she was married in 1922 at the age of 15, the fortunes of both families were still healthy. She even brought with her, as part of her dowry, a little slave girl whose duty, among other things, was to help bath her, wash her feet and put on and take off her shoes. All such symbols of wealth had disappeared by the time I became conscious of my surroundings at the age of 4 or 5. But memories of better times survive in old photographs of me – an infant over-dressed in clothes imported from England, or in an expensive pram. Chua's house in Telok Kurau was a large wood and brick bungalow. He and all the children by his third wife lived in that house, my mother, as the eldest daughter, together with my father and five of us children occupying one big bedroom. Ours was a large and reasonably happy household, all of us living together harmoniously but for occasional friction, mostly over mischievous and quarrelling grand-children. I thus grew up with my three brothers, one sister and seven cousins in the same house. But because they were all younger than I was,

Above: Grandfather or "Kung", Lee Hoon Leong, the Anglophile, complete with waistcoat in the hot tropics.

Opposite: After his return to Dapu, Guangdong province, in 1882: great-grandfather Lee Bok Boon, in the robes of a Qing official Grade 7.

I often played with the children of the Chinese fishermen and of the Malays living in a nearby kampong, a cluster of some 20 or 30 attap or zinc-roofed wooden huts in a lane opposite my grandfather's house. The fishermen worked along Siglap beach, then about 200 yards away.

It was a simpler world altogether. We played with fighting kites, tops, marbles and even fighting fish. These games nurtured a fighting spirit and the will to win. I do not know whether they prepared me for the fights I was to have later in politics. We were not soft, nor were we spoilt. As a young boy, I had no fancy clothes or shoes like those my grandchildren wear today.

We were not poor, but we had no great abundance of toys, and there was no television. So we had to be resourceful, to use our imagination. We read, and this was good for our literacy, but there were few illustrated books for young children then, and these were expensive. I bought the usual penny dreadfuls, and followed the adventures of the boys at Greyfriars – Harry Wharton and Billy Bunter and company. I waited eagerly for the mail boat from Britain, which arrived at Tanjong Pagar wharf every Friday, bringing British magazines and pictorials. But they too were not cheap. When I was a little older, I used the Raffles Library, where books could be borrowed for two weeks at a time. I read eclectically but preferred westerns to detective thrillers.

For holidays, the family would spend up to a week at a wooden house in my grandfather Chua's rubber estate in Chai Chee. To get to the estate from Changi Road, we rode down a track in a bullock cart, its two bullocks driven by my grandmother's gardener. The cart had wooden wheels with metal rims and no shock absorbers, so that half mile ride on the rutted clay track was hilariously bumpy. Fifty years later, in 1977, as I travelled in a Concorde from London to New York and crossed the Atlantic in three hours, I wondered if any of my fellow passengers had ever experienced the joy of a bullock-cart ride.

Myself, age 4, as a page boy at my aunt's wedding, dressed in the traditional costume of the time.

Life was not all simple pleasures, however. Every now and again my father would come home in a foul mood after losing at blackjack and other card games at the Chinese Swimming Club in Amber Road, and demand some of my mother's jewellery to pawn so that he could go back to try his luck again. There would be fearful quarrels, and he was sometimes violent. But my mother was a courageous woman who was determined to hang on to the jewellery, wedding gifts from her parents. A strong character with great energy and resourcefulness, she had been married off too early. In her day, a woman was expected to be a good wife, bear many children, and bring them up to be good husbands or wives in turn. Had she been born one generation later and continued her education beyond secondary school, she could easily have become an effective business executive.

She devoted her life to raising her children to be well-educated and independent professionals, and she stood up to my father to safeguard their future. My brothers, my sister and I were very conscious of her sacrifices; we felt we could not let her down and did our best to be worthy of her and to live up to her expectations. As I grew older, she began consulting me as the eldest son on all important family matters, so that while still in my teens, I became *de facto* head of the family. This taught me how to take decisions.

My maternal grandmother had strong views on my education. In 1929, before I was 6, she insisted that I join the fishermen's children attending school nearby, in a little wood and attap hut with a compacted clay floor. The hut had only one classroom with hard benches and plank desk-tops, and one other room, which was the home of our scrawny middle-aged Chinese teacher. He made us recite words after him without any comprehension of their meaning – if he did explain, I did not understand him.

I complained bitterly to my mother, and she made representations to my grandmother. But a young woman of 22 could not overrule an experienced matriarch of 48 who had brought up nine children from two marriages, and was determined that I should receive some education in Chinese. My grandmother allowed a change of school, however, and I was sent to Choon Guan School in Joo Chiat Terrace. It was a mile away from home, and I walked there and back every day. This school was more impressive, a two-storey wooden structure with cement floors, and about 10 proper classrooms with desks for 35 to 40 pupils in each class. The lessons in Chinese were still tough going. At home I spoke English to my parents, "Baba Malay" – a pidgin Malay adulterated with Chinese words – to my grandparents, and Malay with a smattering of Hokkien to my friends, the fishermen's children. Mandarin was totally alien to me, and unconnected with my life. I did not understand much of what the teachers were saying.

After two to three months of this, I again pleaded with my mother to be transferred to an English-language school. She won my grand-mother's consent this time and in January 1930 I joined Telok Kurau English School. Now I understood what the teachers were saying and made progress with little effort. The students were mostly Chinese, with a few Indians among them, and some Malays who had transferred from Telok Kurau Malay School.

My parents were concerned at my lack of diligence, and my mother gave Uncle Keng Hee the task of making sure I was prepared for the next day's lessons. Three evenings a week before dinner I had to sit with him for an hour. Even then I thought how absurd it was that the least scholarly of my uncles should be deputed to see that I did my homework.

I was given a double promotion from primary 1 to standard I, leap-frogging primary 2. At the end of standard V, after seven years of primary education – six in my case – we all sat an island-wide examination to vie for places in government secondary schools. In my final year, 1935,

I made the extra effort. I came first in school and won a place in Raffles Institution, which took in only the top students.

Raffles Institution was then, and still is, the premier English-language secondary school in Singapore and carries the name of its founder. It turned out small groups of well-educated and outstanding men, many of whom won the Queen's scholarship to go to Oxford, Cambridge, London, Edinburgh and other British institutions, to study medicine, law and engineering.

In 1936, I entered Raffles Institution together with about 150 top students from 15 government primary schools. Admission was on the basis of merit. Students were of all races, all classes and all religions, and included many from Malaya. The early headmasters were Englishmen who modelled the institution on the English public school.

The syllabus prepared students for the empire-wide examinations for Junior Cambridge and Senior Cambridge School Certificates. The textbooks, especially those for English language, English literature, history of the British Empire, mathematics and geography, were standard for all the colonies, adapted I suppose from those used in British schools. The teaching was entirely in English. Many years later, whenever I met Commonwealth leaders from far-flung islands in the Caribbean or the Pacific, I discovered that they also had gone through the same drill with the same textbooks and could quote the same passages from Shakespeare.

There were four grades in secondary school: standards VI and VII, Junior Cambridge and Senior Cambridge. I was not very hardworking, but I was good at mathematics and the sciences and had a solid grounding in the English language. At the end of standard VI, therefore, I was among the better students and promoted to standard VIIA, where I usually came in among the top three without much effort. I was still not very attentive in class, and tried to catch up by peeking into the notebook of the boy who sat next to me. Teo Kah Leong was not only top of the class, he kept beautiful notes of our lessons. But he would cover the pages with his hands. My form master, an Indian named M.N. Campos, nevertheless wrote on my report card these words of praise and encouragement: "Harry Lee Kuan Yew is a determined worker for a place of distinction. He is likely to attain a high position in life."

I went on to Junior A, the best class of the standard. The form master, an Englishman called A.T. Grieve, was a young Oxford graduate with a head of thick, sandy hair and a friendly and approachable manner. He was a bachelor in his late 20s, and doing his first stint overseas. Grieve had no colour prejudice, probably because he had not been in the colony long enough to learn he had to keep a certain distance from the locals, which was deemed necessary for British dominance to be upheld. He improved my English language enormously and I did well, coming in first in school in the Junior Cambridge examinations, my first major examination with papers set and marked in Cambridge. I also won two awards that year, the Raffles Institution and the Tan Jiak Kim scholarships. Together, they yielded the huge sum of 350 Straits dollars. It was enough to buy me a beautiful Raleigh bicycle for $70, with a three-speed gear and an encased chain box—I rode to school in style and still had money to spare. But even better was to come.

I had set my heart on distinguishing myself in the Senior Cambridge examinations, and I was happy when the results in early 1940 showed I had come first in school, and first among all the students in Singapore and Malaya.

I enjoyed my years in Raffles Institution. I coped with the work comfortably, was active in the Scout movement, played cricket and some tennis, swam and took part in many debates. But I never became a prefect, let alone head prefect. There was a mischievous, playful streak in me. Too often, I was caught not paying attention in class, scribbling notes to fellow students, or mimicking some teacher's strange mannerisms. In the case of a rather ponderous Indian science teacher, I was caught in the laboratory drawing the back of his head with its bald patch.

Once I was caned by the principal. D.W. McLeod was a fair but strict disciplinarian who enforced rules impartially, and one rule was that a boy who was late for school three times during one term would get three strokes of the cane. I was always a late riser, an owl more than a lark, and when I was late for school the third time in a term in 1938, the form master sent me to see McLeod. The principal knew me from the number of prizes I had been collecting on prize-giving days and the scholarships I had won. But I was not let off with an admonition. I bent over a chair and was given three of the best with my trousers on. I did not think he lightened his strokes. I have never understood why Western educationists are so much against corporal punishment. It did my fellow students and me no harm.

Nevertheless, I was learning to take life seriously. My parents had pointed out to me how some of their friends were doing well because they had become lawyers and doctors. They were self-employed, and therefore had not been hit by the Depression. My father regretted his misspent youth, and they urged me to become a professional. So from my early years I geared myself towards becoming a lawyer, a professional and not an employee. My plan was to read law in London.

But in 1940 the war in Europe was going badly. France was under severe threat, and about to be occupied. Going to London to study law was best postponed. Having come first in Singapore and Malaya in the Senior Cambridge examinations, I was offered the Anderson scholarship, the most valuable then available, to study at Raffles College. I decided to take it. It was worth $200 more than the other government awards and was enough to pay for fees, books and boarding, and leave something to spare.

∞

Raffles College was founded in 1928 by the Straits Settlements government. It taught the arts (English, history, geography, economics) and the sciences (physics, chemistry, pure and applied mathematics).

The government had designed handsome buildings for it, with quadrangles and cloisters constructed of concrete with mock stone facing, like those at Oxford and Cambridge but with concessions to the tropical climate.

As a scholarship student, I had to stay in one of the halls of residence. It was a difficult adjustment. To suit Singapore's hot, humid climate, the architects had designed big dormitories with high ceilings. Each was divided into 20 rooms with french windows leading to open verandas. Partitions between rooms were only seven feet high, slightly above head level, to allow air to circulate freely. This meant that noise also circulated freely above 20 rooms and around 20 verandas occupied by 20 youthful undergraduates.

Each student had to take three subjects. I read English, which was compulsory for all arts students, and concentrated on it to improve my command of the language, and to help me when I studied law later; mathematics, because I liked it and was good at it; and economics, because I believed it could teach me how to make money in business and on the stock market – I was naive! After the first year, a student had to choose one subject as his major field of study. I chose mathematics.

At the end of each of the three terms in the academic year there were examinations, and for the first of these I was the best student in mathematics, scoring over 90 marks. But to my horror, I discovered I was not the best in either English or economics. I was in second place, way behind a certain Miss Kwa Geok Choo. I had already met Miss Kwa at Raffles Institution. In 1939, as the only girl in a boys' school, she had been asked by the principal to present prizes on the annual prize-giving day, and I had collected three books from her. She had been in the special class preparing to try for the Queen's scholarship two years running. I was disturbed and upset. There were only two Queen's scholarships a year for the whole of the Straits Settlements (Singapore, Penang and Malacca), and they would not necessarily go to the two top-scoring students. Above all, I feared an even-handed geographical distribution designed to give a chance to entrants from Penang and Malacca. The scholarship board might not want to give both scholarships to Singapore students, in which case coming second might just not be good enough.

I did not enjoy my first year in Raffles College as much as my first year in Raffles Institution. Ragging or hazing was then part of the initiation of freshmen and went on for a whole term. Being the top student, my reputation had preceded me, and I suppose as I was also one of the taller and more conspicuous freshmen, some seniors picked on me.

I had to sing. I had to crawl around the quadrangle pushing a marble forward on the ground with my nose. I had to walk at the head of all the freshmen wearing a ragged green tie and carrying a silly green flag. I thought it all stupid, but went through with it as part of the price to be paid for joining an institution that lacked maturity and was developing the wrong traditions. When my turn came in the second year, I turned my face against ragging and tried to discourage it, but was not successful. I strongly disapproved of those who took it out on freshmen for what they had endured when they themselves were "freshies".

We had to attend lectures wearing coat and tie. The lecture rooms were not air-conditioned – indeed, one in the science block was an oven in the afternoons because it faced the setting sun. To be caught in a draught when I was sopping wet with sweat was a sure way for me to get coughs and colds. There was also the disorientation from having to live in strange surroundings, in close proximity with 19 other students in one block, and to eat unappetising institutional food.

After the first year I changed from "C" block to the better-sited "E" block where I was in a cooler and pleasanter room. But the disorientation must have affected my academic performance. I remember that in one term examination I did not come out top even in mathematics. Nevertheless, in the examinations at the end of the academic year (March 1941), I did creditably, and came in first in pure mathematics.

But Miss Kwa Geok Choo was the top student in English and economics, and probably in history too, her third subject. I scored a little better than she did in the statistics paper, which was part of economics. I knew I would face stiff competition for the Queen's scholarship.

There were other problems. It was only in retrospect that I realised Raffles College was my initiation into the politics of race and religion. In a British colony that made no distinction between the races, Singapore Malays were accustomed to being treated the same as others. But in June 1940, for the first time, I met significant numbers of Malays who had been born and brought up under a different system. In the Federated Malay States (FMS) of Perak, Selangor, Pahang and Negeri Sembilan, and even more so in the Unfederated Malay States (Johor, Kedah, Perlis, Kelantan and Terengganu), indigenous Malays were given special political and economic rights. In the FMS, there were only five scholarships to Raffles College open to non-Malays, whereas the Malays had a choice of more, as they did in the Unfederated Malay States. Of the hundred students admitted each year, 20 were Malays from upcountry on scholarships paid for by their state governments.

There was a strong sense of solidarity among the Malays, which I was to learn grew from a feeling of being threatened, a fear of being overwhelmed by the more energetic and hardworking Chinese and Indian immigrants. One Malay in my year was to become prime minister of Malaysia. Abdul Razak bin Hussain attended the same classes in English and economics as I did, but we were not close friends. He was a member of the Malay aristocracy of Pahang, and was therefore somewhat distant from the other Malay students, who looked up to him. Those I got on with more easily were commoners, two of whom played cricket for the college. Because I had many Malay friends from childhood, my spoken Malay was fluent. But I soon discovered that their attitude towards non-Malays, especially Chinese, was totally different from that of Singapore Malays.

One student from Kedah told me in my second year, after we had become friends, "You Chinese are too energetic and too clever for us. In Kedah, we have too many of you. We cannot stand the pressure." He meant the pressure of competition for jobs, for business, for places in schools and universities. The Malays were the owners of the land, yet seemed to be in danger of being displaced from top positions by recent arrivals, who were smarter, more competitive and more determined. Probably because they did better and were self-confident, the Chinese and the Indians lacked this sense of solidarity. There was no unity among them because they did not feel threatened.

One incident stands out in my memory. In my second year, there was much unhappiness over the arrangements for the annual Raffles College Students' Union dinner at the old Seaview Hotel. The non-Malays were incensed at the sharp and cavalier responses of the honorary secretary, Ungku Aziz bin Abdul Hamid, to their complaints. A few students started a move for an extraordinary general meeting to censure him and deprive him of office. But he was a Malay. As the collection of signatures for an EGM gathered momentum, the Malay students rallied round him, and made it clear that if he were removed, they would resign *en masse* from the union. This presented the non-Malays with a challenge. I was approached and asked to make the opening speech setting out their complaints against Ungku Aziz. I had not attended the dinner, and I had no personal quarrel with him. But since nobody wanted to take on this unpleasant job, I decided to do it. The meeting took place on a Saturday afternoon, and all the day students had left, probably because they wished to avoid the unpleasantness. Of those in halls of residence, the Malays turned up in force. The tension was high, and racial feelings strong.

It was my first experience of Malayism, a deep and intense pro-Malay, anti-immigrant sentiment. I made out the case in measured tones, firmly but, I hoped, not aggressively. Ungku Aziz spoke up to refute all the allegations of rude behaviour. I could sense that the crowd of some 80 students felt most uncomfortable about the confrontation. When the votes were cast, the Malays carried the day for Ungku Aziz, and the break-up never came. But the non-Malays felt they had registered their point. This incident faded from my memory. It was only later, between 1963 and 1965, when we were in Malaysia and ran into similar problems with Malayism, that I was to recall it.

But if it was a time of rivalry, it was also a time for forming lasting friendships. Many of those I first met in Raffles College were to become close political colleagues, among them Toh Chin Chye, a science student one year my senior, hardworking, systematic, quiet and consistent, and Goh Keng Swee, a tutor in economics with a first-class mind, a poor speaker but a crisp writer.

When I started my career as a lawyer in the 1950s, therefore, I already had a network of friends and acquaintances in important positions in government and the professions in Singapore and Malaya. Even if one did not know someone personally, just sharing the same background made for easy acceptance, and the old school tie worked well in Singapore and Malaya, even between Chinese, Indians and Malays. Before the days of active politics, when power was still completely in the hands of the British, I did not feel any personal animosity or resentment from the upcountry Malays. I made friends with many of them, including two Malay sessions judges before whom I later appeared.

It was the easy old-boy network of an elite at the very top of the English-educated group nurtured by the British colonial education system. We went through similar schools, read the same textbooks and shared certain common attitudes and characteristics. The British public school was not the only system that encouraged networking through manner of speech, style and dress and a way of doing things.

3. The Japanese Invaders

I was asleep in the "E" Block of Raffles College at 4 o'clock in the early morning of 8 December 1941, when I was awakened by the dull thud of exploding bombs. The war with Japan had begun. It was a complete surprise. The street lights had been on, and the air-raid sirens did not sound until those Japanese planes dropped their bombs, killing 60 people and wounding 130. But the raid was played down. Censors suppressed the news that the Keppel Harbour docks, the naval base at Sembawang, and the Tengah and Seletar air bases had also been attacked.

The students at Raffles College were agog with excitement. Those from upcountry immediately prepared to leave by train for home. Nearly everyone believed Singapore would be the main target of the attack, and it would therefore be prudent to return to the countryside of Malaya, which offered more safety from Japanese bombers. The college authorities were as confused as the students. Nobody had been prepared for this. Two days later we heard that on the same morning the Japanese had landed at Kota Bharu in Kelantan. Malaya was not to be spared after all.

Within days, the hostels were nearly empty. Lectures were suspended, and students asked to volunteer for a Raffles College unit of the Medical Auxiliary Services (MAS). I volunteered for the MAS, and cycled daily from my home (in Norfolk Road since 1935) to my post in the college three miles away. We were not provided with uniforms – there was no time for that – but we were each given a tin helmet and an armband with a red cross on it and paid a small allowance of about $60 a month, for which we worked on a roster round the clock. We were organised into units of six. There was no fear. Indeed there was barely suppressed excitement, the thrill of being at war and involved in real battles.

But the war did not go well. Soon stories came down from Malaya of the rout on the war front, the ease with which the Japanese were cutting through British lines and cycling through rubber estates down the peninsula, landing behind enemy lines by boat and *sampan*, forcing more retreats. Large numbers of white families – planters and civilians with their wives and children – began arriving from across the Causeway. There must have been important Asiatic families too, but they did not stand out. They would have moved into the homes of friends and relatives, or quietly sailed out of Singapore from the Tanjong Pagar wharves, fearing revenge from the Japanese for having helped the British, or for having contributed to the South China Relief Fund supporting Chiang Kai-shek's resistance to the Japanese on the Chinese mainland.

By January the Japanese forces were nearing Johor, and their planes started to bomb Singapore in earnest, day and night. I picked up my first casualties one afternoon at a village in Bukit Timah. Several MAS units went there in Singapore Traction Company buses converted into ambulances. A bomb had fallen near the police station and there were several victims. It was a frightening sight, my first experience of the bleeding, the injured, and the dead.

At about 8 am on 31 January, Maurice Baker, a fellow student from Pahang, and I were sitting on the parapet of the Administrative Block at Raffles College, on standby MAS duty, when suddenly there was an earthshaking explosion. We were both stunned, and I said spontaneously, "That's the end of the British Empire!" Professor Dyer, the principal of Raffles College who was just passing by on his way to his office, heard me, looked away, and walked on.

That same morning all British forces withdrew to the island from Johor. Next day, the papers carried photos of the Argyll and Sutherland Highlanders, the last to march across the Causeway, to the sound of "Highland Laddie" played on their bagpipes, although there were only two pipers remaining. It left me with a life-long impression of British coolness in the face of impending defeat. The Royal Engineers then blew open a gap in the Causeway on the Johor side. That was the explosion Maurice and I had heard. But they also blew up the pipeline carrying water from Johor to the island. The siege of Singapore had begun.

As I cycled home one morning, still wearing my tin helmet and armband, I passed a line of military lorries parked in Stevens Road. Standing beside them were some tall, very dejected-looking Australian soldiers wearing broad-brimmed Aussie hats. They looked frightened and demoralised. I stopped to ask them how close the front was. One soldier said, "It's over; here, take this," and offered me his weapons. I was startled and shaken. Could it be this hopeless? I refused the weapons and tried to comfort him by saying that no battle was lost until it was over. But for that Australian group, the battle was lost. I did not know what horrifying experiences they must have had.

After the war I read that several battalions of Australian troops were sailing to the Middle East when their ships were diverted to Singapore. They arrived just three weeks before the fall of the island, were sent upcountry and quickly beaten back. They had expected to do battle in the deserts of North Africa, probably in Libya against Rommel's forces. Suddenly they found themselves in tropical jungle, facing the Japanese. It was a tragedy for them, and a disaster for the morale of the British and Indian troops they were supposed to help.

Meanwhile, my father, who was working as superintendent of the Shell depot in Batu Pahat, some 100 miles to the north on the west coast of Malaya, had been told to evacuate it. He had returned to the island in his baby Austin before the Causeway was blown up. We still hoped that Fortress Singapore would hold. I believed there would be many casualties, but that the British would dig in and eventually we would be rescued. But every passing day – indeed, every passing hour after the first week of February – I felt more and more in the pit of my stomach that Singapore was not Malta, and it could not support a long siege.

In the middle of January, the schools were closed. As the shelling got nearer to the city, my mother proposed that the whole family move to her father's house, which was further out and so less likely to be hit. I supported the move but told her I would stay and look after the house in Norfolk Road while continuing to report for duty at the Raffles College MAS station. I would not be alone as Koh Teong Koo, our gardener, would stay at Norfolk Road to guard the house while I was on duty at the college. He was also the rickshaw puller who had taken my brothers and sister to and from school every day since 1937. We had built an air-raid shelter, a wooden structure dug into the ground and covered with earth, which my mother had stocked up with rice, salt, pepper, soya bean sauces, salt fish, tinned foods, condensed milk and all the things we might need for a long time. Money was not a problem because the Shell Company had generously paid my father several months' salary when he was ordered to evacuate the oil depot at Batu Pahat.

Amid these darkening horizons I went to the cinema several times when off duty. It helped me to escape the grim future for a couple of hours. One afternoon in late January, I sat through a comedy at Cathay cinema. In one scene a bomb that was supposed to explode fell apart with a small *plop*. It was a dud. As the casing broke open, a sign was revealed – "Made in Japan". It was bizarre. For the past two months Singapore had experienced the devastating power of their bombs and their shells, yet here I was watching this film making fun of the Japanese – they were supposed to be bow-legged, cross-eyed, incapable of shooting straight or building ships that would stay afloat in a storm, able to make only dud weapons. The unhappy truth was that in the two months since 8 December they had proved they had the daring, the power and the military skills to stage the most spectacular successes against British forces. Many years later, Winston Churchill, the war-time British prime minister, was to write of the fall of Singapore, "it was the worst disaster and largest capitulation in British history".

The military took over the entire college on 10 February as British forces withdrew, and two days later the MAS unit had to disband. At first I stayed at home in Norfolk Road, but as the shelling got closer I joined my family at Telok Kurau. The following day we heard distant rifle shots, then some more, closer to us. There had been no sound of big guns, shells or bombs. Curious, I went out by the back gate to Lorong L, the lane abutting the kampong where I used to play with my friends, the fishermen's children. Before I had walked more than 20 yards along the earth track, I saw two figures in dun-coloured uniforms, different from the greens and browns of the British forces. They wore puttees and rubber-soled canvas boots, split-toed, with the big toe in a separate section from the other toes. Later I learnt that it gave them a better grip on soggy or slippery ground. Above all, what made them look strange were their soft, peaked caps, with cloth flaps at the back hanging over their necks. They were outlandish figures, small, squat men carrying long rifles with long bayonets. They exuded an awful stink, a smell I will never forget. It was the odour from the great unwashed after two months of fighting along jungle tracks and estate roads from Kota Bharu to Singapore.

A few seconds passed before I realised who they were. Japanese! An immense fear crept over me. But they were looking for enemy soldiers. Clearly I was not one, so they ignored me and pressed on. I dashed back to the house and told my family what I had seen. We closed all the doors and windows, though God knows what protection that could have given us. Rape and rapine were high among the fears that the Japanese forces inspired after their atrocities in China since 1937. But nothing of note happened the rest of that day and night. The British forces were retreating rapidly to the city centre and not putting up much of a fight.

The following day, 15 February, was the Lunar New Year, the biggest annual festival of the Chinese, normally celebrated with new clothes, new shoes and an abundance of traditional dishes and cakes. It was the grimmest New Year since the Chinese came to Singapore in 1819. There were sounds of battle in the north and near the city, and relatively distant explosions of artillery and mortars, but nothing in the Telok Kurau area itself. The Japanese had swept on towards the town.

That night the guns fell silent. The news soon spread that the British had surrendered. The next day, some friends returning from the city reported that looting had broken out. British and other European houses were being stripped by their Malay drivers and gardeners. This aroused great anxiety in my family. What about 28 Norfolk Road, with all our food and other provisions that would now have to see us through for a very long time? With my mother's agreement, I took Teong Koo, the gardener, with me and walked back some eight miles from Telok Kurau to Norfolk Road. We made it in just over two hours. I saw Malays carrying furniture and other items out of the bigger houses along the way. The Chinese looters went for the goods in warehouses, less bulky and more valuable. A dilapidated bungalow some two houses from ours was occupied by about 20 Boyanese families. Their menfolk were drivers. But they had not yet gone for our place. There were better pickings in the bigger houses, now empty of the Europeans who were assembling for internment. I had got back in time.

In the two hours that I walked from Telok Kurau to Norfolk Road, I saw a Singapore with law and order in suspended animation. The British army had surrendered. The local police – Chinese and Indian junior officers and Malay rank and file – had disappeared, fearing that the Japanese would treat them as part of the British military set-up. The Japanese soldiers had not yet imposed their presence on the city. Each man was a law unto himself.

Out of habit, most people remained law-abiding. But with the bosses gone, the bolder ones seized the opportunity to loot godowns, department stores and shops belonging to British companies for what they saw as legitimate booty. This lasted for several days before the Japanese restored order; they put the fear of God into people by shooting or beheading a few looters at random and exhibiting their heads on key bridges and at main road junctions.

The Japanese conquerors also went for loot. In the first few days, anyone in the street with a fountain pen or a wristwatch would soon be relieved of it. Soldiers would go into houses either officially to search, or pretending to do so, but in fact to appropriate any small items that they could keep on their person. At first they also took the best of the bicycles, but they stopped that after a few weeks. They were in Singapore for only a short time before leaving for Java or some other island in the archipelago to do battle and to capture more territories. They could not take their beautiful bicycles with them.

The looting of the big houses and warehouses of our British masters symbolised the end of an era. It is difficult for those born after 1945 to appreciate the full implications of the British defeat, as they have no memory of the colonial system that the Japanese brought crashing down on 15 February 1942. Since 1819, when Raffles founded Singapore as a trading post for the East India Company, the white man's supremacy had been unquestioned. I did not know how this had come to pass, but by the time I went to school in 1930, I was aware that the Englishman was the big boss, and those who were white like him were also bosses – some big, others not so big, but all bosses. There were not many of them, about eight thousand. They had superior lifestyles and lived separately from the Asiatics, as we were then called. Government officers had larger houses in better districts, cars with drivers and many other servants. They ate superior food with plenty of meat and milk products. Every three years they went "home" to England for three to six months at a time to recuperate from the enervating climate of equatorial Singapore. Their children also went "home" to be educated, not to Singapore schools. They, too, led superior lives.

At Raffles College, the teaching staff were all white. Two of the best local graduates with class one diplomas for physics and chemistry were appointed "demonstrators", but at much lower salaries, and they had to get London external BSc degrees to gain this status. One of the best arts graduates of his time with a class one diploma for economics, Goh Keng Swee (later to be deputy prime minister), was a tutor, not a lecturer.

There was no question of any resentment. The superior status of the British in government and society was simply a fact of life. After all, they were the greatest people in the world. They had the biggest empire that history had ever known, stretching over all time zones, across all four oceans and five continents. We learnt that in history lessons at school. To enforce their rule, they had only a few hundred troops in Singapore, who were regularly rotated. The most visible were stationed near the city centre at Fort Canning. There could not have been more than one to two thousand servicemen in all to maintain colonial rule over the six to seven million Asiatics in the Straits Settlements and the Malay states.

The British put it out that they were needed in Malaya to protect the Malays, who would otherwise be eclipsed by the more hardworking immigrants. Many of the Chinese and Indians had been brought in as indentured labour and were tolerated because the Malays did not take to the jobs a commercial and a plantation economy required, like tapping rubber, building roads and bridges, working as clerks, accountants and storekeepers.

A small number of prominent Asiatics were allowed to mix socially with the white bosses, and some were appointed unofficial members of the governor's Executive Council or the Legislative Council. Photographs of them with their wives appeared in the papers, attending garden parties and sometimes dinners at Government House, bowing and curtseying before the governor and his lady, the women duly wearing white gloves, and all on their best behaviour. A few were knighted, and others hoped that after giving long and faithful service they, too, would be honoured. They were patronised by the white officials, but accepted their inferior status with aplomb, for they considered themselves superior to their fellow Asiatics. Conversely, any British, European or American who misbehaved or looked like a tramp was immediately packed off because he would demean the whole white race, whose superiority must never be thrown into doubt.

I was brought up by my parents and grandparents to accept that this was the natural order of things. I do not remember any local who by word or deed questioned all this. None of the English-educated had any inclination to take up the cudgels on behalf of equality for the Asiatics. I did not then know that there were many Chinese, educated in Chinese-language schools, who were not integrated into the colonial system. Their teachers had come from China, and they did not recognise the supremacy of the whites, for they had not been educated or indoctrinated into accepting the virtues and the mission of the British Empire. After the war I was to learn more about them.

This was the Malaya and Singapore that 110,000 attacking Japanese soldiers captured, together with more than 130,000 British, Indian and Australian troops. In 70 days of surprises, upsets and stupidities, British colonial society was shattered, and with it all the assumptions of the Englishman's superiority. The Asiatics were supposed to panic when the firing started, yet they were the stoical ones who took the casualties and died without hysteria. It was the white civilian bosses who ducked under tables when the bombs and shells fell. It was the white civilians and government officers in Penang who, on 16 December 1941, in the quiet of the night, fled the island for the "safety" of Singapore, abandoning the Asiatics to their fate. British troops demolished whatever installations they could and then retreated. Hospitals, public utilities and other essential services were left unmanned. There were no firemen to fight fires and no officers to regulate the water supply. The whites in charge had gone. Stories of their scramble to save their skins led the Asiatics to see them as selfish and cowardly. Many of them were undoubtedly exaggerated in the retelling and unfair, but there was enough substance in them to make the point. The whites had proved as frightened and at a loss as to what to do as the Asiatics, if not more so. The Asiatics had looked to them for leadership, and they had failed them.

The British built up the myth of their inherent superiority so convincingly that most Asiatics thought it hopeless to challenge them. But now one Asiatic race had dared to defy them and smashed that myth. However, once the Japanese lorded over us as conquerors, they soon demonstrated to their fellow Asiatics that they were more cruel, more brutal, more unjust and more vicious than the British. During the three and a half years of the occupation, whenever I encountered some Japanese tormenting, beating or ill-treating one of our people, I wished the British were still in charge. As fellow Asiatics, we were filled with disillusionment, but then the Japanese themselves were ashamed to be identified with their fellow Asiatics, whom they considered racially inferior and of a lower order of civilisation. They were descendants of the sun goddess, Amaterasu Omikami Sama, a chosen people, distinct and separate from the benighted Chinese, Indians and Malays.

My first encounter with a Japanese soldier took place when I tried to visit an aunt, my mother's younger sister, in Kampong Java Road, just across the Red Bridge over the Bukit Timah canal. As I approached the bridge, I saw a sentry pacing up and down it. Nearby was a group of four or five Japanese soldiers sitting around, probably the other members of his detail. I was sporting a broad-brimmed hat of the kind worn by Australian soldiers, many of which had been discarded in the days before the surrender. I had picked one up, thinking it would be useful during the hard times ahead to protect me from the sun.

As I passed this group of soldiers, I tried to look as inconspicuous as possible. But they were not to be denied attention. One soldier barked *"Kore, kore!"* and beckoned to me. When I reached him, he thrust the bayonet on his rifle through the brim of my hat, knocking it off, slapped me roundly, and motioned me to kneel. He then shoved his right boot against my chest and sent me sprawling on the road. As I got up, he signalled that I was to go back the way I had come. I had got off lightly. Many others who did not know the new rules of etiquette and did not bow to Japanese sentries at crossroads or bridges were made to kneel for hours in the sun, holding a heavy boulder over their heads until their arms gave way.

One afternoon, sitting on the veranda at 28 Norfolk Road, I watched a Japanese soldier pay off a rickshaw puller. The rickshaw puller remonstrated, pleading for a little more money. The soldier took the man's arm, put it over his right shoulder, and flung him up into the air with a judo throw. The rickshaw puller fell flat on his face. After a while, he picked himself up and staggered off between the shafts of his rickshaw. I was shocked at the heartlessness.

The next day, I was to learn another lesson at the Red Bridge. A newly captured car drove past displaying a small rectangular blue flag, the lowest of three ranks – yellow flags were for generals, red flags for majors to colonels, and blue flags for lieutenants to captains. The sentry was slow in coming to attention to salute. The car had gone past, but its driver braked and reversed. An officer got out, walked up to the sentry and gave him three hefty slaps. Taking his right arm, he put it over his shoulder and, with the same judo throw I had seen used on the rickshaw puller, flung the soldier in the air. The sentry fell flat on his face, just as the rickshaw puller had done. This time I was less shocked. I had begun to understand that brutalisation was part of the Japanese military system, inculcated through regular beatings for minor infringements.

Later that same day a Japanese non-commissioned officer and several soldiers came into the house. They looked it over and, finding only Teong Koo and me, decided it would be a suitable billet for a platoon. It was the beginning of a nightmare. I had been treated by Japanese dentists and their nurses at Bras Basah Road who were immaculately clean and tidy. So, too, were the Japanese salesmen and saleswomen at the 10-cent stores in Middle Road. I was unprepared for the nauseating stench of the unwashed clothes and bodies of these Japanese soldiers. They roamed all over the house and the compound. They looked for food, found the provisions my mother had stored, and consumed whatever they fancied, cooking in the compound over open fires. I had no language in which to communicate with them. They made their wishes known with signs and guttural noises. When I was slow in understanding what they wanted, I was cursed and frequently slapped. They were strange beings, unshaven and unkempt, speaking an ugly, aggressive language. They filled me with fear, and I slept fitfully. They left after three days of hell.

While this platoon was camping in the house, British, Indian and Australian forces were marched to captivity. The march started on 17 February 1942, and for two days and one night they tramped past the house and over the Red Bridge on their way to Changi. I sat on my veranda for hours at a time watching these men, my heart heavy as lead. Many looked dejected and despondent, perplexed that they had been beaten so decisively and so easily. The surrendered army was a mournful sight.

There were some who won my respect and admiration. Among them were the Highlanders whom I recognised by their Scottish caps. Even in defeat they held themselves erect and marched in time – "Left Right, Left Right, Left, Left!" shouted the sergeant major. And the Gurkhas were like the Highlanders. They too marched erect, unbroken and doughty in defeat. I secretly cheered them. They left a life-long impression on me. As a result, the Singapore government has employed a Gurkha company for its anti-riot police squad from the 1960s to this day.

The Australians were dispirited, not marching in step. The Indian troops, too, looked dejected and demoralised. They must have felt it was not their fight.

∞

Soon after the Japanese soldiers left my house, word went around that all Chinese had to go to a registration centre at the Jalan Besar stadium for examination. I saw my neighbour and his family leave and decided it would be wiser for me to go also, for if I were later caught at home the Japanese military police, the *Kempeitai*, would punish me. So I headed for Jalan Besar with Teong Koo. As it turned out, his cubicle in his *coolie-keng*, the dormitory he shared with other rickshaw pullers, was within the perimeter enclosed by barbed wire. Tens of thousands of Chinese families were packed into this small area. All exit points were manned by the *Kempeitai*. There were several civilians with them, locals or Taiwanese. I was told later that many of them were hooded, though I do not remember noticing any.

After spending a night in Teong Koo's cubicle, I decided to check out through the exit point, but instead of allowing me to pass, the soldier on duty signalled me to join a group of young Chinese. I felt instinctively that this was ominous, so I asked for permission to return to the cubicle to collect my belongings. He gave it. I went back and lay low in Teong Koo's cubicle for another day and a half. Then I tried the same exit again. This time, for some inexplicable reason, I got through the checkpoint. I was given a "chop" on my left upper arm and on the front of my shirt with a rubber stamp. The *kanji* or Chinese character *jian*, meaning "examined", printed on me in indelible ink, was proof that I was cleared. I walked home with Teong Koo, greatly relieved.

I will never understand how decisions affecting life and death could be taken so capriciously and casually. I had had a narrow escape from an exercise called *Sook Ching*, meaning to "wipe out" rebels, ordered by Colonel Masanobu Tsuji, the staff officer who planned the Malayan campaign. He had obtained the agreement of General Tomoyuki Yamashita, the commander of the Japanese forces, to punish the Chinese in Singapore for collecting funds to support China's war effort against the Japanese, and for their boycott of Japanese goods.

He had another account to settle – with Dalforce, which was part of the 1,000-strong Overseas Chinese volunteer corps organised by local community leaders in Singapore to resist the Japanese. Put together by Colonel John Dalley of the Malayan Special Branch, it brought together Chinese from all walks of life, supporters of Chiang Kai-shek's nationalist Kuomintang (KMT) and of the Malayan Communist Party (MCP), including notably some 500 communists freed from prison by the British at the eleventh hour. Once armed, the volunteers were sent to hold the ground east of Kranji River on the flank of the 27th Australian Brigade. They fought ferociously. Many died, but so did many Japanese. They made Dalforce a legend, a name synonymous with bravery.

On 18 February, the Japanese put up notices and sent soldiers with loudspeakers around the town to inform the Chinese that all men between the ages of 18 and 50 were to present themselves at five collection areas for inspection. The much-feared *Kempeitai* went from house to house to drive Chinese who had not done so at bayonet point to these con-centration centres, into which women, children and old men were also herded.

I discovered later that those picked out at random at the checkpoint I had passed were taken to the grounds of Victoria School and detained until 22 February, when 40 to 50 lorries arrived to collect them. Their hands were tied behind their backs and they were transported to a beach at Tanah Merah Besar, some 10 miles away on the east coast, near Changi Prison. There they were made to disembark, tied together, and forced to walk towards the sea. As they did so, Japanese machine-gunners massacred them. Later, to make sure they were dead, each corpse was kicked, bayoneted and abused in other ways. There was no attempt to bury the bodies, which decomposed as they were washed up and down the shore. A few survivors miraculously escaped to give this grim account.

The Japanese admitted killing 6,000 young Chinese in that *Sook Ching* of 18–22 February 1942. After the war, a committee of the Chinese

Chamber of Commerce exhumed many mass graves in Siglap, Punggol and Changi. It estimated the number massacred to be between 50,000 and 100,000.

In theory, the Imperial Army could justify this action as an operation to restore law and order and to suppress anti-Japanese resistance. But it was sheer vengeance, exacted not in the heat of battle but when Singapore had already surrendered. Even after this *Sook Ching*, there were mopping-up operations in the rural areas, especially in the eastern part of Singapore, and hundreds more Chinese were executed. All of them were young and sturdy men who could prove troublesome.

When I returned to Norfolk Road, I found the house in the mess that the Japanese soldiers had left it, but it had not been looted and some of our provisions remained. A few days later, my family came back from Telok Kurau. Together, we cleaned up the house. Slowly, we got to know the uncertainty, the daily grind and the misery of the Japanese occupation that was to be the lot of the people of Singapore for the next three and a half years.

Within two weeks of the surrender, I heard that the Japanese had put up wooden fencing around the town houses at Cairnhill Road, which had been vacated by the European and Asiatic businessmen and their families who had left Singapore or been interned. It had been an upper middle-class area. I cycled past and saw long queues of Japanese soldiers snaking along Cairnhill Circle outside the fence. I heard from nearby residents that inside there were Japanese and Korean women who followed the army to service the soldiers before and after battle. It was an amazing sight, one or two hundred men queuing up, waiting their turn. I did not see any women that day. But there was a notice board with Chinese characters on it, which neighbours said referred to a "comfort house". Such comfort houses had been set up in China. Now they had come to Singapore. There were at least four others. I remember cycling past a big one in Tanjong Katong Road, where a wooden fence had been put up enclosing some 20 to 30 houses.

I thought then that the Japanese army had a practical and realistic approach to such problems, totally different from that of the British army. I remembered the prostitutes along Waterloo Street soliciting British soldiers stationed at Fort Canning. The Japanese high command recognised the sexual needs of the men and provided for them. As a consequence, rape was not frequent. In the first two weeks of the conquest, the people of Singapore had feared that the Japanese army would go on a wild spree. Although rape did occur, it was mostly in the rural areas, and there was nothing like what had happened in Nanking in 1937. I thought these comfort houses were the explanation. I did not then know that the Japanese government had kidnapped and coerced Korean, Chinese and Filipino women to cater to the needs of the Japanese troops at the war front in China and Southeast Asia. They also made some Dutch women serve Japanese officers.

Those of my generation who saw the Japanese soldiers in the flesh cannot forget their almost inhuman attitude to death in battle. They were not afraid to die. They made fearsome enemies and needed so little to keep going – the tin containers on their belts carried only rice, some soya beans and salt fish. Throughout the occupation, a common sight was of Japanese soldiers at bayonet practice on open fields. Their war cries as they stabbed their gunny-sack dummies were bloodcurdling. Had the British re-invaded and fought their way down Malaya into Singapore, there would have been immense devastation.

After seeing them at close quarters, I was sure that for sheer fighting spirit, they were among the world's finest. But they also showed a meanness and viciousness towards their enemies equal to the Huns'. Genghis Khan and his hordes could not have been more merciless. I have no doubts about whether the two atom bombs dropped on Hiroshima and Nagasaki were necessary. Without them, hundreds of thousands of civilians in Malaya and Singapore, and millions in Japan itself, would have perished.

What made them such warriors? The Japanese call it *bushido*, the code of the samurai, or *Nippon seishin*, the spirit of Nippon. I believe it was systematic indoctrination in the cult of emperor worship, and in their racial superiority as a chosen people who could conquer all. They were convinced that to die in battle for the emperor meant they would ascend to heaven and become gods, while their ashes were preserved at the Yasukuni Shrine in the suburbs of Tokyo.

∞

Day-to-day life had to go on under the Japanese occupation. At first everybody felt lost. My father had no work, I had no college, my three brothers and sister had no school. There was little social activity. We felt danger all around us. Knowing somebody in authority, whether a Japanese or a Taiwanese interpreter with links to the Japanese, was very important and could be a life-saver. His note with his signature and seal on it certified that you were a decent citizen and that he vouched for your good character. This was supposed to be valuable when you were stopped and checked by sentries. But it was safest to stay at home and avoid contact and conflict with authority.

One of my first outings was into town. I walked two miles to the second-hand bookshops in Bras Basah Road that specialised in school textbooks. On the way, I saw a crowd near the main entrance to Cathay cinema, where I had earlier watched the comedy ridiculing the Japanese-made bomb. Joining the crowd, I saw the head of a Chinese man placed on a small board stuck on a pole, on the side of which was a notice in Chinese characters. I could not read Chinese, but someone who could said it explained what one should not do in order not to come to that same end. The man had been beheaded because he had been caught looting, and anybody who disobeyed the law would be dealt with in the same way. I left with a feeling of dread of the Japanese, but at the same time I thought what a marvellous photograph this would make for *Life* magazine. The American weekly would pay handsomely for such a vivid picture of the contrast: Singapore's most modern building with this spectacle of medieval punishment in front of it. But then the photographer might well end up in the same situation as the beheaded looter.

I chanced upon this gory exhibition on my way to Bras Basah Road because I had decided to learn Chinese in order to be literate enough to understand such notices. My English was of no value under the new rulers. Learning Chinese would be better than learning Japanese; at least it was my own language, not that of a hated conqueror. I bought Chiang Ker Chiu's *Mandarin Made Easy*, a thin booklet of some 30 pages that taught a basic 700 Chinese characters, how they were written, and how they were used in combination with each other.

I devoured this in a couple of weeks and went back for the advanced Book Two. Later, I bought a series of four books published by the Prinsep Street Chinese School that reached a higher standard. Working on them every day, I spent the next few months practising to write between 1,200 and 1,500 characters and trying to commit their meanings to memory. But I never learnt how they were pronounced. In Mandarin, each sound has one of four tones. My books did indicate them, but I did not know how to produce them and I had no one to teach me.

In the face of these difficulties, my resistance to the Japanese language lessened over the months. I discovered that it was not made up of Chinese characters alone. It had a syllabary system, written in two scripts: *katakana* and *hiragana*. If the Japanese were to be in Singapore as my lords and masters for the next few years, and I had not only to avoid trouble but make a living, I would have to learn their language. So in May 1942 I registered with the first batch of students at the Japanese language school the authorities had opened in Queen Street.

It was a three-month course. The students were of varying ages and abilities, some from secondary schools, some like me from college, and others young workers in their 20s. I passed and got my certificate. I found Japanese much easier than Mandarin because it was not tonal, but more complicated in its inflexions and grammar.

∞

My grandfather, Lee Hoon Leong, had fallen gravely ill in July, and three weeks after I graduated he died. Before the end I visited him many times at Bras Basah Road, where he stayed with his adopted daughter. I felt very sad for him. It was not just that he was sick, but that he had lived to see his world crash: the British and all they had stood for had been humiliated and defeated. The British navy, the British ships' captains, their discipline, their excellence, their supremacy at sea – these had all been demolished by the strange-looking Japanese. He could not understand how such a slovenly people could defeat straight-backed British officers. How could they have sunk the *Prince of Wales* and the *Repulse*, scattered the British fleet, shot down the Royal Air Force, and captured 130,000 troops with only 110,000 of their own after laying siege to Singapore for only two weeks? As I watched him sinking into a coma, I thought it would have been kinder if he had died before it all happened.

His useful pre-war connections in British colonial Singapore had gone, but he did have one Japanese friend, a Mr Shimoda, whom my father looked up a few days after Kung died. The difficulties of the occupation had sobered my father. He became more responsible in hard times. He had a job with the military department in charge of oil supplies, and also got me my first job. At his request and out of regard for my grandfather, Shimoda offered me work in the new world in which the Japanese were now the masters.

I worked in his company as a clerk for a year, copying documents for internal office use and correspondence with other Japanese companies.

When Shimoda & Co folded up, I moved to the opposite side of Raffles Place where I got another job as a clerk-typist, in the *kumiai* or guild that controlled essential foods – rice, oil, sugar, salt – and tobacco and cigarettes. My salary was paid in currency issued by the Japanese military, bills with pictures of coconut and banana trees on them. These "banana notes", as they were called, had no serial numbers, and were worth less and less every month. The value of my new job lay rather in the payment in kind that went with it – some 10 katis (about 15 pounds) of rice, sugar, oil and, most tradeable of all, cigarettes. These rations were better than Japanese money, for as the months went by they would get scarcer and cost more and more in banana notes.

I worked in the *kumiai* for about eight months, until late in 1943 when I read an advertisement in the *Syonan Shimbun* inserted by the Japanese information or propaganda department called the *Hodobu*, which was located in Cathay Building. It wanted English-language editors. I turned up to be interviewed by an American-born Japanese, George Takemura, a tall, lean, fair-skinned man who spoke English with an American accent and was called Ji-oh-ji by his fellow Japanese. He did not wear the uniform of a Japanese army officer, but of a civilian in the military administration with five blue stars – the equivalent of a captain. He was soft-spoken, and turned out to be a decent man. He was satisfied with my English, and I was relieved to have found a place where it was wanted.

My job was to run through the cables of allied news agencies: Reuters, UP, AP, Central News Agency of China, and TASS. These cables, sent out in morse code, had been intercepted by Malay radio operators. Radio signals were not clear in the late afternoons and early evenings, and because reception was poor, many words were garbled or lost. I had to decipher them and fill in the missing bits, guided by the context, as in a word puzzle. The cables then had to be collated under the various battle fronts and sent from the top floor of Cathay Building to the floor below, where they would be revamped for broadcasting. I worked there for about 15 months until the end of 1944.

It was a strange life. My work would begin at 7 pm Tokyo time, which was 5:30 pm Singapore time and still daylight. Radio reception was poor until about midnight Tokyo time. So the first shift from 7 pm to 12 am was hard work, but one got home early to sleep. The period 12 am to 9 am was broken into two shifts, with a two- to three-hour break in between. Reception was better, and there was less puzzling over missing words or parts of words, but it meant sleeping at awkward hours.

There were two editors on duty at any one time. George Takemura, usually wearing his uniform without the jacket because of the warm and humid weather, would drop in several times in an evening, giving the other editor and me a packet of Japanese cigarettes from his rations. I had to stay awake, snatch some sleep from 4 to 6 am by arrangement with my fellow editor, then work until 9 am, when conditions again deteriorated. Radio reception became hopeless in bright sunshine, so the operators also packed up for the day. I would walk the one and a half miles from Cathay Building to Norfolk Road for brunch, then go off to bed in broad daylight for a few more hours of sleep.

Stranger than its schedule were the psychological implications of the work. For hours my head would be filled with news of a war that was going badly for the Japanese, as for the Germans and Italians. But we talked about this to outsiders at our peril. On the ground floor of Cathay Building was a branch of the *Kempeitai*. Every employee who worked in the *Hodobu* had a file. The *Kempeitai's* job was to make sure that nobody leaked anything.

From the end of 1943, food became scarcer and scarcer. The Japanese navy had suffered defeats with heavy losses at the battles of Midway and Coral Sea. They had lost control of the oceans and their ships were being sunk by Allied submarines. Even Thailand, a traditional rice exporter, could not get its rice to Singapore, either because the Japanese did not want to pay the Thais for it or because they could not transport it to the island.

Reduced to eating old, mouldy, worm-eaten stocks mixed with Malayan-grown rice, we had to find substitutes. My mother, like many others, stretched what little we could get with maize and millet and strange vegetables we would not normally have touched, like young shoots of sweet potato and tapioca plants cooked in coconut milk. They could be quite palatable, but they had bulk without much nutrition. It was amazing how hungry my brothers and I became one hour after each meal. Meat was a luxury. There was little beef or mutton. Pork was easier to buy and we could raise chickens ourselves, but there were no leftovers to feed them.

My mother's resourcefulness was sorely tested during the occupation. When the combined salaries of my father, my brother Dennis and myself became negligible because of inflation, she started all manner of businesses. As a daughter in a Straits Chinese family, she had learnt how to cook and bake. Now she made cakes for sale. Wheat flour and butter were soon unobtainable, so she used tapioca flour, rice flour, sago flour, coconut milk and palm sugar. She also made sweetened condensed milk from fresh milk. She was a good cook. Later, when I was prime minister, she filled in her time teaching Straits Chinese cooking to expatriate wives, including wives of the diplomatic corps. She wrote *Mrs Lee's Cookbook*, which sold well even after she died.

Everything was in short supply. Motorcars had disappeared, except for those used by the military and important Japanese civilians. The few local people who had their own cars could not get petrol for them. Taxis were converted to run on charcoal and firewood. Stocks of bicycle tyres and tubes soon ran out. Local manufacturers could only produce solid bicycle tyres, which made for bumpy going, but that was better than riding on steel rims. Textiles were scarce, so we converted curtain fabrics and tablecloth into trousers and shirts. All imported goods had become precious. Liquor kept well and was much sought after by wealthy black marketeers and Japanese officers.

Meanwhile, inflation had been increasing month by month, and by mid-1944 it was no longer possible to live on my salary. But there was a solution to this. Although I received the usual rations of rice, oil, other foodstuff and cigarettes, there were better and easier pickings to be had as a broker on the black market. There was a lively trade in ever-diminishing supplies of British medicines, pre-war stocks that had been hoarded, the most valuable of which was Sulphonamide Pyridine M&B (May and Baker) 693. Other profitable commodities were spirits like Johnnie Walker whisky and Hennessy brandy, British cigarettes in hermetically sealed tins of 50, jewellery, landed property and Straits Settlements currency.

The brokers operated mainly in High Street or Chulia Street, off Raffles Place. I joined them in 1944, and learnt how to hoard items, especially small pieces of jewellery going cheap. I would buy them, hold them for a few weeks, and then sell them as prices inevitably went up. It was easy to make money if one had the right connections. At one end were those among the old middle class who were parting with family heirlooms in order to stay alive. My mother knew many women from previously wealthy families who needed to sell their jewellery and properties in a Singapore that was running short of food. Brokers like me would sell them to people at the other end who wanted to sell them to Japanese civilians anxious to convert their banana notes into something of more lasting value, or give them to Japanese military officers who handed out contracts.

∽

The key to survival was improvisation. One business I started changed the course of my life. While brokering on the black market, I met Yong Nyuk Lin, a Raffles College science graduate who was working in the

Overseas Assurance Corporation in China Building, in Chulia Street. Nyuk Lin and I both frequented a goldsmith's shop in High Street run by two Hakkas, another Raffles College graduate and his elder brother. The shop was a meeting place for brokers like myself who traded in little bits of jewellery. I had been asked by Basrai Brothers, Indian stationers in Chulia Street, if I could get them stationery gum, which was in short supply – there was little left from pre-war stock. Could I perhaps make some myself? I asked Nyuk Lin whether he could make gum. He said he could, using tapioca flour and carbolic acid. So I financed his experiments.

Nyuk Lin's method was to take a big cylindrical pot, fill it with tapioca flour, and place the pot in a big wok of boiling oil. He used palm oil, which was freely available and cheap. He kept the oil at a constant high temperature to heat the tapioca flour, which needed to be stirred all the while until it became a deep golden brown dextrine. It looked and smelt like beautiful caramel. He added water to the "caramel", which dissolved it into mucilage or gum, and finally carbolic acid as a preservative to prevent mould from setting in. The gum was poured into empty Scotts Emulsion bottles, which I discovered were plentiful and cheap. I marketed the gum under the name "Stikfas", and had an attractive label designed by an artistic friend with the word in light brown brushwork against a white background.

The gum turned a decent profit, and we made it in two centres. One was my home, with my mother and sister helping; the other was Nyuk Lin's home, where he was helped by his wife and his wife's younger sister, Kwa Geok Choo, the girl who had done better than me at Raffles College. I had seen her again when I first looked for Nyuk Lin in his flat in Tiong Bahru, riding my bicycle with its solid tyres. She was sitting on a veranda when I arrived, and when I asked where I could find him, she smiled and pointed out a staircase around the corner. Now we were meeting under different circumstances. She was at home, at a loose end, doing domestic chores as there were no maids. Making gum was one chore that gave her pin money, and my visits to check on production led to a friendship that developed over the months.

By September 1944, we knew each other well enough for me to invite Nyuk Lin, his wife and Geok Choo (now simply Choo) to my 21st birthday dinner at a Chinese restaurant at the Great World, an amusement park. It was the first time I had asked her out. True, she was escorted by her brother-in-law, but in the Singapore of that era, if a girl accepted an invitation to a young man's 21st birthday dinner, it was an event not without significance.

The gum-making lasted for some six to seven months until late 1944. By then, the war was going badly for the Japanese. Few merchant ships came through and trade was at a standstill; business dwindled and offices did not need gum. I discontinued gum-making, but continued to visit Choo at her Tiong Bahru home to chat and keep up the friendship.

∞

By May, the Japanese attempt to invade India from Burma had failed at Imphal and Kohima. This time it was the Japanese who were on the run. They fought tenaciously and ferociously even as they retreated, and I read dispatches of the stubborn resistance they put up as the British advanced towards Mandalay and down the Arakan coast. I felt certain the British would soon push their way down the Malayan peninsula in the same way, and feared that, with the Japanese fighting to the last man, the recapture of Singapore would mean street-to-street and house-to-house fighting to the bitter end, with enormous civilian casualties. It was only a matter of time before it happened – one to two years.

I decided it would be better to get out of Singapore while things were still calm, and I could resign from the *Hodobu* without arousing suspicion over my motives. I applied for leave and went up to Malaya to reconnoitre Penang and the Cameron Highlands, to find out which was the safer place. I travelled from Singapore to Penang and then to Tapah by train, but from Tapah to the Cameron Highlands I got a lift in a vegetable lorry and sat next to the driver. After two nights in the Camerons, I went back to Tapah by the same means. It was a scary ride. To save petrol, the driver switched off the engine and freewheeled for the better part of two-and-a-half hours down the steep, winding road.

In Penang, I stayed with Hon Sui Sen. In 1942, some four months into the occupation of Singapore, Hon had sent his wife and baby daughter back to Penang and boarded with my family in Norfolk Road as a paying guest. We shared a room and became friends, but after nine months he decided it was not worth staying in Singapore. He was the best science graduate of his year, and one of the two annually recruited into the Straits Settlements Civil Service. (He was later to become our minister for finance.) But his government pay was paltry, his rations were inadequate, and he could not earn enough to keep his family. So he joined them in Penang.

Although I saw little military activity as I wandered around Penang, I ruled it out. It would be a logical stepping stone for the British forces on their way down to Singapore. There would be street fighting, building by building. So I went on to the Cameron Highlands where Maurice Baker, my friend at Raffles College, had his home in Ringlet village at 3,200 feet. He and some friends were living off their savings, planting vegetables and root crops. I paid for my whole trip by selling at an enormous profit half a dozen steel hoes purchased in Singapore. The farmers needed them badly. On my return journey I bought a basket of beautiful vegetables unobtainable in Singapore, and spent a day and a half guarding them on the train.

Once back, I discussed the next move with my mother. We decided it would be best to move to the Cameron Highlands. As a first step, we sold the tenancy of the house at Norfolk Road to a group of Japanese men who worked for a *kumiai*. They paid us the handsome sum of $60,000 in banana notes for vacating this rent-controlled property and handing it over to them. Then I gave one month's notice to the *Hodobu*.

As I took the lift down in Cathay Building the day before I stopped work, the lift attendant, whom I had befriended, told me to be careful; my file in the *Kempeitai* office had been taken out for attention. I felt a deep chill. I wondered what could have provoked this, and braced myself for the coming interrogation. From that moment, I sensed that I was being followed. Day and night, a team tailed me. I went through all the possible reasons in my mind, and could only conclude that someone had told the *Kempeitai* I was pro-British and had been leaking news that the war was going badly for the Japanese, and that was why I was leaving. At least two men at any one time would be outside the shophouse in Victoria Street where we stayed after moving from Norfolk Road. My father had obtained the tenancy of this house from his employers, the oil authority in Alexandra Road.

To discover if I was indeed being followed, I asked my brothers Dennis and Fred to station themselves at the upstairs windows and watch the two Chinese men at the corner of Bras Basah Road and Victoria Street with two bicycles parked nearby. Then I cycled around the block. When I came back, they confirmed that the moment I left, so did the men, and when I returned, so did they. My heart sank. I told my mother, and decided that it would be best if I did not leave Singapore after all. If I attempted to do so, the *Kempeitai* would probably pull me in for a nasty interrogation. If I stayed behind and acted openly, leading a harmless life operating on the black market and making gum to get by, they might leave me alone.

I endured this cat-and-mouse game for some eight weeks. At times, in the quiet of the early morning, at 2 or 3 am, a car would pass by on Victoria Street and stop near its junction with Bras Basah Road. It is difficult to describe the cold fear that seized me at the thought that they had come for me. Like most, I had heard of the horrors of the torture inflicted by the *Kempeitai*. They wore white armbands with the two Chinese characters in red for *Kempei*, military police, and their powers of arrest and interrogation could not be challenged, even by high-ranking Japanese officers. They had their headquarters in the YMCA building in Stamford Road, and branches in Oxley Rise, Smith Street and the Central Police Station in South Bridge Road. People living nearby reported hearing their victims' howls of pain, sounds calculated to fill their hearts with dread, and their fears were spread by word of mouth. It was a deliberate method to terrorise the locals; a cowed population was easier to control.

I had no links with any underground or any network for spreading Allied news. I had no reason to listen secretly to any radio broadcast because it was anyway my job to deal with Western news reports. I made up my mind that if I were arrested, I would tell them what I feared: that after clearing Burma, the British would re-invade Malaya and push their way down to Singapore with the Japanese fighting to the last man. I had therefore planned to leave the island to plant tapioca, sweet potato and vegetables in the Cameron Highlands, which would not be in the path of any military invasion. I would provide proof of my visit to Penang and the Camerons, which was followed by that of my mother and my brother some two months later to confirm my assessment that it was the best area for the family to move to. But one day, two months after it began, the surveillance ceased. It was an unnerving experience.

After I stopped making gum for lack of demand, I teamed up with a Shanghainese called Low You Ling. He was a small contractor in the construction business, in his mid-30s. He had no partners. I could speak Japanese; he could not. Between us we got odd jobs from Japanese companies and from the *butai*, the regiments that garrisoned Singapore. To increase my contacts in the civilian sector, I teamed up with a Mr Kageyama, a Japanese civilian, also in his mid-30s, who had been employed by the *kumiai*. When there was little work for him in the *kumiai* because Japanese ships were being sunk and commodities became scarce, he decided to strike out on his own as a middleman between the big Japanese companies, the military and local suppliers. He and I complemented each other, with Low providing the construction capability and the connections with the subcontractors, carpenters, masons and bricklayers whom we needed. Together, we all made something of a living.

I continued to operate on the black market, acting as a broker for anything and everything tradeable. It was a no-lose situation. Every item was in short supply and getting scarcer. Hyperinflation meant nothing ever went down in price. But one needed capital to get richer. I was able to raise some money and quickly accumulated more. I knew that the moment I had cash, the important thing was to change it into something of more permanent value or it would melt away in my hands. In this mad urge to convert banana notes into assets, I bought myself a full-size billiard table, had it restored and revarnished, the green baize top re-covered, and installed it – adjusted and levelled – in the upstairs flat at Victoria Street. In March or April 1945, a friend of my parents had moved out of his flat in China Building and had offered us the use of it. So I was able to use Victoria Street for business and recreation: business, because next to it was a red-brick corner building, a confectionery and bakery, where brokers would gather to exchange information and close deals; recreation, because the billiard table was there. It was an existen-tialist life, with each day another day nearer to a re-invasion that spelt danger for the locals. Meanwhile, one had to live and carry on as usual.

In May, news came of Germany's defeat and surrender. Now the whole war effort would be turned against the Japanese. Everyone knew it was only a matter of time before Japan would be defeated. Having edited the Burma campaign press despatches while I worked for the *Hodobu*, I was fearful of the price civilians would pay. But there was no way out. For me to leave was still to invite detention and interrogation.

Then out of the blue, on 6 August, a strange bomb was exploded over Hiroshima. The news was only carried in the *Syonan Shimbun* of 11 August in the form of a masthead report – "Nippon protests against the attack on Hiroshima with a new kind of bomb last Monday" – but those who had listened to shortwave broadcasts from the BBC spread the news that Japan had been hit with a powerful new radiation weapon. We felt the end was close.

On 15 August, the Japanese emperor broadcast to his subjects and announced the surrender. We heard this almost immediately, because people had become bold and many were listening to Allied radio broadcasts, especially the BBC. The news did not appear in the *Syonan Shimbun* until 20 August, when it published the whole "Imperial Rescript". The war had come to an end without further fighting. We were spared the fiery ordeal that had been the fate of Rangoon and Mandalay.

For three weeks after the emperor's broadcast, there were no signs of the British arriving. It was an unnatural situation. It was different from what had happened three and a half years earlier, when the British had surrendered and the Japanese had not yet taken effective control. Unlike the British, the Japanese troops had not been defeated and demoralised in battle. They were despondent and confused, but still very much in charge, and still had the power to hurt us. When locals who could not contain their elation celebrated their defeat, Japanese soldiers passing by would gate-crash their parties and slap the merrymakers. The Japanese army expected to be called to account by the British and punished for its misdeeds, but it was also resentful and apprehensive that the population would turn on its officers when they arrived. Shots were reported to have been heard from Japanese officers' messes, for several could not accept the surrender and preferred to commit *hara-kiri*, either Japanese-style with a dagger or, less painfully, with a revolver. But the locals were fortunate. The Japanese did not kill civilians, as far as I know, nor were there ugly or brutal incidents. They left the population alone until the British took over. Their military discipline held.

∽

The three and a half years of Japanese occupation were the most important of my life. They gave me vivid insights into the behaviour of human beings and human societies, their motivations and impulses. My appreciation of governments, my understanding of power as the vehicle for revolutionary change, would not have been gained without this experience. I saw a whole social system crumble suddenly before an occupying army that was absolutely merciless. The Japanese demanded total obedience and got it from nearly all. They were hated by almost everyone but everyone knew their power to do harm and so everyone adjusted. Those who were slow or reluctant to change and to accept the new masters suffered. They lived on the margins of the new society, their fortunes stagnated or declined and they lost their status. Those who were quick off the mark in assessing the new situation, and swift to take advantage of the new opportunities by making themselves useful to the new masters, made fortunes out of the terrible misfortune that had befallen all in Singapore.

The Japanese Military Administration governed by spreading fear. It put up no pretence of civilised behaviour. Punishment was so severe that crime was very rare. In the midst of deprivation after the second half of 1944, when the people half-starved, it was amazing how low the crime rate remained. People could leave their front doors open at night. Every household had a head, and every group of ten households had its head, and they were supposed to patrol their area from dusk till sunrise. But it was a mere formality. They carried only sticks and there were no offences to report – the penalties were too heavy. As a result I have never believed those who advocate a soft approach to crime and punishment, claiming that punishment does not reduce crime. That was not my experience in Singapore before the war, during the Japanese occupation or subsequently.

I learnt after the initial shock and drama that life had to go on almost as usual. People must eat; they need medicines and other things like toothbrushes, toothpaste, clothes, shoes, pens, ink, paper. Even razor blades became precious and difficult to get, so that used blades were sharpened and re-sharpened by being pressed and rubbed back and forth against the inside walls of a glass. Tobacco was worth more than Japanese currency. Some professions were reduced in value and earning power. There was little demand for lawyers trained in English law, because there was little commerce, and military law dealt summarily with crimes. Accountancy stagnated because there was little business. On the other hand, doctors and dentists were as essential as ever since people still got sick and had toothache, so they prospered despite shortages of medicines and anaesthetics.

In the first ten months of the occupation, it was not unusual to see British and Australian prisoner-of-war working parties coming to town, with a light escort of Japanese soldiers. Usually they performed tasks like moving goods from a godown to a lorry. They would sneak into the coffee shops looking for food, and the owners and ordinary housewives would pass them bread, canned food and other foodstuffs and money. The Chinese had great sympathy for them. They had grown thin and looked the worse for their confinement. Their uniforms, usually shorts and shirts, were tattered. Towards the end of 1942, they gradually became less visible, and a year later they were seldom seen. People believed they had been sent to work elsewhere, in Thailand, Indonesia and Japan. When they reappeared in Singapore in late 1944 and early 1945, they were just skin and bones, skeletons with ribs sticking out to be counted. They had been working on the Burma railway. Some wore only G-strings, their hip bones exposed. They were pitiful, with sores, ulcers, scars and scabies all over their bodies, especially their arms and legs. Food was scarce, but not so scarce that they could not have been adequately fed. Their sufferings exceeded those of prisoners of war anywhere else in the world.

The switch from English to Japanese as the language of administration and of the bosses put the old at a grave disadvantage. They could not learn Japanese so easily. Those who spoke it, like the Chinese from Taiwan, were at a premium; some were already in Singapore before the occupation, but others followed the Japanese army. Young locals learnt enough Japanese to be employable, but beyond that most people were decent. They did not want to cooperate or collaborate with the enemy. They just wanted to coast along, to give the minimum to the new masters. Only a few dared to oppose them, even secretly.

There were others, the smart and the opportunistic, who went out of their way to ingratiate themselves and to make themselves useful to the Japanese. They provided them with labour, materials, information, women, liquor, good food, and they made fortunes. The lucky ones were contractors whom the Japanese needed to obtain basic supplies, or who were in building construction.

The luckiest and most prosperous of all were those like the Shaw brothers who were given the licence or franchise to run gambling farms in the amusement parks, the Great World and the New World. For a deprived, depressed population facing the prospect of mass destruction and death in one, two or three years when the British returned to oust the Japanese, gambling was a wonderful opiate. The locals patronised these farms to try their luck and punted their fortunes away, while others came to watch and pass the time. It was amazing how much time people spent in these gambling farms and how much money they inevitably lost to the bankers in this simple way. As existence was uncertain, all games of chance were favoured. Life itself had become a game of chance.

But however you made money, the most important thing was how to preserve its value by changing it into tangible goods or the old Straits Settlements dollars. Grains and other foodstuffs were bulky and difficult to store or handle. The items most sought after were those that would retain their value after the British returned, and in the meantime were small and easy to hide. Hence, from 1944, the exchange rate of the British Straits Settlements dollar shot up on the black market with every passing day as more and more banana notes were printed and distributed. The next most desirable asset was jewellery. To deal in jewellery, brokers had to know what was real gold, what was 24 carat and what was only 18 carat, to recognise good diamonds with good colour and few or no flaws, and to learn the virtues of rubies, sapphires, aquamarines, cat's-eyes and other semi-precious stones.

The bolder ones with big money bought properties, but their value did not escalate as much as gold or Straits Settlements dollars because they were immovable. Transfers required conveyancing by lawyers and registration in the Registry of Deeds. The chances were 50–50 that the conveyance would be repudiated or annulled when the British returned. Meanwhile, there was a likelihood of buildings being bombed and destroyed. As it turned out, there was no invasion, conveyances were not annulled and buildings were not destroyed. In the last stages of the occupation, after Germany had surrendered and Japan's defeat was certain, it was possible to sell a case of 12 bottles of Johnnie Walker whisky for enough Japanese banana dollars to buy a shophouse in Victoria Street. Those who negotiated such exchanges became wealthy after the war.

I learnt more from the three and a half years of Japanese occupation than any university could have taught me. I had not yet read Mao's dictum that "power grows out of the barrel of a gun", but I knew that Japanese brutality, Japanese guns, Japanese bayonets and swords, and Japanese terror and torture settled the argument as to who was in charge, and could make people change their behaviour, even their loyalties. The Japanese not only demanded and got their obedience; they forced them to adjust to a long-term prospect of Japanese rule, so that they had their children educated to fit the new system, its language, its habits and its values, in order to be useful and make a living.

The third and final stage, which they would have achieved if they had been given time, was to get us to accept them as our new masters as part of the natural order of things. Morality and fairness were irrelevant.

They had won. They were on top and in command. We had to praise their gods, extol their culture and emulate their behaviour. But it did not always work. In Korea, the Japanese met resistance from the moment they attempted to govern the country. They tried to suppress the instincts and habits of a people of an old culture, people with a strong sense of pride in their history and a determination to oppose their new barbaric oppressors. They killed many Koreans but never broke their spirit.

But that was one exception. In Taiwan – ruled by the Chinese, the Portuguese and the Dutch before the Japanese came – there was no hatred. Had the Japanese stayed on in Singapore and Malaya, they would, within 50 years, have forged a coterie of loyal supporters as they had successfully done in Taiwan. Malaya was too young, its peoples too diverse and its society too plastic and malleable to resist. There were some Malays who joined the anti-Japanese guerrillas in the Malayan jungle trained by British officers of Force 136. But most of them hoped the Japanese would be their new protectors, just as they hoped the British would be when they in turn ousted the Japanese.

The only people who had the courage and conviction to stand up to the invaders were the Chinese who joined the Malayan Communist Party and, in smaller numbers, the Kuomintang-led resistance. Both groups were fired by Chinese nationalism, not Malayan patriotism, and were to prove as much a source of trouble to the British in peace as they had been to the Japanese in war.

∞

In the confused interregnum between the Japanese surrender on 15 August 1945 and the establishment of effective British control of the island towards the end of September, anti-Japanese groups took the law into their own hands. They lynched, murdered, tortured or beat up informers, torturers, tormentors and accomplices – or suspected accomplices – of the Japanese. I remember the thudding of feet as people were chased in broad daylight down the backlanes around our two homes in

Victoria Street and China Building. I heard the sound of blows and screams as they were knifed and killed. But in the last days many collaborators managed to melt away, going into hiding or fleeing up-country to Malaya or to the Riau islands in the south.

The liberation did not bring what everybody wanted: punishment for the wicked and reward for the virtuous. There could be no complete squaring of accounts. Fairness and justice demanded documentation and elaborate investigations. It was not possible to muster the resources to bring every culprit to book. There were too many of them, both Japanese and locals. Justice was meted out to a few, but most went free.

There were trials, but the major Japanese war criminals were not punished. Colonel Tsuji, the man who had ordered the *Sook Ching* massacre, had disappeared. General Yamashita, the "Tiger of Malaya", who as commander-in-chief had agreed to *Sook Ching*, had been transferred first to Manchuria and then to the Philippines, where in September 1945 he surrendered to General MacArthur's forces. He was tried and hanged in Manila for the senseless sacking of the city, not for his approval of the killing of fifty to a hundred thousand innocent young men in Singapore.

Some 260 Japanese war criminals were tried in Singapore, but only 100 were convicted and sentenced to death although hundreds of people in Singapore, among them my own friends, had been detained and tortured in the *Kempeitai* centres in Singapore. One of them was Lim Kim San, who later became a cabinet minister, from 1963 to 1980. He gave me this grim account of his experiences in 1944:

> "I was detained twice at Oxley Rise, first in January 1944 for a fortnight, second in February 1944 for more than a month. A Chinese youth who had come to my shop in North Bridge Road had pointed me out as one who had given money to him for the communists. When I argued that it did not make sense that a capitalist was also pro-communist, I was flogged with a rope, kicked and manhandled.

"I regained consciousness when water was splashed on my face. I found myself imprisoned in a room about 15 feet by 10 feet, shared by about 30 people, male and female.

"There was a lavatory at one corner of the room, a squatting type with the cistern high above our heads. Repeated flushings made the water 'clean' and it was then collected from the gushing outlets in the toilet bowl. It was the water you drank and washed with. If you became sick you would be taken away to God knows where. I was disgusted by the sight of flowing blood from a woman menstruating.

"We were fed with rice gruel mixed with discarded vegetables from an old kerosene tin. I could not stomach it and retched every time I tried to eat. It reminded me of the way we fed our ducks.

"All of us were made to sit on our haunches and we were not allowed to change position without permission from the guards, local boys who were recruited and trained to be cruel.

"One day, an elderly Indian with his leg broken was brought in. He could not sit and he could only move in a prone position, dragging his injured leg along. One of the young *gunpo* (guards) threw a stick and the injured Indian had to painfully drag himself with his injured leg to fetch the stick and return it to the *gunpo*. This was repeated until the poor man was exhausted and almost unconscious with pain.

"Among those detained was a young, strapping, jolly Teochew lad of about 17 or 18 years of age. He was a *gunpo* who was caught after he deserted. One evening, the *Kempeitai* strapped him bare-bodied to the ceiling. His hands were tied behind him and the rope attached to a beam with his feet barely touching the ground. From time to time you could see him stretching his toes to reach the ground, to ease the weight on his shoulders.

"They left him there the whole night without food and water. He yelled profanities and cursed the Japanese in a strong voice in Teochew.

"The next morning, the shouts and curses turned to piteous wails and moans when a *Kempeitai* man used a cane to hit the

Gruesome torture by Japanese soldiers during the occupation.

man's back. It went on for a few hours and the wailings and moanings became weaker and weaker; ultimately, it stopped. He was dead and yet was left hanging for some time before all of us, as a warning to the *gunpo* and to us.

"Another time water was pumped into a man from a hose, and when his stomach was filled with water, the torturer would jump and sit on it. The man vomited and passed out.

"Every morning, we shivered when we heard the sound of heavy boots approaching our cell. It was a sign that some of us would be undergoing interrogation and torture. Some never came back.

"I was released on the intercession of the top Taiwanese liaison officer.

"I have seen the true nature of the Japanese, in and out of prison. The civility and the bowings are a thin veneer under which lurks the beast. The Allied victory saved Asia."

A poignant summation of Japanese bestiality was contained in the opening address of Lieutenant-Colonel Colin Sleeman, the prosecutor in the "Double Tenth" trial, which opened in Singapore on 18 March 1946:

"To give an accurate description of the misdeeds of these men it will be necessary for me to describe actions which plumb the very depths of human depravity and degradation. The keynote of the whole of this case can be epitomised by two words – unspeakable horror.

"Horror, stark and naked, permeates every corner and angle of the case from beginning to end, devoid of relief or palliation. I have searched, I have searched diligently, amongst a vast mass of evidence, to discover some redeeming feature, some mitigating factor in the conduct of these men which would elevate the story from the level of pure horror and bestiality, and ennoble it, at least, upon the plane of tragedy. I confess that I have failed."

Yet, throughout the 50 years since the end of the war, successive Japanese Liberal Democratic Party governments, the majority of leaders of all Japanese political parties, most of their academics and nearly all their media have chosen not to talk about these evil deeds. Unlike the Germans, they hope that with the passing of the generations these deeds will be forgotten, and the accounts of what they did buried in dusty records. When they refuse to admit them to their neighbours, people cannot but fear that it is possible for them to repeat these horrors. It was only when a non-LDP government took office in 1992 that a Japanese prime minister, Morihiro Hosokawa, gave an unqualified apology.

4. After the Liberation

On Wednesday, 12 September 1945, at about 10:30 in the morning, I walked to City Hall, where the surrender ceremony would take place, and waited on the Padang across the road. The wait was worth it. I saw a group of seven high-ranking Japanese officers arrive from High Street, accompanied by British military police wearing their red caps and armbands. They were led by General Itagaki, commander-in-chief of the forces in Malaya and Singapore. Unlike so many Japanese officers, they did not shuffle; they walked properly. The crowd hooted, whistled and jeered but the Japanese were impassive and dignified, looking straight ahead. They had come to sign the formal surrender in obedience to their emperor's orders. Many officers were later seen at various locations laying down their long samurai swords in a pile. They were acknowledging defeat, were disarmed, and became prisoners of war. But the seven generals who now walked up the steps of City Hall represented an army that had not been routed in battle. They would have fought to the death, and they left the people of Singapore who hated them in no doubt that they would have preferred to go down in flames, bringing everyone else down with them, rather than surrender.

Some 45 minutes later, Lord Louis Mountbatten, the British com-mander-in-chief, South East Asia Command, appeared, wearing his white naval uniform. He was accompanied by his generals and admirals, and some seven or eight officers representing the Allied forces, including Indians, Chinese, Dutch and others. He raised his naval cap high with his right hand and gave three cheers to the troops that formed the cordon in front of the steps. He loved uniforms, parades and ceremonies.

These were moments of great exhilaration. The Japanese occupation nightmare was over and people thought the good times were about to return. The signs were favourable. The troops were generous with their cigarettes – Players Navy Cut in paper packets, unobtainable for the last three years. Good quality beer, Johnnie Walker whisky and Gordon's dry gin found their way into the market, and we believed that soon there would be plenty of rice, fruit, vegetables, meat and canned foods. This was not to be for some time. But during those first few weeks, there was jubilation. The people were genuinely happy and welcomed the British back.

By early 1946, however, people realised that there was to be no return to the old peaceful, stable, free-and-easy Singapore. The city was packed with troops in uniform. They filled the newly opened cafés, bars and cabarets. The pre-war colonial business houses could not restart immediately, for their British employees had died or were recuperating from internment. Ship arrivals were infrequent and goods were scarce in Britain itself. It looked as if it would be many years before the pre-war flow of commodities resumed. Even locals who had worked for the government could not just go back to their old offices, and many remained unemployed. It was a world in turmoil where the hucksters flourished in Singapore as they did in Britain (where they were called spivs). Much of the day-to-day business was still done on the black – now the free – market.

There were numerous army jeeps and motorcycles in the streets, but no new motorcars or buses. The trolley buses were dilapidated, and the roads full of potholes; telephones were old and the lines unclear because replacements were not available; electricity was still in short supply. It was going to take some time to put things right. We had lived too much in anticipation of the "good old days" during those years of suffering. Our hopes, based on nostalgia, were too high, and we were bound to be disappointed. The infrastructure had run down, property had been lost or destroyed, people had died, become old or sick. Life had to go on but it was not going to be like the good old days.

Nevertheless, the British Military Administration, whatever its shortcomings, was an immense relief after the terror and oppression of its Japanese predecessor. British officers and civilians knew that the locals welcomed them back, and they reciprocated the warmth we showed them and did their best for us. Many soldiers and officers shared their army rations as well as their cigarettes and liquor with the people they dealt with. Many in Singapore understood the English language, English culture and the English form of government. Even the uneducated were vaguely familiar with those parts of the British colonial system with which they came in contact.

It was to be expected that the Straits Chinese in particular would be happy with the return to a form of society into which they had been for long assimilated. Although they retained much of their Chinese culture, many had stopped speaking their own dialects, and conversed only in Baba Malay. They were the descendants of early immigrants who had not brought their womenfolk with them from China and had therefore contracted mixed marriages with local women. They were for the most part loyal to the British, and they sent their children to local English schools, many in the hope that they would eventually become professionals and government servants in a colony administered in the English language. The most loyal joined the Straits Chinese British Association and were popularly known as the King's Chinese. Their leading members were made knights.

But the King's Chinese formed only about 10 per cent of the community. The remainder were the Chinese-speaking Chinese who had come to Singapore more recently. They spoke not English but their own dialects – mainly Hokkien, Teochew, Cantonese, Hakka and Hainanese. Their children went to Chinese schools, where they learnt Mandarin. Their contact with the British authorities was minimal, they led a separate existence and they were no more assimilated after the war than they had been before it.

Their loyalty was to China, not Britain. It was they who went into the Malayan jungle to fight the Japanese, as guerrillas in the Malayan People's Anti-Japanese Army (MPAJA), the military arm of the Malayan Communist Party. They were looking ahead to the day when they would expel not only the Japanese, but also the British. In the power vacuum created when the Japanese surrendered suddenly before the British could invade, they spelt trouble.

In Malaya, they took over some of the smaller towns, put up arches to welcome the guerrillas as the real victors in the battle against the Japanese, and acted as the *de facto* local authority. Mercifully, they did not try that in Singapore, but they caused turmoil enough. They appeared in the streets in assorted khaki uniforms with cloth caps modelled on those of the Chinese Communist 8th Route Army – soft, floppy, oddly shaped, with three red stars on the front over the visor. In the flush of victory, they were high-handed. They forcibly requisitioned property and set up people's courts to mete out summary justice to collaborators of all races. In one instance 20 Chinese detectives were rounded up and put into pig crates pending trial.

There was extortion and subtle blackmail of businessmen for their past collaboration with the enemy. Many prominent people were psychologically or physically compelled to make generous contributions to the MPAJA to make up for their past misdeeds. Young hooligans went around town openly using MPAJA credentials to wring money or goods from those who had had dealings with the Japanese. The British forces could not reestablish law and order in the face of the MPAJA's aggressiveness and the opportunism of gangsters who pretended to have played a part in the resistance. Fortunately, because they had no means to travel down to Singapore, most of the MPAJA remained stuck in Malaya, where they operated more effectively as it was familiar territory.

The British Military Administration offered the MPAJA $350 for every guerrilla who handed in his weapons. From December 1945 to January 1946, some 6,500 did so, including several hundred in Singapore. On 6 January, the British held a ceremony outside City Hall at which a small, uniformed MPAJA contingent marched past Lord Louis Mountbatten, who pinned medals on 16 of their leaders. Chin Peng, described in the newspapers as a communist guerrilla commander, received the Burma Star (1939/45) and War Star, after which he gave a clenched-fist salute. Official recognition of the MPAJA's contribution in defeating the Japanese gave them a status that they exploited to the utmost to extend their power. Meanwhile, they secretly stored many weapons for future use.

The communists were able to recruit some of the English-educated into the united front they were creating. A group of so-called intellectuals – lawyers, teachers, Raffles College graduates and students back from Cambridge – formed the Malayan Democratic Union, which had its headquarters in some shabby rooms above the dance hall at the Liberty Cabaret in North Bridge Road. They had inveigled Philip Hoalim Senior, a lawyer and our family friend, into lending it respectability by becoming its chairman. They needed him as cover in order to manipulate the organisation, and I became a casual visitor to their proceedings through my acquaintance with him. Its purpose appeared legitimate enough. The British had announced the formation of the Malayan Union, which would include the nine Malay states and the Straits Settlements of Penang and Malacca, but not Singapore. This meant that Singapore would remain a British colony. That was unacceptable, and the Malayan Democratic Union demanded the independence of both Malaya and Singapore as one unit.

Philip Hoalim helped to draw up the proposed constitution, but although I saw the draft, I had nothing to do with it. On their part, the communists considered all talk of constitutional change irrelevant. What they wanted was total power. The Malayan Democratic Union was merely a front organisation to mobilise the English-educated to help them achieve it. But when they resorted to armed struggle against the British in 1948 to get it, the Malayan Democratic Union folded up.

Before that happened, however, there was plenty of action. Very soon after they emerged from the jungle, the communists started to flex their muscles, using the trade unions. On 21 October 1945, they got 7,000 workers in the dockyards at Tanjong Pagar and the Singapore Harbour Board to go on strike. A few days later, they held a mass meeting attended by 20,000 workers at which they inaugurated the General Labour Union. In typical communist fashion, the union took in workers from every conceivable trade and also self-employed groups. When it called a general strike on 29 January 1946, in a demonstration of strength after the British Military Administration had detained a few communists, some 170,000 workers from hospitals, shipyards, the Naval Base, rubber factories, cinemas, cabarets and public transport stopped work, and the shops closed. It was called a *hartal*, a word taken from the civil disobedience movement in India.

This stoppage was neither voluntary nor spontaneous but was enforced by intimidation and fear. The shops closed because if they did not they would be vandalised and wrecked. Workers who reported for work were beaten up. So not only hawkers, but trishaw riders, rickshaw pullers and taxi drivers played safe and took the day off. Life in the city came to a halt. But the communists suspected that they could not sustain the strike for long. Having demonstrated they could command overwhelming compliance for their *hartal*, they called it off after the second day.

My education in the unfairness and absurdities of human existence was completed by what I saw happening in the immediate aftermath of the war. If three and a half years of Japanese occupation had earned me my degree in the realities of life, the first year in liberated Singapore was my postgraduate course. It was very different from my memory of the colonial thirties. Those British civil servants who survived internment had been sent home for medical treatment and recuperation, and temporary officers of the British Military Administration controlled what were improvised departments.

True, they were reinforced with a few of the pre-war generation who had been on leave when the Japanese came, or had got away in time. But they were out of touch with the changes that had taken place. The men now in charge – majors, colonels, brigadiers – knew they would be in power only until they were demobilised, when their wartime commissions would vanish like Cinderella's coach. The pumpkin of civilian life to which they would then be reduced was at the back of their minds, and many made the most of their temporary authority. Their needs, alas, were similar to those of Japanese officers – something small, valuable and easy to secrete on the person to take home to England when their time was up. So the same items were in demand. In return, they granted permits and supplies of scarce materials to the locals, and therefore opportunities to make money. But they were not bullies and oppressors like the Japanese.

With the Japanese out of the way, many houses became vacant, and my mother and I looked for a suitable place to move into, for we had to leave the China Building, and the Victoria Street shophouse was unsuitable. In Oxley Road, a middle-class area where Europeans had vacated their homes in 1942 and Japanese civilians had taken them over, we came across two identical houses – Numbers 38 and 40 – built by a Jewish merchant, who named them Castor and Pollux. They were empty except for some heavy furniture, and we decided to make a bid for the tenancy of Number 38. It was a big, rambling house with five bedrooms, and three others at the back originally used as servants' quarters. I saw George Gaw, a Java-born Chinese friend of the family who was in charge at the office of the Custodian of Enemy Property, and he was happy to let us have it at its pre-war rental. The rent had now to be paid in Straits dollars – some $80 a month, a fairly sizeable sum – but we decided to take it.

My father went back to work for Shell, this time to be in charge of their depot at Pasir Panjang in Singapore. Meanwhile, I had to decide what to do. Trading on the open market was still profitable, but the range of goods had changed and this made it riskier. I could not predict which items in short supply would suddenly become plentiful if they were brought in for the troops. So, as an alternative, I approached various British officers in charge of public works to see whether they wanted any construction jobs done. After two or three attempts, I succeeded in clinching a deal with an Indian brigade that controlled Japanese army warehouses in Alexandra Road. I spoke to a major, a tall lanky Englishman, who needed labourers to move Japanese goods out of the warehouses and replace them with British army stores. My Shanghainese friend Low You Ling and I supplied him with some 100–150 workers at $2 a day, and my younger brother Dennis acted as cashier and paymaster. The army paid us after a head count at the end of each day and we then paid the workers. There were also some construction jobs to be done for which we were paid separately. The work started in October 1945 and kept me busy until May 1946.

In March 1946, Dennis met with a bad accident while cycling home one evening after collecting the money to pay the labourers. A passing lorry caught him and dragged him many yards along the road outside Victoria Memorial Hall. His left arm was almost torn from his shoulder and his face was injured. I dashed off to see him at the hospital. The first thing Dennis asked me was whether the money was lost. I felt a pain in my heart. It was just a few hundred dollars, but he took his job seriously. I comforted him as best as I could. The surgeon operated on him successfully, but he was in pain and incapacitated for many months.

All this while, I had also been preoccupied over what I was to do about my uncompleted education and my growing attachment to Choo. I did not feel optimistic about being able to finish my diploma course at Raffles College soon enough. The college would take at least a year to get restarted. Then I would need another one or one and a half years to graduate. In all, I would lose two to three years. I discussed the matter with my mother. We decided that, with her savings and jewellery, my earnings from the black market and my contract work, the family could pay for my law studies in Britain and those of Dennis. I planned to leave for England as soon as possible instead of returning to Raffles College to try to win the Queen's scholarship.

In October-November 1945, I introduced Choo to the librarian at Raffles Library (now the National Library) and got her a temporary job there. Her family had moved to a bungalow in Devonshire Road, about a mile from our house, and I used to walk her home. Sometimes we would sit at a quiet spot in the grounds of the big Chesed-El Synagogue at Oxley Rise, close to where the *Kempeitei* had had one of their centres. But in November 1945, I could afford to buy a second-hand car, a pre-war Morris refurbished with spares now available from the British army. As my business improved, I sold it at a profit after a few months and bought a pre-war Ford V8, restored to good condition. It must have been used by a Japanese general during the occupation.

On New Year's Eve, I took Choo to a party for young people at Mandalay Villa in Amber Road, the seaside mansion of Mrs Lee Choon Guan, doyenne of the Straits-born Chinese and a very wealthy widow. Just before the party broke up, I led her out into the garden facing the sea. I told her that I no longer planned to return to Raffles College, but would go to England to read law. I asked her whether she would wait for me until I came back three years later after being called to the Bar. Choo asked if I knew she was two and a half years older than I was. I said I knew, and had considered this carefully. I was mature for my age and most of my friends were older than me anyway. Moreover, I wanted someone my equal, not someone who was not really grown up and needed looking after, and I was not likely to find another girl who was my equal and who shared my interests. She said she would wait. We did not tell our parents. It would have been too difficult to get them to agree to such a long commitment. This was the way we dealt with each other; when we ran into difficult personal problems, we faced them and sorted them out. We did not dodge or bury them. The courtship blossomed. I started to plan on leaving Singapore that year, 1946.

In March, I wrote to the Middle Temple, one of the four legal societies in London, enclosing my School Certificate results. Within a month, they replied that they would admit me if I presented myself in person and signed up as a student. With this letter, I approached the British major I worked for and asked him how I could travel on one of the ships that were then beginning to arrive at Tanjong Pagar to take troops back to Britain to be demobilised. The major put me in touch with the army transport officer, and in May I saw one of his staff. I was able to make an impression because in those days few locals could speak grammatical and idiomatic English without a strong accent. I explained my predicament, how my education had been interrupted by the war so that I had now lost three and a half years, but that I had now been admitted to the Middle Temple. I produced the Middle Temple letter and said I urgently needed a sea passage to Britain. He was sympathetic and promised to help. In July, he offered me a priority passage on a troopship that would get me to London by October.

In the frantic two months before I left Singapore, I scouted around with my mother for woollen clothes for the English winter. We found most of them at the Sungei Road flea market, which used to deal in stolen property before the war and had sprung back to life with items pilfered or bought from British troops, many of them flogged by soldiers who had been given them for their return to civilian life, or Civvy Street as they called it. My mother bought a huge wooden trunk with metal caps at the corners and packed in it a rug, a quilt, an overcoat, two sports jackets, flannel bags and a suit made of RAF barathea by the best tailor in High Street.

Before I sailed, she also did her best to make sure I would leave Singapore committed to some Chinese girl, and therefore be less likely to return with an English one. Several students had come back with British wives, often with unhappy results. Their families were upset, and couples broke up or else went off to settle in England because they could not fit into British colonial society, where they were patronised if not publicly ostracised. She introduced me in turn to three eligible young ladies of suitable background and good social status. I was not enthusiastic. They were the right age, their families were comfortably off and they were presentable. But they did not arouse my interest. I was quite happy, having settled on Choo. Finally, I decided to confide in my mother. She was a shrewd woman. Once she realised I had really made up my mind, she stopped her search. Her attitude to Choo changed to one of the warm friendliness of a prospective mother-in-law.

I had earlier told her about Choo, the girl who had beaten me in the English and economics examinations at Raffles College. She had also met Choo during our gum-making days and had visited the family. Choo's father, Kwa Siew Tee, a banker at the Oversea-Chinese Banking Corporation, was a Java-born Chinese like my father and my paternal grandmother. Her mother was a Straits-born Singapore Chinese like my own mother. We had similar backgrounds, spoke the same language at home and shared the same social norms.

Choo had been educated at Methodist Girls' School, and having passed her Senior Cambridge examinations, was only 16 when she went to the special class at Raffles Institution for students competing for the Queen's scholarship, but she did not get it. She told me later she was waiting for her Prince Charming. I turned up, not on a white horse but

Family photo in September 1946, before I sailed for England. Monica, Dennis, me, Freddy and Suan Yew standing behind my parents.

With Choo, in September 1946, at MacRitchie Reservoir. We were young and in love.

a bicycle with solid tyres! In 1940, she went to Raffles College, and we met at dinners and picnics, but at that time I kept my distance as I was in my first year and having a difficult time adjusting. Moreover, I was not eager to get close to any girl because I was not ready for any commitment. The few times we met socially or in lecture rooms, we were friendly but casual. In 1943–44, however, we came together in a different setting – myself older by three years of Japanese occupation and seeing her with different eyes; Choo cooped up in a flat doing housework, learning Mandarin, reading whatever books she could get and ready for our gum-making venture.

She belonged to a large family of eight children and had a happy, sheltered childhood in a conservative home. Her parents were moderately well off and there was always a car to take her to school, to Raffles College or wherever she needed to go. They also had a keen sense of propriety. On one occasion, after they moved to Devonshire Road, Choo arrived home from the library riding pillion on my motorcycle to the consternation of her mother. She was roundly rebuked for such improper behaviour. What would people think! Who would want to marry her! Soon afterwards, her family moved back to Pasir Panjang, where they had lived before. Fortunately, by then I had a car.

In the hectic months before September 1946 we spent a lot of time together. Before I left, I got my cousin Harold Liem, who was boarding with us at 38 Oxley Road, to take a whole series of photographs of us, all within a couple of days. We were young and in love, anxious to record this moment of our lives, to have something to remember each other by during the three years that I would be away in England. We did not know when we would meet again once I left. We both hoped she would go back to Raffles College, win the Queen's scholarship to read law, and join me wherever I might be. She was totally committed. I sensed it. I was equally determined to keep my commitment to her.

When I left Singapore on my 23rd birthday, 16 September 1946, aboard the *Britannic* and waved to her from the ship's deck, she was tearful. So was I. All my family and some friends, including Hon Sui Sen, were on the quay to wish me luck and wave me goodbye.

5. My Cambridge Days

The *Britannic* was a 65,000-ton Cunard Liner that sailed across the Atlantic from Liverpool to New York before the war. No ship as large or as fast did the Southampton to Singapore run. It was packed with troops on their way home for demobilisation. There were some 40 Asiatics on board, most of them Chinese, sleeping twice as many to a cabin as would have been normal for paying passengers. I was glad to be one of them.

I had no law textbooks with me to prepare myself for my studies, so I spent my time playing poker with some of the Hong Kong students. It was a relatively innocent pastime. I was shocked to see the unabashed promiscuity of some 40 or 50 servicewomen, non-commissioned officers and other ranks, who flirted with the officers. One night, a Hong Kong student, his eyes popping out of his head, told me they were unashamedly making love on the lifeboat deck. I was curious and went up to see for myself. What a sight it was! The deck was a hive of activity, with couples locked in passionate embraces scattered all over it. Some were a little less indelicate. They untied the canvas covers of the lifeboats to get inside them for a little privacy. But to see dozens of men and women openly engaging in sex contrasted sharply with my memory of the Japanese soldiers queuing up outside the "comfort house" at Cairnhill Road. "French letters", now called condoms, littered the deck.

I received another shock when the ship passed through the Suez Canal. It proceeded slowly so that the waves would not wash down the loose sand on the banks. As we passed, a group of Arab workers on the shore started shouting obscenities and lifted their *gallabiya* – long garments like nightshirts – to flaunt their genitals at the British servicewomen, who were on the deck watching the world go by in the torrid heat. The women shrieked in surprise and disgust, much to the delight of the Arabs, who put their hands on their penises and shook them. I had seen monkeys in the Botanic Gardens in Singapore do this to visitors who refused them bananas. Later, I learnt that they hated the British. Why, I did not know. It was the first time I had left Singapore to go overseas. I was being exposed to a new world of the hates and loves, the prejudices and biases of different peoples.

Nobody in Britain knew I was coming, so there were no arrangements for me to be met when the ship arrived in Liverpool on 3 October, 17 days after it left Singapore. However, knowing that the Hong Kong students sponsored by their government were being met by officials from the Colonial Office in London, I decided to latch on to them. Our train reached London late that night, and I followed them by taxi to a Victoria League hostel in Earl's Court. There I was given a double-decker bunk like the one on the *Britannic*, in a cavernous room in a basement with no windows. I found myself in the company of some 20 African and Caribbean students. It was another shock. I had never seen Africans before in real life, only in photographs. I was unprepared for their strange body odours, quite unlike those of the racial groups we had in Singapore. I did not sleep well that night.

I had to look for somewhere to live, and after 12 days of temporary accommodation at the YMCA, I found myself a room at 8 Fitzjohn's Avenue. It was a beautiful, quiet, tree-lined road only a short walk from Swiss Cottage tube station and the bus stop for the Number 13 that would take me straight to the Strand near the London School of Economics (LSE).

I still had to get a place at the LSE, which was not easy. Term had started two weeks before, and the universities were overflowing with returned servicemen. But I managed to see the head of the law faculty, Professor Hughes Parry. I explained to him my lost three and a half years, and that I had got onto the earliest possible troopship, not knowing I could have sent my application by post. I produced my Senior Cambridge results as top student in Singapore and Malaya for 1939 to convince him that I would have no difficulty in catching up even though I was starting late in the term. He was sympathetic and took me in.

It was a strange life. The LSE resembled a busy hotel, totally unlike Singapore's leisurely, gracious Raffles College, where students lived in halls of residence, sauntered to lecture rooms, sat around in junior common rooms and attended tutorials of two, three or four students at the most at a time. The LSE was a multi-storey building with students dashing up and down in the lifts, everybody hurrying to do something, somewhere. Lectures were a scramble. After one in the LSE, I would dash across the Strand to King's College for another, and then take either the tube or a bus to Euston for a third at University College, London – the nicest of the three because it was away from the hubbub of central London, and with its hospital grounds had something of the atmosphere of a college.

One interesting incident took place early in the academic year in the entrance hall of the LSE. For about a week, students representing various clubs – the Labour Club, Liberal Club, Conservative Club, Socialist Club – stood by little booths, handing out pamphlets and recruiting new members. The most active in canvassing among the colonial students were the communists. They masqueraded under the name Socialist Club, but I soon discovered their Marxist colours and their trick of having attractive British women students on hand to lobby African, Caribbean and the few Asian undergraduates. I steered clear of them all.

I was suffering from culture shock before the phrase was coined. The climate, the clothes, the food, the people, the habits, the manners, the streets, the geography, the travel arrangements – everything was different. I was totally unprepared except for the English language, a smattering of English literature, and previous interaction with British colonials.

For a large bedsitter, I paid the princely sum of £6 a week, a big amount for someone who had stopped earning. Fortunately, it included breakfast. There was a gas fire and a retractable gas ring in the room, and I had to put shillings into a meter to light the fire and cook for myself. I was desperately unhappy about food. It was rationed, and the restaurants where I could eat without coupons were expensive. I did not know how to use the rations that I bought and they were never enough. I had no refrigerator. The book *Cooking in a Bed-sitter* had not yet been written. I had disastrous experiences with boiling milk, which spilt over, and frying bacon and steaks that shrank and filled the room with powerful smells. The odours refused to go away for hours even though, in spite of the cold, I opened the sash window and the door to create a through draught. They clung to the bedclothes and the curtains. It was awful. Lunches at any of the three college canteens were stodgy and dreadful.

It was cold and lonely at night. As I returned to Swiss Cottage each evening with British white-collar workers, I felt good about not going back to a colonial student ghetto. But I was always alone. In the house itself, everybody went to their own rooms and closed the doors, since there was no common dining room or sitting room, and in the morning they had breakfast brought up to them or made their own. When I ran into difficulties with my housekeeping, I approached some British girls, six young office secretaries who shared a room in the attic. I took advice from them on where to buy meat and how to keep butter and milk fresh without a refrigerator (leave them out in the cold on the window-sill, and not indoors where they would turn sour). From fellow students, I learnt that I could save a laundry charge of sixpence if I washed a handkerchief and left it to dry on the mirror above the washbasin. But I could not do that with shirts and underwear. And shirt cuffs and collars got grubby in less than a day with London soot. I was thoroughly unhappy over the little things I had always taken for granted in Singapore. My family provided everything I needed. My shoes were polished, my clothes were washed and ironed, my food was prepared. All I had to do was to express my preferences. Now I had to do everything for myself. It was a physically exhausting life, moreover, with much time spent on the move from place to place. I was fatigued from walking, and travelling on buses and tubes left me without the energy for quiet study and contemplation.

One day, after a tutorial on constitutional law, I approached the lecturer, Glanville L. Williams. I had seen from the LSE calendar that he was from St John's College, Cambridge, where he had taken a PhD. I asked him about Cambridge and the life there. He said it was a small town whose existence centred on the university, very different from London. The pace of life was more leisurely. Students and dons moved around on bicycles. It sounded attractive and I decided to visit it.

I went up in late November 1946, and met a Raffles College student, Cecil Wong, who had got into Fitzwilliam House, a non-collegiate body for poorer students where the fees were much lower. Cecil took me to see the censor of Fitzwilliam, W.S. Thatcher, who was the equivalent of the master of a college. Billy Thatcher was an impressive man. He had won the Military Cross in World War I for service in Flanders, where he had been badly wounded. His face was scarred, and because his palate had been injured, his speech was affected. He had strong Christian principles and great compassion for an underdog. Thatcher was much respected and loved by dons and students alike. I recounted my problems to him. He took a liking to me and offered to take me in that same academic year when the Lent term started in early January 1947, provided my friend Cecil would share his room with me. Cecil immediately agreed. I was overjoyed and grateful. I returned to London, wound up my affairs and packed my bags. In early January, I took a train from King's Cross station, arrived at Cambridge some two hours later, and caught a taxi to Cecil's rooms at 36 Belvoir Road.

Two weeks later, I wrote to Professor Hughes Parry to tell him I had decided to leave the LSE and go to Cambridge instead. I received an angry reply. "I would remind you that I went out of my way to persuade the authorities of this school to accept you when we had turned others away," he wrote. "Your conduct shows that I was wrong in my estimate of you and that I should not have been so ready to help." On getting this letter, I decided to see him personally, to face him and take my medicine. I turned up at his office and explained how difficult life had been in my first term, that I came from a small town and felt totally lost in a big city of so many millions, so completely impersonal, with everybody hurrying around at a tremendous pace. Furthermore, I could not cater for myself.

He listened to my woes. I must have looked truthful because he relented and said I should have brought my problems to him. He could have arranged for some accommodation in a hostel that would have provided for my needs. Looking back now on those years, I am glad I did not stay on in London. I am sure I would have had a miserable time. But I have always felt remorse at having let him down after the special favour he extended to me. When he became vice-chancellor of London University in the late 1970s and I was prime minister of Singapore, I thought of writing to him but decided it might be better to let it pass. Perhaps I should have, just to tell him I had not forgotten his kindness.

London had its compensations – and its lessons for a future lawyer. One person who made an impact on me in my first term at the LSE was Harold Laski, a professor of political science. Like many other students who were not doing political science, I attended some of his lectures. He was a magnetic speaker, small, unimpressive physically, but with a scintillating mind. His Marxist socialist theories had a profound influence on many colonial students, quite a few of whom were to achieve power and run their underdeveloped economies aground by ineptly implementing policies based on what they thought Laski taught. It was my good fortune that I had several of these failed economies to warn me of this danger before I was in a position to do any harm in government.

The two or three of Laski's lectures that I attended were my first introduction to the general theory of socialism, and I was immediately attracted to it. It struck me as manifestly fair that everybody in this world should be given an equal chance in life, that in a just and well-ordered society there should not be a great disparity of wealth between persons because of their position or status, or that of their parents. I made no distinction between different races and peoples. We were part of the British Empire, and I believed the British lived well at the expense of all their subjects. The ideas that Laski represented at that time were therefore attractive to students from the colonies. We all wanted our independence so that we could keep our wealth for ourselves.

I thought then that wealth depended mainly on the possession of territory and natural resources, whether fertile land with abundant rainfall for agriculture or forestry, or valuable minerals, or oil and gas. It was only after I had been in office for some years that I recognised that performance varied substantially between the different races in Singapore, and among different categories within the same race. After trying out a number of ways to reduce inequalities and failing, I was gradually forced to conclude that the decisive factors were the people, their natural abilities, education and training. Knowledge and the possession of technology were vital for the creation of wealth.

There was much Marxist analysis in Laski's socialism. I agreed with the Marxists that man did exploit his fellow men through his possession of greater capital or power, and that because a man's output was more than he needed to consume to stay alive, there was a surplus for the employer or landlord to cream off. My aversion to the communists sprang from their Leninist methods, not their Marxist ideals. I had seen how ruthless the MPAJA had been in Singapore after the Japanese surrendered, taking summary revenge on all those whom they suspected of having worked for the enemy or otherwise betrayed their cause without any attempt to establish their guilt. They had been repulsive down to their very uniforms, their floppy cloth caps, their body language and their arrogant, aggressive attitudes. Among the student communists at the LSE, I found the same zealous hard sell, that over-eagerness to convert people to their cause. And they used whatever means were at their disposal, like those attractive young ladies ready to befriend lonely colonial students, deceiving the unwary by calling themselves the "Socialist Club".

I had also read in the British newspapers how the Russians had used their armies of occupation to install communist regimes in Poland, Czechoslovakia and Hungary. I was revolted by the way Jan Masaryk, the foreign minister of Czechoslovakia, was killed, found dead after having conveniently "fallen" from a window so that the communists could take over; by the harassment of Cardinal Mindszenty of Hungary, who had to take refuge in the American embassy in Budapest after standing up to them for his Catholic beliefs. Jack Hamson, a Cambridge Law School lecturer and himself a Catholic, was so outraged and sickened by what had happened that he spent a whole hour's lecture on the morning the news broke not on the law of contract, but on the evils of Soviet communism. It made a deep impression on me and increased my antipathy.

But the idea of an equal, just and fair society appealed to all colonial students, and the British Fabians recommended a step-by-step approach to this ideal state that would make it unnecessary to behead the rich and expropriate their riches. By stages, and without disrupting the economy or creating a social upheaval, the rich would be deprived of their wealth through taxation in their lifetime, and through heavy estate duties when they died. Their children would then have to start out in the world on the same basis as those of poorer parents. I could see no flaw in that. I was too young to know how ingenious British lawyers were in constructing trust deeds that made it difficult for the government to get too much out of estate duty.

I was so attracted by the Fabian approach that for years after my return from Britain I subscribed to their magazines and pamphlets. But by the early 1970s, I was despairing of their unworldliness. One particular issue stuck in my gullet. It was about education. Two headmasters had written a serious article to argue that British comprehensive schools were failing, not because they were wrong, but because the best teachers were still teaching the best students. The best teachers should be teaching the weakest students, who needed them in order to become equal. The good students would do well anyway. This Procrustean approach was too much for me. I stopped subscribing.

☙

Cambridge was a great relief after London. In the immediate post-war years it was a blissfully quiet provincial market town. There was little traffic – many bicycles, but only a few private cars and some buses and trucks. Most of the dons, the fellows of colleges, tutors, lecturers and professors, and even the censor of Fitzwilliam rode bicycles. I bought myself a second-hand bicycle for £8 and cycled everywhere, even in the rain. This was a very basic bike handed down from student to student over the past 20 or more years.

I soon got used to my new routine. And I had less trouble with meals. The food in hall was wholesome, with enough carbohydrates and proteins, although very British and very pallid. The deep-sea cod and halibut were tough and not tasty like the inshore fish I was used to in Singapore. There were no garnishes; as aboard the *Britannic*, everything had to be seasoned with salt and pepper. In spite of the cycling in clean but damp fenland air and the adequate meals, when I got back to Singapore, an X-ray of my lungs showed I had had a touch of tuberculosis when I was in England. Fortunately, it had healed and showed up only as a white patch in the X-ray. Still, I was grateful I had got a place in Cambridge. I am sure it would have been worse had I stayed on in London.

For exercise, I decided to join the Boat Club. I had first to practise, not by going out on the boat, but by "tubbing" on the river bank: sitting in a stationary tub, and being instructed how to hold the oar, how to stretch myself and pull it back, where to put my feet. After two practices per week for three weeks, I made it to a boat. On the afternoon of my second scheduled outing, a snowstorm broke and I assumed the practice was cancelled. I was severely reproached. Seven others and the cox had turned up but could not take the rowing eight out because I was missing. I decided that the English were mad and left the Boat Club. Thereafter, cycling around Cambridge to get from my digs to lectures and from lectures to Fitzwilliam House for meals provided my exercise.

The first year Qualifying One class of law students was small, some 30 compared with 200 in London. Most students who came up to the university were ex-servicemen who were given special dispensation to take a degree in two years instead of three, and therefore went straight into the second year. Unlike them, I had to do a Qualifying One first, and take three years. The British undergraduates studying with me were young people of 18 or 19 straight from school. I was 23. There were a few men from Malaya including Yong Pung How, about 20 years old and from Kuala Lumpur. (He was to be the chief justice of Singapore in 1990.) As I had missed the first term, Pung How readily lent me his notes. They were in a neat hand, comprehensive and a good synopsis of the ground I had missed. They were most useful because the Cambridge syllabus had different subjects from my first-year London course. During the Easter vacation, I swotted up what I had missed and caught up with my work. By May, when the Qualifying One examinations were held, I was fairly well-prepared. Three weeks later, in June, when the examination results were posted up at the Senate House, my name was among the few in Class I. I cabled home the good news.

I was glad I had not disappointed the censor, who had taken me in one term late on the strength of my academic record. Billy Thatcher, as

Love to Choo, from Britain's coldest winter, January 1947.

he was affectionately known by all his students, met me outside Fitzwilliam as I was parking my bicycle to go in for lunch in hall. He paused to congratulate me. I could feel that he was pleased. He had told me when I saw him in December 1946, "Lee, when you come up to Cambridge, you are joining something special, like joining the Life Guards and not just joining the army. You have to stand that extra inch taller." When I replied that I would try to get a First Class, he looked gravely at me and said, "Lee, don't be disappointed if you don't. In Oxford and in Cambridge, you need that divine spark, that something extra before you get a First." I was relieved that my Cambridge examiners had decided I had that something extra.

In high spirits, I bought myself a second-hand motorcycle, an old army surplus Matchless, not much to look at but with a lovely engine. It cost about £60. Suddenly I was mobile. I went wandering all over the Cambridge countryside and saw places that were not accessible by bus or railway. I would stop and buy cherries or strawberries where the farmers had put up placards inviting people to come and pick them or buy them.

∞

At the end of June, Choo wrote that she had taken a Class I diploma. She now stood a good chance of winning the Queen's scholarship to study in England. I was optimistic. Towards the end of July came the best news of all, a cable from Choo that she had been awarded the Queen's scholarship. But the Colonial Office could find no place for her in any university for the academic year beginning October 1947. She would have to wait until 1948. Stirred to action, I puzzled over how to get her into Cambridge

I looked up Mr Barret, the chief clerk at Fitzwilliam. He was a tubby, competent and experienced man in his late 40s. He had seen hundreds of young students come and go. He knew that the censor liked me. I told him of a lady friend in Singapore, very bright, who had won the top scholarship to study in England. She wanted to read law. How could she get into Cambridge in time for the Michaelmas term? With a twinkle in his eyes he said, "You know the censor knows Miss Butler, the mistress of Girton, very well. Now, if you could get him to speak to the mistress of Girton, that could make a difference." I was excited at this possibility.

There were only two months to go before the new academic year began. I asked to see the censor. Not only did he see me, he was also willing to help. On 1 August, he wrote to Miss Butler, and for good measure to the principal of Newnham, the other women's college in Cambridge. Both replied immediately. Newnham offered a place in 1948. Miss Butler was more positive. She was willing to offer a vacancy in October 1947 that Girton kept for special cases, provided Choo had the qualifications for admission. Thatcher wrote sending me both replies. I dashed off to the Examinations Syndicate near Silver Street along the river Cam. I gave them the year Choo had taken her Senior Cambridge – 1936. They traced her results and gave me a certified copy – she was the top student of her year.

I then wrote and asked to see Miss Butler at Girton. She was willing to see me, and I turned up at the appointed time on the morning of 6 August. I told her that my friend, Miss Kwa, was a very bright girl, brighter than I was, and that she had come top of the list, ahead of me in Raffles College on many occasions. I added that I had come up to Cambridge one term late and taken a First in my Qualifying One examination, and I had no doubt that she would do likewise. Miss Butler was a friendly, white-haired lady with glasses, somewhat plump and benign-looking. She was amused at this young Chinese boy talking in glowing terms of his lady friend being a better student than he was, and intrigued by the idea that perhaps the girl was exceptional. That same day I cabled Choo: "Girton accepts. Official correspondence following. Get cracking."

She boarded a troopship in Singapore in late August. I was waiting impatiently at the docks when she finally arrived in Liverpool in early October, and was overjoyed to see her after a long year of separation. We went off at once to London by train and after five days there we went on to Cambridge.

By now, I had got myself organised and knew my way around. But there were new problems. Mr Pounds, the junior tutor and bursar of Fitzwilliam, had given me rooms some three miles to the south of Cambridge. I was aghast. Girton was to the north of town. I tried hard to get a room nearer to Choo but to no avail. Mr Pounds was unrelenting. I appealed to the censor. His reply was fatherly, but spiced with a touch of dry humour:

"My dear Lee,

"… You plead that it is a long way to go to see your fiancée, or your wife as apparently you hope she will become. Not really so far as you make out, especially if love supplies the motive power. I don't know whether you read the great myths, but you will remember the gentleman who swam the Bosphorus every night to see his lady love. Going to Girton is a slight thing compared with that. Unhappily, the gentleman got drowned in the doing it (sic) one fine evening, but I doubt whether you need die of exhaustion on the road. If, however, you can find rooms near Girton, we will do our utmost to cooperate with you and get them licensed, so if you like to come up and look round, do so.

"By the way, I am not sure that Girton will appreciate you marrying the young lady so quickly, as they will very naturally and properly assume that in the first light of love there will be very little work done. But I am too old to offer advice between a man and the light of his eyes.

Yours sincerely,
W.S. Thatcher"

A week later, I found a room near Fitzwilliam at Captain Harris' Stables. Captain Harris kept horses and foxhounds. I was his one student boarder. He charged an exorbitant price, some £9 a week just for bed and breakfast, with baths and everything else extra. I had no choice. It was convenient. I was to stay there for the next two years until I came down from Cambridge in the summer of 1949.

Now it was Choo's turn for culture shock. She was not accustomed to the thick woollen suit she had bought with her clothing coupons, the heavy overcoat, and later the fleece-lined boots for winter. They weighed her down. And Girton was two miles from town. She could not cycle, and had to take a bus. Her sense of direction was never good. It was her time for disorientation.

After a few weeks of hectic adjustments, she told me she found me a changed man. I was no longer the cheerful, optimistic go-getter, the anything-can-be-done fellow, bubbling with *joie de vivre*. Despite the favour I had been shown, particularly the kindness of Billy Thatcher, and my happy mood during the glorious summer of 1947, I appeared to have become deeply anti-British, particularly of the colonial regime in Malaya and Singapore, which I was determined to end. One year in London and Cambridge had crystallised in me changes that had started with the Japanese capture of Singapore in 1942. I had now seen the British in their own country and I questioned their ability to govern these territories for the good of the locals. Those on the spot were not interested in the advancement of their colonies, but only in the top jobs and the high pay these could give them; at the national level they were primarily concerned with acquiring the foreign exchange that the exports of Malayan rubber and tin could earn in US dollars, to support an ailing pound sterling.

After Choo's revelation, I began to examine myself to see how it had happened. It may have begun with my experience of the colour prejudice of the British working classes, the bus conductors and conductresses, the salesgirls and waitresses in the shops and restaurants, and the landladies in Hampstead I encountered in my search for digs. Several times I had gone to houses listed in "rooms vacant" notices near Swiss Cottage tube station, only to be told, once they saw that I was Chinese, that the rooms had already been taken. Later, I pre-empted such problems by telling them on the phone that my name was Lee, spelt "L, double e", but that I was Chinese. If they did not want a Chinese, they could put me off then and save me the bother of travelling to their door.

The British people I met at the upper end of the social scale – the professors and teachers, the secretaries and librarians at Cambridge and at the Middle Temple – were cultured, polite and helpful, if a little reserved. The British students were by and large well-mannered, even friendly, but always correct. But of course there was colour prejudice when it came to competition for places on sports teams, for college colours or university "blues" and "half blues". Singaporeans and Malayans were very good at badminton, which rated a half blue, and in fact they did win some; but it was almost impossible for an Asiatic to get into the team for a major sport like cricket, rugby or, most prestigious of all, rowing.

The discrimination may not have been due entirely to colour prejudice. It was the class system – another strange phenomenon for someone coming from a young, mobile society of migrants. Even among the white students, those from the "right" public schools had the advantage. And like the rest, they coveted college colours because they would prove an asset in the future, when they could list them on their CVs. They were stepping stones to great things – anyone with a rowing blue had his career made. Similarly, being president of the Cambridge Union Society helped one to become a prospective candidate for a Labour or Conservative constituency, or to get a job in the research department of one of the parties.

There was also keen rivalry among Asiatics, mostly Indians, for election to office in the Union Society, but in their case it was difficult to understand, since by 1947, India and Pakistan were on their way to independence. One Ceylonese student at Trinity Hall got as far as being elected secretary of the Students' Union. I wondered how that would help him become a leader in a free Ceylon.

I was not interested in these extras. I decided to concentrate on getting my First, because that would make a difference when I went back to Singapore.

∽

Meanwhile, Choo and I discussed our life in Britain with an eye to the future. We decided that it would be best if we got married quietly in December during the Christmas vacation, and kept it a secret. Choo's parents would have been most upset had they been asked; Girton College might not have approved, as the censor had reminded me in his letter; and the Queen's scholarship authorities might have raised difficulties. We were already mature, in our mid-20s, and we had made up our minds. Unaware of our true motive, a friend who came from that part of England recommended an inn at Stratford-on-Avon as a place to spend Christmas and to visit the renowned Shakespeare theatre. Once we arrived, we notified the local Registrar of Marriages of our intention, and after two weeks of residence were duly married. On the way to Stratford-on-Avon we had stopped in London, where I bought Choo a platinum wedding ring from a jeweller in Regent Street. But when we went back to Cambridge, she wore the ring on a chain around her neck.

Despite this change in our lives, we worked systematically and hard at our studies. I wanted to make sure that I kept up the standard I had set for Tripos I. But Choo had a difficult time coping with a second-year course. The examinations came around again in May 1948, and in June the results were posted at the Senate House. I had made my Class I on the Tripos I honours list. Choo was placed in Class II in Law Qualifying Two. She was disappointed. But it was not a Tripos and did not really count. I consoled her, and we decided to take a two-week holiday on the

Continent. Avoiding tour groups, we arranged to spend five days in Paris, then a week in Switzerland.

One particular incident in Lugano has stuck in my mind to this day. The hotel receptionist looked at me and asked whether I was Chinese.

I said, "Yes, but from Singapore."

He said, "Ah, Chiang Kai-shek."

He did not know the difference. I was not very proud of Chiang Kai-shek. He was being chased out of mainland China by the People's Liberation Army. But I had grown to expect this stereotyping of me as a Chinaman by Europeans. We still had the best holiday of our lives, sightseeing, walking, eating, and drinking beer, wine and champagne.

In October, we were back in Cambridge for our final year. We attended lectures, wrote essays and assignments for supervisors, and read in the library or in my room at Captain Harris' Stables. But life was not all work. At weekends and on some evenings I would cycle to Girton, and Choo would cook Singapore dishes on the one gas ring in the gyp wing. I would invite Yong Pung How and Eddie Barker, also a Queen's scholar from Raffles College and reading law. Sometimes, my whole week's ration of meat went into a curry, or Choo would make marvellous fried *kway teow*, using fettucine, chicken in place of pork, and paprika in place of chillies.

By now, we were well-adjusted and had established good contacts. I had arranged to be taught by some of the best law supervisors in Cambridge. They were fellows of Trinity Hall, then the leading law college, but after I was placed in Class I at the end of my first year, I was able to persuade them to supervise me although I was at Fitzwilliam. My best supervisor was Trevor Thomas. He had a crisp, clear, methodical mind.

I also became friends with a few British students. Some were activists in the Cambridge University Labour Club who later stood as Labour Party candidates in the 1950 general election; others went on to different branches of the law and became distinguished professors in international law, comparative law and industrial law. They were a bright bunch and good company.

In February 1949, I represented Cambridge in a moot (formal disputation) at Oxford before a Justice Sellers. The other student lawyers did not seem to grasp the niggling point of law at issue, and once I grappled with it, Sellers' face lit up. When he delivered judgement, he complimented me. But I did not participate in any Cambridge Union Society debate. I did not think it wise to speak my mind before I had settled with my friends the line we must take when we got back to Singapore.

However, when I was in London I went to the House of Commons on several occasions to listen to the speeches. Some of the Labour MPs were friendly towards colonial students (unlike the Conservatives, who frowned on their desire for freedom). Fenner Brockway, the member for Eton and Slough, would meet me in the Great Hall at Westminster to give me my ticket for the Strangers' Gallery. Stanley Awbery (later Lord Awbery) was like Fenner Brockway, a supporter of colonial underdogs. Labour had some notable speakers. I remember, on my first visit in 1947, watching Stafford Cripps cut strips off the Conservative shadow colonial secretary as if with a rapier. He had a brilliant mind.

We took our final law examinations in May 1949, and when the results came out in June, I was satisfied. I had made a First and won the only star for Distinction on the final Law Tripos II honours list. Choo also made a First, and we cabled the good news to our parents. It was a good cachet for the next stage of my life. Before an undergraduate can take his degree, university rules require him to "keep" at least nine terms, in other words to stay in residence in college or in approved digs for about eight weeks in a term. Choo had been in Cambridge for only six terms; I for only eight. Special dispensations must have been granted because we were both allowed to take our degrees that midsummer day, 21 June. Otherwise I would have had to remain in Cambridge for another term, and Choo for another three before we could graduate.

Cambridge makes a point of maintaining hoary traditions that become more quaint with the years, but they add to its mystique as an ancient seat of learning. On Congregation Day, students formed a queue in accordance with the seniority of their colleges and, led by their tutors, entered the Senate House near the law schools. As censor, Billy Thatcher personally led me and the others forward – Fitzwilliam, being non-collegiate, was last in the queue. Afterwards we took many photographs with the dons and other students on the lawn outside the Senate House. Several of the law lecturers, who as supervisors from Trinity Hall had taught Choo and me, were there to share our joy, including Trevor Thomas. Pung How captured the moment with his camera.

We then adjourned to Trevor Thomas' rooms in Trinity Hall to celebrate the occasion with champagne. Another lecturer, Dr T. Ellis Lewis, affectionately called TEL, who had taught both of us, joined us. He was Welsh, with a delightful quizzical face, bald, wispy white hair at the sides and rimless glasses. He said to Choo and me, "If it's a boy, send him to us in Trinity Hall." When Loong, our first child, was born in 1952, I did write to the senior tutor to book a place for him. But 19 years later, when he went up to Cambridge, Loong decided to go instead to Trinity College, which Isaac Newton had established as the premier school of mathematics. Good tutors in Trinity helped him become a wrangler (a student with first class honours in mathematics) in two years instead of the usual three.

The photograph of our graduation that I treasure most is one of Billy Thatcher standing between Choo and me. I had not let him down. Nor had my "lady friend". Thatcher left a deep impression on me. He was a wise, perceptive man who had a lot of time for the students in his charge. One day, when I was having tea with him in his room, he pointed to the road workers who had been digging up Trumpington Street, and said that in the previous three hours they had had two tea breaks. They had been different before and during the war. Now they were not willing to work as hard, and the country would not progress. I thought him a reactionary old man, but he taught economics, and years later I concluded that he knew what made for growth. On another occasion, he told me, "You are Chinese. You Chinese have a long civilisation of several thousand years to back you up. That is a great advantage." Just before we went down from Cambridge in June 1949, he invited Choo and me for morning coffee for the last time. He patted Choo's hand and, looking at me, said, "He is too impatient. Don't let him be in such a hurry." He had read my character well, but he also knew that I had a serious purpose in life and was determined to achieve it.

Having graduated, we took a 10-day holiday, this time touring England and Scotland in a coach. But we were not finished with our law studies yet. To practise in Singapore, even a degree from Cambridge University was not enough. We still had to qualify as a solicitor or a barrister in England. So we had joined the Middle Temple, which was one of the four Inns of Court that together taught and examined students for admission to the Bar. When we came back from our trip, therefore, we tried to live in London and for a while took a flat not far from my old digs on Fitzjohn's Avenue. But for Choo housekeeping and study did not mix well, so we decided to skip lectures at the Inns of Court, and stay at Tintagel in Cornwall to read up and prepare for the Bar finals by ourselves.

We had already spent several vacations there, in an old manor house run by a Mrs Mellor with the help of her three sons. She fed us well, and was reasonable and helpful. We had the whole house to ourselves, except during the summer when there were a few other guests. We took long walks along country lanes and enjoyed the warm, moist southwesterly winds. Our only entertainment was to listen to the BBC Home Service on a Pye radio I bought in Cambridge. It gave us many hours of relaxation and pleasure. For exercise and recreation, I started to play golf, alone most of the time, on a nine-hole course at King Arthur's Castle Hotel that was empty except during the holiday season. The course was hilly and

Cambridge, 1948, with the Bridge of Sighs in the background.

Graduation day, 21 June 1949, with Choo and W.S. Thatcher, censor of Fitzwilliam, who made it all possible.

windy, and exciting for a duffer like me. It kept me fit. Choo and I spent much time looking for my lost golf balls, often finding other, better ones. Choo would also pick wild mushrooms, which Mrs Mellor cooked for us. They were delicious.

Less delicious were the meals we were obliged to take at the Middle Temple. To be called to the Bar, we had to "eat our dinners" in hall three times a term, as was required of all students. That meant a seven-hour train journey to Paddington station. But it was a chance to catch up with Malayan and Singapore friends at Malaya Hall in Bryanston Square. We indulged in talk of the kind students in London from all colonial territories engaged in, of our coming fight for freedom.

Some of my friends from Raffles College were politically active. Among them were Goh Keng Swee, my former economics tutor, who was taking a first degree BSc at the LSE, and Toh Chin Chye, who was doing a BSc in physiology at London University. They and a few others had formed a group called the Malayan Forum, whose object was to build up political consciousness and press for an independent Malaya that would include Singapore. Its members were drawn from all racial groups – Malay, Chinese, Indian, Eurasian – and it was non-ideological, neither left-wing nor right. It was anti-colonial, but committed to non-violence in order to disassociate itself from the Malayan Communist Party (MCP), which had already launched its armed insurrection against the British in Malaya in June 1948. Its members held meetings, sometimes with British politicians – junior ministers in the Labour government like Woodrow Wyatt, or Tory and Liberal MPs – as guest speakers. India and Pakistan had already gained their independence in August 1947, Burma and Ceylon in 1948. The imperial dam had been breached, the British Empire was in retreat, and most of us were confident that we, too, could get our independence. We sensed that the British people and their leaders had lost the will to keep their subject peoples down.

Some members of the Malayan Forum in a restaurant in Soho, London, summer 1950. Standing, left to right: my brother Dennis, Philip Hoalim Jr, Maurice Baker and Lee Kip Lin. Mohamed Sopiee is at my right. Seated, left to right: Chin Chye, Miki Goh, Choo, Kenny Byrne and his wife Elaine.

After plenty of talk, we would go pub-crawling from Malaya Hall to Marble Arch and along Edgware Road. The beer was awful, flat and heavy English "bitters". Even after many years, I never got to like it. But there was nothing else we impecunious students could afford. Light lagers were expensive, the price of whisky was prohibitive. Soused with beer, we talked of the great things we would do on our return. Later, I was to discover that very few would stay the course. Many wives would object to their husbands jeopardising their careers by opposing British colonial authority, and quite a number of the men themselves, faced with cold reality and hard choices, lost their stomach for the fight. Meanwhile, there were others already in the field. At one extreme were the politically effete time-servers, the English-educated intelligentsia. At the other were the communists and their united front, well organised and apparently enjoying support in every key sector of society from schools to trade unions, the press and the Chinese Chamber of Commerce.

I decided before leaving Britain to make contact with Lim Hong Bee, the unofficial MCP representative in London. Lim had been a Queen's scholar in 1934, but had lost interest in his studies and was consumed by the communist cause. He never passed his Bar examinations nor did he get his Cambridge degree. He stayed on in London to produce a stencilled pro-MCP tract called the *Malayan Monitor*. It was dreadful, crude propaganda, but he was a strong-willed fellow. I telephoned him to ask to see him, and he arranged to meet me outside the office of the *Daily Worker*, the organ of the British Communist Party, near Fleet Street. I brought Choo along; she knew him as a friend of her elder brother.

He was a strange man. Instead of going straight to where we could talk, he took us by a roundabout route through narrow streets, making unnecessary twists and turns before finally stopping at a working man's pub-cum-lunch-room, grubby and very proletarian. He lived in a self-created conspiratorial world. After social pleasantries, I asked him point-blank why it was that all communists devoured the social democrat workers in their united fronts, quoting what they had done in Czecho-slovakia and Hungary. He denied this strenuously. He said the social democrats in these countries had become so convinced that the cause of the communists was superior that they had joined them. He was completely out of touch and living in a dream world of his own in which he was a great revolutionary. When we parted, I was convinced that the MCP either did not consider London an important outpost or had no idea what Lim Hong Bee was actually doing there as their unofficial representative.

৵

In February 1950, while I was still at Tintagel, David Widdicombe, one of my Cambridge friends, stood as the Labour candidate for the rural seat of Totnes in Devon, an hour and a half away by train. He needed a driver for his truck and a general assistant. Choo and I spent a fortnight helping him until election night. We were both put up with Labour sup-porters, I with a train driver, Choo with the young wife and children of a man who was away training to be a solicitor.

I learnt how to campaign, and made several speeches in small school and church halls. The audience would be a few dozen strong, with a maximum of a hundred and fifty. I chose one basic theme that I elaborated upon and varied from meeting to meeting. This was that Britain got more dollars every year from Malaya than the US-sponsored Marshall Plan, because Malaya produced half the world's rubber and one-third of its tin. If Britain lost Malaya, there would be heavy cuts in imports of food and raw materials, an increase in unemployment and a steep rise in the cost of living.

In a choice between Labour and Conservative, people from the colonies had no difficulty in deciding which was better. Labour had a colonial policy. Its record since 1945 was impressive. Reforms long overdue had been carried out. But to the Tories, the colonies were simply areas for very profitable investments. A Tory government determined to suppress the new nationalist spirit of colonial peoples in order to preserve the empire would provoke disorder. Then the MCP would become strong enough to drive the British out of Malaya.

The Devon audiences were intrigued to see a Chinese speaking for a British Labour Party candidate. It was a hopeless cause, but it was the way the party made young candidates cut their teeth. On 23 February 1950, the result of the election was declared at the Town Hall. David Widdicombe had been soundly trounced. But he made a brave speech, and his victorious Conservative opponent a generous one, encouraging him to fight another battle in some other constituency. It was useful experience in politics at constituency level.

A month or two later, I received a letter from the Singapore commissioner of police, R.E. Foulger, who was home on leave. He knew my parents, had heard that I was in Cornwall, and invited Choo and me to his house at Thurlstone in Devon. We spent three days there. He wanted to size me up, and I was interested in making contact and seeing what a post-war British colonial police chief was like. We played golf. My golf was still bad, but it was a useful weekend. I knew by then that I had drawn the attention of Singapore's Special Branch and would be on their watch list. I had made some anti-British, anti-colonial speeches at Malaya Hall. They would know I was no dilettante. I thought it best if they also knew that I acted above board, constitutionally, and that I had no communist ties or sympathies. For we would soon be returning to Singapore.

In May 1950, we went down to London to take our Bar finals. We ran into a football crowd that weekend, and they banged the doors of the hotel where we stayed day and night, distracting us from our studies. But it would not have made much difference: we were to pay the price for being out of London and failing to listen to the lecturers who were also the examiners in the major subjects. They had set their questions on new cases they had taught. No one got a First Class. I got a Second Class and was listed in third place. Choo got a Third. But all was well.

On 21 June 1950, wigged and robed as the pageantry demanded, we were both called to the Bar at the Middle Temple dining hall. Life was about to enter a new phase.

∞

I was happy at the prospect of going home, but looked back on my four years in England with satisfaction and some pleasure. I had seen a Britain scarred by war, yet whose people were not defeatist about the losses they had suffered, nor arrogant about the victory they had scored. Every bomb site in the City of London was neatly tended, with bricks and rubble piled to one side, and often flowers and shrubs planted to soften the ruins. It was part of their understated pride and discipline.

Their courtesy and politeness to each other and to foreigners were remarkable. Most impressive was the consideration motorists showed: you waved on the person with the right of way; he waved back to thank you. It was a very civilised society. And I felt a certain nostalgia for the Cambridge where I had studied with that unusual generation of returned warriors in their 20s, some even in their 30s, married and with children. They were serious men who had seen death and destruction. Some had been through hell. One student in Fitzwilliam, who had been badly burnt when his plane crashed, was painful to look at despite repeated plastic surgery. But he overcame his disabilities. He knew his disfigured face frightened and upset people meeting him for the first few times, so he set out to act normally, to be reassuring and without self-pity. Unbowed, he made the best of his life.

It was not the Cambridge of youngsters who wanted to have a good time and to impress each other with their arty-crafty ways. Yes, there were a few of those, fresh from peacetime national service or exempted from it, but they were a minority and they did not set the pace. It was the ex-service students, some carrying the ugly marks of war, who made post-war Cambridge a place for learning and coping with the war's aftermath. I was privileged to have been up with that generation of Britons.

Of course, there were rough bits, friction mainly with people who had to serve me – English men and women who probably resented having to wait on a scruffy and impecunious Asiatic student. But if some landladies were especially mean and difficult, there were gems like Mrs Mellor at Tintagel and Mrs Jackson, the caretaker of the China Institute in London whom I remember most from my years in Britain. The China Institute in Gordon Square was created by the British government and financed from the indemnity the Chinese had had to pay for the damage to British lives and property in the Boxer Rebellion of 1900. It was open to all ethnic Chinese students, and I found it most convenient, a wonderful haven of peace and quiet near the heart of London.

Mrs Jackson was friendly to all the students. But from the very first she was particularly kind to me. During my vacations, as I changed addresses from London to Cambridge to London to Tintagel, 16 Gordon Square became my postbox. It was also a repository for our spare bags and books. Choo and I frequented it because we had no home in London, and at the China Institute we could wash off the grime of a capital sooty from coal fires with hot water, soap and clean basins that cost us nothing. All we needed were our own towels. And since the premises were rent-free, Mrs Jackson was also able to provide good and substantial high teas for just one shilling.

Petty matters? No one who was not a foreign student in England in those years of privation and shortages immediately after the war can imagine how difficult and inconvenient life was for us in a London bedsitter. The landlady supplied only breakfast, after which Choo and I would have to get out of our room to allow her to clean it. We would go to the public library to study, and eat our lunches and dinners in a restaurant. A clean and quiet place to rest and wash was an immense luxury, especially when it was free.

When I was in London in 1956 for the constitutional conference on the future of Singapore, I went back to Gordon Square to visit Mrs Jackson. She was as pleased to see me as I was to see her. But my association with the China Institute had meanwhile produced an unexpected political backlash. Years later, I discovered old reports in files of the Singapore Special Branch claiming that Choo and I had frequented it in order to fraternise with pro-communists from China, where Mao Zedong was then heading for victory in the civil war and on 1 October 1949 proclaimed the People's Republic. One report even said that Choo was a more radical left-winger than I was. My confidence in Special Branch reports was badly shaken.

During my student years, I was eager to make contact with political leaders in the Labour Party, especially those who could assist people like me who wanted an early end to colonial rule and an independent Malaya that would include Singapore. The Labour Party was much more sympathetic to independence for the colonies than the Conservatives, who still spoke of "King and Empire" in rich, round tones when they addressed meetings I attended. I also wanted to develop contacts with British students who were likely to play a role in future in the main political parties, a network that would be useful when I tangled with the colonial authorities in Singapore and Malaya. I therefore studied their political system with keen interest.

Their system of parliamentary democracy seemed to work so well. A tremendous revolution – economic, social and political – was taking place peacefully before my eyes. The voters had thrown out Winston Churchill and his Conservatives in May 1945, although Churchill had won the war for Britain. They had put Clement Attlee and the Labour Party in power on the strength of their promise to bring about the most profound changes in British history. The Attlee government was implementing programmes designed to create a welfare state that would look after Britons of all classes from cradle to grave. Yet there was no violent protest from its opponents, no blood in the streets. Only strong words from Conservatives in parliament and in the constituencies urging moderation and common sense on the question of what was affordable. I was most impressed.

Soon after the National Health Service Act was passed in 1948, I went to collect my spectacles from an optician in Regent Street in Cambridge. I had expected to pay between five and six pounds for them. At the counter the optician proudly told me that I did not have to pay for them, and instead gave me a form to sign. I was delighted and thought to myself that this was what a civilised society should be. A few months later, the same thing happened at the dentist. Again, I only signed a form. The college doctor did not even bother to have me sign a form because I was already registered in his book as a patient. Again, I was enormously impressed. But the newspapers reported that many Frenchmen and other Continentals were coming over to Britain for free dental treatment. I thought this was carrying things too far, but then the French were so much poorer. I admired the British immensely for the transformation they were bringing about.

What struck me most was the fairness of the system. The government was creating a society that would get everybody – rich or poor, high or low or middle class – on to one broad band of decent living standards. And this although there were still shortages. The rationing of food and clothes, introduced during the war, would continue until the Conservatives abolished it in the mid-1950s. It still applied to items like tea, sugar, sweets, chocolate, butter, meat, bacon and eggs. Utility clothes at reasonable prices were available, but needed coupons.

I was too young, too idealistic to realise that the cost to the government would be heavy; worse, that under such an egalitarian system each individual would be more interested in what he could get out of the common pool than in striving to do better for himself, which had been the driving force for progress throughout human evolution. That realisation had to wait until the 1960s, when I was in charge of the government of a tiny Singapore much poorer than Britain, and was confronted with the need to generate revenue and create wealth before I could even think, let alone talk, of redistributing it.

Meanwhile, I knew from letters and from little snippets in the English press that trouble was brewing at home. Labour unrest and social tensions were being fomented by the MCP. There were strikes and political agitation, and by June 1948, communists had started shooting and killing British rubber planters upcountry. The guerrillas were back in the jungle, and the colonial government had declared an Emergency. In the open constitutional arena, on the other hand, there was no political force beyond the weak and spineless English-educated leaders who were only too eager to accommodate and please the British rulers. I felt strongly that when my generation returned, we must fill that arena. I joined the Cambridge University Labour Club and regularly attended their meetings, especially when Labour ministers came down on Friday evenings to talk about the programmes they were pushing through in parliament.

It was a time of great excitement and change. This was democratic socialism in action. And it was all so civilised. On one occasion, British doctors threatened to go on strike, but they were deterred from doing so by their sense of honour and tradition, and the duties and habits of constitutional order. Aneurin Bevan, the health minister, got his National Health Service bill passed after doing nothing more drastic than call the Tories "lower than vermin". The Labour Party was also building more council houses to rent out at very heavily subsidised low rents. They expanded the scope of welfare to make sure the "safety net" caught all families who did not have enough to meet their minimum needs. (These minimum needs looked like luxury compared to what I remembered of conditions in Singapore even before the Japanese impoverished us.) It was a remarkable lesson in how to go about creating social justice.

My generation of Singapore and Malayan students in Britain after World War II were completely sold on the fairness and reasonableness of the Labour government's programme. We were enthusiastic about the mature British system, under which constitutional tradition and tolerance allowed fundamental shifts of power and wealth to take place peacefully. We compared what we saw in Britain with Singapore and Malaya, with our largely uneducated peoples and a feeble press that ignored all the basic issues but reported the comings and goings of important people, mostly white bosses and the locals who hovered around them. The situation looked backward and unpromising.

It was against such a backdrop that Choo and I sailed home on a Dutch liner, the *Willem Ruys*. It was the best ship plying between Southampton and Singapore – new, air-conditioned, with excellent Indonesian and Dutch food, and wonderful service provided by literally hundreds of *djongos*, or Javanese waiters, dressed in native costume. It was a farewell fling. We travelled first class in adjoining cabins, and had a wonderful time – except when I got seasick in the Bay of Biscay and again on the Arabian Sea, and was reduced to a diet of dry toast and dried beef. Otherwise, it was a memorable journey.

By now, I had become highly politicised and anti-colonial, and was repelled by the presence among the first class passengers of several Indonesian Eurasians who fawned upon the Dutch captain and his officers. On the other hand, we were impressed by the bearing of Mr and Mrs Mohammad Razif, a reserved middle-aged Indonesian couple who kept their distance from the captain. We struck up an acquaintance with them, and Razif proved to be a nationalist from Sumatra – he later became the Indonesian ambassador in Kuala Lumpur. He restored my faith in the pride of a colonial subject people, and I had a high regard for him. But it was to be some time before I realised that a country needed more than a few dignified and able men at the top to get it moving. The people as a whole must have self-respect and the will to strive to make a nation of themselves. The task of the leaders must be to provide or create for them a strong framework within which they can learn, work hard, be productive and be rewarded accordingly. And this is not easy to achieve.

We reached Singapore on 1 August. It was good to be home. I knew I was entering a different phase of my life. I was quickly reminded of its hazards. Although we were travelling first class, the immigration officer, a Mr Fox who came on board wearing a natty bow tie, made sure that I knew my place. He kept Choo and me waiting to the very last. Then he looked through Choo's passport and mine and said enigmatically, "I suppose we will hear more about you, Mr Lee." I glared at him and ignored his remark. He intended to intimidate, and I was not going to be intimidated.

Later, I was to discover that among the black marks against me was my suspected attendance at the World Festival of Youth in Budapest in August 1949. During that summer vacation, the Soviet Union used the Hungarians as hosts for this communist-organised rally and the International Students Union in London invited groups in Britain to take part. Some Malayan and Singapore students accepted because it was a chance to have a cheap holiday, everything found for the cost of a return rail fare. Keng Swee, Maurice Baker, my brother Dennis and many others went. Once there, however, Lim Hong Bee and a Singapore crypto-communist named John Eber tricked them into forming a contingent to march with a banner that read "Malaya Fights For Freedom". British Intelligence learnt of this, and since some of them might become troublemakers when they returned home, sent to Singapore Special Branch a list of those who had participated, including "K.Y. Lee". Special Branch interviewed my parents, but as they knew nothing, they could not clarify the position. In consequence, the authorities did not know that their suspect was my brother Dennis, D.K.Y. Lee, and not me – H.K.Y. Lee.

But there were other reports in their file on me to earn me the distinction of being the last passenger on the *Willem Ruys* to be cleared. When I recorded my oral history in 1981, a researcher showed me documents of a meeting on 28 June 1950 at Government House at which Nigel Morris, the director of Special Branch, had recommended that Choo and I be detained on our return from England. However, R.E. Foulger, the commissioner of police who had earlier invited us to spend a weekend with him in Devon, had disagreed. The minutes further recorded that the governor, the general officer commanding and the colonial secretary had supported Foulger, arguing that because we both came from respectable families, public reaction to our arrest would be bad. Instead, they said, more could be gained if we were befriended and won over. The commissioner general for Southeast Asia, Malcolm MacDonald, "was suggested as an appropriate host since he frequently invited students to dinner". In fact Malcolm MacDonald did invite Choo and me a few months after our return.

While Mr Fox kept me waiting in the first class lounge of the *Willem Ruys*, I popped out on deck to wave to my family – Father, Mother, Fred, Monica and Suan – on the quay with some friends, including Hon Sui Sen. Choo's family was also waiting for her, but when we disembarked, we parted company. She went back with her parents to Pasir Panjang, I to Oxley Road. We parted as friends, not giving away the secret of our marriage in Britain.

6. Work, Wedding and Politics

The press reported our return, giving prominence to my academic success in Cambridge, and also to Choo's. The publicity helped me get my first job. While visiting the Supreme Court, I met a Straits-born lawyer, T.W. Ong, who asked me if I was interested in doing my pupillage in his firm, Laycock & Ong. I was, and he immediately arranged for me to see John Laycock, his senior partner, the following day.

Laycock was a Yorkshireman of about 60 who had qualified as a solicitor in England. He had been in practice in Singapore since the early 1930s, and had married a Chinese woman. They had no offspring of their own and had adopted several Chinese children. He had a powerful mind and a fierce temper, but his voice was small for a tubby man with such a big head; his face would flush when he was angry and he would become almost incoherent. He was full of energy, drank heavily, and perspired all the time, wiping himself with a large handkerchief. He offered to take me as his personal pupil. This meant I would sit in his office cooled by two large Philco air-conditioners, which made a powerful racket but were otherwise effective. He would pay me $500 a month until I was called to the Singapore Bar, which would take one year because I had chosen not to read in chambers in England.

I started work almost immediately. I had tropical clothes made – white drill trousers and light seersucker jackets – and bought cellular cotton shirts that could breathe. But it did not help. I sweated profusely, not having acclimatised to the heat and humidity, and every time I went out to the courts I would come back soaked. It was disastrous to be wet in Laycock's draughty air-conditioned room, and I would go down with coughs and colds. I soon learnt that the first thing to do when I got back to the office was to wash my face with cold water, cool down and change into dry clothes.

Having found a job, my next task was to see Choo's father, Kwa Siew Tee. He was a tall, energetic, self-made man who had taught himself accountancy and banking through correspondence courses and had risen to his present position in the Oversea-Chinese Banking Corporation on his own merits, having neither relatives to give him a push nor money to buy promotion. I asked him for his daughter's hand and when we could have the wedding. He was dumbfounded. He had expected the normal ritual of a visit by my parents to broach the subject, but this brash young man had turned up to settle the day himself, taking for granted that consent would be given. However, he did not grumble as much to me as he later did to Choo. We agreed to an engagement, to be followed by marriage at the end of September. Reading the announcement in the newspaper, Laycock offered to take Choo as a pupil and pay her $500 a month too. I told Choo about it, and she promptly accepted. It was most convenient. We could go to work together, and see each other every day.

On 30 September 1950, after being married secretly for nearly three years, we went through a second ceremony at the Registry of Marriages, which was then in the Supreme Court building. The registrar, Mr Grosse, was 15 minutes late. I was furious and told him off. An appointment had been made yet he kept all of us waiting. Later that afternoon, our parents held a reception for relatives and friends at the Raffles Hotel. Tom Silcock, professor of economics at the University of Singapore who had taught both of us at Raffles College, proposed the toast to the bride. He was not a witty, light-hearted speaker, but he did Choo proud. Choo then moved into 38 Oxley Road. My mother had bought some new furniture for us, and we started our official married life. But it was a difficult adjustment for Choo because she had now to fit into the Lee family,

Our wedding at Raffles Hotel, 30 September 1950. The label "Stikfas" in the left corner was placed by Yong Nyuk Lin to remind us of our gum-making during the Japanese occupation.

consisting not only of my grandmother, father, mother, sister, and three brothers, but several relatives from Indonesia who were still boarding with us, supplementing my mother's income.

I joined the Singapore Island Club to keep up the golf I had learnt to play at Tintagel, and was so keen on the exercise that one wet afternoon I drove Choo there despite the rain. On Thomson Road my Studebaker skidded, did a U-turn, and rolled over onto a soft grass slope. I was stunned. So was she. We were lucky. We had absolutely no injuries. Had we gone off the road a little further up, we would have struck a large water pipe instead of wet ground, and that might have been the end.

I was restless. Politics in Singapore made frustrating, even infuriating reading. Power was in the hands of the governor, his colonial secretary and his attorney-general. They all lived in the Government House domain that symbolised it. The governor lived in the biggest building, Government House, the colonial secretary in the second biggest bungalow, the attorney-general in the third, and the undersecretary and private secretary to the governor in two other bungalows. The telephone exchange serving these five buildings was manned 24 hours a day.

This was the real heart of government. There was a Legislative Council, but only six of its 25 members were locally elected. The rest were British appointees and officials, headed by the colonial secretary. In 1951, elected members were increased to nine, but they did not have the power to determine policy. Nor did they have any standing with the people – the turnout for municipal and Legco elections was pitifully small.

My boss, John Laycock, was the moving spirit in the main political party, the Progressive Party, but its nominal chief was another lawyer, C.C. Tan, who looked and sounded feeble. Its leaders were mostly returned students who had read law or medicine in Britain in the thirties and were overawed and overwhelmed by English values. They were like my grandfather – everything English was the acme of perfection. They had no confidence in themselves and even less in their own kind.

Patrick O'Donovan, Southeast Asia correspondent of the London Sunday newspaper *The Observer*, when I was a student in England described the older generation of returned Asian students as emotionally and psychologically incapable of fighting for freedom. Their starting point was that they could not take over immediately and run an independent country, and would require many more years of experience before they could do so. I saw them as unable to stand up for themselves, let alone stand up against the British. The same applied to the Indians from India who had become "Singapore leaders" by reason of their British passports and the political vacuum the MCP revolt had created. The only local of consequence was Lim Yew Hock, the general secretary of the Singapore Clerical and Administrative Workers' Union.

These politicians made supine speeches that never challenged British supremacy. They were inordinately proud whenever they said anything critical of colonial officials. My friend Kenny Byrne described them as "bred in servility". Kenny had come home on the *Willem Ruys* with me; he worked in the government secretariat and we would voice our frustrations when I visited him in his government quarters after dinner. He was a tall, slow-talking, slow-walking Eurasian who had a long memory for insults and loathed some of his British fellow officers in the civil service.

I was determined to do something about this lamentable situation, and anxious that my other friends should return from England, especially Keng Swee and Chin Chye. I wanted their assessment, to compare notes and decide on a course of action. I also wanted to make contact with John Eber and Lim Kean Chye, who had been leading left-wing figures in the Malayan Democratic Union (MDU) before it was dissolved when the Emergency was declared in June 1948. One day in November 1950, without prior notice, John Eber called on me at Oxley Road. I asked him what we could do about Singapore's futile constitutional politics. Why not form a party and do something substantial – stop this beating about the bush and challenge the power of colonial government? He was noncommittal. He said, "Well, there is an Emergency on. We have to be very careful." He had probably heard from Lim Hong Bee of our meeting in London and was sizing me up as a potential recruit.

In January 1951, the newspapers reported the detention of an English-educated group of communists. It included John Eber, who had been vice-president of the MDU, C.V. Devan Nair, secretary of the Singapore Teachers' Union, and Abdul Samad bin Ismail, chief sub-editor of the Malay newspaper, *Utusan Melayu*. This was the first time detention powers under the Emergency Regulations were used against an English-educated group. I had hoped to get John Eber and his friends interested in forming a constitutional political party, but instead he had come to assess me as a possible recruit for his cause. If he and his group had not been arrested for another six or 12 months, Special Branch might well have included me in the clean-up. This turn of events gave me time for reflection, and I soon realised the gravity of this development.

The MCP was waging a guerrilla war against the British in the jungles of Malaya, shooting white planters and locals who supported the colonialists. They were winning many recruits from among the Chinese-educated majority in Singapore, who had been impressed by reports of Communist China's progress, and by the victories the People's Liberation Army had scored against the Americans in Korea. These successes gave a powerful boost to China's stature, and therefore to the conversion of the Chinese-educated to the communist cause.

But it was now clear that the MCP had also won recruits among the English-educated intelligentsia. In spite of the favoured treatment they received, and their monopoly of jobs in the government and the professions, some of the most idealistic had succumbed to the appeal communism had for peoples fighting colonialism. If we did nothing, if we failed to mobilise them into an effective political movement, the MCP would be the ultimate gainer.

∽

I continued my work at the law and followed Laycock to court in his Chancery cases. He stayed sober when he had to appear, but on other occasions it would be something of an ordeal. He would take me out to lunches and dinners, and drink copiously – black and tan (beer and stout) to wash down oysters at the Kallang airport hotel or T-bone steaks at the Stamford Café or the Adelphi Grill. Sometimes he became too inebriated to work effectively in the afternoon, and at night he would drink himself silly on whisky. I ate more than was good for me and drank more than I wanted. Laycock must have thought me a useful recruit for his Progressive Party, for in February 1951, he asked me to be his agent for the Legislative Council election. I agreed. It would give me an idea of conditions and practices in Singapore.

Nomination day was 8 March, but there was no excitement. Small wonder. At the previous Legislative Council polls in 1948, only 23,000 out of a potential electorate of 200,000 had voted, and nearly half of those had been Indians although their community consisted of no more than six per cent of the population. Not unnaturally, therefore, there was a disproportionate number of Indians among those standing for election in 1951 – 15 (including one Ceylonese) candidates out of 22 contesting nine seats. One of them, the first woman to be elected to the Legco, absconded to India the following year with her lawyer husband and a large sum of money belonging to his clients. That did no good to the standing of India-born Indians in Singapore, who were regarded as birds of passage.

With a meagre vote, Laycock secured one of the six seats won by the Progressive Party. Two went to the Labour Party, and one to an independent. The campaign was a parody of what I had seen in England. Laycock contested his home constituency of Katong on the east coast, where there were large numbers of English-speaking Straits Chinese loyal to King and Empire. As his election agent, I paid helpers to put up posters with his photograph, his name and the caption "Vote for John Laycock, Progressive Party". But he also instructed me to arrange evening parties, with professional female dancers to partner the men in the Malay *joget*, and provided food and drink although it was against the law. I had to make sure, moreover, that the headman of the kampong involved was adequately compensated, for he was expected in return to tell his people to vote for Laycock. In the midst of the merrymaking, John Laycock would mount a small platform with a microphone to make a speech in English, promising that he would bring electricity and water to his audience. Few in the audience understood him. We held two meetings in Kampong Amber, a squalid squatter area that is now a high-rise condominium.

As in the 1948 election, only a small proportion of those eligible to vote turned up – 24,693 out of 250,000. The world that the legislative councillors represented was a small segment, isolated from the broad mass of the people. The majority of those on the island had been uninvolved and uninterested in the election for the simple reason that they did not have the vote, and anyway, everything was conducted in English. But the bulk of the population were Chinese-speaking. Their avenues for advancement after going through Chinese schools were negligible, and their political aspirations could only be realised through the MCP. They included the hawkers, trishaw men, taxi drivers and runners for the illegal four-digit and *chap-ji-kee* lotteries. They were the ordinary people who appeared in the outer office of Laycock & Ong, looking for help to get them out of entanglements with the police, the municipal authorities or the government. They spoke no English, and clerks interpreted for them to lawyers who did not speak their dialects.

I felt that this world of colonial make-believe was surreal. Officials catered only to their own interests and those of the English-educated, who could bring some pressure to bear on them through the English-language newspapers. But they were not the economic dynamo of Singapore society. I had a great sense of unease. I discussed these thoughts only with Kenny. I had to get on with my career in law, and had yet to see how the law would help me in politics.

∽

On 7 August 1951, I completed my one year of pupillage. To be called to the Bar, Choo and I dressed in sombre clothes and donned our barrister's robes complete with white tabs and, in my case, a stiff wing collar. It was an important occasion then, for the entire Bar had 140 members, and only some 10 new lawyers were admitted each year. René Eber, a respected old Eurasian lawyer, moved our petition for admission with a gracious little speech. It was his crypto-communist son, John, who had been arrested seven months before. Singapore is a small world.

Because my birth certificate called me Harry Lee Kuan Yew, I could not get either the Middle Temple or Cambridge University to drop "Harry" from my registered name. So on both my Cambridge University degree and my certificate as Barrister-at-Law, I am Harry Kuan Yew Lee. In 1950, I decided to try to have myself called to the Singapore Bar using only my Chinese name, with my surname placed before my personal name: Lee Kuan Yew. This time, I succeeded; Lee Kuan Yew became my public *persona*, what I stood for and saw myself as – a left-wing nationalist – and that is how I appeared in newspaper reports of my cases in court. But through all these years, my wife and my personal friends still call me Harry. In the 1950s, during my early days in politics, I was mildly annoyed to be sometimes reported as Harry Lee. Politically, it was a minus. However, by the middle 1960s, after I had been through the mill and survived, I got over any sense of discomfort. It was not a reflection on me and my values. I did not name myself. I have not given any of my children a Western first name, nor have they in turn given their children Western names.

Three days after being called to the Bar, I was asked by my old friend, the registrar of the Supreme Court, Tan Thoon Lip, to defend four Malays in a case that would have a profound impact on my views about the jury system in Singapore. In December 1950, a Dutch girl who had been converted to Islam by her Malay foster mother was placed in a convent on the order of the High Court while the judge determined the right of her natural mother to reclaim her. The Dutch mother had handed the child to the Malay woman to look after when the Japanese overran the country. The press carried photographs of the girl in the convent, before a statue of the Virgin Mary. This so enraged the Muslims, who considered her a Muslim, that it sparked off several days of rioting during which Muslim mobs in the streets killed white men and women indiscriminately.

The four men whom I now had to defend were among 13 charged with having committed murder by causing the death of Charles Joseph Ryan, a non-commissioned officer in the Royal Air Force. The other nine accused were defended by a more senior lawyer, F.B. Oehlers.

The trial lasted nearly two weeks and was conducted before a judge and a jury of seven. I applied myself to the case more assiduously than Oehlers, a man of 50 years whose reputation at the Bar had already been made. Mine was to be decided. I did most of the cross-examination, setting out to cast doubts on the accuracy of the identification of the persons who took part in the riotous attack that resulted in Ryan's death. It had become dark by the time they got hold of Ryan, dragged him out of the bus in which he was travelling from Changi to the city, beaten him senseless and left him in a deep monsoon drain in the Malay area of Geylang Serai. I got the judge, together with the jury and witnesses, to go to the site at night to see the poor street lighting, which left much of it in shadow. I questioned how strangers who saw a mêlée of some 40–50 Malay and Indian Muslims could in that half-light have recognised the men in the dock as those who had struck the victim. How far away were they from his assailants at the scene of the crime? For how long did they see my clients? What clothes were they wearing? What special marks or features did the accused have on their faces?

After the cross-examinations, Oehlers and I summed up. We pointed out all the contradictions between what the witnesses had said at the preliminary inquiry and at the trial itself, especially about the visibility. It was like pushing through an open door, as Chinese and Indian jurors were never happy to convict if it meant sending a man to his death. The jury were therefore only too relieved to be able to acquit all of the accused on the murder charge. But the evidence weighed heavily on their conscience and they found nine of them guilty of voluntarily causing grievous hurt. Three of my clients got off scot-free. One was only sentenced to five years rigorous imprisonment. There was disgust on the faces of the English judge and English prosecutor.

I, too, was sickened by the result. My duty as an advocate of the Supreme Court required me to do my best for my clients without breaking the law or advancing a falsehood. I had cast much doubt on the prosecution's case and thwarted justice. I had no doubt that my four clients did kill Ryan, that they were highly keyed-up that night and would have murdered any white or partly white person who came their way, anyone associated with the Christian religion and thus, to them, against Islam. I had no faith in a system that allowed the superstition, ignorance, biases, prejudices and fears of seven jurymen to determine guilt or innocence. They were by definition the ordinary man in the street with no special qualifications other than an ability to understand English and follow the proceedings. I had seen juries in British courts. I did not think they deserved the reverence that lawyers and jurists ritually accorded to their collective wisdom.

One difference between cases in England and Singapore was the need for interpreters. Many witnesses were not able to or did not wish to speak in English, if only to have more time to frame their replies to questions. The Malay interpreter, a stout Indian Muslim, was superb. He would mimic the pitch of voice, the body language and the mood of the witness. He produced his most memorable line when one of them quoted the words *Allahu Akbar*. He translated: "He said the men were shouting *Allahu Akbar*. My Lord, the phrase means 'God is Great'. It is also the Muslim battle cry."

But interpreters have other uses, and when our first child was born on Sunday, 10 February 1952, I consulted one of those at the Supreme Court who had helped many lawyers find appropriate Chinese names for their children. The date of birth was the most auspicious in the Chinese calendar, the 15th day of the first moon of the Year of the Dragon. We therefore decided to name our son Hsien Loong – Illustrious Dragon. He was a long baby, scrawny but weighing more than eight pounds, and he gave us great joy.

When I saw Choo in Kandang Kerbau (maternity) Hospital over the next few days, I was able to tell her of my second piece of good fortune – my first union work. It would bring me into the political spotlight and into a head-on clash with the government.

7. My First Clashes with the Government

One afternoon in 1952, a group of three Malays and one Indian in postmen's uniform came to the offices of Laycock & Ong to see me. No longer in Laycock's room, I met them in the outer office – not air-conditioned, hot, humid and noisy with the sound of traffic and hawkers. The Postal and Telecommunications Uniformed Staff Union, they told me, had put forward claims for salary revisions but had so far not been successful, and they had been given permission to engage a lawyer to appear for them. I asked John Laycock whether I should accept the case, given that there would not be much money in it. He told me to carry on for the sake of the goodwill, so I did it without asking for legal fees. This decision to represent the postmen was to be a turning point in the history of the trade unions and constitutional mass action. Little did I know that I would be guiding union leaders in a strike that in two weeks changed the political climate. It put the colonial government on the defensive and encouraged workers' militancy. But it also created the conditions for the communists to reorganise their mass support.

P. Govindasamy, a mail officer (one grade higher than postman), was not well-educated but briefed me in adequate English. He was totally relevant and reliable. He was later to be elected MP in a neighbouring constituency and helped me look after mine. The negotiations with the Establishment Branch of the government secretariat, which lasted from February to May, produced only the same salary revisions that applied to postmen in Malaya although I had argued that the work was more onerous and the cost of living higher in Singapore.

We were coming to a crunch. One Sunday morning, the union held a pre-strike meeting at their quarters in Maxwell Road, where large families lived in one-room flats with communal kitchens and toilets. Nearly the entire union of 450 postmen turned up. My presence was to give them moral courage, and to reassure them that what they were doing was not illegal, especially since no strikes had been held in Singapore since the Emergency was declared in 1948. In bazaar Malay, I got my views across to all, mostly Malays, the rest Chinese and Indians. They decided to give strike notice.

Before the strike began on 13 May, Keng Swee, who had returned from England, arranged a dinner at the Chinese Swimming Club in Amber Road for me to meet an associate editor of the *Singapore Standard*, Sinnathamby Rajaratnam. Raja was a Malayan of Jaffna Tamil origin. He had been in London for 12 years until 1947, associating with a group of Indian and African nationalists and British left-wing personalities, and writing anti-colonial tracts and newspaper articles. He was a good listener. Out in the open by the swimming pool, against the music and the hubbub of the swimmers, I briefed him on the background to the strike. He had been waiting for a good issue on which to challenge the colonial government, and was eager to do battle for the postmen.

While the postmen were picketing peacefully on the first morning of the strike, the government sent a large contingent of Gurkhas armed with revolvers and kukris into the General Post Office in Fullerton Building on Collyer Quay, the most prominent part of the business district. The deputy commissioner of police announced that police with sten guns would stand guard at all post offices until the strike ended.

Next day, the newspapers carried photographs of the Gurkhas and police and, in sharp contrast, a moderate statement by the president of the union saying that the postmen would refrain from picketing until their intentions were clearly understood. Public sympathy swung towards the postmen. The following day, the government withdrew the Gurkhas and the pickets resumed peacefully.

At the government secretariat at Empress Place, leading the negotiating delegation of the Postal and Telecommunications Uniformed Staff Union in May 1952. At far right is mail officer P. Govindasamy, who later became an MP.

The *Singapore Standard* was a locally owned newspaper with a much smaller circulation than the pro-British *Straits Times*, but its voice counted in this contest. Many locals read it, forcing some colonial officials to read it as well. In his editorial, Raja took a sardonic swipe at the racial bias of the colonial government, questioning the right of British expatriates to receive better pay than the locals; they had been given $1,000 in expat pay, but the postmen were refused an extra $10 a month.

Meanwhile, the mail piled up, to everyone's inconvenience. The public had to collect their letters and parcels on their own. In spite of this, the public was for the postmen because of their moderate actions and the statements I drafted for them. Raja's headlines and editorials in the *Singapore Standard* helped enormously. The Malay newspaper *Utusan Melayu* backed the strikers, for most of the postmen were Malay. So did the Chinese dailies, the *Nanyang Siang Pau* and *Sin Chew Jit Poh*, where many communist sympathisers among their reporters and editors always opposed the government.

The *Straits Times*, on the other hand, was British-owned and run. It had a capable editorial writer, Allington Kennard, who tried to be neutral but found it difficult not to be pro-government.

Raja was enjoying the fight. This was crusading at its best – fighting for the downtrodden masses against a heartless bunch of white colonial exploiters. His polemical style was emphatic. Many years hobnobbing with Indian and West Indian anti-imperialists had given him a heavy touch. My three years of sparring with friendly and sympathetic British students of the Labour Club in Cambridge had given me a different diction, and a preference for the understatement. So we played a duet, Raja strong and vigorous, I courteous, if pointed, always more in sorrow than in anger. I phoned him to make suggestions, relaying reactions from our supporters; he checked his editorial pitch with me. He would bring his galley proofs to my home for discussions, or we would talk on the phone, often well past midnight, just before his paper went to bed. The

Singapore Standard forced the pace and the establishment paper, the *Straits Times*, had to publish my letters to keep up an appearance of impartiality.

By the end of the first week, popular opinion turned strongly against the administration. British colonial officers had not been accustomed either to presenting their case in order to win public backing, or to dealing with local men who politely showed up their contradictions, weaknesses and cavalier attitudes. Exposure of the high-handedness of the government officers who dealt with the postmen moved other unions to come out in open support of them. Even the secretary-general of the pro-establishment Singapore Trade Union Congress, who was a close associate of Lim Yew Hock and an executive committee member of the Singapore Labour Party, joined the bandwagon. He announced the launching of a fund "to help the postmen to carry on their strike to a successful end". The *Singapore Standard* invited contributions from the public and collected donations from individual donors.

The government was rattled. The colonial secretary offered "to resume negotiations as soon as the employees return to work". I replied that if the workers called off their strike and the negotiations then failed again, they would face the prospect of a second strike. "This pattern, if repeated several times, will reduce the strike, the union's last weapon in collective bargaining, to a farce."

At a Legislative Council meeting on Wednesday, 20 May, the governor himself warned the postmen that the government would not be forced by strike action into submitting to all their demands. The following day Raja riposted in the *Singapore Standard*:

> "For the first time in the history of the trade union movement in this country, the foremost official in the colony has publicly questioned the validity of the strike weapon. Put more bluntly, Mr Nicoll (the governor) says that the government considers pressure through strikes, whether justified or not, whether illegal or not, as something which the government cannot tolerate."

This hurt. British officials were demoralised by this turn of events. They were taking a pummelling in public. The colonial secretary responded by promising the 500 striking postmen and telegraph messengers that he himself would conduct negotiations with their union representatives if they reported back for work. I persuaded the union leaders to take a fresh position and announced that the strike would be suspended for three days.

That saved the face of the colonial secretary and his officials. Negotiations resumed on 26 May and ended with a satisfactory agreement.

∽

It was the first strike since the Emergency Regulations were introduced in June 1948, and it was conducted completely within the law, with no threats or violence or even disorderly picketing. The fight had been for public support and the union won. After this demonstration of the incompetence of the British colonial officers, the people saw that the government was vulnerable when subjected to scrutiny.

The press exposure and publicity enhanced my professional reputation. I was no longer just a brash young lawyer back from Cambridge with academic honours. I had led striking workers, spoken up for them and was trusted by them. I had delivered without much broken crockery. I gained enormously in the estimation of thousands of workers in Singapore and Malaya without frightening the English-educated intelligentsia. My friends and I were now convinced that in the unions we would find the mass base and, by extension, the political muscle we had been seeking when discussing our plans for action during all those beery nights spent pub-crawling in London after meetings at Malaya Hall. We had found the way to mobilise mass support.

Non-communist groups were encouraged, even emboldened, by this demonstration of constitutional, peaceful, non-violent mass action to redress legitimate grievances. A spate of trade unions and clan associations approached me to be their legal adviser, and I was happy to collect them as potential political supporters. Most paid nominal fees to Laycock & Ong to put my name down on their letterheads as their Legal Adviser. I attended many of their annual dinners or general meetings. I learnt to get along with different Chinese language groups, some Cantonese and Mandarin-speaking like the Chinese Printing Workers' Union, many only dialect-speaking like the Singapore Hakka Association.

It was often embarrassing because my Chinese was totally inadequate. I felt greatly ashamed of my inability to communicate with them in what should have been my native tongue. Once again, I started to make an effort to learn Mandarin. I got myself a teacher and a small tape-recorder. I shared the teacher with Hon Sui Sen, who had now become commissioner for lands, taking lessons at his government quarters at Cantonment Road. But progress was painfully slow. I had little time and, worse, few opportunities to practise the language.

However, I did not need Mandarin for my next major involvement in industrial action. In December 1952, 10,000 mainly Indian members of the Naval Base Labour Union gave strike notice out of the blue, and on 29 December, the workers at the base in Sembawang downed tools, to the discomfiture of the naval officers in charge and of the Singapore government. Royal Navy ships that had reached Singapore from the war in Korea – a carrier, two frigates and a submarine – were held up and could not be repaired. The governor intervened, but after two fruitless meetings, representatives of both sides agreed to send the dispute to an independent arbitrator, John Cameron, a Queen's Counsel from the Scottish Bar. The union asked me to present their case.

I spent a few weeks swotting up salary scales and making comparisons between Singapore government and Admiralty wages for the same or similar jobs. Hearing was in camera at the Registrar's Office in the Supreme Court and lasted for a week in February 1953. Cameron, a seasoned Scottish advocate, maintained an air of impartiality. The Admiralty had an experienced establishment man who knew his salary scales backwards. When Cameron made his award on 11 March, it was clear that he knew the limit of the Admiralty's budget and was not going to breach it. I had pressed for parity with Singapore government pay rates, but Cameron rejected it.

The union officials were disappointed, and the president was under pressure to reject the award. I saw the officials and persuaded them that it would be unwise to resume the strike after they had accepted arbitration as a means of settlement, that this was part and parcel of constitutional struggle. My views prevailed and the episode did me no harm. Although I lost some standing for obtaining only minor concessions, I had established myself as a legal adviser who played by the rules and was prepared to advise his client union to accept an unfavourable award.

∽

Other strikes were brewing in Singapore and in Malaya. The clerks of the Singapore Union of Postal and Telecommunications Workers had given notice that they would strike for higher pay on 23 March 1953. It was to be the first-ever strike by government clerks. The union asked me to be its legal adviser. The government offered arbitration and after discussions with me the union agreed. The government put up the names of six members of the Malayan arbitration panel. One of them happened to be Yong Pung How, my contemporary at Cambridge Law School.

For three days the proceedings received considerable publicity in the press and on radio. I had two objectives: to get a good award; and more important, to expose the high-handed and incompetent manner in which British colonial officers dealt with local public servants. I did this without appearing aggressive. Yong Pung How awarded the 1,000 clerks 28 months' back pay and other increases amounting to about $1 million. This outcome restored my standing with the workers.

Meanwhile, senior government local officers had been getting restive. Kenny was seething with resentment at an unjust award of special family allowances for expatriate officers only. The Singapore Senior Officers

Association had made repeated representations without results. When Keng Swee returned from England at the end of 1951, he worked out a simple strategy that would give them the political muscle to bring the government to heel. Instead of fighting for family allowances, comparable to expatriate allowances, for fewer than 200 local senior officers, Keng Swee proposed that they demand proportionate allowances for all government servants, especially the poorly paid and numerous Division 4 daily-rated workers. Since 1945, wages in government service had lagged behind inflation. After the postmen's strike had shown what mass action could do constitutionally, the daily-rated workers were eager for industrial action.

In July 1952, Keng Swee helped Kenny to form a Council of Joint Action to represent all government unions and associations with a total membership of 14,000. They demanded family allowances equivalent to non-pensionable expatriate pay. At a mass rally in November, the workers turned up in force to express their resentment at the racial discrimination against local public servants. Their handbill asked, "Is this just? Europeans have SMALL families and BIG allowances. We have BIG families and NO allowances."

The elected members of the Legislative Council sensed that there was political credit to be gained from backing the demand for family allowances for the locals, especially the lower paid, and began to speak in support of it in the Legislative Council. Governor Sir John Nicoll, who presided over the Legislative Council meeting, was not amused. He advised them to confine themselves to exercising control "on the higher plane of general policy", and warned the civil servants, "you cannot put pressure on councillors".

The Council of Joint Action denied that they had approached the legislative councillors for assistance, but asked whether as members of the public, government servants did not have the right to discuss matters of principle with their elected representatives. The Singapore Federation of Government Employees' Unions wrote to the colonial secretary to express the "deep distrust which all locally domiciled officers have of expatriate officers in the government".

Faced with growing resistance and a surprisingly rebellious attitude from his government servants and even from previously meek legislative councillors, the governor sought to diffuse the mounting dissatisfaction by appointing a special committee under a well-known economist, F.C. Benham, to "investigate whether the present emoluments of locally domiciled officers are adequate". After three days of consultation, the committee agreed with the unions that they should receive family allowances. The governor was appalled. This would lead to an enormous drain on the budget. When he rejected the report, six unions threatened strike action. To stave off the strike, the governor promised an independent commission under Sir Edward Ritson. In March 1953, Ritson recommended that expatriate family allowances be abolished.

The Council of Joint Action had shaken the colonial system. After 10 months of further negotiations, the government approved a salary scale that gave bigger increases to the higher-paid than to the lowest-paid government workers or those in between. Thus the colonial government denied Keng Swee and Kenny the political credit with the blue-collar workers that they had sought.

8. Widening the Oxley Road Circle

In September 1952 a tall, Indian-looking Malay in his late 40s, with a long, thin, un-Malay nose, arrived at my desk. Speaking English well but in a hesitant manner and with a slight stammer, he introduced himself as Yusof Ishak, owner, editor-in-chief and managing director of the *Utusan Melayu*. His chief sub-editor, Samad Ismail, had been held with other subversives on St John's Island since his arrest in January 1951, but his case would soon come up for review. Would I represent him?

All the hopeless and near-hopeless cases against the government had been coming to me as a counsel of last resort. I had prosecuted on quite a number of fiats (which entitle a private citizen to sue the state), getting convictions against minor officials for bullying underdogs who were prepared to pay me to seek retribution for them – a trishaw rider suing a detective for assault, a dock storeman suing the Harbour Board for unjust demotion. In one illuminating instance, I prosecuted for criminal breach of trust Lieutenant-Commander George Ansel Hardcastle, RNVR, the chief fire officer of the Naval Base Dockyard Fire Brigade, for misuse of the workers' benevolent fund. The case went before an English judge in the criminal district court, who acquitted him. The dissatisfied firemen then took my advice and sued Hardcastle for restitution and damages in the high court in order to publicise the case. However, his fellow officers passed the hat around and produced the $12,000 required for restitution and to pay legal costs just before it was to be heard, thus denying the union the satisfaction of exposing and disgracing him in open court. Such was the atmosphere of antipathy and distrust in which we lived.

But Samad's case was not a matter of law. It was a political action by a colonial administration threatened by a communist armed insurrection, and under growing pressure from nationalist demands for independence. The best approach was to persuade the government that this particular detainee was probably a nationalist who would eventually become an adversary if not an enemy of the communists, even though he might be going along with them for the time being. I decided to take the case without referring to John Laycock. This was work for which the *Utusan Melayu* would pay the bill.

I was unlikely to get results by simply pushing against the government, so I decided to call on the Special Branch officer responsible to find out the real position of my client, and what they had against him. As luck would have it, that took me to Superintendent Richard Byrne Corridon. Corridon, who was in charge of the Indian and English-educated section of Special Branch, was an expert who had been doing similar work in British India, and could tell the difference between Indian communists and Indian nationalists.

We had met before. He had studied my file, and one Sunday morning early in 1952 had visited me at 38 Oxley Road, just for a chat. He said he had read of my activities in London and was interested to meet me to find out more about the communists there, like Lim Hong Bee, and their influence on Singapore and Malayan students. I told him what I thought of Lim Hong Bee, and of the unlikelihood of the communists making much headway with the English-educated in London, but added that after the arrest of Eber and his group in Singapore in January 1951 I could be wrong. At the same time, I disabused him of the suspicions Special Branch had entertained about the Budapest Festival of Youth. I said Dennis had gone to the festival simply for a good holiday, and that he was about as political as a tadpole. Years later, I discovered that this phrase had found its way into their files.

I now saw him at his Special Branch office in Robinson Road. He was completely open. He said Samad was a bright Malay, very active, a first-class operator. I asked him if he was a communist. He said, "The most brilliant communist I know." This did not sound promising until he added, "But people grow up and their minds change with experience. Work on him. He is worth saving."

The police provided a special launch to take me to St John's Island, a courtesy they extended to lawyers who represented the detainees. It was a pleasant 20-minute boat ride on a working-day afternoon, and was followed by a 20-minute walk from the jetty along pathways and up steps to the northern side of the island. There, amid beautiful old tembusu trees, stood some government holiday bungalows, and not far away, long rows of barrack-like buildings surrounded by chain-link fences for opium addicts undergoing rehabilitation. One of the bungalows was also ringed with chain-link topped with barbed wire. This housed the political detainees. In anticipation of my visit, the camp wardens had put a little wooden table with two wooden chairs under a nearby tembusu. I waited while an Indian warder went to the bungalow and came back with a slim, spritely, narrow-faced Malay of medium height, wearing sunglasses and looking quite sinister with his trimmed moustache and a broken front tooth. He smoked incessantly and seemed highly strung. He appeared sceptical about his prospects of release before an advisory committee consisting of a high court judge with two lay assessors.

I told him it depended on whether Special Branch believed he would continue to be a communist, in which case he would probably be detained again and again. But if after his release he operated as a nationalist, they were likely to leave him alone. He gave one of his deep guffaws. This was my first face-to-face meeting with a detained member of a communist organisation. I was ignorant of their psychology, the mental make-up and motivation that made them determined to prove to themselves and the world that they were men of conviction and strength, able to endure great privations and hardships for a cause, worthy to be comrades of the other warriors dedicated to the Marxist millennium.

The review of his case was held in the judge's chambers with no publicity. The chief ground for his detention was that he was a member of the MCP and a leader of the Malay Section of its auxiliary organisation, the Singapore People's Anti-British League. The judge listened to my submission that he was basically an anti-colonialist and a Malay nationalist; that as a Malay he could not accept the chauvinistic appeals of a Chinese-led MCP; and that it was out of friendship and personal loyalty that, in September or October 1950, he had arranged the escape to Indonesia of a prominent communist, Abdullah Sudin, knowing that he was wanted by the police. I do not know if I made any impression on the judge and his two assessors. The judge said nothing, and the hearing was over in less than 20 minutes.

Samad returned to St John's Island, but in April 1953 he and a few other detainees were released, among them C.V. Devan Nair. When I first saw Nair through the chain-link fence, wearing horn-rimmed spectacles and clad only in shorts and Japanese-style rubber slippers, I found him an unlikeable person. He was short, squat, pugnacious and obviously angry with the world. But when Samad noticed that he had caught my eye, he told me that he was a good friend, an official of the Singapore Teachers' Union. "Under detention," he said, "you soon learn to differentiate between the weaklings and the strong men." He referred to another Indian detainee, James Puthucheary, who talked a lot, was superficially clever but unreliable. Nair was a strong man, totally dependable. That might be so, I thought, but I did not like his looks. As it happened, shortly after that, the Singapore Teachers' Union approached me at Laycock & Ong and asked me to represent him. I could not refuse, but did not relish the prospect of trying to win him over. When I next met Corridon, he gave me a rundown on Nair, confirming that he was an angry man, dedicated and determined. He had been converted to communism by P.V. Sharma, the president of the union.

∞

Our small group – Keng Swee, Chin Chye, Raja, Kenny and I – had meanwhile been meeting on Saturday afternoons in my basement dining room at Oxley Road to consider the feasibility of forming a political party. The room was in a hot, uncomfortable part of the house facing the setting sun, and even with three wide-open windows, two open doors, and a powerful ceiling fan whirring it could become extremely muggy. But if the atmosphere was soporific, we were not. We were determined that we would be completely different from the supine, feeble, self-serving, opportunistic parties and individuals in the existing Legislative Council and City Council. We therefore decided to invite Samad to join us to discuss the prospects for waging a constitutional struggle for independence without finding ourselves sucked into the communist movement. We also wanted him in because he could give us access to the Malay-speaking world, and get our views across to the Malay masses through the *Utusan Melayu*.

After two meetings, he asked if he could bring his friend Devan Nair along because he could make a useful contribution. I did not like the idea, but my friends and I agreed that if we only had people we liked in the inner core, we would never expand into a party. So Nair came too, and every week, or at least every other week, we would meet to talk over the situation and what political action we could take.

The British were not unaware of the political pressures that were building up. In 1953, the governor appointed Sir George Rendel, a former ambassador to Belgium, to head a commission to review Singapore's constitution and recommend the next stage. In his report, published on 22 February 1954, Rendel proposed the automatic registration, as eligible voters, of all British subjects born in Singapore. This would increase the electorate fourfold. The new government was to consist of a council of nine ministers, six of them elected members, who were to be appointed on the recommendation of the leader of the majority party. But the key portfolios were to be in the hands of three ex-officio members: the chief secretary, the financial secretary and the attorney-general. Except in the limited areas of foreign relations and defence (including internal security), the governor would be bound to accept the decisions of the council, which would be accountable solely to the new Legislative Assembly. There were to be 25 elected members, six nominated, and three ex-officio. The governor accepted the report for implementation at the next election in April 1955.

It became urgent for my friends and me to decide whether to take part in the election under this new constitution or again to stay on the sidelines. Samad and Nair were for staying out. They wanted independence or nothing at all. Drawing on the lesson learnt from the mistakes of the Malayan Democratic Union, Raja was strongly in favour of participation. So were Kenny and Keng Swee. I was convinced that non-participation would exclude us from the constitutional arena, and we would then end up like the MDU or have to go underground. So we started planning to form a party before the end of 1954 to give us some 6 months before the polls.

⚮

Things always seem to come out of the blue. On 28 May 1954, a group of students at the University of Malaya were arrested and charged with sedition. They wanted me to defend them. I looked at the charges; there was a 50–50 chance of a conviction. They had published in *Fajar*, a small undergraduate magazine that came out irregularly although it was supposed to be a monthly, an article which might have broken the law. I agreed to act for them, and after some reflection, advised them that theirs was a case best treated as a political contest, not a legal one. I proposed that we bring out from London a British Queen's Counsel,

D.N. Pritt, famous for championing left-wing causes. Pritt was in his 60s, and known as a fellow traveller with a waspish tongue who was completely without fear of any judge either in the colonies or Britain itself. He had already been cut off from the British establishment and was treated as a crank, one of those eccentric Englishmen from the bourgeois class who chose to be more proletarian than the poorest worker while still living the good life. In June 1950, Choo and I had visited him in his flat in London to ask him to sign papers sponsoring our call to the Bar, where he was a Master of the Bench of the Middle Temple. I believed he would take the case, provided we could pay his passage and accommodation and give him a small fee. I wrote to him, and he replied promptly. Yes, he would come.

Knowing that Special Branch would be monitoring my correspondence with Pritt, I used Chin Chye's name and address, and Pritt's letters to me were therefore sent to him at his University of Malaya quarters in Dalvey Road. When I was writing this chapter in 1995, I discovered that, as a result, Special Branch thought Chin Chye and Raja had been responsible for bringing Pritt out to Singapore. They were wrong. I also used the address of Choo's sister, so some of his letters went to Kwa Geok Choo at Cairnhill Circle, instead of to 38 Oxley Road or Laycock & Ong. Special Branch apparently never realised this, for their records did not show any interception of mail posted there.

One big problem I had expected was Pritt's admission to practise at the Singapore Bar, which would normally have required him to have completed six months' pupillage in the office of an advocate and solicitor of at least seven years' standing. There is provision for a judge to waive this in unusual circumstances, but I expected the Bar Committee to object to any special dispensation. The Socialist Club of the University had set up a Students' Defence Fund Committee and collected $10,000 to defray the cost of Pritt's air passage, hotel expenses and a small gift. I decided that whether he was admitted or blocked, it was worth flying him out to Singapore, since refusing him the right to appear would be a political defeat for the government. So I took the chance, and he arrived on 11 August. The students and I met him at the airport, and I drove him to the Adelphi Hotel. Big, heavy-set and bald, he was a bundle of energy. After a long flight with overnight stops in Cairo and Colombo, he was able that same evening to sit down at the desk in his warm and uncomfortable room, with an inadequate air-conditioner chugging away, to write up his notes of the case. I gave him the background to it and published materials that could be used in the defence, including marked extracts of relevant books and speeches.

He was obviously well-qualified to represent anyone accused of sedition anywhere in the British Empire and in Britain itself. But the law had to be complied with, so I arranged for him to sit in the office of Osborne Jones, an advocate and solicitor of not less than seven years' standing, as required. After Pritt had graced his office for six days, Osborne Jones was able to swear in an affidavit, "I have instructed the applicant, so far as I am able to, on the differences of the law as it is in England and the law as it is in Singapore." Osborne Jones was being strictly truthful. Pritt then had to appear before three examiners who had to satisfy themselves that he had "an adequate knowledge of the practice and etiquette of the profession and of the English language and is a suitable person for admission". The three were the most eminent members of the Singapore Bar, the solicitor-general and two senior British lawyers. One of them asked him, "Mr Pritt, how would you draw up a conveyance of land?" Pritt replied, "Queen's Counsel, sir, do not draw up conveyances of land." Even the *Straits Times* reported this gem.

Pritt crafted his affidavit so as to leave the judge in no doubt as to his qualifications. He had been admitted to the Bar in 1909, which made him more senior than any lawyer in Singapore, including the judges. He had been a King's (Queen's) Counsel since 1927, and a Master of the Bench of the Middle Temple since 1936. He had appeared before courts around the world, from India to the Cour de Cassation in Algiers. And he "had been offered permission to appear before the Supreme Court of the United States in 1950".

In support of the application, I drafted an affidavit on behalf of the eight accused to affirm that since the case involved difficult and complex questions of law, they had earlier wanted to get another counsel for the defence with more experience in criminal cases and had asked me to approach David Marshall. But on 24 July, one of the students had received a letter from Marshall couched in vehement and colourful language. It read, "It is with growing anger that I have been reading your recent issues of *Fajar*, because through them I have learnt that you are merely masquerading as Socialists whilst spouting a venomous communist propaganda. ... Please remove me from your list of sympathisers."

The students attached this letter as an exhibit to their affidavit, stating, "We then felt that it was no use briefing Mr Marshall. We also felt that if Mr Marshall, the lawyer who had hitherto appeared most sympathetic to our political aims, could be so hostile as to write such an uncalled for letter, the other local lawyers in Singapore would not be less hostile."

Pritt's petition for admission was opposed by the Bar Committee and – unexpectedly – by the attorney-general. The chief justice, who heard the petition with Pritt appearing in person, recognised the furore that would follow if his application was denied, and admitted him.

The hearing started on 23 August and went on for three days. It was, for me, a lesson in advocacy in political trials – instructive, entertaining, even hilarious. Pritt took full advantage of his position as a renowned rebel QC to bludgeon and browbeat his opponents on every imaginable issue, however remotely relevant to the case. Wherever he had the chance, he took a swipe at authority with a big cosh. To begin with, he made great play of the "duplicity of the charges". In essence, the students were all accused equally of publishing with the intention to "libel the Queen or libel the government or to incite the people of Singapore or to promote ill-will". He wanted to know which particular "intent" the prosecution attributed to each individual defendant. He argued that a charge that concealed within itself so many different alternative charges must be bad. He asked the court to strike it out and instruct the prosecutor to frame one that was less ambiguous.

I had already protested along the same lines, but I did not have Pritt's standing as a senior QC, nor his powers of invective. Although the judge ruled against him and found that the charges as framed were not bad, he had scored with the public both in court and in the newspapers.

Mr Justice F.A. (Freddy) Chua was a man with a practical turn of mind and a good sense of the realities outside the court. At the end of the submissions by Pritt and the DPP, and without going into any legal argument, he simply said that the articles in *Fajar* were not seditious. The eight students were all acquitted. For the press, this was an anticlimax. They had expected him to explain why they were or were not seditious, but Chua was a cautious judge who did not want to commit himself more than he had to.

The students and their supporters were jubilant. This had been an unnecessary prosecution; it damaged the government and encouraged rebelliousness among people who enjoyed the spectacle of a colonial attorney-general resisting unsuccessfully the admission to the Singapore Bar of an eminent if troublemaking English QC, and of a colonial deputy public prosecutor getting the worst of the exchanges in court.

Immediately after the case, and while Pritt was still in Singapore, the Chinese middle school students approached me to act for them and brief him to represent them in their appeal against conviction for rioting on 13 May near King George V Park, where they had gathered to protest against the National Service Ordinance. This case would lead me into a totally different world, one teeming with raw energy and idealism.

9. The World of the Chinese-educated

My introduction into the world of the Chinese-educated came after what was called the 5-1-3 incident, named after the riots of 13 May 1954. Five students turned up at my home one evening in 1954, soon after the *Fajar* trial: Robert Soon Loh Boon, a small young man with a crew cut and a front tooth missing, who acted as their interpreter and spokesman, Louis Hwa, who was also competent in English, and three pigtailed Chinese girls. The boys were in shorts, the girls in skirts, their school uniforms. Seven of their fellow students had been convicted for obstructing the police during the riots in which 500 Chinese middle school students, mainly from Chung Cheng High School, clashed with the police. They were marching in support of a delegation on its way to Government House to present a petition against registration for national service when they were stopped and asked to disperse. Instead they threw stones at the police, six of whom were also stabbed. The police charged with batons and hit some students on the head. Twenty-six people were injured; 48 students, including two girls, were arrested.

The trial was held on 28 June. Of the 41 students accused of disobeying police orders to disperse, 26 were found guilty and given a six-month suspended sentence. Seven were tried on the more serious charge of obstructing the police. They asked for their case to be transferred to another court because the judge had shown prejudice in the way he had treated and convicted their fellow students the day before. They refused to say anything in their defence and were sentenced to three months, the maximum for the charge. Their appeal would be heard in October. Would I ask Pritt to take up their appeal?

Their defiance of the law was the immediate concern of the court. But the underlying issues were deep and fundamental. The Chinese-educated had no place or role to play in the official life of the colony, which employed only English-educated locals as subordinates. The government provided primary schools teaching in English and in Malay, and secondary schools teaching only in English.

But immigrant communities were left to fend for themselves. The Chinese collected donations and built their own schools. Completely self-supporting, they used textbooks published in China and employed teachers recruited in China who taught in Mandarin just as if they were in Guangdong or Fujian province. Culturally, they lived in a world apart. Graduates could either continue their studies by switching over to an English school and so make their way up the English-educated ladder, or look for jobs in firms that used the Chinese language – Chinese shops, restaurants and business houses, and the few Chinese-owned banks.

They felt dispossessed, and their lack of economic opportunity turned their schools into breeding grounds for the communists, who had been burrowing away in Malaya and Singapore since 1923, when the Comintern (Communist International) first sent agents from Shanghai to the island. After the war, the record of its resistance to the Japanese gave the MCP a prestige that made it a powerful force among the impressionable young, and it proceeded to build up a network of cells in the classrooms. Many teachers became communist cadres or sympathisers; many overaged students whose education had been interrupted by the Japanese occupation were indoctrinated and co-opted; and the school management committees of merchants and shopkeepers were either sympathetic towards them or fearful of opposing them.

Once the Emergency was declared, the communists in Singapore were superficially dormant, but in fact they were recruiting and expanding. In 1952, the British introduced national service bills in Singapore and Malaya, making all males between the ages of 18 and 55 liable for call-up into the armed services, police, or civil defence forces, and in April 1954, the government started registering them. It needed only 800 for the Singapore Military Forces and 1,200 for the Civil Defence Corps, and was going to choose them by ballot. But registration in the schools was slow, and on 12 May, the closing date, Chinese High School students presented a petition to the acting colonial secretary asking for mass exemption. In response, Acting Governor W.A.C. Goode issued a statement saying that exemptions could be granted only on a case-by-case basis. This led to the demonstration by 500 students, whose leaders the governor had refused to see until they had all first registered.

I did not understand the background of the problem at the time, though I knew something was simmering and bubbling away in this completely different world. The students were well-organised, disciplined and cohesive. They had remarkable self-control and were capable of mass action, of collective demonstrations of defiance that made it difficult for the government to isolate and pick out the leaders for punishment. After the arrests, they set out to blow up other issues that would enable them to engineer clashes with the police, to produce martyrs and so arouse public feeling against the government. I understood their motivations and methods only much later. Many of the English-educated, including the University of Malaya Students' Union, were equally ill-informed and naive. On 18 May, they came out in support of the Chinese demonstrators by calling for an inquiry into the rioting because the police had used improper force. They were as simple-minded as I was.

The communists immediately commemorated the clash on 13 May with the numbers "5-1-3", 5 for May and 13, a Chinese shorthand for famous or infamous incidents – the Tiananmen episode on 4 June 1989 is "6-4", 6 for June. The students mounted camp-ins and protests, and formed a 55-man exemption delegation, which organised different sections to collect information on injured students, provide them with medical treatment and drum up public sympathy.

They fanned out across Singapore to enlist the support of other students, parents, shopkeepers, local Chinese leaders – indeed the entire Chinese-speaking community. Theirs were tried and tested methods of mass agitation that the communists had worked out in China. At the first sign of trouble from the police, they shut themselves up in schools or factories to form a critical mass, attract attention, win sympathy, defy authority and provoke the government into "victimising" them.

So on 14 May, the day after the 5-1-3 incident, they barricaded themselves in Chung Cheng High School, but dispersed after one day when a 12-man committee formed by the Chinese Chamber of Commerce asked them to do so. They had become important, and the elders of the Chinese community had come down to plead with them, promising to intercede with the authorities. In response to pressure from a government faced with growing indiscipline, the chamber brought forward the mid-year holidays by two weeks and closed the school. But its representatives had first to accept a list of six demands from the students for submission to the colonial administration. These called for total exemption from national service, unconditional discharge of the 48 accused awaiting trial, a public inquiry into the incident, and several other concessions. The students had skilfully involved the elders of the Chinese community in their cause, and on 22–23 May, 2,500 of them locked themselves up in Chung Cheng High School again, refusing to leave until all were exempted from national service. They dispersed three days later, but only after the police stopped their food supplies and irate parents forced them to.

And so it went on. The Chung Cheng students demanded that schools be reopened, the Chinese High School students threatened to go on a hunger strike, and on 2 June, a thousand students drawn from various middle schools assembled at the Chinese High School to begin a camp-in during the enforced holidays. It was an act of defiance. They held their own lessons in the classrooms and in the open fields, with senior pupils teaching their juniors mathematics, English, Chinese and geography. Parents brought them food, but it was otherwise a self-organised mid-year holiday refresher camp.

The students also sent more petitions to the governor, but none were answered. When seven schools reopened on 24 June, new disciplinary measures were imposed: among others, teachers would be screened and pupils would be forbidden to use the school premises for extramural activities not approved by the principal. But these orders read well only in the newspapers. They could not be enforced because the management committees and the principals were afraid of the organised underground among the teachers and students.

Then, on 13 September, the government announced that it intended to give itself powers to close down any school that did not comply with the Schools Ordinance. Its supervisor could henceforth be asked to show cause if in the preceding six months it had been used for political propaganda detrimental to Singapore. This was a ghastly mistake. The committees of the Chinese schools had been divided among the anti-communists, the fence-sitters, and the fellow travellers. But once the government proposed to control their schools, they were all united against it, and were supported even by the nationalist Kuomintang press.

Governor Sir John Nicoll was taken aback. Speaking to the Legislative Council on 21 September, he deplored suggestions that the government was adopting an anti-Chinese policy. It did not intend to assimilate the Chinese schools into the colonial system of education. The communists knew that the governor's plan was to stifle their subversive activities, but he had in fact given them a chance to rally all Chinese-educated groups around a patriotic cause, and they cleverly twisted the issue into a threat to anglicise Chinese schools and destroy Chinese culture, language and education. These were a sacred heritage dear to the hearts of all Chinese, especially the poorly educated merchant millionaires and shopkeepers of Singapore. They had been mesmerised by glowing reports from

Communist China, depicting its transformation into a great nation. And now, just when this rejuvenated China should be a source of new pride and dignity to Chinese everywhere, the British seemed out to strip them of their birthright. The colonial government had stumbled into a cultural minefield. If Special Branch had had Chinese-educated officers who could feel the pulse of the chauvinistic communities in Singapore and Malaya, they would have warned the governor to move with greater sensitivity and circumspection.

The Chinese-educated were nothing like the English-educated students who had published *Fajar*. They were resourceful fund raisers. When I approached Pritt on their behalf I told him they could mobilise the financial resources of the merchant community in the Chinese Chamber of Commerce. He suggested a fee of $30,000. I put it to the students. They did not bat an eyelid. Long before Pritt flew to Singapore on 7 October for the hearing of their appeal, which was to begin five days later, they brought the money in cash to my home. (They seemed to feel uncomfortable about going to Laycock & Ong, where an Englishman was the senior partner.)

Having read the record of the appeal, Pritt must have known there was no chance of it succeeding, so with the practised vehemence of years of experience he again made as much noise and propaganda for the students as he could to damage the government. The students gave him a tea party at the Badminton Hall the day after his arrival. Pritt made a speech in English, and his hosts made several in Mandarin, but none of this was translated to him. Not surprisingly, for this was an opportunity for the backroom leaders to mobilise support, work up enthusiasm, and generate more steam for mass action, utilising a perfectly legitimate cause. The proceedings left so deep an impression on him that in his autobiography published 12 years later, Pritt remembered the organisation and logistics that had produced 5,000 students neatly seated in a hall, each one provided with a box of cakes, buns, peanuts and bananas, the leftovers of which were placed back in the same box and carried away by ushers along the aisles, so that the hall was left neat and tidy when they marched off to their buses to go home. And all this in response to crisp orders given over the loudspeakers with great aplomb and self-confidence by boys and girls of only 15 or so who were instantly obeyed. It was a performance that would have gladdened the heart of any staff officer in the army, and I was as impressed as Pritt. That was the first of several such meetings I was to attend. I had never seen anything like it among English-educated students, who spoke diffidently, lacked self-confidence, and were psychologically hobbled when they used a language that was not their mother tongue.

The appeal itself, I knew, would be an anticlimax. But the students saw it as an occasion to organise demonstrations against the government. On 12 October, a large crowd of them gathered on the Padang outside the Supreme Court, and according to the *Singapore Standard*, "a storm of applause" broke out from them when Pritt arrived. The English judge, Mr Justice Knight, asked, "Why has a trivial appeal like this been listed for three days?" Pritt said he was responsible, as he estimated it would not be safe to say that it would be concluded in less. He then ploughed through his grounds for appeal, putting up a stout performance that lasted two days (I would have been hard pressed to keep it going beyond one morning), but with no effect. After submissions were completed at the end of the second day, the judge said that he upheld the conviction. However, he would set aside the prison sentences if the young students would sign bonds of good behaviour for 18 months.

Each student was asked in turn if he or she would sign a bond. Each signified refusal by a shake of the head. The judge was determined to uphold the rule of law, and the students were determined to be martyrs. The judge had no alternative but to send them to prison, although in doing so he had given them another issue with which to work up anti-government feelings among the Chinese-speaking masses.

Knowing now how the communists would exploit it, I would have released them on a bond of good behaviour signed by their parents, whom I could have called to court and dealt with directly before the communist backroom boys could get at them. The government would have scored a moral victory and the parents would have been relieved that their children had been let off with a warning. But at that time I, too, got carried away by the wave of sympathy for them, and on 20 September, the *Nanyang Siang Pau* quoted me as saying, "Until now the authorities have no evidence of any communist activity in the Chinese schools; but they regard opposition to the government's refusal to allow the students postponement of service as communist activity, and under this pretext, they seek to exercise better control over the Chinese schools." I was ignorant, gullible and stupid. I did not know just how efficient the communists were, how their tentacles reached out and controlled every single organisation that was bubbling up against the government.

The appeal to the Privy Council was heard on 15 February 1955 and was dismissed. The case was over, but my initiation into the world of the Chinese-educated had just begun. It was a world full of vitality, of so many activists, all like jumping beans, of so many young idealists, unselfish, ready to sacrifice everything for a better society. I was deeply impressed by their seemingly total dedication to the cause of revolution, their single-minded determination to overturn the colonial government in order to establish a new world of equality and fairness. And I was to grow increasingly fearful of the direction in which their leaders were taking them.

But I was also convinced that if I could not harness some of these dynamic young people to our cause, to what my friends and I stood for, we would never succeed. So far, we had links only with the English-educated and the Malays, who did not have the convictions or the energies to match, never mind the will to resist the Chinese-educated communists. The only "Chinese-speaking Chinese" in our network were small groups in the Naval Base and the Harbour Board, largely Cantonese skilled labourers, and some daily-rated City Council workers. The one union whose members were all Chinese-speaking was that of the night-soil workers in the Municipal Council, who every morning collected human waste in two metal buckets, one at each end of a pole. They were not well-educated, and did not look to me like revolutionary material.

The students must have been instructed to use me as their lawyer, after having employed others who were not very political nor as willing to stand up to the government as I was. They started turning up at Oxley Road looking for advice on a hundred and one problems they encountered whenever they came into conflict with or were obstructed by authority, from schoolboys scalded during their camp-ins to permits for public meetings. They usually arrived in a bright pink Chevrolet with the number plate 1066. (Choo recognised and remembered it: the year of the Battle of Hastings.) One of these pigtailed schoolgirls was evidently using her father's car; he was probably a wealthy shopkeeper or merchant.

I never turned them away, however inconvenient the hour. I wanted to poach in this pond where the fish had been fed and nurtured by the communists, to use hook and line to catch as many as I could. After all, they had fished in our English-speaking pond, poaching John Eber, Sharma, Devan Nair, Samad and others. I was innocent – it was like recruiting police cadets in mafia territory, a hazardous business. I believed then that the discipline of the students and the energy and dedication of their leaders were natural and spontaneous, born of youthful enthusiasm and idealism. It took me two years from 1954 to 1956 to fathom their methods, to get glimpses of their intrigues and deviousness and to understand the dynamics of the communist united front (CUF). Behind the scenes, the anonymous Town Committee of the MCP controlled and ran open front operators like Robert Soon Loh Boon and those section leaders at mass rallies. The communists had a secret network of disciplined cadres grouped in cells of about four, each with a leader who gave the orders (dressed up as the outcome of democratic discussion), who in turn took orders from a leader in another cell of a higher rank.

These orders were disobeyed at the risk of isolation and marginalisation for those on the fringes, of rustication and punishment for those who were members of the Anti-British League or the MCP, and of death by assassination if a party member had committed an act of betrayal. It was a ruthless system in which a past record of sacrifice could count for nothing, and therefore not one to be defied lightly, as the case of Liew Yit Fun should have taught me.

Liew joined the MCP in Malaya in 1942 and operated against the Japanese in Negeri Sembilan in the Second Regiment of the MPAJA. After the war, he became the MCP representative in Malaya for contacts with the authorities, and the publisher of a party newspaper called *Min Sheng Pau*. Just before the Emergency was declared in 1948, he was convicted for sedition and sentenced to 18 months' imprisonment. In October 1949, as his sentence was about to expire, a detention order was served on him, and this was extended three times to 1955.

Asked by his friends to represent him in the judicial review of his case, I saw Liew in Johor Bahru jail and found him a most intelligent, eloquent and dedicated communist. He wanted to be banished to China (or to Jamaica, where he had been born), but there was little I could do for him under the law. So I decided to use the threat of an action for habeas corpus, which would generate adverse publicity. This was about six months after I had brought D.N. Pritt out for the *Fajar* case and, four months later, for the defence of the Chinese students, so my threat was taken seriously. In a letter dated 11 July 1955 and addressed to police headquarters in Kuala Lumpur, the director of Singapore Special Branch paraphrased me as saying, "if the habeas corpus action did not succeed, the facts would become known in the press of the world, and Peking would start taking an interest in this case of one of its nationals". Within three months, the British banished Liew to China. The final twist was yet to come. Like so many communists, he was eaten up by his own revolution. During the Cultural Revolution, Chin Peng, the leader of the MCP, expelled him from the party and he died in disgrace, a disillusioned man. He had been martyred by both sides.

But in 1954, I was still blind to the true nature of the communist adversary, and was not deterred. I believed I could win over some of the non-committed who had open minds and would see that Mao-inspired communism could never succeed in Malaya. I had much to learn.

10. Enter the PAP

Choo was on the veranda with our son Loong, then aged 2, when two men turned up at 38 Oxley Road one Sunday morning in 1954. This was a fortnight after I had told some of the Chinese-educated students that I wanted to meet some leaders in the Chinese trade unions. I came to the sitting room to greet them. They said they were from the Singapore Bus Workers' Union. They were soft-spoken and could understand a little English, but had brought Robert Soon Loh Boon along as interpreter. Their names were Lim Chin Siong and Fong Swee Suan. I had made contact with the activists in the Chinese-educated working class world and was excited at the prospect of exploring it for recruits to our cause of a democratic, non-communist, socialist Malaya. Lim and Fong looked the right type: well-mannered, earnest and sincere in demeanour, simple in their clothes, Fong to the point of shabbiness. Keenness and dedication were written in every line of their faces and in every gesture.

They were in marked contrast to the shallow characters whom my colleagues and I had earlier met at David Marshall's flat, when he and Lim Yew Hock of the Labour Party were discussing the formation of a new political grouping that would later emerge as the Labour Front. That had been part of our probing; we wanted to assess what they were capable of. But we found it difficult to take Marshall seriously. A mercurial, flamboyant Sephardic Jew, he was then the leading criminal lawyer in Singapore, but when he made what he considered a sound proposal, we often could not help laughing at him. He was apolitical and naive. We knew he was a prima donna who loved to be centre-stage and would be uncontrollable. On one occasion, he was so furious when we laughed at him at the wrong moment that he flounced out of the room in a tantrum, and then out of his own flat altogether. We found ourselves left with his friends and a lot of food and drink. We ate, drank, exchanged pleasantries, thanked the maid, and left. After the third meeting, we decided that it would be ruinous to be in any way associated with these people. What we were looking for were serious-minded men for a long-term enterprise, men who would take with equanimity the ups and downs of politics in pursuit of our objectives.

Lim Chin Siong and Fong Swee Suan were the exact opposite of Marshall and company, and I liked what I saw. They were the Chinese-educated equivalent of the *Fajar* boys who were prosecuted for sedition, but more determined, more selfless, more hardworking, the kind of lieutenants we had been searching for. I was hopeful that we could win such people over.

I explained to them my plans for forming a party to represent the workers and the dispossessed, especially the Chinese-educated, not in order to win the coming election, but to gain a significant number of seats so as to show up the rottenness of the system and the present political parties, and to build up for the next round. They were non-committal, but after my experience with the Chinese school students, I was not surprised. I knew that before making any major decision they would have to report back and submit their assessments, whereupon somewhere above or beyond them earnest discussions would be held and they would eventually be given the MCP line. Two weeks later, they returned with another interpreter. Yes, they were prepared to join me, not to seek power but to expose the colonial regime, the inadequacy of the proposed Rendel constitution, and to demolish the parties that would take office.

We planned to launch our People's Action Party at a public meeting on 21 November 1954, and I wanted them both to be convenors. They whispered among themselves and said they would first discuss it. The next time they came, they said that Fong, who was the paid secretary of the Singapore Bus Workers' Union, would be a convenor, but Lim Chin Siong would stay out for the time being. I did not know their reasons. I suspected it was because Fong was the more expendable of the two, and at the same time had been less exposed as a security risk, so that Special Branch would have few traces of him on their records when his name appeared in the press.

But I was satisfied. With Fong in, I felt the new party would have a reasonably broad working-class base. We had the English-educated, the Malay blue- and white-collar workers, and we now had the Chinese clan associations, trade guilds and blue-collar workers as well. We did not want the middle school students to be in any way associated with us. Any political party in Singapore's segmented society had to balance its appeal to one section of the community against the fears or resistance it would arouse in another, and for this reason they would not be an asset. They would frighten off the English- and Malay-educated, who were about 40 per cent of the population.

In October, we announced the inauguration of the party, and in November, pledged ourselves to fight for "a multilingual legislature with simultaneous translation as no elected legislative councillor has the slightest idea what the Chinese-speaking population thinks and feels and this is hardly a healthy state of affairs". This forced the other political parties to do likewise.

To balance the party's radical reputation and the left-wing background of some of the convenors, I persuaded Tunku Abdul Rahman, by then the leader of the United Malays National Organisation (UMNO) and a member of the Executive Council in Malaya, and Sir Cheng Lock Tan, president of the Malayan Chinese Association (MCA), to speak at the inauguration. I had met Tan at several dinners, and the Tunku had consulted me in my office when he wanted to sue a newspaper in Singapore

First PAP central executive committee, November 1954. Back row, from left: Tan Wee Keng, Devan Nair, S. Sockalingam, Lee Kuan Yew, Ong Eng Guan, Fong Swee Suan. Front row, from left: Lee Gek Seng, Mofradi bin Haji Mohd Noor, Toh Chin Chye, Ismail Rahim, Chan Chiaw Thor.

for libel. Later, I had invited him together with the Singapore UMNO leaders to dinner in my home. Thus I had two highly respected Malayan leaders attend the inaugural meeting of the PAP because of their personal links with me, and probably also because they thought I could be a useful ally in future. But while the Tunku did not want me to enter politics in the Federation, Tan did. This fundamental difference between the two reflected basic contradictions in their electoral interests. The Tunku wanted the Chinese in small pockets, disunited if possible, disorganised and easy for the Malays to handle. Tan wanted young men who could bring the Chinese community together, and the MCA was very keen on getting Singapore into the Federation to increase their voting strength.

We started the meeting at 10 am on Sunday, 21 November at the Victoria Memorial Hall and continued until 1 pm, when we had to stop because it had been booked for a concert that afternoon. It was a warm, sticky morning. We filled the hall, but not to overflowing. Everybody was seated on wooden and cane armchairs. The *Singapore Standard* said there were 1,500 present, the *Straits Times*, 800. There was no electricity or magic in the air. Our supporters from the unions filled about two-thirds of the seats, and the rest were taken up by observers from other political parties and interested outsiders. We read set speeches; there was no great oratory. We dressed in open-necked shirts, Cheng Lock Tan in a lounge suit and the Tunku in formal Malay attire – a buttoned-up silk top, loose trousers and a short decorative sarong around his hips.

It was a good but uninspiring meeting. We had formally launched the party, got a decent press, made ourselves known, and were taken seriously. There were no flights of rhetoric, no balloons, no pigeons freed. But we were ready for nomination day when it was announced for 28 February and polling for 2 April 1955. After much intense discussion we had decided on five candidates: for Bukit Timah, Lim Chin Siong; for Farrer Park, Devan Nair (not my preference but a concession to the pro-communists); for Punggol-Tampines, Goh Chew Chua (a 60-year-old contractor friend of Kenny's who had lived in Punggol and was well known in the area); and for Tanjong Pagar, myself. Fong Swee Suan could not stand as he had been born in Johor, but we fielded Ahmad Ibrahim as an independent for Sembawang, where the Naval Base workers would have the decisive vote. We believed he would get more support from Malay and Indian workers in the Naval Base if he was not identified as PAP and therefore too radical.

The PAP organisation was weak, almost nonexistent: no paid staff, branches or grassroots leaders. For canvassing and help at election rallies, we could call upon the unions and Chinese middle school students. But once the campaign started, our candidates went their separate ways, except when better-known speakers like myself made the rounds of all five constituencies to address mass rallies.

On nomination day, my two opponents in Tanjong Pagar constituency – one Chinese-educated, one English-educated – objected to my candidature because I had not resided in Singapore for seven out of the past ten years, as required by an Order in Council issued by the Queen's Privy Council in London for elections under the new Rendel constitution. But it seemed that this ruling could itself be defective, for Singapore had been a separate colony for only eight years and eleven months – before April 1946, it was part of the Straits Settlements. A few Britishers also wrote letters to the *Straits Times*, threatening to take action to unseat me if I were elected, but the returning officer upheld my nomination and advised my opponents that objections on residential grounds could only be made through an election petition if I were returned.

After hearing from me, Keng Swee, then back in London, briefed the Labour MP Stanley Awbery about it, and Awbery put down a question in the House of Commons. In March, Henry Hopkinson, minister of state for colonial affairs, replied:

"Malayan students who were in Great Britain during the qualifying period for the forthcoming federal elections have on their return, if not otherwise disqualified, been allowed to register as electors if during the absence they have continued to regard the Federation as their home. They would no doubt also be treated as eligible to stand as candidates."

Although he referred to Malayan students, those opposing me decided to drop the issue. They knew London would take retrospective action if necessary to put matters right, rather than have an unpleasant political row over rules that were manifestly absurd. As I had pointed out at the time, John Ede, born and bred in England, could qualify as an assemblyman because he had been resident in Singapore for seven years. If I, born and bred in Singapore, and lived here all my life except for four years in England, did not qualify, then the world must be square, not round.

But that was only my first hurdle. I suffered public embarrassment when the newspapers reported that Lam Tian, my Chinese-educated rival in the Democratic Party, had said I could not read or write the language, and was therefore not capable of representing the Chinese voter. I gamely countered, "Logically, since Lam Tian does not read and write Tamil and Malay, it means he does not propose to represent the Malay and Indian population of Tanjong Pagar." I blithely claimed I could read, write and speak Mandarin, Hakka and Hokkien, and that I also spoke Malay. It was election bravado. I had been advised by some Chinese reporters that it would be best not to admit my lack of command of my own mother tongue. I remembered and bitterly regretted that I had not heeded my maternal grandmother's wish that I should study Chinese in Choon Guan School. Now I had to exaggerate my linguistic skills. I could write some characters, but had forgotten most of them because I had not been using them since I gave up my job with Shimoda & Company in 1943. My spoken Hakka and Hokkien were pathetic, almost negligible. I vowed to make up for past neglect.

Lam Tian then challenged me to a debate at a street meeting in the Cantonese-speaking Kreta Ayer area of Tanjong Pagar. I dodged it, and counter-attacked by saying that to get things done in the Legislative Assembly and in the government, a candidate had to have good English, and that I would therefore be a more effective representative than he would. But I made a supreme effort to say a few words in Mandarin at my biggest rally in Banda Street, another Cantonese area. A friendly *Sin Pao* reporter called Jek Yeun Thong drafted two paragraphs for me, and then spent several hours coaching me to read a speech that took only three minutes to deliver. But the crowd was with me, and they cheered me for the effort.

My problems did not end there. The Chinese-speaking left-wing unions and the middle school students concentrated all their efforts on helping Lim Chin Siong at Bukit Timah and Devan Nair at Farrer Park. They did nothing for me or our other candidates. If ever I was in any doubt as to whom they took their orders from, it vanished after this experience. We were a united front of convenience. They wanted their own two men in, and I was only useful as cover for them. I never allowed myself to forget that. I had to speak at one rally for Lim and another for Nair, but my heart was not in it. It was in Sembawang with Ahmad Ibrahim, the unionist from the Naval Base fire brigade, and in Punggol-Tampines with old man Goh Chew Chua, who turned out to be an effective speaker in Hokkien and did well.

The campaign in no way resembled that of 1951 when I was Laycock's election agent in Katong. That was a genteel affair with tea and dinner parties for a limited electorate of 48,000 registered voters out of a population of 1.8 million. In 1955, with automatic registration of the Singapore-born, there were 300,000 voters, about 60 per cent of them Chinese-speaking. Moreover, the communists and their sympathisers had decided to join the fray for the first time since the beginning of the Emergency. The atmosphere was very different: the principal languages were the main Chinese dialects, bazaar Malay, which could reach the largest cross-section of the people, and lastly English, which reached the smallest – the top layer of Singapore society who were close to the levers of power but insignificant in voting strength. The street rallies and the meetings in open spaces had speakers standing on lorries or pick-up trucks with microphones and makeshift loudspeakers, and electric bulbs to light them up. They drew huge crowds where Chinese and Malay-speaking voters predominated. The sedate parlour game politics of 1951 was a thing of the past.

One valuable experience I gained was from the canvassing I did. Tanjong Pagar was the docklands of Singapore where the dock workers, the trishaw riders, the shopkeepers catering to them, and the opium dens were. I visited places like the Singapore Harbour Board quarters for daily-rated Malays in Reclamation Road, wooden houses with no sewerage and no drainage. The stench was overpowering. I retched whenever I went into the area. But inside these homes their leaders maintained a network that kept the Malays a close-knit society. I was introduced to the local UMNO chief, and in no time at all he produced the key men among the few hundred families who lived there. They promised to deliver me their votes.

Another scene of filth and dilapidation was presented by the rows of mean, broken-down shophouses in Narcis Street and the roads leading to it on the site where Tanjong Pagar Plaza now stands. They had not been repaired for many years, and the drains were clogged with rubbish left by roadside hawkers, so that there was always a stink of decaying food. Enormous rats ran fearlessly in and out of these drains, ignoring the cats around. Again, I retched. When I got home, washing my hands was not good enough. Before I could sit down to dinner, I had to bath and have a complete change of clothes.

The biggest single theme that galvanised the Chinese-speaking was Chinese culture, and the need to preserve Chinese traditions through the

Chinese schools. It was not a proletarian issue; it was plain, simple chauvinism. But the communists knew it was a crowd-winner that pulled at Chinese heartstrings, and they worked on it assiduously. In previous elections for the Legislative Council, the speeches were feeble, tepid, dull, delivered without feeling or conviction, usually in English, otherwise in Malay, and only sometimes translated into the different Chinese dialects. This time, Chinese orators took off. Speaking in their own dialects – Hokkien, Cantonese, Teochew – they were superlative crowd-rousers. They could wax eloquent, quote proverbs, use metaphors and allegories or traditional legends to illustrate contemporary situations. They spoke with a passion that filled their listeners with emotion and exhilaration at the prospect of Chinese greatness held out to them. For the Chinese of Singapore, it was never to be the same again.

One man emerged from this election as a powerful public speaker. He was young, slim, of medium height, with a soft baby face but a ringing voice that flowed beautifully in his native Hokkien. The girls adored him, especially those in the trade unions. Apart from Chinese culture, his themes were the downtrodden workers, the wicked imperialists, the Emergency Regulations that suppressed the rights of the masses, free speech and free association. Once he had got going after a cold start at the first two meetings, there was tremendous applause every time he spoke. By the end of the campaign, Lim Chin Siong was seen as a charismatic figure and a person to be reckoned with in Singapore politics and, what was of more immediate concern, within the PAP.

Fong Swee Suan also addressed these mass rallies but he did not have Lim's hypnotic effect. He was at a disadvantage. He had to speak in Hokkien to reach the widest audience, for the Hokkiens formed the largest single Chinese community in Singapore, and as a result their dialect was understood by the other groups – but Fong was a Hakka, like myself. Mandarin could reach only those under 35 who had been to Chinese schools; I was frantically learning it, but after these election meetings, I knew that even if I mastered it, it would not be enough. Yet I balked at the idea of learning Hokkien as well. The other language that could reach a big audience was bazaar Malay. This *Melayu Pasar* was a pidgin with little grammar, but it was understood by all races, and was the only means of trading with the Malays and Indians. However, because it was limited, it was difficult to move crowds in it. There could be no flights of rhetoric.

It was amazing how much personal loyalties counted for in that campaign. Those who came forward to help did so because they already thought well of me and wanted me to win. Under their union leaders, about 20 postal clerks sat for several consecutive days on my front veranda at Oxley Road (which was election headquarters for all four constituencies the PAP was contesting) to address my election manifestos for distribution to voters. Postmen also canvassed on my behalf in Tanjong Pagar and delivered my pamphlets house-to-house. Groups like the Itinerant Hawkers and Stallholders' Association helped us. Some of their members who sold live chickens and ducks in the markets had been charged with packing too many fowls into the baskets strapped to their bicycles at Chinese New Year, and I had got them off lightly by appealing to the magistrate to have a heart – it was, after all, the biggest festival in the lunar calendar.

But the most enthusiastic organisations were the main Hakka Clan Association and its subsidiaries, like the association for my clansmen from our ancestral prefecture of Dapu in China. Total strangers came to Oxley Road to offer their services. They were Dapu Hakkas (one of whom called me "uncle" although he was older than I was), and they expected nothing in return except to share in my glory. Chong Mong Sang, the president of the Singapore Hakka Association, mobilised the clan's resources and helped me with cars. He owned a successful chain of pawnshops in Malaya and Singapore (many pawnshops were run by Hakkas) and was my neighbour in Oxley Road. I was the association's honorary legal adviser, and as a close-knit minority, the Hakkas loyally rooted for me. The Singapore Chinese Liquor Retail Association allowed me to use its premises in Bernam Street as my second election head-quarters. Many anonymous people came there to give money, while others turned up with bales of white cloth for banners. They asked for no favours or rewards. I had none to give. In contrast, of the English-educated left wing, only two of the *Fajar* students assisted by writing addresses on election manifestos.

One big logistic problem that we had was to find transport to carry voters to the polling stations, where they would then feel obliged to cast their ballots for our candidate. This practice, introduced by the British, favoured the wealthy parties whose supporters had cars. I depended on miscellaneous personal contacts – my brothers and sister and my aunts, my Hakka neighbour, and friends like Hon Sui Sen and his brother. I put Dennis in charge of transport arrangements on polling day. It was not an enviable task. He had first to establish order and some sort of system out of the bedlam of vehicles that converged on Oxley Road from all over Singapore, then go on to my Bernam Street headquarters, and run around Tanjong Pagar picking up voters at the behest of my canvassers. He also persuaded some petrol stations to honour his signature and that of my clerical assistant at Laycock & Ong, for my friends had lent their cars with full tanks and we had to return them with full tanks, the petrol paid for out of election funds.

Nor was this all done just for me. Election agents for Lim Chin Siong and Devan Nair made demands on me for cars – an unpleasant man called Kam Siew Yee of the Teachers' Union insisted that I produce 30 for Nair alone. On 21 April, some three weeks after the election, Choo wrote a letter to Keng Swee in England, which was intercepted by Special Branch and thus survived in their files. It vividly illustrates whom the unions and the Chinese students were really campaigning for through their biased behaviour over canvassing and cars:

"Harry's helpers, canvassers, speakers, were honest to goodness straightforward workers – the postmen – clerks, shop assistants – a man who runs a food stall in Chinatown, Printers Union chairman, etc. Towards the last week about 20 brats came to help canvassing between 2 and 5 pm when all the men were still at work and not home, so their canvassing was not of much effect and you can compare that with the hundred and more Louis rustled up for Farrer Park right through the whole month. On polling day, there were a few more kids helping in Tanjong Pagar – pulling chaps out to vote. But if ever you have any doubts as to whether the kids are coming your way – this election will clear those doubts.

"... On morning of polling day Devan made the mistake of sending Kam here to 38 Oxley Road to collect cars destined for Farrer Park. Our transport committee had had a hell of a time finding cars (out of the 100 over lent to Harry) that could be sent to Bukit Timah and Farrer Park, because most people (like our Hakka neighbours opposite) lent cars to Lee Kuan Yew personally and not to PAP and had strong objections to cars going off elsewhere than to Tanjong Pagar. Cars were therefore carefully allotted – those who had no objection being sent away. When cars allocated to Farrer Park were late in turning up – Kam, the lout, had the effrontery to throw a scene and demand cars. Who the hell does he think he is."

Polling day, 2 April 1955: I collected 6,029 votes against 908 and 780 respectively for my two opponents, both of whom lost their deposits. I had won by the largest number of ballots cast for any candidate, and by the widest margin. Lim Chin Siong, Ahmad Ibrahim and Goh Chew Chua were also returned. Devan Nair lost, and I was greatly relieved, for without Nair, Lim would not be able to operate effectively in an exclusively English-speaking Legislative Assembly. He was not fluent in the language, and Nair would have been his crutch. Now he had to depend on me.

The big shock of the election was the rout of the Progressive Party, which had been expected to emerge the largest in the Assembly. The Labour Front won 10 out of the 17 seats it contested, and, to his own astonishment, David Marshall became the chief minister. The PAP won three out of four, and the smaller parties and independents, eight of the remainder. But the Progressives won only four out of the 22 they contested, and the Democrats only two out of 20. Yet their two parties had the most resources in money and election workers. What had happened?

The Progressive Party had been formed as early as 1947, but consisted only of a small coterie of English-educated professionals and Englishmen like John Laycock. But Laycock lost out in his ward like many others because they were now heavily outnumbered by the Chinese-educated – the "Chinese Chinese".

The Democratic Party was formed only in March 1955, after the Chinese Chamber of Commerce realised that automatic registration under the Rendel constitution would bring many Chinese-speaking voters onto the rolls. Broadly speaking, both parties represented the middle and upper middle classes, but while one was part of the British colonial establishment, the other was outside the magic circle. Its members were Chinese who made a good living as importers and exporters, retailers, merchants and shopkeepers, bankers, and rubber or tin magnates. They were the leaders of the Chinese-speaking traditional guilds; they were in charge of the Chinese schools, which they paid for and ran through their boards of management; and they funded and administered charitable Chinese clan hospitals and other welfare organisations. They saw this election as their chance to get at the levers of power that would increase their business prospects. They further believed that they could harness the energies of the Chinese middle school students to their party because the students were their children, and they had been sympathetic to their cause of defending Chinese education.

The cultural divide between the Progressives and Democrats was thus very deep and could not be bridged. In many constituencies, therefore, they split the right-wing ballot, with the English-speaking and Malay votes going to the Progressives and the Chinese-speaking to the

Democrats. If they had worked together, they would have won half of the 160,000 votes polled (seven times the number in the 1951 election).

Once they knew they had lost, they sneaked out of the counting centre at the Victoria Memorial Hall and vanished into the night. They did not understand that when you lose, you have to be defiant, to keep up the morale of your supporters, to live and fight another day. The communists knew this and we, the non-communists in the PAP, quickly learnt it from them. But the two parties had been totally demoralised by our hard-hitting campaign, which introduced a note of stridency into the hustings. We had attacked the Progressives as stooges of the colonial power, and the Democrats as capitalists and exploiters of the people. Our main target, however, had been our white overlords, of whom I wrote in my manifesto, "The colonial rule of the British over Malaya is the basic cause of a great number of social and economic evils of this country."

Marshall, a political greenhorn, criticised the PAP for going a little too far in demanding immediate self-government. "They seem to have been centred on antagonism and attack on the British. Their utterances seem to be unnecessarily anti-British." That might have been the feeling of the English-speaking middle class; it was different with the mass of the Chinese-educated.

Phoenix Park, the British commissioner-general's office, had its own intelligence assessment of the election. It quoted some passages of a speech I made at an election rally:

> "As far as I can see, apart from those over 40, all the Chinese are immensely proud of the achievement of the Mao Tse-tung government. A government that in five years can change a corrupt and decadent administration into one that can withstand the armed might of the Americans in Korea deserves full praise. General Chiang and Kuomintang are finished – except to some stray supporters who talk of the reconquest of the Chinese mainland.
>
> "But I believe there is growing in Malaya a generation of Chinese born and bred here, educated in the Chinese language and

traditions, but nevertheless Malayans in their outlook. They consider Malaya to be their only home. They are proud of China as a Frenchman in Quebec would be proud of France. Of course, there are those who feel that the task of building up a Malayan nation is not worthwhile. These are the young students who go back to China to be re-absorbed into the Chinese stream of life. Those who remain behind are Malayans and will be more and more as the years go by."

British intelligence thought my words worth reporting to fathom my real position.

Earlier, in January, Raja had drafted a PAP statement, which I then issued, proposing a general amnesty for the MCP. It was reasonable and logical, but in retrospect, naive and unworkable. "The past six and a half years have made clear that the Emergency in this country is essentially a political and not a military problem," it said. The sooner it was ended, the sooner could the people avail themselves of the democratic rights that it had curtailed, and without which effective democratic parties could not properly function. The Malayan government should give firm guarantees that if the MCP abandoned its armed insurrection, there would be no reprisals, and if it accepted constitutional methods of political struggle, it should be permitted to operate as a legitimate party.

Raja and I were Western-educated radicals who had no idea of the dynamics of guerrilla insurgency and revolution by violence. Only later did we realise that the communists would never give up their capacity to use armed force whenever democratic methods failed to win them power. But while in part our misguided demands could be put down to innocence, in large measure they could be traced to adroit manipulation of the mass rallies by the pro-communists. They were superb stage managers, and their cheerleaders had orchestrated prolonged applause for all speakers who attacked the Emergency Regulations and made them appear to be a major issue, since they had to be abolished first if the MCP were to break out into the open and be free to organise the ground.

Initially I did not understand this, and was duly impressed because it all appeared to be so spontaneous. But as I attended rally after rally over the next two years, I gradually became aware that these cheerleaders were always scattered among the audience. Furthermore, they would be led by a master cheerleader, from whom they took their cue, and each in turn would have his own claque of 30–40 who would begin to applaud when he did, triggering off a response from the audience around him. It was well-rehearsed. I was to see them play a game of "spot the leader" at their picnics at which 20 to 30 students would sit in a circle, each touching his nose or pulling his ear or tugging his shirt sleeve, the object being to identify the one who changed signals and almost instantly prompted all the others to change with him. With a good team, it was not always easy. But it was the combination of this stage management and his own oratory that made the reputation of Lim Chin Siong during those weeks of electioneering.

Later, I learnt that if any speaker broke the party line, the claques would suddenly go cold on him, however striking his oratory, hissing, booing and making disconcerting noises to distract the crowd. The communists had developed these techniques in mass psychology to a fine art and used them to great effect among the Chinese-educated. So far as I could see, they did not work with the English-educated.

I said many things then that were imprudent, so it was perhaps fortunate that the PAP had not set out to form a government and therefore would not be implementing our proposals. But meanwhile, we had aroused expectations of great changes. We had got the people interested enough to come and listen to our speeches, and then tossed them stirring ideas, instilling in them a spirit of defiance. The campaigning during the five weeks of that election decisively changed the mood in Singapore. But while tea party politics might be a thing of the past, the aftermath of all that rhetoric would soon be bloody violence.

11. Round One to the Communists

Laycock had become increasingly unhappy about my political activities but never complained to me directly. In 1954, after three years of service, he had given me a partnership contract under which I was guaranteed a minimum that was more than what Choo and I earned together. He did not want to continue to employ Choo, who was happy to stay at home to look after Loong – and later Ling, when she was born in January 1955. He knew I was doing my job in accordance with our agreement, and he tolerated me. However, the defeat of the Progressive Party and his own dismissal by the voters of Katong were crushing blows. He might perhaps have thought that the Progressives would form the government and I would be in opposition. But not this. I had become totally unacceptable. He never spoke to me again. Finally, he wrote me a letter asking for our partnership to be terminated as soon as possible, suggesting the end of August 1955. I promptly agreed. Thus ended one phase of my career.

In the five years since my return from England, I had built up something of a law practice and also a base for political support in the trade unions. But I now had two tasks ahead of me: to start my own law firm and to create a party organisation for the PAP. There was no great urgency. I had four months before I would leave Laycock & Ong, and four years in which to get the PAP into shape before the next general election. Together with Choo and my brother Dennis, we set up the firm Lee & Lee in Malacca Street, next to Laycock & Ong.

What I had not anticipated was the impact of the election campaign on the militants and trade unionists. The frenetic activity of the pro-communists, the fierce rhetoric of their speakers on Lim Chin Siong's and Devan Nair's platforms, had generated great heat. Many of the MCP cadres had been lying low, or had been under cover since the Emergency was proclaimed. In the weeks before and during the election, they came out into the open, using their anonymity as campaign helpers to foment feelings against authority among the workers, the rural dwellers in the countryside (mostly Chinese vegetable, pig and poultry farmers) and the Chinese middle school students. They stoked up hatred against the imperialists, the colonial government, the colonial police, the British capitalists and the local compradors who helped the British capitalists exploit the people. They had created a hothouse atmosphere – all those caught up in their circle believed that a successful revolution was just around the corner. And the militancy proved contagious.

Before the *Fajar* case, I had been looking for potential activists among University of Malaya students who would be willing to work with the unions. I had too much to do, and needed lieutenants who would stay on the job full-time. They were not easy to find. Good graduates wanted good careers. Not many were willing to take less than the going rates of pay for men with their qualifications, and work with the unions. There was no glamour in the job. The few who came forward did it for a cause, the idealism of youth. One of these was Sandrasegeram (or Sidney) Woodhull, whom I appointed to the Naval Base Labour Union as their paid (or underpaid) secretary. Another was Jamit Singh, a Sikh who had discarded his turban and trimmed his beard. He had failed his final examinations, but was active enough for the job, although some-what hotheaded. On my recommendation, he became the paid secretary of the Singapore Harbour Board Staff Association. Before I made these appointments, I checked with Corridon to know whether they were secret members of the Anti-British League or were likely to be Marxists or communists. He had nothing on them, but could not vouch for their inner loyalties. He encouraged me to try them out because if I did not get them to work for non-communist causes, their activism would lead them to the communists. It made sense. Neither was pro-communist to start with. Woodhull had only dabbled in Marxism at the university, and Jamit had no interest in intellectual theory.

But the next thing that happened was that the Singapore Harbour Board Staff Association, hitherto a non-militant group of largely English-educated Indian and Chinese clerks, went on strike. Ostensibly, Jamit had called them out because the Harbour Board had not settled claims on overtime rates, working hours, pensions and bonuses. But the truth was that he just wanted a fight, and pressed on even after the Harbour Board offered wage increases. It was all my doing. I had been naive in putting the few English-educated activists that I had into contact with the Chinese-speaking cadres of the MCP. Now even the apolitical Jamit Singh had gone along with Lim Chin Siong and Fong Swee Suan because they were the most active of all the unionists. He had got worked up seeing the Chinese-speaking unions becoming militant, and decided his clerks should not lag behind. Furthermore, now Lim had Devan Nair and James Puthucheary (they had been detained on St John's Island together) in his Singapore Factory and Shop Workers' Union, whose membership had jumped from a few hundred the previous year to more than 10,000. They helped him operate within the law and navigate the Chinese-educated through the English-speaking bureaucracy.

The pro-communist cadres were keyed up with the exhilaration of winning their political battles with a legitimate political vehicle, the PAP, with English-educated leaders who understood constitutionalism. It provided them with cover. Lim Chin Siong's position as a legislative assemblyman also gave him status and respectability with government and police officials. Then there was the hubris arising from the complete and total defeat of the Democratic Party and the rout of the English-educated professionals in the Progressive Party. To face this challenge there was now a Labour Front government consisting of weak opportunists, with a well-meaning but politically innocent chief minister in David Marshall, who did not understand the Chinese-speaking people, but was extremely anxious to live up to his self-perceived role as a liberal and a socialist bent on freeing Singapore from colonialism.

In the Legislative Assembly, I renewed my acquaintance with William Goode, the chief secretary. I first met him in 1953 over a minor grievance of the postmen. This was when the government had given convicts the task of painting red stripes down the sides of the postmen's khaki drill trousers, which they complained made them look like circus attendants. The government insisted the stripes were necessary because postmen were wearing these trousers when off duty, which they were not supposed to do. Goode was a big man with rugged features and a broken nose from boxing in his younger days. He had a long upper lip and spoke in a quiet, modulated voice. He had been educated at a public school and Oxford. But one could feel the steel behind the soft voice, his grey eyes and the firm set of his jaw. He was in the Singapore Volunteer Corps and a prisoner of war from 1942 to 1945, and was sent to work on the death railway in Thailand. He laughed easily and had a bluff manner. We got on well, and settled the problem by having the painted stripes changed to narrow red cloth piping. This made the postmen look smart, not clownish. It cost the government a little more.

Goode now explained that the Emergency Regulations were necessary because murder, arson, acid-throwing and other crimes of violence were part of the communists' bid for power. They had to maintain their acts of terrorism not just against the military, but also against civilians in order to cow them into a conspiracy of silence. The result was that no one who valued his life would appear in court as a witness to any communist-related crime. He recalled the assassination on 17 April of a young Chinese boy who was called out of a music club where he was playing a harmonica and shot dead. As it happened, I was at our Dapu Hakka Association just next door that Sunday afternoon, attending a tea party given in my honour to celebrate my election victory, and had heard the gunshot ring out. It was broad daylight, but nobody came forward to identify the assassin or assist the police, who were always helpless when it came to getting communists arrested and brought to trial.

I knew from my five years of practice at the Bar that Goode was stating hard facts. However, I could not support the extension of the Emergency Regulations because we had attacked them as part of our election platform. We had done so as a matter of principle, believing that if we had independence we could do away with them. By April, I was beginning to have some doubts about this, but it was to be another year and a half before my doubts turned into a conviction that Raja, Keng Swee, Chin Chye, Kenny and I were all wrong.

But I had a role to play in the Assembly, namely to discount the gravity of the security situation and move our agenda forward. In response to Bill Goode's speech, therefore, I said ironically, "That was a thrilling account of what good police and detective work can unravel," adding that there was "not one iota of evidence" that the schoolboy was killed under very mysterious circumstances or was a victim of a campaign of terror, other than the fact that since he had been shot, his fellow students had thought it wise to stay out of the affair.

Neither repealing nor prolonging the Emergency Regulations would solve the problem, I said, adding, "If we are ever to solve it, let us have the courage to say: 'We believe in democracy and we are going to fight for it. We give you this democracy to fight for.' If we then fail we would have to admit, as the French admitted in Indochina, that nothing can succeed." I believed then that had the French given the Vietnamese their full independence they might not have gone communist.

After the first two days of that Assembly meeting, it was obvious to the reporters in the press gallery and to the members present that the two main players were going to be Marshall and myself. He had the personality, a gift for colourful language, and a histrionic bent that could capture the attention of the House. I had a knack for pricking and deflating his high-flown metaphors and rather enjoyed doing it. Although the PAP had only three members in the Assembly plus Ahmad Ibrahim, the Speaker, Sir George Oehlers, placed me where the leader of the opposition would normally be seated, facing the chief minister.

A lawyer in his late 40s, Oehlers was very meticulous and punctilious, determined to be manifestly fair and impartial. He knew that he would preside over more interesting debates if I were seated opposite Marshall because I would stand up to him. What the Speaker did not yet know was that Marshall was easily provoked by sharp needling into making sallies he would later regret. He was soon to face a vital test of his authority, for the momentum of Lim Chin Siong and Fong's activities during the election campaign was carrying them inevitably towards a clash with the police.

Fong had succeeded in getting the Paya Lebar Bus Company workers to join his union in February against the wishes of their employer, and was now trying to win over the Hock Lee Bus Company. But Kwek Sing Leong, the tough managing director of Hock Lee, was not going to give up control of his workers and his business to a group of young communists; what was more, Lim Yew Hock as labour minister supported him, and so did his Singapore Trade Union Congress. Fong was nevertheless determined to teach Kwek and the remaining bus companies a lesson.

The day after the opening of the Assembly in April 1955, he got the supporters of his Singapore Bus Workers' Union (SBWU) to celebrate its first anniversary by picketing the Hock Lee depot in Alexandra Road. He declared an official strike, and urged the employees of all bus companies to come out in sympathy if Kwek did not agree to Hock Lee becoming a closed shop with the SBWU as its only union, and immediately settle their outstanding disputes. Kwek's response was to dismiss all 229 workers belonging to the SBWU, whereupon the workers went on a hunger strike and picketed the depot again the same night.

Then the ubiquitous Chinese middle school students got into the act. The boys and girls turned up to entertain the strikers with songs and dances, and since one of Lim Chin Siong's many disputes was with the Mis-Sino Aerated Water Company, which was not far from the Hock Lee premises, the students were able to shuttle between the two to give encouragement and support. I advised Fong not to call a strike until a 14-day notice had been given and had expired. Fong complied but in a speech in the Legislative Assembly on 27 April, Lim Chin Siong objected to the notice, which was required under the Emergency Regulations.

Kwek was not browbeaten by the threat of strike action and wanted to send his buses out the next day. But 150 strikers of Fong's group had already formed a human barrier in front of the main gate of the depot and refused to move despite repeated police warnings. Water hoses were then used and they were dispersed. Fifteen strikers claimed they had been brutally assaulted, but none had anything more than superficial bruises. Kwek got 40 of his 70 buses onto the road.

In the next two weeks, I received my first lesson in CUF negotiating tactics. Every concession made immediately led to a new demand. Every refusal to give in to a demand led to an increase in heat and tension. Meanwhile, the Chinese students together with supporters from Lim Chin Siong's Factory and Shop Workers' Union continued to visit the strikers in order to increase their sense of solidarity and omnipotence, and their conviction that victory was inevitable. Lim and Fong wanted nothing less than to win control of all the bus workers and be able to paralyse the city's transport system at will.

On 29 April, Marshall intervened, going personally to the Hock Lee depot to bridge the differences and get a settlement. Under pressure from the chief minister, Kwek offered to take back the dismissed workers pending the outcome of the court of inquiry ordered by Lim Yew Hock. I persuaded Fong to accept this. F.A. Chua, the judge who had heard the *Fajar* sedition case, was the chairman of the court of inquiry. Being a pragmatic man, he looked for a workable solution. He gave two-thirds of the buses to Fong's union and one-third to the house union, to be run on separate routes, and recommended that all dismissed workers be reinstated. The buses went out the next day.

But the strike resumed within hours when ticket inspectors from Fong's union refused to register their names with the company before leaving the depot, while other members claimed they were being discriminated against by being allotted vehicles in poor condition. Workers in Kwek's loyal Hock Lee Employees' Union continued to take their buses out on the roads, but strikers slashed the seats and rang the bells incessantly to disturb the drivers. Meanwhile, the pickets were out once more and the police had to use water hoses to disperse them. That was only the beginning. The following day, Fong called a two-day stoppage by all seven bus companies in Singapore, which would bring public transport to a halt. Twenty unions in the group that he and Lim Chin Siong controlled then threatened a general strike unless direct negotiations between the Hock Lee Bus Company and the SBWU were opened within 24 hours. Early on 12 May, crews of the remaining Hock Lee buses and of the Singapore Traction Company were intimidated into stopping work, and since the STC ran the major routes within the city, the city itself was almost paralysed, with only private cars and pirate taxis on the streets. Work also stopped at many other places, as Governor Sir John Nicoll reported to Alan Lennox-Boyd, secretary of state for the colonies, either "in sympathy, fear or plain bewilderment".

On the same morning, the pickets returned to the Hock Lee bus depot. Fong had urged them to be brave enough to stand firm this time, and they linked arms in a human chain as the police moved in with their hoses. The water jets still swept them away, and the buses passed through the gates, to be pelted with stones. But in the afternoon, 20 lorryloads of reinforcements from the Chinese middle schools converged on the depot and a pitched battle took place, with about 2,000 students and 300 strikers pitted against the police. The main weapons were stones and bottles on one side and tear gas on the other, but every now and then cornered policemen had to use their firearms. When darkness fell, the rioting grew more intense.

At about 9 pm, I drove to the junction of Tanglin Road and Jervois Road, which was on a hillock and gave a good view of the Hock Lee bus depot below me. I had my car radio on, and at 9:30, Marshall came on the air. It was sad. He was confused. He was for the people, for the downtrodden workers, yet they were rioting. He extolled them for their past sacrifices, which had made Singapore prosperous, and appealed to them to give him time to put things right. He said, "We have furthermore sought and are still seeking to obtain the services of Professor Arthur Lewis of the University of Manchester, a West Indian Negro of world standing as an economist, and all his life a staunch socialist, in order to assist us in reorienting the economy of this territory for the benefit of the people." I could hardly believe my ears.

I despaired for Marshall and for Singapore. Either he should have left the governor and the chief secretary to tackle this problem, or if he was going to be in charge then he had to govern and tell the striking workers that unless they stopped this violence, he would use force to restore law and order. On 21 May, the governor reported to Alan Lennox-Boyd, "The chief minister, under strong pressure from myself and others, addressed the public over Radio Malaya in a long and unconvincing speech, once more blaming 'colonialism' and 'economic exploitation' for the situation, likely neither to restrain the lawless nor to reassure the law-abiding."

I knew that Lim Chin Siong and Fong were working for a clash with authority, but I did not expect an outburst of mob fury. People assumed there was always some latent animosity in the Chinese-speaking population for their white bosses, but I never realised it was so intense. Raised to fever pitch by the middle school students and the communist cadres in the unions, it exploded. It is probable that even Lim and Fong were not prepared for what was now to take place. But I was to learn again and again that their purpose was never to argue, reason and settle. It was always to engineer a collision, to generate more popular hatred of the colonial enemy. They wanted to establish the Leninist preconditions for a revolution: first, a government that no longer commanded the confidence of the people, and second, a government that had lost faith in its ability to solve its problems as growing lawlessness, misery and violence overwhelmed it.

The rioting spread the next day. By 4 pm, mobs of about 1,000 were attacking the police and had to be broken up with tear gas. After dark, they continued to strike at police posts, road blocks, individual policemen and radio patrol cars. It was hit-and-run throughout the night until 3 am, when the main crowds dispersed. But groups of 10 and 20 were still throwing stones and bricks at policemen who were clearing the roads of obstruction and towing away damaged vehicles. Two policemen were killed and 14 injured, along with some 17 civilians. Whenever violence erupted, the crowd would go for any whites on the scene, since feelings against them were running strong. An American correspondent for UPI was beaten to death, and three Europeans had narrow escapes.

At about 10.35 pm that first evening, a mob had attacked a police patrol car with a British police lieutenant in charge, hurling bottles and stones as they closed in for the kill. The lieutenant radioed for help, but before he and his men were rescued he fired four shots from his revolver. He was not aiming at the crowd, he said, but one shot appeared to have hit a Chinese student of about 17. Instead of taking him straight to hospital, however, the other students put him on a lorry and paraded him around the town for three hours, so that by the time he was brought there he was dead from a wound in the lung. Had he been taken to hospital directly, he might have been saved. But what was one life if another martyr could stoke up the fire of revolution?

After the riots on 13 May 1955, the government decided to get tough and closed three Chinese schools. But the students continued to camp in them and were supported by the trade unions controlled by Lim Chin Siong and Fong; there were more marches through the town by the strikers, and stone-throwing and attacks on cars. The tense situation finally eased after the funeral of the Chinese student on 15 May passed without incident. That night, after four hours of mediation, a happy Marshall broadcast that an agreement had been reached that "might well lead to a settlement of all outstanding strikes of an industrial nature" in Singapore. He appointed as arbiter Charles Gamba, who was known to be sympathetic to the union. Gamba gave his final ruling on 28 May. The SBWU members who had been dismissed on 23 April were to be reinstated. The Hock Lee Employees' Union was to be dissolved, and 160 members retrenched.

Kwek would not give up easily. He still allocated work to members of the officially defunct Hock Lee Employees' Union who had been loyal to him, and the union's leaders threatened to reject Gamba's ruling until the government prevailed upon the company to go along with it. Kwek was bitter and defiant. He was a Hockchia, a Hokkien sub-branch known to be rough and tough. The Hock Lee Bus Company was a family business, and he was confident he could fight and win because many union members were his clansmen and key officials like the inspectors and timekeepers were his blood relatives. But an inexperienced government, not knowing what the game was about, helped the communists to break the most tightly knit of all the bus companies in Singapore.

It was a total victory for Fong and the Singapore Bus Workers' Union and their methods, not least because they now had the full measure of Marshall. They knew they had a swing door to push. The way in which the SBWU had fought and won gave all trade unions – workers and leaders, communists and non-communists – confidence that they had much to gain if they, too, showed fight.

12. Marshall Accentuates the Crisis

Fong Swee Suan and four other union leaders were arrested by the government under the Emergency Regulations on 11 June 1955. Six thousand bus workers came out in protest against their detention. The next day, thanks to what the authorities described as "mob coercion" of the drivers, taxis also disappeared from the streets. But the government mounted free emergency lorry services to important parts of the city, and more than 100,000 labourers and 280,000 others went to work as usual without incident. Despite the paralysis of public transport, the strike failed to bring the city to a standstill. This time the people were out of sympathy with it – it was too political and not related to any of their economic grievances. After four days, Lim Chin Siong and Devan Nair suddenly called it off, and 13,300 workers, men and women in 90 commercial and industrial enterprises, returned to work. The government claimed victory. Fong was not released until 25 July.

I had decided to get away from this madhouse and go on my annual vacation. With Choo and Loong, age 3, I drove up to the Cameron Highlands on 1 June and stayed there for three weeks. We left 5-month-old Ling at home as she was too young.

I played golf at Tanah Rata every day, morning and afternoon. As I walked on the pleasant and cool nine-hole Cameron Highlands course, 5,000 feet above sea level, I soaked in the significance of the events of the previous few months. I felt in my bones that to continue on the course Lim Chin Siong and Fong had embarked upon would end in political disaster. The PAP and the Middle Road unions (named for the location of their headquarters, not their policies) would be banned. But if Marshall were to flinch from taking unpopular action, the whole economy and society of Singapore would be in such a chaotic mess that the British government would have to suspend the constitution.

On 21 June, I drove back to Singapore with the family. The press hinted that I had run away from these troubles, but I knew my presence would have made no difference. When the *Straits Times* asked why I did not return from my leave, I said my executive committee had not asked me to, and I had full confidence in them.

This had been my baptism of fire working with the CUF. I talked the problem over with Chin Chye, Raja and Kenny. (Keng Swee was in London doing his PhD.) We decided that I should read the riot act to Lim and Fong. I told them that if they carried on in this way, they would have to go it alone. That sobered them up, and on 26 September the governor, Sir Robert Black, would write in a report to Alan Lennox-Boyd:

> "The collapse of this general strike did much to discredit the extremist elements in the PAP. Lee Kuan Yew was away from Singapore at the time and I am informed that he departed deliberately in order to have no part in the violence. ... Since then there has been a change in tactics by the PAP. While continuing to foment strikes, in pursuit of their campaign for winning control of labour, they have been at pains to keep within the law."

That did not last long. After a few months, the pro-communists drifted back to their old ways, but they did not provoke bloody clashes with the police or stage a general strike to paralyse the economy. I believed they still thought clashes with the police and the government were the way to arouse more hatred and heighten the revolutionary fervour of the people. There were times when Lim and Fong appeared to listen to my advice to keep to the methods of constitutional struggle with long negotiations and passive resistance to avoid bloodshed. But they came from a different tradition and background from mine and they had different models in mind.

I was in a most difficult position. While I could not and would not defend them, I could not condemn them without breaking up our united front. As I had explained to a correspondent of the *Sydney Daily Mirror* in an interview reported in the *Straits Times*, "Any man in Singapore who wants to carry the Chinese-speaking people with him cannot afford to be anti-communist. The Chinese are very proud of China. If I had to choose between colonialism and communism, I would vote for communism and so would the great majority." I was hoping that I could get enough Chinese to vote with us against the communists and for independence and democracy. But I was not at all sanguine that this could be easily achieved if a successful communist China continued to be their source of inspiration.

And I was under pressure. The chief minister had called for an emergency meeting of the Assembly for 16 May, to capitalise on the revulsion of public feeling against the unions, isolate and turn the heat on the PAP, and make the non-communists in the party split from the communists. This time the chief secretary, Bill Goode, led the attack. He made a powerful speech, recounting what had taken place factually and effectively. He deplored the loss of life, praised the police and condemned the evil men who had exploited the workers and the students, and the failure of the manipulated Chinese newspapers to give any support to the side of law and order. All efforts to promote a settlement were frustrated by people who, Goode said, "clearly do not want grievances to be removed but are out to maintain unrest and are out to exploit the genuine grievances of decent workers for their own evil ends".

He then rounded on me.

"In their lust for power ... the People's Action Party and their covert communist supporters and backseat drivers wanted violence and bloodshed and industrial unrest. ... If the honourable Member believes in orderly progress to democratic self-government, then he must be against communism; and if he is, let him say so loud and clear, with no quibble and no clever sophistry. He has deplored violence after hell was let loose and men were killed. ... I ask him: What did he do to prevent violence before it happened? Is his conscience clear? Or did he lose control to the Member for Bukit Timah (Lim Chin Siong) who sits behind him and drives the party?"

He was followed by John Ede, the expatriate who had won Tanglin for the Progressives. This made my task easier. I rose immediately after Ede to say I was glad it was to two Englishmen that I had to reply. Had it been Marshall,

"he would have weighed his words with more care, with more circumspection, and with more understanding of the difficulties and the dangers of the situation; with more understanding of the hopes, fears and aspirations of people. ...

"We have not come here as prisoners to be accused, or as prisoners who must discharge the burden of their guilt. We have come here as representatives of the people, and we shall speak as such."

(I reiterated the stand of the PAP.) "To destroy the colonial system by methods of non-violence. We abjure violence. ... We are not prepared to fight, perpetuate or prolong the colonial system. But give us our rights and we will fight the communists or any others who threaten the existence of an independent and democratic non-communist Malaya."

Because I had praised him, Marshall again wobbled when he replied, confusing his followers, and saved the PAP from total discredit by saying:

"If the PAP, which consists of responsible, decent, honest men many of them, if they would purge themselves of the communists and fellow travellers that they know they have – if they would face their own responsibility, they could be the organisation that they hope to be that would one day lead this country to win its independence."

Marshall did not know that by his speeches and, worse, by his eagerness to settle and avoid conflict, he had opened Pandora's box. Every worker in Singapore, every leader and every communist cadre knew they had a government they could use for their own purposes, to corner the employers, win benefits, and take over management's prerogatives.

∞

Already their successes were paying off. By August 1955, membership of the Singapore Factory and Shop Workers' Union (SFSWU) had swollen to 23,000, most of them young Chinese. Meanwhile, its English-educated associates, including Nair, Woodhull and James Puthucheary, were helping the Chinese-educated to demolish the British colonial system. Their tactics were both to infiltrate existing unions and to form new ones. They had the Singapore Chinese Middle School Students' Union as a *de facto* affiliate, and their weapon was the sympathy strike. For any single issue in any single company, they would threaten to stop the whole works.

As the communists had done in China, this was to be a united front of workers, students and peasants (such as there were in Singapore) to foment unrest and convert labour disputes into political issues, increase class and racial hatred (of the white man) and breed contempt for authority. Once the SFSWU had become an octopus-like conglomerate trade union, with its membership of Chinese-speaking workers, Lim Chin Siong and Fong targeted the Singapore Harbour Board Staff Association, the Naval Base Labour Union and the City Council Labour Union – non-communist organisations whose Indian, Malay and English-speaking Chinese were prepared to go along with the SFSWU. They realised they could make use of the militancy of the Chinese unions and the threat of sympathy strikes to further their own demands.

Sir Robert Black also recognised that the situation had changed for the worse. On 26 September he wrote to Lennox-Boyd:

"During the elections, ... extravagant speeches were made attacking the government. ... PAP meetings were also packed with organised labour and Chinese students; mass feelings were skilfully roused. All this led to a loss of respect for constituted authority, and increased the prestige of those who ... were openly challenging the government."

Singapore was in the grip of a strike fest – in the nine months between 7 April and December 1955, there were 260 stoppages. This militancy, however, was to work to my advantage.

On 19 June 1955, the City Council Labour Union threatened to walk out over demands for back pay they had made the previous year. The City Council threatened to serve lock-out notices, and to hire contractors to take over essential services if union workers stayed away. Talks failed to settle the dispute and the strike began on 17 August.

Three days later, however, the union asked me to be their legal adviser. The members were mainly Indian daily-rated workers, the majority engaged in city cleansing and garbage collection. It was a big union of several thousands, the leader a shrewd, squint-eyed, uneducated Indian called Suppiah. There had already been some ugly incidents in which they had resorted to violence. I replied that I would be proud to act for them, but stipulated that the strike must be carried out in a peaceful way. They agreed, and the talks became constructive.

The governor reported on 8 September to Lennox-Boyd:

"At one time there were disquieting instances of rowdyism on a familiar pattern, but they ceased suddenly after a few days. Whether Lee Kuan Yew should be given any credit for this is not certain, but it is probably the case." (We had reached agreement on 7 September.) "Contrary to expectations ... the strike did not break down and the union has won substantial concessions. ... There are two main reasons for this outcome. One is the weakness of the City Council ... and the other is the intervention of Lee Kuan Yew, the secretary of People's Action Party, as legal adviser to the union. His intervention was in fact useful to both sides and he has probably improved his personal position as a result of the settlement."

My way of constitutional opposition, working within the law, was in marked contrast to that of the communists, and I got results. But without the communists going beyond the law and using violence, my methods would not have been effective. It was the less unpleasant option I offered that made them acceptable to the British. Just as in Malaya, had there been no terrorism to present the British with the humiliating prospect of surrendering to the communists, the Tunku would never have won independence simply by addressing larger and larger gatherings of Malays in the villages. It was the disagreeable alternative the communists posed that made constitutional methods of gentle erosion of colonial authority effective for the nationalists and acceptable to the colonialists. In prewar India, where there was no communist threat, constitutional methods of passive resistance took decades to work.

∞

While the trade unions continued to simmer away and grow in strength, Marshall stirred up one political crisis after another. He had a knack for creating them. In the midst of all the industrial unrest and agitation, he clashed with Sir Robert Black over his demand for the creation of four junior ministers, and when the governor offered only two, decided to make the dispute public. He claimed that the governor had no right to ignore the chief minister's advice, and threatened to resign if he refused to consult him before taking any action. He also wanted Singapore to be given complete self-government. Emergency Regulations had expired on 21 July, but the governor had extended them for a further three months, subject to adoption by the Assembly at its next meeting: Marshall's price for the extension was that the British grant Singapore self-government "at the earliest possible moment".

The proceedings of that Assembly meeting on 22 July were typical of the silly and irresponsible manner in which the political parties manoeuvred. In putting the motion for self-government, Marshall explained that this was a constitutional matter of principle. At the end of his diatribe against the governor and colonialism, he turned to me – the Member for Tanjong Pagar who "has plagued me so consistently and so vociferously in the past" but is "virtually the leader of the opposition in the eyes of the public" – and asked me to second his motion. He thus negated the charge made barely two months before, on 26 April, by Goode, who had often called the PAP a vehicle for the communists and their willing tool. I certainly could not refuse the honour of seconding the motion!

The Assembly adjourned on 22 July. When it reassembled three days later, a Progressive Party member, Lim Koon Teck, tried to outflank both Marshall and me. "Let us ... ask for a full transfer of power so that we, and we alone, shall be responsible for our own affairs and destiny and the British government need no longer be answerable to us," he proposed, and thereupon moved an amendment to substitute "independence" for "self-government". In other words, he wanted "independence" immediately. The Progressives had always represented moderation, the step-by-step approach to sovereignty. By this sudden manoeuvre, they appeared more radical than the Labour Front and the PAP. I remarked that "Today, we are entertained by the unique spectacle of a mouse turned lion."

The amendment was rejected and the original motion for immediate self-government was passed, well-timed to put the heat on Lennox-Boyd, who was due to arrive just a week later. By their move, however, the Progressive Party had destroyed themselves as a consistent, dependable party. Now there was no longer a coherent right wing or middle-of-the-road political force in Singapore.

Lennox-Boyd arrived in Singapore, met Marshall and went off to Malaya. On 2 August, the Speaker read to the Assembly a letter from the governor, saying that the secretary of state for the colonies had discussed matters with the chief minister, and that the discussion would continue when he returned to Singapore from Malaya on 15 August. Marshall, mollified by a Lennox-Boyd looking and sounding sympathetic, said, "For the time being, perhaps we should rest there and proceed with normal business." I disagreed, pointing out that there was nothing in the governor's letter that materially altered the position since our last meeting "except that on that day, we had a much fiercer chief minister". I then moved to block Marshall's resolution thanking the governor, and the Assembly supported me. Marshall was livid.

But on 18 August, the Speaker read another letter from the governor, which stated that he would act in accordance with the chief minister's advice except on the prorogation and the dissolution of the Assembly. The letter also said that the British government would be glad to welcome to London at a suitable date a representative delegation from Singapore to consider constitutional matters. Marshall declared, "This is indeed a happy day for Singapore. It marks the end of the first phase of our struggle for freedom. It marks the beginning of a new era ... an exhilarating victory." Marshall thrived on adrenaline. He again moved that the Speaker "... request the governor on their behalf to thank the secretary of state for his sympathetic approach to our aspirations". I would have none of this and threatened to walk out – I wanted time to think about the implications of such a thank-you message. Marshall was outraged. My motion against the proposal was defeated.

I was having fun with Marshall, but there was more serious business on hand. The future of Chinese language, culture and education remained a grave problem, although the seething unrest in the Chinese middle schools had temporarily subsided when the All-Party Committee on Chinese Schools "appealed" to the government not to proceed with the expulsion of the students, or with the notices served on the schools to show cause why they should not be closed down. The committee had provided a neat way out of an acute problem of face. By accident, the government had stumbled on a process of quiet consultations that enabled a formula to be worked out without the glare of publicity. Otherwise every defect in any solution would have been reported in the Chinese press and made the subject of contention, lobbying and the scoring of propaganda points.

The recommendations of the committee had long-term consequences that were good for Chinese education and good also for harmony in a multiracial society. But they threatened the future of the communists. About 90 per cent of all adult Chinese were Chinese-educated – if educated at all. But the number of Chinese children going to English schools had been growing dramatically since 1948, when the Emergency was declared. In 1950, there were 25,000 more students in Chinese schools than there were in English schools, but by 1955 the ratio had changed, and there were 5,000 more students in English schools than in Chinese schools. Although the communists did not know the exact figures, they were aware of the trend, and since it would dry up their breeding grounds, they had to halt it. So the battle for the preservation of Chinese education became even more crucial for the MCP.

The problem for the government and for the non-communists in the PAP was complicated by the fact that Chinese culture was also dear to the hearts of many parents, who were therefore not enthusiastic about the introduction of English into Chinese schools. All their administrative costs would be paid by the government, but in return the schools would have to comply with government regulations on syllabuses and discipline. And anyway, they wanted the teaching to be completely in Chinese.

True, about half of them wanted to have it both ways. Many clan leaders on the management committees of Chinese schools placed their own children in English schools and gave them Chinese lessons in the afternoons, to make them bilingual. At the same time they exhorted other parents to send their offspring to Chinese schools in order to carry

In a victory handshake with Chief Minister David Marshall outside the Assembly House in July 1955, after the Legislative Assembly had passed his motion calling for immediate self-government and a new constitution.

on the tradition of classical Chinese scholarship. There was no way of satisfying everyone. The government therefore needed a report from the committee, on which I represented the PAP, that would commit all parties to its findings, so that we would all be obliged to undertake the task of persuading the Chinese-speaking ground to accept it. This gave me the opportunity to shape it, but it also exposed me to the grave danger of having to fight the MCP over a matter vital to its survival.

I decided that, whether or not it was practical, the only politically defendable policy was trilingualism, with Malay as the lingua franca and the future national language of Malaya, English as the language of international commerce and science, Mandarin as the mother tongue of the Chinese, and Tamil, Hindi or Punjabi for the Indians. The chairman of the all-party committee was Chew Swee Kee, minister for education, and its other seven members included a Malay, Abdul Hamid bin Haji Jumat, the minister for local government. Over the next nine months I worked on these two, both of whom were comfortable with my views, and together we produced a report that all could embrace. It included a recommendation for rewriting all the textbooks in the Chinese schools, which up to then had been those used in pre-war China under the Kuomintang government.

∞

Meanwhile, Lim Chin Siong and Fong had not been idle. They had been pursuing a typical united front strategy with which I soon became familiar. Lim had made himself chairman of a Chinese education committee representing 16 trade unions and the All-Singapore Chinese School Parents' Association. But that was only a beginning. He had a far wider list of people and organisations on whom he could call, for the SFSWU was not known in Hokkien as Kok Giap or "every trade" for nothing. The Middle Road group around it now included not only many affiliates with no significant numbers of Chinese-speaking members, and therefore no interest in Chinese education, like the Naval Base Labour Union and the Singapore Traction Company Union, but also miscellaneous associations like those of barbers, tailors, cinema and entertainment workers, and even wooden house dwellers.

That was only one aspect of the octopus. Lim Chin Siong also wanted to co-opt the extensive traditional clan guilds that were under the wing of the Chinese Chamber of Commerce, and to this end he sought and obtained the support of its chairman, Tan Lark Sye. Tan was an illiterate multi-millionaire rubber merchant, a great champion of Chinese language and education, and the biggest single donor to a building fund for a university in Singapore for the education of Chinese from all over Southeast Asia. He was a great admirer of the new China and was willing to go along with the communists so long as they did not hurt his interests. He gave Lim his blessing for a joint mass meeting on 6 June 1955, which was to include the Chinese Chamber of Commerce and the clans associated with it, as well as Lim's "education committee".

The vice-president of the Chinese Chamber of Commerce, Yap Pheng Gek, was an English-educated comprador type with the Oversea-Chinese Banking Corporation. He did not want to play Lim's game, and managed to reduce the mass meeting to one for representatives of six educational bodies, including Lee Kong Chian, a rubber magnate who was chairman of the Management and Staff Association of the Chinese High School.

The object of the meeting was to discuss a memorandum to be submitted to the government, calling for equality of treatment for Chinese and English language schools. It was stipulated in advance that there would be no debate and no new resolutions, but only a straight vote on the submissions to be made. Nevertheless, Lim Chin Siong ignored the rulings of the chairman, Yap Pheng Gek, who was afraid to enforce them against the pro-communists. Lim presented his own memorandum, which demanded not only equal status for Chinese schools and English schools, but an allocation of government funds for building Chinese schools, six years free primary education, and the right to form student self-governing societies (i.e., branches of the militant Chinese Middle School Students' Union) in every school.

When the chairman feebly tried to enforce the rules of the meeting, Fong asked to speak on behalf of the Singapore Bus Workers' Union. Permission was refused. Fong then made a direct appeal to the audience, which had been packed with Lim Chin Siong's supporters. There were tumultuous cheers of approbation to demonstrate solidarity and intimidate the chairman. The chairman duly surrendered. From then on, Lim and Fong controlled the meeting.

In this atmosphere, the hall filled to capacity with representatives of the clan associations and pro-communist trade union activists, the chauvinists took over. Chuang Chu Lin, the principal of Chung Cheng High School and later vice-chancellor of Nanyang University, opposed any revision of Chinese history and geography textbooks, and when he received enthusiastic backing, Lim Chin Siong's short-lived proposal to have textbooks with a Malayan background was abandoned. Otherwise, only those resolutions that favoured the communists were carried. Lim got what he wanted, supported now by the traditional leaders of the Chinese-speaking establishment.

The all-party committee gave this memorandum from the Chinese Chamber of Commerce pride of place in an appendix to its report, but ignored all its recommendations. When, in February 1956, Chew Swee Kee made a statement on the report in the Legislative Assembly, no questions were asked. The report was the best compromise we could craft, and representatives of all parties had signed it.

The proposal was simple. The English-language schools would also teach the mother tongue – Chinese for the Chinese, Malay for the Malays, and Tamil or some other Indian language for the Indians. The students in Chinese schools would learn either English or Malay in primary school, and both in secondary school. The Malay-language schools would also teach English in primary school, and a third language in secondary school if the students wished it.

Underlying this tussle over language and education was a struggle for power. The Chinese merchant classes, clan leaders and tycoons of the Chamber of Commerce wanted an Assembly in which their elected representatives could speak for the Chinese population in fluent Chinese, not inadequate English, in order to increase their influence and wealth. They had already presented a memorandum for a multilingual legislature to the Rendel Committee (which had been rejected), and we had supported their proposals as early as November 1954, even before the PAP had been formally launched. Now the Chinese Chamber was again recommending that Chinese be one of the official languages.

One unavoidable problem in a multiracial, multilingual society is how to organise a functioning legislature and government without creating a Tower of Babel. Every old-established community has one main language, and those who migrate into it have to learn that language, whether it be English in the United States and Canada, or French in Quebec. But when Stamford Raffles founded Singapore in 1819, he demarcated in his first town plan different areas in which the different races and even different Chinese dialect groups would live separately. The British then brought in large numbers of Chinese, Indians and Malays, all speaking their own tongues, and left them to their own devices.

Under populist pressure, Marshall predictably moved a resolution on 9 February 1956 that "this Assembly is of the opinion that for the purposes of oral debate, the languages of the Assembly should be English, Malay, Mandarin and Tamil and that a select committee be appointed to examine the report and make necessary recommendations". Marshall knew he risked becoming irrelevant by this move. He recounted how a Malayan (sic) had told him, "with multilingualism, you are going to hand us over to the Chinese. They will swamp us." "Yes, sir," he had answered, "one must accept the rule of the majority. The Chinese are 76 per cent of our population. Let us not avoid the issue." This was typical of Marshall – half idealist and half (or perhaps more than half) an opportunist anxious to prove he was more Chinese than the Chinese, and therefore acceptable as their champion, at least for another term. The enthusiastic cheers for Chinese speakers during the election mass rallies had left no doubt that anyone who voted against multilingualism in order to exclude their representatives from the Assembly would surely lose votes.

In my speech I said, "When we take this step today, we must understand that it is irreversible, unless at the point of the bayonet, and even that would not work for long. We must remember that there are deeper and wider implications ..." This was February 1956, and many people expected a flowering of the Chinese and Indonesian languages and their literature as a resurgent China and Indonesia became strong and powerful in 10 to 20 years. It was not possible, politically or psychologically, to persuade the mass of the people, then in an anti-colonial mood, to accept the primacy of the English language.

I was acutely conscious that my lack of comprehension, let alone command of the Chinese language, was a tremendous political disadvantage. I recounted my own personal experience:

"I was sent to an English school to equip me to go to an English university in order that I could then be an educated man – the equal of any Englishman, the model of perfection. Sir, I do not know how far they have succeeded in that. I grew up and I finally graduated. At the end of it, I felt – and it was long before I entered politics ... that the whole set of values was fundamentally and radically wrong."

I then quoted Nehru who had said that he cried because he could not speak his own tongue as well as he spoke the English language.

"I am a less emotional man, sir. I do not usually cry or tear my hair, or tear paper or tear my shirt off, but this does not mean that I feel any the less strongly about it. My son is not going to an English school. He will not be a model Englishman. I hope, of course, that he will know enough English to converse with his father on matters other than the weather."

That was how I felt. It probably went down well with the Chinese-speaking masses. Although Lim Chin Siong and the MCP were not happy with the report itself, they could not attack me openly for supporting it (the voting was 29 ayes and no noes) without provoking a breach in the PAP. On the other hand, the president and vice-president of the Singapore English Teachers' Union (Chinese Schools) could. They dubbed it "a shameless piece of colonial prudery" (sic) and demanded the appointment of another committee whose members would have a closer understanding of Chinese education. I ignored this statement. The teachers of English in the Chinese schools – underqualified and underpaid – were as much under the influence of the communists as were the Chinese-language teachers.

The MCP was worried about the discipline the government would impose on the Chinese schools. They feared that it would stop the students from being "misused by political groups to overthrow a lawfully constituted government unconstitutionally". Worse, the English language would open for them a completely different world through newspapers, magazines, literature and films. They would see the world with two eyes, with binocular vision, instead of with only one eye through a Chinese telescope. I had to take a position that would not allow the communists to denounce me as a deculturalised Chinaman. Had I taken a false step on this issue, I would have lost out. If they could show that I preferred English to Chinese as the more important medium of instruction in the schools, it would be impossible for me to retain the respect and support of the Chinese-speaking ground.

In mid-1955, I had sent Loong at the age of three and a half to Nanyang Kindergarten, which taught in Chinese. When I visited it later with the all-party committee, the Chinese press carried a picture of him in the kindergarten, making it widely known that he was being educated in Chinese. My determination that my three children should be educated in the language and culture of their ancestors gave me credentials that the communists could never impugn. My two younger children, Wei Ling and Hsien Yang, followed Loong to Nanyang Kindergarten and on to Nanyang Primary School. Later, Loong and Yang went to the Catholic High School, while Ling continued in Nanyang Girls' High School. They were completely Chinese-educated, but because they spoke English at home with their mother, they became equally fluent in English. And with tuition in Malay, from the age of six, they mastered a third language.

While people in Singapore were distracted by Marshall's recurring crises, troubled by the unrest in the schools and industrial strife in the work place, events were taking place in Malaya that were to alter the future of the island.

13. A Fiasco in London

Tunku Abdul Rahman, the leader of the Malay party, UMNO, in the Federation of Malaya, was the opposite of David Marshall. He was completely consistent and reliable. He did not pretend to be clever but was a shrewd judge of people. Most important of all, he understood power. His father had been Sultan of Kedah, and from the shadow of his father's throne he had learnt how to wield it to get men to do what he wanted of them. As a royal prince himself, he had the unqualified support of the rulers of the nine Malay states of the Federation who had opposed the British government's proposal for a Malayan Union in 1946. Best of all, he was genuinely pro-British and anti-communist. He had spent nine years of his youth in England as a student, three years reading law at Cambridge, where he was quite literally given a degree, and six more trying – but never very hard – to pass his Bar examinations. He enjoyed life and often told me about the wonderful times he had had in England. In him, the British found a leader who commanded solid backing from the Malays and good support from the Chinese and Indians.

In July 1955, the Federation held a general election in which an alliance of UMNO, the Malayan Chinese Association (MCA) and the Malayan Indian Congress (MIC) swept the board. The Tunku and some of his colleagues then became members of the British High Commissioner's Executive Council; as in Singapore, they now had limited self-government, but unlike our ministers they were quite happy to work with colonial appointees. One important difference was that they were fighting a communist guerrilla insurrection that could be put down only with the help of British, Australian and New Zealand forces, and the

British required that the Emergency should end before independence was granted.

In January 1956, the Tunku went to London for a constitutional conference, and on his way from Singapore to England aboard the Italian liner *Asia* told the press he did not agree with Marshall that Singapore should enjoy equal status in any alliance between them. If Singapore were granted equal status, "it would alarm the Malays on the mainland. The British separated the two territories primarily to protect the interests of the Malays in the Federation." However, he agreed with the PAP that discussions should be opened between leaders of Singapore and the Federation on a future alliance. In his lead paragraph in the *Singapore Standard*, Raja interpreted "future alliance" to mean "future merger". Raja could not have been more wrong.

The Tunku had something different in mind, not a union of the two territories but "an alliance", an arrangement between two separate entities. He did not want Singapore as a state in Malaya because it would upset the racial balance in Malaya. Nor did he want Singapore as an independent state equal to Malaya. He wanted the British to stay in control of a Singapore with self-government, and an alliance with a non-sovereign Singapore government. Unfortunately, time was running out for such arrangements. The British knew it; the Tunku did not.

Alan Lennox-Boyd had visited Kuala Lumpur in August 1955 to assess the situation and the Tunku himself. He found in the Tunku someone he could trust, and granted him his date for independence, 31 August 1957. Furthermore, with immediate effect from the end of the constitutional conference in February 1956, the Tunku took over all the portfolios in the Executive Council from British officials and Malaya became *de facto* a self-governing state.

⨯

The Federation's political advance altered the outlook for Singapore. Up to then there had been a chance that Malaya would not be granted independence until Singapore was first a part of it. Now Singapore was out on a limb. The British plan was to have an independent Malaya with Malays in charge – Malays who would nevertheless need them for some time to help govern the country and fight the communists – while they kept Singapore as a colony indefinitely because of its strategic value to Britain, Australia and New Zealand. Singapore was likely to become at best a self-governing territory with all the trappings of independence but without real sovereignty, and the last word on defence, security and foreign policy would stay in British hands.

Marshall's reaction to this was predictable: he was spurred into pressing for the maximum at the constitutional talks due to open in London on 23 April. If he had the chance, he would go for full sovereignty. He would exact complete independence from the British and so be on an equal footing with the Tunku. However, Singapore would sign an agreement guaranteeing the British their bases and giving Britain a decisive voice in foreign affairs. In short, he would have it both ways. With a little encouragement from his friends, including Ong Eng Guan, the treasurer of the PAP, he launched a "Merdeka Week" to collect signatures from the public and demonstrate the massive support there was for independence (*merdeka* in Malay) and for himself as its champion. Because his coalition government was known to be weak, he also decided to take to London a delegation representing all parties for a show of their unity on this issue.

He had been there in December 1955 and was then so encouraged by his meetings with British MPs and ministers that he told the British press there were no more "Colonial Blimps", something he thought worth repeating in the Legislative Assembly on his return to Singapore. He also persuaded all parties to agree that he invite a delegation of Conservative and Labour MPs to visit Singapore during Merdeka Week, which was to climax in a rally on Sunday, 18 March 1956 at Kallang Airport. Some 170,000 signatures were meanwhile collected, and a photo opportunity organised featuring enormous bound volumes to be presented by the all-party delegation to the House of Commons as proof of Singapore's desire for independence.

Six British MPs came, the Labour group led by Herbert Morrison, who had been home secretary in the first Labour government in 1945–50 and number two to Prime Minister Clement Attlee. We met them informally at social functions, and I spent one evening with them at a nightclub in the Capitol Building. The main event was a semi-striptease dance show, inappropriate for a delegation that had come with the serious purpose of assessing our maturity, our burning desire for independence, and our capability to manage it. But to my surprise, Morrison enjoyed himself. He was in a holiday mood, and in his cheerful, chirpy, cockney way he made wisecracks about what he had seen. He did not believe that there was a great burning desire for independence among the mass of the people in Singapore, but shrewdly observed that there was a powerful and well-organised secret group that was manipulating the trade unions, the students, and many others. He might have wanted me to protest, but I did not disabuse him of his views.

When the day of the Merdeka rally arrived, I drove to Kallang with Choo, parked the car some distance away from the airport building, and walked to a platform that had been erected in an open field off the runway. It was a sultry afternoon – I was wearing a short-sleeved shirt – but some 25,000 people waited for about an hour until five o'clock, when Marshall arrived in his open convertible. He drove straight to the platform on which Chin Chye, Ong Eng Guan and I were already standing, and once up there with us, gave the Merdeka salute with a clenched fist. The crowd surged towards him, some of them mounting the stage, which, having been hastily and flimsily constructed of wooden beams and planks, promptly collapsed. The public address system then failed, so that for a few minutes no one could speak to them. When one microphone finally came alive again, I told a section of the crowd to behave themselves, that some "devils" were up to no good among them, while a gesticulating Marshall talked into another microphone that was still dead.

Shortly after this, when the British MPs arrived, Morrison said to Marshall, "Sorry to hear you have got a collapsible stage." They never went out to it, but were shown into the two-storey airport building and introduced to the crowd from the upper balcony. They had been reluctant to come, but Marshall had persuaded them that the people were friendly and they need not fear for their safety. Now he tapped the delegation leader, the Conservative Jeffrey Lloyd, on the back and said, "I think you should all nip out quietly." Lloyd and his party quickly left.

I failed to get the crowd to quieten down, and Lim Chin Siong, speaking in Mandarin and Hokkien, was equally unsuccessful. This was not one of Lim's organised rallies. This was the *hoi polloi*, and his cheerleaders were not in control. Ong Eng Guan suggested that if we got them to sing, they would not become violent. He took a microphone from Lim and belted out *We Love Malaya*, after which came the communist song *Unity is Strength*, sung to the tune of *John Brown's Body*. Then it started to drizzle. I signalled Choo to get the car. She brought it as close to the platform as she safely could, and we drove off.

There was no way anybody could have controlled that crowd. They had become a mob. Soon people were throwing bricks through the glass windows of the airport building, then hundreds dashed forward to bang and shake its metal gates, and but for the arrival of police reinforcements would have captured it. When the police broke them up, they scattered in small groups, rampaging through the nearby streets and stoning a St John's Brigade ambulance treating the injured. By about seven o'clock, order had been restored, but 50 people had been hurt, among them 20 policemen.

There was no loss of life or serious damage to property. But the incident left the six visiting MPs with little doubt about the volatility of the political situation in Singapore, and convinced them that the government, even with a British chief secretary and a British commissioner of police, was not in complete command. That was no less than the truth. Marshall's Singapore was not the Tunku's Malaya. The Labour Front government enjoyed no solid support. It was, as Robert Black wrote to Lennox-Boyd, a "mushroom, all head, thin body, no roots". Black's letter described the communist threat on the island as more insidious than upcountry, and the measures taken to counter it – detention without trial, tear gas, water hoses, deregistration of unions, the banning of associations used for subversive purposes – treated the symptoms but did not cure the disease. Black wrote that although the security forces could prevent a breakdown of public services or major disorders, their methods simultaneously produced more anti-government and anti-British youngsters to join the growing ranks of the CUF organisations. Under a democratic system of one man, one vote, it was only a matter of time before the Chinese middle school students and the young Chinese-speaking workers brought in a legitimate, elected pro-communist government.

⚭

I harboured similar grim thoughts as I weighed the dilemma we, the non-communists, faced. But Marshall had limited knowledge of the real situation on the ground, and was in no way sobered or chastened by his experience. He remained optimistic that he would get something almost as good as the Tunku had obtained from Lennox-Boyd, and on 4 April, he moved a resolution in the Assembly to lay out what he expected of the British government in the constitutional talks. The operative part of this document read:

"The Assembly instructs the all-party delegation ... to seek forthwith for Singapore the status of an independent territory within the Commonwealth, and to offer an agreement between the United Kingdom government and the Singapore government whereby the government of the United Kingdom would in respect of Singapore exercise control of external defence and give guidance in foreign relations other than trade and commerce."

I had argued with Marshall privately many times before he tabled the resolution that as long as Britain had the right to tell Singapore what to do in matters of defence, Singapore could not be independent, whatever the arrangement was. But he could not be deflected from his goal – the appearance and the sensation of independence. In seconding his motion, I said the resolution as drafted was "a euphemistic way of saying that we realised the British will not give us complete independence because then it would mean upsetting international arrangements and international bases in the world defence strategy".

I did my best before the London conference to make sure that the next constitution would not open the gates for a communist takeover, but would give us enough room to build a non-communist government, not as a stooge of the British, but as protector of the interests of the people. Marshall never understood the need for this fine balance: to have enough power to act in the people's interest, but to have the British in a fall-back position if the communists should get the upper hand. And Lim Chin Siong never understood that near-independence without sovereignty meant that sovereignty would be with the British government. What he wanted was quite simply to get a constitution that would enable the communists to grow and become strong.

Marshall led the all-party 13-member delegation, which consisted of five ministers and two Labour Front government backbenchers, four Liberal Socialists (the Progressives and Democrats had amalgamated in February) and two PAP. We flew in separate groups on propeller-driven BOAC Argonauts that took two nights and three days to get from Singapore to London, with overnight stops in Colombo and Karachi. I left in early April to give myself time to meet Keng Swee and to assess the situation from the British end. Lim Chin Siong travelled with me, feeling a little lost. It was the first time he had been out of the country. But he was more fearful of being away from his mentors than of being in a strange land.

Before Lim and I took off in the Argonaut, I issued a formal PAP statement to explain why we had since modified our policy: "We wanted merger even before we reached the self-governing state ... Unfortunately, the Federation chief minister could not agree to our proposal ... Now we seek the maximum political advance we can achieve in Singapore alone, but will strive for a merger with the Federation."

The only flights I had made before then had been to Kuala Lumpur and back in a twin engine Dakota. In those days air travel was for the top few, expensive and not without risk, and every journey merited a send-off by relatives and friends or party supporters. A crowd of several hundred came to see Lim and me off and we addressed them from the top of the mobile steps before entering the plane. I made it quite clear that the delegation's aim was "not to secure full independence but 75 per cent self-government with complete self-government after five years". Lim was standing beside me and I was making quite sure the press got it right and would not misrepresent the PAP stand.

I was to pick up new impressions. When we stopped overnight at Colombo, I was surprised to find it so well-developed. It had not suffered from Japanese occupation and looked more prosperous than Singapore. Karachi, the other overnight stop, was hot and dusty, and for the first time I saw camels working as beasts of burden, trundling loaded carts and liberally dispensing enormous droppings as they flip-flopped along the roads. But an evening outing in town gave me a chance to buy Choo several sheer silk stoles that looked like organza interwoven with gold thread. She still uses them occasionally. After Karachi, we had refuelling stops at Cairo and Rome, and finally landed in London on 17 April.

I had six days to catch up with the political mood before the conference began. The weather was beautiful. It was one of the sunnier British springs and the tulips were already flowering along the Mall.

Britain was beginning to emerge from post-war austerity. London looked cleaner, spruced up in the six years since I left in 1950, and there were many more cars on the road. There was also a new racial equation. I saw quite a few West Indian blacks working as conductors on the buses, and some black dustmen, and I noticed that Asiatics were now referred to as Asians in the papers. I was told that sometime in 1953 the British press had started to use "Asian" because "Asiatic" had a touch of condescension or disrespect, and the change was a concession to the people of India, Pakistan and Ceylon, now independent. I did not understand how this improved their status. When young London children called me a Chinaman or a Chink, it did not trouble me. If they meant it as a term of abuse, my business was to make them think differently one day.

I spent much of my time with Keng Swee and his coterie of lieutenants, active students who had helped him combat and defeat John Eber and his communist group in the Malayan Forum. They included among others Joe Pillay, who was to become chairman of Singapore Airlines, and Chua Sian Chin, who was to become minister for home affairs. I was encouraged that Keng Swee could find young men of their calibre who would serve us well when they got back to Singapore.

He had also made many contacts in the Fabian Society and the Labour Party. Some, like Hilda Selwyn-Clarke, wife of a former governor of Hong Kong, set out to be a friend and champion of colonial students. The Fabians were nurturing nationalists who would be good democrats, good socialists, and supporters of Britain in the new Commonwealth. Keng Swee arranged for me to have dinner with Labour bigwigs, then out of office, including Aneurin Bevan, the former minister who had introduced the National Health Service, a Welshman and a great orator. And I took the opportunity to look up old Cambridge friends of both Choo and myself, several of whom were now practising at the Bar. They gave me a feel of the mood of British society in post-austerity London, which would lead into the swinging sixties.

For over a month from mid-April, I shared a service flat with Lim Chin Siong at St James Court, where the all-party delegation was housed. We had two bedrooms with bathrooms attached and a sitting room. Meals were served in a restaurant downstairs, but breakfast could be ordered in the room. There was an old-world graciousness about that hotel, with its elegant brick buildings and ancient lifts.

I was in familiar surroundings and, being well briefed by Keng Swee and many others, I was able to assess quickly how British politicians had shifted in their thinking and attitudes. But it was otherwise for Lim. He revealed himself to be a pleasant, likeable person with no pretensions but many inhibitions, as had most Chinese-educated. He was very anxious not to commit a *faux pas* and grateful to me for giving him little tips on the social customs of the British, including their table manners – how to handle forks, spoons and knives, and to place your fork and knife together to show you had finished a course. We shared a huge Humber Pullman. There was one for each party in the delegation, but since he had no social contacts in London and his functions were all official ones to which I would also go, I used it most of the time. There was another reason, however: he did not want the driver to know when he met pro-communists on the quiet.

I wondered how he would get about. I suspected that before he left home he must have been given some telephone numbers and addresses. But the MCP did not have reliable cadres in London who were in touch with the situation in Singapore and Malaya. As far as I knew, his most important contact was John Eber, and I was reassured, for that meant he would not be getting good advice. Having no one he trusted to turn to, he was operating at a severe disadvantage, compounded by his contempt for the Labour Front ministers and other delegates. With their new clothes and loud voices, they seemed flashy, out for a good time. Lim Chin Siong was the exact opposite. He had a new suit and had bought himself a trilby because he was advised to, but he never wore it except to go to the airport. He was modest, humble and well-behaved, with a dedication to his cause that won my reluctant admiration and respect. I wished I had cadres like him. He was like a Gurkha warrant officer in the British army – totally loyal, absolutely dependable, always ready to execute orders to the best of his ability.

He probably did not know what to make of me. I was a golf-playing, beer-swilling bourgeois, but he must also have sensed that I was not without a serious purpose. On our side, most of the business of drafting documents was done by Marshall and his Queen's Counsel, Walter Raeburn, for Marshall approached the conference primarily as a legal problem. I considered it entirely a political one, and Lim must have noticed that I would concentrate on the key parts, like the question of sovereignty, responsibility for security and foreign affairs through the Defence and Security Council, and chairmanship of the council.

One day, between conference sessions, he went to Collet's, the left-wing bookshop opposite the British museum, to buy a book by L. Kosmodemyanskaya, *The Story of Zoya and Shura*, which he presented to me. "Lee," he said, "this is a very good book. I read it in Chinese when I was in school. I became different." I was touched. He had not written me off as a pleasure-loving bourgeois after all. I thanked him and flipped through the pages. A hardback subsidised by Moscow and costing only five shillings, it told a heroic story about the German invasion of the Soviet Union and how a boy and a girl did the right thing by their country, their friends, and the Communist Party. Extolling high moral values, it had apparently inspired Lim greatly when he read it in his impressionable teens.

He was well-meaning and seemed deeply sincere. All the applause and adulation of the crowds had not turned his head. But we never developed a close friendship. Instead, we recognised each other for what we were. He knew I was not a communist and I knew that he was one. And we accepted each other as such. He needed me; I needed him. He would trust me to be honest in money matters, and in general not to lie to him. But he did not trust me in political matters. That was the nature of our relationship. We did not deceive each other on where we stood. His English was not good enough for him to plough through the heavy conference documents, but as I wrote to Chin Chye at the time, "He is writing lengthy reports back, God knows to which person." He was probably giving his impressions of people and assessments of their positions on important issues.

I myself was meeting and lunching with British MPs, both Conservative and Labour. The Conservatives tended to be buccaneering types, interested in the world at large and totally different from the Labour MPs, who were well-intentioned and serious-minded but parochial. One memorable lunch I had was with Fitzroy Maclean and Julian Amery. Maclean was famous for his wartime exploits in German-occupied Yugoslavia, and had written of his experiences in a book, *Disputed Barricades*, which I found fascinating. Amery, too, had a swashbuckling personality, and our acquaintance developed into a friendship. Such friends I made were to prove most valuable in the sixties when we had to fight the communists in Singapore, and even more so when we were part of Malaysia and threatened with communal repression by Malay "Ultras". (I called them *Ultras*, after the French term for Algerian extremists.) My stay in London was pleasant and profitable. But the same could not be said of the conference itself.

Marshall, already in London, had read the statement I made on leaving Singapore and thought I was undermining him. He attacked me bitterly in an address to 200 Malayan students, warning them that I was inviting communists into the PAP and preparing the way for a communist capture of power in 1959. But I was not the only person with whom he was to find himself at odds. At the opening plenary session of the conference, the colonial secretary, Lennox-Boyd, laid down the line in a quiet, firm speech in which he made clear Britain's position. Referring to Marshall's visit to London the previous December, he said the chief minister had departed from an understanding agreed then that Singapore would have only internal self-government. "Instead he now seeks full sovereign independence. Her Majesty's Government has not been consulted nor agreed to open discussions from this new starting point."

Marshall did not take the hint. He was too involved in his own emotional processes. Before he left Singapore, he said publicly that he would resign if he failed to get independence. A few days after I arrived in London, I received a memorandum from him dated 21 April, which was circulated to members of the delegation and to the British government. Marshall demanded immediate *merdeka*, i.e., independence. Merdeka, he argued, would rally the people against communism.

But Lennox-Boyd was not impressed and said on 25 April that while Her Majesty's Government was prepared to make substantial concessions to Singapore's aspirations, it intended to retain the "ultimate word" in internal security in the form of a defence council chaired by a British high commissioner.

Far from reading the weather signals and battening down his hatches, Marshall decided to sail ahead. He circulated a new memorandum on 1 May together with the draft of a Singapore Independence Act. Since his earlier proposals had not proved acceptable, he had perversely decided to ask for full independence, this time providing for a Defence and Security Council that "shall be advisory only" and constitute no more than a "transitional phase". During this transitional phase Britain could intervene and suspend the constitution, but otherwise Singapore would have "full sovereignty" in "normal times". Marshall's new proposal would allow the British to intervene only in "abnormal times", in other words only after a period of disorder or after the communists had seized power unconstitutionally and threatened Britain's bases.

Marshall's response to Lennox-Boyd was similar to his response when the governor, Robert Black, rebuffed him over the issue of four junior ministers. He raised the stakes. He did not realise that he was playing against the principal himself, and the principal was not going to yield. At the next session, 4 May, Lennox-Boyd commented dryly on Marshall's point about "normal times", that "present times could hardly be regarded as at all normal", and the argument went back and forth, with Marshall getting more and more tense as Lennox-Boyd maintained a phlegmatic calm.

One incident will always stand out in my memory. In the middle of an impassioned flow from Marshall, a private secretary tiptoed up to Lennox-Boyd's chair to put a cable in front of him. Lennox-Boyd read it and began to write on it. Marshall was miffed. He stopped in mid-sentence, and in a high-pitched voice that showed he was really angry, said, "Secretary of State, we know that you have many important possessions around the world, but we have come 8,000 miles to London to present our case and we demand that you give us your attention."

Without lifting his eyes from the cable, Lennox-Boyd continued writing and said, "Chief Minister, let me assure you that of all our valuable possessions across the world, Singapore is one of our most valuable. It is a precious jewel in the British Crown. I am all ears. You were saying, Chief Minister" – and he repeated verbatim Marshall's last three sentences. It was a virtuoso performance, very British, quite devastating. Marshall was livid and speechless, an unusual state for him.

But it was all getting very tiresome and obviously leading us nowhere despite many interminable meetings and quiet discussions. Marshall was chasing a mirage, "something more than internal self-government but less than complete independence", as he told me when I asked him just what he wanted. Discussions dragged on through the eighth, ninth and tenth plenary sessions, until at the eleventh, on 12 May, we moved to the question of the chairman of the Defence and Security Council. Marshall first suggested that he should be someone appointed by the United Nations, a proposal that guaranteed a British rejection. Then, three days later and acting on the advice of his executive committee in Singapore, he suggested that he should be a Malayan appointed by the Federation government. Lennox-Boyd was taken aback. With three British, three Singaporean and one Malayan on the council, the casting vote would rest with the Malayan and the British would be in a minority. That afternoon he dismissed the idea, saying, "The responsibility of defence is a UK one, and as long as this is so the UK must have the final say in the chairmanship of the Defence and Security Council."

The talks had reached a dead end. Lennox-Boyd decided there was no point in taking the conference any further, and made it clear that this concluded the talks. Marshall was flabbergasted. His face darkened with emotion. Except for Marshall and Lim Chin Siong, all members of the delegation including myself had been prepared to accept what the British had offered – a self-governing constitution with the Singapore government in control of internal security, but with Britain retaining the power to override it through a Defence and Security Council on which the British would have the majority vote. I advised Marshall not to refuse this, but to "go back to the Assembly and debate the matter and then take it one step further". But he rejected it outright – he was not one for cool, quiet calculations when in a tight corner into which he had backed himself.

That evening we were interviewed together on Independent Television. We both denounced Lennox-Boyd, but Marshall used the more picturesque language, protesting that the secretary of state had offered "Christmas pudding with arsenic sauce". He now had to keep his promise to resign.

At about 5:45 that afternoon, the secretary of the delegation phoned to say that Marshall was summoning an urgent meeting to discuss the reopening of the talks. I woke Lim Chin Siong up and told him. He was incredulous.

"Lee, go away, do not play fool with me," he said in his Hokkien English.

"Lim, I am not playing the fool," I replied. "There is a meeting at six."

By his unpredictable and inconsistent twists and turns, Marshall had alienated not just myself and the Liberal Socialists, but his key Labour Front members. His wanting to restart the talks to save himself was too much for them. "You cannot eat your own vomit," as one Liberal Socialist delegate put it in vivid Hokkien. Half an hour into the meeting, Marshall knew that if he tried to resume negotiations, he would have to do so on his own. He had overplayed his hand and was isolated.

That night, he went to a performance of *Madam Butterfly* with Lennox-Boyd and Lady Patricia Boyd, and then on to a Spanish restaurant to dine to the tune of guitars and the stamping feet of flamenco dancers. Meanwhile, I decided to stop him from staging a recovery. At a press conference that same evening at Malaya Hall, I made it clear that the PAP would have nothing to do with a reopening of the conference. I said it was a "final, desperate attempt to hang on to office, a sign of incredible political ineptitude", and rounded it off with "Never in the history of colonial evolution has so much humbug been enacted in so short a time by so erratic a leadership."

I knew that by calling the press conference that very same night, late though it was, I would get into the London papers the following day, with a good chance of making the Singapore papers as well despite the time difference. What I said would get into print and pin down the position of all the other members of the delegation. And that was what happened.

I left London with Lim Chin Siong on 21 May. The conference had proved to be a fiasco. But it was not without value, for it purged Singapore of Marshall's erratic exuberance. Marshall had to resign, and I reckoned that Lim Yew Hock would probably be the next chief minister of a Labour Front government. We would be entering a new phase. I was not sure what Lim Chin Siong thought. He may have been calculating the consequences of Marshall's rashness, which he had encouraged. We were bound to have a government less favourable for the CUF, for Lim Yew Hock would be a different proposition. In the last stages of the conference, I had seen Marshall totally under the influence of Lim Chin Siong. When he had alienated all the non-communists by his sudden shifts in position and his tantrums, it was to Lim that he reached out for support, and he had foolishly taken Lim's advice to reject Lennox-Boyd's final offer.

14. Exit Marshall, Enter Lim Yew Hock

When Marshall finally returned to Singapore on 25 May 1956, he was still sore and angry with me. He ordered me out of the room when I turned up at the airport to greet him, intending to stay on for his press conference. Looking right past me, he said the conference was for friends only. I left.

At his last debate as chief minister on 6–7 June, still wanting to go out in glory, he asked the Assembly to approve the stand of its delegation at the conference in London. The Liberal Socialists rebuked him for his inconsistencies, and for his stupidity in refusing three-quarters of a loaf and coming back with nothing. I decided not to criticise Marshall, but to present a united front against the "wicked" British.

There was an end-of-term atmosphere at the meeting, and I saw little to be gained by rubbing Marshall's face in the dirt. At the end of the two-day debate, Marshall resigned. The following day, on 8 June, Lim Yew Hock was sworn in as chief minister.

I was convinced Lim Yew Hock would have to govern differently. He did not have Marshall's personality or his flair for publicity. He could not live from one crisis to another. He was a stenographer who had risen in the world because he was sensible, reasonable, dependable and valuable to his employers. I felt almost certain he would accept the analysis of his officials, notably Special Branch experts, and act on their advice on how to deal with CUF subversion. The CUF had made wide inroads in so many directions, and his problem was how to curb them without incurring unpopularity. If he attacked Chinese education and language, he would lose the votes of the Chinese-speaking people. If he detained their militant leaders and they were suddenly unable to win further benefits through strikes and demonstrations, he would lose the votes of the workers, including the Malays and Indians, who would demand their release.

Nevertheless, with Lim Yew Hock as chief minister, the situation had become more hazardous for the CUF. I was therefore surprised that, far from retreating or lying low, Lim Chin Siong and company decided to play a more prominent role. In the election for the new PAP executive committee, they contrived to win five out of the 12 seats for their group, Lim Chin Siong scoring the largest number of votes himself, 1,537 against my 1,488. He had left the moderates with a nominal majority, but had made it clear that when it came to mass support, the pro-communists held all the trumps. Their strength was overwhelming and they could easily take over the party whenever they wanted to.

I decided it was time to take my annual fortnight's holiday. I drove up to the Cameron Highlands with Choo and Loong, stopping on the way at the Station Hotel in Kuala Lumpur. We chose it because Loong was fascinated by trains, and we took him down to the platform to see them arrive and depart. But there was a more important reason for staying in Kuala Lumpur. In response to a letter I had sent him earlier, Ong Pang Boon came to the hotel to see me.

My Chinese was still woefully inadequate. Pang Boon spoke Mandarin, Hokkien and Cantonese, and was educated in Chinese and English. He had just graduated from the University of Malaya, and was working in Kuala Lumpur for the Malaya Borneo Building Society. His salary was about $700 per month. He had helped me in Tanjong Pagar during the 1955 election campaign, and I wanted him to be the organising secretary of the PAP, but I could only offer him $450 from my assemblyman's allowance of $500 a month. He replied that he would come to Singapore "if the party orders it". I told him I could not order him to do something that was going to cost him $250 in loss of salary and involve his leaving his home town, especially as his employers had also offered to send him to England for training. He asked for time to consider the offer. About two weeks later, he accepted and agreed to start in mid-August. I was relieved and grateful. I would have been hard put to find someone else as dependable. He had political sensitivity, an understanding of the Chinese middle school students, and convictions that were not communist. Most important of all, I felt I could trust him.

His was no easy task. It was difficult to run a multiracial, multilingual party in Singapore. The PAP activists were Chinese-speaking and their natural leaders were Chinese-educated. So the branches catered for them – songs, dances and classes for cooking, sewing, literacy and radio and motor repair were all in Mandarin. This put off the English-educated Chinese and the Malays and Indians, for even where they were in the majority it was the Chinese-educated who ran everything. The PAP central headquarters held general meetings that the English-speaking members would attend, but there were no social or cultural activities specifically organised for them, for that would have required bigger premises too expensive for a poor party to rent.

Without a man like Pang Boon, I would have had no overview of party activities. Inevitably, the branches reflected the mood of Middle Road, where Lim Chin Siong and Devan Nair were pressing us to take a stand against the increasingly clear-cut anti-communist policies of the Tunku's government in Kuala Lumpur, which gave no opportunity for the MCP to operate constitutionally. I therefore issued a PAP statement attacking the Alliance government in the Federation. It was a momentous decision. For the first time, we were touching upon sensitive issues in Malaya.

We argued that the Tunku's policies would "put race against race and class against class", that the building up of a force of 500,000 to intensify the fight against the communists would make it "clear that the army and gendarmerie will be predominantly if not wholly Malay and that these Malay forces will be used to police predominantly Chinese quarters and workers". The dangers of racial friction and conflict between Malays and

Chinese were already present. The anti-communist stand would also pit the workers of all races against "European, Chinese and Indian employers backed by Malay feudalists in the Federation government". It was "concealed colonial control because after the Tunku's taking over defence and internal security and finance, the British have successfully hidden themselves behind the Alliance ministers", exercising real power through their armed forces and the chief secretary's control of police and administration.

The following day, the Tunku hit back. He made it clear that he would have no truck with the communists or the PAP. It was not his policy to look for "spurious popularity" through facile appeals to anti-British sentiments. "My determination is to see our government function free from interference from subversive elements. I am therefore resolute in my determination to maintain law and order in this country," he said. But the most meaningful response came from Tan Siew Sin, later finance minister, then publicity chief of the MCA: "Tunku Abdul Rahman also realises the indiscriminate use of Malay forces in the prosecution of the Emergency may lead to racial conflict, especially as such forces will probably be deployed in rural areas where the population is predominantly Chinese ..." As the Tunku's Chinese partner, he was alive to the danger to himself and to Malaya if there were a communal bloodbath.

The PAP had touched a raw nerve, but there was no way of avoiding this open clash. We were in a united front with the communists and the Tunku was going to carry out exactly the same policies as the British in suppressing them, using British methods but this time backed by Malay nationalism. I did not understand the strategy of Lim Chin Siong's superiors. They must have known that a purge was coming and their key operators would be swept up. Yet they had taken a more conspicuous position in the PAP, and were pressing the non-communists to adopt a hostile stance against the Tunku, which would only increase the chances of a crackdown. I concluded that the MCP leaders in charge of Lim Chin

Siong and Fong Swee Suan were uncertain what course Lim Yew Hock would take, and had decided to use them to test the ground. For their purposes, the two open-front leaders were expendable. Their key cadres they kept under cover, and their main battleground was not Singapore but Malaya, where the Tunku and his mass base of Malay supporters were their major adversary. If what they wanted in Singapore was a safe haven where they could build up their strength for the fight across the Causeway, their provocative policy did not make sense. My immediate concern was to discover what action Lim Yew Hock and his backroom boys in Special Branch and the chief secretary's office were planning – as he put it on 6 September in the Assembly – "in the best interest of Singapore".

∽

I did not have long to wait before the government moved. On 19 September, it dissolved the pro-communist Singapore Women's Federation and Chinese Brass Gong Musical Society and detained six CUF leaders, including the president of the Singapore Factory and Shop Workers' Union (SFSWU) and three prominent militants connected with the Chinese middle schools – a dean of studies, a dean of discipline (sic), and the chairman of the Singapore Chinese Primary School Teachers' Association, one of whom was to be banished to China. Lim Yew Hock told the *Straits Times*, "We have decided on strong action to counter the growing menace of communist front organisations. We have decided to check the 'covert penetration' of reputable associations by the communists and their sympathisers." In a statement, I declared, "the sudden and arbitrary action gives rise to the gravest concern. We are investigating the matter." Lim Chin Siong and Fong were dissatisfied with the lack of outrage and passion in my statement. They wanted condemnation and opposition by all possible means, but I was not forthcoming.

On 24 September, the government deregistered the Singapore Chinese Middle School Students' Union (SCMSSU) and 5,000 students took over their schools in protest. Masked sentries appeared at their gates, covering their faces with handkerchiefs every time police radio patrol cars cruised by, telling parents who called to collect their children to go home and return with food and clothing for them instead. The press reported that the teachers were "helpless", and one principal, himself a fellow travelling Chinese chauvinist, described the students as "uncontrollable". But when Chew Swee Kee, as minister for education, told them they would have to face the consequences if they did not resume their classes in an orderly manner, some decided to go home. Wisely, for this time the government left no doubt that it meant to sweep the board, and Lim Chin Siong and Fong themselves could not have misread the signals as anything other than the end of one phase in their united front offensive.

The next day, four organisations connected with the Chinese schools were banned, including the Singapore Chinese Primary School Teachers' Association and the Singapore Chinese School Parents' Association. One week later, the police arrested Robert Soon Loh Boon, who was chairman of the banned students' union, and on the same day picked up a paid secretary of the SCMSSU, who was also the first member of the PAP executive to be detained by the government.

At a meeting of the Legislative Assembly on 2 October, I moved to censure the government for the arrests and banishments. It was pro forma. The motion was defeated. I knew Lim Yew Hock had to proceed with the clean-up. He could not waver the way Marshall had without coming to grief. Accordingly, Chew took the offensive. He hit out at parents and others who condoned the student disorders. Two high school teachers were sacked and nine more given warnings, including a principal and a school supervisor. Two boys and one girl were arrested, and one of the boys banished as he had not been born in Singapore. Chew also handed the schools a list of 142 students to be expelled. Meanwhile, 742 others came forward to back the government's campaign to wipe out subversives.

A standard protest camp-in followed on the night of 10–11 October, supported by the SFSWU, and with the writing on the wall, the pro-communists went all out to extract the maximum political price from Lim Yew Hock for the break-up of the CUF. They worked hard to involve the masses emotionally with leaders whom they expected to be arrested and with the organisations they expected to be banned, persuading them to feel personally harmed and dispossessed. To broaden the campaign of agitation, Lim Chin Siong and Nair had got Jamit Singh to call a meeting of a "Civil Rights Convention" of 95 trade unions on 28 September, at which 700 delegates claimed to represent 200,000 members. Nair was elected chairman, and their aim was to rouse the people against the British and their "shameless colonial stooge" Lim Yew Hock, who had had the audacity to ban several CUF organisations that week. But it was the usual collection of pro-communists, the same coterie of old united front supporters.

Undeterred, the government kept up the pressure. On 10 October, the police arrested four student leaders of the deregistered SCMSSU, and three days later, shut down the Chinese High School and Chung Cheng High School. Then, on 16 October, the government opened emergency schools for 400 students to continue their studies, and more joined the scheme in the days that followed. A week later, a delegation representing what it called the Singapore Freedom-Loving Students of Chinese Middle Schools presented Lim Yew Hock with a red banner, and the next day the chief minister himself made a radio broadcast giving an ultimatum to the defiant students still camping in the two schools to clear out by 8 pm the following day.

That evening, 24 October, the PAP held a rally on an open field at the Beauty World amusement park along Bukit Timah Road to protest peacefully against the arrests, with Lim Chin Siong, Nair, Chin Chye and myself on the same platform. But when the meeting dispersed, Lim Chin Siong's union supporters piled into a fleet of lorries and headed for the

Chinese High School two miles down the road. As I drove home later, I saw that the gates of the school were swarming with police and hundreds of parents and relatives were milling around them, their cars parked along the road. The communists wanted the largest possible audience for the showdown, timed for that night. I had a feeling it was going to be a nasty and bloody business. Everybody expected broken heads and broken bones. Yet when I passed the nearby University of Malaya hostels, some students were gleefully blowing football referee whistles, excited at the prospect of the fun and games soon to begin. I cursed the idiocy, ignorance and naivety of those English-educated students. They did not know what a dangerous position they were in. If the faceless men behind the Chinese middle schools won, they would be the first to be brainwashed and become the new dispossessed.

As it happened, the rioting began outside the Chung Cheng High School in Goodman Road, where a mob of four to five hundred clashed with the police and attacked the Tanjong Katong Post Office and Geylang Police Station. Then the restless crowd of more than 4,000 outside the Chinese High School became violent, overturning three police cars and setting two others alight. When the police charged and dispersed them with tear gas, they scattered, but the rioting spread downtown to Rochor Road and other parts of Singapore. At midnight, the government imposed a curfew.

At dawn the next day, the police gave the students ten minutes in which to leave the schools with their parents; when they failed to do so, the police moved in, breaking down the barricades and lobbing tear gas at those manning them. At Chung Cheng High School parents had linked arms to protect their sons and daughters, but now they panicked, some jumping into the school pond and others fleeing. When the students tried to march into the city, they were stopped by roadblocks. Rioting continued throughout that day and night, and Middle Road bus and factory workers went on strike. However, with tight police and military

A car set on fire by rioters during communist-instigated clashes in October 1956.

control at key junctions and helicopters overhead fitted with loudspeakers to intimidate the mob, the situation never got out of hand.

The police and the military had been fully prepared and there was close coordination between them. Helicopters and armoured cars had taken up positions before daybreak. Military roadblocks were in place and mobile riot squads on the alert. There was no real threat to security. But the riots, arson and bloodshed had given the government reason to arrest and detain all their main targets within the next 24 hours, a total of 219 persons that included leaders of the Middle Road group – Lim Chin Siong and Fong, and among the English-educated, Nair, Woodhull and Puthucheary.

The riots left 13 dead, 123 injured, 70 cars burnt or battered, two schools razed, and two police stations damaged. The police arrested 1,000 people, including 256 secret society gangsters. The next evening, Lim Yew Hock made a special radio broadcast in which he declared, "We are liberating trade unionists, farmers, teachers and Chinese associations from a form of political exploitation." The *Straits Times* carried it under the headline "Operation Liberation".

The new chief minister had put himself in a no-win position. I had believed from the start that the government had been making a strategic mistake in focusing action on the middle schools, especially the Chinese High School and Chung Cheng High School. These two were the Eton and Harrow of the Chinese-speaking world in Singapore and Malaya, and parents throughout Southeast Asia aspired to send their children to them as boarders if they could afford it. Why had Special Branch acted as they did? By concentrating their preliminary actions and therefore the limelight on the students, they had led people to believe that Lim Yew Hock was attacking the entire Chinese education system. That perception was disastrous for him.

The Rendel constitution did not give him control of internal security. That was in the hands of the chief secretary and the governor. But for political reasons the chief secretary chose not to act against the communists. Instead, Lim Yew Hock had allowed himself to be persuaded by his security officials to take the responsibility for the clean-up. In consequence it was not difficult for the communists to portray him as a tool of the "colonialist imperialists". The British and Americans compounded his vulnerability by praising his courage and boldness. The first to do so was Lennox-Boyd: "The communist snake has been scotched but not killed ... in Singapore, courageous and competent ministers are facing up to their problems in this vital corner of the free world."

Next to congratulate him in glowing terms was the US State Department, and the Australians were not far behind. Little realising how much damage his reputation had suffered with the Chinese-speaking mass base, Lim Yew Hock made the further mistake of trying to emulate communist tactics. He arranged for a 50-man delegation representing 150 organisations claiming 150,000 members to pledge him their support. But the local participants – the counterpart supposedly of the CUF – were too feeble to be convincing, and when prominent Englishmen like the president of the Ex-Servicemen's Association, the British bishop of Singapore and the British president of the Singapore Chamber of Commerce joined in, it only intensified the impression that he was acting in the interests of the West.

I resolved that if ever a PAP government were faced with this problem, I would never make the same mistakes. I would think of a way of obliging the parents themselves to grab their children from the schools and take them home. Special Branch could pick up the leaders after the students had dispersed. It would have been less damaging if Lim Yew Hock had first arrested the key united front operators in the trade unions and cultural societies. The unions themselves could then have been left to carry on. The leaders left at liberty would want to appear militant and not cowed, and would soon have been tempted to act illegally, whereupon the government could have deregistered their unions.

Marshall had taught me how not to be soft and weak when dealing with the communists. Lim Yew Hock taught me how not to be tough and flat-footed. It was not enough to use administrative and legal powers to confine and cripple them. Lim did not understand that the communist game was to make him lose the support of the masses, the Chinese-speaking people, to destroy his credibility as a leader who was acting in their interests. They were thus able to portray him as an opportunist and a puppet acting at the behest of the "colonialist imperialists". Of the two, the more valuable lesson was Lim Yew Hock's – how not to let the communists exact a heavy price for putting them down.

Only after the dust had settled from the government's purge of the communist ringleaders did the second-tier leaders whom Special Branch had not picked up peek out of their foxholes. They ventured out to see if they were going to be arrested. They were not. Several came to see me in my office at Malacca Street, and I asked Dennis to accompany them to their various branches to take an inventory of the damage, recover whatever property was still there, and put caretakers in charge. Dennis went down to Bukit Timah and Bukit Panjang, where he reported the premises to be in shambles; the smell of tear gas still hung around amid the disorder of ransacked furniture and stationery, and slippers and shoes lost in the mêlée of the arrests.

One leader confessed to being extremely worried – some $120,000 of union funds kept in a tin trunk and locked up in a back room at the Middle Road headquarters had disappeared. The money had been withdrawn from the bank at the last moment. I believed it had been taken out to prevent it from falling into the hands of the Registrar of Societies once the SFSWU was deregistered. That had not happened yet, but as it was only a matter of days before Special Branch would look through the union's accounts and find the money missing, I decided as its legal adviser to report the loss immediately.

Lim Chin Siong had committed a crime by withdrawing almost the total amount for purposes not in accordance with the union's rules, and by not being able to account for it. But when I went to see him at the Central Police Station where he was being held for interrogation, he feigned ignorance. He said the cash was in the back room three hours before the premises were raided in the early hours of 27 October. The only other person who knew it was there was the union treasurer. I had seen the treasurer at Changi Prison before seeing Lim. He said there were only two keys to the locked room, one with him, the other with Lim. As far as he knew, the money was in the room at the time of the police raid.

All interviews with detainees under the Emergency Regulations took place in the presence of a Special Branch officer. I could not understand, therefore, why Special Branch did not pass the interview records to the attorney-general's chambers so that the culprits could be prosecuted for criminal breach of trust. They had withdrawn $120,000, spent $20,000 on items they could not account for precisely, and "lost" the rest. The government could have portrayed Lim Chin Siong, his treasurer and his president as thieves, not the revolutionary martyrs they became once detained for a political cause.

Instead, the Registrar of Trade Unions asked them on 21 November to show cause why the SFSWU should not be deregistered because not only was it "used for purposes inconsistent with its objects and rules" but also as "the funds of the union were not expended on objects authorised by the rules". In his statement to the registrar, Lim said he had decided that the union funds, then amounting to about $150,000, should be prevented from falling into government hands and should be kept aside to be used later for the benefit of the workers. The story he then told was quite different from the one he had given me in front of a Special Branch officer, but in essence the conclusion was the same: "We kept the notes in a metal suitcase in a room at the back of the union's premises in Middle Road. That was the last I knew of the whereabouts of these notes. Someone must have stolen the money from this room since my arrest at 2 am." This would have been no defence had the charge been criminal breach of trust. But the government chose to detain him under Emergency Regulations.

I was less interested in the recent losses of the CUF than in how quickly it could regroup and reorganise in the future. The MCP needed a second team of expendable open-front leaders whom they must now field if they were to retain the following the first team had built up. If among the open-front group of activists they could not find men who could do this, they might have to sacrifice some of their cadres in the underground. I waited to see how they would play it. They played it safe. They decided to field Lim Chin Siong's younger brother, Lim Chin Joo, as the substitute who would carry the flag he had left behind at Middle Road. Lim Chin Joo had also been to the Chinese High School. But he did not have his brother's baby-face. He was broader, grosser, less likeable, but brighter and tougher. He did not have Lim Chin Siong's silver tongue either, which was a relief. But he was the logical choice. He symbolised Lim Chin Siong, whom the MCP wanted to have remembered as a great leader temporarily imprisoned by an unjust stooge government.

Anticipating the deregistration of the SFSWU, on 14 February 1957, the new leaders negotiated a partnership with an existing but inactive union and its affiliates, using it much as business corporations use shell companies. The Singapore General Employees' Union had a book membership of 2,000. Lim Chin Joo took it over, the pro-communists filling 18 of the 21 seats on a joint central committee, and moved it to the old headquarters at Middle Road. Within a matter of months, the membership had risen to more than 20,000.

The branches also came back to life, but were not in the same state of frenetic activity. Some of the new cadres were amateurish; some of those who had worked with the detained leaders had taken fright and were reluctant to involve themselves further, not knowing whether there would be further clean-ups. So the unions did not recover the surge and thrust they had developed from the middle of 1954 to the end of 1956. But I had no doubt that as long as the Chinese middle schools were churning out bright and ambitious graduates whom the political system excluded from good jobs in the public and private sectors, the MCP would have a steady flow of recruits. This was the nub of the problem – the frustration of the able and talented among the Chinese-educated who had no outlets for their energy and idealism, and who were at the same time inspired by the example of the young communist cadres in China. It was only after news of the excesses of the Cultural Revolution percolated through in the 1970s that the communist hold on them weakened.

Meanwhile, an ostentatious display of self-sacrifice by their leading cadres added to the myth. After working the whole day running around making speeches and negotiating with wicked employers, Lim Chin Siong and Fong would sleep on top of the desks at union headquarters. Their spartan lifestyle had a tremendous impact on their followers, who tried to emulate them, infecting each other with the same spirit of self-denial. Even wealthy young students who were not hard-core members wanted to identify themselves with Lim and Fong. One bus company owner's son spent most of his time acting as an unpaid chauffeur for them, using his family car. It was his contribution to the cause. He was proud to be associated with revolutionary cadres who dressed simply, ate at hawker stalls and took very little salary for themselves since whatever was won from the employers was for the workers. How much they pocketed in order to feed more revolutionaries I did not know, but I did not see them take anything for themselves – they certainly did not live as if they had.

It was a competitive display of selflessness that swept a whole generation; the more selfless you were, the more you impressed the masses, and the more likely you were to be promoted within the organisation from the Anti-British League to the MCP, a communist party in the middle of a revolution. With such supporters, the communists could run elections on a shoestring – there was no shortage of workers or canvassers, and cloth for banners was donated by enthusiastic supporters. I suspect that printers, too, would either print their pamphlets for nothing or charge the cost to union accounts. There was also no shortage of girls amid all this puritanical zeal, for in the back rooms of Middle Road, supposedly revolutionary young women gave themselves up to illicit love, only too happy to have such star performers as Lim and Fong as their partners. The less attractive girls settled for the branch leaders of the various unions.

In contrast, when we had to find workers, it was a real problem. We recruited volunteers from the unions and from among friends, but they all wanted to go home in time for dinner, for some function or other, or for a private appointment. There was no total commitment, no dedication as on the other side – one of their devotees would do the work of three or four of our volunteers. I used to be quite depressed by the long-term implications of all this. I failed to realise then that they could not keep it up for long. Revolutionary zeal could only carry them thus far. In the end, they had to live and bring up families, and families required money, housing, health care, recreation and the other good things of life.

One odd thing about them though, was that when they abandoned communism, as some young Chinese middle school student leaders did, they often became extremely avaricious to make up for lost time. They seemed to feel that they had been robbed of the best years of their lives and had to make up for what they had missed. It was a preview of what I was to see later in China and Vietnam. When the revolution did not deliver utopia and the economy reverted to the free market, cadres, with the power to issue licences or with access to goods and services at official prices, were the first to be corrupt and exploit the masses.

15. Three-quarters Independent

Eleven months after the collapse of the first constitutional talks, we were back in London for a second round. This second conference was held in a totally different climate. Inter-party differences had been thrashed out and solutions agreed to in principle. On 7 February 1957, Chief Minister Lim Yew Hock had called an all-party meeting, the first of eight to settle the outlines of a new constitution, and a month later a miscellaneous paper was submitted to the Assembly. Lim's motion was realistic and modest: "To secure from Her Majesty's Government the status of a self-governing state with all the rights, powers and privileges pertaining to internal affairs, and the control of trade, commerce and cultural relations in external affairs".

There was no attempt to disguise the unpalatable fact that this was not independence, and that sovereignty remained with the British. As I was to point out later, that meant they would be able to revoke the constitution at will, and there would be sufficient British military forces in the country to make any such revocation possible. The debate was plain sailing, especially as David Marshall was absent in Borneo on legal business. The Tunku had told Lim Yew Hock that he was willing to have a representative sit on a proposed tripartite Internal Security Council; and Lennox-Boyd was now willing to accept this, subject to a careful definition of what the council could and could not do.

However, Lim Yew Hock had been unwise in committing himself to early polls in August 1957. Only after careful preparations should the dice be thrown again in a general election, especially since this time round the stakes would be higher. The all-party committee had agreed that under the new constitution there should be a multilingual Assembly;

there should also be a new citizenship law that would enfranchise between 200,000 and 300,000 people, most of them Chinese who had resided in Singapore for at least eight out of the past ten years. Speaking in the Assembly on 5 May, I made the PAP position clear: this law must be passed and the new citizens eligible to vote and stand as candidates before general elections were held, even though the process would take at least one year, and possibly a further three months.

After Marshall's experience with a 13-member delegation, Lim Yew Hock reduced his to five – two from the Labour Front, one from UMNO, one from the Liberal Socialists, and myself representing the PAP. This was a nuts-and-bolts conference. The proposed constitution provided for a Legislative Assembly of 51 elected members from whom the prime minister and the other ministers would be chosen. The Assembly would have jurisdiction over all matters except foreign affairs and defence, but where internal security and defence overlapped, the power would reside in an Internal Security Council. This would consist of three British members, one of whom would be the chairman; three Singapore members, one of whom would be the prime minister; and one representative from the Federation of Malaya. Singapore would have a head of state called the Yang di-Pertuan Negara, instead of a British governor.

Lim Yew Hock left the drafting of the proposed constitution to Walter Raeburn QC, but I had to read the documents to make sure that if and when the PAP formed the government, we would be able to work it. There was only one contentious issue. At the 15th plenary session, Lennox-Boyd said that Her Majesty's Government would not allow Singapore to come under communist domination, and that he felt sure the Singapore delegation did not want this to happen anyway. He had therefore introduced a non-negotiable provision to bar all persons known to have indulged in or been charged with subversive activities from running as candidates in the first election to be held under the new constitution. I objected to this, saying that "the condition is disturbing both because it is a departure from democratic practice and because there is no guarantee that the government in power will not use this procedure to prevent not only communist but also democratic opponents of their policy from standing for election".

I was speaking for the record. In fact, Lim Yew Hock had quietly raised this matter with me back in Singapore after he had seen Lennox-Boyd in London in December, and Lennox-Boyd had already invited me to have tea with him alone at his home in Eaton Square to discuss it. After some social pleasantries, he asked me what would happen if my comrades who were in prison, like Lim Chin Siong, were to stand for the next election. I said he would win and his opponents in Bukit Timah constituency would lose their deposits. He expressed surprise.

"In this country," he said, "when we arrest a person under Regulation 18D (the equivalent in wartime Britain of our Emergency Regulations) he is distrusted by the electorate. Oswald Mosley – leader of the pro-Nazi British Fascist party – had been a member of parliament. After he was arrested and detained, he never won a seat."

I looked at him sadly and said, "In your country, such people are considered traitors, collaborating with the enemy. In Singapore, when you are locked up by a government with a British governor and a British chief secretary in charge, you become a martyr, a champion of the people. Your popularity increases."

"Would you agree if I imposed this provision, that they be excluded from the first election to give the first elected government under the full internal self-government constitution a cleaner slate to start with?" he asked.

"I will have to denounce it. You will have to take responsibility for it," I answered.

"My shoulders are broad enough," he said.

Indeed they were, physically and metaphorically. I told him I would have to protest, but emphasised that that would not necessarily be the end of the talks – I thought to myself that Singapore's constitutional progress could not be held hostage by Lim Chin Siong, Fong Swee Suan and the Middle Road group.

I had already had the advantage of observing Lennox-Boyd for over a month at the first conference in 1956. He was an impressive figure. Physically he was a giant of a man, over six foot six tall, broad, big and hefty. His enormous vitality showed in his voice, facial expressions and body movements. He dressed well, always with a flower in his buttonhole. He spoke with a public school accent but, in his very upper-class way, he was friendly and sociable and had a knack of putting people at ease. I respected his intellect and liked his forthrightness. At that time, the Colonial Office was under great pressure, with one colony after another demanding independence. Nevertheless, he found time to host the Singapore delegation one Sunday at Chequers, the prime minister's country home put at his disposal. He had just bought a Polaroid camera, then quite a novelty, and enjoyed taking pictures and giving copies immediately to us. I was given one showing all of us gathered at the door of Chequers with John Profumo, who was then a junior minister, as well as himself.

So when I met him at his home that afternoon, I was confident I could speak my mind. If I had felt he was sharp in his dealings, my reply would have been guarded. As it was, I spoke candidly and he understood that I would not break up the conference because of any bar against the detainees' standing as election candidates. What I learnt only 38 years later from documents was that Lim Yew Hock had already told the governor of Singapore that "neither he nor Lee Kuan Yew could possibly take this up themselves during the March talks", but "neither he nor Lee Kuan Yew would demur if the secretary of state laid down this condition", and this had been passed on to London. When Lennox-Boyd sprang the condition at the session on 10 April, therefore, it was no surprise to either Lim or me or, I suspect, to the other members of the all-party delegation whom he had also been seeing privately.

After Sunday lunch at Chequers with (facing camera) Alan Lennox-Boyd, secretary of state for the colonies, 1957. On the right is John Profumo, secretary of state for war, facing Lim Yew Hock.

After five weeks of talks, the conference concluded successfully but on a sober note. We returned home together this time, not separately as before. When we flew into Singapore at 3 pm on 14 April, we looked not jubilant but serious, in keeping with the low-key results we had obtained. The small crowd at the airport was quiet, and the press commented on the absence of shouts of "Merdeka" normal on such occasions. Lim Yew Hock emerged from the plane first, followed by the other delegates, the last of whom was an "unsmiling Mr Lee Kuan Yew who immediately went into a private conference with Dr Toh Chin Chye", according to the *Straits Times*.

Lim held a press conference, then the delegation left for the Padang in a motorcade, with the chief minister, alone in a green convertible, leading the way. Crowds lined the streets, but they were strangely silent. About 2,000 trade unionists who waited at Merdeka Bridge over the Kallang River burst into shouts and let off crackers, and the Singapore Trade Union Congress presented the chief minister with a framed picture and a Chinese banner of congratulations. But when the cars arrived at City Hall, where the crowd was thicker than along the route, there were no signs of welcome. As we mounted the decorated platform, a few hundred students chanted "Oompah Merdeka!" for several minutes – it was not in support of the delegation, but for those who were detained in Changi Prison.

The chief minister and the other delegates made their speeches in turn, none of them inspiring. When it was my turn, I decided to speak in Malay. I said we had been able to get only *tiga suku merdeka* (three-quarters independence), but that those who believed a small country like Singapore could gain full independence by itself must be mad; the only way to it was through merger with Malaya. I was speaking to the pro-communists, and at that moment about 200 Chinese middle school students, who had arrived in buses and lorries and marched on to the Padang to take up positions right in front of the platform, began chanting slogans for the release of Lim Chin Siong, Fong and the rest of the Middle Road detainees. They also booed from time to time, but stopped at their leaders' signal. It was a reminder of how strong they remained on the ground despite the loss of their bosses.

In my absence, Lim Chin Joo's unions had been putting pressure on Chin Chye to order me to take a tougher stand in London, and to demand early elections so that they could get Lim Yew Hock's government out and their first team of leaders freed. The MCP knew that the second team was not up to the job, but was reluctant to expose its experienced undercover cadres. I was not going to oblige them, nor was Chin Chye. While I was in London, representatives of the pro-communist unions had confronted the PAP's central executive committee in a marathon session. The encounter lasted seven hours until 3 am, everyone sitting on wooden benches with no armrests and no backs. They had three demands: rejection of the Internal Security Council, immediate independence and – most important of all – the early election that Lim Yew Hock had mistakenly promised for August 1957. Chin Chye and Pang Boon slogged it out. The pro-communists got little satisfaction. And when a left-wing cadre I had co-opted into the committee after Lim Chin Siong had been detained reiterated their grievances at the airport on 15 April, I gave him short shrift.

The unions had stayed away from the Padang rally to show their displeasure, but I was not disturbed. A new battle was looming, this time with the second team, but I felt they would be easier to deal with. Jamit Singh was advising Lim Chin Joo on how to work legally within the system, but while Jamit had a strong voice and a fierce public-speaking style, he had no strategic sense. They were flirting with Marshall. They knew he dearly wanted early elections so that he could make a comeback, and they planned to use him to force a dissolution of the Assembly. During the debate on the London conference he was raring for a fight, knowing that this time he had the young students and the pro-communist unions on his side. He was contemptuous of a *tiga suku busok merdeka* (three-quarters rotten independence) through which we could not achieve "human dignity and independence", and denounced the constitution as "this deformed thing we have before us".

He then played the anti-subversion clause. "The PAP is extremely anxious to deprive its left wing of the very people whom it pretends to befriend. We kiss Devan Nair on both cheeks and wait for Lennox-Boyd to hang him from the back!" But unwisely he went on to say that banning subversives was "a normal, intelligent and reasonable precaution ... Why should we not prevent from standing for elections a person who, three of our judges say, is a man who seeks to destroy the democratic way of life we seek to establish?" This was hardly calculated to please his new friends, but he never understood that they wanted him to demand early elections precisely because that would give the first team in prison a chance to win seats, either as candidates themselves or through proxies who had not been detained.

When it was my turn to speak, I stripped Marshall of his anti-colonial rhetoric, quoting his 1956 letters to Lennox-Boyd, in which he had addressed the British secretary of state as "My dear Alan" and signed himself "Yours sincerely, David". He was an actor, but not consistent in the roles he sought to play. I was playing for keeps. So were the communists. I made it clear that the PAP would not take office if it won the election unless the detained leaders were first released. I did not say this for the benefit of Lim Chin Siong and Fong. Chin Chye, Pang Boon and I had concluded that the Chinese-speaking ground would distrust us as tricksters if we ditched our former comrades in gaol and took office without them. The accounts had first to be squared; only then could we break with them and stand a chance in the fight for hearts and minds. It was not a political gimmick. We had no choice. We understood the values and social norms of our people and we had to be seen to have acted honourably.

Marshall hit out at every single item he could find fault with and accused the PAP of double-crossing everyone at the constitutional talks. Then he shouted across the floor to me, "Sir, I wish to go back to the people of Singapore. I will go to his constituency if he will go back to his constituency, and I will challenge him there."

I responded immediately, "Accepted."

The Speaker, not a political animal, ruled this as irrelevant. Unwittingly, he was going to let Marshall off the hook. I was not going to allow that. When Marshall appeared cocky and confident, I guessed he had been assured by Jamit Singh and Lim Chin Joo of their support against the PAP. But we had decided to assert our independence, to defend our party stand, and to defy the second team of CUF leaders who were working through him. He was astounded by my prompt acceptance of his challenge, one he had recklessly tossed out without their prior agreement. He did not know I had seen through his bouncy aggressiveness.

When the House adjourned at 4 pm, I immediately called a press conference at which I announced I would send in my resignation at the end of the present session of the Assembly, and that I expected the by-election to be held within five weeks. I disclosed that, at a central executive committee meeting the previous afternoon, the PAP had already decided to challenge Marshall because we knew the line he would take. Now he had stolen our thunder, but we would still oblige him. "It is a clear-cut issue of whether the people of Singapore are prepared to accept the constitution and reject the clause on subversion or would prefer to accept the clause and reject the constitution." The first was our position, the second was Marshall's, and I made doubly sure that he was pinned down to it, since I knew it must be anathema to the communists.

The next day, 27 April, I announced, "Mr Speaker, sir, at the end of this motion when the votes have been taken, I shall tender my resignation as Member for Tanjong Pagar. I shall be standing in the Tanjong Pagar by-election as the PAP candidate."

My father bringing voters to the polls during the 1957 Tanjong Pagar by-election, in his Morris Minor, the car I drove to meet the Plen.

Less than 48 hours later, after the morning sitting of the Assembly, an ashen-faced Marshall announced he was quitting politics "permanently". He told reporters he would not contest the by-election because he feared "there might be trouble if it were fought on the colonial constitutional issue. I do not want to take the consequences of this dishonest game. Now there is such unanimity the people of Singapore should have the constitution in peace if they want it ... I shall resign after the present sitting."

I riposted, "As far as the PAP is concerned, the by-election position is unchanged. I shall resign at the end of this debate on a new constitution."

Lim Chin Joo and the unions were taken aback. One of them issued a statement addressed to Marshall: "Your continued attacks on the PAP has caused great pain to Mr Lee Kuan Yew, officials and supporters of the party." The union asked Marshall to refrain from fighting me in the Tanjong Pagar ward, and to fight the Liberal Socialist leader C.C. Tan in his own Cairnhill division instead. Lim Chin Joo was taking no chances. The communists did not want Marshall to retire, nor did they want either of us to knock out the other. They wanted both of us in the Assembly, with Marshall baiting, provoking and forcing me into a position more favourable to their cause. With Marshall out of the arena, they would have no prod to use on me; but with me out of the arena, they would be left with an unstable Marshall. He realised, in the 48 hours between his challenge and his retirement, that this time he would not have left-wing support. He knew that if he did not fight me, he would be humiliated but that on his own he would suffer a devastating defeat. He decided to withdraw altogether.

Nominations for the by-election were on 18 May 1957. Two candidates stood against me, a Liberal Socialist and an independent. The non-communists in the central executive committee of the PAP were determined to make this a test of our strength. We wanted to know how much ground support we could hold in Tanjong Pagar on our own, without the communists or even against them. When the Chinese middle school students offered to canvass for me, Pang Boon turned them down. Lim Chin Joo's unions decided to blur the issue by urging their members to vote for me, but Chin Chye made it clear that we did not need them. If they wanted to support us, it was their business. We wanted to fight and win on our own. And on 29 June, we did – with 67.5 per cent of the votes. We had defended our policy, and got it solidly endorsed. I said, "We got a higher percentage of votes in 1955 because we might have been all things to all men; now all men and all women know exactly what we stand for and a decisive majority voted for us."

What was ominous for Lim Yew Hock was the result of the by-election in Cairnhill for the seat Marshall had vacated. The Labour Front candidate not only lost to the Liberal Socialists but polled even fewer votes than the third contender, a former Labour Front member who was standing as an independent. That did not augur well for the chief minister.

16. Flushing Out the Communists

After the PAP won the Tanjong Pagar by-election, Chin Chye, Pang Boon and I decided to tighten constitutional control of the party so that the left wing could not capture it and use us. For instead of accepting the setback and working within the changed situation until conditions became more favourable to his side, Lim Chin Joo had decided to make a bid to take over the party himself. One of the branch secretaries told Pang Boon that the pro-communists were planning to capture eight of the 12 seats on the central executive committee.

This was adventurism, or what Marxist-Leninists would call "left-wing infantilism". The pro-communists wanted to demonstrate their revolutionary resolve, not realising that they needed the respectability of the PAP more than we needed their mass support. In the minds of the people, the PAP was already established as a consistent, radical, pro-workers' party. If we did not misplay our hand, we would always have their general goodwill and support because of the good work we had done so far. Rather than lose control of the PAP and have to start all over again, we were prepared to see the pro-communists abandon us and form another party using David Marshall as cover. Marshall's retirement from politics was brief; he was shortly to launch a new party, the Workers' Party. We knew that with him as leader, they would have enormous problems. He was erratic and temperamental. He did not have the political skills to keep the balance between constitutional and non-constitutional methods, and would soon get their new party proscribed.

Keng Swee, Kenny , Raja, Chin Chye, Pang Boon and I discussed this and decided to leak a story to the *Straits Times* that at the coming conference in August we intended to pass a series of resolutions that would effectively reorganise the PAP and make it stand clearly for "an independent, democratic, non-communist, socialist Malaya". To implement this policy, we would put ourselves up as a block of eight candidates, leaving only four seats for open voting. This was our ultimatum – we were ready to fight the pro-communists and have them leave the party. The *Straits Times* played up the story. But the pro-communists had every intention of capturing the PAP because they knew Marshall was not a viable alternative. He might be useful for sporadic action on the flanks of the party to keep it on their track, but he would not be stable enough for the long term. It was, moreover, absurdly easy for them to organise their raid on the central executive committee. We were still innocents at the game, no match for their low cunning.

It was the practice of union members who joined the PAP not to give their home addresses but those of their unions, and we were simple-minded enough to send their admission cards there. As a result, hundreds, if not thousands, of these cards ended up at Middle Road, then the headquarters of the Singapore General Employees' Union (SGEU) and several other unions and associations, to be used as their leaders saw fit. At the party conference on Sunday, 4 August, therefore, their supporters outnumbered ours, and the vote was split 50–50, the non-communists taking six seats and the pro-communists six.

We were faced with a dilemma. To take over the party would put us in a quandary, for we would not have enough votes to implement our policy. Not to take over would mean losing control to the communists and having the party reorganised further to our disadvantage. I calculated that Lim Yew Hock was unlikely to leave these people in charge for long, certainly not until the next general election, but that would still allow the CUF time to rebuild its strength in the unions and the party. After some discussion, I issued a statement signed by all six of us, the non-communists:

"Because three of the eight retiring members were not re-elected (there was one non-communist newcomer), we do not consider that we have the moral right to assume the offices of chairman, secretary and treasurer and their deputies."

The pro-communists were nonplussed. They had not thought their tactics through. They had expected us to continue to front for them on the central executive committee, especially if they left us in nominal charge, holding the key positions of chairman, secretary and treasurer. But we decided to leave them in charge so that any pro-communist act they committed would be entirely on their own account. I felt certain Lim Yew Hock would never allow them to become a threat to him, but would move against them even if they had Marshall as a cover. So we were happy to let them take over all the top positions. They were not. They pleaded with us to have Chin Chye continue as chairman and myself as secretary-general, and to reassure us, they offered to let us co-opt two members to the committee while they co-opted only one, giving us a tactical majority. When we refused, they became nervous, acutely aware of their vulnerability without us as front men. After some hesitation, they filled the key offices with Tan Chong Kin as chairman and T.T. Rajah, a lawyer and a left-wing poseur, as secretary-general. I gave them six months to a year before they got into trouble. I was wrong.

Lim Chin Joo had other far-reaching plans. Jamit Singh and his working committee had opened discussions with the Singapore Trade Union Congress (STUC) to negotiate a merger with the SGEU and its affiliates at Middle Road. This could only lead to the pro-communists absorbing Lim Yew Hock's own mass base in the trade union movement. With his STUC in imminent danger, he decided to act. On the night of 22 August, Special Branch arrested and detained 35 people – Lim Chin Joo and 12 other trade unionists, four journalists and 18 members of the PAP, including all the pro-communists on the central executive committee except T.T. Rajah. They had been in office for only 10 days. Rajah became sick with fear and worry, and on 3 September, precipitately resigned. Whatever else the second team of CUF leaders had lacked, it was not ambition. They had wanted no less than a united front of the PAP, the Labour Front, and Marshall's projected Workers' Party, plus a merger that would have given them overall control of the trade unions. Instead, they received a lesson on the folly of left-wing adventurism.

By moving so swiftly after the pro-communists had taken over the party, Lim Yew Hock had put us in the dirt. We appeared to have betrayed the pro-communists by openly dissociating ourselves from their actions and leaving them fatally exposed. On 23 August, the government issued a white paper with a section on "communist penetration of the PAP". To clear ourselves of the smear that we were involved in these arrests, I proposed a motion in the Assembly, on 12 September, deploring its inaccuracies. I pointed out that the chief minister had suppressed the most important factor that had made him move, namely that his own STUC, his mass base, was on the point of being captured by Lim Chin Joo. He had not acted as a political favour to the PAP but to save his own position at a time calculated to cause us the maximum political embarrassment.

※

If the communists had been given a lesson on folly, so had the PAP – the folly of adopting a democratic constitution that had left it open to capture through the penetration of its own party branches. We discussed several possible changes to ensure that it could never happen again. But even as Pang Boon and I made a start by cleaning out the branches, we were busy preparing for the City Council election due in December. After Lim Yew Hock's two political purges in 1956 and 1957, this election would be the first test of public opinion. The electorate had increased tenfold since 1951 to about 500,000 after the Citizenship Ordinance was passed in October 1957 to enable all those who had resided in Singapore for eight out of the previous ten years to register as citizens even if they had not been born there.

My major concern was to avoid a clash with Lim Yew Hock and his Labour Front, for that would only increase the animosity of the Chinese-speaking towards him, further reduce his political standing and make him take action to weaken the PAP. By working quietly through the UMNO leader, Hamid Jumat, who was *de facto* number two in the government, I negotiated an electoral understanding whereby the PAP, UMNO and the Labour Front would not fight each other but would share out the 32 seats on the council – 14 for the PAP, two for UMNO and 16 for the Labour Front. We undertook not to attack each other but to attack the Liberal Socialists, blaming all the past shortcomings of the old City Council on their predecessors, the Progressives, who had been in charge of it since the early fifties, when elections were first held. Towards the end of the campaign, we converted these complaints of municipal mismanagement into a broad political offensive and presented it as a confrontation of workers (PAP) versus capitalists (Liberal Socialists).

Polling day was 22 December 1957. That night I was out on the field in front of the Victoria Memorial Hall where counting was taking place. A large crowd of young Chinese school students and workers were squatting on the grass, held back by a line of policemen. At about 11 pm, I saw a tall figure of a white man in shorts strolling through the crowd into the hall. It was Bill Goode, the governor. He was brave. True, the crowd was not yet in an excited mood. Nonetheless, he had been the chief secretary when the first wave of arrests was carried out in October 1956, and governor when the second clean-up of the pro-communists took place. But he showed no trace of fear. My respect for him increased.

The election results were devastating for Lim Yew Hock. Of the 16 seats they contested, the Labour Front won only four; the PAP won 13 out of 14; UMNO, the two they contested (both in Malay majority areas); the Liberal Socialists, seven out of 32; the Workers' Party, four out of five;

and two seats went to independents. The PAP had the best scores, with nearly 30 per cent of the total votes cast and the highest number of votes per candidate.

The most significant contest was in Jalan Besar, where the PAP's nominee was Chan Chee Seng, a non-communist Chinese-educated Cantonese, a judo black belt, well-built, not intellectual but loyal and energetic and a good campaigner. The pro-communists had fielded against him a candidate standing under cover of Marshall's new Workers' Party (which they had duly penetrated, as I had expected), to prove that they could beat us if they chose. And although they lost by a clear margin, obtaining 1,600 votes against our 2,400, it was not a crushing defeat, and their latent strength was evident. They did not attack us openly on the public platform for being soft on Lim Yew Hock and the British colonialists, or for failing to fight for our detained PAP comrades, but insinuated this through word of mouth. They were able to muster a considerable vote through their door-to-door canvassing.

On the strength of the results, we decided to make a bid for the mayorship of the City Council by linking up with the two UMNO members. That gave us 15 out of 32 seats, and we were confident the rest would not be able to combine to defeat us. Lim Yew Hock might have expected us to identify ourselves with him by taking his four councillors into the coalition, but that would have been too heavy a political burden. We would have been associated with a corrupt clique, and the alliance might also have confirmed suspicions that there had been collusion between Lim Yew Hock and me when he arrested the pro-communist PAP executive committee members.

But the danger to the PAP had increased. Until this electoral test, Lim Yew Hock had harboured hopes that his tough action against the communists had won him the support of at least half the population – the Malays, the Indians, the English-educated Chinese and some of the anti-communist Chinese-speaking people.

∽

That was not to be my only worry, however. Our candidate for mayor was Ong Eng Guan, whose emergence as a crowd-puller for the PAP had been an important development during the election campaign. Like Lim Chin Siong, Ong was a Hokkien and spoke the dialect as a native. True, he did not have Lim's earnest, deeply sincere manner; he had a higher-pitched voice and his soft cherubic face was not one that showed strength. But in the course of making speeches during those five weeks, he became a good substitute for Lim Chin Siong.

To my astonishment, he began to show signs of megalomania. The resounding cheers that had greeted his Hokkien speeches at election rallies had gone to his head. Becoming mayor added to his delusions of power. On the way to the inaugural meeting of the new City Council on 23 December, he ran into a crowd of young PAP supporters who had set off firecrackers outside City Hall. A Chinese police officer remonstrated with the youths, whereupon Ong, who was there, intervened. In the ensuing mêlée, he and two other PAP city councillors were arrested, brought to the Central Police Station and released after their particulars had been taken. The meeting had to be postponed to the following day.

The next day, Ong went overboard as a populist. He allowed hundreds of the thousands of people gathered outside City Hall to crowd into the building and even the council chamber itself, including students and young children, many of them barefooted and bare-chested street urchins of seven or eight. Soon this mob was not only standing on the press tables and squatting on the floor, but pushing and jostling and breathing down the necks of the councillors themselves as they sat at their horseshoe table. They had come to clap, to cheer, to be part of the excitement although they did not understand anything of the proceedings. It took outgoing City President J.T. Rea, a professional British officer who was accompanied by the mace-bearer, 15 minutes to force his way into the chamber through a back door so that he could formally open the meeting and hand over office. The officials of the council were in a state of shock.

The new councillors could now exercise their newly granted privilege of speaking in Mandarin, Malay or Tamil, and when a Liberal Socialist member made the first speech in English, the crowd booed, although he was congratulating Ong on his election as mayor. Ong wallowed in the adulation he received. He declared that he would not wear mayoral regalia, nor stay in a mayoral mansion. He did not believe in these trappings of office. He would live and dress like an ordinary citizen. He did not approve of cocktail parties, and he did not smoke, drink or go to the races.

He allowed each of the 31 councillors to speak for two minutes, and then took a snap vote on the removal of the mayor's mace. It was carried 26 to zero, with six Liberal Socialists abstaining, and Ong ordered that it "be hereby disposed of as part of the paraphernalia of the Singapore City Council. This is a relic of colonialism." He next pushed his way through the spectators onto the balcony, where a microphone and loudspeakers had been installed at his request, and addressed the crowd outside in Mandarin for 10 minutes. He ended with three cries of "Merdeka!" The crowd cheered and yelled back in unison. "May God protect Singapore" was the *Straits Times* headline for its Christmas Day edition, quoting a Eurasian Liberal Socialist lady councillor.

"The usual dignity of the proceedings was ruined," Goode wrote wryly to Lennox-Boyd in a report dated 27 December. The officials of the City Council, both white and Asian, were dismayed. The expatriates were fearful for their future. But, as he added, "There has been no criticism of the police action and as yet no agitation against the police by the PAP. Lee Kuan Yew is away enjoying his Christmas holiday!" Indeed, I was away. The evening the ballots were counted, my throat was so dry and burnt by all the cigarette-smoking during the election campaign that I could not find my voice to thank the crowd for their support. The following morning, I packed the family into my Studebaker and drove up to Fraser's Hill for a 10-day break.

For the next 16 months, Ong held sway over the City Council as mayor, mounting one spectacle after another. His arrogant behaviour demoralised its officers and frightened the English-educated clerks and professionals. He played favourites, and gave orders through a crony from his home town of Batu Pahat whom he made his general factotum and who had to be obeyed without question. His good luck was that he did not have to last a full three-year term and thus was not called to account for the damage that he was wreaking on the system. There had to be a general election by May 1959, the end of the four-year term of Lim Yew Hock's government, so Ong's weaknesses would not have time to show up. Moreover, he was able to implement popular programmes, which were not costly, notably in deprived areas of Singapore. He installed street lamps and standpipes, brought drainage and power to the villages, and reduced rates for electricity from 20 cents to 12 cents a unit for the rural poor. He set up a City Information Bureau to publicise these achievements, opened a Public Complaints Bureau, and held "meet the people" sessions.

The English-educated were terrified, but Ong's antics delighted the Chinese-speaking. All their lives they had felt excluded from power; now they had a Hokkien speaking their own language and giving vent to their frustrations. But Ong created problems that were to fester for years. For example, he allowed the hawkers to take over many main roads in the city, especially in Chinatown, where formerly they had been kept to the fringes and been allowed to encroach on them only after office hours. He was like a man possessed, intoxicated with power and mass adulation. He wanted to create a newspaper headline every day. He went on raising expectations with dramatic gestures, as if there were no tomorrow when the bills would have to be paid. I knew that he was doing immense harm to the country and the PAP, but thought it best to let him ride the surf for the time being and to sort things out after the general election. The popularity he lost for us among the English-educated he more than made up for in gains among the Chinese-speaking.

17. Rendezvous with the Plen

I remember 1958 as the year when the intense pressure that the communists had been mounting since 1954 subsided. Things were relatively quiet, and there was little excitement from go-slows, strikes, demonstrations, riots or rallies. I had time for reflection, to think and to plan the next important moves before the coming general election, due at the latest in May 1959. The first question I had to answer was whether it was better for us to win and form the government or stay in the opposition, but with more seats, and use another term to consolidate our position with the people.

After the test in Tanjong Pagar and Jalan Besar, however, I was already confident that, even if the communists opposed us in the election, they would not be able to defeat us unless they were able to rebuild their organisation to what it had been in 1956. To do this, they would have to start new parties, form new fronts, and then establish their credentials with the public. All this would take time. Their cadres and immediate supporters – a few thousand in all – could follow the twists and turns of each manoeuvre of the CUF, but not the mass of the people.

Whether or not we formed the next government, we would have to be completely in command of the PAP itself and able to prevent its reinfiltration and recapture. How were we to take advantage of this period of quiet, while the communists had to keep their heads down, to achieve that? They could still retake the branches, but we must on no account allow them to take over the party as a whole, and with it the symbol that would identify it on the ballot papers beside a candidate's name. In a semi-literate, multilingual country, the candidate's symbol is crucial; it is like the logo of a designer product, and the PAP's blue circle with a red lightning flash across it had already won brand recognition. That was an immediate problem. But if we assumed office the problem would become more acute, for we would have to release Lim Chin Siong, Fong and their lieutenants. How could we then stop them – their prestige enhanced by their detention – from rebounding and threatening a PAP government? I was convinced we could not survive unless we had first won the high ground so that we could not be attacked and demolished like the Labour Front. The answer was plain. Somehow or other I must publicly commit Lim Chin Siong and Fong to our own position before we took power.

I had several other preoccupations. Lim Yew Hock now knew that his standing with the voters had been badly damaged, and that he and Chew Swee Kee would find it difficult to survive the communist onslaught against them for the purges they had mounted. But they continued to commit so many blunders that they seemed doomed. I tried to dispel Lim Yew Hock's fears of sudden political death and assured him I would not press him to hold the early election he had foolishly promised, and that given time his political fortunes could change. I found reasons for him to postpone the polls: registration of new citizens, redelineation of constituencies from 25 to 51, changes to the election law to make voting compulsory and forbid the use of cars to carry voters to polling stations. I convinced him that it would be unwise to let voting remain voluntary, for the communists were better organised and better able to mobilise their followers, and the wealthy parties would find themselves supplying cars only to provide transport for the supporters of their left-wing opponents. Time was needed for the details to be worked out and legislation drafted and passed. He accepted these ideas gratefully because they prolonged the life of his government.

I did not tell him that I myself needed time to clean up the PAP, reorganise it, and select active, young Chinese-educated cadres who could be fielded as candidates but who were not committed Marxists or communists. We wanted a balanced multiracial slate. While we could find English-educated Chinese, Malays and Indians who would be totally dependable and non-communist, it was difficult to identify good Chinese-educated candidates who would remain loyal when the communists opened fire on us, such was their hold on the minds of the Chinese-educated.

I started cadre-training classes to talent-spot idealistic Chinese-speakers with political convictions that were not left-wing, but we were fishing in the same pond as the communists, who exploited both Chinese nationalism and Marxist-Maoist ideas of egalitarianism. The most energetic and dedicated of the Chinese were already imbued with these ideals. I had to swing them over to democratic socialism, to get our own political concepts across to them in my inadequate Mandarin – and then read the papers they wrote in Chinese running script, which is far more difficult to decipher than printed characters.

I believe the experience taught me more than it taught them. Their mental terms of reference were Chinese history, Chinese parables and proverbs, the legendary success of the Chinese communist revolution as against their own frustrating life in Singapore. None of this helped them to understand what I was propounding to them – a parliamentary, democratic, socialist, non-communist society in a multiracial Singapore and Malaya established through peaceful, non-violent and constitutional means. Their whole background led them to believe that a communist society should be brought about both by open persuasion and by clandestine subversion and revolutionary force. I later discovered to my dismay that there were quite a few converted hard-core communists even in the group I had picked. There was no way to filter them out. They were like radioactive dust.

One day in March 1958, a Chinese male in his late 20s came to Lee & Lee, my law firm in Malacca Street, and told Choo that he would like to speak to me personally. It was about 11 am, a busy time of the day when many other young men in short-sleeved shirts and slacks were coming and going, but after checking with me, Choo let him through. He said he had an important request. Would I meet a person who represented his organisation? – meaning, without saying it, the communist underground. I said, Yes. He stressed that the meeting must be secret. I proposed a rendezvous on the road between the Empress Place government offices and Victoria Theatre. This would be safest for me. I could take him to the select committee room in the Assembly House just a few yards away. It was quiet and secluded; I knew it was not going to be used for any meeting on the day I suggested, and that there would probably be no Members in the House since it was not sitting that morning.

When the day came, I walked from my office to the rendezvous and looked out, as instructed, for a slim, fair-skinned person with a pair of spectacles in his shirt breast pocket and carrying a Chinese newspaper. He was there, shorter than me, and leaner. We exchanged passwords and walked to the Assembly House as agreed. There was an air of stealth and furtiveness about him, a nervousness and jumpiness, as of a man on the run. The pallor of his face, arms and hands was that of a person who had not seen sunshine for many months. I felt that I was dealing with someone truly "underground". He had a high forehead with a receding hairline, a long clean-shaven face, a long pointed nose and straight black hair combed back in the style of Chinese middle school students. He was very fair, and I guessed he could not be a Hokkien, but was possibly a Hakka or a Teochew. He was younger than me by some three to five years. He spoke softly, as if not wanting to be overheard, but in a firm voice. He soon impressed me as quick-witted and determined. He started the conversation in Mandarin, so I responded in Mandarin, but I repeated the important parts of what I had to say in simple English to make doubly sure I had made myself clear. From his expression, I knew he had understood me.

He said he represented the MCP in Singapore, and wanted to see me in person in order to establish cooperation between the communists and the non-communists in the PAP. He regretted very much that the pro-communist cadres had attempted to capture the party in 1957. He urged me to believe that that was not communist policy. They were over-enthusiastic young people who meant well and wanted to help bring about a revolution in Malaya. He asked me to believe in his sincerity, that his offer of cooperation in a united anti-colonial front was genuine.

What he was proposing meant that Lim Chin Siong and Fong should be free to do what they had been doing before they were arrested in 1956 – to mobilise the workers, the students, the teachers, the cultural groups, the petty bourgeoisie and friendly nationalists, and to form a powerful united front, which the MCP would lead and control through its cadres planted within their organisations. I did some quick thinking and said I did not know who he was, and had no way of knowing if what he said was true. He said I would have to trust him. I blandly asked him for some proof, not of his identity, but of his authority over communist and pro-communist cadres in Singapore as a true representative of the MCP. He smiled at me confidently, looked me in the eye and again said I had to take his word for it.

I named Chang Yuen Tong, who had won the City Council seat for Kallang. Chang was vice-president of Marshall's Workers' Party and president of the Electrical and Wireless Employees' Union. I was fairly certain from his appearance, behaviour and speeches in the City Council that he was a pro-communist cadre. This time I looked him in the eye and said I believed the communists were using Marshall and his Workers' Party to fight the PAP. They had not only put up Chang in Kallang, but had also fought the PAP candidate in the Jalan Besar division in the City Council election in December. (I did not remind him that the Workers' Party candidate had lost.) I said he could prove he was a real representative of the communist command in Singapore and had spoken in good faith when he said that the MCP did not wish to attack the PAP, by instructing Chang to resign from the Workers' Party and the City Council.

Without any hesitation, he said, "All right, give me some time. I shall see that it is done. If he is a member of our organisation, it will be done." We had talked for an hour. He was assessing my character and my political position, and I was returning the compliment. He was taking a risk in seeing me. But so was I. Because if he was indeed a communist leader and I was caught with him, I would have some explaining to do. I was prepared for that, however. I would say that he had wanted to see me on some constituency matter, and I had met him near the House and taken him to the Assembly to listen to his problem. So I took care to part company with him in the committee room, walking ahead of him down the stairs and out of the main door without turning back to see which way he went. I did not think I would see him again. I did not know who he was and did not want to know. I had to protect my position as the leader of the opposition.

I told only Keng Swee about the meeting, and he was as intrigued as I was to see what the outcome would be. We called the man "the Plen", the plenipotentiary. We knew he must be someone important in the MCP, but how important? And what were their real intentions and potential?

∝

My next major engagement was in May 1958, the third constitutional conference. I flew to London and from the airport went straight to the House of Commons to meet Lennox-Boyd. As we travelled together to the conference, he asked for my assessment of future developments in Singapore and about Lim Yew Hock's chances in the next election. I said they had been sinking by the month. Lim Yew Hock had a weak team, and several of his ministers had poor reputations for honesty and integrity. This made him vulnerable to the smear campaigns the communists had mounted against him and Chew Swee Kee. I expected the PAP to win, and having defended the proposed constitution in the Tanjong Pagar by-election in June a year ago, I asked for nothing more than what had already been agreed. I referred in particular to the Internal Security Council, the safety net that would ensure that the communists could not take over. With a Malayan representative holding the casting vote, any detention order it issued could be better defended politically and would not so immediately compromise an elected Singapore government.

All that remained for the conference to do was the serious but politically quiet business of settling the details. Both on the Singapore and the British sides, there was by now an unspoken acceptance that the PAP was likely to win the coming election, so that what I said carried more weight than the chief minister's views. I had to examine the details carefully to make sure I could work the constitution that was now being reduced to legal language. But I remember only one issue that was mildly sensitive and could render us vulnerable to attack in Singapore.

The British government wanted all pensions for officers appointed by Her Majesty's Government, local or expatriate, to be guaranteed against any future devaluation of the Singapore currency. Only later did I understand that they had to insist on this guarantee to keep up the morale of their colonial service officers in other territories that were heading for independence. But ironically it was the pound that was to be devalued, and by 1995 it had dropped to Singapore $2.20, a quarter its worth in 1958. The officers who had asked to have their pensions paid in sterling were unlucky. How were they to know that Singapore would not go the way of other former colonies?

One afternoon, while still in London, I read on the front page of the *Straits Times* that Chang Yuen Tong, vice-president of the Workers' Party, city councillor, and president of the Electrical and Wireless Employees' Union, had resigned "because the demands of his employment made it impossible for him to find sufficient time for council work".

The Plen had given his orders and had been obeyed. He had proved that he was in charge. I found it unnerving. I thought it might happen, but not so quickly. Here was a man on the run, wanted by the police, probably in hiding in some cubicle or attap hut somewhere in Singapore. He had contacted me through a cut-out, who had given me his business card with the address of a bicycle shop in Rochor Road in case I wanted to get in touch with him. And I was sure the cut-out would not be able to lead the police to the Plen. Yet in a matter of eight weeks, his orders had been relayed to Chang and faithfully obeyed. It was an impressive demonstration of the discipline of the MCP organisation.

These were not men to be trifled with. So many were with them because people expected them to win and therefore climbed on the bandwagon. Since "history was on their side", why be so stupid as to fight them? Yet here was I, with my few English-educated friends, ignorant enough to have the temerity to take on a movement that had established its credentials with successful revolutions in Russia and China.

I did not want to show any anxiety or concern, and as I had never been to Rome, I decided to break journey there for four days. This was the Rome of the occasional Vespa scooter, before it was clogged up with cars and choked with fumes. I spent much of my time walking around the ancient city, visiting the Forum and the Victor Emmanuel Memorial, with its bronze bas-relief showing the expansion of Roman hegemony across Europe and the Mediterranean. It reminded me that all empires wax and wane, that the British Empire was on the wane, like the Roman Empire before it.

I left with one even more vivid impression. One morning, I walked to St Peter's Basilica and was pleasantly surprised when the Pope appeared, carried on a palanquin by his Swiss guards. He was being televised, and as he was brought down the centre aisle, the press of people immediately around him started to cheer and shout "*Vive il Papa*", the nuns standing near the palanquin almost fainting with joy. After my experience with communist rallies I instinctively looked for the cheer-leaders. I found them above me, choirboys on circular balconies up the pillars. The Roman Catholic Church had used such methods of mass mobilisation long before the communists. The Church must have got many things right to have survived for nearly two thousand years. I remembered reading about a new Pope being elected by some one hundred cardinals who themselves had been appointed by earlier popes. That recollection was to serve the PAP well.

When I got back to Singapore, we had to decide on a candidate for the Kallang by-election, which I felt reasonably confident of winning. We fielded a trade union activist, Buang bin Omar Junid. Just before the by-election, the Plen gave me a hard-cover English-Chinese dictionary printed in China on fine paper, sending it through the man from the bicycle shop. On the flyleaf, he had written in Chinese, "To respected Mr Lee Kuan Yew, wishing the PAP success in the Kallang by-election". He signed it in Chinese, "John Lee July 1958" – his messenger had earlier told me that that would be his pseudonym. This meant the communists had not only abandoned Marshall but must have told their followers to support the PAP.

On election day, we had 4,278 votes, the Labour Front 3,566. The Workers' Party won only 304 votes. It was a humiliating lesson for Marshall: without the pro-communists, that was what he was worth. With the Liberal Socialists staying out in order not to split the right-wing ballot, the Labour Front vote was close, but if we had fielded a Chinese instead of a Malay candidate the PAP would have done much better. I felt confident we could defeat a combined Labour Front and Liberal Socialist challenge in the general election.

But we were not out of the woods yet. The Preservation of Public Security Ordinance (PPSO), which gave the government powers of detention without trial, was due to come up in the Assembly for another three-year renewal. It was an important opportunity to make our position clear, but would require meticulous handling since we would be reversing our earlier stand. After thorough discussions with my close colleagues, I prepared a script for the speech.

The PAP could not vote in favour of extending the PPSO on this occasion, I explained to the House, for that would mean going back on our promise in the 1955 election to abolish it. But, I went on to say, that would not be our position in the 1959 election.

> "We state our stand now on the question of the Emergency laws, and it is this: that as long as they are necessary for the maintenance of the security of the Federation, so long will they be necessary for Singapore. ... Those who want the Emergency laws abolished in Singapore should try to help to establish conditions of peace and security in the Federation so that they may no longer be required there."

That clarified our policy on detention without trial *vis-à-vis* the communists. Next we had to safeguard the PAP against any left-wing capture of the party. Soon after I returned from Rome, I proposed that PAP elections to the central executive committee be modelled on the system for electing the Pope. As we worked out the details, on 9 October Pope Pius XII died. The cardinals gathered at St Peter's to choose the new pontiff, and within three weeks announced the election of Pope John XIII. We noted the strength of the system, and at a special party conference on 23 November, we got the necessary changes adopted.

The amended constitution established two classes of party membership: ordinary members, who could join either directly through PAP headquarters or through the branches, and cadre members, a select few hundred who would be approved by the central executive committee. Only cadres who had been chosen by the CEC could in turn vote for candidates to the CEC, just as only cardinals nominated by a Pope could elect another Pope. This closed the circuit, and since the CEC controlled the core of the party, the party could not now be captured.

In December, we published an editorial in *Petir*, the party organ, emphasising that the PAP was non-communist and that the PPSO would remain in force if we assumed office. I did not doubt that the Plen would have read every word I had said in the Assembly debate on the PPSO and the proceedings of the party conference that had closely followed it. He would also have seen this editorial, which was reprinted in the Chinese press. I was not surprised, therefore, when the man from the bicycle shop approached me for another meeting, to which I agreed. At about 8 o'clock one night, I drove my father's small green Morris Minor to Keng Lee Road, where I stopped, as I had been instructed, to pick up a Chinese girl in pigtails wearing a simple blouse and skirt. She sat in the front seat beside me and directed me by a roundabout route to a small bungalow in a housing estate off Thomson Road. She then disappeared, leaving the Plen and me in an inner room.

I spent nearly two hours with him. He assured me that I need not be so suspicious of communist intentions. The problems I had had with Lim Chin Siong, Fong Swee Suan and Lim Chin Joo had been due to their organisation's difficulty in communicating with their cadres. Now that I was dealing directly with the top leadership, there would be no more misunderstandings. I listened, looked at him seriously, and said I hoped that that was so. I felt his options were limited. Whatever he promised, I knew we had to seize the high ground by publicly staking out our positions before the election. If the pro-communists stayed in the PAP and did not dissociate themselves from those positions, they would find it more difficult to attack us once we were the government. But I was certain that whether cooperation between us lasted one, two, or three years, in the end we must break. There must be a parting of the ways because we were determined not to have a communist Malaya, and they were equally determined that there should be one.

I could not be sure what his plans were, but he could see I was publicly adopting policies that would justify our taking strong action against the communists if it became necessary. I believed he was totally confident that once Lim Chin Siong and Fong and his other 150 detained cadres were released, they would be able to rebuild their strength within 12 to 18 months to the level of October 1956, when they had been purged. Then he would dictate the terms. And if I then moved against Lim Chin Siong, Fong and their battalions in the unions, Chinese middle schools and cultural organisations, I would be destroyed electorally like Lim Yew Hock and Chew Swee Kee.

He was not playing tiddlywinks. He was playing the Chinese game of *wei qi* (the Japanese call it *go*) in which two players place seeds on a square board until one of them has surrounded the seeds of the other, a chess game of encirclement. For the time being I was the better placed, but he was patiently trying to encircle me with his superior ground forces. If I did not want to lose, I had to take up strong positions that would give me the advantage in defence, even though he had greater numbers with which to launch his attacks. But if he made a false move through overconfidence, the tables would be turned, and I would have a chance to encircle him.

18. Election 1959 – We Fight to Win

Throughout 1958–59, I had been seeing Devan Nair, Lim Chin Siong, Fong Swee Suan, Woodhull and Puthucheary in their new detention camp, located just outside Changi Prison, once every three or four weeks. I would bring them a large pot of delicious chicken curry that my cook had prepared, freshly baked bread bought from a bakery on the way to Changi and, when permission was granted, some large bottles of Anchor beer. During these meetings, I hinted that I had grave doubts about setting out to win the next election, because a PAP government would soon be in trouble with the MCP. This alarmed them, for unless we won and took office, they could spend more years in detention. Gradually, they came around and offered promises to support the party unequivocally. I knew these promises would be worthless, so I asked them to put down in writing the terms on which they would give us that support. Nair wrote a draft and they argued endlessly over it, as only detainees with time on their hands would do.

Nair, detained since 1956, had begun to lose faith in their cause. After the attempted capture of the PAP by the CUF's second team, he despaired of ever getting them to see sense. One day, Corridon arranged for me to meet him alone in a bungalow on St John's Island where I spent the greater part of a day with him. He told me of his disillusionment and said that he wanted to quit politics. I listened, comforted him and advised him not to do anything precipitate.

I felt that he, as an Indian, would never be comfortable in a movement driven by Chinese chauvinist sentiments. But he was in a difficult position. He was already a member of the Anti-British League, and so a candidate for full membership of the MCP. The MCP had only a handful of non-Chinese who were steadfast members, and Nair was one of the few English-educated Indians they trusted. His defection – possibly betrayal – would be a severe blow to them, and their reaction might be extreme. He knew this and was aware of their elimination squads.

Nair's first draft was not four-square with the PAP policy we intended to announce a few months before the election, so I asked him to redraft it. I told him that Raja, Keng Swee, Chin Chye and I were working on a document called "The Tasks Ahead" whose first chapter would set out our political platform – independence for Singapore through merger with a democratic, socialist but non-communist Malaya. He was torn between our uncompromising stand and the reluctance of his pro-communist fellow detainees to confirm it.

By the beginning of 1959, Nair had his political statement ready for the five principal detainees to sign. It gave unequivocal support to the PAP stand that Singapore would gain independence only through merger with a democratic, socialist, non-communist Malaya. This was funda-mental. Without such a commitment, I could foresee them leading a movement to achieve it outside the Federation. They had no alternative, for Malaya had an anti-communist government with a solid Malay mass base they could neither win over by persuasion nor destroy by force in the face of a rapidly growing Malay army backed by the British military. The day came when Lim Chin Siong was finally prepared to sign the statement, and the others followed suit. I was given a copy a few weeks before nomination day on 25 April on the understanding that when freed they would immediately declare their positions and release the document at a press conference.

What made Lim Chin Siong sign? He might have calculated that without the assurance of their cooperation, we would not fight to win the election. Indeed, it was a serious toss-up. I knew the problems facing the next government would be immense. Unemployment was around

I took this photo when visiting (from left to right) Lim Chin Siong, Sidney Woodhull, Fong Swee Suan and Devan Nair in the Changi detention camp in 1958.

12 per cent. Every year, another 62,000 babies were born. With our population growing at 4 per cent per annum, the economic prospects were grim. We had no hinterland, no large domestic market for new industries, and a bad climate of labour unrest. I was not at all confident we could withstand the communist assaults that would follow.

Raja, ever the idealist and the ideologue, was in favour of our forming a strong opposition. Keng Swee and Kenny, both administrators, were convinced we had to form the government. They argued that the corruption would spread from the ministers into the civil service itself, and that if we sat out another five-year term under Lim Yew Hock, there would no longer be an effective administration to implement our policies. Unlike the communists, we had no cadre of our own with which to replace it. By February, we had decided to fight to win, and in preparation, Keng Swee and Kenny both resigned from their government posts under a special law that allowed former senior civil servants to contest elections and continue to receive their pensions. Our chief adversary would be the Singapore People's Alliance (SPA), a coalition of the Labour Front and the Liberal Socialists that Lim Yew Hock had put together the previous November.

We drafted policy papers on economics, education, housing, health, rural development, labour and women's rights, which we published in a series of pamphlets entitled "The Tasks Ahead".

We launched our election campaign on Sunday, 15 February, with a pre-election rally at Hong Lim Green, at which Chin Chye disclosed that the Americans had given $500,000 to the SPA:

> "It is an open secret that income tax investigation into a half-million dollar account at the National City Bank of New York in the name of a minister was quite quickly and properly choked off because this money, being a political gift, was not liable to income tax."

It was a bombshell.

The SPA denounced the accusation as a lie. The US consulate-general issued a statement denying that the US government had made any contribution to the SPA – it was not US policy to interfere in the political affairs of other nations. So, on 18 February, I gave notice of a motion in the Assembly in which I named Chew Swee Kee as the person who had the account and called for a commission of inquiry. As the motion was about to be debated on 4 March, Chew resigned from his post as minister for education and from the Assembly. In a written statement, he said, "I want to clear the SPA's name ... I have nothing to hide."

In the debate, I said that in 1957, Chew had received $300,000 for his party, some of it for the City Council election, and in 1958, a further $500,000, also for political purposes. I revealed that I had the permission of Francis Thomas to say that it was he who had told me that Chew had received the $300,000. As I spoke, Thomas left the government benches and crossed the floor to sit with the opposition. He later explained to the press that he had not disclosed the matter at the time since it would have wrecked the Labour Party and probably the government, which for all its faults was doing a good job. In the middle of 1958, however, it had become obvious to him that the Front was not going to be cleaned up, and he had told me about the money, asking me to keep it confidential (which I did). By then, he had resigned as minister.

Having achieved our political purpose of discrediting the SPA for taking money from the Americans, I offered to withdraw my motion. Lim Yew Hock unwisely refused. He declared that the government had nothing to hide and that he wanted the commission of inquiry to find out, not if the charges were true, but how the information had been leaked from the Income Tax Department. The commission opened its inquiry on 6 April, under Mr Justice Murray Buttrose, an Australian who had served with the British armed forces in the war, and I appeared on behalf of Kenny and Chin Chye. The details then disclosed did further damage to the SPA government. Chew admitted that, with the $800,000 in question, he had bought a house in Ipoh in the name of his wife for $51,000, invested $250,000 in the Perak Mining Enterprise Ltd in the name of a Mr Chong, a trusted member of his party, and was considering an investment of $30,000 in another mining company in Ipoh with Chong as nominee. He had also given $50,000 worth of shares in the mining company to Mrs Hamid Jumat, wife of the UMNO minister for local government. The representative of the National City Bank of New York refused to name the donor publicly, but wrote his name on a piece of paper and handed it to the commissioner, who did not reveal it.

The findings of the commission released on 25 May substantially confirmed what Chin Chye had revealed in his rally speech. The report was published in the press on 27 May, two days before polling day. It only confirmed what voters already knew – that Lim Yew Hock's government was corrupt, and worse, that it was now in the pay of the Americans.

As I expected, the opposition parties were a shambles when nomination day approached. I knew Lim Yew Hock wanted UMNO and the MCA to be in his SPA along with the Labour Front and the Liberal Socialist Party. He was anxious to prevent a repetition of the split in the moderate vote that had occurred in the City Council election. But it was not to be. The disaster of the Chew Swee Kee affair and the unfavourable fallout from the commission of inquiry had put voters off. Meanwhile, general dissension among the Liberal Socialists had led to total confusion as all its assemblymen and many of its ordinary members left it. Instead of merging into the SPA as they had earlier agreed, the Liberal Socialists went into the election on their own.

On nomination day, 25 April 1959, the SPA put up candidates for 39 seats, the Liberal Socialists for 32, and there were 34 independents. The PAP contested all 51 seats with 34 Chinese candidates, 10 Malays, six Indians and one Eurasian. We had proportionately more Malays and Indians than in the population ratio, but we thought it good for the morale of the minorities.

We held six mass rallies and between 60 and 100 street meetings in the 33 days of campaigning, at the start of which the bookies were already taking bets on the number of seats we would win by, which was a good sign. The other parties knew this, were demoralised, and did not put up a vigorous or coherent campaign. On the other hand, PAP election workers displayed tremendous energy. Many of our candidates were under 30, and their speeches generated great enthusiasm among the younger voters. We had broken Chinese tradition by fielding three Chinese barbers – in Imperial China barbers, together with actors and butchers, were not even eligible to sit for the imperial examinations. We represented the new order that would do away with such feudal attitudes.

In the midst of this hectic, at times hilarious, campaign, I sensed that the Tunku and his colleagues in Kuala Lumpur did not view the prospect of a "non-communist" PAP victory in Singapore kindly. Hamid Jumat told an UMNO rally in Geylang Serai that Malaya was anti-communist while the PAP was non-communist. The Malays never liked people who sat on the fence, and merger with Malaya was therefore a daydream. The next day, after I called this talk "wild", he pressed me to be explicitly anti-communist. This was unlike Hamid, and I believed he had been stiffened by messages from Kuala Lumpur. It was clear which side the Tunku favoured.

On Sunday, 22 March, Keng Swee had delivered his speech "On Economic Policy", as part of the "Tasks Ahead" series, and explained the necessity for cooperation between Singapore and Malaya. "In return for a common market we can offer the Federation joint control of our port, which handles so much of its foreign trade." But Tan Siew Sin, now the Federation minister for commerce and industry, declared, "The PAP does not know what it is talking about. The idea of a common market is not practicable. The PAP should realise that one cannot have a free port and a common market at the same time. You must choose one or the other."

At the time, I thought he was only trying to help the other side in the election. Only much later did I realise how strongly he held these views. Keng Swee was Tan's cousin, but Tan was never going to give anything away to Singapore, as we were to find out. The atmosphere in Kuala Lumpur then was generally hostile to the PAP. The Tunku had elevated Lim Yew Hock with the title of "Tun", the highest award in Malaya, and said that although he would not take part in the election campaign, he would help UMNO from behind the scenes. He was in favour of the anti-PAP line-up, and had warned any pro-PAP members in UMNO that they would be expelled if they stood as independents.

The US government did not favour the PAP either. The *Straits Times* reported the Commerce Department's *Foreign Commerce Weekly's* prediction that Singapore might swing left and abandon its tradition of private enterprise. "This possibility makes it impossible to estimate the city's economic outlook and trade prospects," it continued. Singapore's financial situation was sound, but "in contrast with the Federation, the investment climate in Singapore continues to deteriorate despite the government's announced desire to attract foreign investments".

Inevitably, the English-language press was virulently anti-PAP, unlike the Chinese and Malay newspapers, which were friendly. That animosity had provoked a battle when I fired my first salvo on 15 April:

> "It is an open secret (that if the PAP won) the *Straits Times* editorial staff would scoot to Kuala Lumpur. Those who have followed the paper's views should also scoot with them. (For) If you read what you see in the paper, you will think we are extremists and wild men."

This was at a lunchtime rally at Fullerton Square in the heart of the city, next to the General Post Office, near the big British banks around Raffles Place. The audience consisted mainly of white-collar English-speaking workers. I pointed to an article with bold headlines reporting that the police had refused to allow the PAP to hold a rally at Empress

Place, and then to the last paragraph, where in small type it added the meeting would take place where we now were. I compared this with a prominent report about an SPA rally. This was flagrant bias. "If people try to harm us," I warned, "we will give them as hard as they give us."

At our next rally, Raja followed up with an attack on the *Singapore Standard*. They talked of freedom of the press, but stifled the views of those they did not agree with, he said. He was well-qualified to speak. An associate editor of the paper from 1950 to 1954, he had been told to change his policy or quit. He quit – and the paper turned anti-PAP. One week later, he rounded on the *Straits Times*, for which he had worked after he left the *Standard*. He knew who ran the paper and named the four men, all white, including A.C. Simmons, in day-to-day control. Simmons realised that Raja and I were not joking when we said that if we formed the government, we would take them on. They were already making preparations to move the company and key staff to Kuala Lumpur because they feared a PAP victory. I had no doubts that they were determined to fight us from the federal capital. As I wrote to them:

> "If locally owned newspapers criticise us we know that their criticism, however wrong or right, is bona fide criticism, because they must stay and take the consequences of any foolish policies or causes they may have advocated. Not so the birds of passage who run the *Straits Times*. They have to run to the Federation, from whose safety they boldly proclaim they will die for the freedom of Singapore."

The editor, Leslie Hoffman, replied the same day:

> "I am no bird of passage. I, who am responsible for the policy and editorial content of this newspaper, intend to remain in Singapore, even if Mr Lee and the People's Action Party come to power, and even if they use the Preservation of Public Security Ordinance against me. ... My home will be in Singapore."

But he left for Kuala Lumpur before the election was over.

Five days before polling, Hoffman told the International Press Institute, at its annual assembly in West Berlin of newspapermen, editors and publishers, that our threats could be read as "the outpourings of a group of power-mad politicians". The *Straits Times*, on the other hand, was "written, produced and controlled by Malayans who were born there, who had been there all their lives, and who are genuine in their nationalism and loyalty to their country". He would not admit that it was his British masters who owned the paper and who directed its policies.

Simmons knew he was vulnerable. So he had briefed Hoffman, a Eurasian, to put his case to the IPI. "In this sense it is unique that it gives this assembly the opportunity to stop once and for all an attempt by a party to get popular support and backing for its declared intention to curtail press freedom," Hoffman continued. But that was exactly what the PAP intended to do – to get public support for our policy that the press was not to be owned by foreigners to purvey their line. Hoffman quoted what I had said on 18 May:

> "Any newspaper that tries to sour up or strain relations between the Federation of Malaya and Singapore after May 30 will go in for subversion. Any editor, leader writer, subeditor or reporter who goes along this line will be taken in under the Preservation of Public Security Ordinance. We will put him in and keep him in."

The attitude of the *Straits Times* was all the more unjustified because we, the non-communists in the PAP, were in firm control of the election campaign, a source of great satisfaction to me. We settled the agenda, decided on the themes, made the big speeches. No organised crowds were brought to our rallies by the left-wing union leaders. Although the pro-communists were running around the party branches and some might have become candidates, Pang Boon and I had minimised the risk by selecting our Chinese-educated nominees with great care. There was no Lim Chin Siong to sway the crowds.

Ong Eng Guan was not a bad substitute for Lim Chin Siong as a Hokkien speaker for our rallies. But Pang Boon was also fluent in Hokkien as well as in Mandarin, and my Mandarin had improved; although it was not good enough for a flight of rhetoric, it was now adequate to express my thoughts without any script. I might be repeating what I had said in English or Malay in a less elegant way in Mandarin, but I won the respect of the Chinese-speaking for working hard at their language. The same was true of Chin Chye, a small man of five foot two, but lively on stage. His Mandarin was weaker than mine but he was game, and the crowds cheered us, pleased that we were making the effort to reach out to them.

As vote-winners, our future ministers were a mixed lot. Raja turned out to be a quick learner, speaking forcefully in English and reducing his editorial style to punchy street language. He also spoke bazaar Malay and got his point across effectively in a strong voice and with expressive body language. On the other hand, Keng Swee was dreadful; with a first-class mind, he prepared his speeches meticulously, but delivered them in a dull monotone, mumbling, reading from a script, and looking bored.

In a multiracial society, we had one inescapable problem. Some of our candidates might be natural open-air orators, but no one could make a speech at an election rally and move the whole audience to laugh, or sigh, or cry or be angry together. Whatever language he used and however good he was, only one section of the crowd could understand him at any one time, so he had to reach the others through gestures, facial expressions and his tone of voice.

Bazaar Malay was the simplest and most widely understood language, and our most effective speaker in it was Yaacob bin Mohamed who had a dramatic, brilliant delivery with which he reached the non-Malays. To decry the boastfulness of the opposition, he quoted a Malay proverb from Terengganu, the land of turtles from where he came: "A hen lays one egg, the whole village hears her cackles; a turtle lays eggs by the hundred, not a sound is heard." In other words, the PAP brought much benefit to the workers, but never boasted about it. This drew tremendous cheers from the crowd. Those were the days before television, when a good voice and a strong, commanding presence were distinct advantages.

Yaacob was of humble origins. Born in north Malaya and educated at a local religious school, he had driven a truck for the Indian National Army during the war, and when he came down to Singapore in the early 1950s, had worked as an itinerant barber before becoming a religious teacher. He had joined API, a very radical Malay nationalist party, switched to UMNO in 1954, found it too conservative and not egalitarian enough, and so switched to the PAP in 1957. Later, I was to appoint him a parliamentary secretary, then minister of state. He was a great asset with the Malays. His rise from the bottom of the ladder was a feature of those revolutionary times. The old order had lost its hold, society was in a state of flux, and many uneducated men and women from the working class seized the chance to climb to the top through sheer ability, energy and luck.

The great majority of people were poor, many of them living in slums, and as the party of the workers, we received few donations from the wealthy, forcing us to run our campaign on a shoestring. But we could count on the wholehearted support of volunteers. Candidates who could afford it met their own election expenses; the party provided standard posters and manifestoes that varied only in their photographs and biodata. We hired open lorries, pick-up trucks or light vans to use as platforms at meetings, parking two side by side for big rallies; often they were lent free by transport operators who were our supporters. They might have hoped for future benefits, but many continued to help us out in subsequent elections after we had taken office and done them no favours. At night, we tapped electricity from "friendly" shops to light our platforms with strings of naked bulbs, and although we had to hire loudspeakers, with them came the services of small-time electricians who strung out the wires for us on the trees and lamp-posts (sometimes producing a shrill screech in the middle of a speech).

Electioneering meant going to odd corners of Singapore that the English-educated middle class in general would not normally visit. The smells of sullage, the giant rats and mangy strays, the open drains full of garbage and stale leavings from hawker stalls in Chinatown were what I remembered of Tanjong Pagar in the 1950s. At night the hawkers would appear from nowhere and surround our rallies, expecting good business. On the fringes of the crowd there would be large numbers of children, reminders of our high 4 per cent birth rate, out for an evening of fun, some with parents, many unaccompanied. In rural areas like Punggol, Sembawang and Yio Chu Kang, the powerful smell of pig waste was unforgettable and was easily recognised in 1976 when I passed through the countryside of China.

It was a hot, sweaty campaign. I would make three to four speeches in one evening, driving from one ward to another, at meetings that started at 7 pm and had to stop at 10. Fortunately, I had given up smoking and never lost my voice, but on a sticky night I would be dripping with sweat by the time I had spoken in two, sometimes three languages – Malay, Mandarin and English. When the crowd was large, warm and responsive, I would exceed my allotted 30 minutes, always speaking late or last because the crowds would begin to drift away once the principal speaker had finished. Choo would have a fresh singlet and shirt for me to change into after each speech. And now I travelled in style because once we decided in February 1959 to fight to win, Choo had bought a Mercedes Benz 220 to replace the ageing Studebaker. She wanted us to be seen in it so nobody would doubt that I could afford a Mercedes without becoming prime minister, and she would accompany me to meetings, sometimes driving me herself.

The rallies were demoralising for the SPA and Liberal Socialist candidates. They attracted very poor crowds and did not hold any big mass rallies. The English-educated were comfortably off, not the type to stand around listening to speeches. The Chinese-speaking workers spent most of their time in the streets anyway because they had poor, comfortless homes, often no more than hot, stuffy cubicles. For them, our open-air meetings with speeches in the Chinese dialects and Mandarin were free entertainment and a harbinger of better things to come.

These big rallies could be colourful occasions. Elections bring out the diverse cultural habits and practices of our different races. The Chinese showed support for their candidates by presenting them personally with silk banners with elegant four- or eight-character aphorisms stitched onto them. A banner could measure up to three to four yards across and require as many people to come on stage to help the donor unfold and show to an admiring audience. After the candidate had received it with a ceremonial bow, there would be the souvenir photograph. A popular candidate could collect 50 to 100 Chinese banners, which, when hung up between strings of coloured bulbs, lent a rally a festive air. Each banner would display the name of the donor or donors, perhaps a clan society or a trade association that identified itself with the candidate and, having thus committed its members, would work to help him win.

The Indians presented garlands of fresh flowers, usually white frangipani or marigolds bound with strips of gold and silver tinsel, sometimes weighing as much as two pounds. On occasions, I have had six to 12 garlands placed around my neck by one supporter after another until my head was lost in the flowers, and my neck was severely strained. I was lucky I was not allergic to the flowers they used. (However, worse things can happen. Rajiv Gandhi, India's prime minister, was assassinated by a woman who came up to him at an election rally not only to garland him but also to detonate the explosives concealed on her person.)

The Malays presented *tanjak*, headdresses made from silk brocade woven with silver or gold thread and worn on ceremonial occasions by high-ranking chiefs. These were expensive and seldom given.

Addressing a crowd of about 2,000 workers on an open field just outside the Naval Base in Sembawang on 17 May, I stressed that they need not fear for their jobs when we took office. We were not seeking a separate independence for Singapore, and had therefore agreed that the British would retain sovereignty over their bases until we merged with the Federation of Malaya. This reassured the 45,000 civilian workers employed by the armed services, many of them Indians who had come from India with the British forces, and had the vote because they were British subjects.

At a lunchtime rally at Clifford Pier, I explained why we would keep the Preservation of Public Security Ordinance if we took office, emphasising that the real fight now would be between the PAP and the MCP. I recounted how Marshall had vacillated, been chased from pillar to post, and retreated in the face of each communist-led demonstration; how on the other hand Lim Yew Hock had used the big stick and the gun, until the British and their helicopters took over. I said bravely, "The PAP government will not fall into either of these errors. We shall not be intimidated or browbeaten, nor will we use repression as the means of government. We shall govern with the will and support of the people, firmly, wisely and justly." I wanted to avoid any charge of winning the election under false pretences.

Goode had kept in touch with me after the constitutional conference in London in May 1958, and on matters that concerned the future government he would always give me an opportunity to express my views. For example, he asked me what I thought of the choice of John Wyatt as chief justice to fill the gap until after the election, when the appointment would be in the hands of the new prime minister. The British did not want to make any appointment that we would later cancel or reverse. I did not object to any of them. His secretary, Pamela Hickley, would ring up Choo at Lee & Lee and ask if it was convenient for me to see the governor, usually around teatime. I would meet him in the office wing of Government House on the second floor (which I have occupied since 1971). We would talk for an hour over tea, poured English-fashion from a silver teapot through a strainer and served with fresh milk and sugar. The meetings continued even during the election campaign, when he once teased me with taking support away from Lim Yew Hock and the others like someone taking lollipops from a child. I warned him as the campaign heated up that it was impossible for us to keep to our policy statements in "The Tasks Ahead". The ground was getting worked up, and we had to go along with the mood. I assured him that we would remain firmly committed to our programme.

Polling day, Saturday, 30 May 1959, was quiet and orderly in contrast to the election in April 1955. Under the new laws I had persuaded Lim Yew Hock to pass, voting was compulsory, it was illegal to carry voters to polling stations in motorcars, there was no canvassing and no party workers were allowed to wear party symbols on their persons anywhere near or in the polling stations. There was no undue influence, intimidation, bribery or corruption. The polls closed at 8 pm; counting began at seven centres from 9 pm onwards, and ended at 2:45 am.

We won 43 out of 51 seats, with 53.4 per cent of the votes cast by 90 per cent of the electorate. The SPA won four, UMNO three and independents one (A.P. Rajah). Lim Yew Hock won in Cairnhill (against Marshall) and Hamid Jumat in Geylang Serai. I told a press conference, "The people's verdict is clear and decisive. It is a victory of right over wrong, clean over dirty, righteousness over evil." The candidate with the biggest majority was Ong Eng Guan, the former mayor. His Hong Lim voters in Chinatown fully approved of his excesses, and this solid endorsement added to his megalomania.

19. Taking Charge

It was a victory but I was not jubilant. I had begun to realise the weight of the problems that we were to face – unemployment, high expectations of rapid results, communist unrest, more subversion in the unions, schools and associations, more strikes, fewer investments, more unemployment, more trouble. Lim Chin Siong and Fong Swee Suan would soon work on the Chinese-speaking ground again to undermine us. When Lennox-Boyd sent his congratulations, I replied:

> "Few people know the perils of the journey that the state of Singapore has now embarked upon. How well we come out at the end of the next five years depends upon how well we plan and how hard we work, how well the United Kingdom government understands what is happening and why, and upon the gods, of which there are several varieties in this little island of 220 square miles. The first factor we determine, the second is for you, and the third I leave to the people of Singapore to make such incantations as will bring the blessings of the deities upon us."

There was to be a fourth factor – the attitude of our neighbours to the north. The first person to felicitate me publicly had been the prime minister of Malaya. "The people of Singapore have made their choice clear. I congratulate the PAP on winning such a large majority," he told the press. But that was not the Tunku; it was Dato (later Tun) Abdul Razak bin Hussain, who was standing in for him briefly while the Tunku was on leave. He was less diplomatic:

> "Their victory was expected. Other parties were divided and were not able to form a strong opposition to the PAP. I am glad that my

friend, Tun Lim Yew Hock, has won. He will at least provide a strong opposition to the government. On the other hand if the opposition is going to be effective, it must reunite even outside the council or otherwise the position will be the same."

I received many personal messages from people who had been sympathetic to me, including the prominent anti-colonial champion of the Fabian Society, Lady Hilda Selwyn-Clarke, who had told Singapore's Special Branch officer Richard Corridon that I was a good socialist, not a communist. James Callaghan, Labour MP and later British prime minister, a friend who had visited Singapore in the early 1950s and knew the area, warned in his letter of congratulations, "I know from my contacts here how touchy is the government of the Federation and you will have your work cut out to reassure them. Press reaction here has been mixed. There are fears from those who do not understand the situation."

We had done some hard thinking before the election and concluded that Lim Chin Siong and company must be released from prison before we took office, or we would lose all credibility. But having fought and won this election on our own, we were determined to start off the new government by holding our victory rally before they were released and the contest resumed.

We decided to hold it at the Padang on Wednesday, 3 June. I asked the governor to release the eight detainees the day after the rally, but before we took the oath of office. Goode wanted me to take office at once, but my concern was to have time to sort things out, get the British to agree to the release, settle my cabinet and hold the rally first. Goode protested that he had to refer to London about the release, which meant that with my timetable there would be a hiatus in government as Lim Yew Hock had resigned the moment the election was lost. He was unhappy about the delay, but I was not deterred. I urged him to give me the time I needed to put the non-communists in a stronger position before the next round began. I did not expect any immediate crisis. The following day, he told me he had London's agreement to release the detainees, but when he repeated that he wanted me to take office as early as possible, I said I had to consult my colleagues.

I met the central executive committee at the party's headquarters that afternoon for an hour, and returned to Government House at 4 pm. George Thomson, the director of Information Services, later issued a statement to the journalists waiting at the front gate. It said that after two meetings lasting two hours and "After consultations with Her Majesty's Government in Britain, and in order to have swift and smooth introduction of the new constitution, the governor, with the advice of the remaining ex-officio members of the council, decided to release the detainees concerned." Goode had meanwhile told me he could not wait for that to happen; he would gazette and bring into force the new constitution on 3 June. I again countered that we must be sworn in only on 5 June, after Lim Chin Siong, Fong and the six other pro-communists had not only been released but had duly issued a statement publicly endorsing the non-communist aims of the PAP. I wanted that endorsement to get full coverage in the press; we would therefore take office only on the afternoon of 5 June so as not to compete with it for the headlines. Goode disagreed, but I insisted, and had my way.

Our rally took place in front of City Hall on the night of 3 June without the pro-communists. We had 43 MPs-elect on the stage, all dressed in white to symbolise clean government – there would be none of the corruption that had been rife in the past in Singapore and existed in many other new countries. I introduced my new cabinet of nine, including myself. I made a serious, almost sombre speech. There was a huge crowd of some 50,000 on the Padang – orderly, expectant and in good humour. I chose the occasion to temper and dampen their hopes and to prepare my defences for the attacks I knew would come from the communists. They were bound to push for more freedom to subvert Singapore and to use their strength on the island to help the revolution in Malaya.

I outlined the government's position:

"We begin a new chapter. The powers of the people through their elected government are limited to our internal affairs. It is not what we really want but it is a step towards merger and *merdeka*. ... The good things of life do not fall from the skies. They can only come by hard work and over a long time. The government cannot produce results unless the people support and sustain the work of the government. ... There may be times when, in the interests of the whole community, we may have to take steps that are unpopular with a section of the community. On such occasions, remember that the principle which guides our actions is that the paramount interest of the whole community must prevail."

For the British community, I had this caution:

"Do you know, we wanted to use this Padang for our election rallies at night, but a small group of Europeans who were given this field by the former colonial government refused it, although they only use it in the day for a few people to play games? Well, times have changed and will stay changed."

In a significant speech on the English-educated, Keng Swee said they had been largely conditioned by the English-language press and the churches, especially the Catholic Church. As a class they had voted against the PAP, but they were few, and he warned them that in the course of time they would lose the privileges they had enjoyed under the British and would have to compete on equal terms with everyone else in Singapore. To survive, they must try to understand that the changes taking place were in response to tremendous social forces that lay beneath the surface, not the machinations of politicians.

The *Straits Times* and *Singapore Standard* had never published fair reports of our analysis of the causes of the political turmoil, and in consequence we had never been able to get the English-educated to understand that deep social, economic and political grievances were driving the Chinese-educated to support the communists and to help them overthrow the existing order. Now that we were the government, they had to listen, and the English-language press had to print what we said. So we began to get our message through, a process that started that night with Keng Swee's speech.

∽

On the eve of the rally, Dennis had gone to Changi to tell the detainees they would be freed on Thursday, and at 8:30 am on 4 June, Lim Chin Siong, Fong, Nair, Woodhull, Puthucheary and three others walked out of Changi Prison, to be greeted by 2,000 PAP and trade union supporters who had waited outside, waving banners. They were driven to party headquarters where they met the new central executive committee. At 11 am, they saw the press, Nair acting as their spokesman, and released the document they had signed.

The next day, the newspapers carried their statement:

> "To achieve complete identification with the ideal of a united Malayan nation, and to struggle by peaceful, democratic and constitutional means for the enduring objective of a united, independent, democratic and non-communist and socialist Malaya ... It would be a mistake to regard the non-inclusion of Singapore in the independent Federation of Malaya as being due solely to British chicanery. The British, of course, cannot escape their share of responsibility for this cruel amputation. ... The fact remains, however, that the exclusion of Singapore is also a reflection of the genuine fear of the Malay majority in the Federation that the Chinese majority in Singapore are incapable of a Malaya-centred loyalty, and cannot be assimilated into a Malaya-centred nationalism. ... It is up to us in Singapore to prove that the fears and suspicions of our Malay brethren across the Causeway are groundless."

When asked whether they supported the use of the Preservation of Public Security Ordinance, Nair replied, "Our stand is exactly the same

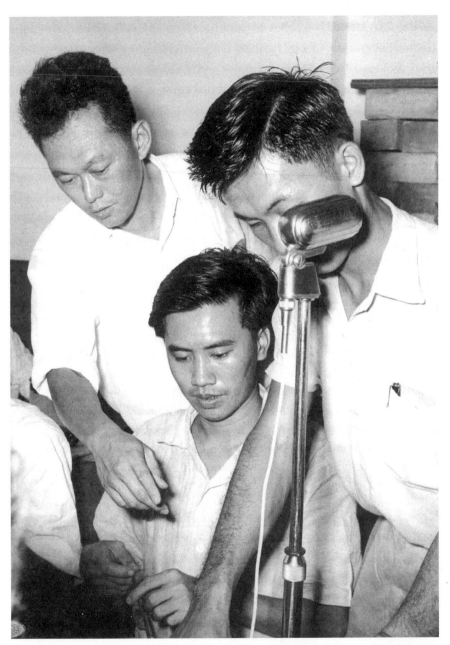

Lim Chin Siong (seated) and Fong Swee Suan at PAP headquarters, releasing their declaration to the press soon after they were freed on 4 June 1959.

as the PAP stand," i.e., that it would stay on the statute books as long
as the Federation of Malaya had laws providing for detention without
trial. As I expected of Nair, the press reports were clear and unequivocal.
But I knew that Lim Chin Siong was not sincere. For him, this was only
a tactical manoeuvre. I hoped that Fong, whom Nair had spent many
hours winning over, would not drift back to Lim. But I could not be
certain. I tried to neutralise them by giving them prominent but powerless
posts – Puthucheary as manager of a new Industrial Promotion Board,
and the other four as political secretaries to different ministers.

These developments were watched closely by the British, who were
anxious to see how the newly elected PAP ministers would shape up in
office. Bill Goode sent Lennox-Boyd, on 12 June 1959, a report on the
election that made interesting reading 40 years on:

"... The PAP concentrated on presenting themselves as a democratic
socialist party which had constructive ideas, and the honesty, energy
and the ability to govern. Their party platform laid great emphasis
on the need to strive for independence through merger with the
Federation of Malaya and the need for harmony amongst all racial
communities in Singapore. They advocated Malay as the common
language to break down communal barriers and put up nine (sic)
Malay candidates. A distinctive feature of their programme was
stress on the need for reorganisation of the government machine
and other public institutions, in particular to abolish the City
Council, in order to eliminate 'red tape, bureaucracy and unnecessary duplication of functions'. In party speeches, candidates
developed various of these themes (sic) to suit the audience. In
doing so, there were often references of a less constructive character
to the alleged shortcomings of other parties, and to the alleged
hostility of the English-language newspapers, of the English-
educated population and of the 'White' businessmen. Condemnation of the Western powers or criticism of the United Kingdom
government were virtually nonexistent in any quarter. ...

"The split of the moderate vote undoubtedly lost the opposition many seats. In 13 constituencies a PAP candidate was returned on a minority vote, ... After the election the PAP publicly admitted that they had not succeeded in winning either the Malay or the English-speaking vote. The Malays generally were frightened of the PAP as Chinese extremists, and were not won over by the bold undertaking of the PAP to make Malay the national language nor by the PAP putting up nine (sic) Malay candidates. In election rallies the top PAP leaders made every effort to win over the English-speaking white-collar workers of the City. Nevertheless, the main residential and suburban areas either returned an SPA candidate or were only won by the PAP owing to the moderate vote being split between the SPA and the Liberal Socialists or an Independent. ...

"Most of the PAP assemblymen are young, many being in their 20s. The average age of the Assembly is 35, and the youngest member a PAP shop assistant aged 22. Three previous ministers, J.M. Jumabhoy, Francis Thomas and M.P.D. Nair, were defeated by PAP candidates in their 20s, Jumabhoy's defeat being all the less palatable in that his successful opponent was a 25-year-old girl, the assistant secretary of the Women's Section of the PAP. ...

"The new Legislative Assembly will thus be dominated by the PAP majority. The following are their professions." (Goode then gave the list: it included among others five teachers, four journalists, eight trade unionists, two hairdressers and a farmer.) "Another change which is more significant is that the first three ministers are establishing their offices in City Hall."

We had indeed decided to make a break with the past by moving the seat of government from Empress Place to City Hall. It was where Ong Eng Guan had started his mayorship amid much tumult and commotion – but had given the underprivileged of Singapore the hope that the PAP government would have their interests at heart and would be honest in trying to advance them.

My colleagues and I were sworn into office on Friday afternoon, 5 June 1959, in the City Hall chamber where Mountbatten had taken the

Leading the PAP government after it had been sworn in at City Hall, June 1959.

surrender of the Japanese military commanders in Southeast Asia in 1945 – and where, just 12 years later, Mayor Ong had thrown out that symbol of British colonial authority, the mace. I decided to superimpose on that image the imprint of the new cabinet. Protocol had hitherto required ministers to present themselves at Government House in lounge suits, to be sworn in by the governor in his white ceremonial dress uniform, complete with a white plumed hat. This time, the governor came from Government House to City Hall for the occasion. He wore nothing more formal than a light fawn suit and tie. We wore open-necked white shirts and trousers. I greeted him at the bottom of the steps and walked with him into the chamber, which was bare except for one table and a few chairs – there had been no time for decorations. Apart from the press, there were 200 party supporters who had worked hard during the election, also in white. But no wives were present, a grievance Choo holds against me to this day. She, too, had worked very hard and expected to be there. I said it would lead to trouble with the other wives, and anyway it was just a minor ceremony. She was not placated. But I could not give way.

After he had sworn us in, Goode, as the first Yang di-Pertuan Negara (head of state) and the last governor of Singapore, extended his congratulations. I replied, "It has been our good fortune, in the last few days, to have had the opportunity to deal with someone most conversant with the hopes and aspirations of our people and the limitations of our situation. ... I hope that in the next six months of your office you will assist us in taking over effectively, smoothly and peacefully the reins of governing Singapore."

After we were sworn in, everyone was keen to get cracking, to get to grips with his job and earn as much credit for us as possible before the euphoria wore off. We feared the communists would soon be busy eroding public support, with Lim Chin Siong and Fong fomenting industrial and social unrest. I knew from experience that enthusiasm was not enough. To give of their best, the ministers had to have air-conditioned offices. That may sound odd, but without air-conditioning, efficient work in tropical Singapore would not have been feasible. After my first year at Laycock & Ong, I was made to sit in the main office. The heat, humidity and noise were hellish, especially in the afternoons. My energy was sapped, the clerks would work at only half the normal pace, typists would make mistakes, and lawyers more errors in correcting them, as well as in dictation. The high court was even worse, for we had to appear with wing collars and tabs and wear a black jacket under our barrister's robes – a dress originally designed for the dank and cold of a London winter. A turning point in my life in terms of comfort and efficiency came in 1954, when Choo and I installed a one-horse-power air-conditioner in the bedroom. Thereafter, we never lost sleep because of the humid heat. So I encouraged air-conditioning for all government offices.

I took over the mayor's office on the second floor of City Hall, sharing with Chin Chye, as deputy prime minister, a general office, a reception room and a conference room; for ease of communication, my secretary occupied the room between us. But Ong Eng Guan did not want to be with us in City Hall; he chose instead public housing premises in his own Hong Lim constituency as headquarters for his ministry of national development. I did not closely examine the reasons for this, and therefore agreed. I did not know that the building was totally unsuitable for a government office and needed extensive renovation; walls had to be knocked down, plumbing and electrical wiring changed, tables, filing cabinets and safes moved up narrow staircases or in small lifts. But these were minor considerations for Ong, administrative details that he ignored in his quest for a separate centre of power. He did not want to share the glory of City Hall with Chin Chye and me. It was only months later that I realised that his megalomania was undiminished. He wanted to outdo everyone else in the cabinet, to keep himself in the public eye as he had when he was mayor. To this end, he announced plans for big expenditure without first clearing them with the finance minister or the cabinet, much to the consternation of other ministers.

Keng Swee had assumed the finance portfolio and moved into Fullerton Building. He was familiar with the workings of the civil service and got started early. Finance was our most important ministry, and I allowed him to have his pick of government officers. For permanent secretary he chose Hon Sui Sen, my good friend since the days of the Japanese occupation, then commissioner of lands. He was to prove a tower of strength.

It was fortunate we could call on men like Sui Sen. We had so much on our plate, so little time, and such scanty resources. So little time, because I expected at most a year's honeymoon before the communists reorganised and turned the heat on us. And scanty resources because there was little in the kitty.

∞

Within a few days, Keng Swee reported that the last government had dipped into the reserves and used up $200 million. He foresaw a budget deficit of more than $14 million for 1959. There could be minor savings but they would not exceed $5 million. Ministers should therefore be warned that there was absolutely no way to finance development schemes over and above what had already been allowed for, and even those would have to be ruthlessly pruned. The steps necessary to balance the budget would prove unpopular not only with the public but also with ministers, but it was imperative that we did not end up in the red in our first year of government.

I agreed, and told him that we had better take the unpopular measures early in our term. On 12 June, the newspapers reported that the finance ministry had ordered that no further expenditure was to be incurred without the finance minister's approval. Among the items likely to be affected were the government's charitable contributions, advances to civil servants for buying cars, and disbursements for scholarships, fellowships and training courses abroad. But that would not yield much. Keng Swee proposed that we cut our own ministerial salaries from $2,600 to $2,000 a month to set an example, and also reduce the variable allowances of civil servants. Again, I agreed. We held a meeting of the General Purposes Committee of the Civil Service Joint Council, but the staff side would not accept the proposal because they had no mandate from their unions. We discussed this in cabinet and decided to proceed anyway. The government announced that allowances would be scaled down from 1 July, but that it would receive representations on the subject from staff unions and associations.

It was a significant but not devastating pay cut, and affected only 6,000 of the 14,000 government servants. All personnel drawing $220 a month and above would lose a part of their variable allowances, but only 10 per cent of them would suffer cuts of more than $250 a month, and only a handful the maximum of $400. The 8,000 employees in the lower income brackets would not be touched. We had to take action quickly if we were to set the tone for thrift and financial discipline right from the start. There was great unhappiness, especially among the senior officers. The English-educated believed we had set out to punish them for having voted against us. That was not our motive. We wanted to show everyone in Singapore, especially the Chinese-educated majority, that for the public good, the English-educated were prepared to make sacrifices, led by the ministers. I thought it not unreasonable that they make this sacrifice to help us get the message across that, in this new era, we would all share hardships and joys equally.

There was another good reason for the cuts. Since 1952, I on behalf of the unions, and Keng Swee and Kenny on behalf of the civil servants, had successfully pressed the government for more and more pay and allowances with scant regard for the economic situation. If the unions carried on like that, we would be in trouble. There was no better way to signal that those days were over. The annual saving would be $12 million. Keng Swee refuted estimates by the newspapers that it would be $20 or $25 million and reminded them that for the remaining six months of 1959 it would thus be only $6 million, reducing the expected deficit from $14 million to $8 million.

A few days later, he announced a freeze on all new appointments, which meant vacancies in government could not be filled without the approval of the minister.

The civil service unions were up in arms. They organised a Council of Joint Action to confront us, just as we had confronted the British colonial government, and to fight for the restoration of full allowances. But we were not a colonial government on the defensive; for the moment at least, the Chinese-speaking majority were solidly behind us, and the council never took off. I was nevertheless exasperated by their reaction. They showed little appreciation of the grave challenges before us, and the fact that we had to prevent the communists from exploiting the grievances of the Chinese-speaking, whose voting strength was now decisive. Some of the senior officers had to give up their maids – too bad, but the country was facing greater hardships and perils, and we had to convince people that this government would govern in the interests of all. Only then would we be able to tackle the lack of a Malayan consciousness among the Chinese, and imbue them with a commitment and loyalty to the country of their adoption; and this was all-important, for they had to change their attitude before the Malay leaders in Kuala Lumpur would agree to merger and enable Singapore to achieve independence as part of Malaya.

When I made my first speech in the Assembly as prime minister on 22 July, I warned, "If the PAP government fails, it will not be the opposition that will be returned to power. They will be fleeing for their lives. Because behind us there is no alternative that is prepared to work the democratic system. In the last analysis, if we fail, brute force returns." I said that we therefore needed the civil servants to cooperate with us in order to deliver what we had promised to the people.

> "Why should we like to hurt and injure people who must work with us? Under the democratic system, there is a civil service that does the bidding of the party that has the mandate of the people. ... If nothing more catastrophic happens than the loss of allowances ... government servants should go down on their bended knees and thank God that their souls have been spared."

Because of history, the English-educated had an important role to play, I said, adding, "They can help us in bridging the gulf between the colonial past and the egalitarian future." If we failed to close the chasm between the Chinese-speaking and the English-educated elite, the result would be painful. For if the Chinese-educated won power, the English-educated would suddenly become the new dispossessed under a government that would be conducted in Chinese.

From time to time, I continued to berate the English-educated and prod them into changing to meet the future. We – Keng Swee, Chin Chye, Kenny, Raja and I – were English-educated and their natural leaders. We did not want them to be a dying breed; together we must carry at least half of the Chinese-speaking with us if they were not to finish us off. But the English-educated were so depoliticised that they did not understand the danger they were in. Although the cuts were fully restored in 1961, the affected civil servants remained resentful for a long time, and had it not been for the tumultuous events that later overtook us, they would have voted solidly against the PAP in the 1963 election. As it was, the threat from the communists was by then so obvious that they could not but support us.

By the end of the year, we were able to balance the budget, and revenue did not continue to fall, as Keng Swee had feared. If I had to pronounce on it again, I would still agree to the cuts, but only one-third as severe. That would have made the point with the Chinese-speaking, and although the English-educated government servants would still be unhappy, they would not have been so shaken. The episode, however, had shown up their lack of political understanding and the need to reorient them, to make them aware of the dangers and difficulties ahead. It confirmed the decision Keng Swee, Kenny and I had taken before we took office, to set up a political study centre to teach top-ranking civil servants about the communist threat and our social and economic problems. To be successful, however, we had to win their confidence and convince them they were not simply being brainwashed.

We chose George Thomson to run the centre. Thomson was in his 40s. He had a good mind, was well read, and was an earnest speaker in his strong Scots accent. He had been a lecturer in history, and an effective one because he was full of enthusiasm for whatever he taught. He understood what we wanted and soon grasped the part he had to play. He chose as his assistant Gerald de Cruz, a former communist who had broken away from the MCP because he could not accept their discipline and disagreed with their policies. He had ended up as paid secretary of the Labour Front, working for Marshall and then for Lim Yew Hock.

As finance minister in charge of personnel, Keng Swee took a large colonial government bungalow in Goodwood Hill for the study centre. I opened it on 15 August. Its objects, I said, were:

> "not only to stimulate your minds but also to inform you of the acute problems that confront any popularly elected government in a revolutionary situation ... Once these problems have been posed to you, you will be better able to help us work out the solutions to them, by making the administration more sensitive and responsive to the needs and mood of the people."

Some of my ministers and I came to the centre to give it a practical approach by discussing real situations we had to wrestle with immediately. At first the civil servants were sceptical, but the lecturers were obviously not communists, and they quickly got over their initial suspicion that this was an exercise in Marxist indoctrination. Because the teachers were of a similar cast of mind as their own, they accepted that the government was on the level, that the problems were real and seemingly intractable, and that we wanted them to work with us to find and implement solutions. Thomson did a good job and over the next four to five years educated the senior echelons of the civil service in the theory of communism, the possible democratic answers to the social ills that fostered its growth, and the practice of guerrilla insurgency. They came to understand what was happening in the wider world, the causes of revolution in Southeast Asia, and the need for a fundamental shift in attitudes and policies to meet the challenges. But for a long time, our relations with them remained uneasy.

One problem I had anticipated was getting used to power. I had seen what happened with Ong Eng Guan in the City Council, how the underdog had misused it when he became the top dog. I warned my ministers, parliamentary secretaries and assemblymen who were assigned to help ministers deal with public complaints not to get drunk on power and not to abuse it. It was easier said than done, and on many occasions we still antagonised civil servants.

We were determined to strike while the iron was hot and exploit our post-election popularity. We mounted a series of well-publicised campaigns to clean the streets of the city, clear the beaches of debris and cut the weeds on unkempt vacant land. It was a copycat exercise borrowed from the communists – ostentatious mobilisation of everyone including ministers to toil with their hands and soil their clothes in order to serve the people. We saw no reason why the MCP should have the monopoly of such techniques and organised drives to enthuse the people and involve them in setting higher standards in civic consciousness, general cleanliness and the preservation of public property. One Sunday, Ong

Setting an example to keep Singapore clean soon after the PAP took office.

Eng Guan would muster government servants to clean up Changi beach. On another, I would take a broom to sweep the city streets with the community leaders.

There were other things we wanted to do. Keng Swee and I planned and formed the People's Association, a statutory board that would embrace all the important voluntary social organisations, clubs and associations for sports, music, ballet, drawing and cooking. We built over one hundred community centres – big ones in the city, small wooden huts in the rural areas – places for education and recreation. Table tennis, basketball, badminton, Chinese chess, lessons in repairing radios and refrigerators and courses in technical trades were some of the activities. We wanted to give people something positive to do, and get them lined up on the side of law and order. Each centre would have a full-time organising secretary to administer it and cater to the needs of those who lived around it. To supervise the centres, the Social Welfare Department would be transformed into a community development department.

We organised a Works Brigade to take in unemployed young men and women, put them in semi-military uniforms, house them in wooden barracks and teach them farming, road building, bricklaying and construction work – generally to put some discipline into them and, most important, to get them off the streets.

But we also had to discipline those already in work, for we badly needed to establish a grip on the unions under communist control to stop their political strikes. We therefore set up an arbitration court. In the 1950s, the Australians had good industrial relations, largely thanks to compulsory arbitration procedures that kept tempers in check. At our request, they sent the permanent secretary of their ministry of labour, Harry Bland, to help us. After the court was set up, the minister could order any major strike, especially one in essential services like public transport or public utilities, to be referred to arbitration. Once referred, it was illegal for a union to continue the stoppage pending the outcome, and if it persisted, it would face deregistration. Before a strike, moreover, there had to be a secret ballot, not just the show of hands at the end of a rabble-rousing speech, which I had too often seen.

On the other hand, we shared the view of the communists that one reason for the backwardness of China and the rest of Asia, except Japan, was that women had not been emancipated. They had to be put on a par with the men, given the same education and enabled to make their full contribution to society. During the election campaign, we had used one of our allotted party broadcasts in four languages – English, Malay, Mandarin and Tamil – to put over our policy on women's rights. But we could not find a PAP woman member who was a good enough speaker to take on the programme in English. After Choo had auditioned the wives of two candidates in Lee & Lee's office, she came into my room, where I was in discussion with Keng Swee and Raja, to tell me that they sounded too soft, not tough enough. When she left us, my two friends suggested that she should do it. I asked her, and after a moment's hesitation, she agreed. Raja wrote the first draft, which she amended so that it would sound like her. It was cleared by the central executive committee and translated into the other languages, and she delivered it in English over Radio Malaya. One paragraph was crucial:

"Our society is still built on the assumption that women are the social, political and economic inferiors of men. This myth has been made the excuse for the exploitation of female labour. Many women do the same kind of work as men but do not get the same pay. ... We are fielding five women candidates in the election. ... Let us show them (the other parties) that Singapore women are tired of their pantomime and buffoonery. I appeal to women to vote for PAP. It is the only party with the idealism, the honesty and ability to carry out its election programme."

This was a serious commitment, or I would not have agreed to my wife making it in a broadcast. I wanted to implement it early, although it meant urgent work for the legal draftsmen in the attorney-general's chambers. They searched for precedents in the legislation of other countries, and drew up the Women's Charter, which we passed into law within a year. It established monogamy as the only legal marital condition and made polygamy, hitherto an accepted practice, a crime – except among Muslims, whose religion allowed a man to have four wives. The charter was comprehensive and altered the status of women. But it did not change the cultural bias of parents against daughters in favour of sons. That has still not been achieved.

There were, in addition, several easy, popular points to be scored that required no planning, including a series of "anti-yellow culture" prohibitions imposed by Pang Boon as minister for home affairs. "Yellow culture" was a literal translation of the Mandarin phrase for the decadent and degenerate behaviour that had brought China to its knees in the 19th century: gambling, opium-smoking, pornography, multiple wives and concubines, the selling of daughters into prostitution, corruption and nepotism. This aversion to "yellow culture" had been imported by schoolteachers from China, who infused into our students and their parents the spirit of national revival that was evident in every chapter of the textbooks they brought with them, whether on literature, history or geography. And it was reinforced by articles of left-wing Chinese newspaper journalists enthralled by the glowing reports of a clean, honest, dynamic, revolutionary China.

Pang Boon moved quickly, outflanking the communists with puritanical zeal. He ordered a clean-up of Chinese secret society gangsters, and outlawed pornography, striptease shows, pin-table saloons, even decadent songs. It did no harm apart from adding somewhat to unemployment and making Singapore less attractive to tourists. But the seamen who had always been a part of Singapore's transient population soon found their way to the amenities still offered in the more obscure corners of the island to which we turned a blind eye. Prostitution continued discreetly; we left it alone because we could not ban it without taking silly and ineffective action.

Our most significant programme was to give every child a place in school within a year. My gum-making brother-in-law, Yong Nyuk Lin, now minister for education, did us proud: in 12 months, he doubled the intake of students, converting each school into two by splitting it to provide a morning and an afternoon session. He ran a crash programme to train the teachers needed, and promoted many of the seniors to be principals, headmasters and headmistresses. He also started adult education classes to teach Malay, now the national language, and launched a Chinese literacy drive, using Mandarin as the common language of all Chinese dialect groups. People wanted to feel they were improving themselves and their prospects, and we gave them the means. We adopted the proven methods of our communist adversaries. As with the mass campaigns, we saw no reason why we should give the MCP a monopoly of such techniques.

20. Glimpses of Troubles Ahead

I was uneasy about taking power at the age of 35. I had no experience of administration – not even of my law office, which I left to Choo and Dennis. I decided to acquaint myself with the structure of the government and obtain an overview of the ministries. I wanted to get the feel of the senior staff, the nature of their work, their attitudes and work style, so that I would know how much had to be changed if we were to solve our political, economic and social problems. I also wanted to assess the resources of each ministry and redeploy them so as to strengthen the most important.

The first I visited was finance, for without financial resources, nothing could be implemented, and the next was home affairs. We needed to have good intelligence on the communists, to be sensitive and effective in dealing with them, and, if possible, to pre-empt their moves. I wanted to know if we had competent men in charge who could help us with the information, the analysis, the thinking and planning necessary to work out a counter-strategy to foil them. And at street level, I wanted the police to be disciplined, but also firm, decisive and robust once we decided to break up a demonstration or an incipient riot. I was determined that they should not act in the dumb, blunt way they had under Lim Yew Hock, when they were simply trained men doing an unpleasant duty and allowed the communists to score all the points with the Chinese-speaking.

I visited the home affairs ministry in October, some four months after taking office, and spoke first to the senior police officers to boost their morale. I told them that I expected trouble from the communists in about a year, after they had regrouped. I wanted them to be well prepared to meet it. The commissioner of police, Alan Blades, was a tall, taciturn man with a white goatee and glasses. A former director of Special Branch who had not done much work as a uniformed police officer, he was well aware of the danger the communists posed, and probably thought I was too close to them for my own good – a view shared by several of his senior officers. I do not know how long it was before he concluded that I knew what I was about, and that I was deadly serious when I said we had to counter them without losing out massively with the Chinese-speaking.

From the police headquarters at Pearl's Hill, I went to the Criminal Investigation Department, and then on to Special Branch to meet the newly appointed director, John Linsell. Linsell had spent most of his career as a uniformed police officer and was more at home with riot control than intelligence-gathering. He did not strike me as having that subtlety of mind necessary to understand communist tactics and strategy. I therefore decided to see him together with his senior staff for regular weekly meetings so that I would hear directly from the officers who were experts in security without Linsell filtering out important nuances. This paid dividends. Two officers, Richard Corridon and Ahmad Khan, were to prove most valuable; without their shrewd and perceptive analysis of information on the communists and experienced handling of sensitive situations, the government would have been much worse off.

My visit to Special Branch was worthwhile. On one unforgettable day in October, I was shown a bundle of files with covers printed in bold red type: "Arrest On Sight". They contained mugshots of important MCP leaders, each accompanied by a short write-up giving essential details of the subject. As I had expected, a photo of Eu Chooi Yip was among them. Very able, completely bilingual in English and Chinese, Eu was a Raffles College graduate, a contemporary of Hon Sui Sen who had visited Sui Sen at my house during the Japanese occupation. He was already a radical left-winger then, and as I later learnt, he was the Plen's party superior.

A few pages on, my heart missed a beat though I hoped my face did not show it. I was looking at the Plen himself. I did not pause too long, but long enough to take in the key facts. He was Fang Chuang Pi, had been educated at Chinese High School, and worked at *Nan Chiao News*, a pro-communist paper shut down soon after the Emergency began. I realised at once from the name that he must be the elder brother of Fung Yin Ching. Fung (Fang in Mandarin) was 25, an active, innocent-looking, sincere, hardworking Chinese middle school girl we had fielded in the election. She was now the PAP assemblywoman for Stamford.

Within two weeks of my taking office, Yong Pung How arrived unannounced at my home early one morning while I was having my bath. The maid mistook him for a Chinese student and told him he should go to the office. At that moment, Choo saw him on the veranda and invited him to wait in the sitting room. He refused breakfast but talked while I had mine. He had come from Kuala Lumpur to ask whether I could make a statement sympathetic to the MCA about their problems with UMNO, their Malay partner in the ruling Alliance coalition. He had just been elected chairman of the MCA's publicity committee at a time when there was rising tension in the Federation over the question of Chinese education. The Chinese felt under threat, for the UMNO leaders seemed to have made up their minds to take over and exercise complete power in the country, with only nominal participation of the non-Malay communities. Since Yong knew me well, the MCA president had proposed that he should get me to express support for their cause. They thought that, as the prime minister of Singapore and the leader of the PAP, I had standing and influence among the Chinese in Malaya, whereas the MCA felt itself pathetically weak.

I was greatly upset and troubled that my old friend wanted me to take a position that would antagonise the Tunku and UMNO. I told him that while I had sympathy for the MCA, it was simply out of the question for me to annoy the Tunku and UMNO in any way, since Singapore's primary objective was merger with Malaya. Thirty-six years later, Yong remembered the incident clearly. He said that I repeatedly stressed, "I have to think of Singapore first." He was not too disappointed, because he had anticipated my reaction. He knew that I was direct and open with him. But I should have listened more carefully to him instead of regarding his request as an unwelcome intrusion into my plans. I should have seen the significance of such strong communal attitudes for Singapore if it was to become a part of Malaysia. If I had inquired into the background to the education problem, I would have had early warning of the kind of major concessions we must be prepared to make if we were going to work with the Malay leaders in the Federation.

∞

While the danger of communist penetration of government and administration was ever-present, our main concern during this period was with those who could not join it – the Chinese-educated of Nanyang University.

For years the idea of a Chinese university had been in gestation as the achievements of the People's Republic of China aroused resurgent pride in its language and culture. The intelligentsia, with the support of the Chinese press, stirred up demand for a university teaching in Chinese. During the colonial era the Chinese disdained the artificial boundaries imposed by its white masters on most of Southeast Asia, and referred to the whole region as Nanyang, or the "South Seas". Because Singapore was predominantly Chinese, it had become a centre for Chinese education. But there was as yet no Chinese university.

The rubber boom during the Korean War in the early 1950s made our merchants rich. When Tan Lark Sye, a rubber baron and chairman of the Singapore Hokkien Huay Kuan, the association of the largest Chinese dialect group, in January 1953 proposed the founding of a

Chinese university, there was widespread and spontaneous support. In May that year the Nanyang Company Limited was registered under the Companies Ordinance. The Hokkien Huay Kuan donated 500 acres of poor quality rubber land in Jurong, a rural area in the west of the island. The Chinese-speaking working class, trishaw riders, hawkers, taxi drivers and ordinary workers, contributed one day's earnings.

In March 1956 Nanyang University was inaugurated with an enrolment of 584 students in three colleges teaching arts, science and commerce in Chinese. This meant more political problems because, without English, the graduates would be unemployable. We also knew it would be only a matter of time before the university, both staff and students, would be captured by the communists, just as the Chinese middle schools had been.

In his last months as chief minister, Lim Yew Hock had appointed a commission with Dr S.L. Prescott of the University of Western Australia as chairman. The commission presented us with a report recommending that the government should not recognise Nanyang University degrees because the standards were too low. This report immediately provoked a furore in the Chinese-speaking community, whose business leaders took it as a slight on their competence – richly deserved, because they had been directing and interfering in the work of the academics, which should have been left to a senate.

In particular, Tan Lark Sye, as chairman of the University Council, was very angry with us. To show his defiance, he appointed Dr Chuang Chu Lin, the pro-communist headmaster of Chung Cheng High School who had been dismissed from his post, to be vice-chancellor of the university, and to cock another snook at the government, he increased the student enrolment for that year. We knew this would give the MCP greater freedom to use the university as a breeding ground, but we were not then in a position to intervene without paying a high political price. I made a mental note to deal with Tan at a later date.

It was my first lesson on the difference between formal constitutional power and the political strength needed to exercise it. Nyuk Lin had submitted a draft bill to the cabinet designed to strip Tan of his ability to meddle with the administration by giving the government the same authority over Nantah (Chinese abbreviation for Nanyang University) as it had over the University of Malaya in Singapore. We roared with laughter in cabinet at the simplicity of this solution. Nyuk Lin had come straight into office after 20 years in the insurance business, and although he proved to be an energetic minister, he had no idea what a hot potato he was handling. I would never forget Sunday, 30 March 1958, when the whole 14-mile route from Nantah down to Bukit Timah Road and the city was one long line of cars inching forward, all heading for the cere-monial opening of the university. I could feel the tremendous emotional commitment of our Chinese-speaking people to this project. Nyuk Lin's proposed bill would have caused riots in the Chinese middle schools.

So we shelved the problem, and it was not until the late 1960s, after we had separated from Malaysia, that we had the political strength to impose administrative discipline on the university's financial accounting, staff appointments and student conduct. To reduce the tension in the interim and buy some time, we appointed a second committee of local academics to review the Prescott report, only to find in February 1960 that they came to the same conclusions. But it would have been politically unacceptable to allow the first batch of Nantah graduates to be without hope of government recognition and employment. We discussed this carefully in cabinet and decided that we had to give a few of them a chance to enter the public service, but at a lower level than University of Malaya graduates.

I drove down the then winding Jurong Road to Nantah in October 1959 to speak to its one thousand students. The first batch of 400 wanted jobs, and I said the government would absorb 70 graduates – 50 for the education service, 20 in other departments. The performance of these

SINGAPORE · POLICE

$2,000 REWARD

The above reward will be paid by the Commissioner of Police, Singapore, to any person or divided amongst persons giving information leading to the arrest of the undermentioned Chinese.

FANG CHUANG PI alias **FONG CHONG PEK**

English and Chinese speaking male Teochiu, age about 24 years, Height 5′ 5″. Slim build. One time reporter of "Nan Chiao Jit Pao".

The information may be given at any time and any place either verbally or in writing, to any Police Officer or by letter addressed to P.O. Box 5000. The identity of the informant will not be disclosed.

This offer of reward is valid until 30th October, 1951.

Dated 17th July, 1951
Ref: No. SSB(P)6949.

Reward Notice No. 12 51

A 1951 Special Branch poster offering reward for information on Fang Chuang Pi, the "Plen", then in the communist underground.

70 would determine the future of those that followed. "If the first batch proves your worth as able and disciplined workers, prepared to compete on par with the English-educated and make your contribution to society, then you will get your worth recognised." We also gave suitable candidates scholarships for postgraduate study in universities abroad, particularly in science and engineering. We believed this would mollify the brighter ones and test their real worth. They were pacified, but only for the time being. The communists continued to burrow away with unremitting energy and they were winning recruits every day.

While our mass support from the Chinese-educated was threatened by the communists, our meagre support from the English-educated white-collar workers was at an all-time low. As I had feared, the running-in process caused more gears to crash. I had put Chin Chye in charge of the Singapore Polytechnic, as he was particularly interested in technical education. That, however, proved two-edged. On finding its courses irrelevant to our anticipated needs, he denounced the board of governors and the principal; and when he summarily dismissed the governors, the principal resigned. This provoked bewilderment and fear, because the staff had no security of tenure, and the teachers, most of them white expatriates, started to look for jobs elsewhere. So did the staff of the Singapore Improvement Trust, the housing authority under the former government, where Ong Eng Guan behaved in his usual autocratic way. Ong continually harassed and tormented white officers. He had told Keng Swee how to "do in" expatriates who held high positions in the City Council, which was still under his control as minister for national development. From above, they would meet resistance from his own trusted lieutenants, while from below he would instigate the clerks and other subordinates to make life difficult for them. Sooner or later, they would capitulate and leave without compensation.

Ong had a deputy secretary called Val Meadows, a most capable officer, stout-hearted, with a distinguished war record. Meadows had been deputy secretary to Hamid Jumat when he was minister for local government, and had drafted Hamid's replies to Ong when they were locked in the altercation that culminated in his suspending the Mayor's powers. Ong bore Meadows a grudge.

Meadows recounted 36 years later that he was "utterly unprepared for the degree of hostility" he encountered. He was physically banished to the southern islands to see what could be done for their improvement and development. As he had already prepared plans for clinics, wells, piers, pathways, schools, community centres and fishing cooperatives when he was with Hamid, this was done expeditiously. But instead of being complimented, he was evicted from his office in the ministry in his absence. When he returned one Saturday morning to write his reports, he found to his utter amazement that it had vanished. Wooden frames and panels, doors, glass windows, air-conditioner, desk, office equipment – all had disappeared without trace, leaving a void in their place. The permanent secretary told him he had acted on ministerial orders. Meadows could use the communal clerical office. At that moment, Ong walked in to savour his discomfiture, but Meadows made a studied effort not to overreact. The following Monday, he handed in his resignation, but was told by the head of the establishment office to hang on as a rescue operation was "in train". That was my taking the portfolio away from Ong and instructing Val Meadows to discharge his duties from my office.

Ong had already made several other mistakes, and the whole cabinet and a large number of the assemblymen had concluded that he was going to be a liability and not an asset to the government. Keng Swee had earlier complained to me in writing that he had asked for $415 million for public housing without submitting any detailed plans or explaining how they were going to be achieved. I therefore moved to take the City Council away from him, instructing him to distribute its various components to other relevant government ministries. Ironically, the excuse given to the public was that he needed to concentrate on public housing, and for the sake of appearances, I also adjusted the portfolio of another ministry.

I made Val Meadows my deputy secretary and put him in charge of breaking up the City Council, creating a statutory board to take over its departments for public utilities, water, electricity and gas, and sorting out what to do with the others. I wanted to signal to expat officers and civil servants generally that I did not approve of what had happened and that I was not afraid of being dubbed their puppet.

I was reluctant to act against Ong, but not because I feared he would displace me. I had not coveted my job as prime minister; whoever held it was going to be the prime target when the communists opened fire, and I did not relish that prospect. I knew Ong would not have the courage to take them on. I had seen him blanch when they targetted him at a party conference in August 1957 and got him voted out of the central executive committee. Later, although he was the minister with the most support among the Chinese-speaking, he declined to move the extension of the Preservation of Public Security Ordinance as the cabinet wanted, and it was left to Chin Chye to make the firm speech we had settled. But Ong was still our best Hokkien speaker. If we downgraded him, we would lower his public standing and be hard put to find someone to replace him.

Ong, the economy, the civil servants, the communists, the language difficulties – these immediate problems allowed little time for us to stand back and evaluate our own performance. But there was one man who was deeply involved, yet could make a dispassionate assessment of our first six months in office, and his last six months in Singapore – Bill Goode, the former governor, who for six months was the transitory head of state, the Yang di-Pertuan Negara. He summed up the PAP's first days in three reports to his secretary of state. His first, on 26 June, started on an optimistic note:

"The new ministers are intelligent men. They have given much thought to their political programme which was put to the electorate in carefully prepared speeches. They are extreme socialists by conviction, but they realise the practical limitations imposed by Singapore's peculiar circumstances as an international trading centre. They also realise the gravity of the economic problem presented by a rapidly increasing population expecting a high standard of living in a city which depends for its income upon winning business against keen competition. Above all else, they are obsessed by the threat of communism.

"To succeed they must retain the support of the Chinese working and student classes. In this lies their weakness, since they will be obliged to indulge in popular gestures which will antagonise the business and commercial class upon whom they depend for economic progress. Their obsession with the political and ideological struggle to win the minds of the masses to democratic socialism in preference to communism is likely to prejudice a competent approach to the other problems of making Singapore's economy work. ...

"The ministers have also decided to restrict attendance at social functions. The general impression which they are trying to foster is that of sober dignified dedication to the task of governing for the benefit of the masses.

"They (therefore) call themselves non-communist and are at pains to show that they are not puppets of the West. They are sensitive even to praise from the West, since they consider that it damages the popular support of the left-wing Chinese population of Singapore which they must firmly retain against the alternative leadership of the communists.

"The MCP are unlikely for some time to challenge a government which undoubtedly commands the enthusiastic support of the Chinese-speaking mass of the population. Mr Lee Kuan Yew himself estimates this period of grace as being probably a year or more."

Two and half months later, on 7 September, he was still optimistic, despite listing my government's shortcomings:

"It is hard to recognise in all this the extremist PAP of the last four years, penetrated by communists and sweeping to power on mass support won by exploiting the grievances of workers, peasants, Chinese middle school students and young intellectuals. But it would be wrong to think that the responsibilities of office have changed these young men.

"I have a regular weekly meeting with Lee Kuan Yew on Thursday afternoons at Government House, at which we talk freely and frankly. I find him greatly matured. He still has his prejudices and obsessions, but he is generally very sensible and always quick and intelligent. I have repeatedly taken him to task for the behaviour of his government, warning him bluntly of the consequences I foresee. Occasionally, he is able to correct my information or present it in a different light. Often, there is a sensible reason for what the government are (sic) doing: it is the way in which it is done that is wrong. Generally he accepts my criticism, particularly over treatment of the public service. His reply is that his ministers must learn the hard way by seeing the results of their own mistakes; that he should not stand over them; and that they will learn.

"While in the big things they are sound and responsible, in the little things they are emotional and tiresome. We shall have constant difficulties and worries in working with them; our tolerance and understanding will be strained. But they have potential to achieve much; and there is no present alternative to working with them. The opposition parties are discredited and possibly even moribund."

On 23 November, he wrote his last or "haul-down" report, so called because British governors used to hand in their final reports as they hauled down the flag.

"It is unlikely that the present leadership of the PAP will ever commit themselves publicly as anti-communist. The government's attitude towards communism is, however, fundamentally sound, and for this fact we have profound cause to be grateful. I remain convinced that to regard the present PAP leaders as crypto-

Bidding farewell to the last British governor, Sir William Goode, and his wife, on 2 December 1959.

With President Sukarno at Merdeka Palace, Jakarta, January 1960.

communists would be an entire mistake. To describe them as crypto-anti-communists would be much nearer the mark.

"Despite the best endeavours of the Singapore ministers to win acceptance by the Federation ministers, the attitude of the Federation remains distrustful. The prime minister now realises that there can be no hope of merger during the lifetime of the present Federation government and he also appreciates that public emphasis on merger in Singapore causes political embarrassment and consequent public rebuffs in the Federation. But he is concerned to hold Singapore to its present constitutional *modus vivendi* and to keep the aim of merger as the decisive influence on Singapore politics. He rightly believes that it would be disastrous for both Singapore and the Federation if merger became discredited as unattainable and Singapore turned elsewhere for its future. It is of paramount importance to all of us that this should not happen.

"So the position today is that Mr Lee Kuan Yew is very much in command of the cabinet and the cabinet are impressively united. They have made mistakes, as was to be expected, and with the exception of the prime minister I doubt they are as able as they first appeared to be. They are finding it much more difficult to run a government than to organise a successful political party. But on the whole they have made a good start to carry out their declared policies. The prime minister tells me to postpone judgement on their competence until they have had a year in office. So far most of what he has said has been proved right.

"Our policy must continue to be to work with the PAP government and to do all we can to secure their goodwill and confidence. Thus we shall be able to help them to give Singapore a stable and competent government, and only thus shall we overcome the constant minor difficulties and provocations which I am sure we shall encounter."

Like my form master at Raffles Institution, Goode gave me a kind report. However, he did not know what troubles were in store for my colleagues and me, and how wrong his assessment would have turned out to be had the cards fallen differently. Goode's haul-down report was to have a decisive influence on the incoming British commissioner, Lord Selkirk, or more accurately, on his deputy, Philip Moore, an officer of the British Civil Service who had been Selkirk's private secretary when he was First Lord of the Admiralty.

Before Goode left on 2 December, I wrote to say that he had done his best for his Queen and country, but he had also served the people of Singapore well. He once remarked to me during one of our teatime sessions, "We are here for the percentage. If there was nothing in it for us, we would have left." He had no pretence, and I respected him the more for it. As he chose to sail, not fly, home, the cabinet lined up on the wharf to bid him farewell.

With the departure of the last British governor, we had to appoint our own head of state. We chose Yusof bin Ishak, the managing director of the *Utusan Melayu*, to be his successor, our first native Yang di-Pertuan Negara. We wanted a distinguished Malay in order to show the Federation that Singaporeans were willing to accept Malays as their leaders, and I knew him as a good man of simple habits who carried himself with dignity. His wife, somewhat younger than himself, was lively, pleasant and sociable. He was sworn in on 3 December at the City Hall chamber, as the cabinet had been six months before. But while the cabinet had been sworn in under bare, makeshift arrangements, on this occasion there was time to organise a protocol guest list of important community and business leaders and members of the consular corps, and make proper seating arrangements. We held the ceremony at 8 am so that it would not be too hot for the one-and-a-quarter-hour parade past the City Hall steps when the new state flag was unfurled and a choir sang the new state anthem, joined by the assemblymen and ministers on the platform, surrounded by the crowd.

There had been much ado over the flag, for again racial sentiments had to be respected. The Chinese-speaking wanted red for good fortune, the Malays red and white, their traditional colours for courage and purity. But Indonesia already had red and white for their flag, and so had Poland. The Chinese, influenced by the five yellow stars on the flag of Communist China, wanted stars. The Malays wanted a crescent moon. We settled for a crescent moon with five white stars instead of the traditional one star for Islam. The five stars represented the five ideals of the country: democracy, peace, progress, justice and equality. Thus we reconciled different racial symbols and ideals.

We had also finally agreed on the state arms, with a lion and a tiger as the supporting animals on two sides of a shield containing a crescent moon with five stars, and a scroll below with the Malay words *Majulah Singapura*, which mean "May Singapore Flourish".

The choice of state anthem had proved easier. A Malay musician, Haji Zubir Said, had composed a suitable tune. It was not a martial, stirring tune like the French *Marseillaise* or the Chinese national anthem *Arise, Arise, Arise*, the song of the revolutionary resistance. The melody was of the region and the lyrics in Malay matched our motto, *Majulah Singapura*.

∞

In spite of the stumbles in our first six months of office, we did lay the foundations of many important government policies, including the first move in a building programme that was to transform Singapore. In February 1960, we dissolved the Singapore Improvement Trust and divided its functions between the Housing and Development Board (HDB), which was placed under the minister for national development, and the Planning Authority, which came under the prime minister. We then made Lim Kim San chairman of the HDB. This was a crucial appointment. Kim San had been Keng Swee's contemporary in Anglo-Chinese School and at Raffles College. He was a businessman, a practical, inventive person who had designed his own sago-processing machine. He managed his father-in-law's pawnshops and his father's petrol stations, besides being a director of one of the bigger local banks. He was a man of many skills. Keng Swee wanted to make sure that any money given to the HDB for housing the people would be well spent, and Kim San would see to it. Ong Eng Guan was not to be allowed to waste public money.

Shortly after he was appointed, Kim San came to see me. As minister for national development, Ong had ordered him to hire construction workers direct and so cut out building contractors who, being middlemen, were "exploiters of the workers". He wanted the HDB to become a model employer. Kim San was nonplussed. He asked me, "Do you want me to build houses or do you want me to be an employer of construction workers? If you want flats, then I know how to get the flats built; you leave it to me, I will produce you the flats. If you want me to hire workers direct, better get another chairman. Every contractor has his own supervisors, his relatives and trusted foremen who are either related to him or old retainers. In turn, they hire their gangs of workers and they know every person in their group and pay according to results."

This was another of Ong's political gimmicks to put himself in a good light. I overruled him and told Kim San to proceed in the way he thought best. He produced the flats. There was a big fire in June 1960, when some 30,000 people in a squatter area, known as Bukit Ho Swee, were rendered homeless. Within 18 months, Kim San had housed them in one-room flats with communal kitchens and communal toilets. He also put up a block in my constituency along Cantonment Road, a prominent location. My voters could see it going up, and were looking forward to moving in. Had it not been nearing completion at the time of the next election, I might not have been re-elected.

All new governments want to prove themselves by passing many new laws and launching many new projects. We hit the ground running, before the phrase was coined. In February 1960, I announced plans for the reorganisation of the Singapore Harbour Board into the Port of

HDB Chairman Lim Kim San speaking at the completion ceremony of HDB flats at Cantonment Road on 10 April 1964. I was seated behind him.

Kim San and me inside a newly occupied three-room flat that evening of 10 April, then a poorer Singapore.

Singapore Authority. Next, we moved the first reading of the Women's Charter to bring Singapore into the modern era of monogamy and equal rights. Then we legislated for an Industrial Relations Court, based on the Australian model, and appointed Charles Gamba, professor of economics at the University of Malaya, as its president. As the arbitrator in the Hock Lee bus strike, he was known to be sympathetic to labour, but was not likely to kill off the employers. We launched a family planning programme with 1,000 volunteers who were trained as lay workers to promote it among the public, keen to reduce the 4 per cent annual increase in the population. Most important was a bill to give ourselves wider powers to combat corruption. It was the first of several that strengthened the law so that offenders could be charged and convicted in court. It led to the creation of a new agency, the Corrupt Practices Investigation Bureau, which has helped to keep Singapore clean.

We announced we would give equal financial aid to the University of Malaya (in Singapore) and Nanyang University, but would require equal standards. Impertinent as always, the Nanyang University Students' Union said in their organ, the *University Tribune*, that while they were happy with equal treatment, they wanted the aid to be unconditional. We were not amused, but did not say so. We improved the prospects of the Chinese-educated by allowing them to advance through the University of Malaya. We started pre-university courses of three terms in the arts, law and science faculties for qualified non-English language students to prepare them as students of the University of Malaya.

∞

However, our economic plans made little headway. In September, we had talks with the Malayans about forming a limited common market, but they were even less forthcoming than before. Things were so bad that when a local manufacturer planned to expand his cotton-spinning textile mill to include weaving and finishing, it was big news because it would increase the labour force by 300. We were desperate for jobs.

Tourism was then an infant industry in Asia, as most tourists visited developed countries. We had a "Visit the Orient" year for 1961 with an air display, television and radio exhibition, motor show, orchid show, photographic exhibition and the State Day celebrations on 3 June, followed by a two-week cultural festival. It was a thin programme of attractions.

We placed our hopes on a United Nations Technical Assistance Board team that arrived in October to survey a proposed industrial site at Jurong and advise on the types of industry suitable for it. We were fortunate in the choice of the leader, Dr Albert Winsemius. A Dutch industrialist, he spent three months in Singapore and made the first of his many contributions that were to be crucial to Singapore's development. He was a practical, hard-headed businessman with a grasp of the economics of post-World War II Europe and America. He was to play a major role in our later economic planning.

We were then heavily dependent on trade, especially entrepot transactions. The previous month, an Indonesian team had arrived to discuss how to eliminate "irregular trade", and to improve their foreign exchange earnings. They wanted us to credit Indonesia with foreign exchange for a substantial percentage of the value of their exports to Singapore, in return for which they would buy an agreed quantity of goods through us. But it would be extremely difficult to get the private sector to cooperate; nobody would declare the value of his imports from or exports to Indonesia, or what or how much he had actually bought or sold and at what price; the Indonesian shippers would under-invoice the value of their goods, and often used the same export permit to send a second consignment of goods; and so it went on.

Aggravated by the employment situation, the threat posed by the communists loomed larger than ever. The Internal Security Council was getting increasingly unhappy about their growing strength in the unions, and wanted the Singapore government to move against them. I refused. If we did that, we could end up like Lim Yew Hock, simply arresting activists, and that would be like lopping off daisies; more would sprout. Goode had admitted this to me before I took office. But I was under constant pressure from the Malayan side to act.

Wearing his other hat as UK commissioner and chairman of the Internal Security Council, Goode had held its first meeting in August. Ong Eng Guan, Pang Boon and I represented Singapore, and Dr Ismail bin Dato Abdul Rahman, minister for external affairs, the Malayan government. Ismail, a doctor, was short, slightly tubby and dark for a Malay. He had curly hair and a moustache, wore horn-rimmed glasses, and a pipe was never far from his lips. He was a quiet, reserved man and a keen golfer. To get along with him, I again took up golf, which I had neglected. I came to like and respect him for his direct and straight-forward manner. He knew what his job was – the security of Malaya. He took advice from his officials who were experts on communism and subversion, and was determined that the Malayan Chinese communists were not going to win. He was sceptical of the PAP policy and tactics against the communists, and it took some time for me to convince him that we had to adopt a different approach because our mass base was a Chinese-speaking majority that was susceptible to communist persuasion and pressure.

As I got to know the Malayan ministers better, he was the one I trusted absolutely. He was honest and sincere in his dealings with me, and I believe he reciprocated my friendship and respect for him. He was number three in the leadership of UMNO, after the Tunku and the deputy prime minister, Tun Abdul Razak. He did not have the Tunku's charisma and status as a Malay aristocrat, nor Razak's quicker mind, but Ismail was the soundest, and a decisive leader. When the Tunku retired, Razak as prime minister made Ismail deputy prime minister. He would have made a very good prime minister had he not died rather young from a heart problem.

At that first meeting, Singapore presented two papers: one from the professionals in Special Branch and the other from the ministers seeking the release of those who were closely associated with the PAP at the time they were detained. Goode pointed out that the Special Branch experts had reported that past events were repeating themselves – there was the same build-up of communist strength to challenge the government – and he asked whether it would not be wise to intervene and crush the monster now before it got too big. I disagreed. Goode pressed me to explain our policy. The broad policy, I said, was not to be outmanoeuvred by the communists. If we did not first prepare the ground so that the neutral Chinese-speaking workers understood that their leaders were being arrested because they were doing harm to the economy and thus threatening their jobs, we would lose them. They must not be allowed to believe that the leaders were detained because they were good trade unionists who happened to be pro-communist.

Ismail did not understand this approach. He explained how a firm line in the Federation had kept down communist subversion. I said Malaya was different from Singapore. The Malayan government could use a heavy hand against the communists and not lose their mass support because it was mainly Malay. However, the Singapore government must try to win over its mass base – the uncommitted Chinese, especially the intellectuals who could influence the uncommitted. Goode was familiar with our thinking, but had brought it out for Ismail's benefit.

We needed steady nerves to stick to our position. At the end of the first six months, the build-up of the communist united front was still continuing. Lim Chin Siong and his comrades were attracting more unions towards the communist camp, and once they were the majority, the Trade Union Congress (TUC), to which both pro- and non-communist unions belonged, broke off from the Western-sponsored International Confederation of Free Trade Unions (ICFTU). As the ICFTU had been created to counter the World Federation of Trade Unions run from

Moscow, the pro-communists used the pretext that the ICFTU was engaged in power politics.

Meanwhile, they had worked assiduously on Fong Swee Suan and won him back into the fold. Devan Nair was dismayed at the ease with which they undid his three years of work on Fong in Changi. Unlike Nair, Fong was Chinese-educated, a prisoner of the legends of the revolutionary movement in China and without a framework of values that could accommodate the concept of revolutionary social and economic change by peaceful means. To the Chinese-educated like Fong, revolution required violence. Without violence, it was, in Marxist dialectics, "mere reformism". In any case, he could not resist the emotional pulls of old friendships and traditional loyalties. Woodhull and Puthucheary soon drifted along with the more powerful and apparently unbeatable side. They isolated Nair who, with my agreement, resigned his post as political secretary in February to engage in serious study and writing designed "to contribute to the consolidation of the ideological and theoretical foundations of the PAP".

Lim Chin Siong and Fong went from strength to strength, winning over to the pro-communist camp in the TUC not only English-educated union leaders but quite a few of the Malay-educated. Emboldened by success, they issued several statements critical of the government's position on detainees and the trade unions, so that in August I had to warn in the Assembly that if they challenged authority, they would meet with a serious rebuff. After that, three of the political secretaries – Lim Chin Siong, Fong and Woodhull – declared formally that their stand was the same as it had been at the time of their release from detention in June 1959: to support the PAP and its policy that independence should be achieved through merger with the Federation.

At that time, they thought merger was in the indefinite future – so did I – but they had nevertheless been stirring up demands for an independent Singapore without merger.

21. Trounced in Hong Lim

I had known that a frustrated Ong Eng Guan was plotting with some of the assemblymen, but paid little heed because I was confident he could never get a majority to support him. But he had become reckless. If he could not be in power, he would ruin us even if the MCP benefited. At a party conference in June 1960, his Hong Lim branch introduced 16 resolutions, four of them designed to win him communist support.

In order to dispel my suspicions, Lim Chin Siong and his comrades had earlier protested that they would have no truck with Ong. The Trade Union Congress had issued a statement that although the PAP had made mistakes, they would not support him. But I believed it was not beyond them to have got hold of his close friends to put him up to this. The resolutions called for a more anti-colonial policy, the immediate release of all detainees, and immediate constitutional revision. In other words, internal self-government was not good enough. So Ong, too, wanted independence. We were set for a showdown. He was isolated in the party, and after two days of argument, the conference suspended him and two assemblymen who backed him – S.V. Lingam and Ng Teng Kian, a Chinese-speaking Hokkien like Ong. All three men then crossed the floor of the Assembly to sit with the opposition.

Ong was restive. He had lost his star status and was not making the headlines. He therefore set out to attract attention by doing the unexpected and the eye-catching. In September, he tabled a motion calling on the prime minister to fight in the Internal Security Council for the unconditional release of all political detainees. This could not help him. Once again, it would only help the communists although they distrusted and despised him. But it would embarrass the government. I was away in Sarawak, so Chin Chye moved an amendment to point out that it was unlikely that the Federation government, which had the deciding vote in the Internal Security Council, would agree to release persons who it was convinced were promoting the cause of the MCP. And since it was the government's business to advance the welfare of the people of Singapore through merger with the Federation, it had no intention of going against the Federation's stand.

Ong's strategy had been to show us up as lackeys of the imperialists, and he now took this a step further. In October, he said George Thomson, director of Information Services, was now my guide and philosopher; I was "a ventriloquist's dummy and George Thomson the ventriloquist". He wanted to diminish my standing with the Chinese-speaking by portraying me as the mouthpiece of a colonial speechwriter and mentor. He alleged that Val Meadows, whose office he had demolished, and Alan Blades, the commissioner of police, were similarly manipulating me. When I challenged him to repeat these statements outside the Assembly, he kept silent.

Instead, at the next Assembly meeting in December, he accused me of nepotism, claiming that I had appointed Kwa Soon Chuan as deputy commissioner of the Inland Revenue Department because he was my brother-in-law. Again, I asked him to repeat what he had said outside Parliament. When he did not do so, Chin Chye, as leader of the House, introduced a motion to condemn him for his dishonourable conduct and to suspend him until such time as he apologised to the Assembly. Ong tabled a motion to claim that the Assembly had no power to condemn a Member. He challenged me to resign with him and stand in by-elections in our respective constituencies, renewed his charges against the PAP, and said that the Public Service Commission was packed with PAP supporters. He agreed to an investigation of these charges by a committee of the whole House, but before the Assembly met on the day fixed for it, he resigned his seat. We announced that a commission of inquiry would be formed with a high court judge as chairman to investigate his allegations, and that after the report had been placed before the House and debated, a by-election would be held in Hong Lim.

On 3 January 1961, Mr Justice F.A. Chua was appointed to head the commission, which held ten sittings between 17 January and 1 February. My main objective in the inquiry was to press him to substantiate all the charges he had made against me. Chua's report, submitted in February, found that there was no truth at all in any of the allegations, that they were groundless and reckless, and that Ong was "not a person to be believed". We debated it for two days in the Assembly and condemned Ong for his dishonourable conduct. I had exposed him as a liar and a petty, vicious person. I hoped that this would shake his hold on the Chinese-speaking in Hong Lim. I could not have been more wrong.

∞

We had a long election campaign of nine weeks from 11 March to 29 April. We fielded Jek Yeun Thong, the newspaper reporter who had written my first speech in Mandarin.

After the first two street meetings in Hong Lim, however, we knew that the ground was cold. Ong's personal popularity had not been dented. He had done the people too many favours by giving whole streets away to hawkers. He had put up standpipes and street lamps and talked about distributing taxi licences freely. The people were willing to overlook his lies and many other failings. They were resentful because we had not given immigration permits to their relatives in China, which he now raised as an issue, although he had never done this when he was a minister. He knew that if we had agreed to do so, it would have caused enormous trouble with the other races, even with the English-educated Chinese, and would certainly have antagonised the leaders in Malaya. The voters were not interested in his four pro-communist resolutions. We discovered all this as we slogged it out. I went around Hong Lim, an overcrowded constituency in the heart of Chinatown, up and down the rickety wooden stairs of dilapidated shophouses to canvas in almost all of them, sometimes visiting the same premises twice or even three times. The people were polite but not responsive. We tried hard, but we knew that they were too committed to Ong. And we had to reckon with Lim Chin Siong, who had been unhappy because we had been changing the law to give the government better control over the pro-communist unions and cultural associations.

Lim Chin Siong wanted to eliminate the Internal Security Council because he knew that if he went beyond certain limits, it would act, and if it ordered the arrest and detention of the communist leaders, the Singapore government could not be held responsible and be stigmatised a colonial stooge. For, this time, the Malayan government representative with the casting vote, not a British governor, would be pulling the trigger. When we refused to budge on the issue, Lim addressed a meeting of a thousand trade unionists at the Victoria Memorial Hall during the campaign along these lines and quietly passed the word around in Hong Lim not to support the PAP. When the votes were counted, Ong had defeated our candidate by 7,747 to 2,820.

This was a stinging defeat, but I was determined to fight on. "The results," I said, "make it imperative that we clearly establish our position of confidence."

One consolation from this gruelling experience was that I gained in confidence as a Hokkien speaker. With the suspension of Ong in June 1960, we had lost our only effective Hokkien speaker to match Lim Chin Siong. Keng Swee suggested that I myself should make the effort to replace him, rather than groom another man who might again give us trouble. So I started to learn the dialect, snatching an hour either at lunchtime or in the evening, three, often five times a week. I had two good tutors, both from our radio station, who first had to teach me a whole new Romanised script to capture the Hokkien pronunciation of

Chinese characters. Hokkien is not at all like Mandarin; it has seven tones instead of four, and uses different word combinations for verbs, nouns, and adjectives. But they are both forms of Chinese, and fortunately my Mandarin had reached a sufficiently advanced level for me to go into it, not from the basement but from the second or third floor of a 25-storey building. Nevertheless, the first time I made a Hokkien speech in Hong Lim, the children in the crowd laughed at my mistakes – wrong sounds, wrong tones, wrong sentence structure, wrong almost everything. But I could not afford to be shy or embarrassed. It was a matter of life and death. It was not just a question of fighting Ong. I was preparing for the inevitable showdown with Lim Chin Siong and the communists. I would lose by default if I could not speak the dialect well enough to get my views across to the uneducated and poorly educated Chinese who were then the majority but whom I could not reach with Mandarin. By the end of the campaign and after innumerable speeches, I spoke understandable Hokkien.

To learn a new language in my late 30s, while snowed under by papers stamped Immediate, Urgent, Secret, Top Secret, and by files with huge red crosses printed on their covers and marked Cicero (for addressee's eyes only), required almost superhuman concentration and effort. I could not have done it without some compelling motivation. When I started, it was, as the Chinese proverb goes, as difficult as lifting the tripod brass urn in front of a temple. Even while I was being driven to meetings, I mumbled to myself in the car, rehearsing new phrases. Sometimes, my teacher would be at my side to correct my mistakes immediately after my first speech and before I made my next. Every spare moment, I spent revising to get the sounds right, memorising new words to get them embedded in my mind so that I could roll them off my tongue without looking at the script. I had to learn quickly.

By sheer practice and repetition over the next few months, speaking without notes, making mistakes and correcting them again and again,

I finally mastered the dialect and could make a half-hour speech without groping for words and phrases or anxiously searching for them in my underlined script. The crowd watched all this and I won their respect. When I started, I was fumbling, awkward, almost comic. But here I was in front of them, suddenly able to express myself fluently in their dialect. I may have been unidiomatic, even ungrammatical, but there was no mistaking my meaning, delivered with vigour, feeling and conviction as I argued, cajoled, warned, and finally moved some of them to go with me.

I had become my own dialect communicator. The PAP did not have a Lim Chin Siong or an Ong Eng Guan, both native Hokkien speakers. People knew I started from zero in 1961 and so had no doubts about my determination and stamina. I am Hakka, and Hakkas as a minority group living among speakers of other dialects are supposed to be great linguists. This added to the myth. They thought it was natural for me to learn languages easily. But Choo knew I sweated blood to master Hokkien.

Soon after the setback in Hong Lim, we were faced with another. About nine days before polling for Hong Lim, our assemblyman for Anson, Baharuddin bin Mohamed Ariff, died of a heart attack. He was a young Malay in his early 30s, a journalist in the *Utusan Melayu* who had been a PAP city councillor, energetic, intelligent and promising. It was a shock, and it meant another by-election. I knew the communists would now try to chase us from pillar to post. They would see Hong Lim as a sign that the Chinese-educated we had won over in the general election were in fact more Ong's supporters than ours, and that we English-educated leaders did not have a real following among the Hokkien-speaking masses.

That May Day, as I went to the Trade Union Congress rally at the Jalan Besar Stadium, I decided to dig my toes in. I quoted Lim Chin Siong's communist phrase, "Seek concord, maintain differences", a neat four-character slogan Mao Zedong had often used when he called for a united front on specific issues. To make clear that the PAP was not going to demand the abolition of the Internal Security Council when the constitution was revised in 1963, I said, "Seek concord if you will, but on the PAP stand, otherwise maintain your differences and seek no concord if you find that the PAP is against your interests." We had believed that key questions on constitutional change could be left open until 1963, but because of the developments before and during the Hong Lim by-election, I decided to tackle them early.

∞

A few days later, a Chinese girl courier came to see Choo in the office with a letter for me. The same courier had earlier that year passed me a note from the Plen, asking me to indicate the pseudonym I would use for him when I communicated with him. I had decided on his surname "Fang" and as first names, "Ping An", meaning "peace and tranquillity". This time he asked if I would meet him, and if so, to ring up the number of the Rochor Road bicycle shop.

I hesitated. The last time we met I was just an assemblyman. Now I was the prime minister. If I was discovered consorting with the enemy, it would be most embarrassing. And I would be going to a meeting at some secret location alone. If I was a threat to their scheme of things, the communists could quietly dispose of me. I decided to take a calculated risk to know what he had in mind. It was also risky for him. I might go to the meeting having first tipped off the police. They might ambush him. But by choosing a pseudonym embodying his surname, I had signalled that I knew who he was, the brother of the PAP assemblywoman Fung Yin Ching. If I wanted to have him arrested, I would not have given this away, and that should reassure him that I was on the level. I had to take a chance that he, too, was on the level and would not take advantage of my vulnerable position.

When I phoned, I recognised the voice that answered as that of the person who had made the first contact with me in 1958. We agreed on the same rendezvous, that I look for a girl in pigtails walking along Keng Lee Road away from Newton Circus at 8 pm on 11 May 1961. I again used my father's little green Morris Minor and picked her up. The Plen might have arranged for my car to be tailed to make sure that nobody followed us, but I did not look into the rear-view mirror in case she reported it and so aroused suspicion and distrust. After taking a round-about route, we ended up in St Michael's Estate, a half-built complex of Housing and Development Board flats off Serangoon Road. The capability and ingenuity of the communist organisation won my admiration. Nobody would be implicated in this meeting but the HDB. I walked up two flights of stairs of an uncompleted block in darkness. Construction materials still littered the place, and there was no electricity or water. When I entered the candlelit room the girl indicated, the Plen was already waiting. It was furnished only with two armchairs and a table standing between them. He knew I was a beer drinker, and provided warm Anchor beer. He opened a bottle, poured me a mug, and topped up his own. He drank first. I hoped I did not show any hesitation before I drank mine. We had to trust each other to talk at all.

He looked leaner, more gaunt than when we last met over two years ago. I asked him how he was. He said it was a hard life on the run, very wearing. I said he did not show it, he looked fine. No, he felt it. He thanked me for helping his sister. (She had been scalded as a child and had her legs so badly scarred that she always wore trousers. In 1960, Choo had arranged for Yeoh Ghim Seng, a professor of surgery and a friend from my London days, to give her a skin graft.) When we returned to the subject of politics, there was anxiety in his voice. He said that I should come around quickly, meaning that if I did not accept his point of view we would find ourselves under attack. As in earlier meetings, I assumed an air of calm. I was not anxious to do a deal with him; I was willing to be conciliatory but would make no commitment. But I was interested to know what he wanted to tell me.

We had a four-hour session, from 8:15 to past midnight, ranging over many subjects. But he would repeatedly come back to "giving the people their democratic rights, their cultural freedom, freer imports of books from China and freer immigration permits" – in short, more opportunities for communist activities, for communist expansion. He wanted us to work together, not for independence or the reversion of British bases – they could have them for a few years – but for the abolition of the Internal Security Council.

He was concerned about my talk of the PAP government throwing in its hand and wanted to know my intentions. I said if I concluded that the present situation would only worsen in the coming years, waiting for the five-year term to end would make no sense. The PAP would fail. And I would only go on if there was a prospect of its policies succeeding. I explained that much depended on the Federation agreeing to a common market so that there would be a better chance for us to industrialise and so create more jobs. He asked whether I was expecting to get merger from the Tunku soon. I replied that there was no imminent likelihood of it. The Tunku had his face set against Singapore. We were too Chinese and the Chinese were too pro-communist.

He pressed me again and again to agree that the immediate target for the 1963 constitutional talks should be the abolition of the Internal Security Council. After observing his body language, his tone of voice, and his keenness to have the PAP carry on, but on his terms, I would have been a fool to go along with him. Put starkly, he wanted to commit us to giving more opportunities to the communists to expand their united front from 1961 to 1963, and then to get the Internal Security Council abolished whatever else the British might not concede.

I decided there was little to be gained by prevarication. I was in government. If I agreed with him now, he would see from my subsequent actions that I had been lying. I did not give him a direct "no", but said it was best for him to assume that the PAP would do what it had publicly stated it would do. In other words, my public statements still expressed my policies for the future. We parted with a handshake. He showed no rancour or animosity. He may have been surprised that I refused to commit myself, when I could have said what was expedient and later gone back on my word.

At the time I felt that he did not fully understand the situation, that so long as the British had not given Singapore independence, they had the power to revoke the constitution. As long as sovereignty and the bases remained in British hands, it was foolish of him to believe he could get the Internal Security Council abolished and build up communist strength in Singapore in order to undermine the Federation. He had got it the wrong way around. The communists could never control Singapore without first controlling Malaya, yet he hoped to use Singapore to overturn the government in Kuala Lumpur. How could he imagine the British would allow that? In fact, I had told Selkirk at an Internal Security Council meeting that the communists wanted by whatever means to make the island a base from which to liberate the whole of the Federation, and they were out to encourage Chinese chauvinism by playing on Chinese fears of Malay domination if there were merger.

I had told Selkirk and Moore that the communists believed there was no need to take action against the British bases for the present since they could easily be rendered useless in time of war. They also disregarded the economic arguments in favour of merger and believed that, as with Cuba and the Russians, they could count on massive Chinese aid. If Singapore did not join the Federation soon, therefore, the situation might get out of hand, but if a proposal for merger could be put to the people within nine months to a year, it would probably be carried. After that, it might be too late. I had emphasised to Moore that we were at a critical juncture, and if the British allowed the communists to believe there could be a pro-communist Singapore, they would be inviting trouble both for Singapore and Malaya. I was absolutely certain that even if the British were to accept the build-up initially, they would suspend the constitution as soon as things got out of hand. There would be riots, violence and bloodshed, and the communists would be quelled by British troops still on the island as of sovereign right.

But it was not my business to spell this out for the Plen.

22. The Tunku's Merger Bombshell

Our clash with the communists was coming to a head, but on the question of merger with Malaya we were making absolutely no progress. The Tunku's attitude towards Singapore was most discouraging, and he repeatedly parried and deflected any proposal for union that was put to him. He was adamant in not wanting merger under any circumstances, and he took every occasion, private and public, to make this clear. In May 1960, he told Malayan students in London that the political thinking in Singapore, like the racial set-up, was very different from that in the Federation, and the addition of the 1.3 million Chinese on the island would confuse Malayans and ruin the calm atmosphere there. "Many Chinese-educated and new immigrants to the country," he said, "will always be loyal to China and they are less Malayan-minded."

His comments were typically Tunku. He could not have been more frank. When I was asked in June 1960 on a radio programme what the prospects were for merger, I decided to dampen expectations by ruling it out for the foreseeable future. I replied that the Federation was anxious not to upset its own racial balance and it suspected that too many Singapore Chinese had communist sympathies; it was therefore up to us to demonstrate in concrete ways that our loyalties were essentially Malayan.

What was particularly worrying was that the Tunku was insensitive to the damage he was inflicting on public sentiment in Singapore by pouring cold water over our hopes. For every time he did so, it was prominently reported in the press, and this meant he was giving the advocates of a separate independent Singapore increasing credibility.

By October 1960, even Lim Yew Hock and the Singapore People's Alliance had come out in favour of establishing Singapore as a sovereign state first, contemplating merger with Malaya only afterwards. But as I emphasised to Selkirk, this was absolute nonsense. A communist-controlled independent Singapore would fight to the bitter end before surrendering its sovereignty to the Federation.

Selkirk, the second son of a Scottish duke, was tall, lanky and slightly bowed, and looked an aristocrat. He had grizzled curly hair, a gaunt face that often wore a puckish expression, and a distracting habit, when seized with a problem, of toying with his denture, one of his upper front teeth, flopping it about with his tongue. He did not have a powerful mind, but had keen social intelligence and the charm of a nobleman out to put a plebeian at ease. He meant well and we got along; but his deputy, Philip Moore, must have sensed my impatience from time to time, and suspected that I did not regard him as a heavyweight. To underline his importance, therefore, he repeatedly reminded me that Selkirk had been a cabinet minister and still had direct access to the prime minister.

Three months later, Sir Geofroy Tory, the UK high commissioner to the Federation of Malaya, told me that the Tunku had confided to him that he found it very embarrassing whenever I, or any other Singapore spokesman, made a public statement implying that union was a possibility. For one thing, it gave comfort and encouragement to his opponents, the socialists, who were mainly Chinese, and who were longing for the day when they could join forces with the PAP across the Causeway. For another, it tended to strain his relations with the Malay nationalists, since any hint that the Alliance government was toying with the idea of some form of *rapprochement* with Singapore might well increase their fears that his policies would allow the Chinese in, to swamp the Malays. Despite all efforts, the Tunku, Razak and Ismail just would not sit down and talk seriously with me about the long-term future of Singapore and Malaya. They did not want to think about the horrendous consequences for Malaya if Singapore were independent and under communist control.

Finally – to keep my hopes alive, I thought – the British encouraged me to put up a bigger formula, a grand design for a federation that would include not only Singapore but also their three dependencies in Borneo (North Borneo, Brunei and Sarawak), so that the ethnic arithmetic would not upset the Malay electoral majority. Selkirk and Moore suggested that I prepare a paper, not for the Tunku, to whom the subject was obviously anathema, but for Razak. I assumed that, through Geofroy Tory, they had talked Razak into considering the concept, and I had a paper ready in early May 1961 to give to Ismail for him. The British had indeed worked hard on him with the support of Robert Thompson, a Malayan Civil Service officer who was secretary of defence in Malaya and had worked closely with Razak as his minister.

But the man who broached the subject with the Tunku, boldly and frontally, was Duncan Sandys, secretary of state for Commonwealth Relations. He came to Singapore in January 1961 on his way to the Federation, to tell both governments that Britain was about to make an application to join the European Common Market. I took this opportunity to spell out to him the danger we faced if there were no merger by 1963, when constitutional talks were due – an independent Singapore that would go communist would be the inevitable result. I must have made an impact on him. Moore told me afterwards that Sandys said he had never met a leader in power who was keener to hand it over to another centre. British records show that Sandys spoke to the Tunku, and Selkirk reported that Sandys had told him the conversation had gone smoothly, although he had no details.

Later, I got to know Sandys well. He could be direct and brutally frank. Son-in-law of Winston Churchill, he did not lack self-confidence. He had enormous determination and courage. He had suffered a leg injury in a car accident during the war and was often in pain, but he took painkillers, limped around with a walking stick, pressed on with life and busied himself with his work. He was a likeable, admirable man if you happened to be on the same side as he was. It was my good fortune that I was. He pushed hard for merger within a greater "Malaysia" and must have got Harold Macmillan, the British prime minister, to support him and to urge it on the Tunku.

⚭

Out of the blue, on 27 May 1961, the Tunku when speaking to the Foreign Correspondents' Association of South East Asia in Singapore said:

> "Sooner or later Malaya should have an understanding with Britain and the peoples of Singapore, North Borneo, Brunei and Sarawak. It is premature for me to say now how this closer understanding can be brought about but it is inevitable that we should look ahead to this objective and think of a plan whereby these territories could be brought closer together in political and economic cooperation."

He said it was the natural tendency of the Chinese in Singapore to try and make the island "a little China". It would be a good thing for all concerned if the people of Singapore and the Federation could decide to make Malaya what it was – our one and only home. This was a bombshell. There had been no earlier indication of any change in his consistent stand that Malaya could not take Singapore in. The moment I read what the Tunku had said, I knew that the Plen would think I had deceived him when we met in May, that I had lied when, in reply to his question, I said that merger was not likely for many years because the Tunku distrusted the Chinese in Singapore.

The Tunku did not explain then why he had changed his mind. Later, in October, he told parliament in Kuala Lumpur that originally he had not favoured merger because integration would spell danger to

Malaya's security, but times had changed. He did not explain how. I could only surmise that the British had convinced him that he had to control security in Singapore in order to safeguard Malaya itself, since the Chinese-speaking majority on the island were susceptible to communist appeals. I believed that Ismail already understood that the problems of subversion in the two territories were closely linked. He had been shown, for example, that although only half of the students at Nanyang University were from Malaya, they formed the bulk of the left-wing leaders and troublemakers, and would cause more trouble after they graduated and went back to the Federation.

Even Selkirk and Moore had not expected the Tunku's volte-face. It came as a "joyful surprise" to them. The British had long discussed the concept of a greater "Malaysia" as one solution to their long-term aim of bringing their colonies in the region together in a federation before they were given independence. But the crucial question had been, would the PAP government in Singapore turn out to be communist-led? They believed I had answered that question when I publicly insisted on merger as the way to achieve independence for Singapore, since this would prevent the MCP from ever winning power. It was then that they began to take the project seriously.

In May 1961, the Tunku seemed at least prepared to consider an association with Singapore within a wider Federation of Malaysia. But there were times during the ensuing six months when this appeared to have been a totally false dawn, for he was still to balk at actual merger. It was fortunate that during this period I was able to get on with most members of the British commission, notably Philip Moore.

By 1961, we were already on the same wavelength. The British had seen the difficulties faced by the PAP government when acting against the communists, and set out to build up momentum for Malaysia and create a sense of its inevitability. Their response to the Tunku's proposal came after two weeks in a coordinated series of favourable statements.

First, Selkirk described it on 13 June as "a sound, long-term plan". A week later, Macmillan, answering a question from Fenner Brockway in the House of Commons, said:

"I have observed with interest the recent striking suggestion of the prime minister of the Federation of Malaya that sooner or later the Federation should have an understanding with the British government and with Singapore, North Borneo, Sarawak and Brunei on a plan which would bring these territories into closer economic and political association. Tunku Abdul Rahman's statement has already stimulated discussion in these countries and the government would wish to take their reactions into account in their own consideration of the suggestion ... I think it is a good thing that this matter has been raised and provoked discussion."

Next Selkirk called a meeting on 27 June of the British governors of Sarawak and North Borneo, the high commissioner to Malaya and the commissioner to Brunei. Goode, now governor of North Borneo, spoke of "the need to seize the right moment to push through the Tunku's 'Mighty Malaysia' plan to ensure its success". On 30 June, soon after the meeting, Selkirk flew to London to discuss the plan with the cabinet.

This public display of British support for merger and Malaysia must have alarmed the communists. The Tunku's initiative was gathering speed, and the Plen would have to take this into his calculations. Their agitation quickly became plain when Lim Chin Siong came back with a series of anti-merger pronouncements. On 2 June, the "Big Six" trade union leaders – Lim Chin Siong and Fong Swee Suan, together with Sidney Woodhull, Jamit Singh, S.T. Bani and Dominic Puthucheary, younger brother of James (four non-Chinese to give it a multiracial appearance) – issued a statement calling for "genuinely full internal self-government not only in name but also in fact", with control of internal security and the abolition of the Internal Security Council. They asked the Anson electorate to vote for the PAP for the sake of victory in the

1963 constitutional talks and the early realisation of their demands. Lim then brought the communist united front into the fray, with 42 trade unions pledging their support for a left-wing, anti-colonial People's Action Party in the coming by-election. In other words, if the PAP were not left-wing and anti-colonial enough for them, it would not get the backing of the unions, which represented the "wishes of the people".

It was a warning to me to play it their way. I replied, "Now independence through merger in a larger unit is clearly before us and will be achieved sooner than anyone imagined two years ago." I made it plain that we would not seek the abolition of the Internal Security Council until our security was assured within the Federation by the electoral weight of its Malay mass base. It was up to the Plen what he would do next.

On 10 June, nomination day for the Anson by-election, the PAP fielded a Malay, Mahmud bin Awang. He was the president of the Trade Union Congress, but the choice did not suit the communists. He had been arrested briefly then released. He was with Devan Nair and therefore one of us. He would face David Marshall, who was the candidate for the Workers' Party, and whom I felt sure Lim Chin Siong and Fong had instigated to stand. Sure enough, on 14 June, the newspapers reported Marshall as saying that he had visited the Federation after the Tunku's announcement to the Foreign Correspondents' Association, and he was convinced there would be no merger within ten years. He advocated independence for Singapore (which must automatically entail abolition of the Internal Security Council), arguing that once Singapore got independence, it would be easier to get merger.

Soon after the campaign began, John Linsell, the director of Special Branch, reported that some communist group wanted to assassinate me. The danger would be greatest at one of the election meetings held in the open, where it would be easy for an assassin to hit the speaker on the stage and make his escape. They left me to decide the degree of security needed and whether I should go on making public appearances at all. I had no choice. To disappear from view during an important by-election campaign just because of an assassination threat would have been politically disastrous. On the other hand, to continue without security cover would have been foolhardy, while too much security would have looked defensive. I told Special Branch to be as discreet as possible but to take maximum precautions.

That same evening, I spoke in my own constituency. It was familiar ground, a neighbourhood friendly to me, and I felt reasonably safe. But there were other public meetings in less friendly neighbourhoods. I did feel twinges of discomfort, but accepted it as part of political life in the terrorist-plagued conditions of Malaya and Singapore of those days.

I was inclined to believe that the communists wanted to inject some fear into me and see how I reacted. I calculated that in fact it would be against their interests to assassinate me when my standing with the public was high. I was not yet regarded as the enemy of the people as Lim Yew Hock had been in 1956. And they could not want the inevitable massive security clean-up against the united front – party, unions and cultural associations – that must follow. If I had lost out in the propaganda battle for hearts and minds and been seen as a "lackey of the imperialists", it would have been different. Bumping me off would then have been politically cost-free, in which case I might have had to decide not to take chances.

As it turned out, Special Branch and the Criminal Investigation Department had mounted a series of raids on 18 June culminating in the arrest of a big-time racketeer and ten others, during which they had found a parcel containing three hand grenades concealed in the compound of the racketeer's residence. But interrogation revealed that an informer had fabricated the assassination plot and planted the hand grenades with the connivance of a Criminal Investigation Department detective corporal. The denouement came as an anticlimax. Nevertheless, until the threat was found to be fiction, I was faced with the real problem of how to respond to it.

Three days before polling, I said that whether the North Borneo states were coming in or not, "we must strive for a merger between Singapore and the Federation under two requisite conditions – freedom in our education and labour policies". I knew that unless we excluded these from federal control, we could never get a majority in Singapore to support us. Malaya's education policy was being implemented against the protests of Chinese schools and Chinese chamber of commerce committees in the peninsula because they would have to replace instruction in Chinese and English with instruction in Malay to qualify for government aid. This would have been totally unacceptable to the non-Malays in Singapore. Even the English-educated would have rejected merger on that basis, and the Chinese-educated would have resorted to violence.

As for labour, Malaya had a tougher policy *vis-à-vis* the trade unions, mainly because they were bent on stamping out communist subversion, but also because they did not believe in militant unionism and had taken harsh measures to curb excesses in picketing and bargaining in industrial disputes. If the ministry of labour and ministry of home affairs in Kuala Lumpur had control of the registration and dissolution of trade unions, the workers and union leaders in Singapore would surely oppose Malaysia.

Suddenly, two days before polling, eight PAP assemblymen signed an open letter asking Chin Chye, as PAP chairman, to declare the party's support for the statement of the "Big Six" and to call a conference of the party's 51 branches to examine its current role in the present political situation. Out to undermine public confidence in the leadership and affect the voting, they repeated Lim Chin Siong's demands: release of political detainees, abolition of the Internal Security Council, genuine full internal self-government. Since I was not giving way, the Plen was determined to make the PAP lose Anson.

On the eve of the election, I publicly asked the three political secretaries – Lim Chin Siong, Fong and Woodhull – to resign. I said these three and the eight assemblymen wanted to force the PAP to accept their line, otherwise they would "overthrow the leadership and capture the party to use it for their purposes ... What is clear is that in order to stop merger, the six trade unionists are prepared to go to any lengths – even to destroying the party with which they are ostensibly associated." In a last-minute effort to swing the votes away from the PAP towards Marshall, they pulled out all the stops. Even my own branch secretary turned against me, and since he worked in the Singapore Harbour Board and had influence in Anson, which is adjacent to the port, he cost us many votes with the Chinese dock workers. On polling night, 15 July, Marshall won by a small margin of 3,598 votes (43.3 per cent) to Mahmud's 3,052 (36.7 per cent), the SPA taking 17.8 per cent. At his flamboyant best, Marshall taunted me in his victory speech: "Resign, and may you in your retirement learn humility and humanities so that in the years to come your undoubted ability may unselfishly and honestly serve our people."

I was too preoccupied with the coming battle to respond to him. The communists had demonstrated once again that they had penetrated the higher ranks of the trade unions and the party so effectively that they could split the PAP vote at short notice, switching popular support to someone known to be unstable and undependable. In a letter addressed to Chin Chye as chairman of the PAP on 17 July, I offered to resign as prime minister. I saw "the opening of a test of strength between the non-communist left and the communist left" together with a danger of "industrial unrest for political objectives". Lim Chin Siong and his comrades would try to coerce the party and the government into abandoning Malaysia, and the party needed to be united behind its leader.

On the same day, Chin Chye replied that the central executive committee had been unanimous in choosing me as prime minister after the general election.

"The call for your resignation as prime minister by our opponents is only to confuse the people over the vital issue of merger between Singapore and the Federation, an objective upon which the party was founded and from which we cannot deviate. Suggestions have been made that I should be the prime minister in your place. Let us not be deceived by this attempt to split the unity of the party and its leadership."

We knew we were headed for a showdown. After we lost Anson, I had to make sure that every PAP assemblyman and party member knew this and would support us. The battle was now joined. We had come to a parting of the ways with our own left wing. We wanted to purge the party of any waverers in the Assembly, and compel the communists to fight us in the open. We decided to call for a vote of confidence and force an open break before they had time to rethink their strategy.

23. Eden Hall Tea Party

I tabled a motion of confidence in the government on 20 July 1961, to sort out the goats from the sheep in the Assembly.

On 18 July, only two days before the vote of confidence, Special Branch had reported that Lim Chin Siong, Fong Swee Suan, Sidney Woodhull and James Puthucheary had been to tea with Selkirk at Eden Hall. This was very odd. Faced with a crisis and an imminent rupture with the PAP non-communists, Lim and Fong were consorting with their arch-enemy, the British. I concluded they were sounding them out to discover whether, if their pro-communist proxies in the Assembly were in the majority, they would be able to take office. Keng Swee, Chin Chye, Raja and I decided that the British would welcome the chance to widen the gap between us so that there could be no reconciliation, no regrouping of the united front between the non-communists and the pro-communists in the PAP in the future. This suited us. The pro-communists had been an albatross around our necks. But we had to be careful how we ditched them. If we appeared opportunistic, dropping them after we had made use of them, we would lose the Chinese-speaking ground. Merger was the perfect issue on which to break.

Since their first statement on 4 June 1959, declaring unequivocal support for an independent, democratic, non-communist Malaya, and for Singapore achieving independence through merger, they had committed themselves to this policy again and again. Now they would be breaching the clear understanding upon which the PAP and the CUF had fought and won the election. If we could not survive a split over such a clear-cut issue, we would never survive anyway. We felt released from a very heavy burden. No longer did we have to give them cover. We would either succeed on our own or pack up. However, we could not thank the British for their ploy to get the communists to bid for power on their own; that would make us appear their accomplices. Instead, we decided to make the British appear the accomplices of the pro-communists. That was the line I took in the debate on the vote of confidence:

> "Dinner parties, cocktails and luncheons led to friendly fraternisation between the British Lion and Messrs Lim Chin Siong, Woodhull and company. The pro-communists were led to believe that the PAP were wicked obstructionists, and that the British, wise and statesmanlike people, were prepared even to envisage a new 'left' government emerging in Singapore even more left than the PAP, provided their military bases were not touched. What has happened is that the British have become their own *agents provocateurs*. And how well they have succeeded! Quietly and insidiously they have instigated the pro-communists to attempt the capture of both the PAP government and the party. Young and inexperienced revolutionaries were so taken in that, in a crisis, Lim Chin Siong, Woodhull and Fong Swee Suan looked to the UK commissioner for consultations last Tuesday, the 18th, at Eden Hall, the home of the British imperialists' representative.
>
> "Sir, we felt that something curious was going on and we therefore kept the residence of the UK commissioner under observation. Lo and behold! The great anti-colonialists and revolutionaries turned up for secret consultations with the British Lion. ... And the British may also have hoped that under attack and threat of capture, the PAP would fight back and finally suppress the communists, something they have so far failed in persuading the PAP to do. Meanwhile, to the PAP, the British had suggested that we should take firm action against the mounting subversion. In fact, a plan was to have been drawn up which would have culminated in an act leading to open collision with the communists in which the PAP either remained in office, and so became committed forever to defend British colonialism, or resigned, in which case a non-communist government not amenable to British pressure would have been got rid off."

Several of our Chinese-educated assemblymen had asked me to withdraw the motion of confidence. I believed Lim Chin Siong and Fong wanted time to consider the implications of all this. I decided to press the issue since I had enough assemblymen to enable us to see merger through by 1963. I wanted PAP assemblymen to stand up to be counted.

Chin Chye made our position clear when he read extracts from a paper that Singapore government ministers had written and presented to the Internal Security Council at its first meeting on 12 August 1959. The paper explained our position as "non-communists", while pinpointing and isolating Lim Chin Siong as our main communist enemy. It identified Lim as someone the British knew to be the most important front man for the MCP, yet the UK commissioner had received him at Eden Hall just two days before his supporters in the Assembly voted against the motion of confidence in the government.

The debate on the vote of confidence went on from 2:30 in the afternoon of 20 July through the night, with only an hour's break for dinner, till 3:40 am the next day before the vote was taken. There was as much activity in the Members' room and in the committee room as in the chamber itself. The pro-communists were hard at work trying to get as many PAP assemblymen as possible to vote against the motion. They already had eight. We expected several more to defect; the question was, how many. We needed at least 26 to govern without a coalition. And a coalition government would have been a disaster. It would mean taking in the SPA or the UMNO-MCA Alliance, both tainted by corruption. We would lose our most valuable political asset, incorruptibility.

We decided to lift the party whip and let all vote as they wished. We needed volunteers, not conscripts, for the nasty fight ahead. The pro-communists soon gave up trying to win over the Malay and Indian assemblymen, and concentrated on the bilinguals and the Chinese-educated. But they needed time, and many approached the whip, Lee Khoon Choy, to ask that the vote be postponed until the next day. We refused. So they filibustered, making long, repetitive speeches to drag out the proceedings.

Among those they were working on were three very disparate Chinese-educated Members who had not succumbed to the lure of communism. The bravest of these was Chor Yeok Eng. He lived in rural Bukit Timah, a communist-infested farming area. He was physically at risk, but he stood firm. So did Chan Chee Seng, a strapping 26-year-old judo black belt who had great courage and was personally loyal to Pang Boon and me. In contrast, Lee Teck Him was a man of 55 who worked as a secretary in the Chinese Chamber of Commerce, a first generation immigrant, born in Fujian. He also stood firm. For some reason, he did not share the young Chinese high school students' zeal for the new China. He might have had word of what had happened to his relatives there. Whatever it was, I was much encouraged that he stood by us.

We were not sure how the voting would go; we thought it might be a photo finish. Chan Chee Seng and I did a head count and were certain only of 25 – one short of a majority. And that was where Sahorah binte Ahmat came in. Sahorah was a large, overweight lady of 36, a good platform speaker in Malay, simple and straightforward. She was sick in bed in the Singapore General Hospital, where she was approached by the Plen's sister – apparently with success, for with only a few hours to go before the vote, several Malay assemblymen also visited her and reported that she had been won over by the rebels. But at a meeting in the Members' room during a break in the debate, Chee Seng said he had visited Sahora only the day before and was confident he could get her to come to the Assembly to vote for us. I had given up and told him not to waste time, but Chin Chye interjected that there was no harm in trying.

Sahora told Chee Seng that her Malay colleagues had been distancing themselves from her at government functions, showing that they despised her. So she had refused to be persuaded by them to support the government. But she liked Chee Seng and agreed to come. Chee Seng immediately arranged for an ambulance to bring her to the Assembly House, where she was carried on a stretcher to the Members' room. From there, she managed to walk the 15 yards into the chamber just in time for the crucial vote.

Twenty-six PAP assemblymen voted for the motion, giving us a clear majority of 26 out of a house of 51 members. Had we lost the vote, the government would have had to resign. Then either the pro-communists could form a government with more defections from the PAP or there would be general elections, which they believed they could win.

Dr Lee Siew Choh, parliamentary secretary to the minister for home affairs, and his supporters who voted against the motion believed that in the long run the communists were bound to win. As we hardened our position and they beguiled him with promises to make him their leader and prime minister, he seized his big chance. He was an inveterate gambler from his days at Medical College. Broadset for a Chinese, he had physical energy and a loud voice that was overconfident and a little boastful. He played rugger and chess. On the rugger field his method was to bulldoze his way through without any deception or diversionary tactics, and he was therefore easily foiled. Keng Swee, who had frequently played chess with him, found him bold to the point of recklessness. He was always initiating some spectacular manoeuvre to break his opponent and crash through, forgetting that an experienced adversary would never be tempted to take risks when he could make a steady, relentless advance against an adventurer. This time he was embarked on his biggest gamble – prime minister or nothing.

Our two barber assemblymen voted against the motion. They were not even remotely communist, but for several months before the Anson by-election, communist cadres had latched onto them and had written speeches and articles for them. When I had summoned them and reprimanded them after hearing their untypical speeches in the Assembly, they had apologised, but after the PAP defeat in the Hong Lim by-election, they felt, like others who defected, that their future lay with the unions and the "masses".

Lim Chin Siong's first objective had been to win enough assemblymen to his side to form a new government. When that failed, he tried various strategies to stop the government from continuing to negotiate merger with the Tunku. He formed a new party, the Barisan Sosialis (or Socialist Front). Dr Lee Siew Choh, its chairman, then called for fresh elections.

Lim Chin Siong was silent for a week after the debate on the confidence motion. Then on 28 July, the *Straits Times* published a letter from him that carried the fingerprints of Woodhull and Puthucheary. "Let me make it clear once and for all that I am not a communist or a communist front-man or for that matter anybody's front-man. ..." he declared. He had not even wanted to re-enter the political arena after being released, and about his appointment to be political secretary to the ministry of finance, he said, "Not only was I reluctant to accept the post, but I had offered to withdraw from politics if he (Lee Kuan Yew) so desired it. He did not desire it. Instead, he wished to show the people that I was identified with the government."

The conclusions I had drawn from his tea with Selkirk he shrugged off as anti-communist hysteria:

> "In their nervousness, they began to shout about communism and chaos, expecting to frighten some people into believing them. The communist left who are supposed to be arch-conspirators have now, we are told, been taken for a ride by the British. How funny can people get? My meetings with Lord Selkirk have been few and far between. If meeting Lord Selkirk makes one a plotter then Mr Lee is the greatest of all plotters for he has dealings with Lord Selkirk more than anyone else in Singapore."

That same day he made a two-hour speech at a union meeting, at the end of which he again touched briefly on the tea party: "Regarding

Lim Chin Siong drinking tea and eating with the British, it is a very common thing. The question is whether the stand is firm or not. We cannot say that when we drink tea with them, then we are in league with them." He must have sensed that the workers were fearful that the British had taken him in. He and his pro-communist followers were now exposed and isolated without a credible non-communist cover. But he was not going to get away with his evasions. If he had been reluctant to re-enter politics and to accept a government post, why see Selkirk?

I hit back on 4 August with a letter to the *Straits Times* in my capacity as secretary-general of the PAP:

> "We ... were extremely concerned with the tremendous problems that would crop up after the election. One of the problems was what he and his friends would do after we had released them. He offered to retire from politics and go away to Indonesia. First, it was not an offer made seriously. Second, we did not think it right and proper that we should make it a condition that he should retire from politics before we decided to contest the election to win. We have to face the communist challenge whether or not Mr Lim personally is in the Singapore political arena. ...
>
> (As for the tea party) "he has still not explained why he went to see Lord Selkirk ... In an explanation published in the Chinese press on July 29, he stated that he met Lord Selkirk for social purposes, giving the impression that his talks with the UK commissioner were purely social. There was no social occasion on Tuesday, July 18. There were no other guests present besides Mr Lim and his friends."

An explanation was to be forthcoming, but not from Lim Chin Siong. In a letter to the *Straits Times* published nine days later, on 13 August, Woodhull quoted a conversation Puthucheary had had with Keng Swee after the Anson by-election. Keng Swee had told Puthucheary that British intervention was imminent, that they would not sit back and see the pro-communists destroy the PAP, and that if the non-communist leadership was opposed in public, the PAP for its part would fold up and let the British finish the pro-communists off.

The following day Keng Swee recounted in a letter the gist of several conversations Puthucheary had with him:

"... After Anson, Mr Puthucheary became progressively more and more agitated. He appealed to me, in the name of sanity, to reverse our policy and to accommodate Lim Chin Siong and his faction. The alternative must be the destruction of the PAP as a political force. This prospect he viewed with the utmost dismay. ...

"It was at this juncture that I entered into a series of serious and sometimes tense and emotional discussions with Mr Puthucheary on the future of the party and the country. I said I knew that Lim Chin Siong had thrown the whole weight of his trade union organisation to defeat the PAP at Anson. I said I also knew that the full weight of Lim Chin Siong's trade union cadres had been deployed against our organising secretaries and branch committee members, as a result of which large numbers had defected. But, I pointed out, the situation was not novel. The same thing happened in 1957, when pro-communist trade union cadres mounted an assault on the party organisation and came within an ace of capturing the party central committee. I said, in 1957, the result of this pro-communist assault against us was to draw openly and clearly the fundamental distinction between the pro-communist and the non-communist groups in the party. This adventure provided the British with a pretext for carrying out the big swipe."

Keng Swee thought that the pro-communists wanted to see Selkirk because they took this as a hint that the British were about to carry out another "big swipe" against them now. In a reply published on 21 August, Puthucheary gave a different interpretation, repeating what Woodhull had already said: what they had sought from Selkirk was clarification of an assumption the PAP had expounded, namely that there could be no alternative government to the present PAP leaders, that they were the only group the British would allow to hold power. But the implications were in fact the same: they wanted reassurance from the British that they could go ahead with their plans with impunity.

Years later, in 1982, Selkirk told an interviewer that Puthucheary telephoned him on the morning of Tuesday, 18 July, to ask if he could see him with one or two friends. Selkirk suggested lunch the following day. Puthucheary said it was urgent and he would like to see the commissioner as soon as convenient. Selkirk "reluctantly invited them to tea" at 4 pm. Selkirk said the essence of what they asked him was:

> "'Was the constitution written for the special benefit of Mr Lee Kuan Yew or was it a free constitution?' I said simply this: 'It's a free constitution, stick to it and no rioting, you understand?' That was really the sum of it. Well, they went away and I then told Lee Kuan Yew, before the debate, that I had seen them."

But I was convinced they had been tricked. Selkirk was no inexperienced politician. He knew the meaning of protocol. For the senior representative of Her Majesty's Government in Singapore to receive Lim Chin Siong and Fong personally during a crisis in which the future of the government was at stake was to signal something significant. The pro-communists were bound to interpret it as a nod that the British were prepared to consider working with Lim, an ex-detainee who, under the 1958 constitution, had been prohibited from taking part in elections. Moreover, none of the four who had seen Selkirk were members of the Legislative Assembly and they therefore had no standing to justify any discussion about the formation of a new government. I could not accept Selkirk's explanation that he had met them out of diplomatic courtesy, merely giving them a constitutionally correct reply. Secretly I was delighted that he had. Now we were free of the albatross.

Keng Swee and I believed that the brain behind this move was not Selkirk but his deputy commissioner, Philip Moore. Moore was a man of energy, vitality and keen intelligence. He was well-built, about six feet tall, with a friendly face and smiling eyes. There was something engaging and open about him. He was British middle-class and educated at a public school. He had served as a navigator in a Lancaster bomber during World War II and been shot down in December 1942 over Germany, where he was a prisoner of war until 1945. After that, he went to Oxford, where he would have taken a First had he not joined the British Civil Service before his finals. He was a rugger "blue" and had played for England; it showed in his athletic frame and his agile movements.

Moore and the other members of the UK commission found it difficult to get to know the PAP leaders because of our self-imposed and much publicised rule that ministers should cut down drastically on attendance at non-official functions. We had seen how Marshall and Lim Yew Hock's ministers had become part of the cocktail circuit and lost their standing with the people, who saw them as social climbers. Moore got around the problem by playing golf with Keng Swee and me after every Internal Security Council meeting for the opportunity of long discussions on the golf course and over drinks after the game. Thirty-four years later, after his retirement, Moore told me that by the end of one year, he had concluded that Goode was right when he wrote in his haul-down report that I was not a crypto-communist but a crypto-anti-communist. Goode's report was crucial in determining British policy because Sir Ian Wallace, then permanent undersecretary at the Colonial Office in London, to whom Moore reported, after talking to me for nearly three hours in 1961, also agreed with Goode's assessment.

From British archives I found documentary support for our deduction that the British had planned to split the pro-communists from the PAP, in a report dated October 1961 from Philip Moore to Ian Wallace, setting out the problem of Singapore and merger:

"Once Lim Chin Siong becomes convinced that the people of Singapore are going to support merger, then I suspect he may well revert to the original long-term policy of the MCP – a socialist government throughout Malaya. The opportunity of overthrowing Lee Kuan Yew and achieving a communist-manipulated government in Singapore seemed, in July, to be so golden that Lim Chin Siong could not resist it."

The "opportunity so golden" Moore referred to in this report was the vote of confidence that came up in July. Selkirk's confirmation that "It's a free constitution, stick to it and no rioting, you understand?" was exactly the same line the British took with the Tunku. Moore reported in the same letter of 18 October that "we had to explain to the Federation that, provided Barisan Sosialis behaved in a constitutional manner, there was no question of preserving Lee Kuan Yew simply by putting the Barisan Sosialis leaders in jail or suspending the Singapore constitution". In other words, the British took the position that, provided the Barisan acted in a constitutional manner, they were perfectly free to take over power under the constitution.

Lim Chin Siong and his comrades took the invitation to tea by the UK commissioner and what he told them as a signal that the British were willing to deal with them, that they would not be locked up to prevent them from taking power. Selkirk spelt out the correct constitutional position and they worked out the implications for themselves and made a bid for power, breaking off from the PAP and attempting to remove it from government.

The seemingly simple constitutional stand Selkirk took achieved three objectives. First, the PAP government had either to take action against Lim Chin Siong and his fellow communists or face the danger of being ousted by them. Second, it offered Lim and his comrades the possibility of a constitutional takeover of power. Third, it showed the Tunku that the consequences for Malaysia would be grievous if he refused to take Singapore in.

Once the Tunku had announced his plan for Singapore and the Borneo territories, and I did not yield to Lim Chin Siong's call for the abolition of the Internal Security Council and more "democratic free-doms", the Plen decided to destroy the PAP and me, because merger had to be prevented by all means. This was revealed years later by Koo Young, who had been Lim's subordinate in the CUF organisation, and was confirmed by Lim Chin Siong in 1984 when he told the Internal Security Department that he had seen the Plen three times between the late 1950s and the early 1960s, and that at one of these meetings, the pro-communists were told to break with the PAP. The Plen evidently thought we would be fearful of the strength of the pro-communists, which was true. He thought that we were soft, bourgeois, English-educated, pleasure-loving middle-class types, beer-swilling, golf-playing, working and sleeping in air-conditioned rooms and travelling in air-conditioned cars. He did not see that there was enough steel inside this bourgeois English-educated group to withstand the heat he could put on us.

24. Communists Exposed

The pressure in the weeks that followed the break with the communists was intense. Every day, we traded statements in the press. On 30 July 1961, the 13 breakaway assemblymen announced the formation of the Barisan Sosialis with exactly the same objective as the PAP: "a democratic, independent, socialist, non-communist Malaya, comprising the Federation and Singapore". Almost simultaneously, similar battlelines were also drawn between the unions. On 3 August, the Registrar of Societies dissolved the Trade Union Congress after the minister for labour had been advised it was no longer possible for non-communist and pro-communist unions to coexist in one organisation, whereupon Lim Chin Siong assembled the leaders of those loyal to him – now 82-strong – to discuss the formation of a new Singapore Association of Trade Unions (SATU).

I wanted to get the feel of the ground, to see whether we were in as desperate a position as Lim Yew Hock had been when he rounded up the communists during the riots in October 1956. So Pang Boon, Ahmad Ibrahim and I took leave from our ministerial duties to go back to our grassroots organisations to check the reactions of people to the sudden turn in events.

I went around my constituency in Tanjong Pagar, met the men and women who frequented the community centre, spoke to its committee members and other grassroots leaders, walked the streets, went to the shops, talked to the ordinary people, and in the evenings visited their homes or chatted with them in coffee shops. I also went to several community centres in other constituencies, and a number of non-communist unions that I had been associated with. I found that the leaders and members were not hostile. Those previously closely associated with me remained friendly and supportive. Most were puzzled, some were fearful. None shunned me or thought me a traitor. I was not in the parlous position Lim Yew Hock had been in.

Within days, Pang Boon and Ahmad reported similar experiences. The ground had not turned against us, our activists were still our supporters, but many in the rank and file were taken aback by recent developments and apprehensive about the future. I did not visit any pro-communist unions. They would have been virulently hostile, or would have simulated rage.

Freed from the minutiae of administration, I had time to take the pulse of the community, to reflect and work out a plan of action for the next phase. I had learnt that when confronted with furious attacks, it was best to ward off the blows, stay calm and rethink the fundamentals. The die had been cast when the vote of confidence was taken on 21 July. The break with the communists was open, the fight was on.

We were not allowed to forget it. Lim Chin Siong was doing as much damage as he could. Once the vote was taken, and they discovered they could not take over the government, the pro-communists wreaked havoc on PAP branches, bent on destroying them. Twenty out of 25 branch organising secretaries and their committees defected and joined the other side, taking with them branch property, including typewriters, sewing machines for sewing classes and furniture. But we now had a cadre membership and they could not capture the party. Together with Pang Boon, I toured the branches to boost morale and show that, unlike the Labour Front, we were not on the run. We managed to get some property returned, items we identified in the homes of left-wing members to which they had been removed. Chan Chee Seng, our judo black belt, acted as our bailiff. He was impervious to intimidation and his loyalty and courage endeared him to both of us.

Among the unions, Lim Chin Siong and his boys were out to do their utmost to stir up trouble and create a state of uncertainty and discontent, the preconditions for mass action. They could not talk government officials into being insubordinate, as they were all English- or Malay-educated, but they could get at the semi-government People's Association (PA) and the Works Brigade, using Chinese-educated activists among whom they had planted pro-communist moles. I knew they would do this, but I had had to take the risk in order to gain a foothold in the Chinese-educated world. To screen them all was impossible; some must get through. What I did not anticipate was the ease with which the few were able to sway the uncommitted majority.

We had built up these two organisations with government resources to reach out to the ground. The PA now had links to clan associations, civic and cultural groups, and about 100 community centres. I had put my parliamentary secretary, Chan Sun Wing, in charge of the operation. But Chan was an MCP member whom Jek Yeun Thong had mistakenly thought he could control. Instead, Chan proceeded to recruit Chinese-speaking activists from the trade unions and the party branches to help staff (and thus penetrate) the community centres and PA headquarters. It was much the same with the Works Brigade, a uniformed group of 2,000 unemployed youths. As planned, we had housed them in camps, drilled them into a semi-disciplined force, and set them to building rural roads, digging drains and ditches, and doing other physical work. But Kenny, as minister for labour, put his political secretary in charge of the brigade, and his political secretary was Fong Swee Suan, who had defected. Wong Soon Fong, our assemblyman for Toa Payoh who was supposedly assisting Kenny, turned out to be another of their faithful cadres who helped Fong plant pro-communist activists in key appointments in the Works Brigade. As a result, the communists were able to break both organisations.

They vandalised the community centres as they had done the PAP branches, breaking fences and stealing fans, cooking utensils and sports equipment. They picketed the labour ministry to where the PA headquarters had moved. Before the strike petered out in November, they had turned violent, assaulted a non-striking employee, injured a Malay and a Chinese worker, and clashed with the police.

Kenny was intimidated by Fong's show of power, so much so that although I had dismissed Fong as his political secretary, Kenny was afraid to take action against him and his unions and the Works Brigade. Against the British, Kenny was fearless; against the communists, he was terrified. I discussed the problem with Chin Chye, Keng Swee, Raja and Pang Boon, and decided we needed a stronger minister to deal with communists. So I crossposted Kenny and Ahmad Ibrahim. Kenny went to the ministry of health, where things were quieter, and Ahmad, former fire-brigade worker, went from health to the ministry of labour, where he soon showed he was not to be intimidated. He deregistered the Trade Union Congress and took action against some of the key pro-communist operators in the Works Brigade.

This provoked a mutiny. In November, militants of the Works Brigade agitated for the formation of a trade union, and 150 of them surrounded the office of the camp commandant. They presented the director with a series of demands, including the transfer of the commandant, and on 24 November, set fire to his bicycle and those of two others whom they considered PAP supporters. We charged seven members with mischief. They formed an action committee, held protest meetings, picketed Works Brigade control centres, and in December, following the dismissal of three of their leaders, 180 barricaded themselves in the Paya Lebar camp.

They were a uniformed paramilitary group with some cohesive discipline and could be destructive if they went on the rampage, so we decided to send in the Singapore military forces, of which there were only two battalions, to take over the camp and enforce law and order. I wanted them to avoid any shooting or violent action that would cause casualties the communists could exploit to gain public sympathy. So I instructed the British officer in charge to display such overwhelming force that troublemakers would not dare resist. I said if we had Gurkha troops to send in, I was certain there would be no defiance and the Works Brigade would melt away, but I was not sure whether they had the same healthy respect for his Singapore soldiers. The officer said that it would not be a problem and ordered his men to surround the camp with fixed bayonets. Confronted with this display of force, 400 Works Brigade members dispersed without offering opposition. We then dismissed them all.

Again they formed an action committee and called for a commission of inquiry. But these were feeble attempts at social disruption compared to the communist agitation in 1955 and 1956. Two factors held them back: first, public opinion could be against them if they artificially engineered violence without people first feeling angry over some grievance, like the threat to Chinese education; second, the violence could provoke the government into taking security action against them.

On the industrial front, I expected Lim Chin Siong to organise widespread unrest and warned at a press conference that we were likely to see a repetition of 1955–56. In 1961, there were 116 strikes, 84 of them after the PAP split on 21 July, and in the 15 months from July 1961 to September 1962, there were 153, a record for post-war Singapore.

⚮

By now I was visiting Kuala Lumpur for discussions with the Tunku about merger, and on the occasions that I came back by air and drove from Paya Lebar airport to my home or office, I would pass six to ten separate groups of strikers with their pickets, idle workers standing outside shops and factory premises with banners and paraphernalia of cooking pots and pans. They held employers to ransom, damaged the economy, discouraged investors, and added to unemployment.

But to hit back mindlessly would do no good. I thought it was better to leave things as they were, and to ride out this rough patch until we had defeated the communists on the merger issue. I felt reassured after my first few days of meeting ordinary people in my constituency, and in the community centres and trade unions. The communists did not have us by the throat. We were free of them and we could now act decisively to consolidate our position without having to consider whether we were causing a split. Lim Chin Siong and his pro-communists were isolated and exposed – Dr Lee Siew Choh as chairman of the Barisan Sosialis was not much of a fig leaf. Their organisation had the capacity to do us great harm through their militant unions and the Chinese students, but if they went beyond a certain limit, the British and Malayan representatives on the Internal Security Council would force us to break up their front organisations and have them detained.

I was not keen to do this before merger. I wanted the Tunku to undertake that task after we had become part of the Federation. But Special Branch was in favour of acting at once. When the Internal Security Council met in the Cameron Highlands in August, Selkirk opened the discussion by inviting my view on "The Chinese Will to Resist", a paper submitted by the professionals of Special Branch that emphasised the need to lock up the leaders at the core of the communist organisation. My view was different. I wanted to compel the communists to explain away their previous commitment to merger, to beat them in open argument, which I was confident we could do. I believed that political, more than security, considerations would decide which side would win.

And the winner would take all. The Chinese-speaking in Singapore, like the Chinese-speaking everywhere in Southeast Asia, traditionally preferred to sit on the fence until they saw clearly which way the wind was blowing. At present they had no confidence in the chances of the non-communist PAP. So they would support even a government that they knew was being manipulated by the communists, if the communists looked like winning in the long run. In their eyes, they did. For they were seen as the political agents of a resurgent China whose influence, they believed, would reach down to Singapore within ten years.

Selkirk handing me a driver at the Cameron Highlands golf course, 1961. Dato Sulaiman bin Dato Abdul Rahman, Malayan minister and brother of Malayan home affairs minister, Dr Ismail, is between us. Goh Keng Swee has his back to the camera.

I cited the case of four education service officers recruited for secondment to Special Branch. They now felt that the future had become more uncertain, that the sudden turn of events had increased the risks of the job and would soon put them on the wrong side of the fence. They refused the appointments. I emphasised that the British themselves had helped create this situation, for the more Selkirk and his UK commission staff fraternised with the communists and their millionaire Chinese chauvinist supporters like Tan Lark Sye, the more the Chinese-speaking believed this meant that the communists would be allowed to take over.

Tan Lark Sye's ambition was to be the successor of Tan Kah Kee, who had been the pre-eminent leader of the Overseas Chinese. When Tan Kah Kee died not long before in China, Premier Zhou Enlai had personally taken charge of the funeral arrangements. The People's Republic was signalling that he was held in high esteem, and by talking with the man who wanted to inherit his mantle, the UK commissioner had reinforced the view that the road to power was open to the pro-communists. There was already a noticeable shift in the two major Chinese newspapers in Singapore. Tan Kah Kee's death and funeral had been given two full pages in the *Nanyang Siang Pau*. If the UK commission miscalculated, we could have a communist front government in six months or less. The British might later be able to rectify the situation with their guns, but by then the will of the Chinese-speaking to resist the communists would have melted away. The Chinese mass base therefore needed a Malayan sheet anchor urgently.

Selkirk retorted that, under the constitution, it was the duty of the Singapore government to govern, but the government had sought to transfer the responsibility for internal security to the Internal Security Council. I countered by saying that the constitution had wisely provided that it should be the British who held the ultimate responsibility for employing the gun. The Singapore government had limited power, by comparison no more than that of an air rifle, and could not use it.

These arguments summed up the dilemma the three governments faced. Each wanted the odium to be carried by the others. Both the British and Malayan representatives wanted the Singapore government to take action against the communists, but the Singapore government contended it could not do this without incurring enormous damage to its support among the Chinese-speaking. What was important now was to show that the communists were not the future masters of Singapore. Because only then could we put merger to the vote. And I had concluded that this was absolutely essential, for to bundle Singapore into Malaysia without it would be disastrous. It would be proof that we had sold out to the Malay-dominated government in Kuala Lumpur.

I preferred a referendum to a general election, whose outcome would not be decided on the single issue of merger. But to win a majority for Malaysia, I had to get the Chinese-speaking fence-sitters to see that we – and not the communists – were the winning side. We could not leave them believing that there was a chance of our losing, for many would then vote against merger or abstain, certain that those who had voted in favour of it would later be punished by the communists. On the other hand, if we convinced people that merger was inevitable and the communists did not have the majority to block it, the people would reason that those who supported the communists would run the risk of being punished by the federal government. I had therefore to create in people's minds the feeling that this was a tide so big and so powerful that neither the communists nor anyone else could stop it. I was sure that if we could get this message across, the Chinese-speaking leaders in the chambers of commerce, cultural associations and schools would not go with Lim Chin Siong. At worst, they would remain neutral, at best quietly support merger.

The surest way to generate this sense of the inevitability of Malaysia was to get people to see that Lim Chin Siong, Fong and the pro-communist cadres themselves realised that they were fighting a losing battle, and it was better not to join them. To foster this impression, I decided it was necessary to give everybody the big picture, the background of how the PAP and the communists had formed a united front, why Lim Chin Siong and Fong had broken their undertaking to fight for independence through merger with Malaya, and why they, the communists, must lose.

To think all this out, I needed peace and quiet, which I could not get in Singapore. On 11 August I left by night train for Kuala Lumpur and then went on by car to Cluny Lodge, a Singapore government holiday bungalow in the Cameron Highlands some 5,000 feet above sea level, taking Choo and our three children. But I also took with me my personal assistant, Teo Yik Kwee, for I proposed to dictate and draft a series of 20 to 30-minute speeches that I would deliver over Radio Singapore, giving the people the whole story.

The Camerons were cool, quiet and remote, a blissful respite from the political hothouse of Singapore. At that time there were no fax machines, not even direct dialling, and as the line was not clear, I had left instructions that I should not be disturbed unless it was extremely urgent. So I was left in peace for nearly a fortnight, playing many rounds of golf on the pleasant nine-hole course. By the time I left I had completed eight speeches but had to write the last four in Singapore in between recording the earlier ones. For a period of one month, from 13 September to 9 October, I was broadcasting three times a week, each time in three languages, two of which – Malay and Mandarin – I normally used only at the colloquial level in my working life. It was a gruelling experience. On one occasion, Radio Singapore staff were alarmed when they looked through the studio's glass panel and did not see me at the microphone. Then one of them spotted me lying on my back, flat on the floor in a state of collapse, as she thought. In fact, I had lain down because it was the best way to recover from my exhaustion and recharge my batteries in between recording the three different versions of my broadcast.

In these 12 talks, I summarised the background to our united front with the communists from 1954 when the PAP was formed, what had happened since, and why the split had taken place, leading to the present fight over merger. I wanted to dispel any suspicion that this was a smear campaign against communists and subversion. I gave the communists credit for the strength and courage of their convictions. In one broadcast I said:

> "We bridged the gap to the Chinese-educated world – a world teeming with vitality, dynamism and revolution, a world in which the communists had been working for over the last 30 years with considerable success. ... We the English-educated revolutionaries were latecomers trying to tap the same oilfield. We were considered by the communists as poaching in their exclusive territory. In this world we came to know Lim Chin Siong and Fong Swee Suan. They joined us in the PAP. In 1955 we contested the election. Our initiation into the intricacies and ramifications of the communist underground organisation in the trade unions and cultural associations had begun.
>
> "It is a strange business working in this world. When you meet a union leader you will quickly have to decide which side he is on and whether or not he is a communist. You can find out by the language he uses and his behaviour whether or not he is in the inner circle which makes the decisions. ... I came to know dozens of them. They are not crooks or opportunists. ... Many of them are prepared to pay the price for the communist cause in terms of personal freedom and sacrifice. They know they run the risk of detention if they are found out and caught. Eventually many of them landed in jail in the purges of 1956 and 1957. I used to see them there, arguing their appeals. Many were banished to China. Some were my personal friends. They believed that I should join them. They believed that ultimately I would be forced to admit that what they call the 'bourgeois' democratic system could not produce a just and equal society, and that I would admit that they were right.

Exposing the communists in 12 exhausting radio broadcasts, each made in English, Mandarin and Malay, 1961.

"On the other hand, I used to spend hours arguing with some of them, trying to prove to them that whatever else happened in China or Russia, we were living in Malaya and, irrespective of communism or democratic socialism, if we wanted to build a more just and equal society in Malaya, we would have to make certain fundamental decisions, such as being Malayans, uniting the Chinese and Indians and others with the Malays, building up national unity and national loyalty, and rallying all the races together through a national language."

I explained why Malaya and Singapore were inseparable:

"Everyone knows the reasons why the Federation is important to Singapore. It is the hinterland which produces the rubber and tin that keep our shop-window economy going. It is the base that made Singapore the capital city. Without this economic base, Singapore would not survive. Without merger, without a reunification of our two governments and an integration of our two economies, our economic position will slowly and steadily get worse. Your livelihood will get worse. Instead of there being one unified economic development for Malaya, there will be two. The Federation, instead of cooperating with Singapore, will compete against Singapore for industrial capital and industrial expansion. In this competition, both will suffer."

In my last broadcast, I re-emphasised the point: "Had there been no drought in Johor and water shortage in Singapore over the last three months, the communists might well have switched their line ... to independence for Singapore alone. But nature reminded them of the utter absurdity of such a move." It had been an exceptionally dry year with little rain and none at all since June. At the end of August, the water pressure suddenly dropped, causing many factories to close temporarily and badly affecting big hotels. Our three main reservoirs were almost empty – one of them, Seletar, had elephant grass covering its floor. Water was rationed to six hours a day. There was no need to remind people that Singapore had had to surrender in 1942 because the Japanese had captured the reservoirs in Johor. Water rationing in 1961 could not be lifted until the end of January the following year. The elements had conspired to help convince people that merger was the rational solution to Singapore's problems.

There was as yet no television in Singapore, and these radio broadcasts reached a wide audience. By the end of the series, I had convinced most people that I had told the truth about the past – the infighting, the betrayals, the Plen – and that I was realistic about the future. I had held their interest. I had told a story that was part of their own recent experience – of riots, strikes, boycotts, all of them fresh reference points in their minds – and I had given them the explanation for mysteries that had puzzled them. It was as if I had gone up on the stage where a magician had been performing and exposed his props and accessories by lighting up the darkened areas they had not noticed before. The talks made a tremendous impact, especially on the English-educated, to whom they were a revelation. Among the young men who listened to them was Cheong Yip Seng, who later became editor-in-chief of the *Straits Times*. He remembered:

> "The broadcasts were a real eye-opener to a schoolboy in his Senior Cambridge year, anxious for a job after his exams to relieve his poor parents. The radio talks laid out the future in stark, real-life terms. I was struck by their candour, the power of the simple, vivid language, most of all, by the inside story of the struggle within the united front against the British colonialists.
>
> "The broadcasts were an unprecedented experience. They were not the typical political ones. They contained real-life experiences. They were happening even as they were being aired. The Plen was real. Every broadcast ended with the listener in suspense, and anxious for the next instalment, the way ordinary folk at that time lapped up the kung-fu serials broadcast over Rediffusion by Lei Tai Sor in Cantonese. A master storyteller was at work. But this was not fiction. This was life and death for Singaporeans."

Soon after my last talk on 10 October, John Duclos, head of the Broadcasting Division, invited Lim Chin Siong to join one of 12 radio forums planned to match the 12 broadcasts I had given. All the others who had been named in these broadcasts, including Fong Swee Suan, Sidney Woodhull, James Puthucheary, Dr Lee Siew Choh and Dr Sheng Nam Chin, were also invited to take part. Duclos wrote, "Any statement made by the prime minister over the air which is untrue and damaging to the reputation of anyone can be challenged." The next day, Lim and Woodhull issued a press statement saying they wanted equal time on the air for their 12 broadcasts. They did not want any face-to-face confrontation. I had put them on the defensive.

Those Chinese-speaking groups already committed to the communist cause showed real anger and hatred for me when I passed their union or society premises. Even Chinese press reporters who were on their side had sullen and sour faces when they covered my press conferences. They looked upon my exposure of their identities, their methods and their intentions as a betrayal. I took this as evidence of the effectiveness of my disclosures.

The highest tribute I received was from James Puthucheary. He came to see me in my office at City Hall after the broadcasts were published in a booklet. He said they were brilliant and asked me to autograph a copy, which I did. I asked him if he would be prepared to take part in a radio forum with me. He looked at me, grinned, shook his head and said, "After you have set up the stage props, I would not stand a chance." More important, he tacitly admitted that what I had disclosed about the Plen and the communists had sunk home. I was satisfied that I had undermined the people's belief in the chances of the communists, and felt more confident that we could paint them into a corner and prepare the ground for later action against them, preferably after merger.

∽

Things had not been standing still on the merger front. A Commonwealth Parliamentary Association conference convened in Singapore, with representatives from Sarawak, Brunei, North Borneo and Malaya, had ended with a communiqué issued on 24 July in which all participants underlined the "necessity and inevitability of the united states of Malaysia", and since its final shape and form would require further discussion, agreed to create a Malaysia Solidarity Consultative Committee to ensure that the momentum towards it was maintained. Ten days later, the Malayan and Singapore governments announced after a meeting in Kuala Lumpur attended by Keng Swee as finance minister that we would seek UN help to study how a common market could be set up.

In August, Keng Swee and I had a three-hour conference with the Tunku and Razak to settle the terms for merger. Ghazali bin Shafie, the permanent secretary of the ministry of external affairs, was present. He was to be their key official in charge of the merger details.

The next month, I spent three days in Kuala Lumpur with the Tunku, discussing further details. On my return to Singapore in mid-September, I told the press, "Merger is off the launching pad and the latest developments have put it in orbit, with June 1963 as the target landing date." I used the vocabulary of a time when the world was enthralled by the Soviet Union's spectacular space flight in 1961 with Yuri Gagarin on board, and with America's efforts to put a manned spacecraft into orbit. On finance, I explained that under the federal constitution, every state gave powers over customs and excise and income tax to the central government, but because Singapore would have control of education, labour, health and social services, we would receive a considerable proportion of them to discharge these responsibilities. Therefore the number of our representatives in the federal parliament had to be adjusted, "otherwise we would be representing ourselves twice over".

Chin Chye had written to the leaders of the opposition parties in the Assembly to ask them to state their stand on the two basic points contained in the agreement in principle, namely that defence, external affairs and security should be in the hands of the federal government in Kuala Lumpur, while education and labour policies would remain with the Singapore government. On 29 August, the day the letters were published in the press, Dr Lee Siew Choh declared in a signed statement that the 13 Barisan assemblymen would accept:

"(1) Full and complete merger with Singapore as the 12th state of the Federation: or (2) As a stage to eventual merger, Singapore as an autonomous unit in a confederation. In a merger, the party seeks the immediate entry of Singapore into the Federation as a constituent state, automatic Malayan citizenship for Singapore citizens, proportionate representation in parliament, general elections in Singapore before merger and pan-Malayan general elections after it. In a confederation, it seeks full internal autonomy for Singapore in internal matters, including security, with external affairs and defence in the hands of the Federation government."

The Barisan had adopted a proposal by James Puthucheary that they go for complete merger in the belief that the Tunku would not agree to it. Keng Swee, Raja, Chin Chye, Pang Boon and I were delighted. They had not rejected it; indeed, they were calling for more and closer merger than we were seeking. It was the ideal issue on which to frame the questions for a referendum: which kind of merger did the people want?

25. Moving Towards Merger

We committed ourselves to holding a referendum in September on merger with Malaysia. To carry out merger just on a majority vote in the Legislative Assembly was out of the question; the people would believe we had sold them down the river, whether or not the terms were fair. They had to be given the facts, have the alternatives explained to them, then choose for themselves. Moreover, that way the Tunku could not take us for granted.

Next, the PAP must remain as the government to achieve this. Hence, the overriding need was to have a majority in parliament. Although that majority was only 26 to 25, I believed that if it came to a crunch, the non-communists in the opposition, with the exception of Marshall (one vote) and perhaps Ong Eng Guan and his two followers – now the United People's Party (UPP), were not likely to vote with the Barisan. And once I had given the background to the present conflict in my radio talks, I was in a much stronger position to press home my arguments.

We now had to pin the communists down on what kind of merger they wanted, not let them wriggle and to call again for an independent Singapore. But wriggle they did. After the split, they equivocated for weeks, using delaying tactics by urging the people to concentrate first on the anti-colonial struggle. Before a cheering crowd of 10,000 at a mass rally on 13 August at the Happy World stadium to mark the formation of the Barisan Sosialis, Lim Chin Siong declared that colonialism was the greatest obstacle to merger between Singapore and the Federation. It was British colonialism that divided Malaya into two separate entities. "Therefore, if we do away with colonialism, we will be closer to a merger, and if merger means genuine reunification, we shall be very happy to support it." Thunderous applause greeted Lim when he spoke in Malay and Hokkien, but I was not so sure that his listeners enthusiastically agreed with this part of the speech. Reunification, genuine or otherwise, would dilute their Chinese-speaking majority and render them vulnerable to security action.

The Barisan was not the only uncertain factor. The British were key players in this drama, for everything depended on their reaching an understanding with the Tunku that he must play a crucial role in the future of Singapore, and that would entail not only an "association", but actual merger. Philip Moore, in his report of 18 October to Ian Wallace in the Colonial Office in London, said:

> "There was never, of course, any question of our not being prepared to deal with the problem of the communists in Singapore in the short term, but we had to persuade the Tunku that he alone, in the present climate of international opinion, could deal with Singapore in the long term. ... It was essential to disabuse him of his illusion that Singapore could safely be left to the British on an indefinite basis."

I believed that after we lost the Hong Lim and Anson by-elections and the communists made a bid to remove the PAP constitutionally and take office, the Tunku must have seen that he had no other choice but to take Singapore into Malaya on special terms so as not to upset the Malay electoral majority in the Federation. He would want to have control of internal security, defence and foreign affairs. The Tunku said publicly on 27 October 1961 that by 1963 "in all probability, Britain will give Singapore a constitution that makes Singapore independent. The day Singapore gets independence, it will establish diplomatic relations with the countries we oppose. Embassies from countries like China, Russia, Yugoslavia and other communist bloc members would be set up. We would then have the communists right at our very doorstep."

But the Tunku had his price for taking in Singapore. As far back as August, his government had given the British six months' notice of withdrawal from the Internal Security Council. The British deduced that since they needed the Malayan government to take over Singapore to keep the communists in order, he, the Tunku, would require that the Borneo territories should be completely integrated into the Federation first. I had of course realised there would be a problem of timing. From my visits to these territories to do cases in their courts, I knew that their level of political consciousness was not high and their leadership still unformed. I had left it to the British to sort this out, and assumed that they had already settled this question with the Tunku.

On 16 November, the Tunku left for London from Singapore for talks on Malaysia with the British government. He was in a happy mood and told the press it was safe to assume that Malaysia was "in the bag" – that is, the three Borneo territories and Singapore would all join the Federation. He was quick to add, as the *Straits Times* put it, with a disarming smile:

> "I would like to be quite honest. I would like it to happen at least simultaneously, otherwise the people of the Federation would be pretty nervous. Singapore is regarded in the Federation as something of a problem child. ... The constitutional proposals are not a complete merger. It would be more correct to say it is a form of very close association."

This remark made my job more difficult.

In London, after his talk with Macmillan for only 80 minutes, he was all smiles as he told the pressmen, "We do not have to wait till 1963." In a joint statement on 22 November, the British and Malayan governments said, "The ministers took note with satisfaction of the Heads of Agreement recently negotiated between the governments of Malaya and Singapore for merging Singapore with the Federation." Why had the Tunku come round? Macmillan had charmed him and virtually promised

Meeting leaders from Sarawak and North Borneo to discuss the Malaysia plan, October 1961. From left: Yong Nyuk Lin, Toh Chin Chye, Ong Kee Hui (Sarawak, later minister in the federal government), myself, Donald Stephens (British North Borneo, later chief minister, Sabah), Rajaratnam and Tun Mustapha Harun (British North Borneo, later also chief minister, Sabah).

him the Borneo territories, subject to the findings of a commission to determine the wishes of the people.

In Singapore, we presented to the Legislative Assembly the main Heads of Agreement for merger in a white paper:

"Singapore will get 15 seats in the federal House of Representatives and two in the Senate.

"The 624,000 Singapore citizens will not lose their state citizenship rights they enjoy in Singapore. With merger, they will automatically become nationals of the larger Federation and carry the same passport as other nationals of the larger Federation. They will have equal rights, enjoy the same protection and be subject to equal duties and responsibilities.

"The free port status of Singapore will be maintained.

"The general direction and control of the government of Singapore will be as at present, by the cabinet consisting of the prime minister and ministers appointed on his advice. ... The present Legislative Assembly in Singapore will continue as a State Assembly, but it will have no power to enact laws relating to defence, external affairs, security and other federal matters.

"Singapore will have autonomy in education and labour policies and generally a larger measure of reserve state powers compared to other states in the Federation.

"Singapore will retain a very large proportion of the state's revenue.

"The special position of the Malays who are Singapore citizens will be safeguarded."

On 20 November, Ahmad Ibrahim tabled the motion that "This House affirms that the first objective of all true patriots of Malaya is to achieve the reunification of these two territories in a merger of Singapore and the Federation of Malaya." The Barisan was in a quandary. They saw that the move towards Malaysia was gathering speed and appeared unstoppable, so they tried to delay proceedings by filibustering, Dr Lee Siew Choh speaking for seven and a half hours over two days. After the first half hour, he spoke gibberish. He had a team of hack writers in the opposition Members' room churning out reams of repetitious drivel that Barisan assemblymen brought to him in the chamber. Often he could not even read what had been written for him. We wondered what advantage he hoped to gain by holding up the proceedings for one or two days since we did not have to meet any deadline. Finally Chin Chye, I and other ministers stood up on points of order to ask the Speaker, Sir George Oehlers, whether Dr Lee should be allowed to repeat himself again and again. But Oehlers was weak at the knees. We were dismayed that the communists could instil such fear even in him that he would stretch all the rules to let the Barisan hold up the debate. We decided that if we won the next election, we must have a Speaker with a stouter heart.

It was just as well that Dr Lee rambled on for so long that he buried several good points in a mountain of trivia. One of the most telling was that Singapore would not get representation in the federal parliament proportionate to its voting numbers. Singapore should have 25–30 seats out of a hundred, he said. I explained that I had asked for 19 seats, but the Tunku was not willing to concede more than 15, the number allotted to the urban centres of Kuala Lumpur and Malacca.

My main difficulty was not with this, or over complete merger, which the people of Singapore did not want. It was with the question of citizenship. Dr Lee described the Federation as taking on three wives in Borneo, while Singapore was not to be a fourth wife, but only a mistress. The children of the mistress were going to be treated as illegitimate with no right to federal citizenship. It struck home. The suspicion that "Malaysian nationals" would not be the same as "Malaysian citizens" caused great unease, and gave the Barisan an ideal issue over which to intensify their campaign of troublemaking on which they were already bent. As I had explained at a press conference on 15 October, while Singapore-born citizens would automatically become federal citizens under complete merger, others – some 327,000 of them, those born in China, India and even Malaya – would first have to meet federal residence qualifications and would also have to pass a language test in Malay before they could become federal citizens. The difference was that under our agreement with the Tunku, all Singapore citizens would become "federal nationals". It was the best "special arrangement" I could get from the Tunku.

The communists launched a determined counter-attack despite their basically weak position, moving away from their call for complete merger to stress that people in Singapore would become second-class citizens. Although Keng Swee rebutted Dr Lee Siew Choh on this, pointing out that they would be able to vote for their representatives in the federal parliament and also stand for election, he was alarmed at the effect of this propaganda on our supporters.

After 13 days of tedious and repetitious debate, the vote on 6 December was 33 for (including two UMNO, three SPA and one independent), 18 absent, nil "noes". The Barisan chose to absent themselves rather than vote against the Heads of Agreement after they had already committed themselves to merger. On 24 January 1962, a second motion was debated to support in principle the plan proposed by the Tunku for the establishment of the Federation of Malaysia comprising the 11 states of Malaya, the states of Singapore and Brunei, and the territories of Sarawak and North Borneo. Voting on 30 January was 35 "ayes" (PAP, UMNO, SPA), 13 "noes" (Barisan), three abstentions and three absent. Ong Eng Guan and Marshall no longer mattered. They had wanted to oppose the motion, but feared they might be treated like the communists if Malaysia came about and the Tunku took charge. So they abstained or absented themselves to avoid a collision with the Tunku.

∞

The debate itself was interrupted by a boycott of examinations by Chinese middle school students. On 29 November, Lee Khoon Choy, parliamentary secretary to the ministry of education and government whip, ran into pickets outside the ministry that prevented him from attending the Legislative Assembly. Raja immediately introduced a motion for the House to call on the police to ensure that those responsible were dealt with according to the law. When the motion was passed by 43–3 votes, the Barisan got the pickets to disperse quietly. The examination issue had been a running sore since June, when the minister for education had proposed the examination system be made uniform in English, Chinese, Malay and Tamil schools. That meant a change for Chinese students. Whereas previously they could fail junior middle school examinations and still go on to senior middle school, we now required them to pass their School Certificate before moving on to take the Higher School Certificate. The pro-communists opposed the new system, and brought matters to a head when 300 of them picketed the examination centres and formed human chains to prevent students from taking their examinations on 27–28 November.

This was part of the general turmoil the communists sought to create. They wanted to get the Chinese school students into the act, as they had done against Lim Yew Hock. But we refused to use the police to break up their pickets. Instead we told parents that if their children missed this examination, they would lose a whole year before they could take it again, and we offered police protection to get them through the pickets. The result was that 60 per cent sat the examinations. The press, including the Chinese newspapers, carried pictures of parents and students escorted by police pushing aside pickets who covered the lower half of their faces with their handkerchiefs, bandit style, to avoid being caught on Special Branch cameras.

I never allowed the communists to exploit Chinese language, education and culture, and in this I gained strength from my children being educated in Chinese. Thus I denied the communists a powerful weapon against me. They could attack my bourgeois middle-class background but could not demonise me as they had Lim Yew Hock, as an enemy who was a destroyer of Chinese culture.

26. Getting to Know the Tunku

The Tunku returned from his trip to London in a happy mood. He was extending his territory. He would take in Singapore on terms that would enable him to maintain his Malay majority and the system of Malay dominance he had established in the Federation. He had got over his deep-seated fears about having to absorb more Chinese.

In mid-December I spent four days in Kuala Lumpur, this time staying with the Tunku at his official residence. I went up alone for tête-à-tête talks – no officials, no ministers, nobody taking notes. That was the way the Tunku felt most comfortable, for he always preferred flexibility when implementing any gentleman's agreement. After our discussions, I told the press that he would like to have Malaysia formed by August 1962, so that the anniversary would fall on an auspicious day. Eight was his lucky number, so he had chosen 31 August as Malaya's Independence Day. August was the eighth month, and 31 was three plus one, which made four, or half of eight, the Tunku explained.

I learnt later from his old friend from pre-war student days in Cambridge, Dr Chua Sin Kah, that he liked me to stay at the Residency because he wanted to know the kind of person I was, my personal habits and character. And he had reached the conclusion that I was "not a bad fellow". I sang in my bath and he approved of my songs, like the lilting Indonesian *Burung Kakaktua* (The Cockatoo), which was then a hit; I played golf and poker; and I drank beer, wine and even took whisky and a little brandy – Three Star Hennessy was the Tunku's favourite drink. He decided I was not a dangerous communist. Indeed I was very human and an agreeable companion – young, a little too smart for his liking, and always too full of ideas, but otherwise all right. I got on with him.

One great advantage was that I could speak Malay and I was completely at home talking to his wife, Puan Sharifah Rodziah, an Arab-Malay woman affectionately called Engku Pah, who was also from Kedah, the Tunku's home state. To add to the impression that I was of sound background, Choo also spoke good Malay. This proved to him that we were Malayans at heart and not Chinese chauvinists.

To negotiate with the Tunku required a special temperament. He did not like to sit down and join issue face-to-face after having read his files. He preferred to leave all tedious details to his deputy, Razak – a capable, hardworking and meticulous man – and to confine himself to making the big decisions and settling the direction of events. Every time we ran into a roadblock with Malayan officials over some matter and could not get the relevant minister or Razak to overrule them, I had to go to the Tunku. This meant getting a word in between long sessions of desultory talk about the world, social gossip and lunches for which he often personally cooked the roast mutton or roast beef – he enjoyed cooking and was good at it. After lunch, he would invariably take a nap, and with time on my hands I would go off to the Royal Selangor Golf Club practice tee to hit 100 to 200 balls while I waited for him to get up. At about 4:30 we would play nine holes of golf, and in between shots or before dinner, when he was in the right mood, I would put the question to him. In this way, one item might involve four days of eating, drinking, golfing, and going with him to dinner parties or weddings. On several occasions I accompanied him to Penang or Ipoh or the Cameron Highlands, waiting for a propitious moment.

He possessed an equable temperament, and almost always appeared serene and tranquil; but he could become quite agitated when he sensed danger. He told me that he would never allow anyone to hustle him into a decision, because when he was not calm and relaxed he could make bad mistakes. If he were pressed, he would postpone making up his mind. But I soon learnt that once he had done so, he never looked back.

The high commissioners who did well in Kuala Lumpur were those who realised this, especially Australia's Tom Critchley and Britain's Geofroy Tory. They humoured the old boy, played golf and poker with him. Critchley might lose a few hundred dollars to him at poker over the months – not big money, but not tiddlywinks either. The Tunku liked winning, or rather did not like losing. It was part of his royal upbringing. I did not mind, as my purpose was to get points of agreement clarified between us; but I robbed him of the sense of satisfaction that comes from winning because my mind was not on it. Once, when I had lost a couple of hundred dollars after taking a third telephone call from Singapore, he said, "Kuan Yew, keep your mind on the game. I don't like winning from you when your mind is not on the game. The work can wait till tomorrow." I laughed, remembering the London talks in 1956 and Lennox-Boyd writing a reply to a cable while listening to David Marshall. "Tunku," I said, "when I went to the telephone, I knew that your bid was $15, I suspected you had three kings, and I did not have enough cards to meet you, so I had to throw my hand in." He was not mollified. He wanted to win only after I had tried my best.

It was different at golf. The Tunku had a 24 handicap and played to 24; mine was 12 (later unfairly reduced to nine) but I actually played to 15. And he would have a strong partner. So it was difficult for me to beat him. Nevertheless, on one memorable occasion my partner and I trounced him by eight holes with seven to play. He was not pleased. Moore, who was at the Royal Selangor Golf Club at the time, took me to task for being tactless.

His friends also humoured him. When his horse was beaten at the races, one of them would often fish some tickets from his pocket and say, "Tunku, I bought these tickets for you. I knew you wouldn't bet on this horse when your horse was running, but I knew it was going to win so I bought them for you." The Tunku would go home a winner by a few hundred dollars in spite of his horse losing. It made his day.

He was a nice man. But he was a prince who understood power and knew how to use it. He did not carry a big stick, but he had many hatchet-bearers who would do the job for him while he looked the other way and appeared as benign as ever. If he distrusted a man, that man was finished with him. But if he trusted you and you did not let him down, he would – in the royal tradition – always find some way of helping a loyal follower, as he did with Lim Yew Hock. When Lim was out of office, the Tunku made him high commissioner to Australia. When he disgraced himself there by getting lost in a striptease nightclub for a few days, provoking a police search for him, and had to resign, the Tunku got him another job in an Islamic organisation in Jeddah (Lim had become a convert to Islam). It was his way of helping a friend in trouble.

And, fortunately, he viewed my parlous position in Singapore with sympathy. There was never a lull in the communist attacks on us. We had chronic industrial unrest, though there were no riots or clashes between workers and police. On 11 January 1962, the opposition in the Dewan Rakyat, the House of Representatives in Kuala Lumpur, put a barbed question to the Tunku as to what would happen after merger since Singapore trade union leaders, unlike their Malayan counterparts, seemed to "flourish in trouble". The Tunku replied that Singapore had more strikes in one month than Malaya had in three years, but he would try to reduce the number and increase the amount of happiness of the people there, adding laughingly, "I don't know how we will do it but our minister for internal security says he will do it. The whole country is with him."

This was a double-edged sword. It was helpful in that it showed waverers in Singapore that the Tunku was confident merger was coming and that after merger he would deal with the communists through Ismail; but it was unhelpful because it spurred the Barisan to more desperate action to stop it. However, the Barisan did not return to violence. It placed its hopes on getting the Chinese-speaking electorate to vote against merger in any form by working on their fears over "second-class citizenship".

To address the issue, the traditional leaders of the Chinese-speaking community (including those of the Chinese Chamber of Commerce) had proposed that I talk to their members. I agreed, and on 13 January, I met over a thousand delegates from 400 guilds, associations and unions at the Victoria Memorial Hall. The chair was taken by the president of the Singapore Chinese Chamber of Commerce and Industry, a successful rubber trader of 51 called Ko Teck Kin who, like most of his colleagues other than Tan Lark Sye, was apprehensive of the communists. He had an economic stake in Malaya, where the rubber came from, and he was not going to side with the communists. After I got to know him better, I found him a sensible, reasonable man, deeply concerned about the future of the Chinese community in Singapore whose interests he felt it was his duty to protect.

I spent three hours answering questions. The audience was not hostile. The majority were practical businessmen. The communists had not been able to pack the meeting and could not dominate it. My answers to several questions drew laughter from the crowd. And when I rounded up the meeting with an account of the historical development of the Chinese communities in Southeast Asia, and of how the clan associations had played a key role in the welfare of the Chinese immigrants, they responded warmly and I sat down to applause.

As I expected, the first question concerned citizenship. This was natural. As one key member of the chamber reminded the audience, they had fought hard for Singapore citizenship, multilingualism and equal treatment for all streams of education. They were therefore anxious to know how these would be affected by merger. I told them that if we sought complete merger as proposed by the Barisan, some 330,000 Singapore citizens would lose all citizenship rights. But Lam Tian, my old opponent in the 1955 general election, later came back to query our alternative. Why couldn't all 600,000 Singapore citizens enjoy the same rights after joining Malaysia under the terms we had agreed with the Tunku? I explained that the rights of all Malaysian nationals, whether Singapore citizens or federal citizens, would be the same, except that Singapore citizens would vote in Singapore for their representatives in the federal parliament, and federal citizens would vote in the Federation. (In fact, the Tunku's object was to exclude Singapore citizens from voting elsewhere in Malaysia.) But the nagging question in the minds of the Chinese-speaking remained – if there was no difference between them, why did the Tunku not agree to use the more familiar term "citizen" instead of "national"?

That distinction was my problem, and my job had not been made easier when the third meeting of the Malaysia Solidarity Consultative Committee issued a statement a few days earlier saying that the special position of the Malays in the Federation would be shared by the indigenous people of the Borneo territories; they would thus automatically become "founder citizens" of Malaysia by operation of law. This emphasised the superior status of "citizens" over the "nationals" in Singapore.

When I met Sir John Martin, another permanent undersecretary at the Colonial Office, with Ian Wallace and Philip Moore at Sri Temasek on 16 January 1962 to discuss Malaysia, they thought that the general opinion in the North Borneo territories ran contrary to the confident assumptions of the Malaysia Solidarity Consultative Committee. Martin and Wallace had been to Borneo and found hesitation on almost all sides. The unsophisticated upriver people knew little of the implications and needed time to think about it. The Chinese were distrustful because they knew it was Malayan government policy to keep them in their place. In Brunei, Azahari, the leader of Partai Rakyat who had considerable support among young Malays, was firmly opposed to joining Malaysia, and was calling for an independent federation of the three Borneo territories. The Sultan of Brunei wanted to know what advantages there were in it for him, and had to be reassured that he could seek special terms in direct negotiations with the Malayan government.

I said that these hesitations of the people who had confided in them should not be taken too seriously. The leaders in the Borneo territories respected authority. Once they saw the Tunku as the ultimate source of power in the Federation, they would accommodate themselves to it. What was important was that the British should give a strong lead and have them understand Britain's support for Malaysia was firm and settled.

Martin concluded that the people of Borneo would come to accept the plan provided the Tunku was wise enough to grant them reasonable safeguards, but more time was needed for preparation to ensure that the administration did not collapse after sovereignty was transferred. I emphasised that we had to keep up the momentum. The Tunku wanted Malaysia by August 1962. I wanted to accomplish merger as soon as possible and so dilute the communist threat in the larger population of Malaysia.

I told them that we had to make haste. The Barisan had made a tactical blunder when they declared themselves in favour of complete merger, and once they knew they could not win, they might decide to launch a campaign of widespread disorders rather than accept Malaysia and their removal from the scene. They might want to go down fighting.

∽

The Barisan's potential for stirring up trouble had not decreased. I was therefore eager to get things moving, and through my impatience and my very different temperament made the Tunku angry with me. I had not been sensitive enough to realise that once he decided to take Singapore into the Federation, his attitude towards me would undergo a subtle change. He was a prince of the royal house of Kedah. Hierarchy was part of his nature. As long as Singapore was outside his domain, he treated me as the leader of a friendly neighbouring country, a lesser leader to whom he was willing to be courteous. But now, I was going to be part of his Federation, and he was accustomed to having courtiers and retainers around him, followers who were faithful and humble. Lim Yew Hock was one of them, and I had been unkind to Lim when he introduced a motion in the Assembly in March to express grave concern at the mounting industrial unrest in Singapore. In the exchange that followed, I had knocked him about roughly, pointing out the differences between his handling of labour disputes in 1955–56 and the way we were dealing with them.

Then Keng Swee aroused anger by announcing that the Singapore government would award equal pay to men and women in the civil service forthwith. Tan Siew Sin, the finance minister of the federal government, was very annoyed and passed his annoyance on to the Tunku. He believed that this change would have financial and social implications for Malaya, since their women employees would demand equal pay.

The last straw was when I told the Tunku that I was planning a tour of Delhi, Cairo, Belgrade, London, Moscow and Beijing. He was appalled. I was on a dangerous course, associating with the enemy. I was giving the impression that the Russian and Chinese leaders were great men when in fact they were "evil fellows" out to destroy the stability of Malaya. He could not understand my reasoning, that after I had visited these countries and been received by them, I would be better qualified to tell the people I was more convinced than ever that the communist system was unsuitable for Singapore and Malaya. That was not the Tunku's approach. I was going to be part of his scheme of things and he did not want anybody in Malaysia to fraternise with the enemy. He was angered by my arguing with him over it, and I finally concluded it was not worth my while to clash with him on the issue.

His irritation showed. On March 25, in Singapore, he opened up on the extremists who looked upon the island as "Little China", opposed merger, and had broken away from the PAP to fight it. If they wanted to create trouble and bloodshed, it would be better not to have merger at all, he said, but in that case he would close the Causeway for Malaya's own safety. On the other hand, he added, extremist groups had nothing to fear after merger as long as they respected the law and worked within the federal constitution – there were already more of them in Malaya than there were in Singapore.

That was typical of him. He had said in the House of Representatives in Kuala Lumpur that his minister for internal security would deal with the communists. Now he said they would be all right if they worked within the constitution. Yet it was obvious he wanted them dealt with. He often indulged in such equivocation. It was the Tunku speaking his mind – not necessarily logical and tight in his presentation but leaving his listeners in no doubt where he stood. However, his intervention this time was more of a help than a hindrance. He had underlined the vulnerability of Singapore, and his determination to have merger. Only two days later, he spoke at a dinner given by Ko Teck Kin, and this time he really let his hair down. "A complete break between Singapore and Malaya might mean war and bloodshed with devastating effect on the people," he said. "War would result if an isolated Singapore sought solace in the company of powers unfriendly to the Federation (meaning China)."

Selkirk reported back to London:

"I feel that the rather hysterical and hectoring note will do harm and will raise the temperature in Singapore politics at a time when we are trying to ease Singapore quietly and inevitably into merger. Threats of closing the Causeway and of war between Singapore and the Federation are futile and will only help the Barisan Sosialis to excite communal feeling against the Malays. ... Perhaps, however, what is more important than the effect on Singapore is the indication of the confused state of the Tunku's thinking. He is clearly puzzled and hurt that his offer of Malaysia has not been welcomed with open arms in both Borneo and Singapore, and part of him is no doubt already regretting the whole enterprise. Nevertheless, I believe he still intends to go ahead with Malaysia and probably the more extreme passages of his speeches should not be taken too seriously."

Selkirk was wrong about the effect of the Tunku's words. They made a considerable impact on the Barisan leaders who realised the Tunku meant business and had now entered the fray. He had painted a bleak picture of the outcome for Singapore if there were no Malaysia. Lim Chin Siong was alarmed enough to write to the Tunku pledging his party's support for merger and Malaysia. The letter was handed over quietly at Federation House in Singapore, but the Tunku leaked the fact through one of his secretaries and the *Straits Times* carried the headline: "Mystery letter. It was from Lim." Pressed by journalists, Lim Chin Siong confirmed that he had written it and said he was grateful to the Tunku for sending him a very courteous reply. Asked what it was about, he declined to answer.

Taunted with dark conjectures voiced by Chin Chye – was it a secret sell-out? – Dr Lee Siew Choh finally produced the letter and the Tunku's reply on 11 July. Lim Chin Siong had written that he thought much of the Tunku's unhappy feelings about Singapore had arisen from a lack of opportunities for free and frank discussion of the "apparently divergent attitudes" between them, which could contribute a great deal towards understanding and national unity. The Tunku in his reply welcomed Lim's assurance that he was completely at one with him on the desire for national unity. He had to leave Singapore the next day, but would be happy to meet him at some future date, and would let Lim know when this could be arranged. But the Tunku, who knew that the "apparently divergent attitudes" were irreconcilable, had offered no date.

Lim Chin Siong had made a serious mistake. Writing the letter and not making it public in the first place was seen by the Chinese-speaking as weakness, an admission that he was in a vulnerable position and wanted to make peace with the Tunku. The letter was a giveaway with nothing gained in return. It implicitly acknowledged that the Tunku was the person most likely to be in control from now on, not Lim Chin Siong and the communists, and I knew the Chinese would take this into account when making their choices in the future. All the Barisan could do in the meanwhile was to keep their cadres busy in order to maintain their morale and stop them from thinking about the hopelessness of their position. Accordingly, Dr Lee announced that 1,500 of them would be out the following Sunday – and every Sunday for six weeks afterwards – on a house-to-house campaign to reject the government white paper on merger.

A week after the Tunku's visit, Tan Siew Sin visited Singapore to open a sub-branch of the MCA, of which he had just become president. He sounded even tougher than the Tunku. Singapore had become the problem child of Malaya, he said. But if there were no merger, it might not be necessary to close the Causeway because Singapore's economy was so vulnerable. A short and simple customs order levying an additional cess on rubber exports would reduce the largest rubber market in the world to a tropical slum. An island smaller than Malaya's hill station, the Cameron Highlands, could not go it alone. He added that the Malayan government was not completely dominated by the Malays and it was not true that the Chinese did not get a square deal. He would not be a member of a government which he felt was hostile to the legitimate interests of the Malayan Chinese.

The threat to fix Singapore through economic measures did not endear him to the Chinese in either territory. A few days later the Barisan countered by warning him that the interdependence of Malaya and Singapore was a grim reality; any attempt by one to impose economic sanctions against the other would be to commit suicide. At the same time, Lim Chin Siong took on the Tunku, albeit obliquely. As it was no longer possible for the British to rule according to the old colonial pattern, he said, they had decided on Malaysia to use local right-wing forces to police and protect their interests in the region.

The Tunku responded by repeating his warning that the Causeway would be closed by the end of the year if Singapore rejected merger, and stressed that he meant it. "If the communists think they can easily dupe the Malays," he said, "they are sadly mistaken." A week later, the Barisan retorted that such threats would only increase public antagonism towards Federation politicians whose attitudes were "most unreasonable, unjust and non-democratic". It said that the Federation wooed the people of the Borneo territories with concessions, but for Singapore it was all threats, coercion and intimidation.

This might well have been so, but the threats had made people realise that the consequences of a confrontation with the Tunku could be devastating. However much it would hurt, Malaya would weather it better than Singapore. The British business community was dismayed, and to underline the precariousness of the situation, the retiring chairman of the Singapore Chamber of Commerce referred to the "orgy of strikes, go-slows, sit-downs, etc, which is termed industrial unrest" and incurred a serious risk that new capital would be kept out of the island, while rising costs would restrict existing trade and create financial difficulties.

The general mood of apprehension all this fostered worked against the Barisan. Meanwhile we had cleared another hurdle. After acrimonious exchanges and a debate that went on for five hours to past midnight and continued the following day, the House passed an amended motion welcoming the introduction of the Singapore National Referendum Bill by 26 votes to 16.

∽

Needing a change after this frenetic activity, I decided it was time to renew my contacts with British leaders, and to meet several Afro-Asian leaders on the way. In April 1962, I flew to London via Rangoon, New Delhi, Cairo and Belgrade.

Prime Minister Pandit Nehru of India fully supported my proposals to merge Singapore with Malaya and form Malaysia. I had a good press. Under the caption, "Prime Minister's blessings for Malaysia secured", *The Times of India*, then India's journal of record, wrote that Malaysia had evoked appreciation in official circles. It was obvious the Indians considered it a sound development because it would help to keep China's influence out of Southeast Asia. At my press conference, I was able to tell journalists that their prime minister was not concerned about the Afro-Asian secretariat's declarations that Malaysia was neo-colonialist.

My next stop was Cairo, from where the secretariat of the Afro-Asian Solidarity Committee issued its statements critical of Malaysia. If I could win President Nasser over, I would make an important breakthrough. I arrived in the morning and was met at the airport by the vice-president and taken to one of ex-King Farouk's smaller palaces, now a guest house. That evening, I was received by President Nasser in his modest, unpretentious but well appointed home. It was a good meeting; the chemistry was right. When I arrived, he was at the front door with photographers in position. I felt he had done it hundreds of times, so photogenic did he look on television and in the papers. All the same, he was most welcoming and friendly. His consul general in Singapore was a great supporter of mine and of Malaysia. He knew we did not want Singapore to become an Israel in Southeast Asia, and had reported this to his foreign minister.

Nasser spent an hour listening to me on the dangers of Singapore going it alone and becoming the odd man out in Southeast Asia, a Chinese entity in the midst of a Malay archipelago of about a hundred million people. I did not want this. The answer was to reunite Singapore and the peninsula, with which it had been governed by the British as one unit for over a hundred years before they were separated. He needed no persuading that Malaysia was not a neo-colonialist plot and assured me that he would support it and that I could say so. All through the five-day visit, the Egyptians laid out the red carpet for me. I was invited to visit Egypt again and see him at any time – it was personal, Nasser said. I had made a friend. I liked the man, his simple lifestyle and his intense desire to change all that was decadent and rotten in Farouk's Egypt.

A big smile of welcome from President Gamal Abdul Nasser of Egypt in April 1962.

Nasser issued a joint communiqué with me, breaking protocol since Singapore was not an independent country. It said that he supported Malaysia and the "unification of all peoples with similar political and social backgrounds ... seeking an end to colonial domination". It was a political plus for Singapore to be understood and supported by Nasser and Nehru, the two leaders who then set the pace in Africa and in Asia.

On May Day, I flew to Belgrade. Tito received me formally. Unlike Nasser, he had a splendid residence, with electrically controlled steel gates that opened silently upon our arrival. I was taken to see him by a minister, Slavko Komar. Tito wore a lounge suit, not one of his resplendent uniforms, and as the cameramen took pictures he looked firm and stern – no smiles, no warmth, completely the opposite of Nasser. I was up against it: the Indonesians had poisoned his mind. But he listened. I took time to explain my background, that I was a nationalist and not a colonialist stooge. I did not agree with the communists in Singapore who took their inspiration from China; they could not succeed in Singapore and Malaya because their brand of communism was not indigenous; Maoism could not succeed in Southeast Asia. I sensed from his body language that I had shifted him. I mentioned an article critical of Malaysia in their party publication, the *Komunist*. Tito said it did not represent the view of the Yugoslav government. I had gained my point.

When I was leaving for the airport and about to meet the press there, I asked Slavko Komar whether I could repeat what Tito had told me. He said the president was a man of his word, and when he had said it was so, it was so. So I quoted Tito's statement and turned around to the minister to ask whether I was right. He nodded and said, "Yes." After my departure, Reuters reported a foreign secretariat spokesman as stating, "the article represents the personal opinion of the author. Premier Lee during his stay in Belgrade informed the president and Yugoslav leaders about desires to create a Malaysian federation, which were received with understanding by the Yugoslav side." It was a plus.

❧

For Choo, the London trip was the first time she had been back since she left in August 1950. The city looked prosperous and Londoners well-groomed. They were going into the Swinging Sixties. Although I had been there three times between 1956 and 1958, I was impressed by the sense of plenty, the shops, the restaurants and the cars. Macmillan had won the general election in 1959 on his refrain, "You've never had it so good", and the popular press had dubbed him "Supermac". It was May, the weather was fine, and we were happy to find the British capital thriving. Several huge Humber Pullmans were parked at Grosvenor House where we stayed, waiting to take us wherever we wished. But I had a tight programme – discussions with ministers, meeting old Labour Party supporters in parliament, and cultivating the British press in off-the-record interviews.

Reginald Maudling, the new secretary of state for the colonies, a large, well-built man with spectacles, was outgoing and easy to get on with. He and his wife saw us socially before our official discussions to make us feel welcome. He also gathered some ministers to meet me for lunch, and Mrs Maudling had what was then called a hen party for Choo at the Hyde Park Hotel.

One major problem was still the old issue – whether the communists should be cleaned up before or after merger. The Tunku had repeated his demand that the Internal Security Council move against them beforehand. He had made it clear to the British and to me that he did not want to take repressive measures the moment Malaysia came into being. It would not be an auspicious beginning.

I was prepared to consider action before merger – with two important provisos. I told Maudling the operation could begin while the United Kingdom still had the responsibility for security, hence under the command of the British, as chairman of the Internal Security Council. My public position would be that it was most regrettable but, from my personal knowledge of the communists, absolutely necessary. Next I insisted that the communists should still be at large when the referendum on Malaysia was held. I believed they would call for a boycott that would not be obeyed and this would discredit them. It would be a fatal mistake to detain them before the referendum; that would completely destroy its worth and open me to accusations that they were arrested to help me win and hand Singapore over to the Tunku. There would be protest riots and public disorder.

A special commission under Lord Cobbold was then visiting North Borneo to determine the attitudes there towards Malaysia. I stressed that whatever the Cobbold report recommended on the subject of citizenship for people in Borneo, Singapore could not be given less favourable terms. The term "Malaysian national" would have been acceptable if it had applied equally to the citizens of both territories, but the Tunku had announced that Borneo citizens would become Malaysian citizens, although Singapore citizens would not.

When Maudling asked about my difficulties with the Tunku, I said, "The Tunku thinks I am clever but wrong and he, though not clever, is right. I win the argument, which embarrasses him, but he feels that my conclusion is wrong though he does not know why." If he would persuade the Tunku that it was folly to believe that every Chinese was a potential communist supporter, it would have more effect than if it came from me. The Tunku's simple belief was that "politics was for the Malays and business for the Chinese". This might have been so in his father's time, but was not realistic in 1962. As for our differences over citizenship, I had also met Lord Cobbold that morning and spent the best part of an hour discussing his recommendations on Borneo, and I told Maudling that I felt happier now that he knew how they could affect Singapore, and how they could increase my problems.

My visit was not all work. We drove up to Cambridge to meet Billy Thatcher for tea at the University Arms Hotel. Thatcher was pleased with what I had done since I went down from Cambridge in 1949 and asked about our children – we had written to him to say how bright Loong was. He gave us a copy of Lewis Caroll's *Alice in Wonderland* for him and said, "He must come soon if I am to be here to see him." He did not look particularly frail but I was glad I was able to meet him. He died a year later. We were both very sad.

The weekend in Cambridge was a welcome break in a full official programme that included a BBC broadcast to Singapore on their Far East Service. I described how the heads of non-aligned nations – India, Egypt and Yugoslavia – had come out in open support of Malaysia. It was not the kind of news that helped the pro-communists.

Press and radio reports of my meetings with Nehru, Nasser and Tito, and my BBC broadcast from London must have done me good because the Barisan attacked me vigorously. To explain why these great leaders of the Afro-Asian world did not think Malaysia was a colonialist plot, they claimed that I had managed to gain their sympathy and support by creating a false impression. They cavilled that Nehru, Tito and Ne Win (unlike Nasser) had not issued joint statements with a discredited prime minister. But they could not deny that they had supported Malaysia.

Meanwhile, the pro-communist Indonesian newspaper, *Bintang Timur*, reported that Lim Chin Siong had said he was in favour of merger with Indonesia rather than with Malaysia. This was foolish, and Lim hastened to deny making the statement, but it had damaged him – the communists were losing that air of irresistible and inevitable victory in their fight against merger, and his denial was unconvincing.

I returned to Singapore feeling the better for five weeks away from the daily grind of public argument and the pressure of industrial unrest. My spirits were sufficiently restored to return to the ceaseless ding-dong with the communists, exchanging vitriol with them in the press and exercising restraint in the face of provocation by their strikes, go-slows and sit-downs while business suffered, jobs were lost and unemployment increased.

Things had not gone too badly. In May, some 3,000 students had gathered at Chung Cheng High School to commemorate the anniversary of the clashes with the police in 1954. They sang songs, condemned the government for setting up a commission of inquiry to investigate the boycott of the secondary four examinations and called for a one-day boycott of classes in all Chinese middle schools on 21 May, the day the commission was to start. But on the day itself, there was 100 per cent attendance at 19 of the 25 morning schools. One hundred students were picked up plastering walls, lamp-posts and traffic signs with protest posters, but at 5 am, when it was still dark. They were not anxious to be noticed and photographed.

And despite the Barisan's canvassing every Sunday, the ground had not turned sour on us.

27. A Vote for Merger

On the question of citizenship though, the Barisan was gaining ground. Its suggestion that Singaporeans would be "second-class citizens" in Malaysia struck a chord and aroused alarm. I was determined to tackle the question head-on. So on 3 June 1962, the third anniversary of Singapore State Day, I spoke at the Padang to a few thousand people gathered there to watch a march past of military detachments, civilian groups and schoolchildren, and cultural displays. I assured them that before Malaysia was implemented, I would make it clear in the constitution that Singapore citizens would be equal to all others in the Federation.

Lim Chin Siong retorted that my pledge was an admission that there was in fact no equality for them under the proposed merger and Malaysia arrangements. The Barisan had narrowed the issue down to this one problem, and I was convinced that if I could get the Tunku to change the term "Malaysian nationals" to "Malaysian citizens", it would be solved. I was determined to achieve this, and then hold a referendum as soon as possible before the Barisan could work up dissatisfaction and discontent over some other spurious objection. But I had no leverage with the Tunku, only the British had, since the Tunku wanted the Borneo territories and also needed their assistance to defend Malaya; I had to get them to exercise it. Moore agreed that we had a legitimate grievance, and I knew he would do his best to get his ministers in London to persuade the Tunku to change his mind on citizenship. But we disagreed about another equally important matter – the referendum.

Moore was worried because the Referendum Bill, which had already gone through a select committee, had recommended that since the submission of blank ballot papers would indicate that the voters concerned did not wish to exercise their right to decide for or against merger themselves, the decision would be taken by the majority in the Assembly (meaning the PAP). I had inserted this provision to counter any communist call for a blank vote. But if people wanted to protest by casting blank votes in large numbers and in that way express their opposition to merger and the referendum, Moore thought I had to give them their choice. He tried to dissuade me from going on with the operation, saying people had labelled it dishonest and phoney. I disagreed. In a report he sent to the secretary of state on 21 June, as acting commissioner, he wrote:

> "In answer to our repeated suggestions over the last six months that he should not hold a referendum, he has always said that he must do so to avoid being labelled as the man who sold the Singapore Chinese to the Malays. ... It seems therefore that he will have to go ahead with the referendum on his terms, which have been carefully calculated to ensure that he does not lose. Probably the only serious risk now is that there will be a large-scale boycott of the referendum."

He was right about one thing: I remained determined that there should be a referendum, and my immediate task was to get the bill through the Assembly. Once the Cobbold Commission report was published, I would have to decide what alternatives to put to the people. There had been endless public discussion in the press, over the radio and in forums at the University of Malaya, and although the debate on the Referendum Bill itself lasted from 27 June to 11 July, with eight midnight sessions, the speeches were heated and repetitious because there were no new arguments, only increasingly vehement reassertions of the respective positions of the opposing sides. An amendment on the key issue was moved by Dr Lee Siew Choh and supported by David Marshall and Ong Eng Guan to propose that only one question should be posed in the referendum – "yes" or "no" to merger. Then Lim Yew Hock intervened to propose that three questions be posed: Do you want merger (A) in accordance with the white paper, or (B) on the basis of Singapore as a constituent state of the Federation of Malaya, or (C) on terms no less favourable than those given to the three Borneo territories? Dr Lee's amendment was defeated and Lim Yew Hock's accepted. I was delighted that Lim had proposed what I had planned to do.

During the debate, every Member of the Assembly received a thinly veiled threatening letter, signed by 39 old boys' associations and university students' clubs led by the Nanyang University Guild of Graduates, telling them to vote for the Barisan proposal – or else. On 29 June, speaking on the supplementary estimates to raise more than a million dollars for a second battalion of the Singapore Infantry Regiment, I warned the Barisan that should wild talk lead to wild action, then the wild men would be put away. If the rules were cast aside for stones and iron bars, then the overriding interests of peace, security and the well-being of the people would require the use of force to suppress force. I felt no qualms about using the Singapore Infantry Regiment against the communists: there was no danger of my being dubbed a colonial stooge. But to encourage them to be on their best behaviour, I assured Dr Lee that no troops would be used as long as they kept to the rules.

On the afternoon of 3 July 1962, PAP assemblywoman Hoe Puay Choo sent me a letter resigning from the party on the grounds that she had not been consulted on important policy decisions. The communists had been hard at work on her and had got her to switch at this, the last moment. The PAP now had 25 Members against the combined opposition's 26. We had become a minority government. I asked Moore to meet Chin Chye, Keng Swee and me. If the PAP had to throw in its hand, Keng Swee asked him, would the British see merger through after we had resigned? Moore thought it would be very difficult, as there would then be no elected government to support it. He urged me to see it through if it was at all possible. I said I would, but asked him to tell London that time was now extremely short. We had to battle on in the Assembly for another eight days of debate before the vote was taken. We carried the motion by 29 votes to 17 – 24 PAP, three UMNO and two SPA against 13 Barisan, one Workers' Party (David Marshall), and three UPP (Ong Eng Guan). Hoe Puay Choo absented herself. We had got the bill through with the support of Lim Yew Hock's SPA and the Tunku's UMNO.

A month earlier, Moore had given me sight of the final draft of the Cobbold report to test my reaction. I was most concerned by its recommendations. "There is no reason for a separate citizenship for the Borneo territories," it said, and set out terms that would include a waiver for a limited period of the language test in respect of persons above a certain age. Thus all those born in the territories could qualify for Malaysian citizenship. This was a disaster. My position would become totally untenable and the referendum would fail. There would be large-scale abstentions or blank votes.

The report had, however, given me one opening. Immediately after the referendum debate, I wrote to Maudling to point out that Singapore citizens could become Malaysian citizens without creating any problems, because the Cobbold Commission had also recommended that electoral rights should only be exercised in the territories where the citizens were normally resident. In other words, Borneo citizens would vote in Borneo and Singapore citizens would vote in Singapore, so the Tunku need not fear being swamped by Chinese from Singapore casting their ballots in Malaya. I then wrote to the Tunku on 12 July, to send him a copy of this letter and to suggest that the solution to the problem was to use similar terms for Borneo and for Singapore, without in any way altering the content of what we had already agreed about limiting voting rights.

I attached an *aide-mémoire* for both him and Sandys, which stated that the main thrust of the attack against the white paper by the communists was that it was anti-Chinese: because the island was 70 per cent Chinese, the Tunku was not prepared to offer Singapore what he was prepared to offer the Borneo territories, which were 70 per cent non-Chinese. This could only be disproved by offering Singapore the supposedly better Borneo terms. I had given the British notice that if they did not press the Tunku to grant us equal citizenship, I would not be able to get merger through the Assembly. What I did not say – and it was something on the minds of Chin Chye, Keng Swee, Raja and myself – was that in that case, we would not even want to go through with it. The Tunku and the British would then have to take the consequences.

Immediately after the Referendum Bill was passed, Dr Lee Siew Choh tabled a motion of no confidence in the government. To this, Lim Yew Hock moved an amendment condemning the government for "not restraining known communists and communist front leaders from manipulating and controlling organisations like the Barisan Sosialis". He waxed eloquent and unburdened himself. It was his chance to show how he had sacrificed everything in order to deal with the communists in 1956–57. Had he known that the prime minister had consorted with the so-called "Plen", he would have sent him to keep Lim Chin Siong company (in Changi Prison). The Barisan wanted to wreck the referendum and merger by this no-confidence motion but Lim Yew Hock would not make common cause with them.

People were becoming less afraid of the all-powerful communists as they realised how vulnerable they were, that it would be the Malayans, not the colonial British, who would soon deal with them. Lim Yew Hock's amendment was defeated as was the original no-confidence motion. After the Barisan had lost the fight on the Referendum Bill and the motion of no confidence, the Tunku left for London in mid-July to finalise the terms with the British over the Borneo territories. Time was running out and the communists searched desperately for some way to prevent merger.

Two days after they lost the debate, a group of 19 assemblymen led by the Barisan Sosialis sent an appeal to the United Nations

Decolonisation Committee, objecting to the way the questions to be put in the referendum were formulated. Only two of the 17 members of the committee were from the communist bloc; the majority were Afro-Asians, most of whose governments had representatives in Singapore and Kuala Lumpur and knew what was going on. As there was nothing to be gained by dodging it, I cabled UN Acting Secretary-General U Thant that the opposition's petition was part of the play of domestic party politics in Singapore, and that if the committee considered the petition, it must hear the government first. I was prepared to lay before it the facts of the situation, which could stand the closest scrutiny.

At first the Indian representative staunchly supported us, in keeping with the view Nehru had expressed in Delhi in April that year, that there was no alternative to Malaysia. Together with Cambodia, Tunisia and other Afro-Asians, he said that since Singapore had a freely elected government, its actions could not come under review by the committee. Then he unexpectedly changed his mind, perhaps because of my willingness to participate. The following day, the UN said the committee, which had earlier voted 10–2 to take no action, had decided it would meet a delegation from the Singapore assemblymen who were petitioning against the referendum and had asked for a UN observer. Dr Lee Siew Choh was jubilant. But I was not unhappy with the outcome; I was confident I could demolish the arguments of the Barisan and Marshall, and on 20 July I made a formal request to the committee to appear before it.

Two days later, Keng Swee and I took off for New York with my personal assistant, Teo Yik Kwee. I wanted to get in the first word with the committee, then leave for London to join the Tunku and Macmillan after they had finished their discussions on the Borneo territories. Our plane was a Superconstellation, a four-engined turboprop and the main intercontinental aircraft then in service. It took nearly two days to fly us from Singapore to New York via Saigon, Guam, Hawaii and Los Angeles. Keng Swee and I worked throughout that flight, preparing a point-by-point rebuttal of the long 19-point memorandum that Marshall had helped the Barisan to draft. Once my bags were unpacked in our Manhattan hotel, I looked for Teo. I found him flat on his back on his bed, fast asleep, fully clothed with his shoes on, totally exhausted. He had been typing endless drafts and redrafts for Keng Swee and me for almost 48 hours.

The British were still in charge of our foreign affairs and an officer from their mission to the United Nations met us at the airport. They were first-rate professionals. They knew every procedural move that had to be taken, and piloted me to the right people for preliminary talks. They advised me not to present any long or protracted argument to the committee but to go back to the position earlier taken by the Indian delegate that there was an elected government in Singapore and the committee should not concern itself with what it decided.

At the hearing, I handed in the memorandum giving our rebuttal to the opposition's charges that the referendum terms denied the people the right of democratic dissent, and in the course of two hours elaborated on every point. They had been guilty of misrepresentation in seeking UN intervention, I said. Their appeal was part of a false alarm designed to maintain an atmosphere of emergency in Singapore in order to boost the flagging morale of their supporters, who saw merger advancing relentlessly upon them. They had also been guilty of seeking to retain colonialism in Singapore for their own purposes, and had petitioned against the duly elected and constitutional government, which wanted immediate independence. It was a paradox. The explanation was that when Singapore joined the Federation, the communist struggle would no longer be against the British colonialists, but against a popularly elected government that had already won independence for the country. Meanwhile, we had a complete mandate to carry out merger without a referendum at all.

After my submissions, Dr Lee Siew Choh made his, and I then requested and was given the right of reply. It was ironical, I said, that both opposition spokesmen, Dr Lee and Woodhull, had been born in Malaya, not in Singapore, and that Woodhull as a Malayan citizen had travelled to New York on a Malayan passport. Furthermore, they did not represent the majority, because when they had challenged the government on a motion of no confidence, they were able to obtain the votes of only 16 out of the 51 Members of the Assembly. Keng Swee and I were both tired from our journey, but we were determined to establish our nationalist credentials as Afro-Asians. By our demeanour, our tone of voice, our gestures and the emphatic way in which we dealt with all questions, we made sure the committee could not mistake us for stooges of the British or the Malays. Sir Hugh Foot, the British permanent representative to the United Nations, was delighted with our efforts. He said the members of the committee were left in no doubt that the PAP was a vigorous outfit with a fighting prime minister, and not by any stretch of the imagination a puppet of the United Kingdom.

∽

We left that very night for London. There was little time to lose. The Tunku was concluding his talks with Macmillan and it was time to press him in the presence of the British to settle the question of citizenship. So I did not stay in New York to hear Marshall make his representations. He made an impassioned plea and evoked a better response from the committee than Dr Lee, but he was unable to remove the deeper impression I had left on its members. The committee decided not to take any action on the petition.

We reached Heathrow Airport on Friday, 27 July, at 11:15 am. Keng Swee and I were exhausted after flying eastwards into the sun all the way from Singapore via New York, but there was no time to rest. After a quick wash at the Hyde Park Hotel, where we were staying, we went down to the dining room in time to have lunch with Selkirk. He briefed us on the progress of the talks with the Tunku on the Borneo territories, and by

3 pm we were seeing Duncan Sandys at the Commonwealth Relations Office. However tired we were, we had to carry on.

The next day, Keng Swee, Stanley Stewart (my permanent secretary) and I had tea with the Tunku at the Ritz Hotel. As usual with the Tunku, we did not discuss the subject of citizenship directly. But he was in a relaxed mood. He had finally settled nearly all outstanding issues with the British over Borneo. The signs were good. On Sunday morning, Keng Swee and I played golf with him and Razak at Swindon, and that afternoon, while the Tunku was resting, Razak represented him at a meeting with Duncan Sandys at the Commonwealth Relations Office, where we discussed the unresolved questions of Malaysian citizenship, the detention of the communists and the plan for a common market. I did not know whether Macmillan had had a quiet word with the Tunku, but Sandys put it bluntly to Razak that these issues had to be settled before the British would sign the agreement on the Borneo territories. Razak conceded Malaysian citizenship in principle, subject to the Tunku's endorsement. It was a great step forward.

I still had worries. Without the British to persuade the Tunku, I would not have got this agreement, and I feared that once Malaysia came into being they would not be able to intervene further on Singapore's behalf. Meanwhile, we had still not established a really sound working relationship with the Tunku and Razak. They had totally different personalities. Razak was always filled with doubts and hesitations, always having second thoughts. He would agree on some item after long debate and discussions, only to ring me up the next day or the day after to revise his decision. He fretted and worried over details, and was a good deputy for the Tunku, who never bothered about them. He was a hard worker, and had finished his Bar examinations, both intermediate and the finals, in a record time of 18 months. He spent time building up a network of friends and supporters among the Malay students in England, including the sons of the nine Malay sultans. But although he himself came from a family of traditional chieftains, he did not have the Tunku's naturally gracious ways, and dealing with him was always more of a strain.

At 10 am on Monday, 30 July, Keng Swee and I went to a formal meeting with the Tunku and Razak at the Ritz and stayed on for lunch. The Tunku duly endorsed what Razak had agreed. I said I would send him a letter setting this out and asked him to confirm what I had written. After lunch, I went back to the Hyde Park Hotel and produced the final draft, of which the key passage read:

"Some persons find it difficult to understand that there is no difference in calling Singapore citizens 'nationals' or 'citizens' of the new Federation of Malaysia. We have, therefore, agreed that, since this question of nomenclature has loomed large in the minds of some sections of the people, paragraph 14 of the white paper should be amended so that citizens of Singapore will be citizens of Malaysia instead of nationals of Malaysia."

I attached a joint statement of the Malayan attorney-general and the Singapore state advocate-general confirming the constitutional position in regard to voting rights, which was that our people would vote only in Singapore, and that this would remain unchanged.

The Tunku replied in a letter the following day, with the Ritz Hotel, London, as his address:

"I confirm that the arrangements for citizenship of the inhabitants of Singapore will be in the form agreed between the governments of the Federation of Malaya and Singapore set out in paragraph 14 of Singapore White Paper Command 33 of 1961, as amended in regard to nomenclature and franchise in the terms of the statement."

This was what I needed. Had the communists not made such an issue of it, they would not have made it so easy for me to turn the tables on them. Now they would have few real grievances left and I was not going to give them much time before the referendum to create new ones to exploit. To this day, I have not discovered how the British – maybe with the help of the Australians – finally persuaded the Tunku to change his mind. Probably Sandys, who could be very firm in negotiations, had told him that if there was no common citizenship, there would be no Borneo territories for him, and no merger. That evening at seven, Sandys held a final meeting with the Tunku, Razak, Keng Swee and me to wrap things up. I asked for the agreement on citizenship not to be published, so that I would have a chance to make a dramatic pronouncement in Singapore at an appropriate time.

There remained the problem of the communists. I had learnt from Selkirk on arrival in London that the Tunku was still insisting that all the troublemakers should be detained before Singapore became a Federation responsibility. But he had repeated that the British were unenthusiastic about taking action against them and would rather that the operation were mounted by the Malaysian government after merger. I was greatly relieved. Now the British could carry the burden of opposing the Tunku. I then adjusted my position to make it clear that once the referendum had been successfully concluded, I would be prepared to support the idea of a clean-up before the inauguration of Malaysia.

But Selkirk had written to Sandys on 27 July :

"I must leave you in no doubt how dangerous I think this policy is for the following reasons:

"(i)   Arbitrary arrest without convincing public proof must strengthen the opposition in Singapore and disturb Lee's colleagues, possibly causing him to fall.

"(ii) It would become abundantly clear that Malaysia was being imposed by the British, regardless of the will of the people concerned. It will then be presented as our plan for preserving our bases with the Tunku allowing himself to be used as our stooge.

"(iii) It will be very difficult to defend action of this character in parliament here or in the United Nations, where the Russians are known to be working hard against Malaysia.

"Nor has any solid argument been advanced why such action as may be necessary for security could not be taken by the Malaysian government after the formation of Malaysia."

What Selkirk left unsaid was that there might be riots and bloodshed, which would bring political odium on the British. Sandys stressed that he could not agree in advance, even in principle, to a series of arrests in Singapore without having had an opportunity to consider the cases of the individuals concerned. A reasonable case must be presented, and it was not for the British government to initiate the matter. But if all concerned showed that they were prepared to take their share of responsibility, the British government would not shirk theirs, and would not let the others down. The Tunku had to settle for this for the time being.

The Tunku often talked openly of his lucky numbers, lucky colours and dreams. He took such otherworldly influences seriously. In London, he had a pleasant dream associated with the animals of the zodiac. This, he said, was auspicious. As the Malaysia Agreement was to be signed on 1 August, his lucky day, he went to a jeweller's near Burlington Arcade to order a gold ring with the symbols of the zodiac on it for the occasion. When he took delivery, however, he was dismayed to discover that it was inscribed with some strange symbols, not those of the zodiac he was familiar with such as the ram, bull, Gemini twins, crab and so on. Keng Swee came to the rescue, assuring him that the symbols represented them, otherwise the ring would have been sent back for alteration and might not then have been ready before the signing ceremony. Such incidents relieved the tedium of being a courtier in the Tunku's court at the Ritz.

The Tunku was nevertheless a liberal-minded Western-educated Muslim of the pre-war generation. He was a bon vivant and was completely open about it. Like other Muslims of his generation in Britain he ate freely, drank liberally and loved horses and women. He was once cited as co-respondent in a divorce suit in England brought by a Eurasian lawyer with whose English wife he had committed adultery. The case, well-publicised in Malaya before he became chief minister in 1955, only increased his popular support. Malay kampong folk admired his prowess. After his retirement from politics in 1970, the Tunku became a devout Muslim, devoting his energies to the furtherance of pan-Islamic unity as secretary-general of the Organisation of Islamic Conference.

The Tunku was altogether a most agreeable dinner companion, full of little stories, often told at his own expense in a most charming manner. His object in life was happiness, and the yardstick by which he measured any situation was whether it made him happy or unhappy. When everything was going fine, he would proudly say, "I am the happiest prime minister in the world." He would add that his aim for Malaya was not wealth, greatness or grandeur, but happiness in a land without hatreds or troubles, and when seeking to reassure the Borneo peoples of their position in the Federation, he told the press that this aim would now be extended to the whole of Malaysia. But it did not go down well with the people of Borneo and Singapore, who were not used to measuring their well-being in that way.

He had no pretensions about his own abilities and no inhibitions in describing the capabilities of his fellow Malays. He was disarmingly frank in his self-deprecation, confessing that his Malay father, the sultan, was a weak man and that his strength came from his Thai mother. The Malays, he said, were not very clever or demanding, and therefore easy to please. All he needed was to give them a little bit more and they were quite happy. These views were similar to those expressed by Dr Mahathir Mohamad in his book *The Malay Dilemma*, published in 1971. He wrote, "Whatever the Malays could do the Chinese could do better and more cheaply", and "they resulted from two entirely different sets of hereditary and environmental influences". Years later, in 1997, when he was Malaysian prime minister, Dr Mahathir said he had reversed his stand and no longer believed what he wrote in *The Malay Dilemma*.

But in the 1960s, the Tunku would often look around at the officials and ministers in his drawing room before or after dinner and say, "These fellows can't do business. They have no idea how to make money. The Chinese will do the business. They know how to make money, and from their taxes, we will pay for the government. But because they, the Malays, are not very clever and not good at business, they must be in charge of the government departments, the police and the army." He had a simple philosophy: the role of the Malays was to control the machinery of the state, to give out the licences and collect the revenue, and most important of all, to ensure that they were not displaced. Unlike the Chinese and Indians who had China and India to return to, they had nowhere else to go. In his soft-spoken, gracious way, he was absolutely open about his determination to maintain the ascendancy of the Malays and ensure that they and their sultans would remain the overlords of the country.

Razak would giggle uneasily whenever the Tunku trotted out his oft-repeated and candid views of his Malays. It made Razak uncomfortable. He thought these views underrated their ability and would not be acceptable to the younger generation – after all, he himself had finished his Bar exams in half the time many Chinese students took to do so. The Tunku might have taken umpteen years to complete his finals, but that was because – as he himself so often said – he had spent much of his time in England on slow horses and fast women.

At 7 pm on 1 August, the Tunku and Macmillan signed the agreement that would bring Malaysia into being, the ceremony having been delayed for one day so that it would fall in the "lucky" eighth month of the year for the Tunku. The governors of North Borneo and Sarawak signed on behalf of the Borneo territories. Singapore and Brunei were briefly referred to in a joint statement, although they had loomed large in the two weeks of discussions that preceded the ceremony. The Sultan of Brunei held out for better terms. So did we.

The Cobbold Commission's report was released at the same time that the agreement was signed. It was well-written, presenting the case in the best possible light. The commission's assessment of the wishes of the Borneo people was that one-third were strongly in favour of Malaysia's early realisation, without concern about the terms and conditions. Another third favoured Malaysia but wanted safeguards. The remaining third were divided between those who preferred to see British rule continue for some years and "a hard core, vocal and politically active, which will oppose Malaysia on any terms unless it is preceded by independence and self-government". In other words, never. On his part, Cobbold rejected a plea from the Borneo territories for the right to secede during a trial period. This was final.

Keng Swee decided to return to Singapore before me, and arrived on 3 August. The press reported him as being in a jubilant mood at the airport. Drinking a toast to Malaysia in champagne, he told journalists that the government had a trump card it would play at the right time.

Although my work was done, I stayed on in London to be with the Tunku, who was a great believer in not being rushed through life. Even during the discussions, he liked to spend time strolling through the Burlington Arcade near the Ritz to buy fancy waistcoats or handkerchiefs as he had done in his misspent youth in England. I tagged along to keep him company and, on one occasion, I joined him in buying a natty grey linen waistcoat I did not need. At a lunch given by Macmillan and attended by Sandys, we were photographed with them outside Admiralty House sporting our new waistcoats. When we were out of the Tunku's hearing, I explained to Macmillan my difficulties in dealing with him, and Macmillan commented, "The Tunku is like a Spanish grandee. That's his world." I could only agree. Macmillan himself acted as a grandee but with a modern mind, calculating the odds at every move behind an urbane demeanour. The Tunku was a grandee who expected the world to fit into his pattern of thought.

On 8 August – a doubly auspicious date for the Tunku – we flew back to Singapore by Qantas, arriving on the ninth. The next day, I accompanied him on a special Malayan Airways flight to Kuala Lumpur, where he received a huge and enthusiastic welcome at the airport. He generously shared his garlands with me, and gave me the opportunity to address my first Malayan crowd. And when he then rode triumphantly to the Residency in an open car with thousands lining the route, he again shared his glory with me by having me stand beside him in the car. I was in his good books.

The following day, I returned to Singapore to make sure of the final preparations for the referendum, including the release of my exchange of letters with the Tunku. When we met the press together, we had made no reference to the agreement we had reached on Malaysian citizenship. I wanted to reserve that for later.

But the Barisan already knew something was afoot. When the agreement was signed in London, Marshall had heard at the United Nations in New York that under British and Australian pressure, the Tunku had agreed to a common Malaysian citizenship. I did not know who had told him, but he could not contain himself. He at once gave the information to the news agencies, and it had reached Singapore. This robbed me of the element of surprise, but as nobody in authority had confirmed it, the suspense remained. Whoever told Marshall in New York might have done so in order to soften his stand against Malaysia. Whatever the motive, the effect on him was profound. He realised that now he was taking on the British, the Australian, and the Malayan governments, and he feared that if he stuck to the anti-Malaysia line of the Barisan, he might receive the same treatment that the Tunku was reserving for them. He was soon to hedge his bets.

He was not alone in this. Lim Chin Siong was in trouble, for all around him his supporters were having second thoughts. On 3 August, a committee member of the Nanyang University Guild of Graduates

With Prime Minister Harold Macmillan and Secretary of State
Duncan Sandys outside Admiralty House, July 1962, after a lunch
for the Tunku and myself, both wearing new-bought grey waistcoats.

The Tunku generously sharing his garland with me on
our arrival at Kuala Lumpur airport after the London
talks, August 1962.

warned him that many people did not agree with the casting of blank votes. According to Special Branch, Lim replied that there was no alternative. Five days later, the editor of the Singapore Socialist Club's journal also told him he could not openly call for blank votes because the club was supposed to be impartial. To do so would antagonise the English-speaking students. He had only been able to insert an appeal for them in the form of a letter from a reader.

On 14 August, I announced two weeks of active campaigning for the referendum on Saturday, 1 September. I assured all Singapore citizens that they would automatically become Malaysian citizens. I read out excerpts of my letter of 30 July to the Tunku and his reply of 31 July confirming it. It was a devastating demolition of the opposition's objections to merger.

∞

Lim's left-wing trade unions and cultural associations ceased all other activities in order to mobilise their members for their campaign for blank votes. Posters, symbols, flags, banners and placards spread across the city on lamp-posts and walls like a pox, and public rallies were held every night, the largest organised by the Barisan. But within 24 hours of my announcement, Ko Teck Kin, as president of the Chinese Chamber of Commerce, pledged support for alternative "A" – the government's formula for merger. He was determined that Singapore Chinese should not lose their citizenship as a result of the political manoeuvring of the Barisan. This was a turning point; the mass of Chinese-speaking people, uncommitted to the communist left and faced with an important decision affecting their personal status and their citizenship, opted to listen to their traditional leaders.

On 14 August, Lim asked one of his cadres, a pro-communist reporter on the *Nanyang Siang Pau*, why his statement on merger had not been published in it. It appeared that the management of the newspaper was now more afraid of the government than of any retribution the communists might mete out to them if we lost the referendum. Lim was getting more desperate by the day, the Barisan even resorting to accusing me of attempting a *fait accompli* in defiance of the United Nations Decolonisation Committee, which, they claimed, would meet in September to consider their appeal against the dishonest referendum. This was nonsense; the committee had already decided to take no action on it.

Meantime, the opposition had suffered another setback. We strengthened our position in the Assembly when S.V. Lingam broke with Ong Eng Guan on 17 August and the UPP and asked to rejoin the PAP. His return restored to the government its absolute majority of 26 to 25. (Lingam's vacillating behaviour was strange. The mystery was cleared up only after we joined Malaysia, when Keng Swee learnt that he had been a paid agent of the Malayan Special Branch. They wanted to know what Ong was up to, but had directed Lingam to return to the PAP when it looked as if the Singapore government was in danger of being overturned. We fielded Lingam as a candidate in the 1963 general election, but when we discovered this, we dropped him.)

Our advantage was short-lived. Ahmad Ibrahim's health had been steadily deteriorating. He had cirrhosis of the liver because of a hepatitis infection years earlier. We had sent him to England for an operation, but the disease had progressed relentlessly, and on 21 August, he died – I was at his deathbed with his wife. Ahmad had great spirit. He had qualities of leadership, which he had displayed to good effect in the Naval Base Labour Union. More important still, he had had the courage to take over the ministry of labour from Kenny to face down the communists. His death was a severe loss, and it left us with 25 votes to 25 in the Assembly once more.

However, the position was far from hopeless. Marshall was wavering and wanted to move away from the communists in order to restore his position with the Tunku. I invited him to take part in a one-on-one radio forum with me. He accepted, and during the question-and-answer session that followed the opening discussion, he conceded that there was no difference between Singapore citizens and the other citizens of Malaysia now that we, too, had got Malaysian citizenship. To keep up the appearance of being reluctant and dubious, he asked for assurances, which I readily gave, that Singapore citizens would have the right to work and own property throughout the Federation, that they would be entitled to jobs in the Malaysian Civil Service, and that the Singapore state constitution would be worded in exactly the same way as those of the other states.

That same day, he met the Workers' Party leadership and got them to welcome the change in citizenship conditions unanimously. Nevertheless, they remained opposed to the referendum provisions, which they considered "so immoral that no honest person whatever his views should participate in it except compelled by law". Marshall knew voting was compulsory, of course, and so advised people to throw in blank votes in protest, since they could not abstain. Once again, this was a typical lawyer's manoeuvre. He was not prepared to oppose and anger the Tunku, but at the same time, he tried to make it appear that he had not broken ranks with Lim Chin Siong.

A few days later, I was able to get him to say during a forum at the University of Singapore, "Let us be precise. The Workers' Party has not changed its stand. The constitutional proposals have been changed to meet the Workers' Party's demand in exactly the formula of the Workers' Party." Yet in a final futile gesture, he asked the government to postpone the referendum until the draft Malaysian constitution had been submitted to the Assembly. Despite the smokescreen he threw around his motives, his unqualified admission, as an antagonist who was both anti-merger and a lawyer, that Singapore citizens would not be second-class citizens in Malaysia was a crushing blow to the Barisan's propaganda line.

There were more blows to come. Following the pledge of support given earlier by Ko Teck Kin, the leaders of 12 trade associations signed a statement on 23 August calling on the Chinese Chamber of Commerce to convene a meeting to advise people not to cast blank votes but to vote for alternative "A". Furthermore, they published their names for easy identification, although their action was in direct opposition to the open letter put out by the MCP.

To give them a further reason for breaking away from the communist line, I decided to add to the fears of the traditional Chinese clan leaders by declaring that if there were large numbers of blank votes, they might well have to be counted as votes for alternative "B" – complete and unconditional merger – for it would mean that the majority had responded to the Barisan's call for them. But in that case all those not born in Singapore but naturalised through registration could lose their citizenship. That sank in. Three days after the first 12 trade associations signed their statement, three more organisations came out in favour of alternative "A", among them the Singapore Chinese School Teachers' Union, which had been communist-dominated.

The next day, Ko led a delegation from the Chinese Chamber of Commerce to my office at City Hall to clarify my statement on alternative "B". I left him in no doubt that he should not take chances with the citizenship of his Chinese-speaking members. He then asked the opposition parties to state categorically what action they would take if at their instigation the number of blank votes cast in the referendum resulted in an acceptance of alternative "B". Lim Chin Siong responded to Ko's query with a threat: the Chinese community would know "how to deal with their so-called leaders who betrayed them", he said, denouncing the chamber for going along with the PAP propaganda line. Not intimidated, however, the council of the chamber itself now asked its members to vote for alternative "A", and on the same day, six more Chinese organisations came out in support of it.

To counter this trend, Lim Chin Siong got 24 trade unions, and then a further 12, to reaffirm that their members would cast blank votes. But their leaders carried little weight; they depended on Lim's prestige, which was fast declining. Exasperated and at his wit's end, he resorted to more threats, became erratic in his speeches, and on 27 August made a major blunder. At a rally at Hong Lim Green, he said "merger and Malaysia had different meanings for different forces. In the struggle for Malayan and Indonesian independence, the nationalist forces in these two territories have brought up the idea of a Melayu Raya, that is, Greater Malaya, or Malaysia, including Indonesia. ..."

This frightened the Chinese-speaking voters, who knew that the Indonesians had been more anti-Chinese than the Malays in Malaya.

Nor did it help when Ong Eng Guan, asked by the press what he would do if blank votes were interpreted as votes for complete merger, refused to comment. It strengthened the traditional leaders' conviction that the pro-communists and the anti-merger group had been boxed into a corner. Taking courage, the Chinese Chamber of Commerce bought space in all the Chinese newspapers for two consecutive days to announce the support of its members for alternative "A". Their earlier fear of the communists was overridden by their fear that 330,000 of the Chinese-speaking who were the source of their strength would lose their citizenship and hence their influence on political developments. Their open defiance of communist threats had a bandwagon effect. Other civic leaders also lost their fear and came out to urge their members to vote for "A", along with 51 commercial firms and trade unions.

The last week before the referendum saw a flurry of street meetings and mass rallies, but I did not believe they would make much of a difference any more. The debate on the merger terms had gone on for a whole year. The issue of nationality and second-class citizenship on which the Barisan had concentrated had been settled. On 30 August, the final rallies were held, the PAP organising its biggest at Hong Lim Green, where we attracted a huge crowd without having to bus them in, as the Barisan had done three weeks earlier. As I started speaking at 9:30 pm, music suddenly blared forth from three loudspeakers on the veranda of the fourth-floor premises of a pro-Barisan trade union. I quipped, "This is Barisan Sosialis democracy. We gave them a year to do their worst. Now they are afraid of us telling you the truth." They turned the music up to drown me out, but I continued. After some minutes a police party went into the building. They found the doors on the fourth floor locked, but the music stopped.

Polling started at 8 am on 1 September and ended at 8 pm, when counting began. By 3 am, it was clear that the Barisan's blank vote campaign had failed. Blank votes amounted to less than 30 per cent of those cast, 70 per cent favoured alternative "A", and there had been scattered support for "B" and "C". There were huge crowds outside Badminton Hall at Guillemard Road, and the atmosphere was tense, for although there were 345 polling stations all over Singapore, the ballot boxes had all been brought to this centre for counting. The Barisan had wanted votes to be counted separately in each electoral division, but we had refused that. We did not want them to know which constituencies had cast the most blank votes, useful information for the next election. But they outsmarted us by getting their supporters to drop their polling cards into the ballot box together with their ballot papers. Those cards clearly stated the district they were from.

At about 6:45 am, just before the results were to be announced, Dr Lee Siew Choh sent a letter to the superintendent of the referendum demanding a recount. The superintendent consented to his demand half an hour later, but the delay prompted Dr Lee to send a second letter at 7:45 in which he claimed that the superintendent had taken his earlier one to the prime minister before answering it, and was therefore no more than his page boy. Moreover, since the first count had been irregular and the same procedure would be adopted for the second, the whole business was as farcical as the referendum itself and he would have none of it. The superintendent had his reply ready an hour later, but on my advice read it out over the loudspeakers for the benefit of the press before he handed it to Dr Lee. It said that the ballot boxes had been opened and the ballot papers mixed and counted before Dr Lee, who was present during the entire procedure but had voiced no objections as to its propriety until it was completed and it only remained to announce the results. However, the superintendent ordered another recount as requested.

Dr Lee's was a futile gesture of protest, and as the recount proceeded he stormed out of the counting station and told the press, "It's lousy. It's farcical." Lim Chin Siong walked out with him and crossed the road towards his cheering supporters to say, "We shall continue unabated our struggle for equal rights for the people of Singapore." But the signal went out for them to disperse. They had lost and they went home with their tails between their legs, not willing to face defeat.

At half past eleven on Sunday morning, the recount was finished: 71 per cent had chosen alternative "A" and 25 per cent had cast blank votes. I was overwhelmed with joy when I spoke to the waiting crowd, and my eyes filled with tears. My words were broadcast live by Radio Singapore from the Badminton Hall:

> "The verdict of the people is a terrifying thing for the politically dishonest. This verdict is decisive. It is the seal of public and popular approval for merger and Malaysia. ... Not to have held the referendum would have been a tragic error, for we would have allowed the communists to make people believe that the so-called masses were against merger. With time and explanation, we can whittle down the remnant pockets of support that they have got by lying, smearing and by intimidation."

"Merdeka Malaysia!" Leading victory cheers outside the Singapore Badminton Hall on 2 September 1962, after winning the referendum on Malaysia. My Hokkien teacher, Sia Cheng Tit, is on my right.

28. Europe Beckons Britain

I left for London on 5 September to attend the 1962 Commonwealth Prime Ministers' Conference convened to discuss Britain's application to join the European Economic Community (EEC). Singapore was not independent, but since the colonies could be affected, we were invited as advisers to Duncan Sandys; I had no right to speak and could only make my views known through him. It was an opportunity for me to renew contacts with the Labour Party. I had met Hugh Gaitskell, leader of the opposition, during my earlier visits to London through John Strachey, the party's shadow colonial and Commonwealth secretary. Strachey was an intellectual, well read and interested in theories and philosophies. He was friendly and wanted to help the colonies make the grade. Keng Swee had invited him to Singapore to witness our referendum campaign. After listening to me speaking at our lunchtime rally at Fullerton Square, he told me I was too intellectual, more of a lecturer than a rabble-rouser. Gaitskell had a different cut of mind: he was less interested in theories, more into practicalities, brisk in his arguments.

The Labour Party held its own conference of Labour and socialist prime ministers of the Commonwealth on Britain's entry into the EEC. Nehru did not attend, but the Indians, represented at a high level, protested strongly that they and the former colonies were being abandoned: Commonwealth preferences for their exports to Britain, especially textiles, would be jeopardised once she was in the EEC. All the other leaders made pleas for continued links and privileged access to the British market, and special consideration by the EEC for their exports. It was interesting to watch them interact. Walter Nash from New Zealand was the only prime minister from the white dominions; the others were from the non-white countries, most of them not yet independent. They all looked to Gaitskell for sympathy and support, since he was against Europe and favoured retaining close economic ties with them.

Addressing the Labour conference, I said that the future was inevitably one of change, but that the changes should not be an excuse for Britain to slough off the responsibilities she had inherited with the empire. If they were abandoned, the consequences could be disastrous, threatening small countries like Singapore. Our closest link with an industrial power was with Britain. If we lost that link, we would suffer a severe setback. I added simply but sincerely that Britain and the empire constituted the world that I had known all my life, a world in which the British were central to our survival; whilst we wanted freedom to decide what we should do with our lives, we also wanted and needed our long historical, cultural and economic ties to be maintained. We especially valued our association with the Labour Party, which had helped us during our struggle for independence.

I struck a chord. After I spoke, Denis Healey, who was the party's secretary for international relations, came up to me to say, "Harry, who taught you to speak like that? That was a powerful speech." I was cheered that I had friends among the Labour leaders. I had dealt amicably enough with Sandys, Maudling and Lennox-Boyd (with whom I got on best), but they were Tories and represented monied interests; they never sympathised with the colonial students who aggressively sought independence. The Labour Party shared our aspirations. They had a similar basic philosophy of support for the underdog and moral principles of equality between men of all nations and races, underpinned by a belief in socialist brotherhood. I had not been in office long enough to understand that when Labour got back into power, their responsibilities would be to the British people and not to the brotherhood of men, that although it might hurt their conscience to abdicate or downgrade their principles, they would nevertheless do so.

The Commonwealth Conference itself was fascinating. Leaders from countries big and small were seated around the oval table at Marlborough House and had equal rights of speech. I was most impressed by Harold Macmillan. He sat there like a patriarch, a great Edwardian figure with drooping eyelids and moustache, a deceptively languid air and an old-world cut to his suit. He greeted all the prime ministers as they came in, including those who were there by courtesy, as I was. As we shook hands, he smiled faintly and congratulated me with the remark that the referendum had gone well. I smiled back and said, "Yes, with the help of the British government in getting the right terms to put to the people." He and Duncan Sandys, who was at his side, both looked pleased. It was one burden off their colonial shoulders.

India was the biggest nation represented but Nehru was a tired man. He had no life, no vigour in his demeanour or his delivery. He was not forceful in opposing Britain's joining the common market. The most memorable speech was made by Robert Menzies, prime minister of Australia, a big, stout, robust figure, with a broad face and a strong, deep voice that rang out in full volume. His bristling eyebrows added emphasis to his delivery whenever he frowned. He spoke with passion, conviction and authority. He brushed aside Macmillan's assurances of continuing close ties with the Commonwealth countries after Britain had joined the common market. "I run a federation. I know how federations work," he said. They were either centripetal, in which case the states came closer and closer together as in Australia, or they were centrifugal, with the states moving further and further apart until they eventually broke away. They were never static. There was no other dynamic at work in such groupings. If Britain joined the EEC, the ties with the Commonwealth would weaken and atrophy.

Looking back over the past 30 years to see how both the old and new Commonwealth have drifted away from Britain as her interests have become more and more enmeshed with Europe's, I have often been reminded how prophetic Menzies was. He knew where Australia's interests lay, and he did not doubt that they were being sacrificed after Australians had shed blood in two world wars for Britain.

For the British prime minister, Menzies' powerful speech was a body blow. It was delivered on a Friday morning, so instead of replying that afternoon, Macmillan adjourned the conference for the weekend in order to meet the Commonwealth leaders separately at Chequers and prepare his reply. On the Monday, an urbane Macmillan gave a polished performance. He was filled with sadness that Britain had to take this path, but the course of history had changed. Wealth was created best in large continents, like America and Europe, where good communications facilitated trade and other exchanges. An overseas empire like the one Britain had built was no longer the way to wealth. For a person of his age and generation, who had been born and bred in it, it would have been so much easier to have carried on with the old ties. But the future had to be faced, and it was his task, however unpleasant, to link Britain to this engine of growth and progress on the continent of Europe. It was a masterly performance, noncombative, even melancholic, with hints of nostalgia for the old Commonwealth. It soothed all the leaders present but left them in little doubt that the prime minister of Britain had a duty to do, and that duty meant responding to a beckoning Europe. He would do his best to keep up the ties of Commonwealth and empire, provided the Europeans (or rather President De Gaulle of France, although he was not mentioned) allowed him to.

I had decided to return to Singapore via Moscow this time, despite the Tunku's displeasure, and left London on 19 September by British Airways. I could not allow myself to be deterred from getting what I felt was a necessary part of my political education: to see the capital of the Soviet Union and the Russians. And I had to do it before we went into Malaysia, when Kuala Lumpur would control my passport. I was greeted by Soviet officials at the level of those deputed to meet leaders from nonindependent countries, notably the vice-chairman of the Committee for Cultural Relations and Foreign Countries. A few Commonwealth diplomats also turned up at the airport, including the British and Australian charges d'affaires and the Canadian ambassador, Arnold Smith, later Commonwealth secretary-general.

I told Western correspondents that I was returning home via Moscow in order to take in the capital of one of the biggest countries in the world. There was no political purpose behind my visit. In fact, the highest official I got to meet was First Deputy Foreign Minister Vasily Kuznetsov. But I learnt much at a dinner given by Arnold Smith at which several foreign diplomats taught me how to interpret what I saw. Moscow was an interesting experience. I had an eerie feeling that whatever I did was being watched. And true enough, as I had been warned, at the city's best hotel – the National, where I was put up as their guest – the washbasin and bathtub had no stoppers. I had brought with me a hard rubber ball, the kind I throw for my dog to retrieve, but it worked only for the washbasin. The hotel service was bizarre. I had arrived at night and been taken out to dinner. The next morning I was served a huge breakfast of caviar, smoked sturgeon, great plates of rye bread, tea and coffee, vodka and cognac – all laid out on a velvet cloth placed over a large, round table. I was out the whole day and taken to the Bolshoi ballet at night. When I got back to my room, I found my breakfast still on the table. I was aghast, and concluded that in this communist paradise, service performed by one human for another must be considered demeaning. So I slept next to the remains.

When I got back to Singapore on 29 September, I told a welcoming crowd of party supporters at the airport that I was still myself. The Russians knew me and were prepared to deal with me and trade with us, but I had gone to Moscow to learn and had not been contaminated. My stand was like that of Prince Sihanouk and President Nasser. We would defend our territorial integrity, our ideas and our way of life. We would be neutral in any conflict between big power blocs. But we were not neutral where our interests were concerned. It was only through intelligent appraisal and understanding of what was happening and why it was happening that we could chart our way forward. For instance, we could see that no single nation, not even one as powerful as Britain, could pretend that a big combination in Europe would not affect it. It would therefore have been utterly ludicrous for Singapore with 1.8 million people to have tried to go it alone.

I explained all this for the benefit of the Tunku, but did not convince him. I was to learn later that he was indeed displeased about my visit to Moscow, and had issued a statement in Kuala Lumpur to say that it had come as a surprise to him. It would naturally nullify what I had said when attacking the communists. He saw me as a disobedient official from a troublesome border province. He had disapproved of my going to enemy communist countries, yet I had gone.

29. Pressure from Sukarno

The Tunku was not in a happy mood. Something significant had happened while I was away. The Malaysia Agreement signed on 1 August had triggered adverse reactions from Indonesia and the Philippines who both coveted the Borneo territories. On 24 September, he had issued a warning to the Indonesians to keep their hands off Malaysia – "we expect others not to interfere with our affairs". He was responding to a statement by Ali Sastroamidjojo, the former prime minister of Indonesia, that Jakarta would not remain indifferent to its formation. This was the first hint that trouble was brewing. Next, the Philippine foreign secretary staked out a claim to North Borneo, asserting that the Republic of the Philippines was the legal successor of the sultanate of Sulu, which owned it, and that North Borneo had never been ceded to the British – they had only leased it.

The Tunku brushed this aside. The British had been masters of these territories since 1878, and for 100 years their right to them had never been questioned. But what he said about us was worrying. He told the UMNO Youth movement that he did not want Singapore, but had to take the island into Malaysia because otherwise the communists would have got into power there. Now he was fearful that if they ever succeeded in doing so in the future, Singapore would refuse to cooperate with the Federation and there would be "trouble galore". His concern was understandable. While I was in Moscow, the Barisan had published an analysis of the results of the referendum, in which they said that their immediate aim was to overthrow the present PAP government in the next general election, and then go on to win the election for Singapore's seats in the federal parliament. Lim Chin Siong went further, calling on the party to marshall all left-wing and anti-colonial forces in order to gain control of the federal government in turn and defeat the "British-Alliance Axis".

Razak responded by warning the people that they must beware of the enemies of democracy, that the Barisan was working not for their real interests, but for those whose loyalty was outside the country. Lim Chin Siong retorted that if the ruling Alliance believed in parliamentary democracy, it must accept the right of the opposition to change the government through the electoral process. Lim's truculence strengthened the conviction of the Tunku, Razak and Ismail that the situation must be brought under control quickly, now that the referendum was over and Singapore's security was going to be Kuala Lumpur's responsibility.

At a meeting of the Internal Security Council held in Singapore on 8 September, a joint report from the commissioners of police of the Federation and Singapore put out by our Special Branch recommended a phased operation against the communists and pro-communists before merger. Razak, who represented Malaysia in place of Ismail, wanted action without delay.

Chin Chye, who represented me as I was away attending the Commonwealth Conference in London, was against anything hasty. Selkirk, for the British, supported Chin Chye, saying that while there was a threat, it was not one requiring violent suppression. A dissatisfied Razak went to London to press Duncan Sandys, who replied that he wanted action postponed until after the legislation for Malaysia had been debated in the House of Commons, which would not be before February the following year. He had to consider reactions in Britain, where he believed the arrests would undoubtedly cause considerable criticism.

After Razak reported this to the Tunku, the Malayans called for another meeting of the Internal Security Council in October. It again postponed taking a decision on the question of arrests. The PAP's main concern now was to consolidate its gains and make sure Singapore was not dominated and kept down by Malay leaders in Kuala Lumpur. I emphasised to Selkirk that ideally we should delay the arrests until after merger. I stressed to Philip Moore that no action should be taken before the election of the 15 Singapore seats in the federal parliament. I wanted the Barisan to be free to contest them because if they were removed and there was no apparent communist threat, the Alliance could win a fair number of the seats. Later, Lord Lansdowne, minister of state to Sandys, referred to my "surprising candour" in telling him that it was to my advantage to preserve a pro-communist rump in the opposition. Indeed I had my reasons.

I had gone to see the Tunku after I returned from Moscow and had spent a few days with him. My explanation for my visit to the Soviet Union mollified him, but I knew he was not satisfied. He was uncomfortable with someone who had a mind of his own and was too ready to argue and, if necessary, take independent action. True, I did not undermine him, but neither did I listen to him, by which he meant obey him. He and Razak were planning for the period after Malaysia; that included who should be in charge of Singapore to do their bidding, and I sensed that the Tunku was writing me off as a compliant caretaker. He wanted someone who was as obedient and loyal as Tan Siew Sin or Lim Yew Hock. He and Razak both liked Keng Swee, but even Keng Swee was not altogether "safe". He was too intellectual and not susceptible to persuasion or temptation.

Things were not going well, therefore, and after another visit to Kuala Lumpur in mid-November, I told Moore that my relations with the Tunku had further deteriorated; his actions had made it clear he wanted to drop me after Malaysia. In Singapore itself, Tan Siew Sin was putting in a considerable effort to rebuild the MCA opposition and Razak was casting around for younger Malay leaders. Most sinister of all, the Tunku had asked me to release Chua Hoe Ann, leader of the biggest Chinese secret society on the island whom we had detained under the Criminal

Law Temporary Provisions Ordinance. Chua had organised thuggery against PAP branch workers during the previous election, and I feared for their personal safety on future occasions, because after merger the Tunku would have the power to release gangsters like him.

I had already told Selkirk that the Tunku intended to resurrect Lim Yew Hock. The Tunku had proposed that the PAP stand aside in the Sembawang by-election necessitated by the death of Ahmad Ibrahim in order to let his candidate fight it out with the Barisan. I had rejected the idea. "It was complete stupidity," I told Selkirk. He must have concurred, for he reported to Sandys that the Tunku was pursuing a doomed policy. Sandys replied, agreeing with Selkirk, that I was at present the best instrument for governing the island.

I took the British into my confidence because I needed their support, or at least their neutrality, in order to implement my plan to demonstrate to the Tunku the folly of trying to install a Lim Yew Hock government that he could control. I told Moore I proposed to inflict a crushing electoral defeat on Lim Yew Hock and the Alliance in Singapore to show the Tunku and Razak that they had to do business with the PAP and no one else. For this, I intended to hold elections for our 15 Singapore representatives in the federal parliament immediately after the signing of the Malaysia treaty in London, which was expected to take place in February, and before its implementation in August 1963, when the Tunku would get control of the police. I would create the 15 constituencies by amalgamating the existing 51 into groups of three or four. I believed UMNO would get only one seat, and the PAP could outdo the Barisan by winning eight or even nine.

I told Moore that Razak and Tan Siew Sin had made no progress in building up the Alliance in Singapore. They were dithering about what to do next, but there was no doubt that they intended to cut the PAP down to size. For example, the *Straits Times* was printing views that its editors knew to be unacceptable to the Singapore government, and this could only mean that they had the full backing of the Tunku. It was a declaration of war on their part, and I would retaliate at an appropriate moment. Again, Kuala Lumpur wanted to control local broadcasting and television, although it had been agreed that Singapore would be responsible for their administration and day-to-day programmes. Their object was to limit the government's political capability, particularly during elections. Meanwhile, Tan, determined to show who was the boss in financial matters, claimed for the federal government a far higher percentage of Singapore's revenue than had been agreed. He had already proved difficult in negotiations over forming a common market, and a decision on it had had to be postponed while experts studied the question.

When I saw Lansdowne on 27 November, I spoke frankly of my problems over merger. On the collection of taxes, Singapore had fully accepted that finance was a federal responsibility, but we could not agree that Kuala Lumpur would collect the taxes and then hand over Singapore's share to us. Singapore must do the collecting and hand over the federal contribution to Kuala Lumpur, otherwise we would find ourselves out in the cold. As for control of information and broadcasting, that was essential for any government if it was to communicate with its citizens. In federal hands, the approach to Chinese problems would be insensitive, go hopelessly wrong, and be politically costly. As an instance, I recounted how the Tunku had created a problem for himself when in India. He had denounced the Chinese as the aggressors in the Sino-Indian frontier war of 1962, when it was far from certain who was in the wrong. Only after someone had pointed out the bad effect this was having on the Chinese of Malaya did he change his vocabulary and refer to the issue as one between Chinese communists and Indian democrats.

After mentioning other points of contention, I told Lansdowne that while my personal relations with the Tunku were good, politically, he wanted somebody more amenable in control of Singapore. I then explained my intention to hold elections for our 15 seats in the federal parliament. He was worried about the effect this would have on the Tunku. I said he would not be delighted, but however resentful and frustrated he might feel, he would learn that his protégés in Singapore were politically finished, and that he could not breathe life into them however much patronage and open support he gave them. Lansdowne urged me to improve our relations by talking candidly to the Tunku about these matters. I said that much as I would like to, the Tunku was not the sort of man one could get to grips with, because conversations with him often drifted into vague pleasantries.

The impact I was making on the British at this time was reflected in Moore's 5 December report to Ian Wallace at the Colonial Office:

> "His plan for the merger of Singapore with the Federation was based on the assumption that he would have a working arrangement with the Tunku whereby the Alliance government would take over the task of maintaining internal security in Singapore while the PAP would run the state government of Singapore. This plan presupposed that the Tunku would be willing to do business with Lee.
>
> "He is anxious to hold the election before Malaysia is implemented because he will still have complete control over the machinery of the government, including especially the police and broadcasting. ... Lee has said that he would much prefer to hold the election with the Tunku's consent. He does not want this to be a declaration of war on the Tunku but he does regard it as absolutely necessary to consolidate his own political position and to demonstrate that the Alliance cannot hope to win power in Singapore. If the Tunku refused to agree to the Malaysian election being held before 31 August 1963, Lee claims that he could hold such elections under Singapore legislation and they would have the necessary political impact whatever their legal validity. Lee has asked us to treat as strictly confidential his idea of holding elections before 31 August 1963 and in particular not to let it be known to anybody in the Federation. ...
>
> "Lee said he was very appreciative of the efforts by Lord Lansdowne, Lord Selkirk and others to persuade the Tunku that it

was in his interest to do business with the PAP and he felt that we had achieved something which was quite impossible for him to do on his own. ... It is an uphill task, particularly in the face of the Tunku's very understandable distrust of Lee, but the best hope of political stability for Singapore within Malaysia still lies in the two prime ministers coming to some effective working arrangement. The alternatives are either a Barisan Sosialis government in Singapore or, if the Barisan Sosialis are destroyed by arrest and proscription, a hostile PAP government with Lee Kuan Yew making an open bid for Chinese chauvinistic support in opposition to the Malays in Kuala Lumpur. I doubt whether the Federation government fully appreciate as yet how dangerous a situation the latter could be. They may find Lee Kuan Yew extremely awkward as a colleague; most people do; but they would find him far more dangerous as an opponent."

I was fortunate in that the British understood and sympathised with my point of view. They saw that the way Kuala Lumpur governed their own Chinese would not work in Singapore. The Chinese of Singapore would not be browbeaten; they were accustomed to conditions in a British colony, they had never been under Malay rule, and strong-arm tactics would be bound to stir up violent resistance. And I needed British support to get the Singapore state constitution promulgated in London through an "Order in Council" in a form that would not prevent me from holding elections for the 15 seats.

∞

Just three days after Moore sent his report, a whole new dimension was added to the situation. Suddenly, on 8 December, a revolt broke out in Brunei. Armed rebels calling themselves the North Borneo National Army and claiming to be 30,000-strong seized the oil town of Seria. The British response was immediate. Two companies of Gurkhas and 300 British troops were air-lifted to Brunei, followed by the balance of two battalions. The troops quickly recaptured Seria, killing some of the insurgents and capturing 500. Meanwhile, a quick-witted British commissioner of police had corralled the first group of rebels in Brunei Town in his tennis court, and kept them there before they could make further trouble. Within 48 hours, the rebellion had failed, and after Seria had been recaptured, mopping-up operations began.

The Barisan issued a foolish statement the day after the news of the revolt had broken, hailing it as a popular uprising against colonialism that merited the backing of all genuine anti-colonialists, and declaring that the Singapore and Federation governments would stand condemned if they did not oppose the British. Coming out in open support of rebellion like this was the second of two major errors on Lim Chin Siong's part. The first was to have met their leader, A.M. Azahari, in Singapore two days before the revolt. As an earnest of what was to come, the Malayan Special Branch arrested 50 people, most of them Chinese, including the organising secretary of the Partai Rakyat of Malaya, and Singapore arrested three members of the local pro-Barisan Partai Rakyat linked to the group. We wanted to take action in conjunction with the Malayans to show solidarity.

The Brunei revolt had far wider implications, however. On 11 December, the Tunku referred in the federal parliament to the financial backing Azahari had received to carry out his rebellion, saying he had close connections with a number of people in countries that were Malaysia's neighbours. He was alluding to Indonesia, where Defence Minister General Haris Nasution had announced that his government would be paying more attention to the areas close to British North Borneo following the Brunei uprising, and the president's own Nationalist Party (the PNI) had expressed support for the Brunei Partai Rakyat. The backing had obviously come from Sukarno himself.

The British were alive to the danger this posed. Dealing with Azahari had been much simpler than dealing with the people behind him would be. The UK commissioner in Brunei, Sir Dennis White, was convinced that the rebels had been certain of Indonesian assistance, otherwise their leaders would not have attacked Limbang (a sliver of land dividing Brunei in two) as it was part of the British colony of Sarawak and the British were bound to retaliate. He believed the Indonesians were encouraging them as a means of wrecking Malaysia, and contrary to press reports that made the revolt seem a comic, amateurish affair, he pointed out that it had been successful in the early stages despite the fact that it had gone off at half-cock. The insurgents had captured a number of police stations and seized many weapons; they had occupied the power station and cut off the electricity supply; they had held the UK commissioner's secretary captive, and in Limbang, imprisoned the British Resident and his wife with other Europeans. Only the prompt arrival of the British and Gurkha troops had saved the situation.

A few days after the Tunku had voiced his suspicions, Sukarno confirmed them by saying, "What is happening there (Brunei) cannot be separated from the struggle of the New Emerging Forces. We take the side of the people who are struggling," and in a live broadcast from Jakarta a few days later, he called on Indonesians to support the rebellion. Those who did not do so were traitors to their souls, he said. The Indonesian people were born in fire and had suffered for their independence. It was right for them to sympathise with those fighting for freedom. They were not like other nations (meaning Malaya) that had obtained their independence as a gift from the imperialists. The Tunku replied by pointing out that the Indonesian government and its political leaders were making fiery speeches although the rebellion in Brunei was now over; their aim was evidently to incite the people of the three Borneo territories to oppose their governments, and this would result in a calamity.

A war of words followed, with the Indonesians once again responding to the rhetoric of their charismatic leader. Working up public emotion through speeches and the media in order to trigger off popular demonstrations was part and parcel of Sukarno's strategy. It had recently proved effective when Jakarta demanded the return of West Irian (West New Guinea) from the Dutch, but now he needed another issue to keep the masses occupied and distracted from their parlous economic situation. On 23 December, several thousand people gathered in Jakarta's Merdeka Square to burn two effigies, one of a Westerner, the other of a Malay with horn-rimmed glasses wearing a *songkok* (the Malay hat) – the Tunku. The Indonesians were gearing up for a campaign against Malaysia, ostensibly in support of independence for Brunei, Sarawak and North Borneo.

Lim Chin Siong joined in the rhetoric, saying that the PAP was souring relations between Singapore and Indonesia over the Brunei revolt by spreading false rumours that Jakarta had engineered it and was anti-Chinese. No one had said this publicly before, and it scared the Chinese-speaking. People could sense that big forces were at work, that Singapore's choice lay between joining Malaysia and going with the Tunku, or joining an anti-Chinese Indonesia to line up with the Indonesian Communist Party, the Barisan's ideological partner. Furthermore, the revolt had now given the wrangling members of the Internal Security Council common ground for action.

30. Bitter Run-up to Malaysia

Five days after the revolt in Brunei, the Internal Security Council met in an emergency session at the Tunku's request. Developments in Brunei had made it necessary to initiate action against the communists, and the statement by the Barisan supporting the revolt had provided the opportunity. I said I understood his position, but it was important that the operation be presented publicly as action in defence of all the territories about to join Malaysia. I could not appear a British stooge, but I was prepared to be seen as a supporter of Malaya.

I advised that Dr Lee Siew Choh should not be arrested but should be given a second chance, provided he did not continue to play the communist game. I would also not move against the pro-communist trade unions once their key figures were destroyed, otherwise it would be said that Singapore had no real autonomy in the field of labour. I further urged that the Singapore Partai Rakyat should not be proscribed so that the remaining communists would gravitate towards it rather than to Ong Eng Guan's UPP, which would take a Chinese chauvinist line. It was agreed that all those arrested who were of Malayan origin would be deported to the Federation except for Lim Chin Siong, who, although born in Johor, would be kept in Singapore. The operation would be undertaken in the early hours of 16 December, and the Internal Security Council would meet in Kuala Lumpur on 15 December to sanction it.

On the night of 15 December, police parties were in position in Singapore and Johor Bahru, from where members of the Federation Special Branch and Police Field Force were to come and help in the operation. That evening, at about 6:30, Keng Swee, who had been in

Kuala Lumpur since the morning, told me on the telephone that he had reached agreement on the texts of two statements, one to be made by Razak to the federal parliament and the other to be broadcast by me over Radio Singapore, giving the reasons for the detentions. Those detained were to include nine of our assemblymen. The day before the round-up, Philip Moore assured me that the Tunku had also agreed to the arrest of two subversive Members of the federal parliament, as I had requested. But when I arrived at the Internal Security Council meeting in Kuala Lumpur at 10 pm, Keng Swee reported that Ismail had told him the Tunku had changed his mind about detaining them. On hearing this, Selkirk proposed – and I concurred – that we should all approach him to urge him not to reverse the decision, and with Ismail and our own aides, we set off for the Residency. At the Residency, all the lights were out and the front door was closed. The Tunku had gone to sleep, and he stayed asleep while we knocked on his front door. We returned to Singapore in the RAF transport plane that had taken us to Kuala Lumpur. The police cancelled the operation.

To forestall any shifting of the blame for this onto us, I wrote to Selkirk to place my position on record:

> "The whole of the case, as set out in the two agreed statements, would become meaningless, when no action is taken against the leading figures in the Federation whose responsibility for aiding and abetting armed revolt in the Borneo territories was as great as the responsibility of those to be arrested in Singapore. ... There was justification last week for action against communist front organisations and their principal leaders. If action against the communists were to be taken in cold blood there would be no alternative for us but to leave it to the British."

That was not the end of it, for the Barisan leaders continued stoking the fires. In their New Year messages, Lim Chin Siong said that Malaya was heading towards the establishment of a fascist and military dictatorship, and Dr Lee Siew Choh said that the Brunei struggle would continue until the people regained their freedom. They pinned their hopes on the revolt and on Indonesia's opposition to the Malaysia plan. These statements were bound to provoke the Tunku into demanding action; despite his refusal to allow federal MPs to be detained, he was becoming impatient and told the British that he would call off Malaysia altogether unless the round-up of the Singapore pro-communists was carried out. Moore saw me on several occasions to urge me to proceed with it, assuring me that it was the only way to get merger. I still had my doubts, but the British were in a better position to judge the Tunku's real intentions, so after discussions among ourselves we concluded that we could not afford to risk ignoring his arguments. A security operation code-named "Cold Store" was set for 2 February 1963.

Some 370 police officers in Singapore, and another 133 Malayan officers from a Police Field Force camp in Johor took part in the raid. The Internal Security Council had sanctioned the operation at a meeting in Kuala Lumpur the night before. (We had removed six Barisan assembly-men from the list because the Tunku continued to oppose the arrest of the two subversive Malayan MPs.) At 3 am, 65 raiding parties fanned out over Singapore to detain 169 persons. They found 115. The rest were not where they had been expected to be. This was always the problem with locating communists. Knowing they were vulnerable, they kept changing the places where they spent their nights.

This time there were no riots, no bloodshed, no curfews after the arrests. Everybody had expected that there would be a clean-up, and the public understood that the communists had it coming to them. It was a severe setback for them. The operation removed some of the most experienced of their united front leaders, and they could recover only if they were prepared to replace them with more leaders from the underground – without being sure that they would be given time to build up their influence with the grass roots before further arrests were made.

I watched anxiously in the days that followed to see whether they would fill the vacancies. There was no sign of this. They were not willing, or not able, to throw more cadres into the open to run the united front.

With the concurrence of the Internal Security Council, I wrote to Lim Chin Siong on the night of the arrests to offer him permission to go to Indonesia or any other country he chose. I said that, unlike the others, he had never deceived me about his communist convictions and his aims, and had told me in Changi camp in 1958 that he was prepared to leave Singapore if his presence prevented me from setting out to win the next election. Lim Chin Siong was not an important communist figure, but he was important as a rabble-rouser. I thought it necessary to make this gesture, which would not do much harm to security, and released my letter to the press. As expected, he turned down the offer. He could not be seen to be abandoning his comrades. But it had served my political purpose, besides signalling to the Plen that I observed some rules of decency and honour towards my former united front comrades in the anti-colonial movement. Unstated was my hope that he would behave likewise. He was aware that I knew of his elimination squads.

Among those arrested were Sidney Woodhull, placed in a first category of hard-core organisers, and James Puthucheary, who was placed in a second category of leading collaborators of the communist conspiracy. Another person in the first category was James Fu Chiao Sian. James Fu was a reporter-translator, a member of the Anti-British League who had once worked on the pro-communist Chinese newspaper *Sin Pao*. His articles were sympathetic to student agitators and strikers, and he was a voluntary publicity agent for Lim Chin Siong and Fong Swee Suan, both former schoolmates from the Chinese High School. But after four months he was released: investigations had shown that his link with the Anti-British League had been broken in 1962. He joined Radio & Television Singapore, and in 1972 became my press secretary, a post he held until he retired in 1993. He was effective since he was bilingual, and totally dependable.

There were quite a few like him who had been drawn into the communist movement when they were young, carried away by idealism and the desire to change the evil society they saw around them. Given time to perceive the ruthless organisational side of the MCP, they recognised the merits of democratic socialism or social democracy – slower and reformist, but fairer and less inhumane. Some, like Lim Chin Siong's brother, Lim Chin Joo, took university degrees while under detention. He acquired an LLB (London external), and on his release was employed in the Registry of Land Titles. He later became a successful and prosperous solicitor.

After the excitement of these detentions subsided, the Tunku proposed that the PAP withdraw from the Sembawang by-election and allow the new SPA-UMNO-MCA-MIC Alliance to have a straight fight against the Barisan. As politely as I could, I told him that they could not possibly win, and that the victory of the Barisan would revive the flagging spirits of the pro-communists. I sensed that his attitude to me had generally stiffened.

I came to the conclusion that the Tunku had raised his sights, that he wanted to make Singapore easier for him to manage, to have more power over the state and to concede autonomy only over matters like education and labour. I had a growing conviction that now that the arrests had been made and the threat from the communists temporarily disposed of, the Tunku would take a tougher line on the detailed terms of merger when translating the white paper into specific clauses in the constitution. My recourse was to threaten the British that I would not go through with it unless the terms we had agreed upon and had put to the people of Singapore during the referendum were observed. Otherwise, I would be selling them out. I could not be party to such a betrayal and, if necessary, I would hold a general election to resolve the matter. That, of course, would put the whole Malaysia scheme in jeopardy if the Barisan and the communists were to win.

On 12 February, ten days after the detentions, I restated my fears to Selkirk that the Federation, not understanding the nature of the communist threat in Singapore, might believe that Operation Cold Store had removed it, and with it the urgency for merger. In Malaya, the majority of voters were Malays, and the MCP – outside the constitutional arena and constantly under attack – knew it could not win power through the ballot box, unlike its counterpart in Singapore. With the urgency for merger removed in the minds of the Tunku and his ministers, I still faced a number of difficulties with Kuala Lumpur, notably over our financial arrangements and the control of broadcasting. It was a time to stand firm. I therefore wrote to Selkirk, "We are not exaggerating the Singapore position if we say that it would not be possible to depart in any way from the terms and conditions that have been publicly debated and endorsed by the people in the referendum of last September."

Both Moore and Selkirk were positive. Selkirk wrote to London on 13 February, "I think we have to take Lee seriously when he says that he will not agree to any deviation from the terms of the merger white paper." But my handicap in dealing with the Tunku was that while I wanted merger, he did not. I had listed the weaknesses of Singapore without it in order to persuade our people to accept it. He took that to be the total truth and became extremely difficult, since he felt that we had everything to gain and he was taking on a multitude of problems. The result was an unequal bargaining position.

He sent down his two top MCA Chinese, the anti-PAP leaders who had organised the Chinese Chamber of Commerce and the Chinese community in Malaya for him, and whom he now wanted to do the same for him in Singapore. T.H. Tan was a former editor-in-chief of the *Singapore Standard* and had turned politician to become a powerful Tammany Hall-type boss of the Malayan MCA. Khaw Kai Boh was a former director of Special Branch in Singapore. He had wanted to have us arrested, especially me, and had left for Kuala Lumpur when the PAP won the election in 1959. The Tunku had appointed both of them senators in the federal parliament and made Khaw a minister. They were gross, looked the fat-cat thugs that they were, and had no success with our Chinese merchant community, who had not been accustomed to having to pay for their business licences, as in Malaya.

The two senators believed that the Alliance would stand a better chance of winning the next election if Kuala Lumpur had control of our finances, and therefore accused me publicly of wanting to keep Singapore's surplus revenue in order to use it to harm the federal government and bring it down. Their ideas dovetailed with the ambitions of Tan Siew Sin, who told the press that he had to take over tax collection in Singapore "on the principle that federal taxes should be collected by federal departments and the revenue regarded as federal". He now wanted 60 per cent of Singapore's total revenue, and I had to remind him of the exchange of letters in which the Tunku had given an assurance that Singapore would be left in charge of its own finances. The Tunku had wanted to control Singapore's security, not its economy. But Tan Siew Sin would not give way and argued adamantly that anything less would be insufficient to defray Singapore's portion of federal expenditure.

In his early 40s, Tan Siew Sin was capable, conscientious, hardworking and honest, free from any hint of corruption. His father was Datuk Sir Cheng Lock Tan, a grand old man of the Straits Settlements and the patriarch of one of Malacca's oldest and wealthiest families, whom I had persuaded to speak at the inauguration of the PAP. But the son was mean-spirited and petty and it showed in the long, pale face behind the rimless glasses. He knew that Keng Swee had the better mind, but he was determined to have the upper hand after merger, and Keng Swee found him impossible to negotiate with. However, I knew it was the Tunku who decided the big issues and I was not going to allow Tan Siew Sin to squat on us, at least not until we were a part of Malaysia, and not even then, provided we had control of our own state finances. His animosity towards Keng Swee and me was reinforced by his desire to cut Singapore down to size. He was out to score points in public and would smirk whenever he thought he had succeeded.

I gave him robust replies, and after he had got the worst of the exchanges, Syed Ja'afar Albar, an Arab Malay who was UMNO secretary-general and a powerful mass rally orator, came to his rescue. Albar warned me in the press not to make my points in public if I wanted to reach a settlement. Razak too came out in defence of Tan Siew Sin and the MCA, saying it was unfair that they were being made to appear responsible for the federal government's demands. The question I asked myself was: where did the Tunku stand? Was he behind Tan, like Albar and Razak, or was he neutral? At first I believed he was neutral, but as the pressure continued, I eventually concluded he was allowing them to push me to the limits. Tan was naturally difficult and needed the Tunku to restrain him, but the Tunku did not.

I believed then that the Tunku never told Tan Siew Sin that he was willing to let Singapore have maximum control of its finances in return for minimum Singapore participation in federal politics. Tan would not otherwise have demanded maximum control over our finances, because the more control the government in Kuala Lumpur exercised over them the more it must expect Singapore to participate in the politics of Malaysia in order to influence its policies towards Singapore. This was a fundamental problem that was never resolved before or after Singapore joined Malaysia. The Tunku left it to fester. In one way, this worked to my advantage. The Barisan berated me for having sold out Singapore and said that my "sham concern" for state finances could not deceive the public. But on the contrary, Tan Siew Sin's haughty, almost imperious demands alarmed the people of Singapore, and my responses, which proved I was not going to be a pushover, were a great relief to them. As the exchanges went on, right up to July, they won me much support. People wanted me to stand up for Singapore.

In mid-June, Kuala Lumpur presented Singapore and Brunei with its final terms for Malaysia, after which "there will be no negotiations". These included provision for a common market in the constitution, and a $50 million grant from Singapore for the development of the Borneo territories. I said Singapore was too poor to play Santa Claus and give away $50 million as its entrance fee to join the Federation. As for the common market, the federal government had announced in October 1962 that a team of experts from the World Bank was to examine its economic implications, in accordance with a decision made in London in July that year. This had held out hopes of our benefiting from professional competence in getting it off the ground. But although the report with the World Bank's recommendations had since been handed to Keng Swee and Tan Siew Sin, no definite terms or conditions had been agreed for bringing it about.

There were other major issues. One was my request that after Malaysia came into being, the power to detain secret society gangsters without trial under our Criminal Law Temporary Provisions Ordinance should be delegated to Singapore. I thought it too dangerous to leave this in the hands of the federal government if we were to stop thugs from meddling in the political life of the state. The Tunku was most reluctant to accede, and Razak appeared to be with him. They also wanted to change the constitution to restrict the movement of our citizens into Malaysia in order to keep out Singapore communists who, as Singapore citizens, would now become Malaysian citizens. In that case, I insisted, there should be reciprocity: the state government should have the same right to stop Malaysian citizens from Malaya from coming to Singapore.

Another issue was my proposal that there should be an amendment in the state constitution to provide that any assemblyman elected on a party ticket who then resigned or was expelled from that party must vacate his seat in the Assembly and fight a by-election. The Malayans were most reluctant to agree to this.

A further concern of mine was keeping corruption down after merger. That would require the Singapore state advocate-general to retain his powers to prosecute under our Prevention of Corruption Ordinance, which made it easier to secure convictions. This law did not exist in Malaya, nor did they have a Corrupt Practices Investigation Bureau. I asked that there should be no changes made in these institutions without the consent of the Singapore government.

The arguments went on and on without agreement, until Duncan Sandys called for a final meeting in London to dispose of outstanding questions. The Tunku was unhappy with me and refused to attend but sent Razak in his place to negotiate with me and to inform him only when a settlement had been reached. He would then come for the signing ceremony. Sandys had meanwhile become impatient with all the bickering. A Commonwealth Relations Office note recorded that he had held a meeting before the negotiations opened to discuss the action to be taken if they ended in deadlock, as they almost certainly would. In that case, he said, three courses would present themselves:

"(1) force Singapore to join Malaysia against its will; (2) abandon the Malaysia project; (3) allow North Borneo and Sarawak to join a reduced Malaysia, leaving the door open to subsequent membership by Singapore.

"The secretary of state thought it would probably be necessary to threaten the Tunku with separate independence for Singapore and it was agreed that this might force the Tunku to reach agreement with Singapore since without her (Singapore) the Malaya Defence Agreement would not continue for long and our free use of the Singapore base would soon be put in jeopardy. ...

"There was, however, some slight evidence that the Tunku was possibly thinking that if he developed more friendly relations with Indonesia, that would serve him better in combating the Chinese influence in Singapore than would the establishment of Malaysia."

Keng Swee and I arrived in London and started what would now be called "proximity talks". In other words, we did not at first meet Razak and Tan Siew Sin. They stayed in a different hotel from us, while the British talked to both sides and narrowed the differences between us. Then I had a working lunch with Razak, and Keng Swee followed this up by seeing him the next day. Finally, Sandys had us sit around a table for a marathon meeting that went on throughout the night. It was his method of dealing with stubborn parties, wringing concessions from both sides until they finally reached agreement. He had done this before to the Singapore delegation, providing strong drinks but little food to wear us down. It was not unlike what the communists did to us at committee meetings, which they would drag out until enough of the non-communists had gone home before the vote was taken.

That evening, anticipating a repeat of this technique, we came prepared with supplies of sandwiches and some bottles of beer, which we brought in typewriter cases to the separate room where we met when we called for breaks for our own delegation discussions. When we ran out of food, our trusted cabinet secretary, Wong Chooi Sen, would telephone Choo at the Park Lane Hotel to order more sandwiches from room service. We did this until Choo reported that room service had run out of sandwiches. To keep our heads clear, we declined Sandys' hard liquor. This prudence and the supply of food kept our stamina up throughout the gruelling night. We believed Razak's side was not as well-provisioned.

Finally, near dawn, it was agreed that we would pay 40 per cent of our "national taxes", or 28 per cent of our total revenue, to the federal government to meet the increased defence expenditure necessitated by the "Confrontation" with Indonesia. In place of a $50 million gift to the Borneo territories, there would now be a $150 million loan, $100 million of which would be interest-free for five years. The common market would be implemented over 12 years, and Singapore would remain duty-free for most important commodities in the entrepot trade. A special board would gradually equalise tariffs over this period. But there was to be no oil-rich Brunei to sweeten the deal for the Tunku. The wily and cautious old sultan was not satisfied with the proposed division of oil revenues between them, and no pressure or threat from Sandys would move him. I saw the sultan in his Grosvenor House suite on several occasions to compare notes on the progress of our respective negotiations. I understood his qualms and reservations and never persuaded him to go against his instincts, which told him to remain under the protection of the British, confident they would not abandon him to the tender mercies of the Indonesians.

The Tunku arrived two days before the signing, which was scheduled for 8 July – another lucky 8 for an auspicious start for Malaysia. But the agreement could not be finalised until I had first got him to accept a number of conditions that had been the subject of earlier wrangling. He conceded that police powers to detain secret society gangsters should be delegated to the Singapore government, and a change in our consti- tution would stipulate that an assemblyman who left the party for which he had stood as candidate would have to vacate his seat. In addition, 50 per cent of the labour for the Borneo projects to be financed from the $150 million loan would come from Singapore.

Since the Tunku's memory was elastic, I scribbled these points on the back of a used envelope I found on a side table in his hotel sitting- room, wrote "Ritz Hotel" as the letterhead, and got him to sign it. This last-minute haggling, and a dinner date with Macmillan, pushed the final ceremony at Marlborough House to late into the night of 8 July. By the time the speeches made by Macmillan, the Tunku, myself and the representatives of Sarawak and North Borneo were over, it was past midnight before the agreement was signed, and it was not dated 8, but 9 July – not an auspicious day in the Tunku's calendar.

The British – Moore, Selkirk and Sandys – were really on my side. They had many cards. I had none. I could not do much myself except

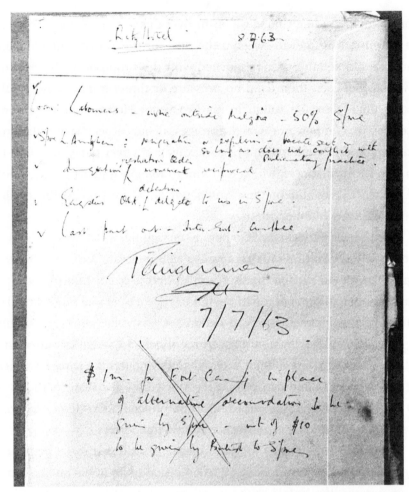

My scribbled points on the back of an envelope that the Tunku agreed
to and signed, 7 July 1963:

Loan: Labourers – when outside Malaysia – 50% Singapore

Singapore Legislative Assemblymen: resignation or expulsion
– vacate seat so long as does not conflict with Parliamentary
practice

Immigration and restriction order, movement reciprocal

Gangsters Ordinance detention, delegate to us in Singapore

Last part out – Inter-Govt Committee

to threaten to throw in my hand and let the communists take over. In those six months, I wrote numerous letters to Selkirk in Singapore and the Sandys in London, urging, entreating and threatening in turn. Without their help, I could not have got my terms. Even so, as I had foreseen, I had much trouble getting them written into the constitution before Malaysia Day on 31 August. In the end, I had to settle for a flexible formula without a guarantee that a common market would come about, and the delegation of powers to Singapore to detain secret society gangsters was agreed upon only in an exchange of letters, which could easily be revoked. We had to go into Malaysia without these guarantees.

As expected, my problems in Singapore did not decrease with the signing of the agreement. The Barisan remained obstreperous, and Lim Yew Hock and the SPA became bolder. Lim Yew Hock helped the Barisan block the Federal Elections Bill on 24 July, because he wanted the elections for Singapore's 15 seats in the federal parliament to be held after the Tunku had taken control of the police. Even on the motion to adopt and support the Malaysia Agreement, the SPA abstained from voting, when it should have increased the majority in favour by seven votes and so shown solidarity on a vital national issue.

31. The Tide Turns

The ten months December 1962 to September 1963 were the most hectic in my life. In addition to constant skirmishing with Tan Siew Sin and the Tunku's ministers in Kuala Lumpur, and with Lim Yew Hock and his SPA and the Barisan in Singapore, there was the growing danger from Indonesia. I had to mobilise support for the next election, which I decided could not be delayed beyond merger. The communists had broken up our party branches when they split away from us, and smashed the People's Association and the Works Brigade. To rebuild a strong PAP organisation would take at least two years, so Keng Swee and I decided on a simple strategy that we thought could make for a quick revival of our grassroots support.

From the Registry of Societies, we obtained the names and addresses of all office-bearers of the grassroots organisations, from Chinese clan associations and benevolent societies to the Chinese Chamber of Commerce and their regional branches, from retailers' associations to sports and chess clubs and the lending libraries in the Naval Base. We excluded all the pro-communist organisations such as the old boys' associations of the Chinese schools and Chinese musical associations.

Once the referendum was over, I began a series of visits to the constituencies, concentrating in the initial phase on those that had cast the most blank votes – rural areas (as they then were) like Jurong, Thomson, Kampong Kembangan and Jalan Kayu. I started with a full-day visit to one constituency every month, then increased it to one every two weeks, then one every week, and as Malaysia Day approached, to two, to three, to four tours a week. Finally, to complete all 51, I went almost every day, sometimes visiting two or three urban constituencies in a single day until late at night.

Before my visits, government officers accompanied by the assembly-man of the constituency (or if it was an opposition constituency, by PAP assemblymen from others) moved in to mobilise the shopkeepers, the community leaders and leaders of all the various local associations, and help them draw up a programme. They would then welcome me to the constituency to discuss their problems and needs with me. I travelled in an open Land Rover, and with a microphone in my hand and loudspeakers fixed to the vehicle, spoke to the crowds that would have gathered and be waiting for me when I made scheduled stops. Our plan worked. Once the communists lost the referendum and people realised all they could muster was 25 per cent in blank votes, everybody took heart. Now they were prepared to stand up and be counted.

The shopkeepers and the grassroots leaders would greet me with huge, heavy garlands of marigolds, frangipani, sometimes even orchids, or paper flowers, bound and decorated with tinsel, if they were poor. The Chinese representatives gave me banners of silk or velvet bearing the names of the donors and adorned with elegant phrases in gold characters expressing their solidarity with us. I would collect dozens of these banners, which were then strung up around the final meeting place where they would give me dinner out in the open. The diners would sit at round tables, ten at each, and there would be at least 20 and often as many as 50 such tables paid for by the successful shopkeepers to honour the leaders of the constituency and me.

The tours were an enormous success. As I argued against the unreasonable demands of Tan Siew Sin and Razak, the people swung behind me. The crowds kept growing bigger and warmer with each visit, the leaders eager to participate in welcoming me and to be seen supporting the PAP government. The officials with me followed up, listening to the people's requests for surfaced roads, drains, power, streetlights, standpipes, clinics, schools, community centres. The easier needs they dealt with quickly; the more difficult ones I promised to study and meet if practical. Community centres were useful for disseminating information to counter communist propaganda, and we started building them – simple wooden structures with corrugated asbestos roofs and cement floors, each equipped with electric bulbs, a ceiling fan, a ping-pong table, a carom table and a black and white television set.

The welcome committees would wait for me for hours if I was held up along the way. Old women and young girls would present petitions asking me to solve their personal grievances. The Indians would take me into their temples, scatter flowers in my path and put a colour mark on my forehead, a gesture of respect for an honoured guest. The Chinese would also bring me to their temples, and greet me at the entrance with lion dancers and the sound of gongs and drums to herald my arrival. It was good for their devotees to see the prime minister honouring their places of worship. I would burn joss-sticks in front of the altars, some Buddhist, others Taoist. The Malays would greet me with their *kompang* bands, 12 or 14 young men with tambourines and hand-held drums, and their elders would place on my head a *tanjak*, the brocade cloth folded into a cap worn by chieftains.

Barisan supporters would line some streets to boo, hiss and taunt me. As I passed the Chinese High School, 40 to 50 schoolboys with handkerchiefs covering the lower half of their faces held up placards denouncing and cursing me as a traitor to the people. In Whampoa one afternoon, Barisan toughs with the tattoos of a secret society on their forearms crowded me and tried to push me into a deep monsoon drain, but my security officer was quick to intervene and deal with them, allowing me to jump clear. Pro-Barisan union members would shout abuse from the upper floors of their premises, and one night in Hong Lim, they yelled threats at me and displayed protest banners from a flat roof. When I told the TV cameraman to turn his lights on them and capture them on film, they switched off their own and vanished. I invited them to come down to show themselves and argue their case with me. They refused, enabling me to point out to the thousands around me that when the communists were confronted with "the masses" out in the open, they switched off their lights and slunk away to hide in the dark.

The tours were physically exhausting and a drain on my nervous energy. I would start off at eight on a Sunday morning or shortly after lunch on a weekday. The afternoons were always hot, and during one tour I would make short speeches of 10 to 15 minutes at every stop, which could add up to between 30 minutes and an hour because I had to speak in two or three languages. Sometimes I made as many as ten speeches in a day, each in Malay, English, and Hokkien or Mandarin. I would sweat profusely. I brought three or four singlets and shirts with me and would nip quietly into somebody's toilet or behind the partition inside a shop from time to time to change into dry clothes, and I carried a small towel to wipe the sweat off my face. I would come home with my right hand bruised and painful from hundreds if not thousands of handshakes, and every now and again a real power squeeze. My back, too, was bruised and blue from bumping against the metal crossbar of the Land Rover. I learnt to offer my left hand to relieve my right, and also to push my thumb and forefinger right up against the other person's to prevent my fingers from being squeezed, and I had a thick pad of towels wound around the crossbar to act as a shock absorber.

But I was young, under 40. My adrenaline was flowing, and I was inspired by the warm response of the crowd. Speaking in Hokkien and Mandarin, I had convinced the Chinese that I was not a stooge of the British, that I was fighting for their future. The Malays backed me because they saw me fighting the Chinese communists. The Indians, as a smaller minority, were fearful and therefore reassured to find me completely at home with all races, speaking bazaar Malay and English to them and even a few words of greeting in Tamil.

News of how each tour had been more successful than the last spread rapidly by word of mouth in the coffee shops and through the press and television. It generated a groundswell of enthusiasm among the people, especially the shopkeepers and community leaders. I became a kind of political pop star. Many of the shopkeepers had been against the young communist toughs, but had been forced to make contributions to their funds. This was their chance to show that they really supported something – me and the government. When I was on stage, they would come not only with garlands and banners but with souvenirs from their display cabinets at home, a red ribbon tied around them and a red card carrying their names and addresses to wish me well. One memorable gift was an exquisite old ivory carving of an imperial Chinese sailing ship resting on a dark lacquered base under a glass case. It was the owner's most precious *objet d'art*. He was a shopkeeper, about 50 years old, greying at the temples, and he wished me happiness and long life in Hokkien. It still sits proudly in my sitting-room, a gift I treasure, reminding me of that great moment when I could feel the people warming to me and accepting me as their leader. The faith that these small shopkeepers placed in me inspired me to fight on.

The success of the tours prompted Lim Yew Hock to question in the Assembly their cost to the state. I was able to reply that no public funds had been misused because not a single dollar had been spent on receptions and refreshments – all had been paid for by the people themselves. The organisers deserved the credit for this and they were proud that they had mustered popular support, with local leaders happy to see themselves on television greeting me, or seated with me on the stage or at table for dinner. I could feel that the tide had turned.

The officials who accompanied me on these tours developed a strong team spirit. After trudging through many tours, listening to my explanations and exhortations on how to improve the lot of Singaporeans, they began to identify themselves with me. In the early days from November 1962 to January 1963, we faced cool, unresponsive and sometimes hostile crowds together, and as I slowly got through to the people, they felt it was as much their achievement as mine. They ranged from the Malay driver of my Land Rover, who had to sit through and listen to hundreds of my speeches in languages he did not understand, perking up each time I spoke in Malay, to officers from the veterinary services, the Public Works Department who looked after the roads and drains, the Public Utilities Board who supplied water and electricity, and the Radio & Television Singapore crew.

They were all cheering for me, including a Chinese television "sound person", Judy Bloodworth. Her experience was recounted by her husband Dennis Bloodworth, then *London Observer* correspondent in Singapore, in the following terms in one of his books:

> "We would arrive in pitch darkness sometimes, then suddenly the lights would go up, the people would cheer and boo, and in the middle of all the noise he would be elated, push his way down among them, laugh at the lion dancers around him, careless of the roaring firecrackers, never showing fear – he was burned in the face once, but took no notice. We really felt like a team, like an army unit; we felt proud of him. You couldn't help it."

Most important for my success was the senior Hokkien language radio programme officer, Sia Cheng Tit. He became my volunteer teacher, noting the major mistakes I made in my speeches, and sitting down with me the next day to point out my errors and provide the correct phrases as others had done before him, sometimes throwing in a few pithy proverbs. But that was not the only way in which he improved my delivery. I would often get hoarse through the sheer physical strain of having to talk so much, and when I was rasping one night at Tiong Bahru, he handed me a packet of neatly sliced ginseng in the paper wrapping of a nearby Chinese medicine shop. I stopped sucking lozenges and, on his advice, put a slice between my cheek and gums and kept it there. It

A visit to the southern islands in 1963 meant getting the feet wet. There were no jetties. Yaacob bin Mohamed, later MP for the southern islands, is third to the left of me, wearing clear glasses and no hat.

Warm crowds greeting me at Geylang Serai (a Malay area) on 9 September 1963. Mr Rahmat Yusak drove me in this Land Rover to every corner of Singapore (1962–63). After listening to hundreds of my speeches, he became my friend and strong supporter.

worked like magic. There was something in it that stimulated the flow of saliva and soothed my throat. Thereafter, I never went out on a tour without a packet of ginseng in my pocket.

The impact of my speeches was also heightened immensely by television. When I was in London in September 1962, Alex Josey, my press secretary, arranged for Hugh Burnett of the BBC to run a mock interview with me and then review my performance on the screen. I had seen an earlier programme in which I had appeared, and had been astounded at how fierce I looked. Burnett assured me that I was a natural. All I needed were a few tips: always look into the camera, never cover your mouth or nose with your hand as you speak, always lean forward in your chair – to lean backwards would make you look slovenly. His main advice: "Be natural, be direct, be yourself." I was reassured. Television was introduced in Singapore in February 1963 and proved a powerful weapon, particularly when turned against the communists. Their techniques were those of the mass rally, where the speaker bellowed, grimaced and exaggerated his gestures in order to be seen by those at the back of the crowd. Captured on the screen with a zoom lens, the speakers looked ugly and menacing. They did not have Hugh Burnett to advise them and did themselves a great deal of harm.

∞

While I was busy gathering popular support, there were troubling developments in the region. On 20 January 1963, the Indonesian foreign minister, Dr Subandrio, declared that Confrontation (*Konfrontasi*) against Malaysia was necessary because Malaya had let itself become a tool of colonialism and imperialism. A few days later, President Macapagal of the Philippines also denounced Malaysia as a new colonial power, and ten days after that, Subandrio told foreign correspondents that if Malaya's hostility to Indonesia spread to the Borneo territories, there could be incidents, including physical conflict. The next day, President John Kennedy publicly expressed his wholehearted support for Malaysia as "the best hope of security in that area", but Sukarno only intensified his aggressive rhetoric. On 1 May, he turned his full attention to the Borneo territories, insisting that they should be given independence first and again condemning Malaysia as colonialism in a new form.

The Tunku responded to these attacks by recalling his ambassador from Jakarta. Malaya then announced an immediate build-up of its army, navy and air force. On 3 May, the British Commander-in-Chief Far East followed this up by saying that he had enough men, ships and planes to meet any emergency in Borneo. The situation was becoming increasingly ominous.

On 31 May, the Japanese prime minister invited the Tunku and President Sukarno to meet in Tokyo. This summit ended with a reaffirmation of faith in the Treaty of Friendship of the two countries signed in 1959, pledging them to settle differences in a spirit of goodwill and neighbourliness. The Tunku was relieved. But Sukarno must have sensed that the Tunku was afraid of him. I myself noted the fear in the Tunku's body language and in his voice when he described this encounter to Razak, Ismail, Keng Swee and me shortly after his return from Tokyo.

The Tokyo summit led to a meeting of foreign ministers in Manila at which Razak conceded that the wishes of the people of the future Malaysia should be consulted again. But after the Tunku signed the Malaysia Agreement in July, Sukarno denounced it and accused him of betraying this Manila Accord. Macapagal contrived to get the two together for another meeting in Manila, and the result was that, on 6 August, the Tunku agreed to amend the date for the founding of Malaysia in order to give time for a UN-conducted survey mission to confirm whether the people of Borneo wanted merger.

The British found themselves obliged to agree that Indonesia, the Philippines and Britain should nominate observers to oversee the work of this mission, but Sandys was furious. He pressed the Tunku for a firm date for Malaysia, determined to stop further backsliding. Hundreds of

Malay youths from Brunei and pro-communist Chinese from Sarawak had already crossed the border for military training on the Indonesian side, and he did not want Indonesian "observers" roaming all over the Borneo territories when Jakarta was embarked on a policy of confrontation and subversion.

The meeting between them was very tense. Sandys reported on 27 August:

> "He (the Tunku) was in a very nervy state and finished by saying, 'I have reached the end of my tether and I do not want to discuss anything further with anybody.' ... He realises that Malaysia is a very small fish compared with Indonesia and he is worried about the prospect of living alongside a powerful and aggressive neighbour who has designs on his territory."

But Sandys was a dogged man and he got the Tunku to agree to announce that whatever happened he would inaugurate Malaysia on 16 September (double eight equals sixteen, another lucky number of his).

The Tunku was never comfortable with his Indonesian neighbours. Sukarno was an orator, the Tunku was not. Sukarno was a dominating personality, the Tunku was quiet and charming. Sukarno represented 100 million Indonesians, the Tunku only four million Malays and fewer than four million Chinese, Indians and others. The Malays generally acknowledge Javanese culture to be superior. But I had never seen the Tunku so fearful. Sukarno must have sensed this and was exploiting his fears to the maximum. It did not augur well.

Sandys had no confidence that the Tunku would stand up to the Indonesian foreign minister. To his relief, it was Razak who met Dr Subandrio in Singapore, not to discuss Malaysia but merely to inform him of the new date.

32. Singapore Declares Independence

As the date for merger drew closer, the Chinese Chamber of Commerce pressed me to get the Japanese to settle their "blood debt". Its leaders wanted it resolved before foreign affairs passed into the hands of a central government that was predominantly Malay, one that would feel less strongly about the atrocities that had been committed almost entirely against Chinese. The government in Tokyo, too, was aware of this and had been dragging its feet.

The chamber also wanted land in which to rebury the bones and to erect a memorial to the victims. I allotted a 4.5 hectare piece of land opposite Raffles Institution for the memorial, but asked the British to pursue the question of the blood debt with the Japanese, since they were in charge of foreign affairs. When I was in Tokyo in April 1962, Prime Minister Hayato Ikeda had agreed to do no more than "seriously consider appropriate steps to make amends and console the spirits of the dead". There were no specifics.

I was not anxious to work up this issue, but the problem was not going to go away. The Chinese Chamber of Commerce had decided to bring the matter to a head, and as I was planning to hold elections just before Malaysia Day, I had to press its demands, whatever the consequences in terms of Japanese investment. On 5 August, the chamber asked for $50 million in compensation, to be devoted to health and education projects. The Japanese responded with an offer of a radiotherapy centre for the treatment of cancer, experimental equipment for educational institutions, and scholarships for Singapore students in Japan, costing $5–10 million.

As president of the Chinese Chamber of Commerce, Ko Teck Kin proposed that a mass rally be held at the Padang in front of City Hall on Sunday, 25 August, "to report on the insincerity of the Japanese government in settling Singapore's demand for compensation". He knew that the PAP government would be unhappy as long as it was purely a Chinese issue, so he persuaded the chambers of commerce of the Malay, Indian, Eurasian and Ceylonese communities to join in the mass rally. I agreed to speak. A few days beforehand, Chin Chye settled with Ko the resolutions to be adopted. One of them was that if there was no satisfactory settlement, the people would carry out a non-cooperation campaign against the Japanese, and the Singapore government should not issue any new entry permits to Japanese nationals.

The Barisan and the communists saw this as another opportunity to show their strength and humiliate me in front of "the masses". The Padang could easily accommodate the 100,000 people the chamber expected, and it was impossible to prevent communist groups from infiltrating the crowds to cause mischief. After meeting officers from Special Branch and the police, I decided to take the risk. They would ensure that if the communists fomented disorder or violence it would be swiftly suppressed. We would deploy 6,000 police and troops – men from the two Singapore regiments – near the Padang and out of sight, but certain to be seen by Barisan scouts. We also decided to install powerful spotlights ready to turn on any section of the crowd that started trouble, especially those in the front row who could most effectively disrupt the meeting. When these spotlights focused on them, photographers and TV cameramen would dash up to take close-up pictures so that the police could later identify the ringleaders.

By that evening, spotlights had been installed on the roof of City Hall and at nearby vantage points. At first the crowd of more than 100,000 was orderly, many gazing at the banners depicting different Japanese torture scenes strung up between palm trees and between the pillars of the building. The Barisan and communist troublemakers were out in front and at the sides of the stage so that any commotion would be amplified by the loudspeakers. When I got to the microphone there was a round of booing and hissing, and as I began to speak the jeer leaders began chanting slogans to drown me out. I kept my patience and appealed for a chance to speak without interruption. But the uproar continued, and after speaking for a few minutes to make sure that the unreasonable behaviour of the rowdies would be obvious to everyone, I signalled to a plain-clothes police officer.

Suddenly, the spotlights came on and focused on the noisiest sections of the crowd, and the photographers and cameramen rushed forward to film them. The effect was instantaneous and salutary. They had not masked their faces with handkerchiefs this time. They knew that officers would pore over photographic enlargements to identify them, and there would be retribution if they persisted. The jeers and chanting stopped. The occasion turned out to be a demonstration of my resourcefulness and resolve to meet their threats when they played it rough, and enhanced my standing as a leader prepared to go to the end of the road in any fight. The thousands on the Padang and others watching television later could see that I was not rattled, that I had no armed bodyguards surrounding me, and that I was prepared to face danger. I made my points quietly in Hokkien – my command of the dialect had become an asset that protected me from Barisan charges that I was betraying the people. People sensed the strength of my convictions.

After this successful rally, I discussed the danger of any further postponement of Malaysia with my colleagues. We did not want the Barisan to recover their spirits at the prospect of merger being aborted. They might decide on direct action in the hope that Sukarno would intervene and scare the Tunku off completely. We therefore decided that on 31 August we would hold our merger rally as originally planned, and announce our immediate independence.

The day before, I wrote to Duncan Sandys to point out that, contrary to what Kuala Lumpur claimed, Singapore had not in fact agreed to a postponement of merger to 16 September. I reminded him that when the Legislative Assembly adopted the Malaysia Agreement at the beginning of the month, it included points conceded by the Tunku in London, some of them contained in an exchange of letters between Razak and me, others written on the back of an envelope, which the Tunku himself had signed. These provisions had still not been ratified or implemented, and I would accept the new date for Malaysia only after they were. In the meantime, I intended to declare Singapore independent within Malaysia on 31 August. I asked him to delegate powers to us in relation to foreign affairs, so that before that date the government could settle with the Japanese the gesture of atonement to be made for atrocities committed during the occupation.

I added that the light-hearted manner in which solemn agreements in writing had been set aside by the Malayans under one pretext or another was most disturbing. They could not be abandoned unilaterally. If I did not receive a categorical assurance from him that Singapore would not be forced into Malaysia unless the outstanding items were settled by Monday, 2 September, I intended to resign and seek a new mandate from the people. They would then become crucial issues in an election and it would be difficult to conceal the fact that Singapore had not agreed to join Malaysia on 16 September.

Sandys did not reply.

On 31 August 1963, at a ceremonial rally at the City Hall steps, I unilaterally declared Singapore independent. The British had tried to dissuade me. Sandys, who was supposed to have turned up if the merger was on schedule, did not. He was on the *Mutiara*, a Malayan naval vessel cruising off the coast of Malaya, waiting for 16 September. Razak also absented himself. But Sarawak had already declared *de facto* independence and North Borneo had proclaimed the establishment of the state of Sabah. I said to the assembled crowd that just as these territories had assumed self-government in advance of merger, confiding federal powers in the interim to their respective governors, so in Singapore all federal powers over defence and external affairs would be reposed until 16 September in our Yang di-Pertuan Negara, who would hold them in trust for the central government. The Tunku and his colleagues believed I had instigated the defiance of the North Borneo states in the face of his express wishes, because the week before, I had met the leaders of the Sabah and Sarawak Alliance in Jesselton. Indeed I had urged them to do something dramatic on 31 August to prevent any further postponement.

Selkirk came for dinner that night as planned but voiced no protest. I did not make a song and dance about it, but I was not going to allow the momentum for Malaysia to falter, especially since I had decided to announce general elections three days later, with nomination day on 12 September. By declaring Singapore independent and holding the federal powers in trust, I put pressure on the Tunku to keep to the date of 16 September. The Tunku did not take kindly to this, and on 2 September, the Malaysian government made strong representations, not to Singapore but to the British. I retorted the next day, "If anybody has to complain it will be the British and Singapore. After all, we run this place." I added that one of the sad things about Malaya was its naive approach in believing that power was handed over on a silver platter with red ribbons by British royalty in uniform. This was insubordinate language, which the Tunku did not approve of, but it was most necessary for me as a Singapore leader not to allow myself to be seen as someone who would only do what pleased the Tunku. He replied by saying that I had hurt the feelings of the people of Malaya.

I told Selkirk on 4 September that if the points of agreement between the Tunku and myself were not honoured by nomination day, I would fight the election on a platform of independence and immediately ask a number of countries for recognition as from 16 September. For any further evasion could only mean that the Malay leaders intended to crush Singapore, and I would be ashamed to accept responsibility for entering Malaysia on such terms. Selkirk reported to Sandys that I showed intellectual arrogance, adding the following day:

> "I consider he is now playing a supreme act of brinkmanship. He believes his position is inviolable. He believes that either he comes into Malaysia on his own terms or he declares independence and can make any terms he likes with us because he is satisfied we would under no circumstances give up our military position in Singapore. He believes, probably rightly, that he could win an election on the slogan of independence interspersed with bitter comments on the Malays and ourselves who he will say are seeking to destroy the hard won position of advantage of the Chinese in Singapore. ... I believe he still basically wants to come into Malaysia. We should therefore press the Malays to meet him fully on the relatively small points still outstanding."

I then declared publicly that I had given Sandys until 12 September "to sort out certain matters with regard to the Malaysia Agreement". I was playing my last card to get the undertakings the Tunku had given me in London written into the constitution or into a proper document. The British took my threat seriously, but after seeing Razak and Ismail in Kuala Lumpur, Geofroy Tory reported on 5 September that "neither ... showed any qualms about going through with Malaysia whatever Lee did". Sandys above all was enraged that things might go wrong at the last moment, and the same day reported to Harold Macmillan, his prime minister, in angry terms:

> "He realises that his declaration has no legal validity and that the British government would not tolerate any attempt by him actually to exercise powers which he purports to have assumed. On the other hand, this act of public defiance towards Britain and Malaya has no doubt helped to strengthen the public image of himself which he wishes to create.

"He is not a man who climbs down. Once he has committed himself to a definite course and has accepted a carefully calculated risk, he is likely to go through with it, for better or worse. Therefore if we were to humiliate him publicly, he would, I believe, retaliate with further acts of defiance of one kind or another and we might very quickly be forced to suspend the constitution.

"If the transfer to Malaysia of sovereignty over Singapore were to take place at a time when the constitution was suspended we would be accused throughout the world of handing over the people of Singapore against their will. Thus it seemed to me that, even at the risk of appearing feeble, it was in our interest to do everything possible to avoid that situation.

"In recent weeks Lee threatened that, if the Malayan government did not give him what he demanded, he would hold elections and seek a vote of confidence from the people. Now he has done it. The Singapore parliament has been dissolved. Nomination day has been fixed for September 12th. Polling day will probably be about ten days later (i.e., after Malaysia Day).

"Lee has so far not announced the issues on which he will fight the election. But he is threatening that, unless the Malayan government give him satisfaction on various points connected with the Malaysia Agreement, he will declare independence on September 12th and will ask the electors of Singapore to endorse this with their votes.

"Tun Razak assured me that the Malayan government were irrevocably committed to Malaysia, and that they would go through with it whatever happened. I believe that he speaks for most of the ministers but I am not so completely confident about the attitude of the Tunku himself. As I told you in an earlier telegram he is suffering seriously from cold feet and although I think it unlikely, it is just possible that at the last moment he might refuse to take over Singapore ... This would obviously face us with a most awkward dilemma which I will not discuss now.

"With these uncomfortable possibilities in mind, it is of the utmost importance to avoid if at all possible a head-on collision with Lee between now and September 16th. I have therefore strongly urged the Malayan government to concede as far as they possibly can the demands which Lee has made regarding the Malaysia constitution. Most of them are not unreasonable and are based upon rather loosely worded undertakings given by the Tunku to Lee in London, though admittedly Lee is trying to interpret these undertakings in a manner excessively favourable to himself.

"But even if he gets his way on all points I do not put it past Lee to think up a new set of demands. I think therefore that it is wise to assume that we are going to have trouble and to prepare for the worst.

"The concessions which I hope to persuade the Malayan government to make may induce Lee to go into Malaysia quietly. But unless I mistake his character, he will bluff, bully and blackmail up to the eleventh hour. In these circumstances it seems to me essential that I should remain on the spot. This will I hope enable me:

(a) To restrain the Malayan government from adopting a provocative or over-intransigent attitude towards Lee.
(b) To try and help the two of them reach agreement and
(c) To stiffen the Tunku's resolve to go through with Malaysia if he should show signs of wavering. It would seem silly for the sake of a few days not to do everything in my power to save Malaysia from the possibility of collapse, with all that that would imply.

"Consequently, if you approve, I propose to remain in this area until we have put Singapore safely in the bag on 16 September. In that case I could stay on the extra two days for the Malaysia celebrations. This would make it unnecessary to find another cabinet colleague to take this on."

But I had no intention of wrecking Malaysia. Having negotiated at several constitutional conferences, I knew the legal position only too well: once I was in Malaysia, not only would the army and the police be under the control of Kuala Lumpur, but Kuala Lumpur could declare a state of emergency and govern by decree. So I wanted as many safeguards built into the constitution or spelt out in official documents as possible in case the federal government decided to do anything stupid.

The British were with me, and the pressure I applied through them worked. By 7 September, the Malayan attorney-general and Razak between them had endorsed all the items in question except the delegation to Singapore of the right to detain secret society gangsters. They did not want this to be in the constitution and I had to be content with a simple letter of authority. On 11 September, I announced that the differences between us had been settled. It could be said that by using the colonial power to coerce the Malayan leaders, I was earning ill-will and storing up trouble for the future. But my unilateral declaration of independence had been necessary in order to warn the British that I could make things difficult for them and for the Tunku if he did not fulfil his promises. My methods succeeded, but at a price. The Tunku and Razak were confirmed in their view that I was a difficult man to handle, and from then on they would always be guarded when dealing with me.

On the very morning of nomination day, I completed my last speech-making tour in the Mountbatten ward after visiting three constituencies during the night. I got home at 7 am to the sound of crackers fired by my neighbours in Oxley Road. They knew there was a critical fight ahead and they were cheering me on. Six hours after the closure of nominations, the government announced that voting would be on 21 September, in other words, five days after we joined Malaysia. If Malaysia had not come by then and the Barisan won the election, then we, Singapore, the British and the Malayans would all be in trouble. Surely this would allow the Tunku no other way but to go through with it on the 16th as scheduled, I argued. I also wanted most of the campaign to take place while we still controlled the police and the administrative machinery of the elections, and the gangsters – including Chua Hoe Ann, Lim Yew Hock's chief supporter – were still in detention. I had earlier turned down the Tunku's request to release Chua.

Two days before Malaysia Day, 16 September, UN Secretary-General U Thant announced that according to the UN survey, a sizeable majority of the people of Sarawak and Sabah wished to join Malaysia. The next day, Indonesia and the Philippines recalled their ambassadors from Kuala Lumpur and declared that they would not recognise Malaysia, and on 16 September huge crowds gathered in Jakarta for an organised display of "popular rage", then the conventional third world protocol for diplomatic protest.

Thousands of demonstrators, screaming "*Ganjang* Malaysia" (Crush Malaysia), stormed the British and Malayan embassies. They burst into the first floor of the British embassy building to destroy furnishings and fittings, and for 90 minutes hurled stones and chunks of concrete from outside, smashing every window. With the missiles falling around him, the British assistant military attaché marched up and down in the uniform of an SAS major, playing his bagpipes in full view of the rioters. Policemen tried to drag him behind a pillar, but he broke free to resume playing. When the British ambassador, Andrew Gilchrist, appeared and was told by representatives of the mob that they would fight for the freedom from imperialism of the people of North Borneo, he responded, "*Hidup* U Thant!" (Long Live U Thant), and speaking in Indonesian pointed out that the United Nations had endorsed Malaysia. These acts of British defiance provoked the Indonesians into setting fire to the embassy, ransacking it two days later, and manhandling members of the staff, including the ambassador himself. The Indonesians also attacked the Malayan embassy, but the ambassador was not available. To return the compliment, angry mobs sacked the Indonesian embassy in Kuala Lumpur.

On 16 September, we held a second ceremony, this time with Sandys representing Britain and Ismail representing Malaya, standing with me on the steps of City Hall as I declared Singapore a part of Malaysia and pledged the loyalty of its people to the federal government. The Tunku was not aware that it was my 40th birthday. If he had been, he might well have changed the date – my birthday could not be his lucky day. The following morning, I flew to Kuala Lumpur for the official ceremony at the Merdeka Stadium. The air was laden with the menace of Sukarno's Confrontation, and the Tunku's dread of what he might do was felt by all his ministers. On the way to the stadium, I ran into Selkirk in his tropical white ceremonial uniform, making his last appearance as commissioner-general for Southeast Asia. He, too, looked somewhat tense and harassed, but I took heart from the resolve of the British, which I felt was firm and strong. I had no doubt they would see Malaysia through in spite of anything Sukarno could do.

The ceremony over, I flew back to Singapore and resumed campaigning for the next four days. The PAP fielded candidates in all 51 constituencies, the Barisan and the UPP 46, the Singapore Alliance 42, the Partai Rakyat three, the Workers' Party three, and independents 16. All parties shared radio and television time in proportion to the number of their candidates. It was amazing the speed with which a relatively tranquil city suddenly came alive with eager beavers scurrying around, putting up posters and banners and distributing pamphlets. The PAP campaign was the climax of my constituency tours of the past 10 months, and Keng Swee convinced the election committee that I should be the focus. I was the target of the MCP's wrath, and the PAP's response would be the more dramatic if it were built around me personally to show people that the communists had failed to destroy me. We had only one campaign poster, a picture of me taken during one of my constituency visits bedecked with a huge Indian garland, my right arm raised, smiling and waving to the crowds.

The Barisan put up posters of their detained leaders, especially of Lim Chin Siong, to arouse the faithful and win the sympathy vote. Once the campaign got going, their supporters went all out to muster votes, and their underground organisations and united front groups sprang to life to throw in everything they could mobilise. They held large rallies at which they poured forth a stream of vituperation against me and – what was new – spewed out hatred against the right-wing reactionaries, namely the Tunku and the feudal Malays. Four days before polling, Dr Lee Siew Choh reiterated his opposition to Malaysia and took the side of the Indonesians against the Tunku. This made our earlier warning that a vote for the Barisan was a vote for Sukarno even more credible. At a huge lunchtime rally, I predicted that the communists would dive underground for cover after we had won. As expected, the election was a fight between the Barisan and the PAP.

My eve-of-poll broadcast nevertheless concentrated on getting the Alliance out of the way to minimise splitting the non-communist vote. The MCA knew by now that they could not win, and preferred to have the Barisan win so that Kuala Lumpur could suspend the state constitution, institute direct rule, and take over lock, stock and barrel – a simple if naive solution to a most complex problem. The Singapore government would have control of a budget half that of the centre, and a radio and television station more powerful than that of Kuala Lumpur. In the hands of communists with links to the Indonesian Communist Party, it would bring calamity upon Malaysia. The constitutional safeguards we had agreed upon would work only if the PAP were in power. The choice before the people was clear and simple.

Philip Moore reported to London:

"... There are very few independent observers now who will confidently predict an overall PAP majority in the Assembly, i.e. 26 seats or more. ... The strength of the PAP seems to lie in the highly effective strong government which they have exercised in Singapore over the last 18 months. ... The weakness of the PAP lies primarily in their lack of party organisation in the constituencies and in particular among the Chinese-speaking members of electorate, who number 63 per cent. ... But Lee himself was full of confidence on the telephone this afternoon. He was, however, furious with the Tunku for having come down to Singapore yesterday (19 September) and intervened in the campaign.

"My own prediction is still that the PAP will get an overall majority, but most of the people whose judgement I respect are less optimistic and do not give them more than 20–24. A Barisan Sosialis majority cannot be ruled out. ... However, even if the Barisan Sosialis did pursue fairly moderate policies in Singapore, it is difficult to see how the central government could tolerate them in power in Singapore for very long."

The Tunku's personal appearance to speak at Alliance rallies had been a most serious development. Whatever his personal wishes, the UMNO leadership and the pull of the local Malays had brought him quickly into Singapore politics. Also, Razak had talked to Selkirk a few months earlier about the possibility of "elections producing an alternative government to replace Lee". All this meant that UMNO did not intend to allow the state to look after itself as we had agreed, and that sooner rather than later we would have to enter Malayan politics to defend our interests. I had hoped to postpone that contest for at least one election term. Now this no longer seemed possible.

The votes were counted on 21 September, and it proved an exciting night for in many constituencies the results were very close. Chin Chye beat Dr Lee Siew Choh by 89 votes and Raja won by fewer than 200. Kenny lost to the Barisan's S.T. Bani by 159 votes. David Marshall, abandoned by the Barisan's communists, lost his deposit in Anson. The hopes of Lim Chin Siong, Fong Swee Suan and the other detainees in Changi, who were listening to it all on the radio, were soon dashed as it became obvious that the PAP was not going to be routed, that the massive crowds at Barisan rallies had not reflected true popular support. We won 37 seats, the Barisan 13 and Ong Eng Guan's UPP one. As one of them was to admit later, the Barisan were completely stunned.

The Tunku's dream of having an SPA-UMNO-MCA-MIC Alliance in control of Singapore also vanished. All 42 of their candidates were eliminated. I was right in not agreeing to a complete clean-up of the communist open front leaders, otherwise the Alliance might have won enough seats to remain a potential force. But the most devastating blow for the Tunku was that the PAP had defeated UMNO in all three of its overwhelmingly Malay constituencies, which he had specially come down to Singapore to address on the eve of the election. Faced with the choice of a weak Alliance, a strong Barisan and a credible PAP, the Malays in the southern islands, Kampong Kembangan and Geylang Serai had voted for the PAP. We had strong Malay candidates, the best of whom was Yaacob bin Mohamed. This result was to have tremendous repercussions. We did not know until after the Malaysian election in April 1964 how ominously UMNO viewed this unexpected PAP victory and how vicious their counter-attacks would be.

After all the results had been announced, and well past midnight, I summed up over radio and television four and a half years of acute conflict and anxiety: "We reached this morning what is for the communists their moment of truth – that their masses were mythical." Their cheer-leaders, slogans, posters stuck all over the place to smother everybody and give an impression of inordinate numbers and invincibility – these "were exposed by you". Next day, 22 September, Moore reported to London:

> "This was a famous victory and the crowning achievement to date of Lee Kuan Yew's career. It is a much more decisive victory than the 1959, since he won then with communist support but on this occasion he fought communists openly and decisively defeated them. ...
>
> "We have always said in Singapore that Lee Kuan Yew is the only man who can run this city and that the Malaysian government would either have to do business with him or put him in jail. The latter is now unthinkable and we must hope that enough moderation

Swearing in as prime minister before Yusof bin Ishak, the Yang di-Pertuan Negara, in 1963.

will be shown on both sides to make a working partnership possible. Lee spoke to me on the phone this morning and I took the opportunity of stressing to him the importance of not gloating too much over the Alliance defeat and concentrating on improving his relationship with Kuala Lumpur. He has made so many mistakes over this in the past and it is up to him to make a genuine effort to strike up a new relationship."

∞

Three men played critical roles in the open fight to defeat the communists. Raja was superb. His fighting spirit never flagged. After the Barisan mounted their attacks on us in mid-1961, when everything looked bleak and we were in the depths of despair, Raja roared like a lion. They reviled the PAP as turncoats and renegades who had sold out the people; Raja answered in terms as pungent, rebutting and debunking them. He put his pamphleteering skills to work, and his robustness stiffened everybody's morale. He was convinced that we were in the right, that we must fight, and that we would win.

Next, Pang Boon – quiet and soft-spoken, dependable and reliable, good in his assessments of who were loyal at PAP headquarters and in the party branches. He kept our loyalists together and in good heart, so that we had Chinese-educated party workers who became the core of an election organisation. Together with the grassroots community leaders, this made up for what had been demolished by the defecting Barisan supporters when the PAP split.

But my most important backroom player was Keng Swee, with his clear mind and sharp pen. He helped me refine the tactics that defeated the communists. For every clever move they made, we worked out a counter-move. Throughout this fight and for the next 21 years until he retired as deputy prime minister in 1984, he was my *alter ego*, always the sceptic, always turning a proposition on its head to reveal its flaws and help me reshape it. He was my resident intellectual *par excellence* and a doughty fighter. There were several other stalwarts, but these three stood out.

33. Konfrontasi

The 1963 election was a watershed for the communists. Soon after the results, two Barisan candidates who won – Chan Sun Wing, my former parliamentary secretary, and Wong Soon Fong, who had subverted the Works Brigade – dived underground. They must have expected to be picked up the moment the Barisan lost. But for the moment our sights were elsewhere. We had decided to make an example of prominent figures who had acted as front men for the communists, believing that their wealth and standing in the Chinese-speaking community gave them immunity. Number one on the list was Tan Lark Sye, then honorary president of the Chinese Chamber of Commerce and the founder of Nanyang University. I had made a mental note to deal with him when the government had the political strength. Now we no longer needed to tolerate his spouting the communist line in the press, using his position in the business world as a shield.

The day after the election, we started proceedings to cancel his citizenship, which had been acquired by registration. A statement from my office read:

> "The government has decided that no man, whatever his wealth, status and standing, shall with impunity play stooge to the communists and jeopardise the peace and prosperity of Singapore and the amity and unity of the races of Malaysia. ... He had openly and blatantly intervened in these elections by signing statements drafted by these communists standing as Barisan Sosialis candidates denouncing the government, using as cover his so-called protection of Chinese language, culture and education."

This action would have been unthinkable earlier. We were then fearful of alienating the Chinese-speaking voters, especially as the vernacular press would distort the issue and make it appear directed against businessmen who supported the cause of Chinese culture. Now the time had come to deal with him. Tan Lark Sye was helpless. No Lim Chin Siong with his unions came to the rescue, there were no protests in the newspapers, no demonstrations. We were neutering him politically. Asked to comment the next day, he had nothing to say. He had gambled and lost. He never regained his prominence.

A few days later, at a lunchtime meeting at Fullerton Square, I cleared the way for the post-election, post-merger situation: "I am giving the Plen two weeks. If he is still here, will he please get out; security is no more in my hands." I added that it was now controlled by the central government, and I had to make his identity known to Ismail. From interrogation of communists who had fled to the neighbouring Riau Islands but later returned, Special Branch discovered years later that the Plen had already left Singapore soon after the referendum. He had remained in the Riau Islands, which were Indonesian, and from there directed his underground subordinates in Singapore through couriers. Travel by ferry or outboards between the two would have taken only two to four hours, and it was easy to escape detection because fishermen sailed to and fro all the time. So I was not exaggerating when I warned that the struggle against the MCP was not over, that they would continue to fight their enemies by fair means or foul and would prove hard and tricky to deal with. Nothing had changed – except one thing; I was no longer in charge of the police.

This point was driven home the next day when Special Branch, now under Federation orders, arrested 20 Nanyang University undergraduates, three of whom had fought unsuccessfully in the election as Barisan candidates. Students on the campus rioted, and a large crowd of them attacked the convoy taking the prisoners away. Two police vans of the riot squad were waiting outside the gates, and, using loudhailers, the police ordered the demonstrators to disperse. When they did not do so, the riot squad moved in; the students threw bottles and stones at them, injuring the two drivers.

They had not yet learnt that Special Branch now took orders from a new government in Kuala Lumpur, based on a Malay majority with no inhibitions about dealing with Chinese students. Several thousand workers from seven big SATU unions, which had already been asked to show cause why their registration should not be cancelled, were driven to a meeting at the university campus in more than 100 lorries and buses. They still acted as if big mass rallies would intimidate the government. Members of the Naval Base Labour Union went on strike, led by supporters of Sidney Woodhull, now in detention, and 500 Nanyang University students sat down on the Padang opposite City Hall while their leaders presented a six-point petition to Chin Chye, talking as if the Barisan were still poised for victory as the next government. The following day, workers in the bus companies and in the many firms with unions affiliated to SATU called a two-day general strike.

A few hours before it began, 14 SATU officials were detained, including S.T. Bani, who had won in the Crawford constituency against Kenny Byrne. A crowd of a thousand workers then tried to march to the ministry of home affairs from the Padang but were dispersed by the riot squad, and by evening, some of the unions had begun to dissociate themselves from the strike. The neutrals were taking heart. They could see no future in playing the old games. As the strike petered out, the leaders called it off.

Dr Lee Siew Choh charged that once again I was using the communist bogey to divert attention from, instead of attending to, the issues at hand. But the world had changed. Woodhull and Puthucheary were released from detention on 28 November. They announced that they were staying out of unions and politics for good. Woodhull declared,

"Experience has shown me that communist activity has mucked things up for the non-communists." As for Puthucheary, he wanted "nothing more to do with communism, to which I am opposed". Woodhull and Puthucheary were leftists who prided themselves on being Marxists. They were not communists; indeed they would never have been accepted into the MCP. They lacked the necessary steadfastness and would have been a security risk to any cell they were part of. They were political dilettantes who enjoyed the cocktail circuit where they held forth.

Violence had also come from another direction. A few days after the election, an Indonesian saboteur had exploded two bombs within 72 hours of each other on the south coast near Katong Park. Confrontation was now a reality. But an even more ominous development was beginning.

The day after the election, the Tunku had expressed shock that Malays in Singapore who had always supported UMNO had voted for the PAP. "I think there must be a few traitors amongst the members who have brought about this change of heart of the people here," he said. On 27 September, he came down to a rally organised by Singapore UMNO at Geylang Serai, a Malay settlement, at which he again criticised "certain Malays" (i.e., pro-PAP) who had "betrayed UMNO" in the election. "In future, I will play an important part in elections," he said. He went on to say that the control of Singapore was not in the hands of Mr Lee or the PAP any more, but with the central government in Kuala Lumpur.

Accompanying the Tunku was Syed Ja'afar Albar, who wanted to make sure that the Malays who had been "misled" into voting for us would be made to return to the fold. In his speech, he warned me that the people could only be fooled once, and vowed that he would fix Singapore at the proper time. Local UMNO leaders began to talk in truculent terms. They felt they were the masters now. The American consul-general, Arthur H. Rosen, reported to Washington that "passions were ... stirred by a violent anti-PAP speech with strong racist overtones by Ja'afar Albar". They burnt an effigy of me before a screaming crowd.

At the time, I did not take much notice. I thought it was just post-election morale-boosting. I did not then understand the nuances of Malay talk and it took me another nine months to grasp the real implications. Little knowing that this was the prelude to a bitter campaign of hate, which would come to a head in Malay-Chinese riots, I had blithely told the crowd at a rally in Fullerton Square that time would heal hurt feelings. I had had to say some harsh things before and during the election, but my task now was to reestablish good relations and mutual confidence with Kuala Lumpur. I was sure Singapore would then hum with industrial activity and be the prosperous hub of Malaysia. I promised that the government would cooperate with the centre on a fair and equal basis, not as servant with master.

I was still talking in terms of UMNO and the PAP fighting our common enemies, the MCP with their united front supporters and Sukarno's Indonesia, which was under communist influence. I did not know that the Tunku's lieutenants, like Albar, thought differently. They left the British to protect them from the Indonesians. For them, it was more important to deal with the enemy within – the PAP, which, unless stopped in its tracks, would start to win over Malays from the kampongs in Malaya itself.

Speaking at City Hall on 29 September, I had said, "We understand that for the next two decades the prime minister of Malaysia must be a Malay. There are 43 per cent Malays, an indigenous people, 41 per cent Chinese, 10 per cent Indians and 6 per cent others. We are not out to capture power in Kuala Lumpur. We want to cooperate and work in the common interest of Malaysia." But I referred to the MCA leaders Khaw Kai Boh and Tan Siew Sin dismissively, and the Tunku disapproved of this. The next day, he responded by saying that although the MCA represented the Chinese community, they had not lost sight of national interests, and their ability to care for both at the same time had contributed much towards the success of the Alliance at elections; UMNO, the

MCA and the MIC must stand together. He was signalling that he was not willing to give up his Alliance partners. I did not understand until nearly a year later that if the PAP wanted to join the Alliance as part of a coalition it must accept the role of an MCA, and bring the Chinese around to cooperating in the national interest to further UMNO's programme, which basically was to help the Malays.

Geofroy Tory's assessment of these political trends in the new Federation was succinctly summarised in his report of 5 October 1963 to Duncan Sandys:

> "But the position of the Alliance in the long term is certainly not unshakeable. Mr Lee Kuan Yew has shown in the recent Singapore elections that he is able to unite all the non-communists of Singapore, including the Malays, in a common front at the Alliance's expense. (However,) much of his success must be ascribed to his performance as a defender of Singapore's interests against Malaya; and it is unlikely, therefore, to bring him much credit elsewhere in the Federation.
>
> "On the other hand, if the tale of communal grievances against the more extreme policies of UMNO becomes too long, and if for this and other reasons the Chinese wing of the Alliance weakens still further, a serious communal Chinese opposition based on the Malayan West Coast, but with assistance from the other Malaysian opposition parties, could begin to develop. Once seriously alarmed, the Malays would certainly not be prevented by constitutional forms from protecting their position, even if the cost were the bitter one of exchanging their present relatively enlightened and moderate form of parliamentary democracy for some kind of more closely guided democracy."

Geofroy Tory was prescient. He more or less predicted what was to happen in 1965, when the Malaysian Solidarity Convention would bring the opposition parties together.

∽

In early October, Choo and I drove up to the Cameron Highlands for a two-week break. The mountain air and the relative isolation helped me to think out our position under the new dispensation. For the next fortnight, I played golf, often alone. Walking around the nine-hole course with Choo, my half bag of clubs carried by an aborigine boy, I pondered over the problems that would now have to be tackled. We faced danger from Indonesia, but we had contained the communists for the time being. They were dazed, keeping their heads down, taking stock of their vulnerability in a new situation. They knew Kuala Lumpur was out to crush them.

We too had to adjust to a central government that openly stood for Malay interests. This we could only accommodate if the Chinese, Indians and others were given enough space. Nevertheless, when I had seen the Tunku in Kuala Lumpur five days before, I had left him in a good mood, and some questions seemed to have been settled amicably, despite all that had happened. He had spoken of closing the Bank of China and the Bank Negara Indonesia (National Bank of Indonesia) in Singapore, but added that he had not taken any firm decision and wanted to discuss the matter again. I was able to tell the press that he had promised to allow them to stay open provided they were not staffed by senior government officials from China or Indonesia.

After my return to Singapore on 14 October, I met Philip Moore and told him I had proposed that we should appoint a Malay as one of our two senators in the federal parliament. The Tunku had been pleased and had suggested the UMNO leader in Singapore, Ahmad Haji Taff. I had agreed. The other senator was to be Ko Teck Kin.

The Tunku had also wanted us to close our trade commission in Jakarta, and although I was unenthusiastic, we recalled the commissioner, leaving a junior officer in charge. Moore himself was worried that we were having secret discussions with the Indonesians in Singapore to find a way to lift the embargo they had announced. I assured him that discussions had taken place only between our traders and their officials, not with Singapore government officers. I added that I was happy with the way things had worked out with Ismail. Kuala Lumpur's security action in Singapore had gone off well. Ismail had phoned to tell me of the planned arrest of the SATU union leaders, and asked me to confirm that this would have the support of the Singapore government. I gave him that assurance. We had then exchanged letters, which kept me in the picture on the internal security situation; my regular Saturday morning meetings with the police and Special Branch were to continue.

It was a period of deceptive calm. The new Legislative Assembly was sworn in on 22 October and the first bill passed was for elections to the House of Representatives in Kuala Lumpur. It was carried on a voice vote and we named 12 PAP and three Barisan assemblymen. As I was leaving for the opening session on 3 November, I described the PAP's role in the federal parliament as that of a "'cross-bencher' – friend, loyal opposition and critic, not like the Barisan or the Malayan Socialist Front, which were destructive and disloyal". While in Kuala Lumpur, I agreed with the Tunku that we should receive an official visit by the Yang di-Pertuan Agong, the king of Malaysia, and when he came, he was welcomed with pomp and ceremony. The Tunku was a great upholder of the mystique of royalty.

I myself was not entirely happy with my time in the federal capital. The Tunku was too busy to have any effective discussion with me on our relationship, and meanwhile, there was renewed discord. In reporting a thinly veiled attack on me by Albar, the Malay press had lashed out at Alex Josey for writing an article in which he had represented me as the leader of the four million Chinese in Malaysia. This had given particular offence. Razak had also taken me to task for describing the PAP as cross-benchers, friendly but critical – how could we be both?

In response to Razak's objection to my idea of the PAP as cross-benchers, I had asked the Tunku where our MPs should sit in the House.

He proposed that some of the 12 PAP MPs sit on the government side and some with the opposition. We were in an equivocal position. On my return to Singapore, I told Moore that our relationship with the Tunku and UMNO would have to be settled one way or another within two or three years of the coming federal election. The Tunku would have to decide either to drop the MCA and work with the PAP, or fight the PAP for control of the towns of Malaya.

Not that we were forgetting the countryside. On 21 December, I spoke for the first time in the House of Representatives during a debate on Tan Siew Sin's budget. I criticised it for its lack of a broader sweep of the Federation's problems. It was good for big business, which was centred in the towns, but would not benefit the have-nots outside them. I stressed the need to bring prosperity to the rural areas where the bulk of Malays lived as farmers. The opposition leaders in Malaya had not talked in these terms before; we had brought our Fabian thinking to bear on Malaysian problems and believed that this was the solution.

Moore reported to London that Keng Swee, who had previously been doubtful about our prospects in Malaya, was now convinced that within a year or so, the PAP would rout both the Socialist Front and the MCA. With Singapore now a part of Malaysia, Moore's reports were sent through the new UK high commissioner in Kuala Lumpur, Viscount Head, who had replaced Geofroy Tory. Antony Head had a totally different cast of mind from his predecessor. He was a political heavyweight. A Sandhurst cadet, he was awarded a Military Cross in World War II and was a brigadier when he entered the House of Commons in 1945. He became minister of defence in Anthony Eden's cabinet at the time of the Suez invasion, resigning when it failed. He was elevated as viscount to the House of Lords. His wife Dorothy was a great character, thoroughly undiplomatic and openly interested in politics. Head had been British high commissioner in Nigeria for three years and she was a great lover of the birds of Africa. Some of the most glorious and exotic of them, including golden-crested cranes, would wander all over the grounds and into the drawing rooms of Carcosa, their official residence in Kuala Lumpur, to leave their droppings on the beautiful chintz-covered cushions. Neither of them batted an eyelid. They would just wipe up the mess with some paper and continue the conversation. I liked both of them and we got on. Whenever I was in Kuala Lumpur, I would have lunch or dinner with him and his wonderfully eccentric wife.

Head had an understanding of the ups and downs of peoples and nations. He thought things through. While the British were resolutely holding the line against Sukarno's now ceaseless incursions into Borneo, he cautioned me that British and Malaysians must both conduct operations in such a way that when all this was over, we would be able to live together peacefully with the Indonesians, that if we rubbed their noses in the dirt, it would make future relations more difficult. British restraint dragged out the conflict, but it did make the subsequent reconciliation easier. When Sukarno had been removed from power in 1965, General Suharto, then the *de facto* ruler, sent emissaries to Kuala Lumpur and Singapore to establish contact and begin to restore our confidence in Indonesia. Head had wisdom, that rare quality of learning from one's mistakes and, better still, from the mistakes of others. He also understood the Tunku and the hierarchical structure of Malay society. It was not unlike what he had found in northern Nigeria.

It was fortunate for me that the British prime minister had decided to send a top-ranking politician from the establishment to Kuala Lumpur instead of a professional diplomat like Tory. The history of Malaysia and Singapore would have been very different otherwise. Head brought to bear his varied experience, including what he had seen of the problems in Nigeria. He knew too well the difficulties in the evolution from colonial rule to self-government and nationhood. In the two years before August 1965, I would have much to do with him. His assessments and reports to London made an enormous difference to the outcome of the tussle

Philip Moore (left) and Antony Head at Eden Hall, the UK deputy high commissioner's residence, Singapore, 1964.

between the Tunku and his Ultras on one side, and my colleagues and me on the other. The Ultras pressed for a completely Malay-dominated Malaysia. We in Singapore – especially those born in or deeply attached to Malaya like Chin Chye, Pang Boon and Raja – were determined to establish a multiracial Malaysian Malaysia. This was the heart of the matter.

Head had a good feel for Africa and for the Commonwealth African leaders. He believed that a visit to them by a mission of ministers from the new Malaysian states would win their sympathy in international forums like the United Nations. He guffawed when I said the Tunku believed the Africans were slow-witted, for Head had met many Africans smarter than the Tunku, quite a few of whom had taken Firsts at Oxford. He sensed that I was a restless, active person who was keen to do something to counter Sukarno's propaganda offensive. He suggested that I get the Tunku to send me to Africa to win their support, which he thought would be useful on the psychological front while the British held the military front. He also foresaw that it would make me better known internationally, which would mean that if things ever came to the point where the Tunku wanted to lock me up, there would be a bigger price to pay.

I put the idea to the Tunku, and to my surprise, he readily agreed. Confrontation had taken a sombre turn. The first burst of excitement and even enthusiasm that had inspired demonstrations outside the Indonesian embassy in Kuala Lumpur had subsided. The Tunku went around the country making speeches to arouse Malayan nationalism, since Malaysia was too new a concept. But from private conversations with him, I knew he was fearful of the pull that Sukarno's rhetoric could have on Malayan Malays, especially recent immigrants, the first- or second-generation descendants of Sumatrans and Javanese.

I myself had complete faith in the capabilities of the British, and was blissfully unaware that their policy of active opposition to Confrontation could not be sustained if the US government took a contrary line. I had paid scant attention when the press reported the US representative to the Malaysia celebrations of 17 September in Kuala Lumpur as saying that America was in no position to take sides in the dispute. But diplomatic documents from the British archives of that period disclose grave concern over the ambivalent attitude of the Americans. Their assessment was that the Americans feared Britain would be overstretched by Confrontation and ultimately the United States would have to shoulder the burden. They also feared that by thwarting Sukarno, the British would be discrediting a non-communist government in Jakarta, thus turning Indonesia over to the communists, which would pose a threat to US bases in the Philippines.

The British must have worked hard to get the Kennedy administration to suspend at least some forms of US economic aid to Indonesia and ban fresh arms deliveries of Lockheed spare parts in November 1963. To show their own total commitment and resolve, the British had announced in December that Australian and New Zealand forces would join them in the defence of Malaysia against mounting Indonesian military incursions.

At the urging of the British, the Tunku had meanwhile stopped wavering in his attitude towards Indonesia. Sukarno had made a speech on 3 December claiming that the first UN survey mission in North Borneo had not been carried out in accordance with democratic procedures. He promised to welcome Malaysia if a second survey showed that its people wanted to be a part of the Federation. A spokesman of the Malaysian ministry of external affairs turned down the offer, but it was clear that it was the Tunku himself who had refused it. A few days later, a big bomb exploded in Sennett Estate, a middle-class suburban area, wrecking a car and killing two men. These were the first casualties of Confrontation in Singapore; we prepared for more trouble. On 18 December, the Tunku disclosed an Indonesian plot to blow up the Pasir

Panjang Power Station, the water mains between the island and Johor, and other vital installations. At the same time, I revealed that an Indonesian naval attaché had been training saboteurs from Singapore, and that the Indonesians had set up dummy firms for the import of weapons.

34. Winning Friends in Africa

Syed Ja'afar Albar opposed my leading a mission to Africa. "Instead of making Malaysia known to the Africans, he would make himself known to the African countries," he said in parliament on 3 January 1964. He wanted a Federation cabinet minister to head it. The Tunku replied that I had asked his permission to explain Malaysia to friends in that part of the world, and he thought it was better for the people from the new territories of the Federation to go on their own to inform the African states that they had joined it of their own free will. If the government was dissatisfied with the results of the mission, it could send another delegation, in which case he would include Albar in it. At the same time the Tunku also took a swipe at me for having answered a letter from Zhou Enlai, even though I had written my reply before merger. This, he said, was very wrong of me. It was very much the Tunku and his oblique style. I had to understand that in Malaysia such conduct was not acceptable. The Federation would have no truck with any communist country, least of all China.

The mission left Singapore in late January 1964 in a chartered four-engine turboprop aircraft, which gave us flexibility of movement. The mission included Sarawak's chief minister, Stephen Kalong Ningkan (who joined us in Lagos in February), and his deputy, James Wong, Sabah's chief minister then, Harris Salleh, and one of his MPs, and from Singapore, Devan Nair and my parliamentary secretary, Rahim Ishak. I wanted every major racial group to be represented – Malays, Chinese, Indians, Dayaks and Kadazans. We had two senior officials from the ministry of external affairs as secretaries, and a team of Malaysian reporters. We planned to visit 17 to 18 countries in some 35 days, and stayed in Cairo and

Alexandria while the arrangements were being made. This was not simple. Malaysia was not represented anywhere in Black Africa, so communications were slow and roundabout, through their London missions for Commonwealth countries, or their Cairo embassies, or UN delegations, and sometimes with help from the British foreign office. That had the disadvantage of making Malaysia appear a protégé of the British, but sometimes there was no choice. Only one country, Libya, refused to receive us.

Our first stop was Cairo. President Nasser had not changed his mind about Malaysia since I saw him in April 1962. Antara, the Indonesian news agency, had reported that the Malaysian ambassador to Cairo had been cold-shouldered by Nasser, who had refused to receive his credentials. The Egyptian foreign minister, Mahmood Fawzi, said there was no truth to this claim. Antara had also said that Egypt sympathised with Indonesia. (The Indonesians had craftily asked the Egyptian embassy in Kuala Lumpur to look after their interests when they withdrew their ambassador.) Fawzi said this was "without foundation". These were blows for the Indonesians. Fawzi, over 70, was a cultivated man of considerable sophistication. He explained why Sukarno was against Malaysia and what he hoped to gain, that he needed an issue to keep his people preoccupied with external ambitions, and if he could break up Malaysia, it would only be a matter of time before Sabah and Sarawak would be absorbed into Indonesian Borneo.

Nasser was warm and friendly during a two-hour discussion, followed by dinner. In a joint communiqué, he stated that he had accepted an invitation to visit Malaysia. In other words, Egypt recognised Malaysia and did not consider it neo-colonialist.

In Tunisia, my next stop, President Habib Bourguiba, a very Frenchified Arab, unexpectedly took a strong anti-colonial line. The problem was that the Tunku, because of his mild personality and his moderate statements, was seen to resemble the typical African tribal chief who had been nurtured by the colonial power and then given independence, and through whom the former rulers still retained their political influence and economic interests. Bourguiba, however, accepted that Malaysia, a country of 10 million with 10,000 troops, had the right to call for help when a nation of 100 million with 400,000 troops attacked it. I repeated this argument with good effect each time I met a leader who had reservations about Malaysia's defence ties with Britain.

From Tunis we flew to Rabat, capital of Morocco. The king did not receive us, and his prime minister did not show much interest, making our talks inconsequential. He was not against Malaysia, and anyway the Moroccans were pro-Western, so there was no danger of their supporting Sukarno's Indonesia.

Then to Algiers, which I had visited in July 1962 on my way home from the London Conference soon after the Algerians had won their independence from the French. Although I had flown in from Paris late that evening, Prime Minister Ben Bella had still given me dinner at 11 pm. This time he had probably been advised by his foreign ministry that the Tunku was not a revolutionary anti-colonialist, but he knew me as a nationalist and was friendly. With the help of Harris Salleh from Sabah and James Wong from Sarawak, I was able to persuade him that we had the right not to be swallowed up by Indonesia but to throw in our lot with the Malayans, with whom we shared a common British colonial past. James Wong and I were then called to an unscheduled second meeting with him. Ben Bella voiced the hope that peace would be reestablished, and said Algeria was willing to support any effort that would bring together Malaysia and Indonesia to resolve their differences amicably. This meeting produced a communiqué drafted by the Algerians that reflected none of the reservations they had earlier expressed in the United Nations Credentials Committee, and recorded that the visit of the Malaysian delegation augured well for the reinforcement of mutual understanding and friendship between the two countries.

My next stop was Bamako in Mali, an arid country, much of it desert. I was surprised to discover that Timbuktu was not a fictitious place. At the airport I was welcomed in the French style, first with a guard of honour, and then by a slim, dark-complexioned, half-Arab half-African girl in a Western dress who bussed me on both cheeks and presented me with a bouquet of flowers. President Modibo Keita received us in flowing Arab robes in his newly built palace, its high-ceilinged rooms opulently furnished and air-conditioned. An official communiqué issued from the presidential palace said that he reaffirmed Mali's attachment to the principles of non-alignment, which were entirely opposed to the presence of foreign military bases, but added that those principles also demanded respect for the sovereignty of states. The communiqué then referred to an invitation to the Mali head of state to make an official visit to Malaysia and stated that he had given it a favourable reply. Like Ben Bella of Algeria, President Keita had signalled that his country was withdrawing its reservations about Malaysia.

As I flew south, I could see how the Arabs and the Africans had met and intermingled in the northern part of the Sahara, where many of the latter had converted to Islam. Black Africa was ethnically a completely different world with a totally different set of cultures.

Liberia was a scream. We arrived at the capital just before dusk. After the dry desert air of Bamako, Monrovia was warm and humid, not unlike Singapore. But Liberia was a parody of a state. An American-style guard of honour was drawn up at the airport, looking most unmilitary and anything but smart. A tall African greeted me in American-accented English and said he was the secretary of state. Most of their institutions were named or modelled after the Americans, but there the similarity ended. As I inspected the guard of honour, I heard the feeblest 18-gun salute ever, sounding like damp squibs.

While we waited in the VIP room for our bags to be unloaded, the secretary of state told us that we were going straight to President William

Tubman's farm, where he was waiting to give us dinner. It was at least two hours away by car. I was appalled. We had been flying for three hours and needed to wash and freshen up. But there was no getting out of it. Off we went. We had seven military motorcycle outriders on huge Harley-Davidson twin-exhaust machines, and the walkie-talkies of the principal rider and the military aide-de-camp in the front seat of our Cadillac crackled ceaselessly. When one of the motorcycles skidded into a ditch, the secretary of state was not at all perturbed. In the course of the three-hour journey, two more bikes went off the road. Whether the riders were badly or slightly injured, nobody cared. I decided not to enquire; from the reactions of the secretary of state and the military ADC, these seemed commonplace happenings.

We arrived and were shown in to be photographed. I had to insist before I was given a few minutes in which to wash. Tubman then held forth at great length. Finally, dinner was served. He rapped the table with his gavel and said, "Mr Vice, grace." The vice-president sitting at the other end of the table then thanked the Lord for the bounty that was to appear. It was not until midnight that we left to make the long journey to our guesthouse in Monrovia.

Worn out, I unpacked my pyjamas, went to the bathroom, and found the washbasin full of water with rusty sediment at the bottom. I cursed and pulled out the plug, but despite my fatigue knew instinctively I had done something stupid and quickly replaced it. Sure enough, there was no water from the tap. With what remained of the rusty water, I did my best to wash off the grease and dust of travel. I looked for a bottle of soda water to brush my teeth. Finding none, I settled for Fanta. It was sweet, but better than nothing; I hoped my toothpaste would counteract the sugar. After all the excitement, I was not sleepy. I picked up some reading material from the bedside table. It was a paean of praise for the president, the star of Africa, the saviour of his country. I folded the pamphlet to take home as a souvenir of how not to impress guests.

There was no need for a joint statement in Liberia, as Tubman was known to be pro-American; he supported Malaysia and accepted the Tunku's invitation to visit the Federation. The next day, I wandered through Monrovia to gaze at the huge presidential palace and the terrible slums around it. I was glad to get out.

After Monrovia, it was Conakry in Guinea, the most anti-French of all the Francophone African states. French President De Gaulle was displeased when Guinea voted to leave the French community. They told us the French had pulled out all the telephones and other fittings before they handed over the country. But even if everything had been left in working condition, the statist policies that President Sekou Toure pursued – socialism based on the Soviet model – were certain to condemn it to poverty. In 1964, the effects were not yet devastating. The delegation was put up in VIP chalets by the coast that looked like large African thatched huts for tribal chiefs, but were built of brick and mortar.

Sekou Toure had been a trade unionist. He was highly intelligent. We spent much time talking about socialism through an interpreter, and he gave me several volumes of his book, *Socialism for Guinea*. He was publicly known to be against imperialist intervention in France's former colonies to support black leaders who favoured French policies, but although he knew little about Malaysia, I was able to make him understand that British troops were necessary for the survival of a small country threatened by a huge neighbour. Whatever his initial views, I left him more receptive and open-minded. He could see that James Wong, Harris Salleh and I were not colonial stooges. He received us with courtesy, gave us an official lunch, and did not denounce Malaysia.

Then we headed for Abidjan in the Ivory Coast (Cote d'Ivoire). The contrast with Conakry was striking. President Houphouet-Boigny, a black Frenchman, had been a minister in the Fourth Republic. Polished in manners, elegant in dress, he received me in a splendid palace attractively sculptured on the slope of a hill, and we dined on exquisite French cuisine with champignons flown in from Paris that day and excellent wines. That he was African was not to be doubted, for he had two wives, both present at dinner, both young and attractive, and sisters!

There was no need to convince him of our case. He said that those African leaders who went the other way and became anti-colonial and pro-communist or socialist would suffer. I was impressed by his realism. He had a French *chef de cabinet* (chief of staff). So did those of his ministers I met. The Frenchmen took notes and looked efficient. The president accepted the Tunku's invitation to visit Kuala Lumpur without hesitation. The Ivory Coast was at that time a member of the UN Security Council, representing the African bloc, and therefore useful to have on Malaysia's side.

Next, Accra in Ghana. Among the ambassadors who greeted me at the airport were those from the Ivory Coast, Egypt and Algeria, which confirmed that the Algerians were with us now. Ghana, better known in my stamp-collecting days as the Gold Coast, was the first of the African states to gain independence (in 1957). Its leader, Kwame Nkrumah, was a great Pan-African, and had set an example to others by taking an Egyptian wife. The local press referred to him as Osagyefo, the man of the times or the torchbearer, and he had his anti-colonial credentials to keep up. On the day of my arrival, Accra's *Evening News* said, "The present Malaysian Federation bears the earmarks of neo-colonialism." The paper compared it to the dissolved Central African Federation and the incorporation of Aden into the South Arabian Federation.

I met Nkrumah on Sunday at the 18th century Christianborg Castle, an old Danish slave-trading post, which was then the seat of government. As I approached his inner sanctum, I walked between Indian-style oil lamps, wicks floating in small brass bowls lining both sides of a red carpet. I found him in a strange state of mind. He had just survived a failed coup and was withdrawn and somewhat dazed. But he was cordial and friendly towards me, and we had an hour's discussion. He told me

– and I had it reported to our press – "If you had not come, you would have lost by default, your fault." The next day, the local newspapers moderated their tone towards Malaysia. Now they said only that it was possible that, perhaps unconsciously, it could be used for neo-colonialist purposes. I spent the day driving 70 miles to the High Volta dam, then being built by an Italian consortium and financed jointly by the World Bank and the US and British governments. But after seeing Conakry and Accra and meeting leaders who talked in socialist terms of the distribution of wealth, I believed they would become paupers.

At Lagos in Nigeria, the Tunku's good friend, Prime Minister Alhaji Sir Abubakar Tafawa Balewa, met me at the airport with a full guard of honour. The ceremony was totally British. His support for Malaysia was forthright and so was the friendliness of the Nigerian people. All along the 15-mile route to the city, they gathered to wave and shout greetings of welcome. Lagos was in much better shape than Accra. Many of the public buildings looked identical with those in Malaya and Singapore. They must have followed the same British Public Works Department design. On leaving, I was able to talk of the unqualified moral support that the prime minister was giving to Malaysia. Nigeria had sent a special representative to the independence ceremonies in Kuala Lumpur.

Lusaka was in Northern Rhodesia, soon to become independent and change its name to Zambia. It had held its first general election in January, just a few weeks before we arrived. Kenneth Kaunda, the prime minister, was away and I was received by his deputy leader, Kamanga. We were put up at the Livingstone Hotel, an attractive, single-storey, rambling building, like a large inn in an English provincial town. The ministers were friendly. They knew very little about Southeast Asia but were very pleased we had visited them to seek their support, and the government accepted the Tunku's invitation for Kaunda to visit Malaysia.

Then on to Blantyre, Malawi. The president was Dr Hastings Banda, whom everyone called Ngwazi, meaning a man to be looked up to like a lion for his power and strength. He had qualified as a medical doctor in Scotland and practised happily there for many years. He did not need any convincing; he was dead set against anti-white xenophobia.

And from Malawi, on to Madagascar, then called Malagasy, and to its capital Tananarive, where President Tsiranana received us with great warmth and hospitality. He was an interesting man, blunt and straightforward. He talked openly of his country's close ties with France. After hearing me, he said, "If one must be colonised, it is at least preferable that the colonising be done by a higher rather than a lower civilisation."

Madagascar was a strange country, an island off the African coast whose people were part-African and part-Malay or Polynesian. Their dances combined the African stomping of feet with Malay and Polynesian hand movements, and there were Malay words in their language. After our discussions in his office, Tsiranana produced a leather pouch from his drawer and spread out a sparkling array of semi-precious stones, all mined in Madagascar. He invited each of us to choose one. I picked an aquamarine for Choo. The other members of the mission each had a different preference. He found great pleasure in seeing the delight on our faces as we made our choice of gems.

Dar-es-Salaam in Tanganyika, later to become Tanzania, was different. Julius Nyerere was a Christian, a humanist and a socialist, and he expressed his support for Malaysia in unequivocal terms. From our first meeting, I liked him for his simplicity of dress, manner and way of life. He put me up at the presidential mansion, formerly used by the British governor and before World War I by the German administrator. He himself preferred to live in a small house nearby. He had his Indian ministers to dinner, making the point that, unlike the other East African countries, he had a place for them in Tanganyika. But alas, his Fabianism and statism, picked up not so much from Marxist tracts as from discussions with other anti-colonial leaders and well-meaning British socialists he had met in Britain, caused his country unnecessary poverty.

When I arrived at Kampala in Uganda, Prime Minister Milton Obote was away and I was received by his ministers. They were friendly and understanding; the Commonwealth ties counted. There was some tension between the government and the Kabaka of Buganda, or "King Freddie" as he was popularly called, but although Obote had met the Tunku at Commonwealth conferences and mistakenly seen him as another "King Freddie", that did not affect Uganda's support for Malaysia. They sympathised with Malaysia and did not support Indonesia.

The next stop, Nairobi, was important. President Jomo Kenyatta was known as Mzee, a term of great respect and reverence for an old man. He had a worldwide reputation as a fighter for freedom who had been detained in shackles during the Mao Mao rebellion in the 1950s against the British government and the white settlers. The governor-general, Malcolm MacDonald, whom I had known when he was the British commissioner-general to Southeast Asia, had briefed the Kenyan government about Malaysia, and all I needed to do was to meet Kenyatta and get his endorsement. Unfortunately, he was away in Mombasa, opening an oil refinery, but Malcolm MacDonald was resourceful and got the government to fly me there.

Kenyatta met me at the airport and we drove together in a convertible to my hotel through throngs of people, all shouting *"Urumbi, Urumbi"*. Kenyatta prompted me to join the chant and point my forefinger to the sky as they did; the gesture, he explained, meant "let us pull as one people". In a joint communiqué, he emphasised Kenya's friendship with Malaysia, welcomed the mission's visit as a step towards strengthening understanding, and thanked me for coming to Mombasa to see him.

My last stop was Addis Ababa in Ethiopia. After my arrival, I went for a drive in the afternoon, had dinner at the guesthouse, and slept. At 3 am, I woke up feeling an enormous weight on my chest. I feared I was about to have a heart attack. I slept fitfully. At breakfast, I asked some other members of the mission whether any of them had experienced this

President Jomo Kenyatta receiving me at Mombasa Airport, January 1964.

February 1964: Visiting Julius Nyerere (centre) in Dar-es-Salaam, Tanzania. Stephen Kalong Ningkan, chief minister of Sarawak, is at right.

strange sensation. None had. I wished we had brought a doctor with us. When the main party arrived in a coach from a hotel in town, I was greatly relieved to find that several of them had had the same experience. It was mountain sickness. Addis Ababa was 8,500 feet above sea level.

To be received in audience by Emperor Haile Selassie, I had to walk past two cheetahs lightly chained to posts on either side of him. It was a scene from King Solomon in biblical times, except that Haile Selassie wore a British-style military uniform. He listened and was unequivocal in his support for Malaysia. But his was not one of the revolutionary regimes of Africa. I was shocked by the deference and cowed demeanour of the people on the streets as my car drove by with flags fluttering. They took off their hats and bowed deeply. The flags represented authority, whether they flew for the emperor, his guests or his officials, and they knew their humble place at the bottom of the ladder. In contrast to the sometimes handsome buildings around them, they looked shabby and poor. I attributed all this to an antiquated feudal system that kept the peasants down and confined wealth to the nobility. I did not feel sanguine about the future of the country.

From Addis Ababa we flew to Aden for a refuelling stop on our way to New Delhi. Aden was in the throes of a civil war, as the British prepared to withdraw. There was heavy security around the airport, with barbed wire and soldiers at strategic points, and talking to RAF officers in the hour we spent there, I could feel the sense of emergency.

In Delhi I was startled to see how much Nehru had aged since I first met him in April 1962. He looked weary and had trouble concentrating. The border war of December 1962 between Indian and Chinese forces across the Himalayas near Ladakh had been a disaster. It had destroyed all that he had hoped and worked for. He had introduced Zhou Enlai to the Afro-Asian leaders at Bandung in 1955 to herald a new age of Afro-Asian solidarity. His dream had turned to ashes. I felt for him. He had lost his vitality and his optimism. His ministers and officials received us with warmth and hospitality and their missions in Africa had been helpful.

My next stop was Kuala Lumpur, not Singapore, for I had to report to the Tunku. He was pleased that I had countered Sukarno's propaganda on the Afro-Asian front, and my press conference was covered on Kuala Lumpur television at great length. I said that the Indonesians had been at the diplomatic game for a long time and were many years ahead of us Malaysians. They had developed propaganda skills; they knew the sensitivities and susceptibilities of the African leaders to whom foreign bases were anathema. There was the problem of the international image of Sukarno who, judged by his rhetoric, seemed a fire-breathing anti-colonial revolutionary while the Tunku, by contrast, was the mild, moderate man of the West. The Indonesians had misrepresented his gentle manners as those of a British stooge.

In the euphoria of the moment, the Tunku forgave me for my insubordinate statements during the election, and suggested that I should go on to New York and Washington to convince the Americans as I had convinced the Africans. I could leave immediately after I had rested. The next day, 27 February, I flew into Singapore to the rousing welcome of thousands at the airport. James Wong, who had left for Sarawak after Dar-es-Salaam, described our mission as a tremendous success on his stopover in Singapore: "We have secured the understanding, sympathy and moral support of all the African heads of state and ministers whom we have met." As I drove home with Choo and the three children in the car, the crowds waved to me along the route. It had been an exhausting trip, but an invaluable part of my political education. I had learnt at first hand about the Arabs and the Africans, and understood what obstacles the new African countries must overcome to educate their tribal peoples and develop their often one-commodity economies.

Throughout my 35-day tour of the 17 African capitals, I was helped by the professionalism of the British embassies. Their diplomats were well-informed, well adapted to their host governments, prominent or unobtrusive as the situation required. At each stop, I was given a short brief of the situation in the country, thumbnail sketches of the ministers I was likely to meet, and a description of the power structure. The briefs were invariably good. The quality of British diplomats was high. Whether they brought Britain economic benefits was another matter.

One of my most memorable recollections was of Government House in Lusaka, where I stayed as the guest of the last British governor of Northern Rhodesia, Sir Evelyn Hone. It was well-furnished and well-maintained, but not luxurious. The toiletries, soap, towels, cutlery and china were similar to those I had found in British government houses in Singapore, Sarawak and North Borneo. They were all part of one well-run system. I wondered what sort of life the governor would lead in Britain, once out of office and without a large retinue of uniformed servants. He carried out his duties as host with grace and style. From his drawing room window, I was delighted to see deer, antelope, red bucks, peacocks, cranes and other African animals and birds in the garden. Government House was like an English country mansion sited in the highlands of Africa, with as much of old England as possible brought in to relieve the homesickness of governors.

I was to go back to Lusaka in 1970 for the Non-Aligned Conference, and again in 1979 for the Commonwealth Conference. Each time was a saddening experience. I remembered the flowers, shrubs, trees and greenery at the side of the roads and at the roundabouts when I was driven in from the airport in 1964. Roses grew in abundance. Six years later, the roses had gone and weeds had taken over. Nine years after that, even the weeds had given up; the roundabouts were covered with tarmac. And there seemed to be fewer animals and birds in the grounds of Government House, now the President's Lodge. I wondered why.

I had received an unforgettable lesson in decolonisation, on how crucial it was to have social cohesion and capable, effective government to take power from the colonial authority, especially in Africa. When the leader did not preserve the unity of the country by sharing power with the chiefs of the minority tribes, but excluded them, the system soon broke down. Worse, when misguided policies based on half-digested theories of socialism and redistribution of wealth were compounded by less than competent government, societies formerly held together by colonial power splintered, with appalling consequences.

35. Venturing into the Malay Heartland

On the day of my departure for Africa, I had called an urgent meeting of the PAP's Publicity and Propaganda Coordinating Committee, of which I was chairman, to discuss how we could safeguard Singapore's interests in Kuala Lumpur. Our economic development could not be held hostage to the political prejudices of Tan Siew Sin, the Malaysian finance minister. I wanted the committee to consider "... the desirability of the PAP intervening in the forthcoming election in Malaysia" by fielding some token candidates. They were to make a decision only after my return.

However, when I was away in Africa, Raja, Chin Chye and Pang Boon – three Singapore ministers brought up in Malaya – persuaded the PAP central executive committee to contest the Malaysian general election. The day after my return, the newspapers reported that the election would be held in April. Chin Chye immediately announced that the PAP would field a small number of candidates. He added that it had no intention of fighting the central government or UMNO, and the PAP's purpose was to cooperate with them to make Malaysia succeed.

Keng Swee was absolutely against any token participation; he believed it would sour relations between Kuala Lumpur and Singapore and jeopardise his plans for our industrialisation within the Federation. I also had my reservations, but since the Tunku had breached his verbal undertaking to me not to participate in Singapore's elections, I felt no longer bound by my return undertaking and went with the decision of the central executive committee.

The response from UMNO was sharp and immediate. Khir Johari, minister for agriculture and a favourite of the Tunku who had been asked to rebuild Singapore UMNO, declared it was prepared to fight the PAP because its ideology was different: the PAP said it was non-communist whereas UMNO was definitely anti-communist. Tan Siew Sin's reaction was angry. For him, this was nothing less than a challenge to the MCA over who should represent the Chinese in the Federation. Chin Chye had said his main reason for contesting was to fight anti-Malaysia parties, but the Alliance (of which the MCA was a member) had the same aim, therefore the PAP's participation could only help to split the pro-Malaysia vote.

I stayed silent. I was prepared to go to New York and come back only in time for the election, but the Tunku would have none of it. After a few days, he said it would be "politically inconsistent" for the PAP to represent Malaysia in the United States when it was competing against the Alliance at the polls. He rejected as sophistry our stand that a few token candidates would be pitted, not against UMNO, but against the MCA. The PAP was trying to supplant the MCA and align itself with UMNO, he said, "but we don't want them". I knew that, but I believed he could be made to change his mind when he saw that it was the PAP, not the MCA, that had the support of the urban voters. I said that the present Malay leadership of the Tunku and UMNO was vital to Malaysia, but the MCA was replaceable. Popular antipathy towards it in the towns had reached such proportions that the (Malayan) Socialist Front, despite its obvious communist links, might make gains in some constituencies where there was no other way to register a protest vote against it.

The PAP election manifesto had two objectives: first, to assist in building up a united democratic and socialist Malaysia based on the principles of social justice and non-communism, and second, to ensure that the Socialist Front did not benefit from substantial protest votes against the MCA. We fielded only 11 parliamentary candidates. The politically better-qualified were Malaya-born federal citizens who had been working in Singapore and had long been associated with the PAP. The best known was Devan Nair, whom I accompanied to his Bungsar ward in the suburbs of Kuala Lumpur on nomination day. The PAP withdrew two candidates in Johor when we found they were facing UMNO and not MCA candidates, but this did not mollify the Malay leaders – we were still challenging their trusted Chinese partners, and they did not want us. I thought I understood them. In fact, I did not. I did not understand that their objection was basic; they did not want the Chinese to be represented by a vigorous leadership that propounded a non-communal or a multiracial approach to politics and would not confine its appeal only to the Chinese.

At the start of the campaign, on the night of 22 March, a huge crowd turned up to listen to us at Suleiman Court in Kuala Lumpur, overflowing the square and the road beyond. The excitement the PAP had generated was enormous. I emphasised in my speech that if elected, our nine PAP candidates would trigger a social revolution far beyond their arithmetical significance. "If you demonstrate positively that you are in favour of an honest party with a dynamic social and economic policy, then the winds of change will begin to sweep throughout Malaysia," I said, borrowing Harold Macmillan's famous phrase. I added that if UMNO leaders wanted the support of the urban voters, they would have to adjust their policies to take into account the wishes of the people. Razak retorted that "terrific" winds of change had already swept through Malaya and people could see the social evolution for themselves.

In a month of campaigning, I motored up and down Malaya to the towns where we had candidates – Penang, Kuala Lumpur, Seremban, Malacca and Kluang – and everywhere we held rallies, huge crowds turned up. They wanted to see and hear us. They gave me a big cheer each time. They had heard, read, and in some cases, seen what we had done in Singapore and appeared keen to have us do the same for them in Malaya.

As if to underline the difference between the two, I spoke in Malacca about Keng Swee and Tan Siew Sin, both Malacca-born: "They shared the same grandfather, but there the similarity ends." As finance minister of Singapore, Keng Swee had pursued policies that had led to financial surpluses, reflecting his harsher and more spartan background. He was a teacher of economics and a social worker. On the other hand, Tan had inherited the family's fortune and was a multimillionaire. A director of many companies, he ran the ministry of finance as if it were one of them – prudently and economically in order to provide the best dividends for the directors. He was a man born with a silver spoon in his mouth who had moved easily into high political positions in the wake of his father's reputation. He represented the rural Malay constituency of Malacca Tengah, and so found it unnecessary to learn to speak or write Chinese. Yet, he claimed to lead the Chinese of Malaysia.

Tan Siew Sin was angered, but the Tunku came to his rescue. Sink or swim, UMNO would stand by the MCA; even if there were only five of them left, he would never throw his partners overboard – unlike the PAP, which came into power with the help of the communists and had now got rid of them, the Tunku said. With the Tunku behind him, Tan retaliated in strong terms. The PAP was capable of stabbing one in the back; principle and honour counted for little with its leaders, and Lee himself was like a chameleon, he charged, whose idea of democracy itself was in doubt, judging by the lack of democracy in the PAP. He called on me to give details to support the allegations I had made that the MCA was corrupt, which were close to libel. I replied that I was prepared to do so if he would agree to a commission of inquiry to follow them up. He did not respond.

While the Tunku, Razak and his ministers took the high road, Syed Ja'afar Albar took the low road. On 25 May, he pointedly asked if I advocated the eventual disappearance of the sultans and the nationalisation of rubber estates and tin mines when I talked of social revolution. Just as British military power had maintained me in office, so the Alliance government had saved me from being eliminated by the Barisan, but I

Capacity crowds at the PAP's first election rally, March 1964, at Suleiman Court, Kuala Lumpur did not translate into votes.

still treated the Singapore Malays as stepsons and antagonised them, he said. "Lee Kuan Yew is so contemptuous of the Malays that his government refused to appoint any Malay to serve on statutory bodies in Singapore," he added. He then denounced me for having said, during a speech made in Chinese in Seremban, that the Tunku was not a politician of high calibre, hinting that his leadership was inept. This was utterly false, but the Tunku was sore, and riposted that while he favoured social revolution, my version was an alien concept unsuited to the genius of the people and therefore unwelcome to them.

I replied in Kluang that half of the Tunku's problems were created by old friends who had skilfully and cynically exploited his personal loyalty to them. I had not smeared him when I spoke in Chinese in Seremban; they should credit the PAP with enough intelligence to know that taking two different lines in two different languages would be the surest way to discredit it. But Albar still accused me of being double-faced, adding, "No one should trust Lee Kuan Yew for he is a man who does not keep his word. There is no place for men like Lee Kuan Yew in Malaya." He had received hundreds of letters from Malays in Singapore, including government servants, complaining about their plight under the PAP, he said. It was a sinister racist line that he was to plug with ever greater venom to make the Malays hate me.

Judging by the response at mass rallies, it appeared to be a month of highly successful campaigning for the PAP. Even our canvassers came back with optimistic forecasts, for they were well received. We became confident of winning six or seven of the nine seats, and fought the campaign vigorously, pulling our punches only against UMNO, despite their attacks, notably those of Albar. At our final rally in Selangor on the eve of polling, I described Malaysia as a ship heading towards troubled waters with the Tunku at its helm; what the MCA needed to survive were not new faces but fresh ideas.

The election results, announced in the early morning of 26 April, came as a shock. By 4 am, the Alliance had won 89 out of 104 seats, doing better than in the previous election. Every Alliance cabinet minister had been returned with a bigger majority. The PAP had won only one seat, that of Devan Nair in Bungsar, and then only by 808 votes.

Where had the PAP gone wrong?

First, we did not have an indigenous party with branches and local leaders in Malaya. We had moved in workers from Singapore, and although quite a few had been born and bred in Malaya, they did not have that rapport with the grass roots needed to win their confidence. Second, we had no experience of campaigning in the Federation. In Singapore, everything was voluntary, and often even our banners were donated by supporters. In Malaya, everything had to be paid for in cash, including the workers who put up the posters and banners. By the end of the campaign, the PAP was over $60,000 in debt, after having spent some $40,000 of its own funds. Third, our token participation did not give people a good reason to switch from the MCA to the PAP. They wanted to retain links with the UMNO-led government that was in charge of issuing the licences they needed. The way to make a dent and change their voting habits would have been to field a large enough contingent to be credible, to make it worth their while to back us in the expectation that we would be strong enough to cut a deal with UMNO. We did not understand the power equation that was uppermost in the minds of the urban voters of Malaya, 75 per cent of whom were Chinese or Indian and only 25 per cent Malay.

Did PAP participation in the election cause relations between Kuala Lumpur and Singapore to deteriorate? Yes, but it made no difference to the main cause of conflict and eventual separation – UMNO's determination to maintain total Malay supremacy.

After we lost, our relations with UMNO ministers did not deteriorate dramatically, but they could not have remained smooth for long because of this fundamental difference between us. They wanted us to confine ourselves to Chinese voters and stop appealing to the Malays. They would not tolerate any challenge to their hold on their Malay political base. The Malay electorate was out of bounds to non-Malay parties like the PAP. The MCA accepted that restriction. We did not.

In retrospect, I believe it would have been worse for Singapore had we postponed participation in Malaysian elections till the next election in 1969. The same problems would have arisen with UMNO, but with Confrontation ended, the restraining influence of the British would have diminished, because their troops would no longer have been needed, and Malay leaders would have been even less inhibited in dealing with the PAP.

UMNO was elated by its victory, the MCA was relieved, and trouble was in store for the PAP. To show the displeasure of the Alliance with our party, the Speaker – probably after consulting the Tunku, for he was an UMNO MP – moved the five PAP ministerial members representing Singapore in the federal parliament, who had previously been seated on the government side, over to the opposition benches to join the seven others already there. Among other things, it looked as if Keng Swee's fears that our industrialisation plans would be aborted by the Alliance were well founded.

On 17 April, speaking in Singapore to the four chambers of commerce at a dinner in my honour after my mission to Africa, I had already given one good reason why we had to contest the federal election: "As long as the MCA believe that they can make a comeback in Singapore using their ministerial position in the federal government, they will be tempted to obstruct or interfere in Singapore," and that would inevitably lead to a repetition of the sharp conflict that had bedevilled financial negotiations over merger.

Until mid-July, things were relatively quiet. Surprisingly, Tan Siew Sin showed magnanimity in victory by inviting me to a Chinese steamboat dinner at the Federal Government Lodge at Fraser's Hill. I accepted the invitation readily. He was affable, bubbling and confident. Our personal relations had not deteriorated to a point where we could not be civil and sociable, and I was determined to keep them on an even keel. His father had been particularly kind to me.

The tragedy of Tan was the tragedy of that whole generation of Straits-born Chinese. They did not understand that the rules were different in an independent Malaya – later Malaysia – from those they had been accustomed to under the British. The Malays were now the rulers. They felt insecure because they believed they could not compete on par with the Chinese and Indians. They were therefore determined to consolidate their hold on power regardless of whether it was fair or unfair to the other races, and the more the Chinese and Indians tried to win enough space for themselves, the more they saw it as a challenge to their position as rulers, and the more insecure they felt. Tan was totally insensitive to this, as were most Straits-born Chinese. In contrast, members of the Chinese-speaking merchant class were quick to realise the dangers in this new situation. They were already beginning to feel the heat, for more out of a sense of insecurity than any desire to kill Chinese culture, the Malay leaders were imposing on them an education policy designed to conscribe and to minimise the learning of the Chinese language and the transmission of Chinese culture through their Chinese schools.

The Indians in Malaysia, like Raja's brother in Seremban, were similarly apprehensive about the future because the English language was being replaced by Malay. They knew they were a minority with no chance of achieving power, and were happy to go along with any group that would leave them the space to live and advance, but they, too, were fearful of the changes that would deprive their children of a good education and fair prospects. They were losing their monopoly of jobs on Malayan Railways as more and more Malays were recruited. Worse still, as time went by, the big rubber estates owned by British companies were being sold to government institutions. Large numbers of Indian rubber tappers who had lived on those estates and had their own schools teaching in Tamil were ill-prepared for re-employment in other fields. They were to become a problem.

For the Malays, too, there were ominous social and political changes, which had intensified their feeling of insecurity. For the first time, the Tunku found he had to defend himself in parliament for giving expatriate officers a 10 per cent pay rise. Not only did the PAP and the Socialist Front MPs attack him, but the Congress of Unions of Employees in the Public and Civil Services and senior government officers in Malaya had also taken a leaf out of the Singapore experience and mounted a protest. A week later, the government backed down. A statement issued after a cabinet meeting said that it had not been made aware of the possibly serious repercussions in the civil service and expressed its regrets for any inconvenience caused. Malaya's cosy politics had taken on a sharper edge, with the PAP bringing Singapore's norms into Malaysia's public debate.

The Tunku's increased electoral support drew a sharp reaction from Sukarno. After a six-hour meeting with the president, Subandrio issued directions to step up the "Crush Malaysia" campaign in all fields. In June, the Tunku met Sukarno and Macapagal in Tokyo. The meeting collapsed, with Sukarno repeating, "I say a thousand times that I cannot accept Malaysia. I say a thousand times this (Malaysia) is a British act. It must be crushed." This threat was countered by the Australian prime minister, Sir Robert Menzies, reaffirming his country's support for Malaysia, and on 26 June, President Johnson said the United States would stand by ANZUS, the defence agreement that linked Australia and New Zealand to the US. America would be involved in the Malaysia dispute if its two allies ran into difficulties. Confrontation could be contained.

But we had more reason to worry about Albar. What he was planning we did not know, and would only learn on Prophet Mohammed's Birthday.

36. Albar Stokes Up Malay Passions

Syed Ja'afar Albar was the hatchet man of the UMNO leaders hostile to Singapore. Originally from Indonesia but of Arab descent, he was small, balding, a bundle of energy with a round face, a moustache and a good, strong voice. In the early 1950s, he had seemed friendly. In February 1955, when I was seeing the Tunku off on the ship that would take him to England for the Constitutional Conference, Albar urged me to get closer to the Tunku so that we could be photographed together for the press, saying in Malay, "take a ride on the old boy's fame". But he was a great rabble-rouser, skilful in working up the mob and, as I was to learn, totally ruthless and unscrupulous in his methods. His English was not adequate for public speaking, but his Malay was superb, his delivery powerful. He did not need to be reported in the English-language press, which would have shown him up as a racist to English speakers not only in Malaysia but internationally. He concentrated on the Malay newspapers, and his most strident lines were confined to them, especially to the *Utusan Melayu*, which was printed in Jawi (the Arabic script) and not read by the Chinese, Indians, British or other Europeans. The *Utusan* had been bought by UMNO, and was Albar's weapon of choice for multiplying the effect of his speeches.

Albar and the Malay press kept repeating the falsehood that I had belittled the Tunku as a leader of little calibre. They now mounted a campaign to work up a sense of grievance among Malays over specific issues, real or imaginary, playing on the fact that theirs was the least successful and the poorest of the different communities in Singapore. The truth was that the Malays were never discriminated against by the PAP government. On the contrary, they were given free education, something not accorded to children of other races, and although there was no Malay quota for taxi or hawker licences as in Malaya, we made sure that there were always Malay shops and stalls to cater for Malay customers in our Housing and Development Board neighbourhoods. Nevertheless, on 13 May 1964, the *Utusan* reported that there was anxiety and unrest among Malays over the allocation of stalls in the new Geylang Serai market, and in June claimed that the PAP's policy on schools had led to Malay education becoming retrogressive.

Albar's offensive had started on 21 September 1963, immediately after Singapore's general election, when Singapore UMNO accused members of the PAP of intimidating the Malays in Geylang Serai on the eastern side of the island, by throwing firecrackers at their homes after the PAP had won in the three Malay constituencies. I did not realise then that this was part of a campaign. If our supporters did throw firecrackers I should apologise, and I did so on television. On investigation, the charges proved completely unfounded. But regardless of the truth, UMNO leaders were able to work up enough feelings to have me burnt in effigy a week later.

More distortions were to follow. For instance, after Chin Chye announced on 1 March 1964 that the PAP was going to take part in the federal election, the *Utusan* ran this headline: "1,500 Malays threatened with quit notices". The reality was that the land they were asked to quit was private property. The owner was within his rights to issue the notices, and he would have to negotiate with the tenants and pay them compensation. It had nothing to do with the Singapore government. The *Utusan* conveniently ignored this, and on 28 May, reported that 3,000 Malays were threatened with eviction from their homes in Crawford, Rochor and Kampong Glam. I toured these constituencies to tell the people that the quit notices were sent to Malays, Chinese and Indians impartially in order to implement a plan submitted by a United Nations expert to rebuild the city, starting from the outer parts and working towards the centre. We had to demolish old buildings and rehouse the people affected by this urban renewal scheme. We would provide them with temporary accommodation nearby, and each family would be given $300 to cover the cost of moving and priority to return once the new buildings were completed.

We were also under attack on more general grounds. On 23 May, an editorial in the *Utusan* accused the PAP and me of inciting non-Malays to demand the abolition of the special rights of the Malays. On 11 June, the paper proclaimed, "Singapore UMNO directed to take steps to save PAP victims". The next day, another headline: "Malays in Singapore today facing threat, pressure and oppression by the government. Do not treat the sons of the soil as stepchildren". A week later, the *Utusan* urged all Malays to "stand solidly behind UMNO in making strong and effective protests against the PAP government", and to call on Kuala Lumpur to take immediate action to protect their special rights. UMNO then published a "white paper" setting out "in detail the sufferings of the Malays under the PAP led by Lee Kuan Yew". Once more, they accused us of treating them as stepchildren, saying that the Malay traitors to their own race who had voted for us were realising their mistake, because now the government intended to turn Geylang Serai into another Chinatown.

That all these were flagrant falsehoods was irrelevant as long as they succeeded in inflaming the Malay ground. A good example of this principle was provided on 4 July, when the *Utusan* twisted a speech I had made in Seremban, in which I had said "40 per cent of Malays in Malaysia cannot drive away the 60 per cent non-Malays". The *Utusan* reported this as: "Those able to drive others away from Malaysia are the Chinese and other non-Malays and those who are driven away are the Malays because their numbers are very small." They repeated this over the next few days, claiming again that the PAP was out to destroy the "special rights" of the Malays, when we had pointed out that the Singapore constitution recognised only their "special position".

Earlier, I had decided to counter this campaign by inviting all the Malay leaders in Singapore to meet me on 17 July for a face-to-face discussion to expose the lies and innuendoes. On 30 June, UMNO pre-empted me; the *Utusan* announced that UMNO would organise a convention of Malay parties on 12 July to "discuss the fate and plight of Malays in Singapore under PAP rule". This meeting was attended by all Malay political parties, although three of them were anti-Malaysia and pro-Indonesia. No matter; this issue demanded the unity of the Malay race, and Albar set out to work up their emotions, saying that the fate of the Malays was even worse than it had been during the Japanese occupation. This excerpt from one of his speeches was typical:

> "I am very happy today we Malays and Muslims in Singapore have shown unity and are prepared to live or die together for our race and our future generation. If there is unity no force in this world can trample us down, no force can humiliate us, no force can belittle us. Not one Lee Kuan Yew, a thousand Lee Kuan Yews ... we finish them off ..." (Handclapping. Shouts. "Kill him ... Kill him ... Othman Wok and Lee Kuan Yew ... Lee Kuan Yew ... Lee Kuan Yew ... Othman Wok.") "However much we are oppressed, however much we are suppressed, however much our position has been twisted and turned by the PAP government, according to Lee Kuan Yew's logic: Hey, shut up, you, you minority race in this island. Here I say to Lee Kuan Yew: You shut up and don't tell us to shut up."

The entire proceedings were shown over Television Malaysia in Kuala Lumpur the same evening. Among the resolutions passed was a call to boycott the government's convention on 17 July at which I was to address the Malay grassroots leaders. The intense racial agitation in the Malay newspapers fanned Malay emotions throughout the Federation. On 14 July, federal police headquarters announced that incidents had occurred as far away as Bukit Mertajam in Province Wellesley, 500 miles to the north of Singapore, where two persons had been killed and 13

UMNO secretary-general Syed Ja'afar Albar, July 1965.

wounded. Malay-Chinese clashes had already taken place on several occasions in this former crown colony of Penang after it was absorbed into the Malayan Federation in 1948 and Malay special rights became applicable there, where it had not applied before.

Despite the call for a boycott, some 900 delegates from 83 Malay organisations and 300 *ketua* (village headmen) attended the government's convention. I spoke in Malay and we discussed problems of Malay education, employment and housing. Not one person raised the question of the resettlement in Crawford, which had been used to trigger the fiery agitation. In five hours of frank discussion, I made it clear that the government would do everything possible to train Malays for top positions, but there could be no quota system for jobs or for the issue of licences for taxis or hawkers.

Kuala Lumpur radio and television blacked out all reports of this meeting. Instead, the *Utusan* carried a mischievous and dangerous headline the next day: "Challenge to All Malays – UMNO Youths, Lee Kuan Yew condemned, Teacher forced student to smell pork – protest". This headline was incendiary, forcing a Muslim to do something abhorrent to them, especially on the eve of Prophet Mohammed's Birthday, a time of great religious significance for all Muslims.

∽

Prophet Mohammed's Birthday was on Tuesday, 21 July 1964, a public holiday. It was the practice for Malays to congregate in some open space in town and march towards their settlement at Geylang Serai with tambourines and drums, chanting religious verses to celebrate the holy anniversary. This time, the procession was to start at the Padang, but instead of the religious sermons that were usually the order of the day, there were political speeches designed to stir up Malay feelings of hatred.

Othman Wok, minister for social affairs, was present at the Padang with a contingent of PAP Malay Muslims. He was already expecting trouble because, nine days before, at the rally in Singapore, Albar had accused all PAP Malay assemblymen of being un-Islamic, anti-Islam, anti-Malays and traitors to the community. At the Padang itself, he felt something would happen that afternoon because, intermittently during the speeches, there were shouts of *"Allahu Akbar"* (God is Great), their voices raised in anger, not in praise of Allah.

Esa Almenoar, an Arab lawyer and playboy who was probably the most nonconforming Muslim at the Bar, referred to the Crawford resettlement by quoting a verse from the Koran: "Allah forbiddeth you not that ye shall deal benevolently and equitably with those who fight not against you on account of religion nor drove you from your homes, verily Allah loveth the equitable." He explained its meaning in this way: "It is clear that Allah does not stop Muslims to be friendly with non-Muslims ... but in everything that we do there must be a limit that such people who are non-Muslims who have disturbed our religion and who have driven us from our homes then Islam says such people are cruel wrongdoers."

I had just finished my round of golf at the Royal Singapore Golf Club at about 6:20 pm when the police alerted me that Malay-Chinese riots had broken out during the procession and the trouble had spread. I dashed home to change and went to police headquarters at Pearl's Hill, where Keng Swee and I were briefed by John Le Cain, the police commissioner, and George Bogaars, the director of Special Branch. As reports of casualties continued to flow in, first of Chinese victims, then of Malays when the Chinese hit back, Le Cain conferred with police headquarters in Kuala Lumpur and ordered a curfew from 9:30 pm to 6 am. In a radio broadcast at 10:30 that night, I described how, according to the police, the riots had started:

"Sometime after 5 pm, the procession of some 25,000 Muslims passed by the Kallang Gas Works in a predominantly Chinese area. A member of the Federal Reserve Unit (police sent down from peninsular Malaysia) asked a group who were straggling away from the procession to rejoin the main stream. Instead of being obeyed, he was set upon by this group. Thereafter a series of disturbances occurred as more groups became unruly and attacked passers-by and innocent bystanders. The disturbances have spread rapidly throughout the Geylang area. By 7:30 pm, trouble broke out in the city itself."

I urged a return to sanity:

"What or who started this situation is irrelevant at this moment. All the indications show that there has been organisation and planning behind this outbreak to turn it into an ugly communal clash ... But right now our business is to stop this stupidity ... Rumours and wild talk of revenge and retaliation will only inflame men's minds."

But racial passions had been aroused, and mayhem had broken loose. The news, distorted and exaggerated, soon spread by word of mouth. All over the island, Malays began killing Chinese, and Chinese retaliated. The casualties came to 23 dead and 454 injured, and when the body count was made at the mortuary there were as many Malay as there were Chinese victims. Secret society gangsters had stepped in to protect the Chinese and exact revenge, not least for the harsh behaviour shown towards them by the men of the Malay Regiment and the Federal Reserve Unit, who were mainly Malay. The riots raged on intermittently over the next few days, during which the curfew was lifted for short periods to allow people to go to the market. It ended only on 2 August.

Despite the bloodbath, the *Utusan* continued its agitation. On 26 July, it published a report from an Indonesian newspaper with the head-line, "Lee responsible for Singapore riots", even as both the federal and Singapore governments were appealing for calm and harmony. Six days later, Albar said they had occurred because "there is a devil in Singapore who sets the Malays and the Chinese against each other. ... why is it that under the British, Japanese, David Marshall and Lim Yew Hock governments no incidents happened in Singapore ... It is because Lee Kuan Yew has been trying to challenge and chaff at our spirit of nationalism. You remember ... how he ridiculed us by saying, You have received your independence on a silver platter ... You can see for yourselves how he has challenged the Tunku: 'Tunku Abdul Rahman has no calibre'."

The Tunku himself was away in America, after attending a Commonwealth Prime Ministers' Conference in London. Speaking over Radio Malaysia from the United States, he said he was shocked by the events, and in a TV interview, said that this was the "most unhappiest moment of my life". As acting prime minister, Razak flew to Singapore, and I received him at the airport. He told the press that the situation was under control, but serious, and the curfew would go on indefinitely. The cause of the disturbances had been a mischief-maker who had flung a bottle at the procession, he declared. He knew from the reporters that this was not true. I was still hoping the central government would put a stop to all the racist politicking.

I announced over radio and television that plans were afoot to return things to normal, and added boldly that they would include arresting key members of the secret societies and proscribing activities of extremist elements. Meanwhile, we set out to form goodwill committees in all constituencies, getting together grassroots leaders from the Chinese, Malay, Indian and Eurasian communities to restore confidence in each other and discourage the repeating of rumours. I toured the badly affected areas to show that the Singapore government was present, and tried to give people the impression that we could still get things done and restore peace although we were no longer in charge of the police and army. Deep inside, I felt frustrated for I had lost control of the instruments of law and order and could not deal with these blatant racists. Methodically and meticulously, however, we assembled all the

Receiving acting Malaysian Prime Minister Tun Abdul Razak at the airport on 22 July 1964, the day after the riots. Goh Keng Swee is on the right.

Urging a crowd in Hong Lim to be calm after racial clashes, August 1964.

data available to expose beyond any doubt their systematic exploitation of the media to work up communal feelings through lies and malicious distortions.

Later the government published a memorandum setting out the events that had led to the riots. It read:

> "It is the submission of this memorandum that, unlike in the past, influential political leaders and newspapers were allowed to carry an open and sustained communal and political propaganda for many months. The purveyors of communal propaganda were not obscure fanatics with little resources and facilities to spread their message ... This time, the propagandists of aggressive communalism included people and newspapers closely associated with the central government and with the ruling party of Malaysia."

The memorandum concluded that at no time did those in authority in Kuala Lumpur restrain those indulging in inflammatory racist propaganda. Nobody put a stop to it, and nobody was prosecuted for sedition, as they could so easily have been. The evidence produced clearly showed that the riots were not a spontaneous and unwilled manifestation of genuine animosities between the races. The purpose of the campaign was principally to reestablish the political influence of UMNO among the Singapore Malays. An even more important objective was to use the Singapore Malays as pawns to consolidate Malay support for UMNO in Malaya itself. By placing the blame for the riots on our government and depicting it as oppressing the Malays of Singapore, the perpetrators hoped to frighten those elsewhere in the Federation into rallying around UMNO for protection.

A week after the riots, Othman Wok, who had been deputy editor of the *Utusan Melayu*, was told by a senior reporter of *Utusan* in Kuala Lumpur that at 2 pm on 21 July, he already knew something was about to happen. Othman asked, "But the riots did not start till 4 pm, how did you know beforehand that riots would take place?"

The *Utusan* reporter replied, "We knew beforehand. We have our sources."

Those responsible wanted to reserve the front page for the big news.

Chin Chye called for a commission of inquiry to investigate the reasons for the riots. But in Kuala Lumpur, federal minister Khir Johari said the government would conduct a post-mortem on the disturbances, not an inquiry. They did not want to put Albar and the *Utusan's* role under scrutiny. That was not reassuring. Nor was the atmosphere between the communities. It was important that the Chinese population should not be cowed, or else the extremists and those in UMNO whom they represented would have achieved their objective – a compliant and browbeaten people, submissive when they were treated as second-class citizens. However many Chinese were intimidated as a result of the open bias of the Malayan troops and police during the riots, and one effect of the senseless violence was to segregate the two races. The Chinese felt persecuted and looked at their Malay neighbours with apprehension and suspicion, while the Malays who lived in a predominantly Chinese part of the island were afraid of being vulnerable in a race riot. Chinese families that formed minority pockets in a Malay area quietly moved out to stay with relatives elsewhere, even if it meant selling their homes to incoming Malays at a discount. The same process occurred in reverse, with Malay families moving out of mainly Chinese areas to seek refuge in schools and community centres under police protection.

It was terribly disheartening, a negation of everything we had believed in and worked for – gradual integration and the blurring of the racial divide. It was impossible to dispel or overcome the deep-seated distrust evoked once irrational killing had been prompted simply by the mere appearance, whether Malay or Chinese, of the victim. At one rural community centre I visited, a terrified Malay woman of 35 clutched my arm as she recounted how several Chinese men had wanted to rape her, while a Chinese man outside the local police station came up to complain that he had been abused by Malay policemen and ordered to masturbate because some Chinese men had raped a Malay woman in the vicinity. People did foolish and vicious things to each other when the enemy was identified only by race, as if it were a uniform.

On 14 August, the Tunku returned from America. He broke out in tears when he spoke of the riots in Singapore. "I have always asked that leaders be careful in what they say to avoid any quarrel amongst themselves. But some of them have been careless in the speeches leading to these incidents," he said. He sounded like the Delphic oracle. Who had been careless in his speeches, Ja'afar Albar or I? I hoped he meant Albar, but was not at all certain. He had left it vague enough for the *Utusan* to keep pointing the finger at me. Maintaining a bold front, I said I trusted that the Tunku would keep the extremists in Malaysia under control, urged everyone to make his job easier, and stressed that there was no alternative to peaceful cooperation between the communities.

A few days later, the Tunku came to Singapore to study the situation. Speaking to Malays at Geylang Serai, he assured them that plans would soon be drawn up to "raise their economic and social position", the euphemism for catching up with the living standards of the Chinese and Indians. I was present and said that the success of Malaysia rested on more than constitutional and legal rights and obligations. It depended on faith and trust, and I believed the Tunku was capable of solving the problems now confronting it. I was signalling to him that I trusted him to do the right thing. I had to. Power was now in his hands.

A day later, he ended his visit with a speech to a thousand people at St Patrick's School on the east coast, a very mixed area of English-educated Chinese, Eurasians, Indians and Malays. He asked every Malaysian to help relieve him of his burden, appealing for harmony so that every race could live according to its customs and religion. I promised that the Singapore government would do its best to solve the social problems that had disturbed communal relations. When he left the next day, he said he was leaving with "peace in my mind", while I bravely spoke of the "beginning of a thaw".

The riots had struck a blow not only against Malaysia at home. Before they broke out, international opinion had been developing in Malaysia's favour. It was folly for the UMNO leaders to allow Albar to mount racial clashes in Singapore and so give Sukarno a propaganda advantage – evidence that Malaysia was a neo-colonialist arrangement with serious racial conflicts threatening its unity as a federation. It was a heavy price for the Malaysian government to pay to teach the PAP a lesson for taking part in the Malayan election and to regain the Malay ground they had lost in the 1963 Singapore election. UMNO leaders knew what Albar was up to from reading the *Utusan Melayu*, but allowed him to go on.

The diplomats, both in Singapore and Kuala Lumpur, reported back home what had happened. Head told London he had "no doubt that this extreme element of UMNO played a considerable part in stirring up the first communal riots which took place in Singapore".

The British high commission in Kuala Lumpur reported:

"The riots had a political rather than a religious origin; there had been a similar, but less serious, outbreak the previous week in Penang state. Communal tension has been sharpened during the past few months by a propaganda campaign (conducted primarily by the leading Malay newspaper, *Utusan Melayu*) accusing the PAP government in Singapore of unfair treatment of Malays there. *Utusan Melayu* often acts as the mouthpiece of UMNO, and in particular of its extremist secretary-general, Syed Ja'afar Albar. The loss of the Malay seats in the Singapore Legislative Assembly last September to the PAP rankled, and UMNO resentment was increased by the PAP intervention in the Malayan general election in April (unsuccessful though it was), and by the PAP's continuing efforts to set up a grassroots organisation in all the main Malayan towns."

A report prepared by the Joint Intelligence Committee (Far East) for the British Chiefs-of-Staff Committee said "The campaign against the PAP was carried on by UMNO branches in Singapore with the active and open support of UMNO headquarters in Kuala Lumpur."

The American consul-general in Singapore, Arthur H. Rosen, in his airgram to the State Department, said that the riots were "politically inspired" and the "logical outcome" of the "long period of anti-PAP political agitation, with strong communal overtones, by UMNO leaders".

Donald McCue, charge d'affaires at the American Embassy in Kuala Lumpur, corroborated this in his despatch to the State Department:

"Dato Nik Daud (the permanent secretary of the ministry of internal affairs) has told me that his ministry [was] convinced riots [in] Singapore were caused by Malay extremists. He admitted [that the] July 12 Syed Ja'afar meeting and speeches [in] Singapore had further increased communal uneasiness which already existed. Daud, a Kelantanese, is a Malay Malay. If there were any doubt regarding Malay extremists being responsible for Singapore riots Daud would give them the benefit of the doubt."

W.B. Pritchett, the Australian deputy high commissioner in Singapore, reported to Canberra: "There can be no doubt that the responsibility for the riots rests squarely with UMNO whose members ran the communalist campaign or condoned it."

The New Zealand Department of External Affairs concluded:

"[T]he fact remains that UMNO (and ultimately UMNO's leaders) must bear the main burden of responsibility for the recent outbreak by virtue of their recourse to the excitation of Malay racial sentiment. It appears to us that Razak and other UMNO leaders did not act soon enough to curb the excesses of extremists like Ja'afar Albar and we [were] left in even more disturbing doubt by the reaction of the federal government to the riots."

Sukarno made a radio broadcast urging Singapore Chinese not to support Malaysia, which had been formed to oppress them. Then, on 17 August, Jakarta landed 30 armed men on the west coast of Johor opposite Sumatra, to stir up trouble. Fortunately, they were neutralised. Two weeks later, the Indonesians sent in 30 more men in two airdrops. Most were caught. Jakarta claimed that they were Malaysian freedom fighters and Indonesian volunteers. In fact, most were Indonesian paratroopers. Sukarno had overstepped the mark. Malaysia lodged a formal complaint with the UN Security Council and the British assembled two carrier groups with additional air and naval support. Sukarno promised to cease these operations.

On the same day as the Indonesian airdrops, Malay-Chinese clashes broke out in Geylang. A trishaw rider was murdered and the driver of a car attacked. Despite a curfew, rioting went on for three days, during which 13 people were killed and 109 injured. Again, the casualties were about equal between Malays and Chinese. I was away in Brussels attending the centenary celebrations of the Socialist International. Chin Chye, as acting prime minister, said that Indonesian agents had caused the riot. The situation had become so volatile that all it needed was for Malay toughs to beat up some Chinese and retaliation would follow.

After this second outbreak of race riots, the Malaysian cabinet, under growing pressure from public indignation in Singapore, ordered a commission of inquiry, with Mr Justice F.A. Chua as chairman, to investigate the causes of the disturbances here, and also the earlier ones at Bukit Mertajam in Province Wellesley. The federal government, however, ordered it closed to the press and public. The commission did not start its hearings until 20 April 1965, seven months later.

In his opening address, counsel for the Malaysian government said he would show that the two disturbances were the work of Indonesian agents in Singapore. He had subpoenaed 85 witnesses to provide the evidence of this, but the evidence of the five main witnesses he produced did not show that it was so. All of them firmly denied that Indonesia was in any way connected with the disturbances. The cross-examination of a star witness ran as follows:

QUESTION: If during the months of May, June, July, we have all these various things that I have just been telling you – this propaganda, which is opened and sustained, would you agree that the feelings of the Malays would have been very high?

ANSWER: Yes.

QUESTION: And it was so on the day of the riots, was it not?

ANSWER: Yes.

QUESTION: Would you agree that this highly charged propaganda was the factor with regard to the riots?

ANSWER: Yes.

Of greater importance was the light thrown on the riots by Keng Swee. He met Razak in Kuala Lumpur on 28–29 July 1964, one week after the first riots. Razak told him that he saw a way out. He was willing to set up a national government of Malaysia in which the PAP would be represented in the federal cabinet – on condition that I resigned as prime minister of Singapore; I could take up a post at the United Nations and make an effective contribution from there. After two or three years, the position might be reviewed.

Keng Swee asked whether, as a quid pro quo, Albar would be removed. Razak answered, "No." Razak was emphatic when he told Keng Swee that he had Albar and the *Utusan Melayu* completely under his control and gave a clear undertaking to Keng Swee that he could control *Utusan*. Keng Swee made a note immediately after the meeting: "Razak admitted that his opinion was sought whether or not trouble would break out in Singapore and he had given as his opinion that trouble would not break out. He admitted that he had made an error of judgement. Had he foreseen it, he would have taken action."

Keng Swee recorded in his oral history in 1982:

"Now, this amounts to an admission that he was involved in this whole campaign to whip up Malay racist and religious feelings in Singapore. And Albar's entry into Singapore and his campaigning in Singapore and the support given to *Utusan Melayu* had the full backing of Razak. It could not have been otherwise.

"Now, when Razak said that in his opinion, trouble will not break out, I mean, that's ... I frankly don't accept that. No one in his senses would have believed that this shrill racist campaign coupled with a well-organised procession of the Malays in which the *bersilat* (martial arts) groups came out in force, no one could have believed that. The outcome must be racial riots.

"In fact, some days, perhaps more than a week before the riots broke out, I remember Mr Lee was extremely worried and felt in his bones that there was going to be race trouble. Discussed it with me. I was too engrossed on economic and financial matters. I was not fully informed and appeared quite sceptical about this. Again, this is a matter of political judgement – getting the feel of the situation – which I had not. When I questioned Mr Lee very closely, he just sighed and changed the subject. He must have thought that I was very dense on these matters. And indeed I was. Well, whatever the outcome was, the riots took place, Razak was involved in it and it was clearly his intention to remove Mr Lee from office. That was the purpose of Albar's campaign."

37. Singapore-KL Tensions Mount

I was in Brussels for the Socialist International celebrations when the second wave of rioting broke out on 2 September. Should I rush back to deal with the situation? I decided against it. Dashing back would not make the slightest difference to how events unfolded. Once a riot had started, there was a certain dynamic and momentum to it and one needed strong police action to suppress it. So I stayed on in Brussels.

On Sunday, 6 September 1964, there was a march past of contingents from the Socialist International in Europe. I was struck by the large number of war veterans in mufti, many wearing their medals, and by the appearance at the head of each contingent of a small brass and wind band playing martial music that was obviously giving them a lift. My mind went back to February 1942, when two remaining pipers of the Argyle and Sutherland Highlanders had played, first for the Australians and then for the Gordon Highlanders, as they marched across the Causeway into Singapore and captivity.

We had not been allowed to use the police band for our Singapore State Day parade in June 1964. The federal government, now in charge of the police, had decided to shut us out. We were frustrated but could do nothing about it. Seeing this great array of bands from many countries in Brussels, I decided to form them in our schools and the People's Association. I had to keep up the morale of the people.

On my return, I told the director of the People's Association to look for retired bandsmen from the Singapore Infantry Regiment, and got my violin-playing contemporary at Raffles College, Kwan Sai Keong, now permanent secretary at the ministry of education, to mount a crash programme for brass bands in all secondary schools. My plan succeeded. On Singapore State National Day in June 1965, the PA band was on parade, and so were bands from a few secondary schools. We had shown Kuala Lumpur they could not hold down a resourceful and determined people. Later, we expanded the programme downwards to take in the primary schools, and then upwards to the university. Soon we had a youth orchestra. I believed music was a necessary part of nation-building. It uplifted the spirits of a people.

There was more to Brussels than brass bands. Addressing the congress, I stressed that democratic socialists in Asia could meet the challenge posed by the organisational and propaganda techniques of the communists only if they could achieve two conditions: first, reasonable living standards, and second, effective administration. Otherwise they would not survive in newly independent countries. Willy Brandt, the mayor of Berlin and the best known of the many socialist leaders I met in Brussels, heard my speech and congratulated me. The man who reacted most warmly was Anthony Greenwood, the Labour shadow cabinet's minister for colonial affairs who was then in charge of the International Department of the party.

Greenwood was a tall, lean man in his early 50s, well-dressed and conscious of his smart appearance, yet friendly and approachable, with no superior airs. He was the right person as spokesman for colonial affairs, for he instinctively sympathised with the underdog. His father, Arthur Greenwood, had started life as a trade unionist, ended up in the House of Lords, and was proud of his antecedents. Anthony himself went to public school and Oxford, which made him an Establishment figure, but he was never apologetic about his proletarian background. A likeable man, he had a big heart. I liked him.

He spent some time talking with me about the race riots in Singapore, asking why I had not rushed home. I hinted that some Malay agitators with high-level connections were behind these troubles. He understood and expressed approval for my cool, rational approach. He invited me to meet other British Labour leaders and attend a dinner at the House of Commons on 11 September, when all the Labour MPs and party candidates would be present. It was the annual dinner of their Parliamentary Association and would be held on the eve of nominations for the general election. I accepted and flew to London.

Earlier, in January, I had met the Conservative defence secretary, Peter Thorneycroft, in Singapore and told him that however resolute his government might appear, the Indonesians knew that the Labour Party could be the government after the general election in the autumn. I said that if Harold Wilson as the party leader made it clear he would honour Britain's defence commitments, it would kill any hope Sukarno harboured that a Labour government would find intolerable a long-drawn-out campaign of harassment and give up. Thorneycroft agreed to speak to Harold Wilson on his return, and with his concurrence I wrote to Wilson in those terms.

This was now to bear fruit. Before the dinner on 11 September, I met Wilson in the room he had in the House of Commons as leader of the opposition. We talked for 40 minutes. Indonesia's Confrontation of Malaysia was much on his mind, as were the Malay-Chinese riots in Singapore. British troops were helping to defend Malaysia and he wanted to know if the new Federation was viable in the long run. We had met more than once before and, face to face, I was able to be very frank when analysing our problems. I told him that apart from Confrontation, which accentuated the Tunku's sense of insecurity, the Tunku and his colleagues found it difficult to give up their policy of total Malay dominance for a more balanced position between the races, although this was necessary now that the composition of the electorate had altered with the addition of Singapore, Sabah and Sarawak. I said that my colleagues and I accepted that this would take time to change, that we did not envisage a non-Malay multiracial party taking power for at least 20 years. I added that we could not and would not accept a Malay-dominated Malaysia in which the non-Malays were there on sufferance. That would be contrary to the constitution we had agreed with the Tunku. Like Greenwood, he was reassured by my rational and objective approach.

Wilson was in high spirits. He expected to win the general election, and assured me that a Labour government would continue to support Malaysia against Indonesia's Confrontation. He wanted Britain to do its share of containing Soviet mischief-making in Southeast Asia, and Confrontation was one such mischief that the Soviets had created by supplying arms to the Indonesians. He looked to me and the PAP in Singapore to make it easier to get this policy supported by Labour MPs. It was a warm, fraternal meeting. He poured himself a double whisky. I settled for a single, and as it was a beautiful September evening, still light around 6:30, we walked onto the terrace overlooking the Thames to enjoy our drinks. He was in an expansive mood and spoke animatedly of how he intended to run his new government. He had some of the ablest men of his generation in his shadow cabinet. He would get Britain going again by using her lead in science and technology.

It was one of the most important meetings in my life. If Labour won the election and Wilson became prime minister, I believed the Tunku would know he had to moderate his racial policies against the PAP. With Alec Douglas-Home, the 14th Earl of Home who had succeeded Harold Macmillan as prime minister, the Tunku had felt a certain affinity as between two noblemen. He was sure Douglas-Home would understand his needs and his style of government. But the Tunku would suspect Harold Wilson and his bunch of radical Oxford dons of regarding him as an anachronism, akin to the tribal chiefs of Africa. I therefore had more than a passing interest in the results of the election due that October.

There were over 600 British Labour Party MPs and prospective candidates at the dinner. Wilson, prompted by Greenwood, asked me to speak during the dessert. I recounted the problems of Indonesia's Confrontation of Malaysia and how stability in the region and Malaysia's survival depended upon British resolve to prevent a larger nation from swallowing up its smaller neighbour by force. If Labour formed the next government, I hoped it would honour the obligations that the British Conservative government had undertaken. I said that given time people in developing countries would evolve a fairer and more just society, like the one in Britain of which they had read. This theme resonated with the prospective MPs, and consolidated my standing with Wilson. That was to make a crucial difference to events in Singapore in the coming year. Later that evening Greenwood told me he had given me a captive audience and I had done a superb job in winning their support for Malaysia.

I returned home on 13 September, reassured that if Labour became the government I would have friends in the party, with some of whom my ties went back to my Cambridge days in the 1940s. Most of the MPs would have heard me speak that night and, I hoped, would remember me. I was reassured by my visit to London. But when my aircraft landed in Singapore, I found a very different atmosphere. The airfield was ringed with riot police armed with tear gas and guns, while many more plain-clothes men mingled with the crowd that lined the road from the airport. The day before, the Barisan had tried to mount a demonstration of some 7,000 youths, but the police had dispersed them before they could gather, and 77 people, including one Barisan assemblyman, were subsequently charged with rioting. The demonstrators had planned to give me a hot reception.

Nor was that all. I found uneasiness within the cabinet itself. Several ministers came separately to see me, to tell me they were unhappy with the way the troubles had been handled in my absence. Chin Chye, as acting prime minister, had been nervous and imposed a curfew suddenly, without a grace period, while people were at work and students were in schools, increasing alarm and causing chaos as everyone had to rush home. I took note of their reservations, but decided to leave things as they were. I was terribly depressed, but determined not to allow the situation to get worse by showing any sign of despair. If we were to fight and win this battle, the morale of the population and their will to resist was of the utmost importance.

A week after my return, I was to officiate at the opening of the new building of the Singapore Chinese Chamber of Commerce in Hill Street. The Chinese merchants were down in the dumps, and Ko Teck Kin came to see me one evening at Sri Temasek, looking most worried. Having appealed to the Chinese-speaking to vote for alternative "A" in the referendum to join Malaysia, he felt keenly responsible for their present predicament, their helplessness when caught between Malay rioters and a Malay police force and army that were openly anti-Chinese. What could be done?

He looked at me intently and said, "We cannot let down the Chinese people."

I told him we had our rights guaranteed in the constitution, and I had no intention of allowing this to be ignored. It was our business to unite and mobilise the people to ensure that the constitution was respected. There would be no discrimination between races, other than what was provided for in that constitution, which entitled Malays to special quotas for education, jobs, licences and contracts only in peninsular Malaysia.

He said, "You have good relations with the British Labour Party, can you not get them to help us out of this difficulty? Let us be on our own. It is terrible to live like this."

He sensed that if Labour formed the government, they would be more sympathetic to a non-communal socialist party in Singapore than to a Malay communal right-wing party in Kuala Lumpur. He shared the mood of the Chinese-speaking community who found it intolerable to live in a constant state of fear. The first communal riots had been engineered, with emotions stoked up over months and then sparked by Malay *bersilat* groups from the peninsula. Once the senseless beating and killing of innocent passers-by had taken place, it was easy to provoke them a second time. Everyone felt this. The poison of racial suspicions had spread. Relations had become tinder-dry and it would not take much to ignite them again.

When I opened the new Chinese Chamber of Commerce building, I gave a boost to their morale. I had to exude confidence myself in order to instil confidence in them. I was certain there was a future for the Chinese in Malaysia "if we are Malaysians and as long as there is a Malaysia", I said. I compared the two riots – in July and in September. In the first, the leaders in Kuala Lumpur might not have acted in concert with the leaders in Singapore, but in the second, we had worked in unison to fight communalism.

On the same day, the Tunku spoke at a reception given by the Singapore Alliance. On most occasions, he struck the correct note, and he now urged all Singapore leaders to play down communal differences, to come together with the Alliance "to fight in this land of ours" against a common enemy. He would be setting up peace committees, as the existing goodwill committees had not functioned properly. I wondered how this change could make any difference – I did not know what he could do that would be effective, short of arresting the extremists. But that was the Tunku's way. He was trying to play the role of the father of the nation. I had to help him as best I could.

On 25 September, I went up to Kuala Lumpur with Chin Chye and Kim San to see him. We met for talks in the morning, and our discussions continued that night when the Tunku gave us dinner. Chin Chye said that neither goodwill nor peace committees would be effective in maintaining law and order if groups of militant youths went on the rampage. He added, "In such a situation, firm police action is necessary. We believe that action must be taken against all those persons who were responsible for making one community fight against another." This was the nub of the problem. If the police acted promptly and fairly, without discriminating between the races, it would be difficult for riots to gain momentum.

The next day, Chin Chye told the press that complete accord had been reached between the state and central governments after the recent misunderstandings. More in hope than in confidence, he said the discussions had helped to banish all doubts and fears about their ability to work together to make Malaysia succeed. Party differences would be relegated to the background; Malaysia's interests must come first. I said that both sides had promised to avoid sensitive issues regarding the respective positions of the communities in Malaysia, and the greatest effort would be made to mobilise the people against Indonesian aggression and subversion. There was to be a two-year truce between the Alliance and the PAP. I had proposed, and the Tunku had concurred, that to stop the deterioration in the situation, we should both abstain from expanding our party branches and activities. I was hoping for some respite to the politicking.

∞

At about 5:30 in the morning on 17 October, I got up at Singapore House in Kuala Lumpur to listen to the BBC. The final British election results were announced: the Labour Party had won. I was greatly relieved. Harold Wilson was to be the prime minister. My position had improved. The Tunku would have to deal with a British Labour government that would not be sympathetic to feudal chiefs who put down a democratic loyal opposition that abjured violence.

Things seemed to be working out. But my optimism was soon clouded. That same day, Tan Siew Sin said, at a dinner given in his honour by the Hokkien Clan Association, that Singapore could not secede from Malaysia as the constitution did not provide for it. He was confident the island would progress and prosper, but it could not be "the sole oasis of prosperity in a desert of poverty". Secede? When I returned to Singapore, I rebutted his remarks, saying that the people of Singapore were more interested in making Malaysia a success, and it was unfortunate that he had talked of secession when we had agreed to a two-year truce to halt the communal drift that could break it up. Tan responded that he had made the statement to kill strong rumours that Singapore was nonetheless contemplating separation. They were not the only rumours; such was the distrust that I had to kill another rumour that I had been detained by the federal government in Kuala Lumpur.

One week later, Khir Johari announced a major shake-up in the Singapore Alliance, designed to end PAP rule in the next state election, due in 1967. Chin Chye promptly asked the Alliance to clarify the position on the two-year truce, stressing that it could not be applicable only to the PAP. Khir denied any knowledge of the truce, and after a meeting with the Tunku the next day, the Singapore Alliance issued a statement claiming that the agreement to abandon party politics for two years referred only to communal issues; it did not mean that the Alliance should not be reorganised into an effective body. This was troubling. The Tunku expected all accords to be interpreted in his favour. Chin Chye was angry and bitter. But since Khir and the Tunku had said in effect that we were free to expand our respective political parties, Chin Chye, Raja, Pang Boon and Khoon Choy began contacting friends in their home towns on the peninsula to build up grassroots support, and Chin Chye announced that the PAP would be reorientated so that it could mobilise popular backing in Malaya; the party had members all over the mainland, and when the time came he would organise them into branches.

Indonesian intelligence set out to exploit these tensions, and put out feelers to me through our Chinese traders, promising that Indonesia would resume trade with Singapore if we withdrew from Malaysia. To scotch such attempts to divide us, I disclosed Jakarta's overture in the Legislative Assembly in Singapore on 12 November and dismissed it, saying that the Indonesians would eventually understand that Malaysia was not easily digested and learn to live and trade with it.

But morale in Singapore had sagged. The city looked scruffy. With the weakening of law enforcement, Indian herdsmen had allowed their cows and goats to graze on playing fields and even on the grass verges of roundabouts. A lawyer drove his car into a cow one night just outside the town centre and was killed. From my office window, I could see cattle on the Esplanade. After the two riots, the place was slovenly, with more litter, more cows and goats meandering on the streets, more stray dogs, more flies, more mosquitoes, more beggars. Even the grounds of the Singapore General Hospital were unkempt. I was determined to check this decline. I called a meeting at the Victoria Theatre of all officers concerned with public health, and with full press and television coverage urged them to restore standards of cleanliness and tidiness. We gave the herdsmen a few days grace to take their cows and goats back to their pens; any found at large thereafter would be slaughtered for consumption at welfare homes. This had a salutary effect. The city spruced up.

Then Tan Siew Sin struck again. In his budget speech on 25 November, he announced tough new measures to increase revenue, including a one-half per cent turnover tax on gross earnings and a 2 per cent tax on the total payrolls of all trading and other business houses. This would hit Singapore most. We needed to create more jobs, and increasing the cost of the work force would discourage labour-intensive industries. I pointed out that the measures would not help Malaysia's industrialisation, and were likely to widen the gap between the haves and the have-nots. In his first speech in the federal parliament, Keng Swee also said that the taxes were regressive and the timing unfortunate. Singapore would be paying 25 per cent of the national turnover tax and 40 per cent of the payroll tax yields, which was manifestly out of proportion to its population and economy. And when the Singapore Trade Union Congress with well-reasoned arguments objected to the new taxes as anti-labour,

Tan accused our government of using all the machinery at its disposal to inflame mob passions against them.

Tan said he wanted our financial arrangements to be reviewed soon, claiming Singapore's tax burdens were the lightest in the whole of Malaysia. He looked to a time when Singapore would pay 60 instead of 40 per cent of its revenue to the central government.

The Tunku himself sounded ominous at a Medical College dinner in Singapore on 9 December, saying Singapore was "full of politics. In Singapore, for instance, you will find there is less harmony than elsewhere in Malaysia. ... That was why I was not very anxious to bring Singapore into the Federation." Our criticisms of the turnover and payroll taxes had struck home, for he added:

> "If we find that any particular kind of taxation appears to be either unworkable or objectionable, then we can make changes. ... If the politicians of various colours and tinges and flashes in Singapore (the lightning flash is the symbol of the PAP) disagree with me, the only solution is a breakaway, but what a calamity that would be for Singapore and Malaysia."

38. Constitutional Rearrangements?

The Tunku must have felt that Malaysia was headed for trouble. When I met him in Kuala Lumpur on 19 December, he was not his normal relaxed and serene self. He skipped his usual pleasantries and jokes, went straight to business, and talked seriously for half an hour. He was direct, and for the first time proposed constitutional "rearrangements". He had spoken to his inner circle – Razak, Ismail, Tan and Khir Johari – about this after a cabinet meeting the day before.

He repeatedly stressed that defence was vital to him. Trade and commerce would continue as usual, but we must help to pay for defence. Singapore was to be "in partnership, independent, but part of the peninsula". He wanted both Singapore and Malaysia to be in the United Nations. We could share embassies and perhaps our UN representations. He did not appear to be clear in his mind as to what he wanted, but he said the target date for completing these changes would be before the next budget, and in the meanwhile I could think about the problems.

I said that as long as he was alive, he could hold the different forces.

He replied, "In Singapore there are too many Chinese chauvinists, too many Chinese communists. You have to do many things for the Chinese because it's a Chinese state but there are repercussions in Malaya. Lee Siok Yew (MCA minister for education) now wants a Chinese college in Malaya. Once we separate you can be different. You can recognise Nanyang University; your language policies can be different. After we are clear in our minds we can inform the British."

I pointed out that British interests must be protected if they were to continue to maintain their bases in Singapore and defend Malaysia.

I asked whether Singapore would be like Northern Ireland or Southern Ireland. He replied, "Somewhere in between."

On 31 December, I met Ismail for an hour. He was more specific and logical. "The Tunku feels these things intuitively. He wants to go back to the original plan, that you will look after Singapore for the Tunku."

When I asked for details, he said, "You can think these things out more properly. You know now what we want," and repeated three times, "I'd better not say too much, better keep quiet. They are all so suspicious of me. I have been circulating Special Branch impartial reports but they are now being ignored in favour of our own private intelligence, UMNO private intelligence. After the Tunku there will be trouble because the extremists and chauvinists are active in all camps. As long as the Tunku is there, with his personality, people will listen to him. He is above the cabinet and rules of joint cabinet responsibility do not apply. So it is easier for the Tunku because we can do the dirty work. He can disown us if he wishes."

As I was leaving, Ismail said, "Better keep these things quiet, otherwise it will be a big shock to the public, a flight of confidence, investors will flee, Sukarno will be the victor, and he will go on with Confrontation. Best put things down on a piece of paper and discuss. Best for me not to talk as they distrust me. There is now a deepening rift, UMNO distrusts MCA. MCA has to compete with PAP, so more chauvinist line. So back to the old position, trouble over Chinese education. In the end whether PAP or MCA, there is no difference, it's Malays versus Chinese. Before the election, Tan Siew Sin suggested the Alliance merge into one party. Now he refuses as he knows the Chinese following will go to the PAP."

He repeated several times, "Talk with Toh and Raja, their non-communal line we can agree in principle for next generation, but now the ground is communal. Let's go along parallel lines for 15, 20 years, then merge the two societies. Singapore and Malaya, our histories are different, composition different."

I stressed that a big obstacle was that Chin Chye, Raja, Nyuk Lin and Pang Boon were from the Federation, with families still there. Emotional ties made it very difficult for them to withdraw from Malaya. Ismail nodded in agreement.

Much as we tried to keep talks of new constitutional arrangements quiet, the bitter disputes we were engaged in did not go unnoticed by the British. They were wary of any move that might weaken the Malaysian merger and play into Sukarno's hands.

On 28 July 1964, soon after the first communal riots, Keng Swee had met Antony Head, who commented that the UMNO leaders knew that in a political fight based on ideology and doctrine they would lose out to the PAP in the long run. Keng Swee outlined to Head Razak's proposals for cooperation or coexistence. Head thought them unworkable. He said my resignation would not do any good. Demanding the dismissal of the boss of Singapore for trouble the Malays themselves had created might inflame Chinese feelings and in fact do considerable harm.

Head wanted the Tunku to return quickly from the United States and announce immediately the formation of a government that would, on the contrary, strengthen national unity in the face of Indonesian aggression. He had given London his views and it was likely that his prime minister would press the Tunku on this. He also viewed the situation in Sabah and Sarawak with grave concern because they were not adequately represented in cabinet; there was no point in Britain defending the frontiers while the rear disintegrated.

The Tunku came to Singapore on 18 August and told me that on his way back from Washington, he had stopped in London and seen the British prime minister, who had advised him that the best way to consolidate Malaysia after the communal riots in Singapore would be to form a coalition with the PAP. The Tunku said UMNO would never accept this, because, on our side, we could not accept the fundamental condition Razak had laid down, that we stay out of the Malay world.

By December 1964, both sides were groping towards a looser arrangement within the Federation. The Tunku asked me to put the ideas he had discussed with me in a paper in order to clarify what we were prepared to settle for. My memorandum, completed by 25 January 1965, proposed that we return to the position just before merger: all constitutional powers that were under the jurisdiction of the Singapore government would revert to it, the central government would be in charge of defence and external affairs in consultation with us, and we would share responsibility for security in the Internal Security Council. While these constitutional arrangements prevailed, Singapore citizens would be prohibited from participating in party political activities outside Singapore and likewise for Malaysians on the mainland.

The person most vehemently opposed to any temporary withdrawal from Malaysia was Raja. It would mean our isolation, he protested, and eventually we would be finished off by the extremists. He thought we should stay in the Federation to rally the people against extremists and thus stand a better chance of countering them. True to character, Raja never flinched from a fight, however nasty, when he was convinced we were in the right. Chin Chye was with him, but the majority of the cabinet supported me. I gave my memorandum to the Tunku a couple of days later and discussed it with him at the Residency for three hours on 31 January.

∽

Chinese New Year and Hari Raya Puasa, the two biggest festivals of the Chinese and Malays, fell on the same day, 31 January, in 1965. In my message, I made a strong pitch for racial harmony to counter Indonesian propaganda, which had aggravated Malay-Chinese feelings. The appeal Sukarno was making to pan-Malayism had made UMNO emphasise its "Malayness" to outdo him. My message provoked a sharp response from the Tunku the next day:

"There are politicians who are charging the government with the use of strong-arm tactics to impose our will on others. We realise we are not only a strong government and also a just and good government, but to say that we employ strong-arm methods is not true. ... These politicians talk of strife and strain, of trouble and bloodshed ahead, they talk of war ... they produce gloom in the minds of the people wherever they go. ... In this hour of trial and tribulation, such talk is indeed foolish and harmful and dangerous, and I say shame on them."

I replied four days later, at a dinner given by the goodwill committees, that if we faced up to the unpleasant facts of life, we were more likely to resolve them than if we pretended they did not exist. Things were being said which, if allowed to go on, would lead to great unhappiness. I was referring to articles in the *Utusan Melayu* that continued to stoke up Malay feelings against me, the PAP and the Chinese. We published translations in English, Chinese and Tamil of these daily diatribes, and broadcast excerpts in all languages on radio and television. The Tunku knew I had seen through their tactics. He wanted me to keep quiet and talk things over with him privately. But I had first to expose to everyone the vicious racist campaign that Ja'afar Albar and the *Utusan* were conducting.

While the hard-hitting public exchanges continued, Keng Swee and I had private discussions with the Tunku, Razak and Ismail. I had proposed a disengagement for a few years, with a loosening of federal ties and the granting of more power to the Singapore state government, especially over police and internal security matters.

The alternative to cooperation in a national government would be a state of coexistence: Singapore would not be represented in the cabinet, but both governments would operate independently within their respective spheres of influence, which were to be agreed. However, their fundamental precondition for either cooperation or coexistence was that, not only in Malaya but even in Singapore itself, the PAP should stay out of the Malay world and leave it entirely to UMNO to deal with the Malays through Khir Johari. UMNO must have the monopoly of Malay leadership, even in Singapore.

After several attempts at compromise arrangements, I concluded that the Tunku had hardened his stand. He was now determined to get us out of the federal parliament. He did not want us taking part in its debates at all. We were becoming too much of a thorn in their side, especially over finance. Singapore should start collecting its own taxes before the next budget, he said, but should pay a contribution to Malaysian defence since it would become prosperous, thanks to their common market.

"If you are out of parliament, we can be friends," he said. "Better that way – if you are in parliament, you must criticise."

But he appeared determined to have control of defence and external affairs. His argument was simple. "What will happen if Singapore opens up diplomatic relations with China and other communist countries? It will make nonsense of defence."

From the very beginning, he had wanted the association with Singapore to be on a partnership basis, not a merger. His idea of our position was that of dominion status – "like Rhodesia", Ismail said.

I told the Tunku that if we were to pay towards defence then we must be in parliament. There could not be taxation without representation. But he was emphatic; as I wrote to my cabinet colleagues, "his desire to get us out is implacable". When I added that I might not be able to persuade them to accept my views, the Tunku burst out with considerable heat, "You tell them that I will not have Singapore, that is all. I do not want Singapore in parliament and they can do nothing about it."

I asked Ismail the next day whether the Tunku understood my point, that he could not have us out of parliament and expect us to contribute towards defence and external affairs. Ismail replied, "Yes, the Tunku has appreciated that point. We can't have it both ways."

Not surprisingly, we made no progress with the "rearrangements" within the Federation that I had proposed in my memorandum of 25 January. After a meeting with the National Defence Council on 9 February, Razak told Keng Swee that it was impossible for the two sides to depart from political positions that had more or less solidified over the years. What was suitable for Singapore was not suitable for Malaysia and vice versa. Merger had been a mistake. There ought to have been a transition period to avoid a collision and it was now necessary to establish a looser form of confederation.

Keng Swee said that any constitutional rearrangement must not make Singapore appear a semi-colony. If Singapore left the federal parliament, it would be relinquishing its status and rights, and that would be a serious matter. He reiterated my idea that we should work towards the position that existed before Malaysia, and this time Razak agreed that something along those lines would be worked out.

These discussions about "rearrangements" were confusing and frustrating because the Tunku and Razak went backwards and forwards in their successive proposals. In the end nothing came of them, for one overriding reason: the British wanted no weakening of Malaysia during Confrontation, and Head had skilfully intervened, working on the Tunku, Razak and Ismail to block them.

On 15 February, Chin Chye, Kim San and I played golf with the Tunku. I mentioned casually that the British had guessed what was going on because a short while before, Lord Mountbatten, who had been visiting Kuala Lumpur and then Singapore, had expressed concern on behalf of his prime minister. The Tunku said he had told Mountbatten not to worry as he was fully aware of the danger of Indonesia benefiting from news that Malaysia was breaking up. But when we retired to his study, we discovered that his thinking on the rearrangements had changed after Mountbatten and Head had worked on him. Singapore would continue to be represented in the federal parliament, he now said. State finances and powers of taxation would go back to Singapore, removing a major source of friction between us. As already proposed, defence and external affairs would be in the hands of the central government, while control of the police force and matters of local security would be vested in the Singapore government. But national security and intelligence (the Tunku referred to MI5 and MI6) must remain with the centre because otherwise – he repeated this three times – "What would happen if the PAP were not in power and some extreme-left party like Barisan were to take over? Singapore would become a Cuba."

He then asked me to draft a letter he would write to Harold Wilson, to inform him of these arrangements and reassure him that Malaysia was not splitting up. I sent him a draft the next day.

All three of us from Singapore were convinced that the British had successfully scotched any idea he had of allowing the island to "hive off", as the Tunku put it. He would later tell Keng Swee and me at the Residency that he now wanted to go about things slowly. He was afraid of any public disclosure that would give Sukarno an advantage.

Claude Fenner, the inspector-general of police, then came down from Kuala Lumpur to see me. He appeared resigned to giving Singapore control of its uniformed force, and satisfied we could maintain civil order in case of riots if we raised our own reserve units. He was convinced that once Malay extremists in Singapore knew the state government was in charge of security and could take action against them, there was likely to be little trouble. He seemed sincere, but I was mistaken in thinking that this was his final position. Five days later, he showed me a paper he had prepared for Ismail, arguing the exact opposite: neither the police nor state security should be handed over to Singapore. Like the Tunku, he had completely changed his position. He had brought Sir Roger Hollis, the head of MI5 who was visiting Kuala Lumpur, to see Ismail, and Hollis had convinced him that it was inadvisable, from a professional point of view, to divide the police in Singapore and the Federation. So

Ismail, in turn, suggested that the federal government should continue to look after law and order in Singapore, as at present. I asked whether the Tunku had also changed his mind. Ismail said he had not, but he had a duty to give him the professional advice he had received.

Soon afterwards, I had lunch with Head at his residence, Carcosa, with serious discussions 20 minutes before and 20 minutes after it. He had met the Tunku, Razak, Ismail and Tan earlier that day, and said the Tunku had set his mind on the latest rearrangements, but there were three spanners in the works. First, Tan was opposed to giving up control of finance. Second, Ismail objected to handing back to us control of police and security. Third, Singapore UMNO did not want to pipe down, let alone pack up. I told him that it was Fenner who had put the spanner in the works as far as control of the police was concerned. Unperturbed, Head said he had not gone into the matter with Fenner, but perhaps could do so later.

He proposed that there should be a standstill while negotiations were going on, a kind of truce. I reminded him of what had happened to the last truce. I suggested that the Tunku and I should issue a statement to say that we had agreed in principle to stay out of each other's hair for the period of Confrontation, and to emphasise that details were being worked out as to how this could be achieved administratively so as to leave the fundamentals of Malaysia unchanged. Head concurred, but did not mean it. He told me that the rearrangements would be a major victory we should not give Sukarno, because it would only encourage him to persist with Confrontation. He advised me to be patient and wait for that to end. It could not go on for long because the Indonesian economy was suffering and hyperinflation was destroying it. Once it was over, I could press the Tunku on constitutional issues.

I listened carefully, discussed it with my colleagues, and concluded that the British would not want Malaysia to take any risk by adopting a looser arrangement that would only work with a PAP government in

Singapore, and would lead to serious problems if the Barisan were the government. I also decided that we stood a better chance of getting a reasonable constitutional rearrangement if I pressed my case with the Tunku while the British were defending Malaysia against Indonesia and could still influence him. Head had said that while he would rather we sorted things out for ourselves, he had been given wide discretion by his government, and it could bring enormous weight to bear if necessary.

The next day, 24 February, I asked him to see me at Singapore House in Kuala Lumpur. I told him I could not get the Tunku to issue a statement because he (Head) had frightened him against saying or doing anything. The position was bound to deteriorate with both sides slugging it out, and we might find ourselves with a third riot on our hands. Head said he would get the Tunku to announce that he was thinking of making minor adjustments to Malaysia for smoother working, but not fundamental or radical changes. Negotiations over the police and finance would take at least six months; the position meanwhile had to be held.

I gave a written assessment to the cabinet: not only were Mountbatten and Head putting pressure on the Malaysian leaders, but British officials trusted by the Alliance ministers, like Fenner in the police and Gould in the federal treasury, were doing their utmost to thwart the Tunku on the rearrangements. The British wanted no changes while Confrontation was still on, and if there were to be any, they must be minimal. The police, both uniformed and Special Branch, were to remain under the control of the centre. My conclusion: "From my experience of the merger negotiations, this is characteristic of British methods. Never head-on assault to say that there will be no changes, but a gradual piecemeal erosion of the other man's point of view. ... I do not know whether he (Head) intends to wear us down." I did not rule out the possibility that if we failed to heed Head's advice, he might indicate to the Tunku that the British would be prepared to connive at his eliminating our challenge in the Federation altogether.

Our bargaining asset was the political strength we derived from our party branches in Malaya and our presence in parliament, which enabled us to rally the non-Malays and progressive Malays throughout Malaysia. But for that, and our ability to call mass rallies and campaign in Malaya, Tan Siew Sin would have just ignored our attacks on his budget and brought his bill for the turnover tax before parliament.

The behind-the-scenes discussions had nevertheless kept the situation from boiling over. Both sides wanted to avoid a collision. Both wanted a looser arrangement to end the constant friction that in the long term would weaken Malaysia's position internationally and internally. But the British would have none of that, and worked strenuously to keep Malaysia intact; the Australians and New Zealanders supported the British. The Australian high commissioner, Tom Critchley, and his deputy in Singapore, Bill Pritchett, both urged me to leave things completely unchanged constitutionally and administratively, get out of Malayan politics and close the PAP branches in the peninsula in return for having two ministers in the federal government. I told Critchley that we could not withdraw the PAP from Malaya while UMNO operated in Singapore and the Malay extremists could be used as a stick to blackmail us with the threat of communal unrest. UMNO could not have their cake and eat it.

One saving grace in the midst of the growing tension and bitter altercation between Singapore and Malaysian leaders was that confidential dialogue was still possible between Keng Swee and myself on the one hand, and the Tunku and Razak on the other. Razak was comfortable with Keng Swee but not with me; the Tunku also preferred Keng Swee but did not find me unacceptable and would talk to me, so our private and frank exchanges at a personal level were able to prevent disaster.

But since the public altercation between Kuala Lumpur and Singapore was causing disquiet in Australia and New Zealand, their high commissioners (after clearing it with the Tunku) extended official invitations to me to tour their countries in March and April 1965. I would be able to explain why, despite internal differences, Singapore was solidly behind Kuala Lumpur against Confrontation. This would help to reassure their peoples that their governments should support Malaysia against the Indonesians.

So on 5 March, I found myself landing in Auckland.

39. Seeking Support Down Under

New Zealand was a welcome break. Choo and I stayed in a delightful little hotel in Auckland where white maids, dressed like their English counterparts just after the war, brought us morning tea with bread and butter in bed before offering us a huge breakfast of steaks and lamb chops, which we declined. We drove from Auckland to Wellington, making two overnight stops. At every town along the way, the mayor, wearing his chain of office as he would in Britain, greeted us, gave us lunch or tea, and made a short speech of welcome.

In Wellington, I called on Keith Holyoake, the prime minister, at his office in parliament. After our discussion, he took me to meet his cabinet for a free-ranging exchange of views. They were reassured that I was solidly behind Malaysia. They sympathised with my views and supported a multiracial solution to our problems. At a state luncheon at Parliament House, Holyoake spoke in warm terms. "There are more than military ties which bind New Zealand to Malaysia," he said. He expressed admiration for the progress Singapore had made under me and said that I had worked tirelessly in the service of the new state of Malaysia, "a state troubled by the growing pains common to young countries – pains aggravated by the bullying threats of its larger neighbour, Indonesia. I have no doubt Mr Lee will refuse to be intimidated by such threats, and will continue to work unremittingly to ensure the stability, prosperity and progress of the country he was so instrumental in creating." As if to underline the threats, while I was still in Wellington, a bomb placed by Indonesian saboteurs went off at MacDonald House in Singapore, where the Australian high commission and the Hong Kong and Shanghai Bank were located, killing two and injuring 35 others.

The next day, I spoke to the students and academic staff of Victoria University. I complimented Britain for having the wisdom to know when it faced an irresistible revolution mounted by communists and by nationalists. Instead of trying to stamp out both, Britain had allowed the nationalists to provide the non-communist leadership. On the other hand, when trying to stamp out communism in South Vietnam, the United States had relied on people like Ngo Dinh Diem, and in 11 years had failed to find a group who could lead the nation. So South Vietnam was going through its death throes and the Americans were in an unenviable position. The South Vietnamese themselves had lost confidence and were opting out of the conflict. This left the Americans with only two alternatives – to increase their military occupation or make a calamitous withdrawal. (By April 1975, ten years later, they had done both.)

From Wellington, we flew to Christchurch, drove to Dunedin and Invercargill, then flew back to Wellington. I found New Zealand fascinating. In speech, manners and way of life, they were much more like the British than were the Australians. The country was green and wet, like southern England. And they were friendly and hospitable.

My next stop was Sydney, the starting point of an 18-day tour of Australia that would take us to Canberra, Melbourne, Adelaide and Perth. In Canberra, I spoke to members of the National Press Club. Indonesia's Confrontation of Malaysia was very much on their minds:

> "We have a common neighbour, bigger in numbers than both of us, poorer than either of us and likely to be in a state of unrest and turbulence for a long while yet … We know that military and economic aid cannot guarantee us our ultimate success, but at least it will buy us time."

But the situation in South Vietnam showed that however massive the military cover, however enormous the economic assistance, if the leaders did not set out to secure their own salvation, the end result would still be perdition, both for the helper and the helped. I said:

"The more Malay leadership in Malaysia talks in terms of Malay nationalism, the more non-Malays in Malaysia will be in doubt as to their future. Theoretically, there would be three possibilities if disintegration set in:

(1) Malaysia's absorption or conquest by a third power;

(2) Supremacy of one community over the others in Malaysia; or

(3) A drift towards segregation and ultimately partition.

"All three have gruesome implications."

A large crowd of journalists and diplomats applauded my frankness and realism.

I then met Sir Robert Menzies, the prime minister. Menzies carried weight with the Tunku. Unlike Harold Wilson, he was a Conservative, and had always supported the Tunku. The Tunku had spoken of him in warm terms, and if Menzies would now urge him to seek a solution for Malaysia through political accommodation and not force, he was more likely to succeed than if Wilson did so. He was interested in what I had to say and our meeting lasted for 75 minutes, twice as long as scheduled. After that he took me to meet his whole cabinet for a free-ranging discussion.

I explained the pressures the Tunku was under. Sukarno was appealing over his head to the Malays of Malaysia, a large proportion of whom had come not so very long ago from Sumatra and Java. But by trying to outbid Sukarno's pan-Malayism, the Tunku was alienating the Chinese and the Indians. It was crucial that somebody he trusted, like Menzies, should explain to him that the long-term future lay not in squatting on the Chinese and Indians, but in giving them a place under the Malaysian sun. I pointed out that the three major races in Malaysia – the Malays, Chinese and Indians – had the wellsprings of their culture outside Malaysia, in Indonesia, China and India. The leaders in those countries could pull at their heartstrings as much if not more than could the Malaysian leaders themselves. Menzies was sympathetic. He took my analysis seriously and asked me to give him a note on what I saw as a

With Australian Prime Minister Sir Robert Menzies in Canberra, March 1965.

solution to the problem. I promised to do this when I got back to Singapore. My meetings with him and with his cabinet were not reported in the Malaysian press, probably to avoid annoying the Tunku.

It was a gruelling trip. In every city I made speeches, gave interviews on radio and television, and addressed university audiences and the press. It was well worth the effort. I put across a realistic picture of Malaysia and left New Zealanders and Australians in no doubt that we needed and valued their help, that they were right to help us, and that together, we could succeed.

When I returned to Singapore on 3 April, I found the Alliance leaders angry, alleging that I had been critical of the federal government and the Tunku. Even while I was still in Australia, V.T. Sambanthan, the MIC leader and the Tunku's minister for posts, works and telecommunications, hit out at me "for speaking indifferently" about the Alliance. He said I had got what I wanted, namely Malaysia, and now spoke of the government as being ignorant of politics and run by princes, sultans and chiefs. But I had not said this in any of my speeches.

As the attacks on me continued in the Malaysian papers, several Australians and New Zealanders wrote to the *Straits Times* to defend me. An Australian journalist protested that he had heard me speak several times to university audiences, and at no time had he heard me say anything disparaging about the Malaysian leaders. The president of the Asian Studies Society of Victoria University in Wellington also wrote in to say he was surprised to hear reports from Malaysia that I had been criticised for making "irresponsible statements attacking leaders of the central government". Nothing he had heard supported these allegations.

The truth was that my first sin in the eyes of the Alliance leaders was to have received a favourable press in New Zealand and Australia. They also knew from the Malaysian high commissioners in Wellington and Canberra that I had been warmly received by both prime ministers and their cabinets. But their main grievance was that my arguments and my analysis of the situation had carried weight with both governments. Following the barrage of accusations that I had maligned the Tunku, his ministers and Malaysia generally, I issued a statement that everything I said had been recorded on tape, it was available for checking, and I stood by every word of it. I specifically denied accusing the central government of working only for the Malays as Dr Lim Swee Aun of the MCA, the federal minister for commerce and industry, had claimed, and released a verbatim extract of what I had said on special Malay rights in answer to a question from a Malaysian student in Adelaide:

> "No, I don't think that the issue at the moment is the clause providing for special rights for the Malays. ... And if the immigrant communities of people of immigrant stock do not see the problems, if they can't feel what it is like to be a poor Malay, and don't feel for him, then I say very soon he will manifest his disaffection in a very decisive way and the whole country will be thrown into turmoil."

My charge was not that there were special rights for the Malays, but that they would not solve the problems because they favoured only a few at the top:

> "How does giving bus licences or licences to run bus companies to one or two hundred Malay families solve the problem of Malay poverty? The Malays are farmers. In Australia and New Zealand, all the farmers are wealthy people. How is it that in Malaysia farmers are poor? Because there is no agricultural research, seed selection, fertilisation, improvement in double-cropping techniques, what cash crops you can grow."

My statement was reported in the Chinese and English language newspapers but not in the Malay press. Nor was it carried on Radio & Television Malaysia. So as far as the Malays were concerned, there was no denial by me, and the *Utusan Melayu* was able to keep on stirring up the ground against me.

The Tunku was angered, and warned Singapore leaders that the central government would not be pushed around by any state government on any matter. Singapore, he said, had come into the Federation "with their eyes wide open and on their own accord". He added:

> (Singapore) "would perhaps have been made a second Cuba and the position for us would be untenable … and that was why the central government supported the PAP. With the return of the PAP into power, we considered that Singapore was safe from the communists. But little did we realise that the leader of the PAP had in his mind a share in the running of Malaysia. This we considered as unacceptable since the Alliance is strong enough to run the country on its own."

Two weeks after my return to Singapore, I wrote a letter to Sir Robert Menzies summarising the difficulties of making a success of a multiracial society like Malaysia. In this letter, dated 20 April 1965, I set out the position as my colleagues and I saw it in April 1965. We felt in our bones that if things carried on as they did, something disastrous would happen.

Menzies' reply in May 1965 was supportive but carefully balanced:

> "I can assure you that I want to see, for all our sakes, a sensible and friendly settlement, which I am sure would make Malaysia a living and secure structure. Meanwhile, I urge patience as the constant companion of your unquestioned abilities.
>
> "I will not need to tell you that, if my own influence is to have significance, I must not form any judgements in advance and it must not be made to appear that I have done so."

He recognised that the Australian government would be hard put to justify to its electorate why they should defend a repressive Malay government that was putting down non-Malays – non-Malays who had willingly joined the Federation with a multiracial constitution to which the Tunku and Razak had agreed in London in July 1963.

40. UMNO's "Crush Lee" Campaign

Beneath the increasingly acrimonious exchanges between Singapore and Kuala Lumpur lay a deeper and more fundamental clash between Tan Siew Sin and Keng Swee. Tan was out to block Singapore's economic progress, and this became clear over the issue of pioneer certificates. The Singapore Economic Development Board (EDB) had to send to Kuala Lumpur for approval all applications of prospective investors in the island for pioneer certificates that would entitle them to tax-free status for between five and ten years. But during the two years we were in Malaysia, out of 69 applications, only two were approved, one of which had so many restrictions attached that it amounted to a refusal. To make doubly sure that Singapore would be thwarted, on 16 February, Tan publicly advised all industrialists to consult the central government before investing in Singapore so as to avoid "disappointments and misunderstandings" due to wrong assumptions and calculations. He gratuitously added that "assurances given by experts (in Singapore) were not always feasible".

Not satisfied with blocking us, Tan wanted to take over our entire textile quota. The federal government had claimed quotas for woven textiles and made-up garments when they did not even have factories in which to produce them. Meanwhile, three Singapore textile factories had already been forced to retrench nearly 2,000 workers. Keng Swee said ironically that Singapore was being treated not as a constituent state of Malaysia, but as a dangerous rival to be kept down at all costs. The central government wanted to use the Singapore quota to establish a new garment industry in Malaya while depriving large numbers of unemployed garment workers in Singapore a chance of re-employment.

In the end, under gentle pressure from Antony Head, Kuala Lumpur was shamed into giving back the quota to Singapore. By then, Keng Swee was convinced not only that we would not get a common market, but that Tan would seek to siphon off all industrial investments into Malaya regardless of what the investors wanted. He felt totally frustrated.

Keng Swee recounted in his oral history (1981):

"Tan Siew Sin acted on his own to spite us. Tan was very jealous of Singapore and very envious of Mr Lee. He saw the PAP as a threat to the MCA's leadership of the Chinese in the peninsula and therefore did not want Singapore to succeed. They (MCA ministers Tan and Lim Swee Aun) acted in utter bad faith. And that is why the longer we stayed in Malaysia, the more doubtful we became that we did the right thing."

Keng Swee then referred to a conversation he had had with Leonard Rist, the World Bank expert who advised the Malayan and Singapore governments on the common market and had recommended that it be implemented in progressive stages.

Keng Swee asked, "Suppose he (Tan) does not play the game and the common market does not get off the ground – what happens?"

Rist answered, "In that event, Mr Minister, it's not the common market which should be in danger; the whole concept of Malaysia would be in danger."

Keng Swee was completely disenchanted. Although he had been against our taking part in the 1964 election in Malaya, he now recognised that it was as well that we had, for it enabled us to rally political opinion, which could restrain the excesses of the central government. He had given up any hope of cooperation. He expected no good to come out of Malaysia. Indeed, he expected endless problems. His gloom made Chin Chye even more determined to build some counterweight to the arbitrariness of the centre. Tan's spite was one powerful reason why we had to mobilise the ground throughout the Federation.

∞

The race issue overshadowed everything else. During a session of the federal parliament in November 1964, Dr Lim Chong Eu, MP and leader of the opposition United Democratic Party (UDP) based in Penang, commiserated with me over the two race riots we had suffered in Singapore. He said he had experienced it all. From his description of the disorders in Penang in the 1950s, I realised that what Albar and his UMNO Turks had applied in Singapore was a well-tested method. The police and the army held the ring while favouring the Malay rioters – usually *bersilat* groups, thugs and gangsters let loose to make mischief. Once passions were aroused and enough Chinese counter-attacked, even ordinary Malays joined in. When the Chinese hit back, they were clobbered by the police and army: law and order were enforced against them, not against the Malays. The result was a sullen, cowed population.

We had jumped out of the frying pan of the communists into the fire of the Malay communalists. We had to find a counter to this system of intimidation through race riots, with Chinese being killed and maimed wherever they dared to resist Malay domination. We decided that one effective defence would be to link the opposition in all the towns in the Federation in one network, so that a riot in one major city triggered off riots in others to a point where the police and army would be unable to cope, and all hell would be let loose. So we set out to mobilise fellow sufferers who could together put up this counter-threat. If we could find them in Sabah and Sarawak as well as on the mainland, the Chinese in Kuching, Sibu and Jesselton (now renamed Kota Kinabalu) would also riot, and any communal intimidation by Kuala Lumpur would risk tearing Malaysia apart.

Our moves to unite did not escape attention. On 24 April 1965, the Tunku disclosed in a speech that there were plans for an opposition get-together. He knew the non-Malays were combining forces to make a stand for a multiracial Malaysia, as against a Malay Malaysia, and he suspected I was to be their leader. He warned, "But the people should, however, make a study of this man before they give their heart and soul to any such move. The Alliance and Mr Lee Kuan Yew have worked together for Malaysia, but we found it difficult to carry on after Malaysia." The Tunku had good reason to be concerned. The opposition MPs in the federal parliament had been getting increasingly restive as they listened to the racist speeches made by Albar and the young UMNO Malay leaders. Dr Lim Chong Eu of the UDP in Penang, the two Seenivasagam brothers of the People's Progressive Party (PPP) in Perak, Ong Kee Hui and Stephen Yong of the Sarawak United People's Party (SUPP) and Donald Stephens and Peter Mojuntin of the United Pasok Momogun Kadazan Organisation (UPKO) in Sabah had all by then made overtures to suggest a link-up with the PAP.

The process had begun in January when Dr Lim and Stephens had come to see me separately. Neither meeting had been entirely satisfactory. Dr Lim wanted me to become president of his consumers' association in order to bring about a broad united front of all non-communal parties in Malaysia. I declined. If we came together it must be done openly, not surreptitiously through a consumers' association, or we would lose credibility. Stephens was proposing to leave the Alliance, quit his token appointment as federal minister of Sabah affairs, and get his UPKO members to resign from the Sabah cabinet to prepare for the coming state election. He wanted the PAP to merge with UPKO before that in order to help him win over the Chinese votes in the towns and thus ensure him of a majority in the Sabah State Assembly. The son of an Australian father and a Kadazan mother, he was a big, affable, overweight, pleasure-loving journalist who owned a newspaper in Sabah; chief minister until he joined the federal government, he was the ablest of the Kadazans of his time. But he was not interested in my wider project for a united front that would take in the other opposition parties.

Despite these false starts, I circulated a note to all ministers:

"If we miss this moment, it may be years before we are able to get an equally dramatic occasion for a realignment of forces within Malaysia. On the other hand, taking such a step by which all non-communal parties get together must mean a broad opposition led mainly by the non-Malays against the Alliance led by the Malays in UMNO. Once such a convention has been called and a chain reaction triggered off in men's minds, we can be sure that the fight would very quickly become sharp and acute."

When UMNO already treated us as an opponent and clearly would not cooperate with us, it was a waste of time to postpone a decision. As far as UMNO was concerned, the fight was on, and unless we gathered strength to meet it, UMNO would always have its own way.

On 12 February, Malaysian opposition leaders had met Chin Chye, Raja and myself at Sri Temasek in Singapore, and again on 1 March at Singapore House in Kuala Lumpur, where Stephens turned up in his official car with a flag fluttering and a bodyguard. We thought him rather brave to have done this, until the Tunku came out with his statement on 24 April when we deduced that Stephens had leaked our plans to him. We had decided to move with caution and had sent Lee Khoon Choy and Eddie Barker (my old friend and former partner in Lee & Lee, then minister for law) to assess the political situation in Sarawak and Sabah. They came back convinced we should not open PAP branches in Sarawak. The Chinese there were very strongly left-wing as in the days of the Barisan in Singapore; they were still resentful at having been bundled into Malaysia, and at the PAP for having helped to bring it about. In Sabah, we were likely to get Chinese support and it was feasible to open PAP branches, but we would have to form a coalition with Stephens' UPKO, whose Kadazan supporters were in the majority. I decided not to move into East Malaysia directly, but to work with the present leaders of the opposition there. Chin Chye invited them to a meeting in Singapore on 8 May. Stephens absented himself, but the heads of the UDP, PPP and SUPP of Sabah and of the Machinda Party of Sarawak attended and signed a declaration with us calling for a Malaysian Malaysia:

"A Malaysian Malaysia means that the state is not identified with the supremacy, well-being and interests of any one particular community or race. A Malaysian Malaysia is the antithesis of a Malay Malaysia, a Chinese Malaysia, a Dayak Malaysia, an Indian Malaysia or Kadazan Malaysia and so on. The special and legitimate interests of different communities must be secured and promoted within the framework of the collective rights, interests and responsibilities of all races.

"The growing tendency among some leaders to make open appeals to communal chauvinism to win and hold their following has gradually led them also to what has been tantamount to a repudiation of the concept of a Malaysian Malaysia. ... If people are discouraged and denounced for abandoning communal loyalties because they have found common ground for political action with Malaysians of other races, then the professed concern for a Malaysian Malaysia is open to serious doubts."

The declaration ended:

"A Malaysian Malaysia is worth fighting for because only in such a Malaysia is there a decent and dignified future for all Malaysians. It is in this spirit and expectation that we, the undersigned, appeal to all Malaysians to support this convention."

Although I had been away throughout this period attending a Socialist Youth Conference in Bombay and then visiting Laos and Cambodia, UMNO decided that I had been the moving spirit behind the convention and attacked me vigorously. Albar and the *Utusan Melayu* were getting bolder and wilder in their accusations. Angered by an article in the *London Observer*, Albar sent an open letter in mid-April to Dennis Bloodworth, its Far Eastern Correspondent, which was published in the *Utusan* and included this paragraph:

"As you know the Malays are having a rough time in Singapore and are now being oppressed by the PAP. Lee Kuan Yew is continually challenging their national sentiment with provocative statements, yet in spite of all these, it was not the Malays who started the 1964 riots. The riots were started by *agents provocateurs*, who may even be in the pay of Lee Kuan Yew. Lee's intention is to create disorder in Singapore at a time when the Malays are gathering to celebrate the birth of Prophet Mohammed, so as to give the impression to the world outside that the Malays are already influenced by Indonesia."

I decided on a libel action to check these excesses, and my lawyers took the opinion of a leading Queen's Counsel in London. He had no doubt that it was a libel, and when Albar and the *Utusan* refused an apology and a retraction, my solicitors took action against them. In their writs they spelt out the innuendo of the libel as meaning that I was a hypocrite, an enemy of and a traitor to my own country, a criminal in that I was responsible for the disturbances and incidents of violence resulting in death and injury to members of the public, and that I was unfit to be prime minister of Singapore.

In the action, I cited a story the *Utusan* published on 25 March 1965: "Lee is accused of being an enemy of Malaysia and an agent of Indonesia. WALK OVER MY DEAD BODY FIRST – ALBAR … Tuan Syed Ja'afar Albar, General Secretary, UMNO Malaya last night accused the PM of Singapore, Mr Lee Kuan Yew as being an enemy of Malaysia and an agent of Indonesia." I also cited an article on 27 March: "Albar accuses Kuan Yew of being an agent of the communists. … The PM of Singapore, Mr Lee Kuan Yew, is an agent of the communists and the Djakarta regime which has the evil intention to destroy Malaysia … Lee Kuan Yew has the evil intention to destroy Malaysia and pit the Malays and Chinese against each other".

Now that those words would be scrutinised in a court of law, they became more circumspect. (In 1966, after separation, Albar and the

Utusan agreed to apologise in court through their lawyers and pay for all the costs of my action.)

Not only was I meeting Albar's poison with reason, but my message was also getting through to secondary UMNO leaders at Menteri Besar (chief minister) level. To Albar's shock, the Menteri Besar of Perlis, the northernmost state of Malaysia, welcomed a statement I had made, repeating my argument that special privileges for the Malays would only help a small group of bourgeoisie, whereas what was needed was to enable the mass of Malay have-nots in the rural areas to increase their earning capacity.

Then Razak attacked me for a "statement" I had never made and had already denied making – that the Malays were not the indigenous people of Malaysia. Saying that this was mischievous and dangerous and had created a serious situation, he issued an ultimatum that the Alliance government would not work with me and "if the people of Singapore wish to maintain their relationship with us, they must find another leader who is sincere". Two days later, a group of UMNO youths in Kuala Lumpur burnt me in effigy, and on 16 May, another group picketed the Language Institute where the general meeting of UMNO was due to be held. They carried banners in Malay reading "Suspend Singapore Constitution", "Detain Lee Kuan Yew", "Crush Lee Kuan Yew", and when the Tunku arrived, they shouted "Detain Lee Kuan Yew, detain Lee Kuan Yew!" At the meeting, several delegates demanded my detention, but Ismail said, "This is not the way to do things in Malaysia. We must act constitutionally." The Tunku subsequently described my alleged remark about the Malays not being indigenous to the country as childish, again ignoring the fact that I had never made it.

Tan Siew Sin again warned us that Singapore could not go it alone. "I would ask them to remember that Singapore cannot exist by itself. Even secession from Malaysia cannot eliminate the fact that less than 1.5 million Chinese there are surrounded by over 100 million people of the Malay race in this part of the world." On my return from my visit to New Zealand and Australia, I replied that secession was out, but this, too, was ignored, and the *Utusan Melayu* reported that, on 24 May, Albar had again urged Ismail to take action against me:

> "'If Lee Kuan Yew is really a man, he should not be beating about the bush in his statements and should be brave enough to say "I want to secede from Malaysia because I am not satisfied." He had entered Malaysia with his eyes open and the present Malaysia was the same Malaysia he had endorsed. Why did he not think of all these objections before? Why only now has he regretted? Why?' asked Albar in a high-pitched tone. His audience replied, 'Crush Lee, crush Lee,' and several voices shouted 'Arrest Lee and preserve him like entrails in pickle.' Dato Albar smiled for a moment and then replied, 'Shout louder so that Dr Ismail can hear the people's anger. I want to make quite sure that everybody hears the people's anger.'"

Albar was using the same technique he had employed in Singapore before the 1964 riots. The next day, the *Utusan* carried a story quoting the Menteri Besar of Selangor, headlined "Lee Kuan Yew is the enemy of the people of Malaya", and another Malay paper, the *Berita Harian*, reported that the Menteri Besar of Perak had labelled me "the most dangerous threat to the security of the country." They were working things up to fever pitch.

The attacks reached a climax when Dr Mahathir bin Mohamad, an UMNO MP (later, prime minister of Malaysia), denounced the PAP in the federal parliament as "pro-Chinese, communist-oriented and positively anti-Malay", saying Singapore had retained multilingualism while paying only lip-service to the national language, and that "In some police stations, Chinese is the official language, and statements are taken in Chinese." The national language schools, he said, were the worst-treated on the island, and until very recently had been given only the most

At the opening of the Malaysian parliament, Kuala Lumpur, 25 May 1965, two days before I was to make my last and fateful speech there. Behind me are Ong Kee Hui and Stephen Yong, MPs from Sarawak.

primitive facilities. "In industry, the PAP policy is to encourage Malays to become labourers only but Malays are not given facilities to invest as well." Mahathir was speaking in the debate on the address of the Yang di-Pertuan Agong, the king.

The next day, I made my most important speech in the federal parliament to a hostile and tense audience, including a large number of Malay MPs who had been fed daily with anti-PAP, anti-Lee Kuan Yew and anti-Chinese propaganda by the *Utusan* over the past year. I moved an amendment to express regret that the king's address did not reassure the nation that it would continue to progress in accordance with its democratic constitution towards a Malaysian Malaysia. I quoted from it: "We are also facing threats from within the country." I hoped the Tunku would explain the meaning of this passage. I gave him this firm assurance: "We have a vested interest in constitutionalism and in loyalty because we know – and we knew before we joined Malaysia – that if we are patient, if we are firm, this constitution must mean a Malaysian nation emerges."

But Dr Mahathir's speech implied that this could never happen. I quoted what he had said the day before about the Chinese in Singapore: "They have never known Malay rule and couldn't bear the idea that the people they have so long kept under their heels should now be in a position to rule them." To rule them? I drew a distinction between political equality and the special rights for the economic and social uplift of the Malays. I accepted the special rights, but if the other peoples of Malaysia were denied political equality with the Malays, we would not need Sukarno and Confrontation to crush us. Waving a copy of the Malaysian constitution in my right hand, I said, "Once you throw this into the fire and say 'be done with it', that means you do it for a long time; and history is a long, relentless process." I said Albar wanted us to secede and leave our friends in Sarawak, Sabah, Penang, Malacca and other parts of Malaysia to UMNO's tender mercies; we would not oblige.

I demolished the accusation that we were pro-Chinese. If we advocated a Chinese Malaysia, we could not attract majority support, as the Chinese were only 42 per cent of the population. If I had been going around saying about the Chinese what Albar had said about being a Malay – "wherever I am, I am a Chinese" – where would that have led us? On the contrary, I kept on reminding people, "I am a Malaysian, I am learning Bahasa Kebangsaan (the national language) and I accept Article 153 of the constitution (on the special rights of the Malays)."

Having reached the most sensitive part of my speech, in which I would expose the inadequacy of UMNO's policies, I decided to speak in Malay. Although my Malay was not as good as my English, I was fluent compared with other non-Malay MPs. I said that while I accepted Malay as the sole official language, I did not see how it could raise the economic position of the people. Would it mean that the produce of the Malay farmer would increase in price, that he would get better prices? Would he get improved facilities from the government? I added that if the Alliance did not have real answers to current economic problems, it should not stifle the opposition. Because we had an alternative, and it would work: "In ten years we will breed a generation of Malays, educated and with an understanding of the techniques of science and modern industrial management".

It was at this point that I quoted what Dr Mahathir said earlier in the debate:

> "'It is, of course, necessary to emphasise that there are two types of Chinese ... the MCA supporters to be found mainly where Chinese have for generations lived and worked amidst the Malays and other indigenous people, and the insular, selfish and arrogant type of which Mr Lee is a good example. This latter type live in a purely Chinese environment where Malays only exist at syce level... They have in most instances never crossed the Causeway. They are in fact overseas Chinese first, seeing China as the centre of the world and Malaysia as a very poor second.'"

I continued, "What does that mean, Mr Speaker, sir? They were not words uttered in haste, they were scripted, prepared and dutifully read out, and if we are to draw the implications from that, the answer is quite simple: that Malaysia will not be a Malaysian nation. I say, say so, let us know it now."

As for the Malays "only existing at syce level", I said that the Tunku had frequently said in public and in private that the Chinese were rich and the Malays poor, but I used some simple examples to highlight a few points, still speaking in Malay. Special rights and Malay as the national language were not the answer to this economic problem. If out of four and a half million Malays and another three-quarters of a million Ibans, Kadazans and others, we made 0.3 per cent of them company shareholders, would we solve the problem of Malay poverty?

"How does the Malay in the kampong find his way out into this modernised civil society? By becoming servants of the 0.3 per cent who would have the money to hire them to clean their shoes, open their motorcar doors? ... Of course there are Chinese millionaires in big cars and big houses. Is it the answer to make a few Malay millionaires with big cars and big houses? How does telling a Malay bus driver that he should support the party of his Malay director (UMNO) and the Chinese bus conductor to join another party of his Chinese director (MCA) – how does that improve the standards of the Malay bus driver and the Chinese bus conductor who are both workers in the same company?

"If we delude people into believing that they are poor because there are no Malay rights or because opposition members oppose Malay rights, where are we going to end up? You let people in the kampongs believe that they are poor because we don't speak Malay, because the government does not write in Malay, so he expects a miracle to take place in 1967 (the year Malay would become the national and sole official language). The moment we all start speaking Malay, he is going to have an uplift in the standard of living, and if it doesn't happen, what happens then? ... Meanwhile, whenever there is a failure of economic, social and educational policies, you come back and say, oh, these wicked Chinese, Indians and others opposing Malay rights. They don't oppose Malay rights. They, the Malays, have the right as Malaysian citizens to go up to the level of training and education that the more competitive societies, the non-Malay society, has produced. That is what must be done, isn't it? Not to feed them with this obscurantist doctrine that all they have got to do is to get Malay rights for a few special Malays and their problem has been resolved. ..."

Such arguments put in down-to-earth social and economic terms, and in Malay, had never been heard before in the Malaysian political debate. The PAP had brought crucial, sensitive issues into the open in a rational way to expose the shallowness of UMNO's political argument, that because Malay leaders (mostly the aristocrats and educated elite) worked together with Chinese leaders (mostly the successful merchants) and Indian leaders (mostly the professionals), all would be well.

It was the most significant speech I had ever made in Malay, and I made it to an audience of Malay MPs, many of whom represented rural areas, and to a strangers' gallery, which was packed with more Malays. I had spoken without a script, and for that reason it had all the more impact. As I spoke, there was a stunned silence. The air was electric.

Twenty-five years later, on the anniversary of Singapore's independence, Eddie said of me in an interview: "He spoke for about half an hour. There must have been about 500 or so in the House and in the gallery but you could hear a pin drop. I think if they could have cheered, they would have. Looking back, I think that was the moment when the Tunku and his colleagues felt it was better to have Singapore and Mr Lee out."

My Malay cabinet colleague, Othman Wok, was in the chamber. He recalled: "The chamber was very quiet and nobody stirred. The ministers of the central government sunk down so low in their seats that only their foreheads could be seen over the desk in front of them. The backbenchers were spellbound. They could understand every word. That was the turning point. They perceived Lee as a dangerous man who could one day be the prime minister of Malaysia."

I had no such illusions. Malaysia would not have a Chinese prime minister for a very, very long time.

The Malays present did not expect me, the supposed anti-Malay Chinese chauvinist out to destroy the Malay race, to speak in Malay with no trace of a Chinese dialect accent that most Chinese would have. I had been born and bred in Singapore, speaking the language from childhood. I could trace my ancestors for three generations in Singapore. They had made as big a contribution to the country as any Malay in the chamber. And I was on their side, not against them. I wanted to improve their lot.

The Tunku and Razak looked most unhappy. I was meeting them on their own Malay ground and competing for support peacefully with arguments in an open debate. I was not rattled by their strident, shrill and even hysterical cries of abuse and denigration. I could hold my own. If allowed to go on, I might begin to win over some Malays. They could see that among the MPs wearing the Haji skullcaps of those who had made the pilgrimage to Mecca, heads were nodding in agreement when I pointed out that simply having Malay as the national language would not improve their economic lot. They needed practical programmes directed in the fields of agriculture and education.

The speech aroused such unease among the Alliance leaders and MPs that, contrary to standing orders, the Speaker ruled I could not reply to arguments made against it. It was a backhanded tribute to my effectiveness in Malay. Instead, he called on Razak, in place of the Tunku, to wind up the debate. Razak launched into a long spiel of accusations: I was out to create chaos and trouble and hoped to emerge as the leader who could save the country. I was an expert in creating situations that did not exist. I twisted facts and cast doubts in the minds of people. I planned to split the country into two – "one Malay Malaysia, and one

Lee Kuan Yew's Malaysia". Razak was at his most bitter when he concluded, "The gulf that divides the PAP and the Alliance is now clear. PAP means Partition and Perish."

I had not expected my speech to play so crucial a part in the Tunku's decision to get Singapore out of Malaysia. Twelve years later, 1977, in his book *Looking Back*, the Tunku wrote, "The straw that broke the camel's back, however, was a speech Mr Lee Kuan Yew made in Parliament, when he moved an amendment to 'the motion to thank the King for his speech in May, 1965'. He brought up many issues which disturbed the equilibrium of even the most tolerant Members of the House." He sent me a copy of the book, inscribed:

> "Mr Lee Kuan Yew
>
> "The friend who had worked so hard to found Malaysia and even harder to break it up.
>
> > Kindest regards
> > Tunku Abdul Rahman
> > 26.5.77"

Five years later, in 1982, the Tunku told the author of a book on Singapore, "He (Lee Kuan Yew) would think himself as legitimate as I was to be the leader of Malaya because he speaks Malay better than I do." I did not speak Malay better than the Tunku. Even if I did, I was still not a Malay and could not be the leader of Malaysia. But when he heard me that day in parliament, he realised that I was getting my message through to his own backbenchers. That was unacceptable.

41. The Quest for a Malaysian Malaysia

The mood of the debate in the federal parliament carried over naturally to the Malaysian Solidarity Convention rally the following week in Singapore. On a warm, breezy Sunday morning, 6 June 1965, at the National Theatre, a large open-air amphitheatre with a cantilevered roof but no side walls, 3,000 people packed the seats and filled the grass slopes behind them. It was a buoyant meeting. After their unspoken fears had been aired in parliament, the leaders of the five political parties in Malaya, Singapore and Sarawak felt released from their inhibitions and talked freely about the issues of race and a multiracial society, hitherto taboo subjects.

The convention was Chin Chye's baby. Although he was not a great orator, he spoke with conviction in his opening speech:

> "This convention is embarked on a crusade to preach interracial unity, to propagate the basic rights of all races which form our multiracial society. The force that will unite all our races into a Malaysian Malaysia is more than language, more than external aggression. Experience has shown that in similar countries, a united nation can arise only if one race does not aspire to be the master race but instead all citizens are equal irrespective of his race."

D.R. Seenivasagam of the People's Progressive Party in Perak was direct and blunt. The convention had become necessary because of a calculated attempt by UMNO leaders to stir up racial feeling. In the face of this threat, other political leaders could not sit back and do nothing. He accused the Alliance of using Article 153 of the constitution on special rights for the Malays to "bully non-Malays".

Ong Kee Hui of the Sarawak United People's Party (later a minister in the federal government) was equally pointed:

"We see an attitude of intolerance and mounting signs of denial of political equality to people who are non-Malays. For the sake of our country and for ourselves, this must be stopped and the drift to narrow racialism checked. Political equality should be accorded to all who live here and make this country their home irrespective of their racial origin."

Dr Lim Chong Eu of the United Democratic Party, moderate and cautious by nature, was not known for his outspokenness. But he felt strongly enough to say:

"If we fail now to act on what we resolve, there may be no future, and there may be no equitable society for us, or for our children. The most important and the most fundamental attitude which this convention must manifest is the spirit of resolve and steadfastness in the face of the extremely vicious and near-hysterical criticisms which are hurled against us."

Michael Buma of the Machinda Party in Sarawak was brilliant. He spoke simply but with tremendous effect. His speech was so devastating that the English newspapers were afraid to publish his punchlines. He said that every time he listened to a radio broadcast from Malaya, the announcer gave the time as *Waktu Tanah Melayu* – the Time of the Land of the Malays. Why was it not *Waktu Tanah Malaysia*? So, too, Malayan Railways was known as *Kreta Api Tanah Melayu* – Railway of the Land of the Malays. Again, why? Simply but effectively, he highlighted the racism.

The mood of the audience was set before it was my turn to wind up the convention. I referred to the

"growing truculence, or a heavy racial accent, the intimidatory postures and snarling guttural notes on which they sent out their signals to their followers on the basis of race ... if this goes on,

Malaysia will not belong to the Malaysians. ... They speak on two different wavelengths – one wavelength for multilingual, multiracial consumption, the other, a special VHF meant for their followers. The good men, multiracial men, the top leaders from time to time completely dissociate themselves from this special VHF, but the wild men keep up the pressure."

I quoted Dr Lim's advice to us, based on many years of intimate knowledge of their methods and tactics: "Be resolute, be firm. Never be intimidated."

To give heart to the non-Malays, I tabulated the population figures from the last census: 39 per cent Malays, 42 per cent Chinese, about 10 per cent Indians and Pakistanis, 7 per cent Ibans, Kadazans, Kayans, Kelabits and others in North Borneo, and the rest Eurasians, Ceylonese, etc. Whoever played a communal line would be confined to his own racial group, whether it was Chinese or Malay or another. But those who appealed to the people on a non-racial basis stood a fair chance of winning over the 20 per cent minority. I reduced it to a simple formula: 40–40–20. If the Chinese appealed to 40 per cent, using Chinese slogans, they must lose. I left UMNO to conclude what would happen in the long run if they appealed only to the Malays.

I quoted the chief minister of Malacca, Ghafar Baba (later deputy prime minister), who said, "Look how non-communal the Malays are in Malacca. In a Malay constituency, they voted for Mr Tan Siew Sin." The chief minister, I said, was an honest man, but

"every time Mr Tan Siew Sin goes around beating his chest, this is what he represents, the Malays who voted for him. ... So, too, with Dato Sambanthan (MIC). He is another honest man. ... He said Ja'afar Albar is a good man. Not communal. Do you know why? 'In my constituency, which is in Perak, Sungei Siput, 90 per cent of the people are Malays, and Dato Albar goes around and tells them to vote for me. So they voted for me.' Therefore Albar was not a communalist – because he had told the Malays to vote for UMNO's

Speaking at the fateful gathering of the first Malaysian Solidarity Convention at Singapore's National Theatre, 6 June 1965.

favourite Chinese and Indian leaders in order that they can then lead the Chinese and Indian communities in the direction UMNO wanted to go!"

I exposed their tactics again:

"Get the truth out, and we will know that we have no reason to be afraid, no reason to be intimidated. ... If we are ... woe betide us. (To) a people that are cowed, frightened, intimidated, they will say: Riots coming, blood will flow. So we will all go home, close our doors and take the blankets and cover our heads. And they march up and down the streets shouting slogans. The next day, peace!"

According to Dr Lim, that had been happening for a long time in Malaya.

I stressed that we must not be against special rights for the Malays and the indigenous people. On the contrary, we should compete to raise their economic level in society.

"(But) they (UMNO) don't want to compete. Competition is bad. We are told, 'Lay off. Don't try and do anything good.' They say they are worried about the Malays? I say, so are we. We want to raise their standard of living, and we will, and faster than they can. At the end of 5, 10, 15, 20 years a new generation will grow up that will no longer respond to the special VHF they use. They will be tuning into the multilingual network. They will be thinking like us, working like us, trained like us, prepared to live with us like Malaysians ..."

Albar had called us *orang tumpangan*, meaning lodgers who were staying temporarily in their house. But Lim Swee Aun, the federal minister for commerce and industry, had said, no, "we are co-owners, not lodgers, not guests", and in the one sensible balanced speech made by a Malay minister in the federal parliament, Ismail had spoken of two stages: "one stage – separate communal parties; second stage – non-communal". Therein lay hope, I said.

It was a rousing meeting that brought hope to all those who heard it on Radio Singapore or read about it in the press. We had broken the spell of silence and met their communal intimidation head-on.

The next day, Senator Dato T.H. Tan, in a speech to the federal senate, called upon the central government to take constitutional measures to exclude Singapore from Malaysia or to put Mr Lee Kuan Yew away to sober him. "There appears to be little doubt that Mr Lee, through his words and deeds, is stirring up emotions and causing dissension." A few days later, the minister for information and broadcasting, Senu bin Abdul Rahman, who was from the Tunku's home state of Kedah and close to him, said, "The PAP should note that there is a limit to our patience. … Push us, corner us … then the PAP will be responsible for the consequences. Let them be warned." He asked PAP leaders to come out into the open and state exactly what they wanted for Malaysia. "We know the PAP wants to partition this country. Does it want to set up a republic? Does it want to get rid of our rulers, our so-called privileges? Tell us, spell it out, come out in the open."

Raja, ever the protagonist, replied that I had been prepared to come out in the open in parliament and argue my case, but the Alliance ministers would not allow me to do so. The Tunku responded, in what I thought was an effort to cool tempers, saying he was prepared to spend hours listening to me, to find out what was worrying me.

"Mr Lee used to be sitting with me at this table," he said, tapping his conference table in the Residency. "We spent many late hours discussing many problems. In spite of everything, he still insisted on joining us. Now why bring up all these issues? It is very bad." The Tunku said he had to fight against speaking in parliament because if he did so, he would have to attack me and he did not want to do that.

I read that as a ray of hope and responded immediately by saying, "Let's talk and resolve our difficulties, but these talks should touch on certain important and fundamental objectives." I chided the "hatchet men", the slogan-shouting communal extremists, for their "rough talk and strong abrasive words. ... To these people I make this plea, be like the Tunku, talk nicely, politely and calmly and win the hearts of the people of Singapore."

∽

On 16 June, the Tunku left for London to attend the Commonwealth Prime Ministers' Conference.

That same day, Ong Eng Guan suddenly resigned from the Legislative Assembly, giving the reason that "the Assembly served no more useful purpose". He had been silent and inactive, completely sidelined by the events that had overtaken Singapore since merger. There had not been a squeak from him during the two communal riots, nor on any issue. The following day, he asked the government not to delay the by-election as he wanted to stand again. When he did not, he lost all credibility and sank into obscurity.

We believed that the federal government had influenced Ong Eng Guan to resign, through an MCA member who was Ong's former political secretary when he was mayor, in 1957–59. They wanted a by-election to test how much support the PAP had. If the Barisan could defeat us, they could neutralise PAP leaders using the Internal Security Act, without much agitation against our detention.

On nomination day for the by-election, 30 June, we fielded Lee Khoon Choy and the Barisan nominated Ong Chang Sam, one of the PAP assemblymen who had defected. It was a short campaign of nine days with polling on 10 July. The mood of the people had completely changed. They knew all in Singapore were in deep trouble, and that they had to choose between the PAP and the Barisan after deciding which party could better safeguard Singapore's survival and future. We put to the electorate the choice between the PAP's "Malaysian Malaysia" and the Barisan's "Crush Malaysia", so that the by-election would prove to the Alliance government that Singapore was for a Malaysian Malaysia.

Dr Lee Siew Choh denounced it as a communal and neo-colonial slogan. Yet when asked by the press, Razak said it did not matter whether the PAP or the Barisan won. That confirmed our suspicion that UMNO and the MCA were indeed testing the support the PAP had in Singapore among the Chinese-speaking, of whom the Hong Lim constituency in the heart of Chinatown would be representative. Further evidence appeared in *Utusan Melayu* editorials urging people to vote for the Barisan candidate, although there were few Malays in the ward.

In the middle of the by-election, Ismail issued an expulsion order against Alex Josey on the grounds that it would be "conducive to the good of the Federation". When asked about it in London, the Tunku said Josey had indulged in activities aimed at disrupting interracial harmony. In an article published in the Australian monthly *The Bulletin*, he had given undue emphasis to differences in leadership between the Tunku and me. We suspected the worst, and Chin Chye called a press conference to say that Josey's expulsion was linked to further repressive measures that would follow if the central government continued to placate the Ultras. Chin Chye disclosed:

> "We know that soon after the last meeting of parliament and the first public rally of the Malaysian Solidarity Convention in Singapore on June 6, instructions were given to make a case for Mr Lee's arrest. We urge the central government not to believe that with Mr Lee out of the way, the ministers of the PAP government will quietly acquiesce in his detention."

Every minister knew that removing me would not remove the problem – Malay domination over the other races – and all of them sat together with Chin Chye at the press conference to show solidarity and that none of them was prepared to take over from me. On 10 July, Razak described Chin Chye's allegation as "too wild and mischievous to merit any comment", but we had had the information from George Bogaars, director of Special Branch in Singapore. Razak's denial came on polling day. That night, Lee Khoon Choy won 59 per cent of the ballot in the Hong Lim by-election, a sharp reversal of the result two years before when the PAP gained only 26 per cent. We had more than doubled our votes.

The next day, Senu said in a speech directed at me that non-Malays must not take advantage of the hospitality extended to them in Malaysia. I replied that I was enjoying no one's hospitality; I was in Malaysia as of right. A week later, Malaysian Solidarity Convention leaders met in Singapore to issue a statement warning that the nation would head for serious trouble once a distinction was made between Malaysians "as a matter of right" and Malaysians "as a matter of hospitality". They viewed with concern the "naked and open exploitation of religious and racial emotions against those who mobilise opinion for a Malaysian Malaysia", and announced plans to hold a series of rallies throughout the Federation.

Responding to this, Senu protested, "We have explained this a thousand times. We work for all Malaysians regardless of their origin. Otherwise there won't be the Alliance Party. ... Of course, we want a Malaysian Malaysia. We formulated that concept." Razak followed Senu on 24 July when he referred to the People's Action Party's "Malaysian Malaysia" slogan and said that it was the Alliance and not the PAP that had first conceived the idea, and in an interview in the official organ of UMNO, Ismail made it clear that the Alliance government wanted a Malaysian Malaysia, though not one on the lines advocated by the PAP government. The Alliance concept was based on two factors – racial harmony and a unified non-racial Malaysia.

I welcomed these developments. They represented a great advance on the position UMNO had earlier been taking. They now agreed with our position, albeit without sincerity except for Ismail. Things were on the move. Everyone felt that they were never going to be the same again.

Razak had earlier sent word that he wanted to talk to me, and on 29 June I saw him in his office at the defence ministry in Kuala Lumpur. He was tense, fidgety and ill-at-ease. I deplored the damage the *Utusan* had done and was still doing, pouring out racist poison day after day. I complained about the double-faced policy of UMNO, that while the top leaders reached reasonable agreements and political truces with us, the secondary leaders kept up a screech of hate in the *Utusan* and the *Malayan Merdeka*, which circulated in the villages. I said any future agreements must be in writing and made known to all, including the secondary leaders, and that the clamour in the Malay press must stop. Otherwise, any political accommodation was meaningless. Razak replied that this was very difficult and they would have to think it over.

The most significant statement he made was that "we must decide whether you are going to work with us or to fight us". I said he knew the attitude of the PAP, that we had always wanted to work with UMNO, but that UMNO, and in particular the Ultras, were determined that we should be crushed. I had seen how they had broken up multiracial parties in Sabah along communal lines and were attempting to do the same in Sarawak. I had no doubt that once they had settled the two North Borneo states, they would turn the heat on Singapore and break us up too. They had fixed Donald Stephens, chief minister of Sabah, and were fixing Stephen Kalong Ningkan, chief minister of Sarawak. I reminded Razak that I was present at the Residency in Kuala Lumpur when the Tunku himself had laid down these conditions for Stephens to remain in office: henceforth, the Chinese in Sabah would join SNAP (Sabah National Party), the Kadazans, UPKO (United Pasok Momogun Kadazan Organisation) and the Malays, USNO (United Sabah National Organisation). Razak replied feebly that UMNO had had nothing to do with that – it had been the wish of the Alliance leaders in Sabah. I said this was not so, because when I discussed the fragmentation with Stephens, he had been very unhappy about it.

It was a most uncomfortable two hours. Razak did not want to face the issues I raised and there was no meeting of minds. He left me with a clear impression that UMNO would not budge from its basic principle of a Malay-based political system that would not tolerate encroachment by other races on its exclusive Malay domain. It was Singapore that had to adjust and accommodate itself to the communal structures that had existed in Malaya before merger, and these could not change. Razak was rigid on this, but we could not accept it. I still hoped that the Tunku might be strong enough to be different.

It was not to be. A year later, Razak gave a completely different account of what had taken place. In an article published in UMNO's 20th anniversary souvenir, he wrote that just after the riots in July 1964, I had urged the Tunku and himself to take us into the Alliance government as the only way to ensure communal harmony, since it was the PAP that represented the Chinese of Malaysia. But they had rejected my request outright, whereupon we had started to attack UMNO and the Malays by coining the irresponsible slogan "Malaysian Malaysia" in order to win the support of the non-Malays, creating tension between the Malays and Chinese that could endanger the security of the country. Razak had forgotten that less than a year earlier, in July 1965, Senu and he had publicly claimed that the Alliance had conceived and formulated the concept of a Malaysian Malaysia. He added that once I saw the danger, I pretended to find ways of easing the situation in order to save Malaysia. That had led to the meeting between us on 29 June, six weeks before we left the Federation. Razak wrote:

> "Strangely, at the meeting, Lee Kuan Yew had no intention to find a way out of the impasse, but strongly insisted that the Tunku and I should cast off the 'extremists' in the UMNO if the central government wanted his cooperation. ... He mentioned the names of the so-called 'extremists' alleged to have been responsible for the tense atmosphere. I rejected his allegation about the 'extremists' and told him that UMNO was a disciplined party, and if he wanted to cooperate either with the Alliance or UMNO, he should have confidence in the Tunku, myself and others. I asked him for an

assurance that he and his friends would not make provocative remarks against the Malays or interfere with UMNO's domestic affairs. Unfortunately, he declined to give the assurance."

In response, I published extracts of the note I had made immediately after my meeting with him. I pointed out that I could not have suggested a coalition to the Tunku in July 1964 after the riots. The Tunku had come back to Kuala Lumpur from London only on 14 August, and told me the next day that the British prime minister, Sir Alec Douglas Home, had advised him to form a national government to include the PAP. I added that it was not the desire of the Singapore government to revive old controversies, but inaccurate accounts of such top-level discussions made it impossible for Singapore ministers to remain silent.

There was no reply from Razak. Many years later I read in the Tunku's official biography by Mubin Sheppard that Razak had reported to him in London that he could not get through to me and persuade me to stop politicking. That, the Tunku said, had confirmed him in his determination to get Singapore out of Malaysia.

42. The Tunku Wants Us Out

The Tunku was struck by an attack of shingles while he was in London in mid-June 1965. Lim Kim San, whom he had taken along as a member of his delegation to the Prime Ministers' Conference, visited him in hospital and wrote to me on 23 June:

> "The old boy is confined in bed with shingles and is in low spirits. He is surrounded with people all the time but I managed to have a word with him. He still thinks of having a rearrangement but does not know what form it should take but at the same time he thinks there is no urgency at all and it could be undertaken after Confrontation.
>
> "He has not discussed this with anybody here and I quite believe him, for when I met Arthur Bottomley (secretary of state, Commonwealth Relations) at the Commonwealth Conference, he told me that his report from Malaya indicated that things are OK and that the Malays, with exception of a few of the Ultras whom he considered to be well under control by Tunku and/or Razak, are now less sensitive and that the situation is less explosive. He was told that even the extremists are holding their horses and that with Tunku away none of them will start anything for fear of being accused of taking advantage of Tunku's absence and illness. I told him (Bottomley) that trouble started every time he was away. But he said not to worry ... He was friendly and pleased to see me and we broke off the discussion just before the meeting was called to order. ..."

After he returned from London in early July, Kim San met me to describe the Tunku's condition and mood. The Tunku had said, "You can tell your prime minister he can attend the next Prime Ministers'

Conference on his own." I asked him what the Tunku meant by that. Would there be a rearrangement? Would Singapore become a special state in a confederation? Kim San could not quite fathom what the Tunku had in mind. Years later, recording my oral history in 1981, I sent him a copy of his 23 June 1965 letter. He commented, "On reflection, as I have told you several times, Tunku indicated indirectly that he would give Singapore independence. I was too obtuse then to catch the significance of some of his remarks." Kim San had concentrated on the possibility of a rearrangement and missed the bigger implications of the Tunku's cryptic statements. In London he had met the Tunku only once, which meant that as early as 23 June 1965 the Tunku was thinking in terms of a total separation.

In the meantime, Keng Swee had been away in Germany for more than a month for medical treatment. In mid-July he saw me to say he had just met Razak at his residence and unexpectedly found Ismail and Ja'afar Albar there as well. He said Razak wanted to discuss a rearrangement that would allow both sides to disengage from what would be a disastrous collision.

I discussed with Keng Swee all the possible alternatives and decided that anything was worth trying if we could avoid a racial collision. Keng Swee saw Razak and Ismail again in Kuala Lumpur on 20 July. He told them that only I, Lim Kim San and Eddie Barker knew of his discussions with Razak. Chin Chye and Raja were too deeply involved in the Malaysian Solidarity Convention to consider any rearrangement. He assured Razak that I should be able to carry the PAP if the business was properly handled, but that any premature leak would jeopardise it.

Keng Swee then asked me for a written authorisation to continue the discussions and conclude the rearrangements that he could reach, including, he said, a "hiving-off" from the federation. I feared trouble if the talks leaked prematurely, first, with the British, who had opposed any rearrangement, and next, with Raja, Chin Chye and Pang Boon, who would be against any disengagement from the political contest in peninsular Malaysia where they came from and their families were. But the stakes were high and a collision would be bloody. I wrote a note authorising Keng Swee to discuss with Razak, Ismail and such other federal ministers of comparable authority concerned in these matters in the central government any proposal for any constitutional rearrangements of Malaysia.

Keng Swee came back to report that Razak wanted a total hiving-off. Razak had made two points: first, he wanted Keng Swee to confirm I was in favour. Keng Swee said, "Yes, provided it is done quickly before Lee's commitment and involvement in the Solidarity Convention makes it impossible for him to get out." Ismail accepted this point. Razak appeared both relieved and incredulous because, according to Keng Swee, he half-expected me to reject the idea. Keng Swee said I was realistic enough to see that a collision was imminent and that the consequences were incalculable.

The second point Razak made was that the hiving-off must be a concerted move. In other words, the PAP must support it. He proposed that the Federation and Singapore jointly tell the British of their intentions. He felt they would agree if we stood firm together. Keng Swee pointed out that this course of action must fail. The British would adamantly oppose a separation. He reminded them of how thoroughly Antony Head and his team had thwarted the less radical rearrangement we had agreed with the Tunku in February. Keng Swee urged that the separation be presented to the British as a *fait accompli* when parliament reassembled on 9 August. The necessary constitutional amendments must first be made granting Singapore independence, with all three readings taking place on that day. Ismail readily agreed to this. Razak was greatly amused and said that perhaps PAP tactics were the best. Keng Swee added that he saw no objection if, as an act of courtesy, Lord Head, as British high commissioner to Malaysia, was informed of our intentions at 9:30 am on the day, just half an hour before the independence bill was introduced. This was received with great merriment.

Ismail said two documents needed to be drawn up: an amendment to the constitution making the secession of Singapore possible, and an act giving Singapore independence under that amendment. In the interests of security, civil servants should not be brought in to prepare these, and he asked if we could do the work. Ismail and Razak must have thought through the necessary constitutional procedures. Keng Swee said Eddie (Singapore's minister for law) would try to produce a draft for them in a week to ten days, and that was agreed. Keng Swee impressed upon both of them the imperative need for secrecy and added pointedly to Ismail that his expatriate civil servants, in particular, should not be told anything about the matter either.

Keng Swee sensed that Razak felt greatly relieved and grateful to him for his part in promoting this solution. He really believed it would not only avert the calamity that was now dangerously impending, but also put an end to the tension and misery he had had to endure in recent months. It had all taken just half an hour but they spent another 20 minutes exchanging pleasantries, as Razak insisted that Keng Swee should not leave too early. He also arranged for a police car to take him to the airport transit lounge so as to avoid any journalists.

Immediately after Keng Swee reported to me on that meeting, I saw Eddie in my office. The work was so sensitive that I was not certain our state advocate-general was the best person to undertake it. He might not be able to keep it secret. Eddie himself went to the law library of the University of Singapore to look for precedents, and found one in the break-up of the Federation of the West Indies. To limit the number of persons who needed to know, he dictated his drafts not to his own personal assistant but to Wong Chooi Sen, the cabinet secretary, an officer whose loyalty and discretion were beyond doubt. The only others involved were Stanley Stewart, as head of the civil service, and George

Bogaars, as head of Special Branch. I had called in Bogaars to be quite certain he was confident we could contain any threat from the communists in an independent Singapore as long as we did not allow them to rebuild their organisation. He assured me that we could.

Eddie drafted the two documents, but I asked him to draw up a third, a proclamation of independence. I showed his drafts to Choo. I was still not satisfied with them. I wanted our agreement with the state of Johor, upon which we depended heavily for our water supply, to be included in them and endorsed by the two governments as a formal treaty to be honoured as such. I was too hard-pressed, and told Choo, who was a good conveyancing lawyer, to find a neat way to achieve this. Once she had done so, I approved the drafts for Eddie to submit to Razak. Despite all the uncertainty, I decided to stick to my planned holiday and wait to see whether the Tunku wanted to go on with hiving-off or would change his mind.

There were reasons for doubt. Just the week before, Tan Siew Sin had visited Singapore for a meeting of the University Students' Union to say that the central government would go ahead with their decision to close the Bank of China in Singapore the following month. Despite unofficial protests broadcast over Radio Peking, he denied that the closure would affect trade between Malaysia and China. This indicated no inclination to disengage, let alone have Singapore leave Malaysia altogether. Next, Razak, while touring the southern islands on 25 July, made tendentious statements calculated to stir up Malay sentiment against the PAP, saying that the uncooperative spirit of our government made it difficult for Kuala Lumpur to extend its rural development programme to the local Malays. This unnecessarily mischievous move also made me wonder whether Keng Swee had correctly read and reported Razak, that he really wanted Singapore to hive off. Something was up. Could they, in fact, be testing the ground with a view to suspending the constitution and appointing a governor? Or planning something else unpleasant?

Keng Swee was also worried. He was uneasy about the burden and the blame he would have to bear if the scheme leaked or was aborted. When I was preparing this book in 1994, he gave me permission to read his oral history recorded in 1980–81, and I learnt that he never pressed Razak for a looser rearrangement as I had asked him to. He knew they wanted Singapore out of their parliament and went along with their desire to have us hive off. Keng Swee also said that he wanted that written undertaking from me because he feared I would balk at separation.

Keng Swee called on Razak at Federation House in Singapore on 27 July, to discover that he indeed had second thoughts about the hiving-off. Keng Swee again found him hesitating and constantly reversing his position. He complained of insomnia and appeared morose and despondent. In a rambling 90-minute conversation, he said he had written to the Tunku about their discussions three days after their last meeting, and it was now up to the Tunku to decide, but he would return from London only on 4 August. Razak did not expect him to rush matters, and it was doubtful if the independence bill could then be arranged for the 9th – for one thing, there were various interests to consult, like the sultans.

He then expressed misgivings about the consequences of independence for Singapore – supposing the government entered into a deal with Peking? Razak also put up totally unacceptable ideas about defence, saying Malaysia would have to run the Singapore army. Keng Swee told him that could not be. We would raise and maintain our own army, but for operational purposes it would be put under whoever commanded all Malaysian forces opposing Indonesia. Razak said, "Oh. So the present system will be retained, that is, we command your army?" In order not to deepen further his doubts on the subject, Keng Swee did not point out that this arrangement would hold true only during Confrontation.

Razak next said independence for Singapore meant a resounding victory for Sukarno. Did we want to give Sukarno a boost? Why not have a partial disengagement? Keng Swee told him we were willing to have it any way he liked, even going on as at present. Keng Swee said Singapore's position was strengthening by the day with support from Commonwealth countries. This depressed Razak further, and he reverted to saying that there was no solution other than complete separation – but then backed off again and talked about some kind of confederation whereby Kuala Lumpur controlled defence and foreign affairs.

Keng Swee stressed the need for an early decision before our commitment to the Malaysian Solidarity Convention became irreversible, but while he readily agreed to this, Razak continued to harp on various objections to the whole scheme: Tan Siew Sin was against separation, and UMNO's general support for it could not be taken for granted. He feared opposition. But, on the other hand, the available police and military forces would not be enough to bottle up widespread disorders if Singapore remained in Malaysia, so, after all, perhaps hiving-off was the only solution. He asked Keng Swee if he could suggest another way out. Keng Swee said he could not.

Yet through the press, Razak called upon the Singapore government to work hard hand-in-hand with Kuala Lumpur to carry out development schemes for the Malays. I began to fear that we were again on a collision course.

I was still uncertain as to what would happen, whether there would be a rearrangement, a separation, or a collision, when Philip Moore paid me a farewell call on 30 July; he was to be posted to the ministry of defence in London. It was a highly charged, emotional parting. The British, above all, had to be kept in the dark about our discussions and I had to make sure I did not give any hint of the changes we were secretly negotiating to Moore who had been so understanding and supportive. I was grateful for all he had done, I told him, but I had to go on with Malaysia regardless of the consequences. I had persuaded the people to join the Federation and I could not abandon them. It was my responsibility to see that the constitution was honoured. I could not back out. His expression showed grave concern for my personal safety and the future of Singapore.

On 31 July, I left Singapore to attend a PAP rally in Kuala Lumpur and go on to the Cameron Highlands for my annual holiday with Choo and the children. Before I left Kuala Lumpur, I called on Antony Head at Carcosa for half an hour. I was apprehensive that he might have got a whiff of what was going on. I knew that if he had the slightest hint of it, he was resourceful and strong enough to unscramble whatever we had agreed upon, just as he had thwarted our plans for rearrangement in February. He showed no sign of suspecting anything was amiss, and I was satisfied that this time Razak and Ismail had not leaked anything to Fenner, who would certainly have informed him.

In fact, on 6 August, Head sent this assessment to London:

"Future prospects are gloomy. There is little chance of a political *détente* since neither side trusts the other. A modified form of disengagement without altering the constitution is possible but not likely. Lee's employment overseas now seems to be ruled out and the Malay extremists are growing increasingly powerful. The most likely outcome is renewed racial riots possibly of a much bigger scale than before. ... One of the main causes of the present trouble is the more extreme Malay chauvinists who are led by Senu, the minister for information, Khir Johari, the minister for education, and Ja'afar Albar, the secretary-general of UMNO; Senu and Ja'afar Albar in particular are involved in a competition to be more Malay than each other. If they could be squashed or silenced it would be most helpful; but Razak has shown that he is not prepared to be at all tough with these men, no doubt fearing that they might, by the appeal of their chauvinism, outflank him in his present position of heir apparent to the Tunku. He has therefore cautiously decided to move sufficiently in their direction to safeguard his own political position. ..."

On British policy, Head wrote:

"As long as a hostile Indonesia threatens Malaysia's independence and territorial integrity, our interest in the stability of Southeast Asia, our obligations under the Defence Agreement, and Malaysia's need for help against a greatly superior enemy, seem certain to require our continued presence here. ... But to stay could cause difficulties for us, for I think it would be both unwise and improvident for British policy to assume that there will be a prolonged period of comparative stability in Malaysia."

The day after the rally at the Chin Woo Stadium in Kuala Lumpur, I drove to the Camerons, where I rested, played golf and walked with the children, while I waited for the telephone call from Keng Swee and Eddie to say that I should meet them in Kuala Lumpur. I did not want Head to suspect that I was back in Kuala Lumpur and up to something.

Keng Swee went to Kuala Lumpur for a meeting with Razak on 3 August, the day before the Tunku was due home. Razak came to the point quickly. He said he had received the Tunku's reply. The Tunku was in favour, subject to two conditions: (a) Singapore was to make an adequate military contribution to our joint defence and enter into a defence agreement with Malaysia, and (b) no treaty was to be entered into that would contravene the objectives of that agreement. Keng Swee recorded that many detailed proposals were made in the course of the discussion: there should be a defence council; all Singapore forces should be under a joint military command for operational purposes, and the central government would help to train them; Singapore should raise an infantry brigade, and patrol Singapore waters with our own craft. Ismail also wanted Malaysian embassies and high commissions around the world to conduct Singapore's external relations.

Keng Swee assessed their object was to limit the size of our armed forces and have a voice in controlling them. Ismail was open about this but Razak dissembled. Keng Swee said we could not afford an extensive military establishment anyway – four battalions and some patrol boats would be the most we could contribute. Razak appeared very pleased and said Keng Swee should be Singapore's defence minister, but the question of overall command remained vague and the peacetime status of the Singapore forces after Confrontation was still not raised. This was to lead to trouble later.

They asked if Keng Swee had the drafts prepared. He said he had and showed the papers to Razak. Razak read the agreement, skipped the proclamation, but carefully scrutinised the amendment bill. He appeared satisfied and returned the documents, asking that the points about our defence arrangements and external treaty be incorporated in the second draft. They then discussed the timetable. Razak wanted his attorney-general to examine the texts. Keng Swee suggested that if we produced them on 6 August, after the Tunku's return, and they put up any counter-proposals or amendments the following day, agreement could be reached on 7 August, the documents signed on 8 August, and the whole exercise could be wound up on the 9th.

They pointed out that the Menteri Besars of the Malay states and the chief ministers of Sabah and Sarawak had to be informed. Ismail said that the latter must be detached from their British advisers, and it would be best to summon them to Kuala Lumpur – the welcoming party for the Tunku could provide the pretext. Keng Swee asked if they could count on the Sabah and Sarawak votes. Razak had apparently done his arithmetic and said they didn't expect any trouble.

Ismail then raised the question of the need for time to print the agreement, the bill and the proclamation. Keng Swee concluded that they wanted to go through with the exercise as quickly as possible, but a number of tricky problems stood in the way: for instance, would there also be time to get the Sabah and Sarawak chief ministers to Kuala Lumpur on 8 August? Flight schedules might make it impossible. Keng

Swee felt he should insist on sealing the agreement before anybody was informed; it was evident that without the utmost good luck and efficiency it would be tough going to push everything through by 9 August. After an hour's meeting, Keng Swee phoned me in the Cameron Highlands from Singapore House (in Kuala Lumpur) to tell me the outcome, in Mandarin. It was not his strongest language, but there was no direct dialling to the Camerons in 1965, and trunk calls had to go through operators who spoke no Mandarin.

On the morning of Friday, 6 August, I travelled by car to Kuala Lumpur. Choo and the children stayed behind in the Camerons until Saturday so people would see them and think I was still there. Neither Keng Swee nor Eddie was sure that the Tunku, who was now back, had not changed his mind, in which case everything was off. But when I arrived in Kuala Lumpur that afternoon, they were there with the documents. After I had studied and approved them, they went to see Razak, Ismail and Kadir Yusof, the attorney-general. The meeting went on for hours and hours as I waited impatiently and alone at Singapore House. Late in the evening, Eddie phoned to say that Tan Siew Sin wanted amendments included whereby we would take over the guarantees that the central government had given the IMF and the World Bank for loans granted to Singapore, a niggling detail. I agreed to that, and Eddie and Kadir Yusof started work on the drafts. More hours passed before Eddie phoned again to say that Razak's stenographer was so unaccustomed to legal documents that the typing was getting nowhere. As Wong Chooi Sen and my personal assistant Teo Ban Hock were both at Singapore House, Eddie called them to Razak's home, where they did the typing and completed the job, amendments and all. But it took them until well after midnight. When he returned to Singapore House with Keng Swee, Eddie said they had all got drunk while waiting, and when the documents were finally ready, he was the only one sober enough to want to read them before he signed. Razak, who liked Eddie from their hockey-playing days in Raffles College, said, "Eddie, it's your draft, it's your chap who typed the final document, so what are you reading it for?" So Eddie, too, signed without further ado – "*sign buta*" (signing blindly), as he told me in Malay. Keng Swee was so soused that he had gone straight to bed. But Eddie went through the documents, was greatly relieved to find no mistakes, then handed them to me.

After I had quickly scanned the amendments myself, I looked at Eddie and said, "Thanks, Eddie, we've pulled off a bloodless coup." It was a coup against the British government and their vigilant proconsul Head, a constitutional coup engineered right under the noses of the British, Australians and New Zealanders who were defending Malaysia with their armed forces. At very little notice, we had thought of a way to achieve what the Tunku could not accomplish with his own staff because it had to be carried out in great secrecy and the shortest possible time, including three readings of the bill in one session of parliament on a certificate of urgency, or it could never have succeeded.

I had been apprehensive that Head would probably have advised his government to acquiesce at extra-constitutional measures to neutralise the PAP if he had found out in time to stop it. But with the documents signed, even if the British persuaded the Tunku and his colleagues not to take it through parliament, once I had published the agreements and the proclamation of independence in the government gazette, Singapore's relationship with Malaysia would change irrevocably.

Now I had to get my other colleagues to agree. I telephoned Chin Chye to ask him to come up to Kuala Lumpur, although it was after midnight. Next I spoke to the Istana telephone operator. The Istana exchange was manned 24 hours a day, and the man on duty that night was a most reliable retainer from the days of the British governors. I told him to get a car to pick up Chin Chye immediately and bring him to Kuala Lumpur by early next morning. I then spoke to Raja and asked him to drive up. I did not want them to come together because that would arouse speculation that something was up, and also because they would stiffen each other's resolve to oppose any rearrangements of Malaysia, let alone a clean break.

Chin Chye arrived early that morning. As he came in by the front door, Eddie left by the back to avoid meeting him. I brought Chin Chye up to date and showed him the documents. He was upset and disturbed. Shortly afterwards, Raja arrived. Othman Wok, our minister for social affairs, had driven him up in his car. Then Keng Swee joined us, and we sat down and talked. For a few hours Chin Chye and Raja contemplated the painful decision confronting them. They did not want to sign.

At about noon on 7 August, I went to the Residency to see the Tunku. I waited for some 30 to 40 minutes in the sitting room while he was conferring with some of his officials in the dining room – I could see them in deep conversation through the glass door. Then he came out and sat with me alone for about 40 minutes.

I began, "We have spent years to bring about Malaysia. The best part of my adult life was to work towards Malaysia, from 1954 to 1963. We have had only less than two years of Malaysia. Do you really want to break it up? Don't you think it wiser to go back to our original plan, which the British stopped, a looser federation or a confederation?"

But from his body language, I knew the Tunku had made up his mind. He said, "No. I am past that. There is no other way now. I have made up my mind; you go your way, we go our own way. So long as you are in any way connected with us, we will find it difficult to be friends because we are involved in your affairs and you will be involved in ours. Tomorrow, when you are no longer in Malaysia and we are no longer quarrelling either in parliament or in the constituencies, we'll be friends again, and we'll need each other, and we'll cooperate."

I dropped the subject. I had prepared myself for a long session, but once I saw he had closed his mind to any alternative, I told him that my difficulty was with Chin Chye, Raja, Pang Boon and all those Singapore ministers whose families were in peninsular Malaysia. He told me that I had to settle that problem myself. I sought his help; would he see them?

"No. It is unnecessary," he replied.

I returned to Singapore House to report our discussion to the others. Chin Chye sat at the desk by the foot of the stairs near the dining room, writing something. As I walked up the stairs, I saw that he had drawn a line down the middle of a piece of paper; on the left, he had put the arguments for, and on the right, the arguments against separation. It was Chin Chye, the careful academic. Raja, a chain-smoker, was outside on the patio puffing away. I drew Othman aside to ask if he would sign. He was a Malay and would again become a member of a minority if he did. He had no difficulty in signing, he said, but he was worried about the communists in Singapore. Twenty-five years later, in an interview on the anniversary of our independence, he recalled that I assured him, "Don't worry, that's my problem. I'll handle that."

After making no progress with both Chin Chye and Raja for some hours, I said to Chin Chye, "Why not see the Tunku? The old boy says he can't hold the situation. You'd better see him, because I have seen him and I have come to the conclusion that this has gone beyond argument." He agreed, so I went to the Tunku again that afternoon and told him that I had two ministers, Chin Chye and Raja, who were not going to sign and were absolutely adamant about it. Their families were in Malaya and they wanted to see him.

The Tunku was firm. "No, I don't want to see them. Nothing more to discuss. You tell them."

I said, "I have told them. At least you must write to them. Then they will take your word as final."

The Tunku went off to his desk and wrote a letter to Chin Chye, which he handed to me, saying, "Here, give this to him. There is no need to discuss anything. It is finished."

The Tunku's unsealed letter read:

"Dear Chin Chye,

"I am writing to tell you that I have given the matter of our break with Singapore my utmost consideration and I find that in the interest of our friendship and the security and peace of Malaysia as a whole, there is absolutely no other way out. If I were strong enough and able to exercise complete control of the situation I might perhaps have delayed action, but I am not, and so while I am able to counsel tolerance and patience I think the amicable settlement of our differences in this way is the only possible way out. I request you most earnestly to agree.

Yours sincerely
(Sgd) Tunku Abdul Rahman"

As I was leaving, I met Tan Siew Sin. I was angry and bitter at his short-sightedness and stupidity. He had thwarted our industrialisation and brought about the separation almost as much as had the Malay Ultras. He had been determined to frustrate us at every turn. Apart from his personal dislike of Keng Swee and me, he believed that any concession to Singapore would help the PAP to win over the Chinese in Malaysia. He could not see that without Singapore, the position of the Chinese in Malaysia must weaken.

I could not help telling him that day, "Today is the day of your victory, the day of my defeat; but in five to ten years, you will certainly feel sad about it."

He smirked. I do not think he understood me then, or later. He was only relieved and happy that his position as leader of the MCA and the MCA's position in Malaysia were now secure. The threat from the PAP and the Malaysian Solidarity Convention had been removed. The MCA would be supreme. But secure and supreme were relative terms in this case. Four years later, in May 1969, Malay rioters in Kuala Lumpur would kill and maim hundreds of Chinese and burn their homes and cars. In 1973, when Ismail died, Prime Minister Razak promoted Hussein Onn to be his deputy. Loyal though Tan had been to the Alliance and to UMNO, he was a Chinese, and he discovered that he could not be deputy prime minister. He resigned in 1974, overcome with shame and bitter disappointment. He did not understand that he had already lost out when he had unwittingly helped to get Singapore expelled from Malaysia the decade before.

In his book *Looking Back* (1977), the Tunku wrote:

> "What he [Tan Siew Sin] succeeded in getting went far beyond my idea, for not only did the Central Government exercise important powers in the State's administration, but Singapore found itself committed to financial development in the Borneo States on a very substantial scale. I felt that once we were enmeshed in Singapore's day-to-day life and administration, and controlling the finance of the State, the inevitable consequence would be that the Singapore Government would want to take a full share in the Malaysian administration; and if we were not prepared to give Singapore the right, then Mr Lee Kuan Yew's attack on Malaysia was justified."

When I returned to Singapore House after running into Tan, I gave the Tunku's letter to Chin Chye. Only then did he and Raja realise that we had indeed reached breaking point. To cut short further arguments, I told Chin Chye that if he did not accept separation I would not go through with it, because it would split the PAP leadership and cause confusion among our followers both in Singapore and in Malaysia. I would abide by the majority decision not to sign, and not to secede. But Chin Chye and Raja must take the responsibility; if blood was spilt, it would not be on my conscience. Soon after that, Chin Chye signed, then Raja.

Not unnaturally, my ministerial colleagues were divided according to where they were born and brought up. Those from Singapore accepted the separation, but those from Malaya were very upset. Chin Chye had been born and brought up in Taiping, Perak, and was attached to his family, whom he visited regularly. Raja had been born in Ceylon but raised in Seremban, Negeri Sembilan, where he had many relatives and friends. Through him, they had all become politically involved with the PAP during the general election in April the previous year; his brother had stood as a PAP candidate, but lost. By agreeing to the separation, however reluctantly, Raja and Chin Chye had let down those close to them. Worse, they felt keenly, as I did, that they had betrayed the other leaders of the Malaysian Solidarity Convention. They had been the moving force behind it. For those left behind in Malaysia, separation was a disaster because it changed the racial arithmetic. With Singapore out, it was no longer 40 per cent Malay, 40 per cent Chinese, 20 per cent others. The Malays were again in the majority, and there was now little hope of any multiracial party winning power constitutionally even in the very long term.

Pang Boon was also very emotional about the break. He had been born and educated in Kuala Lumpur, had strong roots in Selangor, and like Chin Chye and Raja, was deeply involved in the work of the Malaysian Solidarity Convention, for which he was just then busy organising a meeting in Kuala Lumpur. When I told him of the break, he was very distressed. Chin Chye helped persuade him to accept the unavoidable, but he signed with the utmost reluctance. Lee Khoon Choy had been born and bred in Penang; on 8 August he, too, was in Malaya organising a Malaysian Solidarity Convention meeting for two weeks later. When he arrived in Kuala Lumpur on the morning of 9 August, he was shocked when told by Chin Chye that the convention was finished.

My next problem was to return to Singapore without running into any British, Australian and New Zealand diplomats, and get the other ministers to sign. It was a very contentious issue, and I wanted to avoid a split in the cabinet. I explained the problem to the Tunku, who arranged for a small RMAF propeller-driven plane to fly me down the next day, Sunday. I had arranged through the Istana telephone operator for all ministers who were not in Kuala Lumpur to meet me at Sri Temasek. The Singapore-born ministers were neither jubilant nor relieved. They accepted that this was the way it had to be, and they signed. Kim San was relieved it had happened. Eddie, who had prepared and signed the documents on the night of 6 August, was from Singapore. Nyuk Lin was from Seremban but had settled in Singapore after marrying there before the war. His family was no longer in Malaya and he was less affected.

By then, it was late afternoon and I had one of the two sets of separation documents sent back to the Tunku by his RMAF plane, duly signed. Stanley Stewart was standing by with the government printer and his staff. He gave them the other set and locked them up inside the Government Printing Office, where they were held incommunicado until the documents were ready to be issued as a special government gazette and a proclamation at 10 o'clock on Monday, 9 August.

Meanwhile, I had arranged for Choo and the children to come down by car from the Cameron Highlands to Kuala Lumpur on Saturday afternoon and leave first thing Sunday morning for Singapore, arriving late in the afternoon. We decided to spend that night at Sri Temasek. We would be safer there if any UMNO Malays in Singapore should riot when the news broke the next morning.

I had a busy time that evening, meeting Le Cain, the police commissioner, to discuss the necessary precautions to be taken, and George Bogaars, to make sure Special Branch was on the alert for any trouble from any quarter. I also saw Stanley Stewart to arrange for all permanent secretaries to be assembled and briefed the next day.

Razak had wanted the PAP MPs to be present in parliament on 9 August to vote for the bills. Keng Swee and Eddie told Razak that no PAP MPs would attend. It would have been too painful for us to face the other Malaysian Solidarity Convention leaders we were leaving behind. We instructed those of our 12 PAP MPs who were not ministers and therefore not in the know to stay away. Then I settled with Bogaars the encoding of similar messages to be sent to the three Commonwealth prime ministers to tell them of the separation and why there was no other way. The one to Australia read:

"By the time you have decoded this message you will know that the Tunku has proclaimed and I have agreed and simultaneously also proclaimed Singapore as a separate and sovereign nation. But for your staunch support for democratic practices in Malaysia, I and my government would have been scrubbed out by near-fascist methods although non-communist we may be. Because of your moral support we were spared and given the choice either to leave Malaysia whilst remaining under the umbrella of the Anglo Malaysian Defence Treaty or face the consequence, which in the Tunku's own words is communal trouble and bloodshed, leaving unspoken the inevitable consequence, which is either (that) fascist methods temporarily succeed in holding the situation or chaos results in eventual communist victory. You can depend on my colleagues and me to ensure that Singapore will remain a non-communist nation so long as we are in authority and whatever the sacrifice we have to make. We will always want to work on terms of honour and friendship with Australia. It is ironic that because of your personal concern for me and my colleagues and what we represent, such an unfortunate result has ensued. However but for your concern more catastrophic results would have taken place for all of us."

The codes were dictionary-based and by the time the messages were decoded it would be after 10 am in Singapore.

Finally, all I had to do was to sleep. This was difficult because I was fretting; had I overlooked any important item that needed to be buttoned up? I did not look forward to facing our supporters in Malaysia who would feel we had let them down; we had aroused many people's hopes, and they would think that we had made use of them to get Singapore out of a nasty mess. And I was not proud of repaying with this separation the staunch support given me by Harold Wilson, Robert Menzies and Keith Holyoake and their ministers, especially Arthur Bottomley. Most of all, I hoped that nothing would go awry before 10 o'clock the next day.

43. "Talak, Talak, Talak" (I Divorce Thee)

I got up very early on that morning of 9 August 1965 after a fitful night. I had awakened several times to scribble notes of the thousand and one things I had to do. Everything had been timed for the proclamation of independence at 10 am on the radio. I had decided against reading the proclamation personally. I had too many other things to do in quick succession. First, I had to brief government officials in the ministries and departments hitherto under Kuala Lumpur that would now revert to the authority of Singapore. Then, just before the deadline, I met those diplomats who could be assembled at short notice to tell them of Singapore's independence and ask for recognition from their governments. It was emotionally exhausting.

At 10 am, the government gazette containing the two proclamations signed by myself and the Tunku was issued together with other documents connected with the separation. Simultaneously, all radio programmes in Singapore were interrupted for the proclamation to be read out. The word spread like wildfire that Singapore had separated from Malaysia and was now independent, stunning millions of people. Even as the proclamation was being broadcast in Singapore, the Tunku stood up to announce the separation in the federal parliament in Kuala Lumpur. The House had been convened for the three readings of a resolution moved by Razak to enact the Constitution of Malaysia (Singapore Amendment) Bill, 1965 immediately. I had feared unexpected delays, but the Tunku and his colleagues were determined that nothing should stop them. By that evening, both parliament and the senate had completed the readings and the Yang di-Pertuan Agong had given his royal assent. Singapore was out.

The Tunku was blunt and to the point. There were only two courses of action open to him: to take repressive action or to sever all connections with the Singapore state government, which had "ceased to give a measure of loyalty to the central government". Repressive action against the few, he said, would not solve the problem, because the seeds of contempt, fear and hatred had been sown in Singapore. Razak had sought without success to reach an understanding with its leaders, but as soon as one issue was resolved, another cropped up.

When it came to the vote, 126 were in favour and none against. Ja'afar Albar ostentatiously absented himself and at a press conference in Parliament House announced his resignation as secretary-general of UMNO "to save the Tunku from embarrassment". He was fiercely opposed to separation, he said, because it would free Singapore from the control of the central government and make Malaysia illogical.

Talking to the press after his speech in parliament, the Tunku gave an undertaking that "separation will be on the understanding that we shall cooperate closely on matters of defence, trade and commerce", and when I met journalists later that afternoon at Radio & Television Singapore (RTS), I responded by saying, "we shall need each other and we shall cooperate. It is my earnest desire that this be so." Before that I had held a TV press conference at RTS at noon at which I was overwhelmed by my emotions and stopped the cameras for 20 minutes until I recovered my composure and could continue.

I had let down many people in Malaya, Sabah and Sarawak. They had responded to our call of a Malaysian Malaysia. Had they not done so and there was no danger of widespread racial collisions if the Malaysian government arrested us, Singapore would not have been expelled. Because they rallied round and felt as passionately as we did about a Malaysian Malaysia, we were expelled. By accepting separation, I had failed them. That sense of guilt made me break down. It was my moment of anguish. The deed was done, but I was overwrought at the thought of all the

Meeting the press on the morning of Singapore's separation from Malaysia,
9 August 1965.

Talak, Talak, Talak" (I Divorce Thee)

shattered hopes of the millions we had aroused. But while I felt crushed and distraught, there was rejoicing in Chinatown. The merchants let off a barrage of Chinese firecrackers to celebrate their freedom from communal oppression, but in the city itself, office workers were apprehensive that there could be communal trouble, and by four in the afternoon it was unusually quiet – people had gone home early.

For me, it was a very full day, with people I had to meet, and work I had to attend to. My last visitor was Antony Head, who flew in from Kuala Lumpur to see me that night at Sri Temasek. I kept up a bold front, asking him whether he had instructions from his government to extend recognition to Singapore. Of course he had not – there had not been time. Inwardly, I was sorry to have repaid his unremitting efforts to keep Malaysia on track by concealing from him any hint of the impending separation. But I had had no choice. When the news reached London, Harold Wilson was on holiday in the Scilly Isles and Arthur Bottomley, secretary of state for Commonwealth Relations, was in West Africa. The foreign secretary, Michael Stewart, flew to the Scillies for discussions with Wilson, and on 10 August, I received the following message from Wilson through the acting deputy British high commissioner in Singapore:

"I wanted to let you know that we have decided to recognise Singapore as an independent state right away, and that we are announcing this in tomorrow morning's papers. I have seen your message and I much appreciate your kind words. I am glad to know that you want to work on terms of friendship with us. I must say that I was disappointed that we were not consulted before this important step was taken, because, of course, it has major implications for us. We are now thinking very urgently about these. But you may be sure that we wish you well. I am concerned that Sukarno may try to use this development for his own ends. I am sure you will agree that we must all be careful to avoid anything which might help him to make capital out of it."

Wilson's decision had been swift, and once the British government recognised our independence I was confident that we would not have any difficulty in winning international acceptance. But feelings abroad were divided along Cold War lines. While there was jubilation in Jakarta, Moscow and Beijing, there was deep disappointment and anxiety in Britain, Australia, New Zealand, the United States and the West in general.

The reaction of Indonesia was uncertain. On 9 August, Dr Subandrio, the foreign minister, was euphoric: separation proved that Malaysia was a British neo-colonial creation, and Indonesia was now prepared to open diplomatic relations with Singapore. But the next day, after a 90-minute meeting with President Sukarno, he said his government found it difficult to accept the independence of Singapore because of the presence of British military bases there. He did not completely rule out eventual recognition, and authoritative sources confided that Indonesia would have no objection to the bases as long as they were used solely for the island's own defence. In that case, Jakarta might exclude it from Confrontation until the situation crystallised. Indonesia was ready to welcome Singapore as a friend if she could prove she would not allow herself to be used as a stepping stone for aggression by foreign powers.

I replied that Singapore needed the British bases, that if they were closed, 44,000 workers would lose their jobs and the island would be defenceless. Then on 17 August, Indonesia's Independence Day, Sukarno made a powerful and virulent speech in which he told the United States and Britain to get out of Southeast Asia and warned them that the axis of Jakarta, Phnom Penh, Hanoi, Beijing and Pyongyang would defeat imperialism in the region. Next, he ordered the seizure of all American capital in Indonesia. He was living dangerously – as he put it, "*Viva perilissimo*". The Indonesian economy was unravelling by the day, with hyperinflation making the people's lives impossible.

The reactions of the opposition in Singapore revealed their political immaturity. The Singapore Alliance said they were shocked that the PAP had agreed to secession without a fresh mandate from the people, because it did not conform to the wishes they had expressed in the 1962 referendum. Singapore UMNO called for a general election and said that they would fight for the reincorporation of the state into Malaysia. But the most ludicrous response was that of the Barisan Sosialis, who refused to accept the island's "phoney" independence on the grounds that it was a British plot to maintain their domination over it.

The day after separation, Chin Chye and I saw three leaders of the Malaysian Solidarity Convention in the Cabinet Room. It was one of the most painful meetings of my life. I explained how it had all happened, but whatever the reasons, we had let them down and let them down badly. I had to sum up the future publicly by telling the press that since it was necessary for us to be "very correct in our relations with our neighbour and one neighbouring government did not interfere in the political affairs of another", the PAP could no longer be a member of the convention. I was emotional as I went on:

"But for a very small number of people, what we stood for could easily have done a great deal of good for Malaysia and established it for many centuries to come as a stable and viable multiracial nation. ... Kinship and feelings for one another cannot be legislated out by a political decision."

Chin Chye was full of bitterness and remorse.

The most sincere and thoughtful statement on the separation came from Ismail. He spoke at the United Nations when Malaysia, Jordan and the Ivory Coast sponsored Singapore's application for membership on 20 September:

"Notwithstanding the separation, there is the fullest awareness in the leadership both of Malaysia and of Singapore that, constitutionally separated as the two states may be from each other, the identity of their interests and the intertwined activity of the people in every facet of human life, having been pulled together by the

Choo and I, Malaysian Deputy Prime Minister Tun Ismail Abdul Rahman and his wife at Sri Temasek, Istana, April 1972, seven years after separation.

inescapable incidence of geography, subjected to a long and common administration by the accident of history, will, as in the decades past, create the incentive and provide the encouragement to live together as good neighbours. In a variety of common tasks, we share the same attitudes and prize the same ideals. The constitutional bond has been severed; the human bond remains."

It was Ismail who understood and sympathised most with what I wanted to do. But he was only number three, and even if he had been number one, I doubt whether he would have been strong enough to control the Ultras and carry out his policy: the gradual reduction of the privileges of the Malays as they progressed until there was a non-communal society with all races on an equal footing.

One man who almost understood what had happened and why it did was Antony Head. On 11 August, the day after London extended recognition, he said in Kuala Lumpur that the defence agreement by which Britain held military bases in Singapore and Malaysia would now have to be rewritten: this would be only a formality, however, if there were no policy changes. I had great respect for Head, his strength of character, his wisdom and insight into the ways of men and nations. He was to return to Britain although he had been in Kuala Lumpur for less than two years. I wrote to him on 14 September:

"I write to tell you that although we have not always seen eye to eye on the solutions to our problems in Malaysia, I never thought, as you once said over lunch, that you were a fool. On the contrary, I knew you were an exceptionally perceptive and shrewd observer, and furthermore a rugged representative of Her Majesty's Government.

"I am sorry that you will be going in January. Your successor will be in greater need of the qualities of ruggedness which from time to time did not endear you to the Tunku.

"May I thank you for having helped to prevent the Tunku from scrubbing out my government and myself. I happen to have other sources of information, and knew that you were doing your utmost for your government to dissuade the Tunku from doing what comes naturally. That was also what the Ultras wanted him to do."

∞

What were the real reasons for the Tunku, Razak and Ismail to want Singapore out of Malaysia? They must have concluded that if they allowed us to exercise our constitutional rights, they were bound to lose in the long run. The Malaysian Solidarity Convention would have rallied the non-Malays and, most dangerous of all, eventually made inroads into the Malay ground on the peninsula. The attitudes and policies of the PAP had already won the unswerving loyalty of our Malay leaders in Singapore; they never wavered even under the stress of the race riots in 1964, nor did they respond to appeals to race, religion or culture, or to the usual blandishments offered to draw them back into the UMNO fold.

This was the nub of the matter. The PAP leaders were not like the politicians in Malaya. Singapore ministers were not pleasure-loving, nor did they seek to enrich themselves. UMNO had developed to a fine art the practice of accommodating Chinese or Indian ministers in Malaya who proved troublesome, and had, within a few years, extended its practice to Sabah and Sarawak. Razak once offered Keng Swee 5,000 acres of the best quality rubber land, to be planted with seedlings of the best high-yielding strains from the Rubber Research Institute. With an embarrassed laugh, Keng Swee protested that he would not know what to do with it and ducked the inducement.

Nor was it easy to compromise us. Keng Swee and I once accompanied the Tunku and Tan Siew Sin to a "mess" in Kuala Lumpur run by wealthy Chinese merchants. These "messes" were men's clubs where excellent food was provided by the best restaurants, where members and their friends could gamble at mahjong or poker, and where attractive call girls and even starlets were available. We had a good meal, and when they played poker afterwards, I joined in. But as soon as the girls arrived,

Keng Swee and I pleaded pressing engagements and made ourselves scarce. We could not afford to give hostages to fortune. If we had stayed, we would thereafter have been open to pressure from the Malaysian leaders. They considered us difficult, almost as dangerous and elusive to handle as the communists, and much too ideological. Worse, we always acted constitutionally and hence were difficult to fix.

If there had been no Indonesian Confrontation, the Tunku and his colleagues would not have had to depend on the help of British, Australian and New Zealand defence forces, and the outcome would have been different. Because these forces helped to defend Malaysia, their parliaments would have reacted strongly if Malaysia had used unconstitutional methods against Singapore.

This was how Harold Wilson saw the break-up, which he wrote about in his book *The Labour Government 1964–1970*:

> "But a new and potentially dangerous problem was developing in Southeast Asia. Some three or four months earlier, we had received a warning that Tunku Abdul Rahman, the prime minister of Malaysia, was losing his patience with his parliamentary colleague, Lee Kuan Yew (Harry Lee), the Singaporean leader, to the point where Lee was in danger of being arrested and imprisoned. ... The Tunku was becoming more and more incensed with his lively opposition. Some weeks before the Commonwealth conference we had received news of an impending crisis, involving a possible coup against Harry Lee and his colleagues. I felt it necessary to go so far as to let the Tunku know that if he were to take action of this kind, it would be unwise for him to show his face at the Commonwealth conference, since a large number of his colleagues – including myself – would feel that such action was totally opposed to all we believed in as a Commonwealth.
>
> "In the event nothing happened, but on the weekend of 13th–15th August (sic) news came through that the Federation had broken up. There had been angry scenes between the Tunku and Lee. This had led to Singapore being virtually expelled from the

Teeing off on a course near Chequers with British Prime Minister Harold Wilson, April 1966.

Federation and told to set up on its own account. Lee was in a desperate state, bursting into tears in front of the television cameras and regretting the break-up. Nevertheless, he was determined to make a go of the newly independent Singapore. ... We took the necessary decisions and made the dispositions that had to be made, sending very strong messages to both leaders to avoid any action that could lead to an outbreak of hostilities, or, indeed, of internal subversion. We authorised talks to take place to review the Anglo-Malaysian defence agreement, on a basis fair to all the parties concerned."

Wilson was a good friend.

Nothing happened because Head had reported on 15 May 1965 to his minister, Arthur Bottomley, that

"some of UMNO would like to warm things up to the extent that they might find a pretext for what they term 'dealing with' and I mean locking up Lee. I stressed that Lee has now quite an international reputation and that, unless there were cast-iron grounds for 'dealing' with him, such a course would do Malaysia great damage. Although the Tunku said nothing, I have a feeling there is some plot in the back of their minds."

On 17 May, a note was sent to the Commonwealth Relations Office that the prime minister had read the telegram, had underlined the last sentence and minuted: "On X (the quote above), if there is a plot, I hope the Tunku realises this would mean an agonising reappraisal for us. H.W."

On 1 June, Head cabled that he had asked the Tunku if he could still treat with Lee Kuan Yew and bring about some kind of *détente*.

"The Tunku said no, he was determined never again to try and treat with Lee Kuan Yew, whom he did not trust a yard and about whom he was completely disillusioned. I said how was all this going to end, to which the Tunku replied 'I know my duty and I shall not hesitate to do it.'

"This sounded sinister, so I thought it was a good moment to dive in and said that among other things the British government were very worried to have heard about discussion in the press concerning Lee Kuan Yew being put inside. Was the Tunku referring to this? He said that he was.

"I said that if Lee Kuan Yew were put inside for any reason other than for treasonable activities, it would much shock and embarrass the British government and would undoubtedly have far-reaching effects among world opinion.

"When I said that I thought that such a step, if done without due cause, might bring a serious reappraisal of Britain's attitude to Malaysia, he said 'very well then, I should have to make peace with Indonesia.' ...

"An hour after I had seen the Tunku, Lee Kuan Yew came to my house. I found him in a very emotional state. I told him that I was deeply worried about present course of events. It seemed to me that unless an initiative were taken present course could only lead to two directions. One was increasing political bitterness and controversy leading to intensification of communal tension and strife; the other would be situation in which federal government felt that increasing political tension could not continue unchecked and might therefore lead to Lee's detention. I felt that some way must be found to avoid continuation of present trend and its seemingly inevitable consequences. Lee said that time had now come to fight for a Malaysia that would not be dominated by Malays. This, in his view, was why he had created new opposition grouping and if federal government decided to put him inside he would welcome it because it would strengthen his position.

"Lee said time for patience and delay was over and that anyway he had gone too far now to adopt such a course. There is, unfortunately, both truth and force in Lee's reply. ...

"Without, I hope, being over-dramatic, it is my view that we are now confronted with a serious crisis. Unless something can be done to take heat out of present situation course we are now following will, I think, eventually bring about serious trouble."

The Commonwealth Relations Office message to Head on 3 June said:

> "If Lee were arrested, it could not be assumed that this step would quietly be accepted in Singapore. The Tunku may have other indications, but in our view there is every risk of serious trouble there, which might well affect the Borneo territories. ... Should the situation following Lee's arrest so seriously deteriorate as to require the use of British troops in Singapore, it would be extremely difficult to secure the understanding and support of British public opinion."

On 4 June, Head reported on his meeting with the Tunku:

> "Reading between the lines it became evident that the Tunku has told his people to make enquiries to see if there is any chance of displacing Lee from PAP leadership and getting a prominent alternative PAP leader to take over from Lee. Lee is already aware of this and had already told me about it. I told the Tunku I had little hope for this manoeuvre. He then said, 'Tell your government not to worry. This is an internal situation which I have got to settle. You must not get involved in our internal affairs. Americans did in Vietnam and look what a mess they made of it.'"

On June 5, Head received a telegram:

> "The prime minister has seen telegram No. 960 of June 1 ... He has made two comments:
> (1) Should I send a message to the Tunku?
> (2) Should High Commissioner quietly suggest to Lee he gets lost (goes abroad) for a week or two. We do not want him put inside before PMs' Conference.
> H.W."

Thereafter there were few new developments for Head to report. The Tunku was away in London and Razak was quietly talking to Keng Swee about Singapore "hiving off".

Soon after the separation, on 21 September, George Thomson, the British Commonwealth secretary, sent this message about it to Lord Caradon (Hugh Foot), the UK representative to the United Nations:

> "Our general comment is that, however provocative Lee may have been from time to time ... nevertheless it is likely that the present break-up and the preceding tension could have been avoided if the Tunku and the Malays had shown some reasonable flexibility in their relations with Lee and Singapore."

Thomson, a Scotsman, did not understand the Malay mind. Neither did I at first, even though I had lived with them all my life. I did not realise how deep were their suspicions of the immigrant races, especially the Chinese, and their fears of being overwhelmed. They had to be totally in charge of the powers of the state, especially the police and the army. Any compromise must be on their terms.

The Tunku, in an interview in 1982 with a British researcher, said that he could not recollect any warning from Wilson, but admitted he had been under considerable pressure to sanction my arrest. He added, however:

> "There was no point in arresting Kuan Yew because the Chinese would, in my part of the world, have also been in sympathy with him because he was Chinese. I did not want trouble because of him, just because of Singapore. If you have a bad leg, the best thing is to amputate it. That is what I did. ... I knew that Kuan Yew would be the best man to take over the government of Singapore. ... His ambitions knew no bounds (in Malaysia)."

There were other considerations. If we had remained in Malaysia, the commission of inquiry into the 1964 race riots would continue to hear damaging evidence against Ja'afar Albar and UMNO, which would receive widespread publicity. Then there would be the hearing of my libel action against Albar and the editors of the *Utusan Melayu*, who would be thoroughly cross-examined in court on all the incendiary passages they had published about me. That would mean a devastating exposure of key UMNO leaders' methods of incitement to racism and bloody riots.

The Tunku's solution to these problems was separation. Singapore would be out of Malaysia and he would control Singapore through the supply of water from Johor and other levers of pressure. He told Head on 9 August, "If Singapore's foreign policy is prejudicial to Malaysia's interests, we could always bring pressure to bear on them by threatening to turn off the water in Johor." Head commented to Bottomley that this was "a startling proposal of how to coordinate foreign policy".

Also on 9 August itself, the Tunku told Tom Critchley, the Australian high commissioner, "We hold the upper hand and Singapore will have to consult with us in dealing with foreign governments."

The Tunku and Razak thought they could station troops in Singapore, squat on us and if necessary close the Causeway and cut off our water supply. They believed, not without foundation, that Singapore could not exist on its own – what better authority than the speeches of the PAP leaders themselves, myself included, and the reasons we had given for it? As Ghazali bin Shafie, the permanent secretary, external affairs ministry, said soon after separation, after a few years out on a limb, Singapore would be in severe straits and would come crawling back – this time on Malaysia's terms.

No, not if I could help it. People in Singapore were in no mood to crawl back after what they had been through for two years in Malaysia, the communal bullying and intimidation. Certainly Keng Swee and I, the two directly responsible for accepting this separation from our hinterland, were not about to give up. The people shared our feelings and were prepared to do whatever was needed to make an independent Singapore work. I did not know I was to spend the rest of my life getting Singapore not just to work but to prosper and flourish.

Chronology of Events

16 September 1923	Lee Kuan Yew (LKY) born in Singapore.
1936–39, 1940–42	Studied at Raffles Institution and Raffles College.
15 February 1942	Japanese captured and occupied Singapore.
September 1945	British returned to Singapore.
1946–50	Studied in Cambridge and London.
December 1947	Married Kwa Geok Choo in England (kept it secret).
June 1948	State of Emergency declared in Malaya and Singapore. Malayan Communist Party went underground.
August 1950	Returned to Singapore.
September 1950	Married Kwa Geok Choo again in Singapore.
1950–59	Practised Law, active as legal adviser to many trade unions.
November 1954	Inauguration of People's Action Party (PAP).
April 1955	Elected to the Legislative Assembly under new Rendel constitution. PAP won three seats. LKY became leader of the opposition.
	Hock Lee bus riots, instigated by communist united front organisations.
May 1956	Member of First All-Party Constitutional Mission to London, led by Chief Minister David Marshall. After talks failed, Marshall resigned. Lim Yew Hock became chief minister.
October 1956	Arrest and detention of communist united front leaders, including Lim Chin Siong, Fong Swee Suan and Devan Nair.

March 1957	Member of Second All-Party Constitutional Mission to London, led by Lim Yew Hock. Agreement on self-government.
31 August 1957	Federation of Malaya became independent.
December 1957	PAP won 13 seats in the City Council election.
March 1958	First of four clandestine meetings with communist underground leader Fang Chuang Pi (the "Plen").
May 1958	Member of Third All-Party Constitutional Mission to London. Constitution for a self-governing Singapore settled.
May 1959	PAP won 43 out of 51 seats in general election under the new constitution.
4 June 1959	Communist united front leaders Lim Chin Siong, Fong Swee Suan and Devan Nair released from detention.
5 June 1959	At 35, sworn in as prime minister of the self-governing state of Singapore.
February 1960	Established Housing and Development Board with Lim Kim San as chairman. Beginning of massive public housing programme.
July 1960	Formed People's Association to mobilise grassroots support to counter the communists.
May 1961	The Tunku called for closer political and economic cooperation between Malaya, Singapore and the Borneo territories.
July 1961	PAP survived motion of confidence vote in the Legislative Assembly.
August 1961	Thirteen pro-communist PAP assemblymen broke off to form the Barisan Sosialis.
September 1961	LKY gave series of radio talks, "Battle for Merger", to expose communist conspiracy and urge support for merger with Malaysia.

September 1962	Singaporeans voted for merger with Malaysia in a referendum.
February 1963	Operation Coldstore: detention of the communists and their supporters.
31 August 1963	Singapore declared independence, ahead of the formation of Malaysia.
16 September 1963	Malaysia formed, comprising Malaya, Singapore, Sarawak and Sabah. Indonesia mounted "Confrontation" against Malaysia.
21 September 1963	PAP won general election in Singapore. Singapore UMNO lost all three Malay-majority constituencies to PAP.
March 1964	Nine PAP parliamentary candidates fought in the Malayan general election, but won only one. Difficulties with federal government increased.
12 July 1964	UMNO-sponsored convention of 123 Malay/Muslim bodies; UMNO secretary-general Ja'afar Albar stirred up Malays against LKY.
21 July 1964	Communal riots in Singapore on Prophet Mohammed's Birthday, the culmination of racist agitation by Ja'afar Albar.
September 1964	Second outbreak of communal violence.
January–February 1965	Unsuccessful discussions between LKY and the Tunku for "rearrangements" within Malaysia.
May 1965	PAP organised Malaysian Solidarity Convention to promote a "Malaysian Malaysia". UMNO called for LKY's arrest.
July 1965	The Tunku, in London, decided that Singapore must leave Malaysia.
9 August 1965	Singapore's separation from Malaysia.

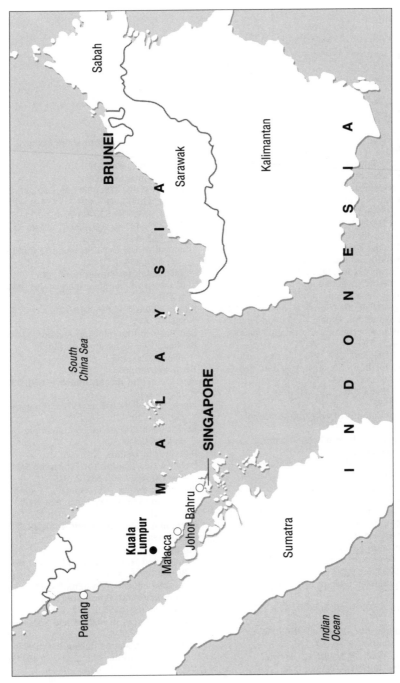

We were a Chinese island in a Malay sea. How could we survive in such a hostile environment?

Index

Abdul Hamid bin Haji Jumat (Singapore minister for local government, leader of UMNO Singapore), 216, 272, 296, 305, 336

Abdul Razak bin Hussain, Tun (deputy prime minister, Malaysia), 14, 41, 306, 348, 363–4, 411, 437–8, 442, 461–3, 471, 477, 485, 493–4, 498, 500–1, 503, 507, 518–19, 543, 559–60, 566, 568–9, 599, 607, 614–15, 624–7, 649, 656
- and Eddie Barker, 638–9
- constitutional rearrangements for Singapore, 581, 583, 585, 587, 589, 591
- "hiving-off" negotiations, 17, 629–38, 661
- merger negotiations, 437–9, 477–80
- suggests Lee Kuan Yew's resignation, 568

Abdul Samad bin Ismail: *see* Samad Ismail

Afro-Asian movement: countries and leaders, 15, 422, 536

Ahmad Haji Taff, 517

Ahmad Ibrahim, 182, 184, 189, 199, 385–6, 388, 406, 447, 463

Ahmad Khan, 329

Algeria, 527

All-Party Committee on Chinese Schools, 213–14, 216–18, 222

All-Singapore Chinese School Parents' Association, 216

Alliance party and government, Malaysia, 17, 223, 461, 465, 476, 515, 543, 547–8, 597

Alliance party, Singapore, 463, 474, 505–6, 508, 576, 652–3

Anti-British League, 159, 175, 255, 290, 473

ANZUS (Australia, New Zealand and US defence agreement), 550

Australia, 16, 17, 225
- defence forces in Singapore and Malaya, 46, 52, 55, 223

Awbery, Stanley (Labour MP, Britain), 117, 182

Azahari, A.M. (Partai Rakyat), 415, 467

Baharuddin bin Mohamed Ariff, 356

Baker, Maurice, 45–6, 69, 122, 132

Balewa, Alhaji Sir Abubakar Tafawa (prime minister, Nigeria), 532

Banda, Dr Hastings (president, Malawi), 532–3

Bani, S.T., 367, 507, 513

Bank of China, 517, 632

Barisan Sosialis, 378, 383, 385, 390, 401–3, 406–9, 413–14, 416, 418–21, 427–8, 429, 432–4, 444, 446–52, 460–2, 463, 471–2, 474, 477, 483–4, 486, 496–7, 505–8, 511, 574, 622, 653
- appeal to UN Decolonisation Committee (1962), 433–4
- declaration on Brunei revolt, 467
- in favour of complete merger, 401, 414, 416

Barker, Eddie, 116, 604, 613, 629, 631–2, 636, 638–40, 645

Ben Bella (prime minister, Algeria), 527–8

Benham, F.C. (committee on family allowances), 155

Berita Harian, 608

Bevan, Aneurin (health minister, UK), 130, 231

Black, Sir Robert (UK governor, Singapore), 202, 206, 209–11, 213, 228

Blades, Alan (Singapore commissioner of police), 328–9, 352

Bloodworth, Dennis, 489, 605

Bogaars, George (director, Singapore Special Branch), 557, 623, 631–2, 645

Bottomley, Arthur (UK secretary of state, Commonwealth Relations), 628, 647, 651, 663

Bourguiba, Habib (president, Tunisia), 526–7

Brandt, Willy, 571

Britain:
- Argyll and Sutherland Highlanders, 45, 55
- Brunei revolt, 466–8
- colonial education system, 36, 43
- Commonwealth Prime Ministers' Conference (1962), 454, 456–7
- defence forces in Malaya and Southeast Asia, 20, 223–4
- defending Malaysia during Indonesian Confrontation, 493, 522–3, 548, 567, 572–4, 590, 636, 657

PHOTOGRAPHS
The publishers wish to thank all those who
contributed photographs. Photographs in the
book were scanned by Straits Times and
Superskill Graphics Pte Ltd and came from:
Internal Security Department, Singapore: 334
Lee Kuan Yew: 30, 31, 33, 95, 96, 109, 120,
122, 136, 148, 292
Ministry of Information and the Arts: 491, 609
Philip Moore: 391, 521
Nanyang Siang Pau: 555
National Archives, Singapore: 482
Straits Times: 2, 180, 215, 248, 260, 265, 311,
314, 323, 340, 345, 396, 405, 423, 445, 453,
490, 509, 535, 544, 560, 561, 596, 619, 650,
654, 657